The Translator

G. J. RACZ is Professor of Foreign Languages and Literature at LIU Brooklyn, review editor for *Translation Review*, and a former president of the American Literary Translators Association. In addition to the plays included in this volume, Racz has published *Rigmaroles*, his translation of Jaime Salom's *El señor de las patrañas* in *Three Comedies* (University Press of Colorado, 2004) and *Dark Stone*, his rendering of Alberto Conejero's *La piedra oscura* (ESTRENO Contemporary Spanish Plays 39, 2016).

The Editor

BARBARA FUCHS is Professor of Spanish and English at the University of California, Los Angeles, where she directs the Working Group on the *Comedia* in Translation and Performance and the Diversifying the Classics project. She is the author, most recently, of *The Poetics of Piracy: Emulating Spain in English Literature* (University of Pennsylvania Press, 2013), and translator of Cervantes' *The Bagnios of Algiers* and *The Great Sultana* (University of Pennsylvania Press, 2010) and Lope de Vega's *Women and Servants* (Juan de la Cuesta, 2016). She is also one of the editors of *The Norton Anthology of World Literature*.

NORTON CRITICAL EDITIONS
Renaissance

CASTIGLIONE, The Book of the Courtier
CERVANTES, Don Quijote
DONNE, John Donne's Poetry
Elizabeth i and Her Age
ERASMUS, The Praise of Folly and Other Writings
The Golden Age of Spanish Drama
JONSON, Ben Jonson's Plays and Masques
KYD, The Spanish Tragedy
Lazarillo de Tormes
MACHIAVELLI, The Prince
MARLOWE, Doctor Faustus
MIDDLETON & DEKKER, The Roaring Girl
MORE, Utopia
SOR JUANA INÉS de la CRUZ, Selected Works
Seventeenth-Century British Poetry, 1603–1660
SHAKESPEARE, Antony and Cleopatra
SHAKESPEARE, As You Like It
SHAKESPEARE, Hamlet
SHAKESPEARE, 1 Henry IV
SHAKESPEARE, Julius Caesar
SHAKESPEARE, King Lear
SHAKESPEARE, Macbeth
SHAKESPEARE, Measure for Measure
SHAKESPEARE, The Merchant of Venice
SHAKESPEARE, A Midsummer Night's Dream
SHAKESPEARE, Othello
SHAKESPEARE, Richard III
SHAKESPEARE, Romeo and Juliet
SHAKESPEARE, The Taming of the Shrew
SHAKESPEARE, The Tempest
SPENSER, Edmund Spenser's Poetry
WEBSTER, The Duchess of Malfi

For a complete list of Norton Critical Editions, visit
wwnorton.com/nortoncriticals.

A NORTON CRITICAL EDITION

THE GOLDEN AGE OF SPANISH DRAMA

NEW TRANSLATIONS
BACKGROUNDS AND CONTEXTS
CRITICISM

Translated by

G. J. RACZ
LIU BROOKLYN

Edited by

BARBARA FUCHS
UNIVERSITY OF CALIFORNIA, LOS ANGELES

W • W • NORTON & COMPANY • *New York* • *London*

W. W. Norton & Company has been independent since its founding in 1923, when William Warder Norton and Mary D. Herter Norton first published lectures delivered at the People's Institute, the adult education division of New York City's Cooper Union. The firm soon expanded its program beyond the Institute, publishing books by celebrated academics from America and abroad. By midcentury, the two major pillars of Norton's publishing program—trade books and college texts—were firmly established. In the 1950s, the Norton family transferred control of the company to its employees, and today—with a staff of four hundred and a comparable number of trade, college, and professional titles published each year—W. W. Norton & Company stands as the largest and oldest publishing house owned wholly by its employees.

Library of Congress Cataloging-in-Publication Data

Names: Racz, Gregary Joseph, translator. | Fuchs, Barbara, 1970- editor.
Title: The golden age of Spanish drama : a new translation, backgrounds and contexts, criticism / translated by G. J. Racz ; edited by Barbara Fuchs.
Description: First edition. | New York : W. W. Norton & Company, [2018] | Series: A Norton critical edition | Includes bibliographical references.
Identifiers: LCCN 2018001462 | ISBN 9780393923629 (pbk.)
Subjects: LCSH: Spanish drama—Classical period, 1500-1700.
Classification: LCC PQ6221 .G65 2018 | DDC 862/.308—dc23
LC record available at https://lccn.loc.gov/2018001462

W. W. Norton & Company, Inc., 500 Fifth Avenue, New York, NY 10110
wwnorton.com

W. W. Norton & Company Ltd., 15 Carlisle Street, London W1D 3BS

1 2 3 4 5 6 7 8 9 0

Contents

Introduction

From the late sixteenth century and well into the seventeenth, Spain produced one of the most vibrant and popular dramatic canons in the history of theater. As Madrid grew into a sophisticated imperial capital, the *comedia** vividly reflected the fashions and predilections of its citizens, while also probing their deepest anxieties. Across the Spanish empire, both lay and religious theater flourished, in the streets and in the courts.

As they built on medieval traditions of minstrelsy and liturgical drama, as well as *commedia dell'arte* and Renaissance innovations from Italy, Spanish playwrights of what is generally known as the "Golden Age" produced hundreds of increasingly sophisticated texts that were played by professional actors for an insatiable audience. The *comedia* was an urban phenomenon that also staged urbanity: wit, rather than force, frequently carried the day. Women, country folk, and servants were often central to the plots. Playing outsize roles on the stage, these figures transcended their social positions.

Early Modern Spain in a Global Context

Over the course of the long sixteenth century, the various kingdoms that made up the Iberian peninsula in the medieval era became the most powerful empire in the world. Iberian consolidation began with the union of Castile and Aragon under Isabella and Ferdinand, known as the "Catholic Monarchs." In their service, Columbus explored the "New World"—the lands that would eventually be known as America—in a series of voyages beginning in 1492, and claimed the territory he "discovered" for Spain. With Isabella and Ferdinand's conquest of the Muslim Nasrid kingdom of Granada in the same year, Spain completed its territorial consolidation at home, as its rulers abandoned medieval models of religious tolerance and instead advocated for a nation identified solely with Catholicism. Forced conversions and expulsions of Jewish and Muslim populations that had coexisted with Christians for centuries in Iberia, as well as the persecution of Protestants in the wake of the Reformation, all furthered this transformation. Although many voices were raised in protest, arguing for the long and venerable place of Judaism and Islam in Spain, the Counter-Reformation confirmed Spain's role as a Catholic power and bulwark against Protestantism. Over the course of the sixteenth century, the newly consolidated monarchy expanded its reach in Italy and the New World, bringing with it a mixture of religious orthodoxy and, where expedient, an openness to hybrid forms of Catholicism and outreach in indigenous languages.

---

*Comedia is a term used for both individual plays, whether comic or tragic, and the Spanish Golden Age corpus as a whole.

When the Habsburg king Charles I of Spain was crowned Holy Roman Emperor in 1519, Spain became the heart of his empire, which extended *plus ultra* (Latin for "even farther," as Charles's motto put it), far beyond the boundaries imagined by the ancients. His son Philip II inherited a global empire that stretched to Mexico and the Philippines (named after the sovereign), which grew only larger when Philip annexed Portugal and its possessions in Asia and South America in 1580. In 1561, Philip made the small but centrally located town of Madrid his capital; the remarkable growth of the city over the decades that followed would be intimately tied to the development of the theater. Imperial power led to the literary and artistic preeminence of Spain in arts and letters, with Philip himself serving as a key patron as he built and decorated his masterpiece, the impressive palace-monastery of El Escorial.

Yet with his endless empire Philip also inherited the restiveness of Protestant lands—including the long and bloody revolt of the Netherlands (1568–1609, 1621–48)—and the costs of defending Catholicism on multiple fronts. At the same time, he faced the ongoing threat of the expanding Ottoman empire to a fragmented and internally divided Christendom. The wealth of the New World paid in part for Philip's military expenses, but also brought with it crippling inflation in Spain. As Francisco de Quevedo notes in his satirical poem "Sir Money Is a Mighty Lord," included in this volume, gold is born in the New World and lives in Spain, where it plays havoc with social hierarchies. In the end, however, it is buried in Genoa, where the king's creditors must be paid off.

The economic upheavals and the influx of New World gold introduced new possibilities for social mobility over the course of the sixteenth century. The *comedia*, concerned with problems of identity and representation, frequently turned to these as it sought to work out the connections among wealth, power, and value.

As an urban phenomenon, and one particularly associated with the capital city, Madrid, the *comedia* served as a shared experience for thousands of people and as an important forum for social and political questions. As the theater took on complicated issues of power and its limits, it also reflected more or less obliquely on the central questions of its time: the proper balance of authority in a society, the possibility of rethinking hierarchies in a time of profound transformations, and the importance of order versus personal liberty.

Theater Comes of Age

The late sixteenth century saw enormous transformations in Spanish drama, from the shorter, simpler eclogues of Juan del Encina and the farces of Lope de Rueda, to classicizing plays such as the *The Siege of Numantia* of Miguel de Cervantes, to the lively new theater of Lope de Vega and his contemporaries, including Tirso de Molina, Guillén de Castro, Ana Caro, and Juan Ruiz de Alarcón. As the seventeenth century progressed, theater expanded into the court, under such figures as Calderón de la Barca and Luis Vélez de Guevara. The *comedia* also crossed the Atlantic to Mexico City, where the remarkable nun Sor Juana Inés de la Cruz wrote for the vice-regal court and commoners alike.

Scholars continue to debate the sources of the fantastic explosion of Spanish theater in the late sixteenth century and early seventeenth century. Although there were hardly any medieval plays per se in Spain, scholars have identified elements in religious devotion, university education, and the long medieval tradition of traveling performers (*jongleurs*) that laid the groundwork for the theatrical revolution (Burningham). At the same time, the Catholic church gradually began commissioning performances for feast days such as Corpus Christi (the Feast of the Sacrament), which took place in public spaces in towns and cities. As the guilds (medieval associations of merchants or artisans) became involved with these performances, they grew in size and importance. Cities and towns competed with each other to host the most impressive Corpus performances and often attracted desirable companies by allowing them to present plays beyond those marking the religious observance (Greer 80).

The early sixteenth century also saw increased cultural traffic between Spain and Italy, where urban theater had already appeared, as well as localized experiments in university and court settings, often following classical models. By the mid-sixteenth century, Italian troupes visited Spain regularly to present the vibrant *commedia dell'arte*, in which performers improvised from stock roles and situations. The writer, actor, and impresario Lope de Rueda (c. 1505–1565) provides the clearest link between these early and imported forms and the theater that followed. In 1554 he formed the first traveling Spanish troupe, which performed both Italian plays in translation and his own short farces. As Jodi Campbell notes, with this mobility and popularity "drama ceased to be linked to particular occasions or messages, and it began to pick up broader themes not limited by region or social class." Eventually, the *comedia*'s popularity provided it with economic support from an increasingly wide and diverse audience (32–33).

The later sixteenth century saw the development of more elaborate plays, often tragic and based on classical sources, such as Cervantes' *Numantia*. The great revolution came with the arrival on the scene of Lope de Vega, whom contemporaries quickly identified as a "prodigy of nature" (Cervantes, "Prologue") and an "Apollo for all poets" (Agustín de Rojas Villandrando, *The Pleasant Journey*). Lope presided over an explosion in playwriting and playgoing, as the *comedia* became a vital, central public art form across Spain.

Over four hundred plays survive by Lope de Vega alone, and experts generally agree that he wrote more than twice that number. His contemporaries also produced dozens, if not hundreds, of plays in an effort to meet the huge demand from theatergoers. Hundreds of plays survive either in manuscript or in early printed editions. The size of this massive corpus—of which only a small subset is regularly studied or produced—makes it difficult to generalize about the *comedia*'s formal or ideological investments, although there are common threads.

The plays are almost always in verse and use different metrical forms to convey various registers or moods (G. J. Racz's translations in this volume are in rhymed verse, in order to approximate the formal qualities of the original plays). Many of these forms—ballads, songs—would have been familiar to audiences as part of popular culture and were readily adapted to the stage. Sources for the *comedia* vary widely and include national and religious history; classical, medieval, and Renaissance literature; popular forms such as ballads and proverbs; and even current events. The *comedia* is a realistic theater, representing a world that is recognizably that of its audience, even when the time and place are transposed elsewhere.

Lope's own witty treatise on how to write *comedias*, *The New Art of Writing Plays* (1609), foregrounds the practical. Tongue firmly in cheek, Lope insists that if the audience pays, they deserve to get what they enjoy. Lope is not far off: the *comedia* was the first real commercial theater, with plays designed to please the broadest possible audience instead of a commissioning patron or occasion. Instead of worrying about Aristotelian precepts, Lope tells us, playwrights should focus on what works and what the audience likes. Unity of time, of place, and of action are far less important than a powerful plot and subplots to keep the audience engaged. Love and honor make for the most effective plots, as they provoke the strongest feelings.

Yet, beyond the theory expressed in Lope's treatise, how did the new *comedia* achieve its remarkable popularity? Three acts give it a compact structure: exposition, crux, and dénouement in around three thousand verses. Upper-class protagonists are generally accompanied by a lower-class comic sidekick, or *gracioso*, who often manipulates the action as well as acerbically comments on it. The verse is lively and varied, ably harnessing models from popular song to the Petrarchan tradition of idealizing love poetry. Subplots multiply and echo the action of the main plot; something is always happening. Yet although Lope clearly hit on a winning formula for playwriting, his plays are hardly formulaic, spanning the gamut from the tragic to the comic and transcending any distinction between high and low forms of entertainment.

Perhaps one way to envision the transition between the older and the newer theater is by considering how Cervantes and Lope render the collective in *Numantia* and *Fuenteovejuna*, respectively. Both plays mine episodes in the history of Iberia, mobilizing powerful analogies between *then* and *now*. While Cervantes follows individual characters at times, he relies heavily on allegorical figures that speak for Fame, for Spain, and even for its rivers as he charts Numantia's fate. Lope dispenses with the allegorical, instead showing us the political volition—and shame— that makes the inhabitants of the town act as one in order to take revenge on their abusive lord. As his figures speak with the voice of prophecy, Cervantes conveys millennia of history, only to complicate our understanding of them. Lope, for his part, is most interested in the immediate, interpersonal tensions that animate the villagers' actions and in their capacity to become the protagonists of their own story.

Even though this account might seem to map a trajectory of modernization for the theater, things are not quite so simple. Cervantes also wrote raunchy, irreverent short plays—*entremeses*, or interludes—that are far from the allegorical stateliness of *Numantia*, while Lope wrote allegorical figures into the few ponderous plays commissioned from him for important public milestones. Though one could certainly trace a path of increasing agility and immediacy through the *comedia* corpus, there are plenty of detours and reversals. The sheer magnitude of the corpus makes it difficult to define any simple progression; plays with very different aesthetic aims and ideological assumptions appear early and late in the Golden Age. Moreover, despite the survival of hundreds of plays, there are playwrights whose entire output has been lost, so that ours is at best a partial and primarily textual reconstruction of a vibrant theater scene. Early modern Spaniards recognized that they lived in an exceptional era of theater. Agustín de Rojas Villadrando begins his survey of recent theater history in Spain by connecting its greatness to imperial grandeur. As he wraps up, he reflects that his own moment "might / by rights be called the Golden Age," including, as it does, "adept performers, splendid plays, / great intrigues, lessons and conceits, / inventive plots, light interludes, / sweet music, lyrics, novelties, / displays of genius, dances, masks, / fine clothing, pomp, rich spectacles, / engagements, tournaments and jousts" (393) unmatched in the history of theater, and difficult, Rojas claims, to surpass.

Corrales, *Companies, and the City*

Theater's new purchase on Spanish society led to the development of the first permanent theaters, the *corrales,* by the late sixteenth century. With the Corral de la Cruz (1579) and the Corral del Príncipe (1582), Madrid featured two permanent, centrally located theaters that replaced the hired courtyards in which earlier, more improvised performances were given. Other cities and towns followed suit, with noted *corrales* in Valencia, Seville, Córdoba, and elsewhere forming a dense network across Iberia and beyond. Twenty-seven cities and towns across Spain had permanent theaters in the period, as did Mexico City, Puebla, Lima, and Potosí in the New World (Greer 80). After performing in Madrid, companies would often take their plays on tour. Actors also continued to perform for religious festivals and in more informal settings, particularly if they were not members of a company.

Corrales were rectangular courtyard theaters located between two- or three-story houses, with the balconies and windows of those houses adapted to seat viewers. Special galleries accommodated nobles and clergymen in separate areas, while ordinary folk (the rowdy *mosqueteros,* or groundlings) stood in the patio itself, or sat on stools and bleachers. While upper-class men and women sat together in the boxes, there was also a segregated section for women of the lower classes, the *cazuela* (stewpot), with its own dedicated entrance and grilles in front of it. A raised stage at one end of the patio generally consisted of two levels: a lower one with doors for entrances and exits and a central discovery space for effects; and an upper one that served for balconies and all other raised locations. There was no lighting, very few props, and not much scenery. Minimal sets might be painted onto the wall of one of the houses or hung as curtains. Cervantes' prologue to his published plays (1615) recalls how simple the earliest productions were and how stage machinery gradually became more complex, bringing the theater to its current "lofty pinnacle." As the theaters gradually incorporated trapdoors and other special effects, playwrights used them to include spectacular moments in their texts. The space of the *corral* embodied many of the tensions between public and private, seen and unseen, and secret and spectacular that would inform the *comedias* presented within it.

The *corrales* were managed by religious brotherhoods, with profits from the plays largely destined for charitable causes, primarily the city's hospitals. This arrangement provided important cover for the theater: when accused of immorality, as it often was, it could point to its undeniable charitable contributions and its deep involvement in municipal concerns. Cities generally supported the theater, while the Crown perennially investigated whether it did more harm than good and charged state officials with figuring out how to regulate it. Moralists kept up a steady chorus of disapproval, and from 1615 on individual plays had to be licensed by the civic and state authorities in Madrid in order to be cleared for performance. The censors were often playwrights, however, and they tended to focus their censorship on religious or sexual matters rather than political ones (Campbell 54). The Inquisition also stepped in to prohibit plays or insist on cuts, generally focusing on heresy and profanity rather than immorality (McKendrick 185). Yet churchmen had specially designated boxes at the *corrales*, suggesting that, however loud the moral condemnation of the theater in some quarters, even the Church made peace with it.

In the reign of Philip III (r. 1598–1621), theater gradually made its way into the court, with private performances in the king's household and other noble houses. Yet at least initially it was the popular theater that was invited in, via commissions to existing companies and replicas of the public theaters set up in palace courtyards. Although court theater eventually evolved into spectacular masquelike extravaganzas, in spaces purposely designed and with no expense spared, its roots lay in the urban, popular *comedia*.

With the permanent theaters, companies also became more established. They operated continuously except during Lent, and actors were hired on annual contracts to play certain types of characters. The companies consisted of about ten or twenty actors, as well as musicians and support personnel. Theatrical companies were licensed and regulated, with actor-managers (*autores de comedias*) appointed every two years by the authorities to serve as "impresario, producer, director and actor rolled into one" (McKendrick 189). The total number of licensed companies was also limited, although smaller, unlicensed companies continued to perform. *Autores* commissioned specific plays for their companies, so that the plays were to some extent determined by the available actors. Records survive for around seven hundred theatrical companies, twenty of which would have been active in any given year, and for almost five thousand actors and actresses in the period to the early eighteenth century (Greer 81).

The presentation of a single *comedia* was a multifaceted, rich event. In addition to the main play, music was omnipresent, and a number of shorter pieces entertained the audience. Before the play began, music would play and the *loa* (a brief praise piece) served as a dedication of sorts. Between the *jornadas* (acts), the audience would be treated to *entremeses* (interludes), *sainetes* (short satirical pieces), *bailes* (dances), *mojigangas* (short carnivalesque farces), or other short pieces. After the play proper, there was often a *fin de fiesta*, literally the "end of the festivities," with more music and dancing. These shorter pieces might be unconnected to the main play or could comment upon it obliquely.

In some cases, playwrights wrote all the short pieces that would accompany their play, perhaps as a way to control the possible effects of the shorter forms on the main piece, as in Sor Juana's *Trials of a Noble House*, which was commissioned to celebrate the 1683 arrival in New Spain of the new viceroy and his wife. Certain playwrights, including Cervantes and Calderón, excelled at writing interludes, which often featured races, classes, and professions less frequently portrayed on stage, and offered a more ribald response to social pieties. In a sense, our understanding of *comedias* as texts is always incomplete in that the plays as performed would have expressed their meaning and negotiated their reception amid a number of other, perhaps challenging representations. Interludes might well have complicated the meaning of a play, ironizing its message or taking down its seriousness. At the same time, song and dance would have enhanced the experience for viewers, providing a powerful sensorial dimension to the performance. Research on the physicality of *comedia* performance is still very new, but the more we learn, the more we must remind ourselves that the texts we read were designed to be performed, and negotiated a multidimensional dramatic universe at every performance.

In Spain as in England, early modern theater emerged in part from the coincidence of newly expanded urban centers and a more mobile and flexible society. Humanism led to wider literacy and education for boys from the artisan classes, who might pick up a smattering of Latin and a familiarity with classical texts. Lope, himself the son of an embroiderer, imagined characters whose education allowed them to transcend their places, as does the secretary Teodoro in *The Dog in the Manger*. The influx of gold and silver from the New World completely transformed Iberian society in the sixteenth century, as Quevedo mordantly notes in "Sir Money." As social mobility became a reality in early modern Spain, the theater proved uniquely well suited to exploring the self-fashioning of characters who could expect to transform their circumstances. The *deus ex machina* in a number of plays from the period is the *perulero*, the rich adventurer returned from Peru, whose wealth changes everything. But even in plays such as *Dog*, in which no *perulero* makes an appearance, social hierarchies become newly permeable, more susceptible to self-fashioning or even imposture.

Part of what the theater achieves in this context is to model urbane behavior, providing for a wide range of viewers a vision of what it would mean to behave like their social betters. Jane Albrecht has argued that theater was not actually cheap enough for just anyone to attend: those below the artisan class, she argues, had neither the time nor the resources to go to the theater regularly. But a wide range of people associated with noble households might accompany their masters to performances. Both their social status and their connection to the upper classes would have made these audiences particularly receptive to the theater's message about the new flexibility of identity and class.

The growth of the city and the development of the theater were fully intertwined. Many *comedias* were set in contemporary Madrid: they addressed the fashionable city, its opportunities for self-display and self-fashioning, and the possibilities of anonymity and female agency that urban space afforded. Despite its wide range of subgenres and very different plots, the *comedia* returns again and again to what we might term problems of *impersonation*: how fixed is identity, and how is it to be negotiated in a society with newfound mobility? Who may claim agency, and on what terms? What new spaces for self-definition become available amid the transformations of the period, whether in political, economic, or intellectual terms? How does the private life of the emotions intersect with the public life of status and display?

Performing Gender

One of the most striking aspects of the *comedia*, particularly for audiences accustomed to Shakespeare, is the importance of female characters. This is no doubt due to the fact that, with some exceptions, professional actresses were the norm on the Spanish stage. Their strong presence and centrality encourage a reconsideration of gender mores in the period. The theory of female morality, as expressed in sermons, antitheatrical tracts, or conduct books such as Luis de Leon's *The Perfect Wife*, differed significantly from the actual roles occupied by women, both as actors on the stage and in society more broadly. The moralists' condemnation of theatricality itself, particularly its dangers for and from women, must be juxtaposed with the undeniable female agency displayed onstage. As historians have reminded us, the representation of conflicts over "honor" in theatrical works—including, crucially, plots about women's sexual behavior and its impact on their men—bore little relation to the way gender actually operated in society or in the criminal courts (Taylor).

Long considered a central tenet of the *comedia*, honor is in fact ironized as often as it is set in motion. If, at its most reactionary, the stage mobilizes concerns about women's chastity as the key to male honor, as in the attacks on the town's women in *Fuenteovejuna*, it also offers strong visions of female agency, as in Laurencia's own response in that play, or, in an alternative, comic vein, the poised and articulate Leonor of *Trials of a Noble House*, or the powerful Diana of *The Dog in the Manger*. With enormous variation among specific plays, the corpus at large portrays women not simply as the victims of a patriarchal system that renders them sexual objects to be conquered or defended, but also as agents fully capable of manipulating that system to their own ends.

But surely, if there were actresses on the Spanish stage, there was no need for cross-dressing? Although moralists were particularly exercised by the thought of women in tights, playwrights found that audiences loved the titillation and adventurousness of cross-dressing plots. Thus Calderón's Rosaura, in *Life Is a Dream*, spends the first act dressed as a man; far more scandalously, in Sor Juana's *Trials of a Noble House*, the dark-skinned *gracioso* Chestnut dresses up as an upper-class white woman.

The appeal of the actresses themselves was considered socially disruptive, and many laws were passed to minimize their effects: unmarried women and widows were not legally allowed to act; masculine costume for women was restricted; actresses were not to receive any male visitors except their husbands (McKendrick). Yet in his memorandum to King Philip II against the reauthorization of *comedias*, Lupercio Argensola focuses on the scandals caused by actresses so irresistible and available that noble lords are led astray by them. Although we should not take Argensola's examples at face value, they tell us a lot about how the life of actors, their companies, and their motives were perceived and remind us that laws, even those passed repeatedly, were not necessarily followed.

Print, Performance, and Translation

Our main access to Golden Age theater, of course, is through the printed record of the plays. The *comedia* was very popular in print: playwrights sold their plays to *autores de comedias*, who guarded them jealously and published them once they were no longer new enough to attract audiences to the *corral*. Cervantes notes that his plays were published because no *autor* would produce them for the stage, yet in general publication seems to have depended on the acclaim for the play as performed (Campbell 21). Print publication was also widely perceived to expand the range and effect of the *comedia*: in the 1620s, the state attempted to stop the publication of *comedias* in Castile as a way to restrict their effects.

The extant corpus of hundreds of Golden Age plays is preserved in collections of around a dozen texts, called *partes,* or in unbound quartos of single plays, known as *sueltas,* which generally include only the main playtext and omit the other dramatic forms that might have accompanied it. Only a small subset of these texts have been the focus of critical attention, and there is wide recognition among critics that any generalizations about the *comedia* must acknowledge the range of texts still to be analyzed.

In addition to this embarrassment of riches, current criticism on the *comedia* grapples with the complexity of reconstructing it as a performance genre. Since the 1954 rediscovery of Almagro's *corral de comedias*, now the site of Spain's largest classical theater festival, archival research has made great strides in mining documents—official records, contracts, maps—for information on the material conditions of early modern theater. Research into props, costumes, and scenery has also allowed critics to flesh out staging practices in the period, even if, as Laura Vidler notes, "Without the benefit of time travel, every bit of documentary evidence is by definition a secondary source" (12).

At the same time, critical awareness of the complexity of performance has meant questioning or at least qualifying the totalizing view of José Antonio Maravall (himself a product of the twentieth-century Franco dictatorship in Spain), who conceived of the *comedia* as an instrument for social control that reinforced existing hierarchies and made them palatable to audiences. Modern understandings are more flexible, noting the layered, ironic, or contradictory meanings of the texts and the additional complexity of reimagining their performance and differential reception.

Even as critics and theater historians examine the conditions of early modern performance and attempt to reconstruct its reception, they have begun to argue for the relevance of modern performance, in its contemporary context, to our understanding of the plays. *Comedia* performance in Spain, though hardly a continuous tradition since the seventeenth century, has grown tremendously in the post-Franco era, as practitioners, too, question the idea that the *comedia* was itself reactionary because it had emerged under an *ancien régime*.* The Compañía Nacional de Teatro Clásico (founded in 1986) and its more recent offshoot for actors in training, La Joven Compañía; the Almagro classical theater festival (founded in 1978); and newer regional companies—all make the *comedia* their focus and are rapidly adding to a contemporary performance tradition that engages audiences and critics alike.

In this volume, Duncan Wheeler's account of *Fuenteovejuna* examines how a relatively recent classic functions in varying political Spanish

---

* *Ancien régime* (French for "old regime") refers broadly to the monarchial and aristocratic political systems of Western Europe before the French Revolution (1789).

contexts over the course of the twentieth century and into the twenty-first, as it is harnessed to varying ideological purposes. As Wheeler's study confirms, *comedias* are hardly antiquarian artifacts, but vibrant texts whose multilayered political potential is negotiated in productions across the Hispanic world and beyond.

In the United States, the *comedia* has been presented for over forty years at the Siglo de Oro Drama Festival at the Chamizal National Monument, on the U.S./Mexico border near El Paso, Texas. The festival began as a goodwill gesture at the border and has evolved into an international event, with productions by companies from the United States, Spain, and Latin America. There are productions both in Spanish and in English, with additional performances across the border in Ciudad Juárez. Regional theaters such as Gala Hispanic Theater in Washington, D.C., and Repertorio Español in New York have regularly produced *comedias* as part of their broader commitment to Hispanic programming, with occasional productions by other regional theaters.

Translation has enabled more productions of the *comedia* in the English-speaking world, where the strong tradition of Shakespearean performance has gradually made room for some of Shakespeare's contemporaries. While some plays, such as the ever-popular *Life Is a Dream* and *Fuenteovejuna*, have been translated multiple times over the past century, there is new attention by critics and theater practitioners to the need to broaden the corpus available in English. And though recent initiatives to "translate" Shakespeare into modern English have proved controversial, translations of the *comedia* offer a powerful solution, making it available to modern audiences in an idiom at once linguistically and historically proximate. Although translation might challenge the idea of the original, authoritative, classical text, recent performance criticism reminds us that every contemporary production—in whatever language—already transforms the original (Fischer).

The internationalization of *comedia* productions has offered important opportunities for a mode of translation embedded in performance contexts. The long-term collaboration between Laurence Boswell, director and translator, and David Johnston, critic and translator, in the United Kingdom offers a compelling model. So, too, does the Royal Shakespeare Company's 2004 Golden Age season, which produced new translations of the multiple plays performed, in consultation with scholars and specialists. In her essay in this volume, Catherine Boyle describes the intricate connections among translation, critical reading, and performance as she worked on a London production of Sor Juana's *Trials* (translated in that case as *The House of Desires*) in 1997.

In the United States, increased dialogue among performers, director, translators, and critics under the auspices of the Association for Hispanic Classical Theater has led to a renewed interest in *comedia* studies and a palpable energy in the field. At the University of California, Los Angeles, I direct Diversifying the Classics, a project to promote the *comedia* through translation, adaptation, and outreach, in collaboration with theater practitioners and students at the university, in the broader Los Angeles area, and beyond.

While this volume is aimed primarily at readers—scholars, students, and anyone interested in the *comedia* as text—our hope is that the encounter with these texts, and the rich documentary and critical contexts that surround them, will also inspire them to support, attend, and perhaps even perform or direct the plays.

Acknowledgments

I would like to thank my wonderful research assistants on this project, Payton Phillips Quintanilla and Laura Muñoz, who did so much to bring the various pieces together. Laura's translations made it possible to include a number of crucial primary texts that were only available in Spanish. Enrique García-Santo Tomás generously pointed me to valuable critical sources, while Margaret Greer graciously read this introduction and offered invaluable suggestions. At Norton, Carol Bemis, Thea Goodrich, and Rachel Goodman were instrumental in bringing the project to fruition. Gary Racz was a model of collegial collaboration throughout. My mother, Susana Schuarzberg, recites with vim the Calderón that she remembers from her schoolgirl days and has a fine eye for copy-editing. I thank them all for their assistance.

BARBARA FUCHS

WORKS CITED

Albrecht, Jane. *The Playgoing Public of Madrid in the Time of Tirso de Molina*. New Orleans: University Press of the South, 2001.
Burningham, Bruce. *Radical Theatricality: Jongleuresque Performance in the Early Spanish State*. West Lafayette, IN: Purdue University Press, 2007.
Campbell, Jodi. *Monarchy, Political Culture, and Drama in Seventeenth-Century Madrid: Theater of Negotiation*. Burlington, VT: Ashgate, 2006.
Fischer, Susan L. "Aspectuality, Performativity, and 'Foreign' *Comedia*: (Re)Iteration of Meaning for the Stage." In *The Spanish Golden Age in English: Perspectives on Performance*, eds. Catherine Boyle and David Johnston. London: Oberon, 2007. 31–48.
Greer, Margaret. "Place, Space and Public Formation in the Drama of the Spanish Empire." In *Making Space Public in Early Modern Europe: Performance, Geography, Privacy*, eds. Angela Vanhaelen and Joseph P. Ward. New York: Routledge, 2013. 76–97.
McKendrick, Melveena. *Theatre in Spain 1490–1700*. Cambridge: Cambridge University Press, 1989.
Rojas Villadrando, Agustín. *El viaje entretenido*, ed. Jacques Joset. Madrid: Espasa Calpe, 1977. 2 vols.
Taylor, Scott K. *Honor and Violence in Golden Age Spain*. New Haven: Yale University Press, 2008.
Vidler, Laura. *Performance Reconstruction and Spanish Golden Age Drama: Reviving and Revising the Comedia*. New York: Palgrave, 2014.

Translator's Note

The reader of the five translations of Spanish Golden Age *comedias* published in this volume may be surprised to find that these renderings employ meter and rhyme. The analogical-form method used here attempts to convey a greater sense of the constitutive poetic structures so essential to these verse dramas, yet too often neglected in modern prosified versions. Using a form that, according to James S. Holmes, fulfills "a parallel function" within the target language, these translations seek to lend an otherwise lost historicity to these sixteenth- and seventeenth-century works while "naturalizing" them for English-language audiences. Thus, the typical Romance-language verse line, the eleven-syllable *endecasílabo*, appears throughout in iambic pentameter. This conversion of a syllabic into a syllabic-stress meter to which the target-language reader/viewer is more accustomed similarly takes place when the shorter eight-syllable *octosílabo* is rendered in iambic tetrameter (with corresponding rhymes whenever four of these lines combine to form a *redondilla*). I have divided the longer, narrative *romance* passages, in which the same assonantal rhyme occurs in alternating octosyllabic lines, into more easily digestible quatrains with off rhymes, sometimes having to forge a six-line unit when there is a two-line remainder. Sonnets, where they appear, should be recognizable as such.

As one might imagine, effecting a desirable balance between content—still the principal focus of translation, including that of verse drama—and other textual features encompassing not only questions of form but also of style, tone, sound, and so forth, can be a challenging task. To achieve this goal, the translator must inevitably resort to what J. C. Catford calls "shifts," or later translation studies scholars such as Gerardo Vázquez-Ayora call the "procedimientos técnicos" (technical procedures or operations) of translation. These include such strategies as omission (the deletion of a source-text element), amplification (the use of more elements in the target text), modulation (a shift in perspective), equivalence (finding a functional correlative for a saying, expression, etc.), explicitation (the addition of interpretive or explanatory words), and adaptation (cultural correlation). More useful still are transposition, a simple shift in grammatical categories, and compensation in place or kind, which permits translators to introduce source-text features and elements at different points in their rendering, thus affording themselves greater flexibility than that proffered through rigid "rank-bound" correlation (Catford again). Translators similarly do well to allow themselves a more expansive "unit of translation," eschewing the limitations of needing to match word with word, phrase with phrase, line with line, and so forth, while ensuring that all features they wish to convey appear somewhere (appropriately, one would hope) in the target text at large. Of course, these procedures involve primarily linguistically based decisions and do not take into consideration the equally important issues of cultural siting, textual function, and (a prevailing concern of mine) aesthetic reception.

That all five translations here are retranslations should not be lost on the volume's reader. Their plain intent is to serve effectively as versions to be read for classroom instruction as well as used for performance onstage as living scripts. In the case of Pedro Calderón de la Barca's *La vida es sueño*, perhaps Spain's preeminent Golden Age drama (and the best known to English-language audiences), some thirty English translations predate my own. In the case of Félix Lope de Vega's *Fuenteovejuna* (perhaps the second play on this imaginary list of canonical favorites), there are somewhat fewer, but still two dozen or so translations, followed by Lope's *El perro del hortelano*, Miguel de Cervantes' *La destrucción de Numancia*, and Sor Juana Inés de la Cruz's *Los empeños de una casa*, with a handful each. Revised somewhat for this critical edition, *Life Is a Dream* and *Fuenteovejuna* previously appeared in *The Norton Anthology of Drama*, Vol. 1, for which J. Ellen Gainor, the skilled editor with whom I worked most closely at that time, posited four main criteria: "linguistic accuracy, stylistic accuracy (as much as possible), readability (for the contemporary student), and playability (from a theatrical perspective—especially acting)." I believe these same standards remained very much in play under the editorship of Barbara Fuchs for the present volume, and that the recent analogical-form renderings of all five of these dramas were commissioned by W. W. Norton & Company to achieve precisely these goals.

Barbara's expertise in Spanish Golden Age theater has proved invaluable for the present collaboration. For this nearly four-year project, with editor and translator residing on opposite coasts of the country, I would send Barbara each translation only upon completion of a draft. After having consulted numerous Spanish-language editions of these works (as did I), Barbara would send me her comments for revision, a long process that took place entirely through e-mail correspondence. Sometimes, I am humbled to admit, her requested emendations concerned my simple misprisions of Renaissance Spanish, which I was only too happy to correct. Other times, Barbara would variously ask me to remain closer to a passage's meaning, or simplify my structure and syntax, or capture an expression in a more nuanced way, or pay closer attention to the tone of a speech by, say, a child or servant or character in emotional throes. Barbara's trove of knowledge and insight regarding her specialization additionally relieved me, as translator, of the difficult duties of assigning lines to characters or inserting stage directions when the various editions we consulted differed on these matters. In one instance in which no amount of translational skill could have justified a rendering, Barbara pointed out to me that a section of Spain's speech in Act I of *The Siege of Numantia* likely referred to mining; in another, that the Countess of Belflor in *The Dog in the Manger* did not reside in an isolated castle but a mansion in the heart of Naples. Her understanding of diverse historical periods thus led to considerable revision, and this volume owes a great debt to her patient guidance and steady stewardship. Any perceived shortcomings in the translations remain, of course, my own.

It may sound strange that a theater translator would expect his/her rendering to serve both reader and actor equally well, but a page/stage divide regarding the intended use and audience for theater translation has been in existence since at least the early nineteenth century. Three lines of the sorcerer Marquino in Gordon Willoughby James Gyll's 1870 translation *Numantia, a Tragedy*, too comically illustrate this dread impasse: "Of Hades' king, who, in the gloomy realm / Of souls perverse, dire ministers betwixt, / Does thee retain to reign o'er lot and chance." Clearly, the qualities embodied by the coined words "speakability" and "playability"—key to the methodology informing the five renderings published here—have been absent in some earlier versions. Phyllis Zatlin thus distinguishes between the translated "theatre" or "performance text" to be used for staged productions and the "drama" or "literary text" to be used for publication and reading. I concur with her judgment that for a translation of a theatrical work to be considered viable, it must be created with performance in mind, although this in no way precludes its alternative function as a pedagogical tool or reading text. Indeed, my versions of both *Life Is a Dream* and *Fuenteovejuna* have to date enjoyed full stagings. It is my hope that all five retranslations of Spanish Golden Age plays in this volume position themselves effectively against earlier English-language renderings as the contemporary versions that best historicize and poeticize their now distant source texts.

As such, they invite future collaborations with directors, dramaturges, and actors for the English-speaking stage. These first two categories of theater practitioners might well prefer adaptations to fit an ensemble cast and/or particular performance spaces, and thus to have begun collaboration with the translator at an earlier stage—perhaps even before a rendering is undertaken. This tendency to consolidate creative control over not only the staging but also the language of the translation, though, too often results in the current vogue for a flat, prosy, modernized diction that severs the source text from its cultural and historical provenance. Since form and content are less easily divisible in practice than in theory, this leveling of poetic discourse can have a negative effect on meaning as well. The retranslations here thus unabashedly demonstrate what Sirku Aaltonen calls "reverence" for the canonical source text in that each effects the translation of the Spanish-language original in its entirety (requisite shifts, including omissions, notwithstanding). As with past productions of the works in translation cited above, a director or dramaturge will always be free to pare lines and/or (re)focus attention on any part(s) of these living scripts for performance. For this reason, and because of the ever-shifting horizons involved in textual enactment, both reader and theatergoer should experience a fresh take on each of these plays during every encounter.

G. J. RACZ

WORKS CITED

Aaltonen, Sirku. *Time-Sharing on Stage: Drama Translation in Theatre and Society*. Clevedon: Multilingual Matters Ltd., Topics in Translation 17, 2000.

Catford, J. C. *A Linguistic Theory of Translation*. London: Oxford University Press, 1975 (1965).

Gainor, J. Ellen. E-mail correspondence of September 23, 2006.

Gainor, J. Ellen, Stanton B. Garner, Jr., and Martin Puchner, eds. *The Norton Anthology of Drama*, Vol. 1: *Antiquity through the Eighteenth Century*. New York and London: W. W. Norton & Co., 2009.

Gyll, Gordon Willoughby James, trans. *The Voyage to Parnassus; Numantia, a Tragedy; The Commerce of Algiers*. By Miguel de Cervantes Saavedra. London, 1870.

Holmes, James S. "Forms of Verse Translation and the Translation of Verse Forms." In *The Nature of Translation: Essays on the Theory and Practice of Literary Translation*. Ed. James S. Holmes. Mouton, The Hague, Paris: Publishing House of the Slovak Academy of Sciences Bratislava, 1970. 91–105.

Vázquez-Ayora, Gerardo. *Introducción a la traductología*. Washington, D.C.: Georgetown University Press, 1977.

Zatlin, Phyllis. *Theatrical Translation and Film Adaptation: A Practitioner's View*. Clevedon: Multilingual Matters Ltd., Topics in Translation 29, 2005.

The Texts of
THE PLAYS

MIGUEL DE CERVANTES SAAVEDRA
The Siege of Numantia† (*Numancia*)

CHARACTERS

The Roman Camp	*The Brave Numantines*	
SCIPIO	MARANDRO	PAGES
JUGURTHA	CARAVINO	MAN
CAIUS MARIUS	THEOGENES	MILVIO
QUINTUS FABIUS	LEONCIO	BODY
1ST SOLDIER	LYRA	1ST WOMAN
2ND SOLDIER	MARQUINO, a sorcerer	2ND WOMAN
HERMILIUS	1ST AMBASSADOR	3RD WOMAN
LIMPIUS	2ND AMBASSADOR	4TH WOMAN
	1ST HIGH PRIEST	1ST BROTHER
Allegorical Figures	2ND HIGH PRIEST	2ND BROTHER
SPAIN	1ST GOVERNOR	MOTHER
DOURO River	2ND GOVERNOR	STARVING SON
THREE CHILDREN, representing rivulets	3RD GOVERNOR	BOY, Lyra's brother
	4TH GOVERNOR	SOLDIER
DEMON		WIFE of Theogenes
WAR	PAGE	SON of Theogenes
ILLNESS	BARIATO, a boy	DAUGHTER of Theogenes
HUNGER	SERVIO, a boy	
FAME	NUMANTINE	

The action takes place in and around the Spanish city of Numantia near the end of the second century B.C.E.

† Translated by G. J. Racz for this Norton Critical Edition.

3

Act I

[*The Romans* SCIPIO, JUGURTHA, CAIUS MARIUS, *and Scipio's brother* QUINTUS FABIUS *enter.*]

SCIPIO   This arduous and difficult campaign
   The Roman senate's left to my command
   Has brought me such fatigue and mental strain,
   What further rigors can my mind withstand?
   I've seen so many Roman soldiers slain   5
   In this uncommon war, still much at hand.
   Who wouldn't wish to see it over, then?
   Oh, who'd not fear to lead the charge again?
JUGURTHA   Who, Scipio? Who besides you boasts the force
   And valor requisite to end this fight?   10
   Your venturousness alone will be our source
   Of triumph here as Rome asserts its might.
SCIPIO   Though power steer a more judicious course,
   It still may level mountains from their height,
   But when such strength, demented, knows no bounds,   15
   A rocky heap replaces once smooth grounds.
   Our challenge hardly lies in lack of zeal,
   The present army showing that and more,
   Abjuring victory and the common weal
   As they licentiously carouse and whore.   20
   It's time I instituted an appeal
   To turn their motivations back to war.
   Before we can defeat our enemies,
   Our friends must leave off their debaucheries.
   Where's Marius?
CAIUS MARIUS   Sir!
SCIPIO   Go out and spread the word   25
   Among the troops that I would have them all
   Appear forthwith before me, undeterred
   By any circumstance that might forestall
   Their coming. I've a speech I would they heard
   About my plans.
CAIUS MARIUS   Sir, I'll put out the call.   30
SCIPIO   Be off, then, for it's best the soldiers knew
   Their conduct hinders all we've yet to do.
                                    [CAIUS MARIUS *exits.*]
JUGURTHA   There's not a Roman soldier to be found
   Who doesn't feel for you both love and fear
   So, as your valor's known the world around   35
   From southern pole to northern hemisphere,
   Each one of these who hears the trumpet sound
   Will rouse his martial spirit and appear
   Desirous to surpass brave feats of yore,
   The stuff of legends entered into lore.   40
SCIPIO   Jugurtha, it remains of uppermost
   Importance that this license be restrained.

Should it run rampant, which of us could boast
A reputation properly attained?
If such a common evil to our post   45
Takes root among the troops, its fire unchained,
We'll find the enemy we've on our hands
Is vice and not the people of these lands.
[*Drums sound, leading the* SOLDIERS *to assemble, and the*
following command is read aloud offstage.]
By order of the general:
All soldiers with their arms repair   50
For muster to the army square
Where absence won't be answerable.
Should it be learned a man has missed
The discourse Scipio would declaim,
As punishment he'll have his name   55
Deleted from the squadron's list.
JUGURTHA   I've no doubt, sir, that there's a pressing need
To harness forces with an iron bit.
A short rein's best employed when soldiers lead
The lives that their intemperance will permit.   60
An army's power weakens when it's freed
To vice, which renders fighting men unfit.
Not all the pennons or the flags we fly
Could ever give this patent truth the lie.
[*An array of* SOLDIERS *enter, armed in the ancient fashion, with*
CAIUS MARIUS. SCIPIO *mounts a boulder to address them.*]
SCIPIO   By all the noble bearing that attends   65
The martial pomp emblazoning this throng,
I recognize you all as Romans, friends—
Yes, Romans, I say—spirited and strong!
But seeing hands so delicate offends
Along with pasty faces that belong   70
On pallid Britons with their lack of swarth
Or offspring of the Flemish in the north.
Your riotous revelries, which late suppose
Disinclination on your part to fight,
Have given life again to fallen foes   75
And cast doubt on our military might.
These unbreached city walls that still enclose
The Numantines shed more unflattering light
Upon the dissipation of your fame,
Renown distinctly Roman but in name.   80
Hold you our rank so worthy of disdain?
The whole world trembles at it in respect
But for your middling efforts here in Spain,
Where Rome now sees its skill in warfare checked.
Why this strange negligence? I can explain   85
Such laxity, if I'm not incorrect,
As born of sloth allowed to reign at length,
The mortal enemy of martial strength.

No, steely Mars can never cede his heart
To tender Venus like a lover yields,   90
For she pursues sweet treats and he the art
Of bloody war with all that power wields.
So let the Cyprian goddess[1] here depart,
Absconding with her son from out these fields,
For army lodgings will seem harsh and spare   95
To ones more used to feasts and savory fare.
More arms exist for breaking down a wall
Than battering rams rough-hewn and metal-tipped,
And more's required when raging battles call
Than hosts of soldiers heavily equipped.   100
Devoid of reasoning, which senses all,
Sheer force will find its powers largely stripped.
What good are all the squads, then, in the world
Or all the weaponry our men have hurled?
For even when a modest army's lines   105
Deploy in concert toward a common end,
You'll see as clearly as our own sun shines
The gains in war for which our troops contend.
But should a little world of men show signs
It lacks the fight on which campaigns depend,   110
That force will be defeated by a side
Not larger, but with discipline and pride.
You ought to be embarrassed as a corps
To see your battle-tested selves so pressed
To crush this haughty remnant of the poor,   115
Brave Spaniards who defend Numantia's nest.
For sixteen years or more we've waged cruel war
And still this motley band can boast they best
A Roman force that numbers thousands here
By dint of murderous hands that show no fear.   120
You're vanquishing yourselves! You'll see all lost
Succumbing to these tempting female charms.
With Venus smitten and with Bacchus[2] sauced,
You're barely of a mind to take up arms.
So be ashamed if blushes haven't crossed   125
Your faces while this small contingent harms
Rome's vast renown by staving off defeat,
Insulting us by spurning to be beat.
From this day forth, I hereby do decree
All prostitutes be banished from this space.   130
I deem their presence mid your ranks to be
The major cause impelling our disgrace.
One cup of wine per soldier, you'll agree,
Will also do, while each man will replace
The bedding where once harlots could be found   135

---

1. Venus (Aphrodite), the Roman goddess of love, was supposedly born on the island of Cyprus.
Mars (Ares): the Roman god of war.
2. Roman god of wine.

With mattresses of straw upon the ground.
The only perfumes I'll permit a man
To smell of will be rosin and black tar.
Now, woe to him who'd tote around a pan
Obsessed with thoughts of where the mess tents are!   140
Indulge yourselves by flouting what I ban
And you'll soon find that armor feels bizarre.
I'll have no mincing ways or courtships thrive
While there's a single Spaniard left alive.
Don't think that by these edicts I abuse   145
My just command with impudent disdain,
For in the end you'll see how men who choose
Such moral codes win all they'd hoped to gain.
Bad habits, once ingrained, are hard to lose;
Yet better, new-found customs hence will reign.   150
Should past proclivities endure, this war
Will just drag on, to Rome one insult more.
Between soft sheets, mid frolic or drunk spree,
Hard-driving Mars can hardly lie sedate.
He seeks some other road and way to be,   155
Some other arms to raise his flags of state.
Each person fashions his own destiny,
As fickle Fortune plays no role in fate.
Bad luck is brought about by indolence;
Empires and monarchies by diligence.   160
So confident am I that in my sight
Stand naught but stalwart Roman citizens,
I hold these Spaniards' walled resistance slight,
A desperate endgame of barbarians.
I promise you, upon my word and might,   165
Should your hands equal your souls' regimens,
My hands will mete out what rewards you've won
While praises from these lips shan't be outdone.
        [*The* SOLDIERS *look at one another and gesture for* CAIUS MARIUS
        to respond for them all.]
CAIUS MARIUS   Illustrious general, as your eyes have gazed
Directly on the faces of the men   170
Who did attend your speech, which justly raised
Concerns that should be brought within their ken,
You doubtlessly saw none of them unfazed,
Some ashen-white, some reddening now and then,
Both signs of fear and shame the soldiers feel,   175
Demoralized, rebuked and down at heel.
Perceiving how their roguish acts reduce
A soldier's standing, sir, explains their shame.
Reproached thus, they're abashed they've no excuse
For faults for which they've no one else to blame.   180
Their fear stems from their guilt for a profuse
Inaction and misconduct they'd disclaim.
They'd sooner die than see themselves abide
Malfeasance that has left them mortified.

There's time and place enough to compensate   185
For chronic ailments born of wayward bents,
A consolation that should mitigate
The gravity of any past offense.
Our lowest-ranking soldier shan't await
A second call to prove his mettle hence.   190
Each pledges here his honor, life and home
To dutifully and loyally serve Rome.
Accept this offering of our wherewithal,
The stout assurance of these valiant bands,
For, in the end, the general will recall   195
That it's a Roman legion he commands.
Now, as a sign you here agree with all
I've said on your behalf, raise your right hands.
1ST SOLDIER   We swear that everything's as you've averred.
2ND SOLDIER   We swear it.
ALL   Yes, it's true upon our word.   200
SCIPIO   My growing trust in you affords me ease
And this commitment's pleasing to my ears,
A fire growing in you by degrees
As you reform the lives you've led for years.
Don't let these vows be borne off by the breeze;   205
Affirm them on the points of stalwart spears.
The more your valor backs these oaths for you,
The more my own espousals will come true.
1ST SOLDIER   Two envoys from Numantia come this way,
Sir, with safe-conduct, for an audience.   210
SCIPIO   So let them enter. Why the long delay?
1ST SOLDIER   They seek your leave first, out of deference.
SCIPIO   If they're ambassadors, they'll have their say.
1ST SOLDIER   They are, sir.
SCIPIO   Show them in. One consequence
Of talks with foes who put aside their shields   215
Is gleaning the intelligence it yields,
No matter how unfrank a front they mount.
What falsehood ever covered truth so well
The smallest crack did not provide a fount
Of facts for those who know what secrets spell?   220
In meeting with your rivals, you can count
On learning more than they would freely tell.
My many years in war will, in effect,
Prove everything I tell you is correct.
        [*Two* AMBASSADORS *from Numantia enter.*]
1ST AMBASSADOR   If your consent to hear our pleas be shown,   225
I've motions from the city to convey.
Would you prefer we spoke with you alone
Or here before your soldiers straightaway?
SCIPIO   No matter. Speak and let your thoughts be known.
1ST AMBASSADOR   Most noble sir, as your frank words allay   230
Misgivings for our safety, I'll disclose

The nature of the offer we propose.
Illustrious general, as a native son
Of our aggrieved Numantia, I've been sent
To you, Rome's bravest officer bar none—   235
Whom night nor day has ever seen relent—
To offer friendship's hand and see us done
With this long strife in which lost years were spent,
Preventing future woe that yet betides
Our wretched peoples suffering on both sides.   240
Numantia never would have flouted laws
The Roman Senate essayed to enforce
Had tyrant consuls here not given pause
Through savage rule, our uprising's true source.
Harsh statutes joined with avarice were the cause   245
Of our proud city's following this course,
Which placed upon us such an onerous load,
We sloughed off both its yoke and legal code.
In time, we didn't think it possible
That cruelties like these would be cut short   250
Until you came, the first real general
To entertain a truce of any sort.
So now that Fate has deemed it best to pull
Our raging craft toward your pacific port,
We've gathered in our sails of war to ease   255
A quick cessation to hostilities.
Don't think we sue for peace as people prone
To fear, although our urgency's acute.
Through harsh travails these many years we've shown
A fortitude that's far beyond dispute.   260
Your virtue and your gallantry alone
Embolden the besieged to bring this suit,
Convinced that we'd attain no better end
Than having you our master and our friend.
That's why we've come and where our council stands.   265
We make bold now to ask for your thoughts, too.
SCIPIO   This late repentance of beleaguered bands
Is no enticement to be friends with you.
Go back to waging war with rebel hands—
I'd like to size up what my own can do   270
As these now hold in trust what Fortune craves:
Rome's glory built upon your city's graves.
Your call for peace is hardly recompense
For shameful insurrection these long years.
Let casualties ensue from your offense   275
Until our past dominion reappears.
1ST AMBASSADOR   Delusion follows from false confidence,
So heed the course your prideful answer steers:
Deriding such a reasoned truce outright
Will only harden our resolve to fight.   280
This turning down of peace our city tried

Negotiating earnestly today
Will make our cause appear more justified
In heaven's eyes, where views of justice lay.
You'll feel, before you ever step inside   285
Numantia's limits, just how far away
The fury of a foe may be discerned
When cast into a friend and vassal spurned.

SCIPIO   So, have you more to say?

1ST AMBASSADOR   In deeds, not speech,
But only, sir, because you'd have it so,   290
Rejecting the proposals we beseech
And tarnishing this grandeur you would show.
The legions you command will feel our reach
The moment you decide to strike your blow,
For coming here as envoys for a truce   295
Is different far from letting violence loose.

SCIPIO   That's true, but just so you four comprehend
How much I've learned of treaties from command,
I'd never deign to call your kind our friend
Or ever look with friendship on your land.   300
You'd best turn back. This meeting's at an end.

1ST AMBASSADOR   Your final word, are we to understand?

SCIPIO   I've spoken! Now, be off!

2ND AMBASSADOR   We'll hear no more,
For Numantines were bred with zeal for war!

                      [*The* AMBASSADORS *exit.*]

QUINTUS FABIUS   Our former lack of discipline imparts   305
A certain swagger to the rant you gave
Although the new time now upon us charts
Our path toward glory on Numantia's grave.

SCIPIO   Yes, idle bluster ill suits noble hearts,
For Fortune backs the honorable and brave.   310
Your own bluff, Fabius, would be best concealed;
Display your valor on the battlefield
Although I'm strategizing other ways
Of vanquishing Numantia absent force,
Some means of winning yet the highest praise   315
Through their surrender. Left but this recourse,
Demoralized and reeling in a daze,
They'll turn their furor inward on its source:
We'll dig a ditch so deep and of such breadth
Around their city, they'll all starve to death.   320
No more shall any Roman soldiers bleed
Their lives out just to stain this foreign earth
And what these Spaniards shed here is indeed
Enough. Of long, cruel war there's been no dearth.
Begin the excavation and proceed   325
To make the ditch of proper width and girth.
Daub one another, comrades, with this mud
Instead of being caked in rivals' blood!
Let no man be exempted from this toil,

However high his rank amid our corps.   330
Work side by side with soldiers shouldn't roil
Decurions[3] deployed on that same score.
I'll likewise show how I can break this soil
And make a shovel seem an arm of war.
Allied thus, you'll see, doing as I do,   335
That I can keep up with the best of you.
QUINTUS FABIUS   My brother and most worthy general,
Sagacious and astute as all can see!
You're right that it would be a terrible
Mistake or simple lapse of sanity   340
To fight this godforsaken, pitiful
And crazed lot holding out so fractiously.
Yes, let's confine them midst their city walls
Until their endless lust for combat palls
And leave them no escape on any side,   345
Except, perhaps, along the riverbank.
SCIPIO   Then help us carry out this rarefied
Design to hem them in on every flank.
If all goes well and heaven is our guide,
We'll only have propitious skies to thank,   350
For Spain will be Rome's vassal, tamed once more,
If we can break her haughtiness in war.
    [SCIPIO *and* QUINTUS FABIUS *exit, and* SPAIN *enters, crowned*
    by towers. She carries in her hand a castle meant to represent
    the land she portrays.]
SPAIN   Oh, mighty heavens, vast, serene, and grand,
Whose nurturing rays and rains have fertilized
My territory's swaths of fecund land,   355
Thus making it above all others prized,
Be moved again to lend your helping hand,
As it's your wont to aid the tyrannized,
And shower me in grace, as you've been prone:
I'm still your Spain, forsaken and alone.   360
For wasn't it enough in years gone by
To scorch my limbs with daylight's fiery streaks
Or so expose my vitals to the sky
That one could see the damned and hear their shrieks
Or let cruel tyrants drain my riches dry,   365
Subdued by the Phoenicians, then the Greeks
Because my subjugation either served
Your plans or made plain what my vice deserved?
Can it be possible that Destiny
Ordains me as these other nations' slave   370
Or that I'll never have the chance to see
The flag of all my freeborn people wave?
Alas, you've every right to burden me
With woes in light of how my sons behave.

---

3. Roman cavalry officers who commanded ten men.

Though brave and worthy, each obeys the laws   375
His soul desires, eschewing common cause.
These brothers haven't once in word or deed
Conjoined their mutual interests with accord;
In fact, the greater one might judge this need,
The more their disharmonious spirits warred.   380
Their quarrels all but ushered in the greed
Of conquest shown by each barbarian horde
That reached here in successive waves to seize
My treasures, lucre, wealth and properties.
Now only brave Numantia makes a stand,   385
Its shining swords unsheathed against cruel foes
To safeguard liberty within its land
While townsmen perish as their brave blood flows.
But, oh! I see its sorry end at hand
And glimpse its death forthcoming mid these throes.   390
Its life may cease for now, but not its fame,
A Phoenix[4] poised to rise from out its flame.
It seems these fearsome Romans, who once fought
For victory, opt now slyly to contain
The Numantines and win a war not fought   395
But one avoiding any rough campaign.
If only these maneuvers came to naught
And all their tactics proved to be in vain!
Then my small city could be left to thrive
And, thus escaping sure defeat, survive.   400
But sadly now its enemies beset
These vulnerable walls as they surround
The city with an even greater threat
Than that for which the Romans are renowned:
A ditch, the likes of which has never yet   405
Begird a city's plains upon dry ground
And offering but one way to be defied,
An undug sector on the riverside.
So here, then, are the tragic Numantines
Ensconced within the confines of their walls,   410
Protected from assaults by war machines—
No sallies or sorties, so warring stalls.
They bristle realizing they've lost the means
To fight in self-defense and unleash calls
In strident tones, all clamoring with one breath   415
For combat on the battlefield or death.
Here where the Douro River in this hour
Of need meets land to form the city's marge
Now seems the only place that might empower
These prisoners to fight again at large,   420
Before Rome builds a catapult or tower
Within your waters, mighty surge, I charge

---

4. The phoenix was a mythical bird that immolated itself on a self-built pyre and was reborn from
its own ashes.

You, river, famed for this great length you span,
Assist my people any way you can.
May you, oh noble Douro, whose sleek turns   425
Have laved my heartland's soil since days of old,
Much like my pleasant Tagus[5] still discerns,
Observe beneath your own flows sands of gold
And have swift-footed nymphs that traipse the ferns
These verdant woods and meadows now enfold   430
Live mid your stream and, when its glass impels,
Give freely of their favors mid your swells.
May you, too, lend an ear to my lament
And bend it closer to my plaints although
It move you from the place you're most content.   435
I beg of you, hence, not to halt your flow
For, if with your continuous ascent
You can't avenge me of this savage foe,
What other self-defense might we assume
To save Numantia from impending doom?   440
        [*The* DOURO *River enters with three children dressed as the*
        tributary rivulets that flow into it near Soria, which was
        Numantia at that time.]
DOURO   Dear Mother Spain, I haven't heard dismay
From you for years, but see whence these woes stem.
If I've been slow to leave my waterway,
It's just because I've no response for them.
Behold the advent of this fatal day: 445
Numantia's now a place the stars condemn
And, as this is the case, I fear it's sure
The city's maladies will find no cure.
Urbion, Revinuesa and Tera[6] clear,
All tributaries that increase my height,   450
Have filled my watercourse to bursting here
And nearly covered up my banks from sight.
The Romans, though, as if I were a mere
Millstream with currents cause for little fright,
Foresee new dams and towers to speed this war,   455
The likes of which you've never seen before.
As it appears harsh Destiny ordains
That your beloved Numantia will soon meet
The end dread fate's prescribed, as war's cruel strains
Have rendered its demise all but complete,   460
One cheering consolation yet remains:
The sunshine of heroic deeds will beat
Back shadows of oblivion on this stage
And be recalled in every coming age.
So while it's true your fertile fields may sense   465
Their subjugation under Rome's cruel heel,
A dire oppression and reviled offense

---

5. The Tagus and the Douro are two of the main rivers of the Iberian Peninsula.
6. Smaller rivers that flow into the Douro.

Our foes discharge with excess pride and zeal,
The time will come, since I foresee events
As Proteus[7] did, when History will reveal   470
The grandeur of these haughty Romans checked
Precisely by the Spain they now subject.
From distant nations, peoples will aspire
To reach your fecund plots and settle down,
Then, in accord with what you most desire,   475
Expel the Romans for a different crown.
The Goths, arrayed in splendorous attire,
Will leave signs everywhere of their renown
As they seek nurture in your bosom's store
And highlight their heroic feats once more.   480
In future years your humbling injuries
Will be avenged by fierce Attila's hand.
His Huns[8] will bring the Romans to their knees,
Enthralled to foreign laws in their own land.
With aid from men abroad, your sons will seize   485
Once sovereign Rome and take their fervent stand
Outside the Vatican, whose papal head,
The helmsman of God's ship, will just have fled.
The time will come again when Spanish swords
Will rightly hover over Roman necks[9]   490
Which, through the goodness of their overlords,
Will live to breathe again the air's effects.
The Duke of Alba will retreat, then, towards
A more secure locale when he suspects
A lack of parity with Rome's vast force—   495
In numbers, not in bravery, of course.[1]
Once all your stout inhabitants will know
Who's rightful Maker of the earth and sky,
God's one true viceroy here on earth below
Will be installed as pope, whereby   500
He'll give your kings and queens a name to go
Along with all their faith and zeal imply—
The "Catholic"[2]—whose sure rule of your domain
Will worthily succeed the Goths' long reign.
The one, though, who'll attain the sort of fame   505
That shouts your honor loudly through the streets,
Assuring that the status of your name
Surpasses all with which your state competes,
Will be another king my visions frame

---

7. Charged with tending Neptune's (Poseidon's) aquatic flocks, the mythological sea-god Proteus was rewarded for his efforts with the gift of prophecy.
8. Attila was the leader of the Hunnic empire, a confederation of nomadic tribes including Huns, Ostrogoths, and Alans that invaded both the Eastern and the Western Roman Empires in the fifth century.
9. An allusion to the sack of Rome by the troops of Charles V, king of Spain and Holy Roman Emperor, in 1527.
1. The Duke of Alba was general of the Spanish forces in Italy. In 1557, he marched on Rome after his victory against the French at the battle of St. Quentin.
2. Alludes to Ferdinand of Aragon and Isabel (or Isabella) of Castile, fifteenth-century rulers who unified Spain and were known as the Catholic Monarchs.

As one who'll carry out the greatest feats.   510
The world his, he'll be known to everyone:
The second Philip[3]—second, though, to none.
Your separate realms, whose self-rule up to then
Afforded you good reason to bemoan,
Will be united as one empire when   515
He comes to rule them from a common throne.
That strip of Lusitania will again
Be part of your whole fabric, rightly sewn
Back into glorious Castille's frontiers,
Restoring your expanse of former years.[4]   520
A thousand foreign lands will envy you,
Beloved Spain, as well as live in fear
Your swords, tinged red with blood, may run them through
As waves of your triumphant flags appear.
Let inklings of these happier times in view   525
Console you for a present that looks drear:
As cruel Fate has ordained Numantia's fall,
There's no escaping Destiny at all.
SPAIN   I thank you, lauded Douro, for you've brought
My current suffering a dose of ease.   530
Indeed, I can't imagine there'll be aught
That proves deceptive in these prophecies.
DOURO   Yes, you may rest assured that there'll be naught,
Though glad times may not come for centuries.
Farewell! My nymphs attend upon the rill.   535
SPAIN   May heaven make your waters clearer still!

Act II

[THEOGENES *and* CARAVINO *enter with four* GOVERNORS *of
Numantia and the sorcerer* MARQUINO. *They sit in council.*]
THEOGENES   It does appear a fact, good gentlemen,
That Fate's dark signs and contrary displays
Bode ill for each and every citizen.
The fabric of our resoluteness frays   540
The more these Romans basely close us in
To seal our ruin using craven ways.
Our one means out remained to kill or die,
But now we'll have to all sprout wings and fly.
Not only does our enemy awake   545
To steal back victories we'd thought complete,
They're even joined by traitors who partake
In slitting Spanish throats from street to street.
May heaven curse the fealty they forsake
And hurl down lightning bolts to strike the feet   550
Of treasonists who'd turn against their friends,

3. Philip II of Spain (1527–1598).
4. In 1580, Philip II annexed Portugal—the Roman province of Lusitania—to the Spanish
Crown.

A perfidy the sky above forfends.
What tactics can our governors contrive
To stay Numantia's course toward certain doom?
Extended sieges end with none alive   555
And send all rivals to an early tomb.
This Roman ditch's breadth and depth deprive
Our troops of staked positions they'd assume
On battlefields, where strong arms make it possible
To overcome whatever obstacle.   560
CARAVINO   If sovereign Jupiter[1] but found it meet
To see our youths unleashed against this foe,
They'd deal Rome ignominious defeat,
Each army trading blow for fearsome blow.
Our forces' courage in the field would greet   565
The scourge of death with scarce a worried show
And forge a pathway offering some means
Of health and surety for all Numantines.
But since we tarry locked up in this place
Like women jealous husbands keep from sight,   570
Let's muster all our strength to shun disgrace,
Reveal our spirit's mettle and invite
A champion from out their ranks to face
In single combat one we'll choose to fight.
Fatigued by so prolonged a siege, they may   575
Just wish to end the conflict in this way.
Should said proposal not meet with success,
However just its premises appear,
We'd have one other recourse nonetheless,
Although it's far more arduous, I fear: 580
That ditch and wall preventing our egress,
Which stay our contact with the Romans here,
Could well be stormed at nighttime on a raid
So we might seek out friends who'll lend us aid.
1ST GOVERNOR   It's but through death, then, or this
        ditch's breach   585
That we create an opening for our lives.
Since death's horrendous pain extends its reach
The more a person's will to draw breath thrives,
Death's cure may be what miseries beseech
Before the moment we submit arrives,   590
Though dying can be most magnificent
When honor warrants its ennoblement.
2ND GOVERNOR   How much more honor can our souls display
In staunchly shuffling off this mortal coil
Than entering once again the Roman fray   595
And, spilling blood, thus prove their worthy foil?
Let any coward here among us stay
Within the confines of our city's soil
As I, for one, would much more happily yield

---

1. Chief Roman god, also known in English as Jove, or Zeus in Greek mythology.

To death in Roman ditch or open field.   600
3RD GOVERNOR   This hunger hounding us on every side
     And certain to consume us to a man
     Compels assent to all you've signified,
     Though yours does seem a rash and risky plan.
     In death we'd one less insult to abide,   605
     So let those souls averse to starving span
     This ditch's breadth with me and forge a path
     To cure our ills with lances, swords and wrath!
4TH GOVERNOR   Before this grueling course of action goes
     Ahead as planned, as now I fear it must,   610
     I think it wise we proffer to our foes
     That chance for single combat we've discussed.
     Let our man and the champion they propose
     Be led to open field on terms of trust
     Where either soldier's death will mean we're done   615
     With battle and the victor's camp has won.
     The Romans, arrogant and overproud,
     Will deem the challenge one they can't ignore.
     Their answering this call, both sides unbowed,
     Will mean our cares may well end with this war,   620
     For there's one here among us who's endowed
     With combat skill and bravery to his core.
     Were he dispatched to fight not one, but three,
     He'd still deny the Romans victory.
     As we've a seer, too, famed near and far,   625
     The sorcerer Marquino, let's devise
     He survey every planet, moon and star
     For augurs of escape or dread demise
     And thus determine what our chances are
     Of living through this dubious siege, just skies,   630
     And fully vanquishing our dogged scourge
     So we end up the victors that emerge.
     First, though, I recommend Marquino make
     A solemn sacrifice to Jupiter,
     An act of reverence we should undertake   635
     To reap the many favors he'd confer.
     Let's pause to heal our own deep wounds and break
     These habits born of vice so we might spur
     An inauspicious heaven's forces thus
     To look down more propitiously on us.   640
     The opportunity is always there
     For anyone who's desperate to die,
     As dying grants a soul the chance to bare
     Its valor when both time and place comply.
     Should we proceed as planned, then, or prepare   645
     Another course, in that the hours fly?
     If you've a different aim in mind, don't stall,
     But let it be a better road for all.
MARQUINO   I hear you and wholeheartedly endorse
     The actions that the governors find meet.   650

We'll make all fit oblations in due course
And lay our challenge at the Romans' feet.
I'll not lose any chance to show the force
Of this dark science that I now entreat:
I'll pluck a soul from out the depths below   655
Who'll forecast better days or future woe.
THEOGENES   Then let me be the first to volunteer
To meet whichever champion they choose
If you still think they'll send a soldier here
And have sufficient faith that I won't lose.   660
CARAVINO   To all us gathered round, your valor's clear.
Your prowess, though, is such that we should use
These talents you possess for greater deeds,
The best of men our city sorely needs.
So, since our people to a man stand fast   665
In claiming that you rightly hold this post
And, you being first, I deem myself the last,
I'll pose our challenge to this Roman host.
1ST GOVERNOR   I stand with all our people in my vast
Desire to carry out what Jove loves most.   670
I'll see what votive offering imparts,
As sacrifice flows freely out pure hearts.
2ND GOVERNOR   Let's, then, depart from here in all due haste
And press those acts we hope will end this war
As savage hunger's laying savage waste   675
To multitudes already at death's door.
If heaven has decreed we be effaced
Before our troops can settle this long score,
May these late acts of penitence revise
The firm determination of the skies.   680
      [*They exit. The Numantines* MARANDRO *and* LEONCIO *enter.*]
LEONCIO   Marandro, where is it you go
And what is it that moves you, friend?
MARANDRO   If even I can't comprehend,
How is it something you could know?
LEONCIO   These constant thoughts of love abate   685
The sounder workings of your mind.
MARANDRO   That can't be so, for now I find
They lend my reason greater weight.
LEONCIO   Experience makes it plain to see
That love confers a share of pain   690
On all who serve it. Thus, each swain
Must reason with more gravity.
MARANDRO   Your pointed words aren't motiveless,
As witty as they're bluntly rude.
LEONCIO   You understand my attitude   695
And I your simplemindedness.
MARANDRO   Who's simple, me? For being in love?
LEONCIO   Yes. As the what and where aren't good,
This ill-timed love's an urge you should

Let reason get the better of.   700
MARANDRO   You think that love's controllable?
LEONCIO   When reason regulates man's flaws.
MARANDRO   Those precepts may be reasoned laws,
    But don't tell me they're beautiful.
LEONCIO   Well, reason hardly rules the day   705
    With all the pleasures love bestows.
MARANDRO   It isn't true the two are foes,
    Though love would rather go its way.
LEONCIO   Beset like every one of us,
    Don't you, once far more soldierly,   710
    Diminish reason's primacy
    By sneaking round enamored thus?
    When you should seek the confidence
    Of Mars, the god of war, above,
    You spend these crucial hours with Love   715
    And bide your time with blandishments?
    The Romans cast a deadly pall
    Upon us mounting this cruel siege
    Or, now that love's become your liege,
    Is this a fact you don't recall?   720
MARANDRO   This awful foolishness you spout
    Is gnawing at my body's core,
    For when has love turned men from war
    Or kept brave hearts from staying stout?
    I've never fled the sentry yard   725
    Or tarried where my lady led;
    I've never romped with her in bed
    And left my captain standing guard.
    When have you known me not to give
    My charge full due or else to slight   730
    Our cause for vice's sweet delight,
    Much less the love for which I live?
    If you see nothing, then, beyond
    This love for which I'm not ashamed,
    Why is it you would see me blamed   735
    For having one of whom I'm fond?
    If you suppose the way I speak
    To be irrational at best,
    Go place your hand upon your breast—
    You'll find the rationale you seek.   740
    You don't remember all those years
    I wooed fair Lyra in despair
    Until that day when my last care
    Dissolved along with all her tears,
    Her father finally content   745
    To have me join his family line,
    Uniting Lyra's love to mine
    And giving us his full consent?
    Then you'll recall as well, my friend,

That all this happened just about   750
The time this bloody war broke out,
Which brought my glory to an end.
Our wedding, therefore, was postponed
Till peace uplift our attitude
And bring about a festive mood   755
When marriage feasts might be condoned.
You see what little hope I've left
To claim the passion I pursue
As victory seems to me run through
By Roman spears, and I'm bereft.   760
With nothing anyone can do
To end the starving state in which
We're trapped behind this wall and ditch,
Outnumbered and encircled, too,
I've all but seen my fondest hope   765
Borne off on adverse winds today.
That's how you caught me on my way,
Unhappy and inclined to mope.
LEONCIO   Buck up, then, and dispel your grief—
We need our old Marandro back!   770
Perhaps, we'll find another tack
For bringing our besieged relief
When Jupiter, the heaven's lord,
Reveals a more effective means
By which to free our Numantines   775
And slough off this vile Roman horde.
In that sweet peace, then, your desire
Will thrive beside the wife you claim,
Extinguishing this tortuous flame
That burns in you with amorous fire.   780
And so, in order to entice
All-thundering Jove to see this done,
Numantia now will act as one
In offering him a sacrifice.
Look, all the city folk draw near   785
With incense and an animal.
Oh, Jupiter all powerful,
Have mercy on our people here!
[*Two* HIGH PRIESTS *from Numantia enter holding a ram between
them by the horns. The sacrificial beast is crowned with olive
branches, ivy, and other flowers. The priests are accompanied
by a* PAGE *carrying a silver platter and another heaped with
incense. A second* PAGE *brings firewood and a live flame.
A third covers a table with a cloth, and all these items are laid
upon it. The citizens of Numantia enter, at which the* 1ST HIGH
PRIEST *lets go of the ram.*]
1ST HIGH PRIEST   That signs of doom I've glimpsed en route portend
No good for any grieved petitioner   790
Has caused this silver hair to stand on end.

2ND HIGH PRIEST   My flawless foresight as a presager
Sees bodeful tidings vexed gods have decreed.
Numantia, could your fate look gloomier?
1ST HIGH PRIEST   Then let's officiate with all due speed,   795
As baneful auguries demand such haste.
Come, move the table here and we'll proceed.
2ND HIGH PRIEST   The water, wine and incense may be placed
There now. Repent and go, so they'll be none
Who's not renounced the evils he's embraced.   800
The first and best oblation anyone
Can make the gods in heaven will be found
In that pure-hearted state in which it's done.
1ST HIGH PRIEST   You mustn't light the fire on the ground.
The ceremonial brazier brought here stands   805
Prepared to aid those who are ritual-bound.
2ND HIGH PRIEST   First, though, the cleansing of our necks and
hands.
The water, please. Why won't the fire light?
NUMANTINE   Will it not follow anyone's commands?
2ND HIGH PRIEST   What trials has elusive Fate in sight   810
For us, oh Jupiter, if things be so?
I wonder why this torch will not ignite.
NUMANTINE   It's kindling, sir, although the flame is low.
2ND HIGH PRIEST   Oh, weakling wisp of fire, get thee hence!
Your dark response occasions me much woe!   815
Its smoke ascends, but in a western sense
With patent speed continually increased
While yellow flames that burn at our expense
Incline toward the direction of the East—
A fateful message and unhappy sign   820
Of future harm now foolish hopes have ceased.
1ST HIGH PRIEST   Although Rome will defeat our noble line,
Their victory will turn to smoke before
Our glory's living flames will cease to shine.
2ND HIGH PRIEST   The time has come to take the wine
and pour   825
Some drops upon the sacred fire's wood
While others burn the incense that they bore.
    [*He sprinkles wine on and around the fire before lighting the
    incense.*]
Oh, Jupiter, I pray you, for the good
Of all Numantia, lift from us this yoke
Our ill-starred fate foresees can't be withstood   830
And just as this hale fire turns to smoke
The holy incense coaxed to kindle bright,
Reduce our vile foe's power at a stroke,
Eternal father, such that all their might
And glory vanish, mid these fumes contained,   835
As only you, I deem, can bring such blight.
May heaven see their forces as restrained

As we this sacrificial victim here
And may they share one fate by god ordained.
1ST HIGH PRIEST   The offering augurs ill and thus I fear   840
We'd give false hope to say we might yet flee
The terrible ordeal that's drawing near.
    [*The noise of rocks clanging in a barrel is heard beneath the
    stage and a rocket fires.*]
2ND HIGH PRIEST   You hear that sound? Say now, did you not see
A flaming bolt of lightning pierce the sky?
This surely presages catastrophe!   845
1ST HIGH PRIEST   I quake with fear to feel our end so nigh.
What fateful omens! If I understand
These right, it's doom they prophesy.
Look—do you spy that fierce, unsightly band
Of savage eagles battling other birds   850
To subjugate the weal to their command?
2ND HIGH PRIEST   It's overpowering force alone that herds
Their foes within the circles they design.
Surrounded, they're all preyed on afterwards.
1ST HIGH PRIEST   I cannot praise, but only curse this sign.   855
Do these imperial eagles tell our end?[2]
You'll soon attend Numantia's sad decline!
2ND HIGH PRIEST   Oh fly away, vile eagles who portend
These starving, half-dead citizens no good!
Our days are numbered sure as you ascend.   860
1ST HIGH PRIEST   Regardless of these auguries, I should
Dispatch this guiltless ram now and dispel
The grim-faced god's wrath mid his nether wood.
2ND HIGH PRIEST   Almighty Pluto, fortunate to dwell
Amid the precincts of your dark abode,   865
Grand ruler of that mournful realm of Hell!
Reside in peace, sure that the love you showed
Sweet Ceres's most sacred daughter[3] will
Return as pure as that which you bestowed
By favoring the petitions of this ill-   870
Affected remnant of Numantia's lot,
Who do expect like mercies from you still.
Close up that lightless and infernal spot
Out which the Fates, those three stern sisters,[4] rise
To send each mortal to his burial plot   875
And end these acts that bring on our demise.
Let their intents to hurt us float away
Like ram's wool wafting harmless toward the skies.
    [*He pulls some wool from the ram and throws the tufts into
    the air.*]

2. The eagle was a symbol of imperial power in ancient Rome and was adapted by the Habsburgs into the double-headed eagle.
3. Pluto (Hades) was the Roman god of the underworld. He abducted Proserpina (Persephone), daughter of Ceres (Demeter), goddess of agriculture, and kept her in the underworld for much of the year, thereby giving rise to the seasons.
4. In Roman mythology, fate was personified into three female figures who spun, measured out, and cut the thread of life.

1ST HIGH PRIEST   As I do bathe this dagger here today
 In blood most pure, a ritual I assume   880
 With cleansed soul absent any thoughts that stray,
 So let Numantia shunt aside clear doom
 And make each Roman spilling blood throughout
 Our land soak ground that will become his tomb.
 [*A demon appears up to his waist through a hole in the stage
 and seizes the ram. The flames flare and the sacrificial items
 topple over.*]
2ND HIGH PRIEST   What's this? Who snatched that animal
 from out   885
 My hands? Oh blessed gods, can you make sense
 Of what these dire omens are about?
 Do you remain unmoved by the laments
 These poor, distressed, bedraggled people raise?
 Will their soft hymns rate no just consequence?   890
 The deities seem angered by our praise.
 How else might we explain the solemn dread
 These portents prompt mid din and smoky blaze?
 Our living remedies bring death, instead,
 And all our earnest efforts serve for naught.   895
 Our goodness flies; our evils seem inbred.
NUMANTINE   The skies declare an end for us that's fraught
 With bitter forecasts of defeat in war.
 To what avail's this mercy that we've sought?
 Let's weep, then, for we've only to deplore   900
 This losing battle whose heroic feats
 Posterity will sing of evermore.
THEOGENES   Marquino, summon all your vast conceits
 Of sorcery and say if it appears
 That Fate spells our destruction as it metes   905
 Out clues that turn our laughter into tears.
               [*All exit except* MARANDRO *and* LEONCIO.]
MARANDRO   So, what's your view on all of this,
 Leoncio? Do these omens show
 The sky's reversal of our woe
 Or is there something else amiss?   910
 I fear I'll spend the whole war gripped
 By this mischance in which I'm bound
 Until what was our battleground
 Provides me with my peacetime crypt.
LEONCIO   Marandro, no true soldier lets   915
 Himself be thoroughly nonplussed
 By shows like these, but puts his trust
 In all that bravery begets.
 Such would-be signs don't agitate
 His mind because a fearless arm   920
 Protects his life and home from harm
 While courage prophesies his fate.
 But if, good friend, you're still intent
 On countenancing this deceit,

Marquino's magic's not complete—   925
He's still some sorcery to present,
The finest spellcraft to be had
By one unmatched in conjuring.
He'll tell us if our harrowing
Despair will turn out good or bad.   930
Look, here he comes, and quite the sight!
MARANDRO   We shouldn't be surprised, I guess,
To see him don such frightful dress,
As he performs a frightful rite.
Would it be wise to tarry here?   935
LEONCIO   I think we should, as there's a chance
He'll need us in some circumstance
And we can be of use when near.
    [MARQUINO *enters barefoot, wearing a black buckram robe*
    and wig of flowing black hair. His waistband very visibly holds
    three phials of liquid—one black, one yellow, the other
    clear—and he grips a black-lacquered lance in one hand and
    a book in the other. MILVIO *accompanies him.* LEONCIO *and*
    MARANDRO *go off to one side as they enter.*]
MARQUINO   So, Milvio, where's the poor youth's resting place?
MILVIO   We just now laid him in his sepulcher.   940
MARQUINO   You're sure you're not mistaken in this case?
MILVIO   I'm sure. To leave a marker, as it were,
I placed a stone here mid the funeral dirge
When no one could have been unhappier.
MARQUINO   What caused the boy's death?
MILVIO   Malnutrition's scourge.   945
Consuming hunger cut the youth's life short,
The cruelest bane from hell to yet emerge.
MARQUINO   You're saying, then, no wound of any sort
Provoked this cutting of his vital thread?
No murderous scars or cancer to report?   950
I ask because, when dealing with the dead,
Black arts can only act on souls below
When bodies are entire, from feet to head.
MILVIO   I buried him myself three hours ago,
His person whole, if lifeless and supine.   955
He starved to death. I swear to you that's so.
MARQUINO   Exquisite, as it seems that every sign
Announces that the right time is unfurled
For me to summon forth the most malign
And dark of spirits from the underworld.   960
Fierce Pluto, you whose lot it is to reign
Mid ministers of twisted souls in hell's
Immutable and tenebrous domain,
Attend to my incantatory spells!
Though you may be averse to what I'd fain   965
Attempt, do everything my voice compels
At once this fateful day as I implore
Your powers, lest I importune you more.

Restore the soul to one whom breath has quit
And let young life reanimate his shanks   970
No matter whether Charon's ferried it
Across the Styx to dank and blackened banks
Or Cerberus's[5] gullets must remit
This anima to vivify his flanks.
Pray, let him see the light of day on earth;   975
He'll dwell anon forever mid hell's dearth.
Now, when this wraith should rise, let him walk out
With forecasts that will leave all disabused
Regarding how this war will end, without
A cryptic phrase or silence slyly used.   980
His speech should bring us clarity, not doubt
Or puzzlement that might leave us confused.
Produce him now—why tarry when we're here?
I don't know how to make these hests more clear.
Reneging gods, will you not move this stone?   985
False ministers, would you see me deterred?
What, haven't you sent signs to me alone
To signal you'd comply and keep your word?
Is this more wickedness to which you're prone
Or do you seek the pleasure you've deferred   990
Not witnessing this practice of black arts
That moves your most unpitying of hearts?
Don't answer, cursèd pack, if that's your choice,
But be prepared for harsher treatment, then.
You know there's ample power in my voice;   995
Enraging you lies well within my ken.
Vile husband of a wife who must rejoice
The six months of the year she lies with men
To cuckold you routinely at her ease,
Why is it you stay mute before my pleas?   1000
My black lance, bathed in limpid liquid here,
Not having touched the earth the whole of May,
Will strike this stone and, when it does, make clear
The full force of these powers on display.

> [MARQUINO *sprinkles the lance's iron tip with the clear liquid
> from one phial and strikes the table with it, after which
> rockets fire and a great din is heard.*]

Oh feckless gods, this cowering proves your fear   1005
Of even this clear philter's magic sway.
List, vile ones! Where lies this great clamor's source?
I see you've come around, if but by force,
So lift this stone, rank spirits foul and base!
Reveal this most unfortunate young man!   1010
What's this—demurral? Gone without a trace,
Are you, just when my menacing began?
If threats won't put your covey in its place,

---

5. In Roman mythology, the boatman Charon ferried the souls of the dead across the river Styx into the underworld. Cerberus: three-headed dog who guarded the entrance to the underworld.

You faithless band, I have another plan:
This blackish water from the Stygian lake   1015
Should make short work of snapping you awake!
Oh, ink-like waters from the horrid Styx,
Collected on a gloomy, moonless night,
Loose forces that in you alone admix,
Unconquerable by any other might,   1020
And make the nether region's devilish cliques,
Along with he who brought about man's plight
In serpent form, come flying to my side,
So ordered, summoned, pressed or woe betide!
    [MARQUINO *sprinkles the black liquid on the sepulcher and it*
    opens.]
Oh, ill-starred youth, emerge from your dark grave   1025
And see the sun once more in earth's clear air!
You lie where naught's to be expected save
The lack of gladsome days spent absent care.
It's time you rose, as you now can, and gave
A true account of all you've seen down there   1030
To answer my incantatory spell
With this and more, if more remains to tell.
    [*A shrouded body emerges with a deathlike face. Entering very*
    slowly, it collapses and lies motionless on the stage.]
What, no reply from one my arts revive,
Too pleased to have of death a second taste?
Let's see if pain will make you feel alive—   1035
You'll talk, no matter how much time you waste.
You're in my power now, so don't contrive
To hold back anything I crave. Make haste,
For I've still sorcery within my reach
To move your mute and stubborn tongue to speech.   1040
    [MARQUINO *sprinkles the body with the yellow liquid and*
    whips it.]
Malignant spirits, wait if you mistrust
This sorcery! As these yellow droplets drip,
My machinations will be realized just
As your inane resistance starts to slip.
For though this flesh before me once was dust,   1045
He'll be revived by that one lash of whip,
However tenuous a life may be
Infused with torment though necromancy.
    [*The body twitches and quivers.*]
Rebellious soul, return now to that inn
Of human form inhabited of late!   1050
Yes, I can sense you filling out that skin
You left behind but now reanimate!
    [*At this, the body trembles and begins to speak.*]
BODY   Leave off this frenzied show in which you've been
Engaging here and let these blows abate!
My being's sad enough amid this doom   1055

Without your adding suffering to my gloom!
Marquino, you deceive yourself to think
Me glad to have returned to this world's bleak
And somber life, once more upon the brink
Of hurried exit even as we speak.   1060
This harm you've brought, from which I can't but shrink,
Has only guaranteed that Death will sneak
A second victory over me this day
And place both palms it's won upon display.
So Death and all that otherworldly crew,   1065
Forever bound to execute your will,
Await, amid the venom that they spew,
My dire relation of Numantia's ill-
Divined and inauspicious end to you,
A prophecy its people will fulfill,   1070
For those residing now within its lands
Will lay the city low by their own hands.
Nay, neither will the Roman hordes defeat
Our brave Numantia nor this city know
Resounding triumph it would hold complete,   1075
Both sides composed of stout men, friend and foe.
There'll be no memory of a peace where heat
Of battle glowed in warring armies so.
Numantia's vanquisher will be the knife
Its people wield to compass death and life.   1080
But wait! Be still, Marquino! Those who dwell
Below would bring my discourse to an end
And, though you may well reckon what I tell
Here can't be true, you'll see all I portend.
        [*The body leaps into the grave.*]
MARQUINO   Oh, ill-starred signs from out the depths of hell, 1085
If all must be as we're to comprehend,
I'll follow this cadaver to the tomb
And bear no witness to our coming doom.
        [MARQUINO *also leaps into the grave.*]
MARANDRO   See what I mean, Leoncio, when
I say that, so far, every sign   1090
Predicts an outcome so malign
I've lost all hope to live again?
No road is open to us save
Calamity, so if you don't
Trust me on this count, then you won't   1095
The corpse, Marquino or the grave.
LEONCIO   Bah, these are just illusions, see?
Black magic and demonic art
Designed to scare the faint of heart,
Fake spellcraft and cheap sorcery.   1100
This divination isn't worth
Your credence, much less your despair.
The truth is that the dead don't care

About the fate of those on earth.
MARANDRO   Marquino never would have done   1105
  The things he did had he not viewed
  Our future hopeless and construed
  No chance this battle could be won.
  We'll need to tell the city this,
  A duty you nor I would choose.   1110
  Though no one likes to bear bad news,
  Not doing so would be remiss.

Act III

    [SCIPIO, JUGURTHA, *and* CAIUS MARIUS *enter.*]
SCIPIO   It pleases me no end that all we've aimed
  To do has followed on what hap permits:
  To see this proud and haughty people tamed   1115
  Without a fight through naught but Roman wits.
  Still, any chance to triumph must be claimed
  Before it slips away and promptly quits
  The field, where one propitious moment lost
  Can bear disgrace and corpses as its cost.   1120
  You'll not regard encircling foes ideal
  And may consider this unsensible,
  A true diminishment of Roman zeal
  To use designs so unconventional.
  Though it's been said by many, I still feel   1125
  That, of all fighters, those most practical
  See grandeur in a victory increased
  Precisely when men's blood is shed the least.
  What more exalted glory can there be
  In all the times that regiments have warred   1130
  Than fully vanquishing an enemy
  Without once ever having drawn a sword?
  A triumph that's recorded gorily
  Through comrades' blood, which cannot be restored,
  Will not be vaunted as a wish fulfilled   1135
  As much as one in which no blood is spilled.
    [*A trumpet sounds from the walls of Numantia.*]
JUGURTHA   Unless my ears deceive me, sir, I hear
  A Numantine who sounds a trumpet call
  That looks to draw you nearer, as it's clear
  Our siege permits him no egress at all.   1140
  The city would, indeed, have you appear;
  There's Caravino standing on the wall.
  Let's move a little closer, then.
SCIPIO   Here's far
  Enough. We'll listen to them where we are.
    [CARAVINO *is seen atop the wall holding a spear with a white flag.*]
CARAVINO   Hail, Romans! Do my accents carry past   1145
  This wall so that our message will be heard?

CAIUS MARIUS Just stop your shouting and don't talk so fast;
   I'm sure we'll understand your every word.
CARAVINO A politic proposal will at last
   Resolve this war, but it's to be referred   1150
   To Scipio alone.
SCIPIO   What's this about?
   I'm Scipio.
CARAVINO   Brave general, hear me out:
   Numantia speaks as one, sir, by this means
   To ask you, wise commander, after years
   Of Roman war against the Numantines,   1155
   To end the fighting, stem this standoff's tears
   And not increase its many tragic scenes
   As pestilential conflict perseveres.
   The motion that we'd have you entertain
   Bids single combat settle this campaign.   1160
   Our side will choose a champion to meet
   Within the confines of a palisade
   The finest warrior from your elite
   So each might halt this warring with his blade.
   Let that poor wretch the cruel Fates would defeat   1165
   Lie slain upon the pitch, an ill-starred shade.
   Should he be ours, Numantia, then, will yield;
   If yours, then Rome will quit the battlefield.
   To show good faith, we offer as our pledge
   A group of hostages, if they're required.   1170
   No doubt you'll take our gage without a hedge,
   Aware how much your forces are admired
   And knowing that your soldiers have the edge,
   Their sweat-drenched foes left overwhelmed and tired.
   The lowest of your low could beat our best   1175
   And thus emerge victorious in this test.
   If you agree to this, sir, let us know
   So we might sooner learn whom Fate selects.
SCIPIO You must be jesting to have spoken so;
   Your proposition's mad in all respects.   1180
   Why not just beg us with your heads bowed low
   If this is an attempt to save your necks
   By shunning Roman swords and all the harms
   Our legions can inflict with seasoned arms?
   If some wild creature locked inside a cage   1185
   For sheer ferociousness and savagery
   Can be made docile over time with age
   By reasoned methods and like strategy,
   That man who'd let it loose again to rage
   Would hardly be accused of sanity.   1190
   You're animals, confined and aptly named,
   Pent up where I can see that you'll be tamed.
   Numantia will be mine despite your stand
   And this without another soldier lost.
   Let he your city deems its ablest hand   1195

Inform you if this ditch may yet be crossed.
If you think this has weakened my command,
A compromise that bears too great a cost,
Let shame be borne off by a powerful gale—
The winds of fame will blow when I prevail.   1200
            [SCIPIO *and his compatriots exit.*]
CARAVINO   Done listening, coward? Run away and hide!
Does single combat cause offense to you?
These actions leave your valor much belied
And lower your esteem in others' view.
Is that your craven answer? Where's your pride?   1205
You're all poltroons, you Romans—bullies, too!
It's your superior numbers in the fray
And not your martial skills that win the day!
You pack of sneaking, prissy, treacherous,
Despotic, trouble-making, criminal,   1210
Ferocious, unrelenting, villainous,
Ungrateful, malformed, unappeasable,
Adulterous, hateful scum! How dubious
To think you bold when you're equivocal!
What glory can there be in killing all   1215
Of us here basely trapped behind this wall?
In closed formation or in lone attack
On open fields where not one soul will find
A towering wall or deep ditch holding back
Combatants with true warfaring in mind,   1220
I think it best no sword should here lie slack
Nor any man retreat or lag behind
Without your vaunted army meeting ours,
A ragtag bunch with far diminished powers.
Our method, now confronted with your way   1225
Of vanquishing through guile instead of skill,
Requires concerted action, not delay,
So serves the bravery of our forces ill.
You're timorous rabbits dressed as beasts of prey,
So praise your ancient glories all you will!   1230
I've no doubt Jupiter will back our cause
And subjugate you to Numantia's laws.
        [CARAVINO *exits, then returns with* THEOGENES,
        MARANDRO, *and others.*]
THEOGENES   So here we gather, close to our last breath,
Good friends. If only this cruel fate would save
Our city pain by hastening each soul's death!   1235
You saw the signs our sacrifices gave,
Forecasting future doom and misery
Before Marquino leapt into his grave.
Our foes, too, treat our words dismissively.
What's left for us? I can't see what road's best   1240
Except to move along our destiny
Or let that flame still burning in his breast
Ignite his spirit, answering the call

To muster more resistance, whose first test
Must be to batter down this hindering wall   1245
So we can perish on the battlefield
And not enclosed like cowards in Rome's dread thrall.
I know the only heft this act could wield
Would be to change the means by which we'll die,
For, either way, it's all our pains will yield.   1250
CARAVINO   Now there's a plan that I can ratify!
I'd be too glad to leave my life behind
If we could bring this wall low on the sly,
Though one recurrent doubt still plagues my mind:
If our wives learn of this, there'll be no need   1255
For undertaking plots of any kind.
Remember when the men here all agreed
To sally forth and leave them while we fought?
With each already mounted on his steed,
Our women, seeing our intentions, thought   1260
The scheme so daft they took the reins from us,
Preventing any charge we'd fondly sought.
They blocked our exit then and would do thus
Again today if we but tried to span
The ditch beyond this wall mid all their fuss.   1265
MARANDRO   That's right. Our wives already know our plan
And have affirmed once more that they're averse
To such a sortie. That's why they began
Protesting that, for better or for worse,
They'd fight beside us, grossly out of place,   1270
Their vexing presence there a seeming curse.
     [Four women from Numantia enter, each holding a child in
     her arms and others by the hand. The maiden LYRA enters with
     them.]
Look, here they come on cue to plead their case,
Concerned their men might leave them in a spot.
They'll melt that steely toughness you embrace.
How sadly they produce each sorry tot   1275
Before its father! Don't you gather how
Their hugs may be the last these moms allot?
IST WOMAN   Most noble lords and masters, after now
What seems a thousand injuries endured
Without the peace that mortal blows allow   1280
Much less the wonted peace this war's obscured,
We've always stood beside you, faithful wives
To husbands of whose love we rest assured.
Why is it, then, now that the sky contrives
To burden all so cruelly with this fate,   1285
You'd show us such scant love and end your lives?
We've just found out your plan to infiltrate
The Romans' camp and hurl yourselves upon
Their far superior arms to liberate
Numantia rather than just waiting on   1290
A torturous death from hunger's pangs, in whose

Gaunt grip, I fear, we'll starve until we're gone.
This perishing in battle that you choose
Will also end the virtuous lives we've led,
As lives and virtue both we're sure to lose.   1295
Don't leave us helpless—cut our throats, instead,
With your own swords, a mercy that will spare
Each grave dishonor in a Roman bed.
My firm intention, which I here declare,
Remains to act as deftly as I know   1300
So, where my husband dies, I'll, too, die there.
The wives assembled here all wish to show
That fear of death alone cannot compete
With offering lifelong love we'd still bestow
No matter whether times are hard or sweet.   1305
2ND WOMAN   Are those your thoughts, illustrious men?
Will you assure us that you're not
Still set upon this desperate plot
To leave behind your women, then?
Could it, by chance, be your desire   1310
To make each virgin here inside
A sacrifice to Roman pride
To live with misery more dire?
Or should the children of these lands
Be left this conquering army's slaves?   1315
You'd best consign your heirs to graves
By strangling them with your own hands!
Would you abet this warring host's
Injustice, servicing their need
To carry off, in wanton greed,   1320
The best of which our city boasts?
Our foes will level these sweet homes
Where happy families once were housed
While forlorn maids will be espoused
To not our strapping lads, but Rome's.   1325
You'd err thus while our foes would reap
A hundred thousand gains from this,
Bad shepherds who see naught amiss
With having no one guard their sheep!
If it's the ditch you hope to span,   1330
Then let us join you in the breach.
We'd hold existence cheap lest each
Of us could die beside her man.
Don't hurry to cavort with death
For thinking that starvation's knife   1335
Is bound to cut your thread of life
And leave you absent vital breath.
3RD WOMAN   Do you not see your mothers' woe,
Poor children? Why hold back your tears
And hide from your own sires the fears   1340
You'll face if they decide to go?
Let murderous hunger finish you

With all the anguish it demands—
Harsh treatment at the Romans' hands
Is nothing you'd look forward to.   1345
Go tell them you were all conceived
Free citizens and inasmuch
As your proud mothers thought you such,
You were not raised to live aggrieved.
Yes, tell those same dear sires who gave   1350
You life in better days, before
Your destinies were shaped by war,
To send you to an early grave.
If you could but communicate,
Mute city walls, say this and then   1355
Repeat it countless times again:
"Stay, Numantines, and liberate
These temples and fine homes you built
Mid harmony and civic weal!"
Your wives and children wish you'd feel   1360
More mercy toward them, blent with guilt.
So men, sweet husbands and kind sires,
Do let your hard resolve give way
And, though bold Numantines, display
The softened hearts your kin desires.   1365
Don't think that by this wall's mere breach
You'll remedy the greater ill
That dwells within our city still
And threatens certain harm to each.
LYRA   Hear, too, these maidens' desperate pleas!   1370
Your presence is the sole defense
Our women can enlist and, hence,
A check on Roman liberties.
Don't let such precious bounty fall
To greedy, lustful hands like theirs.   1375
You know these wanton legionnaires—
They're savage, ravishing wolves all!
It's History's renown you'd claim
In desperate sorties of this kind,
Bold acts in which you're sure to find   1380
Both instant death and lasting fame.
Let's say the blockade's overrun
And you break through to reach the plain—
What city in the whole of Spain
Would favor you for what you've done?   1385
My simple wit would have you know
If you go through with this, you see,
You'd give strength to our enemy
And bring our dear Numantia low.
Rome's force will only mock you when   1390
They gather what your ploys entail.
How can three thousand souls prevail
Against some eighty thousand men?

Suppose your wild plan to breach
This wall works—this offensive will   1395
But lead them, unavenged, to kill
Whomever falls within their reach.
It's better that the skies decide
Our fate, whatever this may be,
And that our destiny decree   1400
We die or otherwise abide.
THEOGENES   What cause is there for tears? Come, wipe your eyes
And see, beloved wives, how much your woes
Have forced our hardened hearts to empathize:
Our brimming love for you now overflows.   1405
Though grief erupt yet or despair arise,
May your pain lessen as our mercy grows.
We'll stay till each man takes his dying breath
To serve you faithfully in life and death.
It's true we thought to cross the ditch, aware   1410
We'd sooner perish fighting than survive
And if we'd die exacting vengeance there,
Though dead, we'd somehow strangely be alive.
Our plot discovered, we would hardly dare
To bring this madness off now as we strive,   1415
Beloved wives and children, your true men,
To consecrate our lives to you again.
We must be sure, though, that the Romans seize
No plundered spoils of which their camp might boast
But make eyewitnesses of enemies   1420
Who'll chronicle our stand against their host.
If you're agreed, a thousand centuries
Could scarce obliterate Numantia's ghost.
Let nothing our great city can provide
Be left a trophy for their thieving side.   1425
We'll light a bonfire in the public square
And burn the lavish pelf our homeland claims
With all the worldly goods that we can bear,
The more to feed its greedy, white-hot flames.
Once you're informed of how we're all to fare   1430
Anon, you'll take these acts for fun and games.
Yes, we'll soon leave our enemy bereft
And see to it no precious bounty's left.
But first, so we may share at least one nice
Last meal and make these pangs inside us fade,   1435
We'll slay our Roman prisoners and dice
Their flesh up so our hunger is allayed.
Serve young and old, so long as it suffice
To ease the anguish caused by this blockade
Though this unprecedented, cruel repast   1440
Leave all who must partake of it aghast.
CARAVINO   What say you, citizens? Are we agreed?
I must admit I'm satisfied for one,
But think it all-important we proceed

To execute all quickly once begun.   1445
THEOGENES You'll know our whole plot soon in word and
    deed,
Though not before this feast I've planned is done.
Now let's as one community unite
And make this fire's flames burn tall and bright.
1ST WOMAN The moment's come to see this action through.   1450
Let's bring our goods here while the fire starts.
Dear spouses, we devote our lives to you
As we in gladder times had pledged our hearts.
LYRA We'll feed the flames with anything in view
The Romans might well haul off in their carts.   1455
No spoils of war should fall into their hands
And they should gloat of nothing in their lands.
    [As the other Numantines exit, MARANDRO takes LYRA by the
    hand and detains her. LEONCIO enters and goes off to one side
                        where he can't be seen.]
MARANDRO Don't rush away from here so fast,
Sweet Lyra! Let me still delight
In this brief bit of joy our blight   1460
Affords me, though it be my last.
Yes, stay and let my eyes feast on
Your loveliness, the sole reprieve
On earth I know that can relieve
The miseries I've undergone.   1465
I dream of you both night and morn,
My darling, and that peace you bring
Remains an ever-living thing
In which I glory, if forlorn.
What's wrong? What are you thinking of,   1470
You, glory of my every thought?
LYRA I think our joy may come to naught
As we live out the end of love.
It's not the Romans' siege, you see,
That's bound to bring about our death.   1475
I'm sure I'll take my final breath
Before this war can finish me.
MARANDRO What are you saying, my heart's heart?
LYRA This hunger cuts my vital thread
And, craving palms to crown its head,   1480
Will take this life I'll soon depart.
Is there to be a marriage cup
From which, as man and wife, we'll drink?
I fear there won't and lately think
I'll die before an hour's up.   1485
My brother perished yesterday,
Succumbing to starvation's wrath.
He followed, thus, our mother's path,
For she, too, met her death that way.
If hunger's yet to run its course   1490
In wrecking what I've left of health,

It's due my youth, which boasts a wealth
Of strength to counteract its force.
Though many drawn-out days have passed
Since I've effectively fought back,   1495
My next defense from its attack
May, from attrition, be my last.
MARANDRO Oh Lyra! Dry your crying eyes
And let these rivers from my own
Provide the waters to bemoan   1500
The woes for which their levels rise.
Though cruel starvation's misery
Has left you weak with lassitude,
You won't die from a lack of food
As long as there's still life in me.   1505
I volunteer to scale this wall
And cross the ditch now that I've cause
To hurtle into death's black jaws
And see you rescued from their pall.
I'll risk my life to snatch the bread   1510
That sates the Romans' gluttony
And won't be stayed until I see
Their food sustaining you, instead.
My valor, then, will forge a place
Where you can thrive, though I expire.   1515
To see you thus is far more dire
Than any death a man could face.
If these two hands are still the same
I'll be possessed of birth to tomb,
They'll bring you something to consume   1520
And that despite the Romans' aim.
LYRA You've spoken like a man in love,
Marandro, but it isn't fair
For me to find consolement where
Relief leaves you in danger of   1525
A violent death and what you'd steal
Could hardly bolster me in time.
You're surer to be killed than I'm
To profit any from your zeal.
Enjoy this final bloom of youth,   1530
Life's tender and florescent spring.
No value that my life can bring
Our city rivals yours, in truth.
Your strength can undo this blockade
And lead us in a staunch defense.   1535
Your staying put makes much more sense
Than perishing for this doomed maid.
So cast that thought aside for now,
My love. I cannot have you lost
Or even wish for food whose cost   1540
Would mean such sweat from that dear brow.
You see, then? Even though you might

Delay my death by one full day,
This hunger no one can allay
Will cast all into endless night.   1545
MARANDRO   You waste your breath deterring me,
Dear Lyra, for I won't be swayed.
I'm pressed to make this daring raid
Through pure resolve and destiny.
So, while I'm absent, pray the skies   1550
Will shelter me till I return
With food enough, I trust, to spurn
My anguish and your quick demise.
LYRA   Marandro, dear heart, don't rush toward
This certain death I see ahead,   1555
Your precious blood cascading red
Off some pernicious Roman's sword.
My all! I beg of you to set
Aside this plan, for if it's hard
Just slipping past the Roman guard,   1560
Returning will prove tougher yet!
I'd cool these boiling passions some
As heaven witnesses I yearn
For your wellbeing, my sole concern,
And not things I might profit from.   1565
Should my petitions be denied,
Take with you on your stubborn chase
This token of my fond embrace
And think me ever by your side.
MARANDRO   The gods be with you, Lyra. Go,   1570
For now I see Leoncio here.
LYRA   Love, may they also keep you near
And free of danger from our foe.
                                                    [LYRA *exits.*]
LEONCIO   This dreadful course of sacrifice you chart,
Marandro, makes it plain for all to see   1575
How love keeps men from being faint of heart,
Though your staunch virtue and stout bravery
Bid greater hope for all. Still, I'm afraid
Our looming fate will prove more niggardly.
I listened keenly as that starving maid,   1580
Your Lyra, spoke of how her death draws near—
Unjust for one who's braved this long blockade—
And how you promised she'd be free and clear
Of menace once you'd made her hunger end
By boldly charging Roman sword and spear   1585
Alone. I want to come with you, my friend,
To join you in this just and furious fight,
Affording you what help these hands can lend.
MARANDRO   Leoncio, you're my soul's true half! What plight
Could ever cleave our lasting bond in twain   1590
Much less some rivalled pleasure or delight?
Enjoy your waning youth, friend, and remain

Within these city walls. I couldn't bear
To murder you in blossoming youth's reign.
I'm heading out alone and trust I'll fare   1595
Well in accord with my sworn loyalty,
Returning with the bread that's ours from there.
LEONCIO   I've bared my fond desires for you to see,
Though yours remain our measure and true gauge.
No matter how pre-signed our destiny   1600
Or how this constant threat of death may rage,
No peril could stop me fighting at your side,
Much less a fear of war these Romans wage.
I'll go with you, in common cause allied,
And come back safe unless the Fates protest   1605
And I, in your defense there, will have died.
MARANDRO   I do beseech you, friend—heed my behest
To stay among our people should I fall
And be no aid to them in this, a quest
So fraught with risk you may be left to call   1610
Upon a grieving mother to condole
Besides that promised wife, who was my all.
LEONCIO   You're kind to think I'd have the self-control
Required, if I learned of your demise,
To soothe these women sad in heart and soul   1615
When I'd, too, be so moved to agonize
I couldn't hope to comfort either one.
If you meet death, my person also dies;
I have to follow now your plan is spun.
There's no deterring me, try as you might—   1620
My course is set and cannot be undone.
MARANDRO   Since nothing will dissuade you from this fight,
Be ready, then, for we'll begin our raid
Quite soon, beneath the cloak of dark this night.
Bear light arms, for we'll only find more aid   1625
If Providence should come to our defense
And not in mail with armor overlaid.
Our mission is to steal, for all intents
And purposes, whatever there's of bread
Or food their mess halls lavishly dispense.   1630
LEONCIO   Lead on, Marandro! I'll be gladly led.
            [MARANDRO *and* LEONCIO *exit.* TWO BROTHERS *enter.*]
1ST BROTHER   Dear brother, let your soul flow forth in tears
To start the bitter weeping of our woes!
May death come soon and cart off on its biers
The spoils of lives that languish in the throes.   1635
2ND BROTHER   Our suffering won't last long, as it appears
That looming death will silently dispose
Of every haggard Numantine in sight,
Souls whisked away in dreamless sleep's short flight.
The clear beginning of our certain end   1640
Is coming ever closer into view,
An ill we can't directly reprehend
The Fates, war's ministers, for seeing through.

It seems we citizens, whose lives portend
No ease we can envision or construe,   1645
Have sentenced our own selves to perish here
By means as laudable as they're severe.
A bonfire in the city's central square
Already rages greedily and burns
With clouds of smoke that vanish into air,   1650
The riches Numantines have brought in turns.
Those still alive rush sorrowfully there,
Unsure mid their forebodings and concerns,
But quick to keep this sacred fire fed
With sumptuous goods from lives once richly led.   1655
It's stoked by pearls from out the pink-skied East,
All sorts of vessels fashioned from pure gold,
Fine diamonds, rubies red and, not the least,
Brocades with purple fabrics to behold.
All this potential bounty has increased   1660
The flames and made the fire overbold.
No Roman hand will ever touch these spoils
Nor bosom claim these guersons for its toils.
  [*Two Numantines enter, each carrying a bundle of clothing.*
  They walk across the stage and exit on the other side.]
Look back again and view this tragic scene:
The city of Numantia, to a soul,   1665
Comes hurriedly to burn their chattels, keen
To watch the fires surge beyond control
Not stoked with mere dry grass or wood yet green
Nor anything consumed as fast as coal,
But their belongings, ill enjoyed of late,   1670
Which they've consented to incinerate.
IST BROTHER   If burning our effects could ease our pains,
We'd patiently consign the lot to fire.
I fear, though, that a crueler fate remains
For all of us, a sentence far more dire.   1675
Before each outstretched neck here ascertains
How Rome's barbaric justice will transpire,
Our hands will be our executioners
And not these cursèd foreign murderers.
No woman, child or aged soul, it's been   1680
Decreed, is henceforth to be left alive.
The state that gnawing hunger's left them in
Would bring a death worse than we men contrive.
Here comes a woman wasted, weak and thin,
Whom I once fancied and believed I'd wive,   1685
As pretty then when she was loved by me
As blemished now by signs of misery.
  [*A woman enters cradling a baby and holding a small boy's*
  hand. She brings clothing to throw into the fire.]
MOTHER   When ever will we find repose
From this dread anguish and despair?
STARVING SON   Won't anybody anywhere   1690
Give us some bread for all these clothes?

MOTHER   Bread, child? Not bread or anything
  Like that, much less a piece of meat.
STARVING SON   But mommy, look: if I don't eat,
  I'll die from all this hungering!   1695
  One piece of bread—a little one—
  I promise not to ask for more.
MOTHER   I've never felt this sad before!
STARVING SON   Why don't you want to feed your son?
MOTHER   I want us all to have our fill,   1700
  My love, but here food can't be found.
STARVING SON   Just buy whatever's lying round.
  If you won't shop for some, I will.
  Here, watch me find someone ahead,
  A random person walking by,   1705
  Who'll see our clothing piled high
  And trade it for a piece of bread.
MOTHER   Poor babe, what are you suckling there?
  My body's tried its very best,
  So can't you see that mommy's breast   1710
  Spouts blood, but has no milk to spare?
  Feed off my flesh, then, if you would
  And sate your hunger bite by bite.
  My weakened arms don't have the might
  To hold you as a mother should.   1715
  I love you, darlings, endlessly!
  But what am I supposed to do
  If I can't even nourish you
  With this same blood that flows in me?
  Grim hunger, I've no way to stave   1720
  You off and, so, you'll take my life.
  Oh, War! What else has all this strife
  Accomplished but to dig my grave?
STARVING SON   I'm tired, mommy. Let's not talk.
  Come on, what are we outside for?   1725
  The more we stand around, the more
  My stomach hurts me when we walk.
MOTHER   We're drawing near the city square
  Where you can ease your burden, son,
  By tossing these fine garments one   1730
  By one upon the fire there.
    [*The woman exits with her children, leaving the two brothers
    alone onstage.*]
1ST BROTHER   The woman scarcely has the strength to budge
  So fiercely has starvation laid her low.
  It's bleak to watch a hapless mother trudge
  On nearly lifeless with her kids in tow.   1735
2ND BROTHER   This same slack-footed, painful pace, I judge,
  Will lead us to the death we'll undergo.
  Now pick your own pace up and follow me.
  Let's find out what the senators decree.

Act IV

[*A call to arms is hurriedly sounded in the Roman camp, at which*
SCIPIO, JUGURTHA, *and* CAIUS MARIUS *enter, flustered.*]
SCIPIO   Here, captains! What's that noise? Who sounds
    the call   1740
  To arms at this late hour? Could rowdy knaves
  So heedless as to show no sense at all
  Have stumbled on our camp and, thus, their graves?
  I hope we've no rebellion to forestall
  Nor any mutiny the bugler craves   1745
  Mid such tight quarters, where experience tends
  To make me sure of foes, but less of friends.
    [QUINTUS FABIUS *enters with his sword drawn.*]
QUINTUS FABIUS   There's no need for alarm here, general.
  The reason for the call to arms is known:
  It marks the loss of soldiers laudable   1750
  For all the heart and gallantry they've shown.
  Two dauntless, brazen Numantines, so full
  Of grit they'd well be praised for this alone,
  Have somehow scaled their wall and crossed our ditch
  To slay us in this battle that we pitch.   1755
  At once they charged the watchmen standing guard,
  Then threw themselves at lances mid the fray.
  Outmanned, though raging valiantly and hard,
  They sighted our encampment, fought their way
  Inside a tent and, showing no regard   1760
  For brave Fabricius there, went on to slay
  Six troops, whom they courageously ran through,
  Their strength and valor everywhere on view.
  No lightning bolt flares faster out the sky
  While slicing through the air mid hurried flight   1765
  And no relucent comet hurtles by
  Illuminating darkling spans of night
  More quickly than this daring pair did fly
  Across our rows of barracks, tinging bright
  With Roman blood the earth on which they tread   1770
  As flailing swords turned all around them red.
  Fabricius, cut deep, bears grievous harm.
  Eracius's head wound looks severe.
  Olmida, after losing his right arm,
  Is not much longer for this world, I fear.   1775
  Nor could Estacius, with his speed, disarm
  These two or even scurry free and clear
  Of threat: his swiftness on this road to death
  Just meant he'd sooner draw his final breath.
  So, going tent to tent, then, to complete   1780
  This venturous raid, they stayed until they found
  Some biscuits, which occasioned their retreat,
  As home, and not our fury, turned them round.

The one who slipped our grasp appeared more fleet;
The other lies there slain upon the ground.   1785
Their boldness makes me think that hunger led
The pair to infiltrate our camp for bread.
SCIPIO   If this is how these scoundrels rage when penned
Inside their walls, half-starved and left to die,
How fiercely, freed and fed, would they contend   1790
Against us with their strength in full supply?
Unbroken beasts! We'll tame you in the end!
Your wild savagery can hardly vie
With artful Roman diligence and skill,
Which always breaks a haughty people's will.   1795
    [*All exit. The alarms sound in the city, at which* MARANDRO
        enters, wounded and covered with blood, carrying a white
        basket of bread in his left hand and a bloodstained biscuit
                                                  in his right.]
MARANDRO   We made it out the combat zone,
Leoncio. Come on. Where'd you go?
I can't just leave you here, you know,
And reach Numantia all alone.
Have you decided to remain?   1800
Was staying always on your mind?
You wouldn't have left me behind,
Yet I forsook you on this plain.
Could one whom I abandoned, dead,
His bloodied body hacked and bent   1805
By brutal Romans, represent
The precious cost of this stale bread?
And could that wound, mid all this strife—
That heinous thrust that laid you low—
Not deal me, too, a mortal blow,   1810
Forswearing me bereft of life?
Cruel Destiny was not yet done
Tormenting me, so in the end
It's I who'd be the treacherous friend
While you'd emerge the faithful one.   1815
The palms you've won this day extol
Your fervent comradeship while Fate
Impels me to exonerate
My acts by sending forth my soul
To join you on the other side   1820
And soon, as Death's dark pull commands,
Just once I've placed in Lyra's hands
This bitter bread for which you died.
I almost said, "the bread we took
Triumphant from the foes we fought,"   1825
Although, in truth, this bread was bought
With blood of friends the skies forsook.
    [LYRA *enters carrying clothes for the fire.*]
LYRA   Good heavens, what's this monstrous sight?
MARANDRO   A specter who won't tarry more

Than injuries sustained in war   1830
Allow when they conspire to smite.
Look here, I've kept my pledge to you
By doing all I could contrive
To see to it that you'd survive
The plights you'd suffered hitherto.   1835
I mean to say, you'll come to see
That, while I've at the very least
Brought surplus rations, I can't feast,
So little life remains in me.
LYRA   What's that you say, beloved friend?   1840
MARANDRO   Hush, Lyra dear, it's time you ate,
But as you do, observe how Fate
Has willed that my life's thread should end.
Come—mixed with blood from my ordeal,
This bread, which one could hardly bake   1845
More tragically, will surely make
For one forlorn and bitter meal.
Yes, here's the bread that fed their host,
Some eighty thousand soldiers strong,
And cost us, friends our whole lives long,   1850
Those very lives we cherished most.
Be certain of this bond I've sealed
With blood. My time on earth is brief
And good Leoncio's come to grief,
His corpse strewn on the battlefield.   1855
Accept this gesture, then, with love,
For it's become my dying wish
And good will makes the finest dish
The heart has ever tasted of.
In calm and storm, you've always been   1860
The queen of all my fond desires,
So take this flesh that now expires,
As you've the soul that dwelt therein.
    [MARANDRO *falls to the ground, dead, and* LYRA *cradles his head*
    in her lap.]
LYRA   Marandro, tell me, dear, what's wrong?
Do you feel ill? What lays you low?   1865
Where did that manly swagger go?
You always were so big and strong!
I can't believe my loved one's died!
Now what is to become of me?
What other sorrow here can be   1870
More dire than that which I abide?
What mischief-maker could entice
So excellent a man-at-arms
And my life's love to face such harms,
Ensuring his own sacrifice?   1875
You launched a raid, my promised groom,
Expecting to preclude my death,
But holding you bereft of breath

Has all but sentenced me to doom.
How could I sate myself on food   1880
Bedewed with blood Marandro's shed?
No, I don't even think you bread
But venom for my solitude.
If this should ever touch my lips,
It wouldn't be for sustenance   1885
But as a sort of reverence
To kiss the blood with which it drips.
        [A BOY enters, Lyra's brother, so faint he can hardly speak.]
BOY   Our mother's dead and father, too,
    Grows weaker as his forces lie
    So very close to death he'll die   1890
    Quite soon, as I'll most surely do.
    They fought, but hunger won the fight.
    Hold on—that wouldn't be the bread
    We've all been yearning to be fed?
    Right now, I couldn't down a bite: 1895
    My throat is so constricted from
    Starvation, water wouldn't flow
    Into this shriveled stomach, so
    I couldn't gobble up a crumb.
    Yes, eat without me what you've found.   1900
    It seems ironic that our store
    Should grow so when I'm at death's door
    And I should starve when loaves abound.
        [He falls to the ground, dead.]
LYRA   Don't you die, too, dear brother, please!
    His candle's vital flame's gone out.   1905
    Oh, things are bad enough without
    The need for them to come in threes!
    Cruel Fortune, what induces you
    To heap these injuries on me?
    You've made this girl and bride-to-be   1910
    A widow and an orphan, too!
    And you, grim Roman host, what doom
    Your ruthless swords now make complete
    By leaving lifeless at my feet
    A brother and my future groom!   1915
    For which one should my keening start?
    I don't know whom to pity first.
    Before our fortunes were reversed,
    I cherished both within one heart.
    My husband and my brother fell,   1920
    So I'll put equal love on view
    By quickly following the two
    Toward heaven or, if need be, hell.
    I'll use the ways and means that led
    Both corpses to their graves too soon—   1925
    A steely blade or hunger's swoon
    Will quickly see to it I'm dead.

I'd rather put this knife in me
Than bread that's prompted such despair.
For one whose life is fraught with care,   1930
Kind death's a gentle remedy.
What holds you there, you craven louse?
Can you have lost your nerve, slack arm?
I'm coming once I've come to harm,
So wait, good brother! Wait, dear spouse!   1935
[*A* WOMAN *enters fleeing a Numantine* SOLDIER, *who pursues
her with a dagger.*]
WOMAN   Help, merciful Jupiter! Look on me
With sympathy and aid a woman's plight!
SOLDIER   No matter how light-footedly you flee,
This ruthless hand will cut you down in flight!
[*The* WOMAN *runs offstage.*]
LYRA   Come wield your blade against this wretch you see,   1940
Brave soldier, and your battle-tested might.
Spare those among us who'd still cling to life
And end my bleak existence with your knife.
SOLDIER   Now even though our senate has decreed
The city's men should have the women killed,   1945
What savage heart could make such beauty bleed
To guarantee this mandate be fulfilled?
I'm not so fierce a man I feel the need
To be the one who sees this vision stilled.
Some other hand will have to run you through,   1950
For I was born to feast these eyes on you.
LYRA   This gallant attitude you'd fain display
Toward me, most worthy soldier, might appear
More courteous—heaven vouch for all I say!—
Were it shown elsewhere. Here, it seems severe.   1955
I'll take you for my newfound friend the day
You, valiant and undaunted, see it clear
To pierce my bosom with that knife you bare
And liberate me from this life of care.
Today, though, should you wish to make plain how   1960
Compassionate you are toward my disgrace,
Come help me bury my poor husband now
And lay him in his final resting place.
My brother needs a grave, too, you'll allow,
The living color banished from his face.   1965
My man met death in bringing me some bread
While sheer starvation left my brother dead.
SOLDIER   I'll do what you request of me, of course,
Provided that you tell me as we go
Which individuals were at the source   1970
Of those events that laid your loved ones low.
LYRA   I've scant reserves for talking left in force.
SOLDIER   This siege is dealing you a fatal blow.
Pick up your brother, for his corpse is light.
Your spouse's heft will likely need my might.   1975

[*They drag the two corpses offstage and a woman representing*
WAR *enters, armed with a spear and holding a shield. She is
accompanied by* ILLNESS *and* HUNGER. ILLNESS *leans on a
crutch, head wrapped in bandages, with a yellow mask for
a face.* HUNGER, *carrying a figurine of a naked cadaver, wears
a yellow buckram robe and a mask of faded colors.*]

WAR   Come, Hunger, Illness, you who carry out
   My baleful orders claiming common cause,
   Consuming lives and bringing death about,
   Not thrall to mankind's pleading, rule or laws.
   You know my mind so well now I've no doubt   1980
   You'll execute my will without a pause,
   Apprised that fealty is best displayed
   When like commands are speedily obeyed.
   The force of Destiny's beyond compare,
   So nothing it intends results in vain.   1985
   I'm thus compelled to back in this affair
   The Roman troops, who mount a shrewd campaign.
   They'll win the day for now, though unaware
   These Spaniards will, in time, rule this domain.
   The hour will come, though, when I change my course   1990
   To blight the strong and aid the weaker force.
   Yes, I'm all-powerful and baneful War,
   Abhorred by mothers' hearts the world around,
   The scourge men wrongly curse at and deplore
   Not knowing how much value can be found   1995
   In me as I know glory lies in store
   For Spain, whose name on earth will be renowned.
   A Carlos, Philip or a Ferdinand[1]
   Must first, though, be enthroned to rule the land.
ILLNESS   If Hunger, our most faithful friend, had not   2000
   So doggedly discharged its fatal role,
   Cold-bloodedly dispatching this brave lot
   Of Numantines that die here soul by soul,
   It would have been my duty, then, to blot
   Their lives out so that victory might extol   2005
   This Roman force with lavish spoils instead
   Of what lies unpropitiously ahead.
   Unleashing these dread powers in excess,
   Cruel Hunger's struck Numantia's folk so hard
   That those who once envisioned some egress   2010
   Now watch as every exit road is barred.
   Still, Fury's lance has dealt with them no less
   Adversely than a fate that's proved ill-starred,
   Which seem together to have so conspired
   That suffering and starvation weren't required.   2015
   Its henchmen, Rage and Fury, scorn to cease
   Their infiltration into each soul's core
   And made this city's thirst for blood increase

---

1. Ferdinand of Aragon, Charles V, and Philip II, the kings associated with Spain's imperial
expansion from the late fifteenth century to the late sixteenth century.

Not gradually like the Romans' lust, but more.
Here then, attacks and casualties are peace   2020
While Numantines exult before death's door
Resolved to snatch this win from Roman bands
By murdering themselves with their own hands.
HUNGER   Now cast your eyes upon the city's fate,
Its towering roofs aflame against the skies,   2025
And hear the growing doom proliferate
As lovely women heave their final sighs
In howling desperation, though too late
To save the skins that make these fires rise.
What man or thing could stay the town's decrees?   2030
Not fathers, friends, true love or frantic pleas.
Like lambs who feel a shepherd boy's neglect,
Abandoned to the wolves and dashing round
In fear as there's no pastor to protect
Their simple lives from dangers to be found,   2035
Frail women and poor children here expect
Their looming deaths by sword, yet flee unbound
Throughout the city's streets—oh, fate unkind!—
In vain attempts to leave this purge behind.
Impassive husbands sink their polished steel   2040
In loving wives in spite of their despond;
Dazed sons strike dead their mothers with a zeal
Denuded wholly of their filial bond
While fathers—what cruel mercy they must feel!—
Dispatch their children to the great beyond,   2045
Eviscerating those their own loins sired,
Bereaved, yet pleased, by acts so undesired.
Numantia's left no corner, square or street
Devoid of blood or not piled high with dead.
What steel blades kill the fire consumes with heat;   2050
This pitiless assault will only spread
Until you'll see in ruins at your feet
Those lofty ramparts once high overhead
While stately homes and sacred temples crash
Unto the ground in clouds of dust and ash.   2055
Step forward, then, and watch Theogenes,
Who's whet the double edges of his sword,
Test out its sharpness on the cervices
Of both the wife and children he adored.
As he's about to slay the lot of these,   2060
His life now seems a bane to be deplored.
See how he casts about for some strange means
Of dying, fateful to all Numantines.
WAR   We'll go, then, but let neither of you be
Neglectful spreading blight throughout this land.   2065
Attend to my commands unerringly
And everything will go as I have planned.
                    [*They exit.* THEOGENES *enters with*
            his two small SONS, *his* DAUGHTER, *and his* WIFE.]

THEOGENES   If deep paternal love will not restrain
  My zeal in executing this intent,
  Dear children, know that nothing can detain   2070
  My hand in seeing through this dire event.
  When taking lives forestalls a deeper pain,
  What horrid prospects must these hurts present?
  How strangely softer, then, my own must loom
  To have to slay you three in your first bloom.   2075
  My darling little ones, superior though
  The Romans' forces be, they'll never claim
  Our line as slaves or deal the final blow
  That would concede them laurel leaves and fame.
  The heavens' true compassion will bestow   2080
  On us a road to freedom all the same,
  And has apprised our city from on high
  That liberty, for us, means we must die.
  Thus you, sweet consort, my beloved wife,
  Will likewise be released from that dread fear   2085
  With which these Romans would have plagued your life
  And from that lust in which they'd persevere.
  My sword will save you from this wretched strife
  So hands won't paw at you and eyes won't leer.
  Our foes may covet spoils, but won't desire   2090
  Numantia once it's been consumed by fire.
  For it was I, my precious spouse, who first
  Proposed that all should perish here before
  Succumbing to the rule of these accursed
  Besiegers, who respect no law in war,   2095
  And that my brood and I would yield life erst
  The last of us was gone.
WIFE   Were there a more
  Auspicious means to thwart this destiny,
  The heavens know how happy I would be!
  As there appears, though, to be none in sight   2100
  And certain death approaches me with speed,
  It's better you snuffed out our living light
  Than for foul Roman swords to do the deed.
  If we're to die, I ask, then, that you smite
  Us in Diana's[2] temple. You may lead   2105
  The way there now and bind our hands, proud sire,
  Before we're killed and burnt upon the pyre.
THEOGENES   Let's not drag out a trial I must complete.
  Death beckons—it's what cruel Fate will bestow.
SON   Why are you crying, mommy? Why this street?   2110
  Don't go so fast—I'm tired and walking slow.
  Could we stop here to have a bite to eat?
  This hunger's worn me down and laid me low.
MOTHER   I'll carry you so you can catch your breath.
  As I've no food, you'll make a meal of death.   2115

---

2. The Roman virgin goddess of wild animals and the hunt, associated also with the moon.

[*They exit. The boys* BARIATO *and* SERVIO *enter, fleeing.*]
BARIATO   Which way would be the best to try
Now, Servio?
SERVIO   Pick a route you know.
BARIATO   You look thin. Never mind, let's go—
Our stopping only means we'll die.
Just turn around—two thousand men   2120
Pursue us with their naked swords!
SERVIO   No one direction here affords
Us hope that we'll escape again.
Is there a place we both can hide
Or secret spot where we can cower?   2125
BARIATO   My father's dwelling has a tower
Where I can wait things out inside.
SERVIO   Then, go ahead, my friend, be gone!
It strikes me, even as I speak,
That I've been left so thin and weak   2130
From hunger I can scarce go on.
BARIATO   So, you're not coming, then?
SERVIO   I can't.
BARIATO   If it's true you can't move from here,
You'll only meet a death that fear,
The sword or hunger's grip can grant.   2135
I'm off, then, dreading all that aims
To steal my youth amid this strife:
The blades that thirst to end my life
And fires with their consuming flames.
                    [BARIATO *exits to the tower.* THEOGENES *enters*
            holding two drawn swords, his hands covered with blood.
                        SERVIO *sees him and runs offstage.*]
THEOGENES   You've watched my very blood as it was spilt,   2140
For what coursed through my children's veins was mine,
And seen me strike with honorable guilt
At innocents while blotting out my line.
As Fate's conspired against me to the hilt,
Sweet skies, devoid of sympathy divine,   2145
Confer a way to make my sorrows cease
So I may find quick death and be at peace.
Here, valiant fellow Numantines! Pretend
Your townsman is a Roman renegade[3]
And reap revenge by bringing to an end   2150
His life with vengeful hand or bloody blade.
May either sword here let you comprehend
The grief I feel and fury I displayed,
For dying thus in battle, as it were,
Would stay these pangs so they don't reoccur.   2155
Let he to whom these pleadings may concern
Discharge this charity and be so nice
As to consign me mid the flames to burn,

---

3. I.e., a soldier who has changed sides.

A piety by which you'd serve me twice.
Come on, what's keeping you? Step up and turn   2160
What's left of me into a sacrifice,
Then take this mercy that a comrade shows
And cast it into rage against our foes.
         [A NUMANTINE enters.]
NUMANTINE   Whom are you calling on, Theogenes?
What novel brand of death would you devise?   2165
How could you urge us to indulge in these
Unheard of fantasies you authorize?
THEOGENES   Brave townsman, if foreboding doesn't seize
That bold and gallant spirit you so prize,
Come take this sword and challenge me to fight   2170
As if I were a Roman you would smite.
To perish so is all I could desire
In light of things you've heard me just relate.
NUMANTINE   What finer way to die could we conspire,
Dictated as this seems to be by Fate?   2175
Now let's all to the plaza, where the fire
Craves corpses so, its flames can scarcely wait.
The victor, then, could throw the lucky dead
Amid the crackling blaze to keep it fed.
THEOGENES   Well said, friend. Let's proceed there while
     we've still   2180
The time to meet our deaths by this design.
A glorious end by sword and fire will
Look reputable, be it yours or mine.
        [They exit. SCIPIO, JUGURTHA, QUINTUS FABIUS,
     CAIUS MARIUS, HERMILIUS, LIMPIUS, and other SOLDIERS enter.]
SCIPIO   Unless my mind is playing tricks on me
Or all the signs conveyed by those dread sounds   2185
Just emanating from Numantia's soil
Prove false—those crackling flames and piteous wails—
I fear, without the slightest hesitance
Or doubt, that our barbarian foes have turned
Their fell brutality against themselves.   2190
No longer do their guards patrol the wall
Nor do the usual martial clarions blare.
A silence and a calm shroud their domain
As if these savage Numantines at last
Had found relief amid some tranquil peace.   2195
CAIUS MARIUS   Let me dispel whatever doubts remain,
Sir, and, with your permission, volunteer
To scale this towering wall to ascertain,
Regardless of the dangers I may face,
What's quelled the obdurate ferocity   2200
Of these proud, unrelenting Numantines.
SCIPIO   Proceed, then, Marius. Lean some ladder up
Against the wall and execute your plan.
CAIUS MARIUS   Hermilius, go fetch a ladder, then,
And while you're at it, have a soldier bring   2205

My buckler and white helmet with the plumes.
I'll either solve this mystery for our camp
Straightway or forfeit life in the attempt.
HERMILIUS   Look there—your shield and helmet lay close by.
Stout Limpius sets the ladder on the wall.   2210
CAIUS MARIUS   Commend my soul to Jupiter sublime
As I discharge the mission I've proposed.
SCIPIO   Just hold your buckler higher, Marius!
Draw in your body and protect your head!
Have courage, now—you've almost reached the top!   2215
Do you see something?
CAIUS MARIUS   Gods above, what's this?
JUGURTHA   What causes you to marvel so?
CAIUS MARIUS   A pool
Of blood stands where the city streets
Once lay and, strewn about, a thousand dead,
All mercilessly run through by cruel swords.   2220
SCIPIO   What, not one living?
CAIUS MARIUS   Not a single soul,
At least as far as I can tell from here
With what my field of view encompasses.
SCIPIO   Upon your life, jump down inside and take
A better look! Jugurtha, go with him.   2225
          [CAIUS MARIUS *leaps over the wall into Numantia.*]
Come, let's all follow.
JUGURTHA   Sir, it isn't meet
For someone of your rank to join this search.
Just wait here calmly until Marius
Or I return. We'll soon have answers as
To what befell these mighty Numantines.   2230
Now hold that ladder tight. Judicious skies!
I've never seen so horrible a sight
In all my life! How could this come to pass?
Blood, still warm, covering every speck of ground
And lifeless bodies in the square and streets?   2235
I'll need to view this massacre up close.
          [JUGURTHA *leaps over the wall into the city as well.*]
QUINTUS FABIUS   It's clear to me these savage Numantines,
Incited by the rage pent in their breasts
And facing ignominious defeat,
Preferred surrendering up their lives to swords   2240
Their own hands brandished rather than to these
Triumphant hands of gloating enemies
They couldn't possibly have hated more.
SCIPIO   If we might find but one of them alive,
My victory will be recognized in Rome.[4]   2245
Then I'll be hailed the conqueror of a land

---

4. To honor victorious generals on their return from their campaigns, Romans held elaborate festivals called triumphs, which included parading captives through the streets. The Numantines' self-inflicted death deprives Scipio of this possibility.

Whose men opposed our glorious empire's name,
Unbreakable in will and prone to hurl
Themselves headlong into the perilous fray,
Fierce adversaries whom no Roman here   2250
Can boast of having scattered into flight,
Stout hearts whose bravery and skill in arms
Have duly forced me to resort to this
Expedient of encaging them like beasts
Untamed, to win through art and strategy   2255
What never could be realized by our strength.
But look—it seems that Marius returns.
    [CAIUS MARIUS *climbs down the ladder.*]
CAIUS MARIUS   Illustrious general, our army's force
Has been expended all this while in vain
And vainly have you steered a prudent course,   2260
Expecting triumph in this long campaign
As patient diligence replaced sheer might.
These hopes have fled; just smoke and wind remain.
This tragic ending to Numantia's fight
Will live on as historians repeat   2265
These deeds for every age in which they write.
Securing victory from their sure defeat,
They've snatched the very laurels that you'd sought,
Resolved to die and make your glory fleet.
Now all our martial plans have come to naught;   2270
Self-murder's seen their honor will prevail
Despite the costly war we Romans fought.
These weary denizens refused to fail
In terminating lives we couldn't take,
Thus bringing to a close this drawn-out tale.   2275
Numantia's now a stagnant, bloody lake,
Its sacrifice of bodies piled high,
A thirst mass suicide alone could slake.
So did its crafty citizens defy
The chains of slavery, which boast no peer,   2280
And our abuse, from which they scarce could shy.
A fire still burning in the plaza here
Is grimly fed yet by the last of these
Dead souls and what possessions they held dear.
I came in time to see Theogenes,   2285
That bravest of all Numantines, berate
An ill-starred destiny which, by degrees,
Compelled this valiant soul to terminate
His life, consigning flesh and blood to flame
In one mad rush to seal his sorry fate.   2290
Before he died, I heard the man exclaim:
"Has ever an heroic act so earned
The merit and regard of lasting fame?
Now reap your spoils, cruel Romans, for we've burned
All, leaving naught but dust and smoke behind.   2295

Pluck thistles, not the flowers for which you've yearned."
I set out, then, exploring with a mind
To search for what had caused the sights I'd seen
Through every lane and alley I could find,
But didn't glimpse a single Numantine   2300
That I could usher back to camp alive
For us to question as to what machine
Of baneful war could lead them to contrive
This plot to blight the city as a whole,
A rush toward death no person would survive.   2305
SCIPIO What, did our enemies suppose my soul
So murderous and filled with savage pride
That mercy lay beyond my self-control?
Did they think lenience toward the losing side
A bent with which my heart was scarce imbued,   2310
My wish to see the rules of war defied?
How badly has my valor been construed
Throughout this land—I, born to conquer men,
Yet treat all prisoners with rectitude.
QUINTUS FABIUS Jugurtha might provide more answers when   2315
He comes regarding all you wish to know.
He's there, perturbed by scenes within his ken.
        [JUGURTHA enters, climbing down the same wall.]
JUGURTHA You're famed for valor, general, although
That futile gallantry has reached its end
And would be best placed elsewhere now on show.   2320
Here nothing's left to which you might attend.
The citizens lie dead but for one last
Stout soul on whom your triumph may depend
Up in that tower, where he shelters fast,
A mere boy, if my inkling is precise,   2325
Alarmed, though otherwise of noble cast.
SCIPIO Our capturing the lad, then, should suffice
For Rome to recognize my victory,
An honor I still crave at any price.
Let's all go to the turret, then, and see   2330
If we might urge the child to end this war
At once, surrendering to the enemy.
        [BARIATO appears at the top of a tower.]
BARIATO Ho, Romans! What could you be looking for?
If entering Numantia's your desire,
There's no one left to stop you anymore.   2335
Just know that I here, high above the fire,
Remain sole guardian of the city's keys,
For Death's consigned my neighbors to the pyre.
SCIPIO My men and I have only come for these,
Dear boy. I promise that you won't be hurt.   2340
Such clemency should set your mind at ease.
BARIATO This offering of mercy you assert
Comes too late now for any Numantine.

It isn't my intention to avert
A doom the likes of which has not been seen   2345
Before on earth to which my mom and dad
And homeland marched, not all serene of mien.
QUINTUS FABIUS   Oh, come now! Things can hardly be so bad
That you'd deprive yourself of youth's fresh age
In reckless disregard of life, huh, lad?   2350
SCIPIO   He's right, son. Temper this inclement rage,
For how is bluster from a boy to fare
Against this seasoned strength it would engage?
Upon my faith, from where I stand, I swear
You'll be the master of your destiny   2355
If you'll but climb down from that tower there.
You'll live amid the lap of luxury
For all your days, just reveling with delight
From every treasure you could wish from me
If you surrender now without a fight.   2360
BARIATO   Here festering inside my seething soul
Burns all the rage of citizens now dead,
Mere piles of dust left only to condole;
Here flares the rancor at the pacts they fled,
False treaties over which they'd no control,   2365
Lodged with me now safeguarded in their stead.
Poor, charred Numantia's turned my bluster hard;
Your venture showed Rome's reckless disregard.
Beloved homeland, this small refugee,
No matter what you're thinking, still adheres   2370
To that obeisance you've instilled in me
In spite of former fealties or fears.
Now that no heaven, soil or destiny
Abets me as this band of brigands nears,
It's possible you'll ultimately find   2375
That I can't pay your valor back in kind.
If I've been driven to this parapet,
Afraid my bold escape would come too late,
Watch Death remove me with more daring yet
As I resolve to share your noble fate.   2380
My worst fears realized, I discharge this debt
I owe unflinchingly to ones so great,
Relinquishing my callow youth's last breath
By bravely joining all of you in death.
You have my word, departed people: your   2385
Intent to thwart these Romans' victory must
Not languish from a duty I ignore,
Unless they mean to triumph over dust.
I'll foil their pompous cause for waging war,
Then, whether they now choose to mount a thrust   2390
Or, suavely promising me everything,
Assure that I'll be treated like a king.
Enough, toy soldiers! You may stand at ease
Instead of laboring so to scale this wall.

I promise you, your forces couldn't seize   2395
Me were they ten times greater overall.
Now watch my true intentions shine, as these,
Which stem from that pure love for what to all
Was once our home, I hereby bring to light
By leaping to my death within your sight.   2400
    [BARIATO *jumps from the tower.*]
SCIPIO I've never seen so memorable an act!
Such classic valor in so young a boy!
The fame you've brought Numantia will attract
A glory Spain forever will enjoy.
Your awesome, manly feat will counteract   2405
My claim of triumph, which like deeds destroy.
This mortal fall will raise your name's renown
As surely as it brings my own name down.
Were it to rise again above this plain
As your abode, I'd judge Numantia sweet.   2410
Of all combatants in this long campaign,
It's you alone who've brought me vile defeat,
So revel in the glory of this gain
Which heaven proffers, as is only meet
For one who, falling, soared yet higher, though   2415
Above him, he who triumphed was laid low.
    [*A trumpet sounds, and* FAME *enters.*]
FAME Ring out, oh clarion voice, so all may hear
Your dulcet tones and reassuring sound!
Fill souls with ardent yearning far and near
To hail this lofty deed the world around!   2420
Lift up your bowed heads, Romans, now and clear
This hero's mangled body from this ground.
That tender youth could manifest the power
To steal your honor leaping from a tower!
As I am Fame, recording all of name,   2425
I'll see to it that, while the blazing sun
Still warms the earth with life's eternal flame,
Providing vital strength to everyone,
I'll rightly, as is only fair, proclaim
The valor of Numantia on my run   2430
From Bactria to Thule[5] and extol
This singular display from pole to pole.
So brave a final stand, unseen before
On earth, foreshadows that same gallantry
Spain's daring sons will boast in peace and war,   2435
Heirs worthy of such bold paternity.
No, neither fearsome strokes from Death's scythe nor
Time's tireless march through every century
Could stop my singing of Numantia's praise
From now until the end of living days.   2440

---

5. Bactria was a province of Central Asia, roughly where Afghanistan is today. Thule was a far
northern land, identified variously with Norway or with islands in the North Atlantic.

Numantia's stalwart qualities belong
In paeans history's annals will rehearse.
Its brave resistance merits endless song,
Its doom such fame as no one can asperse:
With force unvanquished and with valor strong,   2445
Due tribute be its crown in prose and verse.
As Time's remembrance is what Fame bestows,
We bring this drama to a happy close.

FÉLIX LOPE DE VEGA Y CARPIO

Fuenteovejuna[†]

CHARACTERS

Fernán Gómez de Guzmán, COMMANDER of the Order of Calatrava

FLORES ⎫
ORTUÑO ⎭ his retainers

Rodrigo Téllez Girón, MASTER of the Order of Calatrava

LAURENCIA ⎫
PASCUALA ⎪
JACINTA ⎪
FRONDOSO ⎬ villagers
MENGO ⎪
BARRILDO ⎭

ESTEBAN ⎫
ALONSO ⎭ village magistrates

CUADRADO, village alderman

JUAN ROJO, village councilman

Queen ISABEL of Castile

King FERDINAND of Aragon

DON MANRIQUE, a courtier, Master of the Order of Santiago

JUDGE

LEONELO, a University of Salamanca graduate

CIMBRANOS, a soldier

BOY

ALDERMEN from Ciudad Real, SOLDIERS, VILLAGERS, MUSICIANS

The action takes place in 1476.

† Translated by G. J. Racz for *The Norton Anthology of Drama*, Vol. 1 (2009) and revised for this Norton Critical Edition.

Act I

[SCENE: A room in the palace of Rodrigo Téllez Girón,
MASTER of the Order of Calatrava. The palace is located in Almagro,
a town near Ciudad Real in central Spain.]

[*Enter the* COMMANDER, *Fernán Gómez de Guzmán, with his
retainers* FLORES *and* ORTUÑO.]

COMMANDER   The Master[1] knows I mark my time
Awaiting him.
FLORES   Indeed, he does.
ORTUÑO   He's more mature, sir, than he was.
COMMANDER   Enough to be aware that I'm
Still Fernán Gómez de Guzmán?   5
FLORES   He's just a boy. Don't take this wrong.
COMMANDER   He has to have known all along
The title that's conferred upon
Me is Commander of the Ranks.
ORTUÑO   His counselors undoubtedly   10
Incline him toward discourtesy.
COMMANDER   This stance will win him little thanks,
For courtesy unlocks the gate
Behind which man's goodwill resides
As surely as offense betides   15
An enmity fomenting hate.
ORTUÑO   If only men so keen to slight
Knew how they were abhorred by all—
Not least by sycophants who fall
To kiss their feet and praise their might—   20
They'd much prefer to die before
Insulting anyone again.
FLORES   Mistreatment from unmannered men
Is harsh and something to deplore,
Yet while discourtesy between   25
Two equals is a foolish game,
When men aren't peers, it's not the same
But vile, tyrannical and mean.
No sense to take offense, my lord.
He's still a boy and ignorant of   30
The need for your auspicious love.
COMMANDER   The obligation that the sword
He girded on when first this Cross
Of Calatrava graced his chest
Bids courtesy be shown all, lest   35
Our noble Order suffer loss.
FLORES   We'll know soon if his heart's been set
Against your person or your cause.
ORTUÑO   Leave now if all this gives you pause.

---

1. Leader of the Order of Calatrava, a Spanish military and religious order founded by Cistercian
monks in the twelfth century to defend against Moorish attacks.

COMMANDER I'll take the stripling's measure yet.   40
   [*Enter the* MASTER *of Calatrava,* Rodrigo Téllez Girón,
   with retinue.]
MASTER Dear Fernán Gómez de Guzmán!
   I've just been told that you were come
   And rue this inattention from
   My heart's own core.
COMMANDER I looked upon
   The matter ill, with wounded pride,   45
   As I'd thought my affection for
   You and my standing would ensure
   More noble treatment by your side,
   We two of Calatrava, you
   The Master, I Commander, though   50
   Your humble servant, well you know.
MASTER I only was alerted to
   Your presence here at this late hour,
   Fernán, and join you now in fond
   Embrace.
COMMANDER You honor well our bond   55
   As I've done all that's in my power—
   Nay, risked my life—to ease affairs
   For you, petitioning the pope[2]
   To disregard your youth.
MASTER I hope
   That, by this holy sign each wears   60
   Upon his chest, as I repay
   Your kindness with respect, you'll own
   Such honor as my sire had known.
COMMANDER I'm satisfied with what you say.
MASTER What news have you about the war?   65
COMMANDER Attend these words and soon you'll learn
   How duty makes this your concern.
MASTER It's this report I've waited for.
COMMANDER Rodrigo Téllez Girón, this
   Illustrious station you've attained   70
   Derives from the profound esteem
   Your sire claimed for your family name.[3]
   When he relinquished, eight years past,
   The rank of Master to his son,
   Commanders joined with kings to pledge   75
   The cross should pass to one so young
   While further confirmation came

---

2. Pope Pius II (1405–1464), elected to the papacy in 1458. Before his death he issued a papal
bull granting Master Pedro Girón's request that he be allowed to relinquish his post and
appoint his illegitimate son, Rodrigo, to the position of Master. Pius's successor, Paul II, reaf-
firmed Pius's decree (see line 80, below), and in 1466 the eight-year-old Rodrigo was appointed
Master and his uncle, Don Juan Pacheco, coadjutor (see lines 81–83). In 1474 (not long before
the action of the play unfolds), Rodrigo attained his majority and was able to assume full command of the Order of Calatrava.
3. The historical father of Rodrigo Téllez Girón, Pedro Girón, relinquished leadership of the
Order of Calatrava in order to marry the Infanta Isabel, sister of King Henry IV of Castile, but
died before the marriage could take place.

From papal bulls that blessed soul
His Holiness Pope Pius wrote,
Which Paul[4] did follow with his own.   80
Your uncle, Juan Pacheco,[5] then
The Master of Santiago, was
Appointed your coadjutor
And, when he died, we placed our trust
In your ability to lead   85
Our Order at your tender age.
Upholding past allegiances
Is vital in the present case
To honor these progenitors,
So know your kin, since Henry's[6] death,   90
Support Alfonso,[7] Portugal's
Good king, who has inherited
Castile, your blood contend, because
His queen, they vow, was Henry's child.
Prince Ferdinand of Aragon[8]   95
Disputes this claim, and through his wife
And Henry's sister, Isabel,[9]
Asserts his title to the throne
Against your family's cause. In short,
Yours see no treachery imposed   100
By Juana's[1] just succession here.
Your cousin keeps her under guard
Until the day when she will reign.
I come, then, with this counsel: charge
Your Knights of Calatrava in   105
Almagro here to mount their steeds
And capture Ciudad Real,[2]
Which straddles the frontier between
Castile and Andalusia, thus
Strategically commanding both.   110
You'd hardly need a host of men
To have it fall to your control;
Their only soldiers left there are
Its landowners and citizens

---

4. Pope Paul II (1417–1471), elected pope in 1464.
5. Marquis of Villena (see line 125), first duke of Escalona and leader of the chivalric Order of Santiago.
6. King Henry IV of Castile (1420–1474; r. 1454–74).
7. King Alfonso V of Portugal (1432–1481; r. 1438–81), who married King Henry's daughter Juana in 1475 (see lines 94, 101).
8. The future King Ferdinand II of Aragon (1452–1516; r. 1479–1516) and King Ferdinand V of Castile (r. 1474–1516); he claimed the Castilian throne through his marriage to Isabel and was known as "Ferdinand the Catholic."
9. Queen Isabel (sometimes Isabella) of Castile (1451–1504; r. 1474–1504), half-sister of King Henry IV. Following her marriage to Ferdinand of Aragon in 1469, Pope Alexander VI named them the "Catholic Monarchs."
1. King Henry IV's only child (1462–1504); because of the alleged infidelity of her mother, Princess Joana of Portugal, Juana was considered illegitimate by many, and upon her father's death the crown of Castile passed not to Juana but to her aunt, Isabel of Castile, sparking the War of the Castilian Succession (the backdrop of *Fuenteovejuna*).
2. A city in south-central Spain whose name means "royal city." Almagro: a town near Ciudad Real and the seat of the Order of Calatrava.

Who still defend Queen Isabel   115
And follow Ferdinand as king.
How grand, Rodrigo, to avail
Yourself of such a siege and prove
Those wrong who think these shoulders far
Too slight to bear the cross you do!   120
Your gallant ancestors, the Counts
Of Urueña,[3] beckon from
Their eminence in proud display
Of all the laurels they have won;
The Marquis of Villena,[4] too,   125
And countless other captains, ones
So noble that the wings of Fame
Could scarcely bear them higher up!
Come, bare the whiteness of your sword
And stain its blade in fierce assaults   130
With blood red as our Order's sign
So that you may be rightly called
By all men Master of that Cross
You wear upon your chest! If white
It stays, that title stays unearned.   135
Yes, both the weapon at your side
And that dear cross must shine blood-red.
Thus you, magnificent Girón,
Shall be at last enshrined the first
Among your line and most extolled!   140
MASTER   Fernán Gómez, it's my intent
To side with blood in a dispute
Whose rightness seems beyond refute,
So rest assured of this event.
If Ciudad Real, then, must   145
Be leveled by my hands, I'll burn
Its walls with lightning speed and turn
The city into ash and dust.
The friend or stranger who insists
That with my uncle died my youth   150
Could not be farther from the truth:
The spirit of my years persists.
I'll bare this still-white blade and lead
My forces by its dazzling light
Till, like these crosses, it shines bright   155
With blood the reddened wounded bleed.
Do any soldiers now subsist
Among your village retinue?
COMMANDER   They're loyal servitors, though few,
But should you summon them to list   160
With you, they'll fight like lions, for
In Fuenteovejuna all

---

3. Among these ancestors was Alfonso Téllez Girón, the father of Juan Pacheco and grandfather of Rodrigo.
4. That is, Juan Pacheco (see line 81 and note above).

The townsfolk heed the humble call
Of agriculture, not of war,
And farm to reap their daily fare. .   165
MASTER You've quarters near?
COMMANDER   It pleased the crown
To grant me land once in that town
So, mid these perils, I dwell there.
MASTER I'll need a tally of our strength.
COMMANDER No vassal there shall stay behind!   170
MASTER This day you'll see me ride, and find
My couching lance atilt full length!

                   [*Exit* COMMANDER *and* MASTER.]

      [SCENE: The town square in Fuenteovejuna]

    [*Enter the village women* PASCUALA *and* LAURENCIA.]
LAURENCIA I'd hoped that he was gone for good!
PASCUALA To tell the truth, I really thought
The news of his return here ought   175
To have perturbed you . . . and still would!
LAURENCIA I wish to God, I swear to you,
That we had seen the last of him!
PASCUALA Laurencia, I've known girls as prim
And tough as you—nay, more so—who,   180
Beneath the guise of harsh facades,
Have hearts as soft as cooking lard.
LAURENCIA You couldn't find an oak as hard
And dry as I am toward these clods!
PASCUALA Go on, now! You don't mean to say   185
You'd never drink to quench your thirst?
LAURENCIA I do, though I won't be the first
To have to protest in this way.
Besides, how would it profit me
To yield to all Fernán's false woo?   190
I couldn't marry him.
PASCUALA   That's true.
LAURENCIA I can't abide his infamy!
So many girls were gullible
In trusting the Commander's plights
And now live days that rue those nights.   195
PASCUALA Still, it would be a miracle
If you don't wind up in his grasp.
LAURENCIA Pascuala, one full month's gone by
Since you first saw this scapegrace try
In vain to land me in his clasp.   200
His pander, Flores, and that knave,
Ortuño, came by with a hat,
A jerkin and a choker that
Their master had assumed I'd crave.
They started off regaling me   205
With vows his lovelorn heart declared,

Which left me all a little scared,
Though just as disinclined to see
Myself his latest vanquished maid.
PASCUALA   Where did they speak to you?
LAURENCIA   Down by   210
The brook six days ago, as I
Recall.
PASCUALA   Laurencia, I'm afraid
They'll end up getting what they wish.
LAURENCIA   From me?
PASCUALA   No, from the priest—yes, you!
LAURENCIA   The meat on this young chick he'd woo   215
Is still too tough to grace his dish.
I mean, good lord, Pascuala! Look:
You know how much I'd rather take
A slice of ham when I awake
And place it on the fire to cook;   220
Then eat it with a hunk of bread
I baked and kneaded by myself
With wine pinched off my mother's shelf
From jugs that tightly store her red;
And how much happier I'd be   225
At noon to watch beef frolicking
With heads of cabbage, rollicking
In frothy pots of harmony!
Or, when I come home peeved and tired,
To marry eggplant in full bloom   230
With bacon—there's no rasher groom!—
For just the pick-me-up required.
Then later, for some toothsome snacks
To hold me till our supper's served,
I'd pick grapes off my vines, preserved   235
By God alone from hail attacks.
For dinner, I would eat the lot
Of spicy peppered meat in oil,
Then go to bed content with toil
And give thanks with a "lead us not   240
Into temptation"[5] of sheer praise.
But you know how men are: until
They get their way in love, what skill
They use in finding crafty ways
To make us, in the end, forlorn!   245
When, worn down, we give up the fight,
They take their pleasure in the night
And leave us wretched on the morn.
PASCUALA   You're right, Laurencia! It's no joke!
Once men are sated, they grow rude   250
And show us more ingratitude
Than sparrows do to villagefolk.

5. From the Lord's Prayer: see Matthew 6.13, Luke 11.4.

In winter, when the weather keeps
Our snowy fields devoid of crops,
These birds swoop down from off the tops   255
Of houses, all sweet coos and cheeps,
But indoors, head straight for the room
Where they can feed upon our crumbs.
Then, once the warm spring weather comes
And sparrows see the fields in bloom,   260
We hear the last of all their coos.
Forgetting our benevolence
And cutting off their blandishments,
They chirp accusingly: "Jews? Jews?"[6]
Yes, men are like that, too. As long   265
As they desire us, we're their soul,
Their heart, their everything, their whole
Life's being, and can do no wrong,
But once the fire of passion's spent,
They start to treat us worse than Jews   270
And what were once seductive coos
Now chastise us for our consent.
LAURENCIA   You can't trust any of their kind.
PASCUALA   Laurencia, sweetheart, I'm with you!
        [*Enter the villagers* MENGO, BARRILDO, *and* FRONDOSO.]
FRONDOSO   Barrildo, argue till you're blue,   275
You'll never change old Mengo's mind!
BARRILDO   Now, here's a person who could bring
An end to this discussion, men.
MENGO   Let's all be in agreement, then,
Before you ask her anything: 280
If she concurs that I'm correct,
You promise that you won't forget
To hand me over what we've bet?
BARRILDO   That's fine with me. I don't object,
But what do we net if you lose?   285
MENGO   My boxwood rebec,[7] which I hold
More precious than a granary's gold,
If I may be allowed to choose.
BARRILDO   That's good enough.
FRONDOSO   Then, let's not wile.
God keep you, lovely ladies both.   290
LAURENCIA   Frondoso, "ladies"? By my oath!
FRONDOSO   Just keeping with the latest style:
These days, a college boy goes by
"Professor," "one-eyed" means you're blind,
The cross-eyed "squint," lame are "inclined,"   295
And now a spendthrift's a "good guy."
The dumbest person is called "bright,"

6. Intolerance for all non-Christian religions increased during the Reconquest of territories from Muslim forces, and Jews who did not convert to Catholicism were expelled from Spain in 1492.
7. A bowed string instrument of medieval origin, played while held against the arm or under the chin like a violin.

The none-too-brave are "placable";
No one has thick lips—lips are "full"—
And beady eyes are "piercing," right?   300
The nitpicker is "thorough," while
The meddler is "engaged." In speech,
A windbag is "well-spoken," each
Annoying bore said to "beguile."
Thus, cowards are "dispirited"   305
And blowhards "full of fight." With twits,
The useful catchword "fellows" fits
While loons are "uninhibited."
The cheerless are alone "discreet";
"Authority" falls to the bald.   310
If silliness is "charm," who called
"Well-grounded" someone with big feet?
A "chest cold" means the pox in code;
The haughty now are "self-possessed";
The shrewd are "sly," but here's the best: 315
The humpback "shoulders quite a load"!
So maybe now you'll comprehend
Just how you're "ladies," and although
I've more examples, I'll forego
Reciting all of them on end.   320
LAURENCIA   Well, that may pass for courtesy,
Frondoso, with the city folk,
But I've heard other people cloak
Their thoughts in language that strikes me
As far more coarse in every phrase   325
They use and every cutting word.
FRONDOSO   Give us a taste of what you've heard.
LAURENCIA   It's just the opposite of praise:
You're "tiresome" if you're serious
And "brazen" if you look well heeled.   330
You're "somber" if you're even-keeled
And "spiteful" if you're virtuous.
Give counsel and you "interfere";
You "lavish" when you freely give.
Love justice and you're "punitive,"   335
Show mercy and be "inaustere."
The steadfast now are "dull as sin,"
Politeness is "sheer flattery,"
Sweet charity, "hypocrisy,"
And Christian faith "the sure way in."   340
"Dumb luck" is hard-won merit's name
While truth-telling is "recklessness."
Forbearance is deemed "cowardice"
And misadventure now means "blame."
A decent woman's called a "ponce,"   345
A proper, lovely girl is "plain,"
A chaste . . . Why should I wrack my brain
More? Let this serve as my response.

MENGO   The devil! That was quite a list!
BARRILDO   She's not a half-bad orator!   350
MENGO   I bet the priest who christened her
   Laid on the salt, fist after fist!⁸
LAURENCIA   What quarrel is it brings you here,
   If I have heard you right, today?
FRONDOSO   Just listen, on your soul.
LAURENCIA   Tell, pray.   355
FRONDOSO   Laurencia, lend me but your ear.
LAURENCIA   I'll give it to you out and out,
   A special present, not a loan.
FRONDOSO   I trust your judgment as my own.
LAURENCIA   So, what's this famous bet about?   360
FRONDOSO   Barrildo casts his lot with me.
LAURENCIA   And Mengo?
BARRILDO   He insists upon
   Denying a phenomenon
   That's clearly real.
MENGO   It cannot be;
   Experience refutes its name.   365
LAURENCIA   Which is . . . ?
BARRILDO   That love does not exist.⁹
LAURENCIA   Love's vital and would sure be missed.
BARRILDO   Yes, vital; it's a silly claim.
   This world has a most pressing need
   For love, or life would fade away.   370
MENGO   Philosophy's not my forte
   And now I wish that I could read,
   But here goes: if the elements¹—
   Earth, water, fire and air—all live
   In endless discord and then give   375
   Our very bodies sustenance—
   Their melancholy and, let's see,
   Blood, choler . . . phlegm²—I've proved my point.
BARRILDO   This world is nowhere out of joint,
   Dear Mengo; all is harmony³   380
   For harmony is love distilled
   And love, pure concert from above.
MENGO   I don't dispute that natural love

8. Prior to the Second Vatican Council (1962–65), Roman Catholic baptisms often included the
   placing of a small amount of salt on a baby's lips as a symbol of purification and wisdom.
9. The following is a comic pastiche of tenets of classical philosophy.
1. That is, the four elements that make up all matter (earth, air, fire, and water); this theory of
   matter, still current during the Renaissance, was first propounded by the Greek philosopher
   Empedocles (ca. 493–ca. 433 B.C.E.).
2. According to the humoral theory of psychology and physiology, elaborated by the Greek physician Galen (129–ca. 199 C.E.) and dominant for centuries, imbalances among the four humors,
   or bodily fluids, determined health and personality. An excess of black bile, a cold, dry substance in the body corresponding to the earth, made people melancholic; while blood and air
   were associated with the sanguine; yellow bile and fire, with the choleric; and phlegm and
   water, with the phlegmatic.
3. The harmony produced by a balance in bodily systems; "pure concert from above" (line 382)
   also suggests the harmony produced by the music of the spheres, a concept generally credited
   to the Greek mathematician and philosopher Pythagoras (sixth century B.C.E.) but taken up
   more literally in the Middle Ages.

Abides on earth, as God has willed.
Love does exist, but of the sort   385
That rules relations in advance—
Compulsory ties, not bonds of chance—
Among all beings these realms support.
And never once have I denied
That each man's humor finds some fit   390
With love that corresponds to it
To keep his being unified.
If someone tries to punch my face,
I block the impact with my arm
And when I'm facing bodily harm,   395
My feet run to a safer place.
My lids and lashes likewise move
To counter danger to my eye
And all from natural love, I vie.
PASCUALA   What point is it you seek to prove?   400
MENGO   I mean that we should be agreed
That only self-love rules the day.
PASCUALA   That's not true, Mengo, if I may,
For isn't there a vital need
A man experiences when   405
He loves a woman, or a brute
Its mate?
MENGO   Yes, but without dispute,
It's self-love and not true love, then.
Now, what is love?
PASCUALA   It's a desire
For beauty.[4]
MENGO   And why does love pursue   410
Said beauty, in your humble view?
PASCUALA   For pleasure.
MENGO   Right! May I inquire,
Then, whether this enjoyment might
Serve love itself?
PASCUALA   I'm sure that's so.
MENGO   So, self-love, then, will make love go   415
And seek what causes it delight?
PASCUALA   Why, yes.
MENGO   Then, as I'm claiming, there
Can be no love but of the kind
That everybody seeks to find
By courting pleasure everywhere.   420
BARRILDO   I seem to have some memory of
A sermon I heard by and by
Regarding Plato,[5] some Greek guy
Who taught humanity to love,

---

4. A position drawn from Plato's *Symposium* (ca. 384 B.C.E.). See line 423 and note.
5. Greek philosopher (ca. 427–ca. 347 B.C.E.), whose themes were much debated in the fifteenth
century by Neoplatonists.

Although the love he felt was aimed   425
At virtue and his loved one's soul.
PASCUALA   This line of thought has, on the whole,
Both stumped great intellects and shamed
Top scholars in our 'cademies
Who fry their brains debating it.   430
LAURENCIA   She's right; don't fly into a snit
By arguing for such fallacies.
Go thank your stars for leaving you
Without love, Mengo, in this sphere.
MENGO   Don't you love?
LAURENCIA   Just my honor here.   435
FRONDOSO   I hope God makes you jealous, too.
BARRILDO   So, who's the winner?
PASCUALA   You can take
That question to the sacristan.
If he won't tell you, the priest can
And that should settle what's at stake.   440
As I've not much experience
And our Laurencia loves not well,
I wonder how we'll ever tell?
FRONDOSO   To suffer such indifference!
    [*Enter* FLORES.]
FLORES   God keep you, good folk! As you were.   445
PASCUALA   So the retainer's sent to talk
For the Commander.
LAURENCIA   Chicken hawk!
What brings you here today, fine sir?
FLORES   You see this uniform, don't you?
LAURENCIA   So then, Fernán is coming back?   450
FLORES   The battle's won, though our attack
Entailed the loss of not a few
Brave men and blood of good allies.
FRONDOSO   Do tell us how the fighting raged.
FLORES   Who better to, since war was waged   455
Before these witnesses, my eyes?
To undertake this swift campaign
Against a city by the name
Of Ciudad Real, our most
Courageous, noble Master raised   460
An army of two thousand men—
All loyal vassals—with whom rode
Three hundred more of mounted troops
Comprised of friars and laymen both
For anyone who wears this Cross   465
Must rally to its battle cry,
Including priests, especially when
The foes are Moors,[6] you read me right?

6. North African Muslims had conquered Spain and Portugal in 711 and ruled for centuries over
much of the Iberian Peninsula (see line 500 and note).

Thus did the gallant youth ride forth
Bedecked in an embroidered coat   470
Of green with golden monograms.
His glistening brassards[7] alone
Shone through the openings in his sleeves
Held fast by hooks with golden braids.
A sturdy charger rode he, bred   475
In our fair South and dapple-gray,
Which drank from the Guadalquivir[8]
And grazed upon the fertile spots
Nearby. Its tailpiece was adorned
With buckskin straps, its curled forelock   480
In pure-white bows resembling cloth
That expert weavers deftly wove
To match the patches on its hide,
Or "flies on snow," as they are known.
Your liege lord, Fernán Gómez, rode   485
Beside him on a honeyed steed
That bore some white upon its nose,
Accenting its black mane and feet.
Atop a Turkish coat of mail
His armor breast- and back-plate shone   490
Both bordered with an orange trim
Relucent with pearls set in gold.
And from his burnished helmet waved
A crown of plumes that seemed to stretch
In orange-blossom whiteness down   495
To meet his orange vestment's edge.
A red and white brace held his lance
In readiness, although this bore
More likeness to a huge ash tree
To petrify Granada's[9] Moors.   500
And so the city took up arms
In affirmation of the stance
That it obeyed the rightful crown
And would defend its king and lands.
The Master mounted an attack   505
And, after fierce resistance there,
Decreed that all who'd wagged their tongues
Against his honor be prepared
To die beheaded for their crime,
While those who rallied round the flag   510
Among the simple city folk
Were flogged in public, bound and gagged.
There in the city he abides,
As well loved as he is well feared;
A man who battles, castigates   515

7. Armor for protecting the arm, usually from elbow to shoulder.
8. A river that passes through the southern Spanish cities of Córdoba and Seville.
9. A city in southern Spain; the site of the Alhambra, the palace of the Moorish kings, it was the Moors' last stronghold, from which they were expelled in 1492.

And crushes foes, still raw in years,
The town believes will come to be
The scourge of Africa some day,
Subjecting blue and crescent moons[1]
To that Red Cross his garb displays.   520
So many gifts has he bestowed
On our Commander and on all,
It seems that he's despoiling not
The city, but his private vaults.
But listen! Hear the music play?   525
Come welcome your great hero home,
For no wreath suits a victor like
The good will shown him by his own.
   [*Enter the* COMMANDER *and* ORTUÑO, MUSICIANS,
   village magistrates ESTEBAN *and* ALONSO, *and*
   village councilman JUAN ROJO.]
MUSICIANS [*Singing.*]   *All hail, victorious*
   Commander! Thy bold deeds be praised!   530
   For thou hast slain our foes
   And left their rebel cities razed!
   Long life to thy Guzmáns
   And to our Master's proud Giróns!
   In times of peace thy speech   535
   Is couched in calm and measured tones
   Though thou wouldst battle Moors
   Courageous as an oak is strong.
   From Ciudad Real
   To Fuenteovejuna throng   540
   Thy still triumphant troops
   And here thy lofty pennants wave!
   Fernán Gómez, God grant
   A thousand years to one so brave!
COMMANDER   Kind villagers, I thank you for this true   545
   Outpouring of affection I've been shown.
ALONSO   'Tis but a fraction of our love for you
   And scarce reflects the sentiments you're known
   To merit.
ESTEBAN   Fuenteovejuna deems
   Your presence here an honor, and our own   550
   Town council begs you to accept what seems
   No doubt a paltry offering conveyed
   By cart to one the village so esteems
   And tendered in goodwill mid poles arrayed
   With ribbons, though the gifts themselves be small. 555
   To start, glazed earthenware our potters made.
   Next, an entire stock of geese—see all
   Their heads protruding through the mesh to voice
   Praise for your valor with their cackling call!
   Ten salted hogs, each specimen more choice,   560

---

1. Islamic insignia.

Jerked beef, rich delicacies, and pork hides
Which, more than perfumed gloves, make men rejoice.
A hundred capons and plump hens, the brides
Of future widowed roosters of the same
Sort dotting these lush fields, are yours besides.   565
You'll not fetch arms or horses for your fame,
Nor trappings here embroidered with pure gold
Unless you take for gold the love you claim.
And having said "pure," may I be so bold
As to suggest these wineskins bear such wine   570
That poor bare soldiers scarce would mind the cold
As they patrolled outdoors if they could line
Their stomachs with this, steelier than steel,
For wine can cause the dullest blades to shine.
I'll skip the savories and the cheese you'll feel   575
Most tempted by, except to say it's right
That we should pay you tribute for our weal
And wish your household hearty appetite.
COMMANDER   For this, much thanks, good councilmen.
You may retire with all my best.   580
ALONSO   We bid you, sir, enjoy some rest
And welcome you back home again.
This sedge and bulrush at your door,
A touch of grace our town unfurls,
Might well have been oriental pearls—   585
Though surely you deserve far more—
Had we but means to furnish these.
COMMANDER   Kind folk, I doubt not what you say.
May God be with you.
ESTEBAN   Singers, play
Our song of triumph once more, please.   590
MUSICIANS [Singing.]   All hail, victorious
Commander! Thy bold deeds be praised!
For thou hast slain our foes
And left their rebel cities razed!
            [Exit MUSICIANS. The COMMANDER turns toward
                    his residence but stops at the entrance
                    to speak with LAURENCIA and PASCUALA.]
COMMANDER   Here, bide a while, the two of you.   595
LAURENCIA   What can we do for you, good sir?
COMMANDER   Why, just the other day you were
Aloof toward me, is that not true?
LAURENCIA   It's you he's coming to harass.
PASCUALA   Oh God, no! Let it not be that!   600
COMMANDER   I'm talking both to you, wildcat,
And to this other lovely lass,
For aren't you mine?
PASCUALA   Good sir, no doubt,
But hardly for such things as these.
COMMANDER   Just come inside and be at ease.   605
You see my servants are about.

LAURENCIA Well, had the magistrates come, too—
　　For one's my father, you may know—
　　It might have seemed correct to go.
COMMANDER You, Flores!
FLORES　　　　　　　Sir!
COMMANDER　　　　　　　Can it be true　　　　　　　610
　　That they refuse what I implore?
FLORES He said, go in!
LAURENCIA　　　　　Stop grabbing, man!
FLORES You're being foolish.
PASCUALA　　　　　　　While you plan
　　To lock us in and bolt the door?
FLORES He only thought you'd like to see　　　　615
　　The spoils he gathered in this batch.
　　　　[*The* COMMANDER *turns to enter his dwelling.*]
COMMANDER [*Aside to* ORTUÑO.] If they do enter, draw the
　　latch.
LAURENCIA I told you, Flores, leave us be!
ORTUÑO You mean the two of you are not
　　More booty?
PASCUALA　　　Let it rest awhile　　　　　　　620
　　And get out of my way or I'll . . .
FLORES Enough, for now. You see they're hot.
LAURENCIA How much more tribute would it take
　　To make him happy with these meats?
ORTUÑO Your meats would be the sweeter treats.　　625
LAURENCIA I hope they make his belly ache!
　　　　　　　　　　[*Exit* LAURENCIA *and* PASCUALA.]
FLORES He'll give us both an earful when
　　We dare return without the girls
　　And curse us like a pair of churls
　　While we take his abuse again.　　　　　　　630
ORTUÑO Well, masters sometimes grow annoyed.
　　To prosper in the servant class,
　　You have to let their foul moods pass:
　　Be patient or be unemployed.
　　　　　　　　　　　　[*Exit* FLORES *and* ORTUÑO.]

　　　[SCENE: A room in the palace of the Catholic Kings]

　　　[*Enter King* FERDINAND, *Queen* ISABEL, *the courtier*
　　　DON MANRIQUE, *and retinue.*]
ISABEL You would do well to heed the threat　　　635
　　Alfonso's army now presents.
　　His Portuguese have pitched their tents
　　In nearby fields and must be met
　　With troops who'll counter this deceit
　　By striking ere these foes attack　　　　　　640
　　For if our men don't drive them back
　　Our side will suffer sure defeat.

FERDINAND   Navarre and Aragon[2] both aid
  Our righteous cause and shall until
  We steel our forces in Castile   645
  And see their re-formation made,
  A measure which should guarantee
  Our triumph in an allied thrust.
ISABEL   Your Royal Majesty, we must
  Be certain of this victory.   650
DON MANRIQUE   Your Highness, there are aldermen
  From Ciudad Real here who
  Request an audience with you.
FERDINAND   Brave Don Manrique, show them in.
  [*Enter two* ALDERMEN *from Ciudad Real.*]
1ST ALDERMAN   Great Ferdinand, most Catholic king,   655
  Whom Heaven's sent with grace to reign
  Through all Castile and Aragon,
  Our noble succor and true aid,
  On Ciudad Real's behalf
  We've come to sue for royal help   660
  In true humility before
  Your valiant and all-powerful self.
  We'd held our own selves fortunate
  To be the subjects of this crown
  Till adverse fortune intervened   665
  And turned our destinies around.
  Rodrigo Téllez Girón, sire,
  Famed bearer of his family name
  Whose courage on the battlefield
  And strength belie his tender age,   670
  Of Calatrava Master, has
  Assailed our city to expand
  The Order's power and estate,
  His lands erstwhile by royal grant.
  We bravely readied our defense   675
  In hopes resistance would rebuff
  His forces, but our streams ran red,
  Discolored with the fallen's blood.
  In short, he took the city but
  He never could have had Fernán   680
  Gómez withheld his counsel, troops,
  And guidance in this treacherous plot.
  He bides still in our captured town,
  His vassals and sad subjects we
  Who suffer this loss with regret   685
  And hope it soon be remedied.
FERDINAND   And where is Fernán Gómez now?

---

2. Provinces of northern Spain. Following the events depicted in this play, Ferdinand succeeded
his father as king of Aragon in 1479; in 1511 he conquered the southern half of the Kingdom of
Navarre, uniting it with Spain.

1ST ALDERMAN   In Fuenteovejuna, sire,
The village where he makes his home
And where his seat of power resides,   690
The cruel Commander acts unchecked,
More freely than we care to state,
And keeps his vassals there as far
From happiness as they can stay.
FERDINAND   Have you no captain in your ranks?   695
2ND ALDERMAN   It's sure we haven't anymore,
As every nobleman they seized
Was wounded or has faced the sword.
ISABEL   This matter begs a quick display
Of strength, for cautious remedy   700
Would only make this enemy
The bolder given our delay.
Thus Portugal might view this stall
A chance occasion fortune yields,
Thrust through Extremadura's³ fields   705
And so bring grievous harm to all.
FERDINAND   Manrique, take two companies
Of soldiers to their bivouac
And launch a merciless attack
To quell such excesses as these.   710
The Count of Cabra, widely famed
For bravery and a Córdoba,⁴
Will ride with you, and never a
More valiant soldier has Spain claimed!
This seems the most expedient   715
Proceeding we can now effect.
DON MANRIQUE   Your judgment, sire, is most correct
And this dispatch most provident.
As long as life runs through my veins,
I'll see them all put in their place.   720
ISABEL   I'm confident success shall grace
Our cause with such men at the reins.

                                                          [*Exit all.*]

[SCENE: An open field in Fuenteovejuna]

[*Enter* LAURENCIA *and* FRONDOSO.]
LAURENCIA   I had to leave the wash half wet,
Frondoso, just to keep the town
From gossiping. The brook's no place   725
For men to gallivant around.
The villagers are whispering
About how you persist. They know
I've caught your eye as you have mine
And keep their eyes now on us both.   730
As you're the type of brazen swain

---

3. A province of southwest Spain bordering Portugal.
4. Diego Fernandez de Córdoba (b. 1438), count of Cabra and marshal of Baena.

To strut throughout the village clad
In elegant attire that costs
Far more than any other lad's,
There's not a girl or guy about   735
These woodlands, meadows, groves, and brush
Who isn't saying to himself
That we two are already one.
They all await that blessed day
When Juan Chamorro, sacristan,   740
Will leave the church's organ long
Enough to carry out our banns,
Though they'd be better off by far
To see their granaries duly stuffed
With heaps of autumn's golden wheat   745
And have their wine jars filled with must.
The rumors that the villagers
Keep spreading here have caused me pique
But aren't so irritating as
To have deprived me of dear sleep.   750
FRONDOSO   Your harsh disdain so flusters me,
Laurencia, that I fear each time
I see your face or hear your voice
I place existence on the line!
For if you know my sole desire   755
Is that we marry, why repay
These good intentions with such scorn?
LAURENCIA   I know but one way to behave.
FRONDOSO   How can it be you feel no pain
To see me in the grip of grief   760
When, at the merest thought of you,
I lose desire for food and sleep?
How can that sweet, angelic face
Bring such hardheartedness with it?
But, Lord, how rabidly I rave!   765
LAURENCIA   Then you must seek a curative.
FRONDOSO   The cure I seek resides in you
So we can be like turtledoves
That perch together rubbing beaks
And coo contentedly in love—   770
I mean, provided that the church . . .
LAURENCIA   Go ask my uncle from your heart,
The good Juan Rojo. Though I feel
No passion yet, I sense a spark.
FRONDOSO   Oh, no! Look over there—it's him!   775
LAURENCIA   He must be hunting deer nearby.
Quick, run and hide within these woods!
FRONDOSO   It's jealousy I need to hide!
        [*Enter the* COMMANDER.]
COMMANDER   I can't say it displeases me
To set out for a fearsome buck   780
And come upon a lovely doe.

LAURENCIA   I left my pile of wash half done
For this brief respite from my chores
But now, I fear, the brook awaits
So, by your leave, I'll go now, sir.   785
COMMANDER   The brusqueness in your cruel disdain,
Laurencia, is a sharp affront
To all the grace and comely looks
The heavens have bestowed on you
And makes you seem unnatural.   790
You've managed in the past to flee
The loving of my arms' embrace
But now this field, our silent friend,
Has pledged to keep our secret safe.
Come, there's no need for diffidence   795
Or any reason to avert
Your gaze from me, your rightful lord,
As if I were some peasant churl.
Did not Pedro Redondo's wife
Sebastiana gladly yield,   800
And young Martín del Pozo's, too,
Although the latter's wedding seal
Had scarcely dried, our happy tryst
But two days after she was wed?
LAURENCIA   These women, sir, could by that time   805
Claim much experience with men
As that same road you took to them
Had been well traveled for some years
By all the lads with whom they'd lain.
God keep you as you hunt your deer;   810
Were you not costumed with that cross,
I'd take you for the devil's spawn
To hound me so relentlessly.
COMMANDER   What haughty insolence you flaunt!
I'll lay my crossbow on the ground   815
And use these hands to put an end
To all your mincing ways.
LAURENCIA   How now?
You don't mean you'd be capable . . .
          [*Enter* FRONDOSO, *who picks up the crossbow.*]
COMMANDER [*Not noticing* FRONDOSO.]   Don't try to fight me off.
FRONDOSO [*Aside.*]   I pick
His weapon up, but hope to God   820
I'll have no cause for using it.
COMMANDER   Relent already!
LAURENCIA   Heavens, help
A girl in need!
COMMANDER   We're all alone.
There's no need now to be afraid.
FRONDOSO   Commander, you've a generous soul   825
So leave her be or rest assured
I'll make a bull's-eye of your chest

Though, even in my rage, that cross
Elicits my profound respect.
COMMANDER   Vile dog!
FRONDOSO   I see no dogs round here.   830
Quick, run, Laurencia!
LAURENCIA   Careful now,
Frondoso!
FRONDOSO   Off with you, I said!
                                        [*Exit* LAURENCIA.]
COMMANDER   The fool who'd lay his own sword down
Deserves the trouble he incurs.
I feared my prey would hear its clap   835
So I pursued the hunt ungirt.
FRONDOSO   By God, don't make me loose the catch
Or you'll be pierced like game, my lord.
COMMANDER   She's gone! Come, give the crossbow up,
You thieving, treacherous, peasant rogue!   840
Just give it here, I said!
FRONDOSO   For what,
So you could take my life with it?
Remember, sir, that love is deaf
And, from that day it reigns supreme,
Will not be swayed by argument.   845
COMMANDER   Am I to turn my back upon
A village churl? Shoot! Shoot, you knave,
But be prepared to stand on guard,
For as a nobleman I break
Chivalric code to challenge you.   850
FRONDOSO   No need, sir, for I'm satisfied
With my low station here on earth
But, as I must protect my life,
I'll take this crossbow as I flee.
COMMANDER   He plays a rash and perilous game   855
But I shall have my vengeance for
This crime of standing in my way!
Why didn't I just attack the clod?
The heavens see how I've been shamed!

Act II

[SCENE: The town square in Fuenteovejuna]

[*Enter* ESTEBAN *and village alderman* CUADRADO.]
ESTEBAN   We've still abundant stocks of wheat reserved   860
But really mustn't raid our granaries more.
These recent forecasts have us all unnerved
And I believe our strength lies in this store
Though some don't see what good these stocks have served.
CUADRADO   I've always been of one mind on this score;   865
Abundance means there's governance in peace.

ESTEBAN We'll tell Fernán Gómez, then, this must cease.
These fool astrologers do irritate!
Though ignorant of the future, they've a hoard
Of unconvincing prattles that relate   870
Grave secrets vital only to the Lord.
They think they're theologians and conflate
Before and after into one accord:
Ask any one about the present, though,
And you'll soon learn how little any know!   875
What, do they own the clouds that dot the air
Or the trajectory of the heavens' light?
How can they see what's happening up there
To give us all an endless case of fright?
They tell us when to plant our crops and where—   880
Wheat there, now greens, your barley to the right,
Here mustard, pumpkins, now cucumber beds—
I swear to God that they're the pumpkin heads!
First, they predict a herd of cows will die
And die they do—in Transylvania![1]   885
They forecast that our wine yield won't be high
But see beer flowing in Westphalia.[2]
The cherry frost in Gascony[3] they spy
And hordes of tigers in Hyrcania.[4]
Plant what we will, though, blessed by them or cursed,   890
The year still ends December thirty-first.
        [*Enter the university graduate* LEONELO *and* BARRILDO.]
LEONELO Looks like the gossip corner's doing well;
The tardy pupil can't be teacher's pet!
BARRILDO Was Salamanca[5] grand?
LEONELO   I've much to tell.
BARRILDO You'll be Law's second Bartolus.[6]
LEONELO   Not yet.   895
More like a barber, maybe. What I'd dwell
Upon is doctrine for the jurist set.
BARRILDO I'm sure you studied with the utmost care.
LEONELO I tried to gain important knowledge there.
BARRILDO So many volumes are in print today   900
The multitudes imagine they are wise.
LEONELO Yet they know less, it saddens me to say,
For so much wisdom's hard to summarize
And all their vain attempts to find a way
Just make the letters swim before their eyes.   905
The more a person reads the printed word
The more the letters on the page look blurred.

1. A region of present-day Romania, invoked here as a place remote from Spain.
2. A region in the west of present-day Germany.
3. A region of southwest France.
4. An area of ancient Persia (present-day northern Iran), associated in classical and later literature with tigers.
5. A city in western Spain where the country's oldest university was founded in 1218.
6. Bartolus of Saxoferrato (1313–1357), Italian jurist, author of influential doctrines based on
   Roman civil law.

I don't doubt that the art of print has saved
The best cuts from this cloth of rhetoric
By salvaging sage works from Time's depraved   910
Consignment of all earthly things to quick
Oblivion; this the printing press has staved.
To Gutenberg[7] we owe this curious trick,
A German from the town of Mainz whose fame
Is more than any Fame herself can claim.   915
Some writers who were once deemed erudite,
Though, lost their erudition on the page
While dumber men who never learned to write
Have published using names of men more sage.
Still others have penned treatises so trite   920
That, overcome by jealousy and rage,
They've signed their rivals' names to these poor works
To make their readers think these authors jerks!
BARRILDO   They couldn't do such things!
LEONELO   It's natural
For fools to reap revenge on real success.   925
BARRILDO   Still, Leonelo, print is notable.
LEONELO   We've lived for centuries without the press
And I don't see these modern times more full
Of St. Augustines or Jeromes,[8] do you?
BARRILDO   Let's sit a while before you start to stew.   930
    [*Enter* JUAN ROJO *and a* VILLAGER.]
JUAN ROJO   If what we've seen is true, you couldn't raise
A dowry out of what four farms would yield.
Now anyone who'd know the truth can gaze
Upon our town's disruption unconcealed.
VILLAGER   Peace, friend. What news of the Commander's days?   935
JUAN ROJO   He cornered poor Laurencia in a field!
VILLAGER   That lecherous animal! I'd love to see
The villain hanging from that olive tree!
    [*Enter the* COMMANDER *with* ORTUÑO *and* FLORES.]
COMMANDER   God keep you, townsfolk, in His grace.
CUADRADO   My lord.
COMMANDER   Good villagers, at ease   940
Now, as you were.
ESTEBAN   Your lordship, please
Be seated in your wonted place.
We'll stand, as this suits everyone.
COMMANDER   I'll order you to sit down, then.
ESTEBAN   You honor us as only men   945
Of honor can, as men who've none
Can scarcely proffer what they've not.
COMMANDER   Come, sit. I'd like us to confer.
ESTEBAN   Have you received the greyhound, sir?

---

7. Johannes Gutenberg (ca. 1400–1468), inventor of the movable-type printing press.
8. Two revered church fathers: St. Augustine (354–430), bishop of Hippo and author of many
commentaries and the *Confessions*; St. Jerome (ca. 347–419 or 420), author of ecclesiastical
histories, exegeses, and a Latin version of the Bible (the Vulgate).

COMMANDER   The dog continues to besot   950
  My valets, magistrate, and stuns
  The servants with its noble speed.
ESTEBAN   A fine example of its breed!
  Good lord, that noble creature runs
  As fast as any suspect or   955
  Delinquent that the law pursues.
COMMANDER   Well, given but the choice, I'd choose
  To have you point the dog straight for
  A certain frisky little hare
  Too swift for any but this hound.   960
ESTEBAN   I will, but where might she be found?
COMMANDER   I'm speaking of your daughter there.
ESTEBAN   My daughter?
COMMANDER   Yes.
ESTEBAN   How could she be
  A consort suitable for you?
COMMANDER   Do give her a good talking to.   965
ESTEBAN   Why, pray?
COMMANDER   She's set on vexing me.
  A lady here in town you'd call
  Distinguished noted my designs
  And, at the first sign of my signs,
  Succumbed.
ESTEBAN   Then she disgraced us all.   970
  If you don't mind me saying, sir,
  Your language ought to be less free.
COMMANDER   The rustic speaks so loftily!
  Ah, Flores! Have this villager
  Read one of Aristotle's tomes,   975
  The *Politics.*[9]
ESTEBAN   We of the land
  Are glad to live by your command
  And seek but honor for our homes
  As Fuenteovejuna, too,
  Can boast distinguished residents.   980
LEONELO [*Aside.*]   To hear that villain's insolence!
COMMANDER   Has what I said offended you
  Or any gathered here today?
CUADRADO   Commander, this is most unjust.
  You're wrong to say such things and must   985
  Not stain our honor in this way.
COMMANDER   Your what? Who do you think you are,
  The Friars of Calatrava, then?
CUADRADO   No doubt that Order numbers men
  Who wear the cross with bloodlines far   990
  Less pure than simple townsfolk own.
COMMANDER   So should our lines mix, theirs would be
  Forever fouled?

9. A treatise on the city-state by the Greek philosopher (384–322 B.C.E.).

CUADRADO   Iniquity
Defiles, not cleanses—that's well known.
COMMANDER   Whatever reasoning you seek,   995
Your women should be honored so.
ESTEBAN   Such words do shame us all, and no
One thinks you'd do the deeds you speak.
COMMANDER   These peasants can be tiresome!
In cities they know how to treat   1000
A man of qualities and meet
His every wish when he is come.
There, husbands deem it flattery
When other men pursue their wives.
ESTEBAN   You say this so we'll all live lives   1005
Of equal moral laxity.
God still inhabits cities, though,
Where vengeance is more swift and clean.
COMMANDER   That's it! Be on your way!
ESTEBAN   You mean
You wish the two of us to go?   1010
COMMANDER   No, I don't want to see a soul!
Now clear the square and don't come back!
ESTEBAN   We're leaving then.
COMMANDER   Not in a pack!
FLORES   Sir, please, a little self-control.
COMMANDER   They'll plot against me left alone,   1015
Each boor a co-conspirator.
ORTUÑO   Have patience with these rustics, sir.
COMMANDER   I marvel at how much I've shown.
Now head off home, the lot of you—
I won't have anything amiss.   1020
LEONELO [Aside.]   Just heavens, will you suffer this?
ESTEBAN   It's time that I returned home, too.
                                    [Exit VILLAGERS.]
COMMANDER   Men, don't you find these clods absurd?
ORTUÑO   They know you scarcely deign to mask
Your condescension when they ask   1025
That their petitioning be heard.
COMMANDER   So now they think us peers of sorts?
FLORES   Who equals whom does not pertain.
COMMANDER   How does that crossbow thief remain
At large, unsentenced by our courts?   1030
FLORES   I thought I'd spied him lingering near
Laurencia's doorstep late last night,
Though now I know I wasn't right:
I slit some knave's throat ear to ear
When I mistook his cloak to be   1035
Frondoso's in the eventide.
COMMANDER   I can't imagine where he'd hide.
FLORES   Oh, he'll turn up eventually.
COMMANDER   Would anyone who tried to kill
A man like me remain close by?   1040

FLORES   The heedless bird will blithely fly
　　Into a snare lured by a trill,
　　The foolish fish swim toward the hook.
COMMANDER   To think a clod, a boy at best,
　　Could point a crossbow at the chest   1045
　　Of this brave captain, whose sword shook
　　Granada and Córdoba both!
　　It's at an end, this world we knew!
FLORES   He acted as love bid him to.
　　You're still alive, so by my oath,   1050
　　I think you're in the peasant's debt.
COMMANDER   I swear, Ortuño, had I not
　　Disguised my feelings toward this lot,
　　Two hours would not have passed by yet
　　And I'd have run the whole town through.   1055
　　Until I judge the time is right,
　　I'll keep the reins on vengeance tight
　　And then do what I need to do.
　　What says Pascuala?
FLORES　　　　　　　　She replied
　　That any day now she's to wed.   1060
COMMANDER   If she'd still care to lend her bed . . .
FLORES   She's sending you where they'll provide
　　Your lordship with such things for cash.
COMMANDER   What says Olalla, then?
ORTUÑO　　　　　　　　　　　　The girl's
　　A lively one.
COMMANDER   Her quips are pearls.   1065
　　To wit?
ORTUÑO   She and her husband clash
　　Of late because, she'd have you know,
　　He's jealous of the notes I bring
　　And mad that you'd go visiting
　　His wife with manservants in tow.   1070
　　Just wait until he drops his guard
　　And you'll be first inside again!
COMMANDER   This knight is glad upon it, then.
　　The peasant watches her but hard.
ORTUÑO   It's true, though his attention strays.   1075
COMMANDER   And sweet Inés?
FLORES　　　　　　　　Who?
COMMANDER　　　　　　　　　　　Anton's bit.
FLORES   Her offer stands most definite
　　And ought to liven up your days.
　　We spoke in the corral outside—
　　Go round the back and in that door.   1080
COMMANDER   Loose women I've a soft spot for
　　But less so once I'm satisfied.
　　Ah, Flores, if they only were
　　Aware of what their charms are worth!

FLORES As letdowns go, there's none on earth   1085
  Like plain capitulation, sir.
  A woman's quick surrender blights
  The pleasure men anticipate,
  Though certain girls corroborate
  A wise philosopher[1] who writes   1090
  That females crave male company
  As form desires material shape,
  Which shouldn't leave your mouths agape
  For this is but reality.
COMMANDER A man whom ardor's heat lays waste   1095
  Is glad to have his pleasure sealed
  By lady friends who readily yield,
  Though he disdain them for this haste.
  The surest course for love to run
  Once all delight has been bestowed   1100
  Is down oblivion's well-worn road
  Of favors far too easily won.
      [Enter CIMBRANOS, a soldier.]
CIMBRANOS Is the Commander hereabouts?
ORTUÑO What, don't you see him standing there?
CIMBRANOS Oh, brave Fernán Gómez! Throw off   1105
  Your hunter's cap and be prepared
  To strap your battle helmet on!
  Replace your cloak with armor now!
  The Master of Santiago and
  The Count of Cabra's troops surround   1110
  Young Don Rodrigo Girón in
  Support of the Castilian queen
  At Ciudad Real. Good sir,
  I'm certain you can plainly see
  That all the blood your Order's lost   1115
  Will be for naught should they succeed.
  Our forces can already glimpse
  The figures on their coats of arms:
  Castile's two castles paired with lions
  By Aragon's heraldic bars.[2]   1120
  So while the King of Portugal
  Would like to honor staunch Girón,
  The youth would do well just to reach
  Almagro and be safely home.
  Quick, saddle up your charger, sir;   1125
  They'll head back to Castile as soon
  As you ride boldly into sight.
COMMANDER Be still while I think what to do.
  Ortuño, have the trumpet sound

1. That is, Aristotle, who expresses this idea (in less sexualized terms) in his *Physics* and *On the Generation of Animals.*
2. The symbols of two formerly autonomous kingdoms joined by the marriage of Isabel of Castile and Ferdinand of Aragon.

So all may hear it from the square.   1130
How many soldiers have I here?
ORTUÑO   Some fifty horsemen stand prepared.
COMMANDER   Inform them that we sally forth.
CIMBRANOS   If we don't start out now, good sirs,
Then Ciudad Real will fall.   1135
COMMANDER   Fear not, we shan't let this occur.

                                                             [*Exit all.*]

[SCENE: An open field in Fuenteovejuna]

[*Enter* MENGO, LAURENCIA, *and* PASCUALA, *fleeing.*]
PASCUALA   Oh, please don't leave us here alone!
MENGO   How can these fields inspire such dread?
LAURENCIA   I think it's best for us to head
To town now, Mengo, on our own—   1140
Just women, unaccompanied—
In case we should cross paths with him.
MENGO   He couldn't make our lives more grim
Were he the very demon's seed!
LAURENCIA   He's sure to hound us till we're his.   1145
MENGO   Oh, lightning bolts, cast down your fires
And purify these mad desires!
LAURENCIA   A bloody beast is what he is,
Our arsenic and pestilence
In town.
MENGO   Laurencia, I've been told   1150
That poor Frondoso grew so bold
In championing your innocence
He aimed at the Commander's chest.
LAURENCIA   You know how much I've hated men
But, Mengo, I confess since then   1155
I've realized he's not like the rest.
How valiant Frondoso was!
I fear this bravery might mean
His death.
MENGO   He never can be seen
In town, whatever else he does.   1160
LAURENCIA   I love the man, although it's plain
That I, too, know that he must flee.
Still, he responds to such a plea
With raging anger and disdain
While our Commander wastes no breath   1165
Affirming he'll hang upside down.
PASCUALA   I hope he chokes and spares our town.
MENGO   I'd rather see him stoned to death.
Sweet heavens, if I only knew
Some way to use my sling, I vouch   1170
Just stretching back this leather pouch
Would good as crack his skull in two!

You wouldn't find depravity
Like his in Rome's own Sabalus.³
LAURENCIA   You mean Heliogabalus,⁴   1175
Whose reign surpassed indecency.
MENGO   Sir Gawain's⁵ misdeeds were no worse.
Though history's outside my ken,
Our own Commander's crueler than
This legendary rogue of verse.   1180
Has nature spawned another fiend
Of Fernán Gómez's brute ilk?
PASCUALA   It had to be off tigress milk
That such a furious man was weaned.
    [Enter JACINTA, a village woman.]
JACINTA   For God's sake, if you hold our oath   1185
Of friendship dear, just help me hide!
LAURENCIA   Jacinta, you look petrified!
PASCUALA   You may rely upon us both.
JACINTA   The vile Commander's men head towards
Old Ciudad Real, a place   1190
Where, armed with their innate disgrace
Far more than with ennobled swords,
They'd take me to him as he bade.
LAURENCIA   God free you from the wrongs they'd do,
But if he'd be so free with you,   1195
How cruelly would he treat this maid?
                                    [Exit LAURENCIA.]
PASCUALA   A man might help you to escape;
I can't defend you in distress.
                                    [Exit PASCUALA.]
MENGO   I'll have to act like one, I guess,
As I'm a man in name and shape.   1200
Come by my side and never fear.
JACINTA   But have you arms?
MENGO   The oldest known
To man.
JACINTA   A sling without a stone?
MENGO   Jacinta, there are stones right here.
    [Enter FLORES and ORTUÑO.]
FLORES   Thought you could run away, did you?   1205
JACINTA   Now I'm as good as dead!
MENGO   Good sirs,
How can these honest villagers . . .
ORTUÑO   So, mustering up the derring-do
To champion a lady's cause?

---

3. A chieftain in North Africa (first century C.E.) who unsuccessfully revolted against Roman rule.
4. The Roman emperor Elagabalus (r. 218–222), whose reign was marked by sexual decadence, cruelty, and his devotion to a non-Roman god.
5. One of the legendary Knights of the Round Table (and King Arthur's nephew); Gawain is generally presented in English versions of the tales as heroic, courtly, and brave, but in some French works he is cruel and treacherous.

MENGO   I'd first defend her with my pleas,   1210
　　As I'm male kin, but failing these,
　　Would look to force and nature's laws.
FLORES   Enough, now. Run the beggar through.
MENGO   Compel me to unsling my sling
　　And you will rue the day I fling   1215
　　A volley of these rocks at you.
　　　　　[*Enter the* COMMANDER *and* CIMBRANOS.]
COMMANDER   A person of my rank alight
　　To settle such a petty case?
FLORES   The rabble in this horrid place,
　　Which you could purge by every right   1220
　　For giving you no end of grief,
　　Now brandish arms against our own.
MENGO   Good sir, if you cannot condone
　　Such conduct, as is my belief,
　　Then punish these vile soldiers who'd   1225
　　Abduct this woman in your name.
　　Her husband's and her parents' fame
　　Bespeaks the highest rectitude.
　　Now, by your leave, I'll take the girl
　　Back home where all her family wait.   1230
COMMANDER   My leave, you want? Retaliate,
　　Men, by my leave, against the churl.
　　Come, drop the sling.
MENGO   My lord, they bade . . .
COMMANDER   Peace! Flores and Ortuño, bind
　　His hands. Cimbranos, help in kind.   1235
MENGO   You'd act thus, called to virtue's aid?
COMMANDER   What do the townsfolk think of me
　　In Fuenteovejuna, cur?
MENGO   How has our village or I, sir,
　　Offended you so grievously?   1240
FLORES   Are we to kill him, then?
COMMANDER   Why draw
　　Your swords to sully steel you'd grace
　　With honor in a better place?
ORTUÑO   What are your orders?
COMMANDER   Whip him raw.
　　There, lash the peasant to that oak   1245
　　And, when his back is bared, go seize
　　Your horse's reins . . .
MENGO   Have mercy, please,
　　Sir! Mercy! You are gentlefolk.
COMMANDER   . . . And flog this man relentlessly
　　Until the studs fly off the straps.   1250
MENGO   Do heaven's righteous laws collapse
　　To grant these deeds impunity?
　　　　　　[*Exit* FLORES, ORTUÑO, CIMBRANOS, *and* MENGO.]
COMMANDER   You, girl, what are you running for?
　　You find a clod that tills the earth

More pleasing than a man of worth?   1255
JACINTA   Is this the way you would restore
Lost honor when it was your plan
To have me carried off by force?
COMMANDER   So, I desired you?
JACINTA   Of course,
Because my father is a man   1260
Well spoken of, though not your peer
In birth, with manners gentler still
Than any you possess.
COMMANDER   This shrill
Effrontery will not, I fear,
Assuage my wrath or aid your plight.   1265
Now, come along at once.
JACINTA   With you?
COMMANDER   Correct.
JACINTA   Pay heed to what you do.
COMMANDER   I'll heed your detriment, all right.
Who needs you? Why should I deprive
The troops of coveted supplies?   1270
JACINTA   Not all the force beneath the skies
Could make me suffer this alive!
COMMANDER   Come on now, strumpet, move along.
JACINTA   Have mercy!
COMMANDER   Mercy won't exist.
JACINTA   Then I've no choice but to enlist   1275
The heavens to redress this wrong.
          [*The* COMMANDER *exits as soldiers carry* JACINTA *off.*
     Enter LAURENCIA *and* FRONDOSO.]
LAURENCIA   How can you show your face around
Here unafraid?
FRONDOSO   I thought that some
Such recklessness would make you come
To see the troth to which we're bound.   1280
I watched the dread Commander part
While hiding in the hills above
And, seeing you deserve my love,
Lost all the fear that plagued my heart.
I hope he goes far off to thrive!   1285
Good riddance, too!
LAURENCIA   Don't waste your breath.
Besides, the more men wish your death,
The longer you'll remain alive.
FRONDOSO   If that's so, then long life to him,
For both sides profit by this quirk: 1290
I live while our best wishes work
Against him in the interim!
Laurencia, is there any place
For me in your affections, dear?
I need to know if my sincere   1295
Devotion's found its port of grace.

I mean, the village speaks as one
By now, considering us a pair,
And it astounds the townsfolk there
To see our coupling left undone.   1300
So put aside these harsh extremes
And tell me if there is or not.
LAURENCIA   I swear to both you and that lot
That all will soon be as it seems.
FRONDOSO   For this great mercy, let me kiss   1305
Your lovely feet, my future wife!
You've granted me a second life,
I must confess, in saying this.
LAURENCIA   Enough with blandishments! We mince
Words when it's evident to us   1310
That you have only to discuss
The matter with my father since
He comes now with my uncle, see?
Frondoso, don't lose faith, for I'm
To be your wedded wife in time—   1315
That much is sure.
FRONDOSO   God bolster me!
        [*They hide. Enter* ESTEBAN, ALONSO, *and* JUAN ROJO.]
ALONSO   So, in the end, the townsfolk rose
In vocal protest on the square,
And rightly so, for they'll not bear
More crimes from him resembling those.   1320
The scale of his intemperance
These days can scarcely fail to stun
While poor Jacinta's now the one
Who suffers his incontinence.
JUAN ROJO   All Spain will soon be governed by   1325
The Catholic Kings, whose well-earned fame
For piety bestows their name,
Which they do both exemplify.
Soon, too, brave Santiago will
Reach Ciudad Real's razed lands   1330
And win it back from Girón's hands
By marshaling his general's skill.
I'm sorry for Jacinta, though,
A stalwart lass in every way.
ALONSO   They whipped old Mengo's hide, you say?   1335
JUAN ROJO   No ink or flannel that I know
Of ever looked more black or blue.
ALONSO   Enough! You know my blood begins
To boil just picturing the sins
That make his reputation true.   1340
Why should I carry this baton
Of office if it serves no use?
JUAN ROJO   His men inflicted the abuse,
So why should you feel woebegone?

ALONSO   Well, what about the time they found   1345
Redondo's wife in this deep glen,
Left raped by the Commander's men,
Among whom she'd been passed around
Detestably when he did cease
To take by force what she'd deny?   1350
JUAN ROJO   I hear someone! Who's there?
FRONDOSO   Just I,
Who look for leave to speak my piece.
JUAN ROJO   Frondoso, as my house is yours,
Speak freely if you feel the need.
You owe life to your sire's seed   1355
But I'm owed what your grace ensures.
You're like a son to me; I reared
You with much love.
FRONDOSO   Then, sir, I seek—
Based on this love of which you speak—
A gracious favor volunteered.   1360
You know who fathered this proud son.
ESTEBAN   Were you aggrieved by that crazed beast
Fernán Gómez?
FRONDOSO   To say the least.
ESTEBAN   I thought as much—another one.
FRONDOSO   This pledge of love that you confide   1365
Now moves me likewise to profess
I love Laurencia and express
My wish here that she be my bride.
This tongue deserves a reprimand
For hastiness, which you'll excuse,   1370
As usually another sues
The sire for his daughter's hand.
ESTEBAN   Your swift return here is a boon,
Frondoso, and prolongs my years.
Dispelling what my heart most fears,   1375
Your coming is most opportune
And so I thank the skies above
That you've emerged to cleanse my name
And thank your passion just the same
For showing purity in love.   1380
It's only right that your good sire
Should learn at once what you've proposed.
For my part, I am well disposed
To help you realize this desire.
I would consider myself blessed   1385
If this sweet union came to pass.
JUAN ROJO   Well, first we'd better ask the lass
To verify she's acquiesced.
ESTEBAN   You needn't go through all that fuss;
In this case nothing is untoward: 1390
The two were firmly of accord

Before he pled his case to us.
We may as well, then, at our ease,
Discuss the dowry that is due.
The sum I gladly offer you   1395
Was saved up in *maravedís*.[6]
FRONDOSO   If I decline, don't feel forlorn;
What I don't need can pass unwept.
JUAN ROJO   You should be thankful he'll accept
The girl as bare as she was born.   1400
ESTEBAN   That may be, but in any case,
I'll ask the maid if she approves.
FRONDOSO   Good thinking, as it ill behooves
Your pressing what she won't embrace.
ESTEBAN   Sweet child! Laurencia!
LAURENCIA   Father dear.   1405
ESTEBAN   I'm sure she will, though you decide.
You see how promptly she replied?
My child, Laurencia! Only sheer
Love urges me to ask today—
Come closer, girl—would you commend   1410
Frondoso marrying your friend,
Good Gila? He's some fiancé,
The most upstanding of our men,
Proud Fuenteovejuna's son.
LAURENCIA   What? Gila wed . . . ?
ESTEBAN   If any one   1415
Among our maids deserves him, then . . .
LAURENCIA   I do commend their union, yes.
ESTEBAN   Yes—though she's ugly, which makes some
Believe Frondoso should become
Your husband. That we all could bless.   1420
LAURENCIA   Oh, father! Still inclined to jest
And gibe at your advanced age, too!
ESTEBAN   You love him, child?
LAURENCIA   He knows I do
And, though his love's likewise professed,
Unpleasant actualities . . .   1425
ESTEBAN   Should I inform him you consent?
LAURENCIA   Yes, bring him news of my intent.
ESTEBAN   So then it's I who hold the keys?
Well, said and done! Let's all away
To seek our good friend in the square.   1430
JUAN ROJO   Let's go.
ESTEBAN   My lad, as for a fair
Amount in dowry, would you say
Four thousand might work like a charm?
I've that much in *maravedís*.
FRONDOSO   How can you speak of such things? Please,   1435
You do my honor grievous harm.

---

6. Relatively low-value Spanish coins.

ESTEBAN   Come now, son, you'll feel otherwise
Within a day for, by my word,
A dowry that's left unconferred
Goes wanting in some other guise.   1440
         [*All exit except* FRONDOSO *and* LAURENCIA.]
LAURENCIA   Frondoso, are you happy, dear?
FRONDOSO   Just happy? I'm so overjoyed,
The state I'm in leaves me devoid
Of all my senses when you're near!
The smiles to which my heart is prone   1445
Pour out in gladness from my eyes
To think, Laurencia, my sweet prize,
That I can claim you as my own.
         [*Exit* FRONDOSO *and* LAURENCIA. *Enter the* MASTER,
               the COMMANDER, FLORES, *and* ORTUÑO.]
COMMANDER   Sir, flee! We can't do more to hold our ground!
MASTER   The weakness of these city walls before   1450
Their army's forces brought about our fall.
COMMANDER   The blood it's cost them, and the countless lives!
MASTER   They failed to seize our standard, though, to count
The Calatravan colors mid their spoils,
Though it had brought great honor to their toils.   1455
COMMANDER   Your stratagems are at an end, Girón.
MASTER   What can I do if turns of fate from night
To morn appear to be blind Fortune's will?
VOICES [*Within.*]   A victory for the monarchs of Castile!
MASTER   Our foes now crown the battlements with lights,   1460
Emblazoning the windows in the towers
Above with standards marking victory.
COMMANDER   And well they might, for all the blood it's cost.
Their joy seems tragic given what they've lost.
MASTER   I'll set back out for Calatrava, then.   1465
COMMANDER   And I to Fuenteovejuna while
You ponder whether to support your kin
Or pledge allegiance to the Catholic king.
MASTER   I'll write when I'm resolved of my intent.
COMMANDER   Here Time itself will be your guide.
MASTER   Ah, youth!   1470
May your deceptions keep me not from Truth!

            [SCENE: ESTEBAN's house]

    [*The wedding is in progress. Enter* MUSICIANS, MENGO, FRONDOSO,
     LAURENCIA, PASCUALA, BARRILDO, ESTEBAN, ALONSO, *and* JUAN ROJO.]
MUSICIANS   *Oh, many happy years*
   To you, sweet bride and groom!
   Oh, many happy years!
MENGO   You dashed that off in seconds flat,   1475
Now didn't you? It's not much good.
BARRILDO   What? You don't mean to say you could
Compose a better song than that?

FRONDOSO   He's more familiar with the lash
Than with the melodies of verse.   1480
MENGO   Don't shrink, but some have suffered worse.
One man that blackguard didn't thrash
Was taken to the vale one day . . .
BARRILDO   Stop, Mengo, please! Be merciful!
That homicidal animal   1485
Dishonors all who pass his way.
MENGO   A hundred soldiers—not one less—
Administered my pummeling.
I'd nothing on me but my sling
And never suffered such duress.   1490
But, as I was just saying, a
Fine man whose name I won't evoke,
Esteemed by all the village folk,
Was given quite the enema
Of ink and pebbles all in one.   1495
Who'd stand for vileness of that sort?
BARRILDO   The savage looked on it as sport.
MENGO   Well, enemas are far from fun
And, while they are salubrious,
I'd rather that my death come fast.   1500
FRONDOSO   So, may we hear now at long last
The ditty you've composed for us?
MENGO   *Oh, many happy years to you,*
Dear newlyweds! God's grace decree
That envy and vile jealousy   1505
Should never come between you two!
And when your years on earth are through,
Depart this life from satiety!
Oh, many happy years!
FRONDOSO   A curse upon the rhyming hack   1510
Who dashed off such a poor refrain!
BARRILDO   It did sound hasty.
MENGO   Let me deign
To say a word about this pack:
You know how fritter-makers throw
Their bits of batter in the oil   1515
And add more as they watch it boil
Until the kettle's filled with dough?
How some look swollen when they're turned,
Misshapen and a sorry sight,
Some lumpy on the left or right,   1520
Some nicely fried but others burned?
That's what I've come to understand
A poet does to draft a strain,
Material sprung from his brain
Like dough he forms with pen in hand.   1525
Then, whoosh! He plops the poetry
On sheets—the role the kettle plays—
Assuming that a honey glaze

Will mute the public's mockery.
Though once the audience takes a look,   1530
There's scarce a buyer to be found
Because the only one around
Who'll eat that rubbish is the cook!
BARRILDO   I think we've heard enough of this;
It's time the lovers made a speech.   1535
LAURENCIA   Give us your hand, sir, we beseech.
JUAN ROJO   Sweet child, my hand you wish to kiss?
First ask your father for this grace
On both yours and Frondoso's part.
ESTEBAN   I pray God sees it in His heart   1540
To fold them in His fond embrace
And bless the new life they've begun.
FRONDOSO   May you both bless us all life long.
JUAN ROJO   We shall. Come, lads, let's have a song
For now these two are joined as one!   1545
MUSICIANS   *The maid with flowing tresses roamed*
Through Fuenteovejuna's vale
And all the while, unknown to her,
A Knight of Calatrava trailed.
She hid within the leafy wood,   1550
Pretending she had spied him not
And, by turns bashful and abashed,
Concealed herself amid the copse.
"Why do you steal away, fair lass?"
He asked the maiden in the grove,   1555
"You know full well my lynx-eyed love
Has penetrated walls of stone."
The knight approached the maiden who,
Abashed and quite disquieted,
Began to fashion jealousies   1560
From boughs entangled overhead.
But just as anyone who loves
Will think it insignificant
To cross the mountains and the seas,
The knight asked his fair maid again: 1565
"Why do you steal away, fair lass,
My lovely maiden in the grove?
You know full well my lynx-eyed love
Has penetrated walls of stone."
    [*Enter the* COMMANDER, FLORES, ORTUÑO, *and* CIMBRANOS.]
COMMANDER   Don't stop the feast on my account.   1570
Calm now, no need to be distraught.
JUAN ROJO   We recognize you're in command,
But this, sir, is no game you halt.
Sit here if you would stay. What cause
Is there for such warlike array?   1575
Had you some triumph? But, why ask?
FRONDOSO   Stars, I'm a dead man! Send me aid!
LAURENCIA   Frondoso, flee while you've the chance!

COMMANDER   Not this time. Bind the peasant tight.
JUAN ROJO   Resign yourself to prison, son.   1580
FRONDOSO   I'll never leave the place alive!
JUAN ROJO   Why? What is your offense?
COMMANDER   I'm not
    The sort to kill without due cause
    For, if I were, this cur who stands
    Before us would by now have lost   1585
    His life, run through here by my guard.
    Confine him to a prison cell
    Until his father should pronounce
    The punishment his crime compels.
PASCUALA   Please, sir, not on his wedding day.   1590
COMMANDER   Why should these nuptials change my mind?
    Are there no other men in town?
PASCUALA   You're able to forgive his crime;
    You have that power.
COMMANDER   Were I the one
    Aggrieved, Pascuala, then I could.   1595
    But Master Téllez Girón was
    Insulted by this criminal,
    His Order and his honor both,
    And it's imperative that all
    Bear witness to this punishment   1600
    In case some other foe feels called
    To raise a standard versus his.
    You may have heard one afternoon
    He aimed a crossbow at the chest—
    My vassals, such a loyal group!—   1605
    Of your esteemed commander here.
ESTEBAN   Sir, if a father-in-law may
    Defend a deed of his new son,
    It isn't hard to contemplate
    How someone so in love as he   1610
    Might well have rankled with chagrin
    If it is certain you conspired
    To take his wife away from him.
    What swain would not have done the same?
COMMANDER   You're talking nonsense, magistrate.   1615
ESTEBAN   I speak for your own virtue, sir.
COMMANDER   I'm innocent of all you claim;
    She wasn't yet his wife back then.
ESTEBAN   You're guilty, sir. I'll say no more
    But rest assured the king and queen   1620
    Who rule Castile will issue forth
    New orders for disorder's end.
    They'd be remiss, though now at rest
    From war, to suffer that their towns
    And far-flung villages let men   1625
    As powerful and cruel as you
    Display a cross so grandiose.

This sign is but for noble breasts
So let it grace the monarch's robes
And not the cloaks of lesser men.   1630
COMMANDER   You, there! Relieve him of the staff.
ESTEBAN   Obedient, I surrender it.
COMMANDER   [*Striking* ESTEBAN.]   I'll use it on you as I'd lash
An untamed and unruly horse.
ESTEBAN   As you're my lord, I must submit.   1635
PASCUALA   You'd cudgel an old man like that?
LAURENCIA   He thrashes him because he is
My sire. Avenge yourself on me!
COMMANDER   You, take her to the prison grounds
And station ten guards at her cell.   1640
                    [*The* COMMANDER *exits with his men.*]
ESTEBAN   Sweet heavens, send your justice down!
                                          [*Exit* ESTEBAN.]
PASCUALA   The wedding has become a wake!
                                          [*Exit* PASCUALA.]
BARRILDO   Who'll speak? Are there no men around?
MENGO   I took my licks, thanks much! The welts
Are red as cardinals[7] on my back   1645
So save yourselves that trip to Rome!
Let someone else provoke his wrath.
JUAN ROJO   We'll speak to him as one.
MENGO   Perhaps,
Though now we'd best let silence reign;
Don't you recall they whipped my cheeks   1650
Till they were pink as salmon steaks?

Act III

[SCENE: The Council Chamber in Fuenteovejuna]

[*Enter* ESTEBAN, ALONSO, *and* BARRILDO.]
ESTEBAN   What's keeping them?
BARRILDO   They know full well we wait.
ESTEBAN   Assembling here grows riskier by the hour.
BARRILDO   Most everyone's heard why we congregate.
ESTEBAN   With poor Frondoso captive in the tower   1655
And my Laurencia under such duress,
If God does not do all within His power . . .
          [*Enter* JUAN ROJO *and* CUADRADO.]
JUAN ROJO   Why raise your voice, Esteban, when our chief
Aid must be stealth if we're to have success?
ESTEBAN   It's shocking I'm not louder, to be brief.   1660
          [*Enter* MENGO.]
MENGO   I'll slip into the meeting hall as well.

---

7. Newly invested cardinals of the Catholic Church are given a scarlet cap, and other scarlet garments also signify their rank. In Spanish, *cardenal* also means "bruise."

ESTEBAN   An old man whose gray hairs are bathed in grief
  Asks you, good villagers, how best the bell
  For our dear town's lost honor might be tolled
  Now that she's been so ravished and abused.   1665
  And how, if these be honors, can we hold
  Such rites? Is there a single man left here
  Whom that barbarian has not unsoulled?
  Why don't you answer? Is it, as I fear,
  That you've all had your honor basely used?   1670
  Then, make your firm commiseration clear
  For, if this common loss can't be excused,
  What stays your hand? Or have these blows been slight?
JUAN ROJO   The world knows none more wretched and diffused
  Though news now reaching us appears more bright: 1675
  The Catholic kings, who brought peace to Castile,
  Will stop soon in Cordova, where we might
  Dispatch two aldermen who'll sue until
  They're pledged redress, bowed at their royal feet.
BARRILDO   Before the monarchs do come, though, we will   1680
  Still need to find a remedy to meet
  This enemy in that our king, who smote
  So many foes, has others yet to beat.
CUADRADO   If anyone here asks me for my vote,
  I vote that we forsake this baneful town.   1685
JUAN ROJO   We haven't time; besides, they might take note.
MENGO   If the Commander hears the noise, he'll frown
  So on this council, he might kill us all.
CUADRADO   Our tree of patience has come crashing down,
  Our ship of fear floats lost beneath this pall.   1690
  For such an upright man, who leads this land,
  To watch his daughter dragged away in thrall
  To brutes, and have the staff of his command
  So splintered on his head, I ask of you,
  What slave endures more from his master's hand?   1695
JUAN ROJO   What is it you would have our village do?
CUADRADO   Die, die or put those tyrants to the sword.
  We've many villagers, while they are few.
BARRILDO   Rise up in arms against our rightful lord?
ESTEBAN   The king's our only lord by heaven's laws,   1700
  Not that barbaric and inhuman horde.
  If God assists us in our righteous cause,
  What have we all to lose?
MENGO   Take care, good sirs,
  Rash actions such as these should give us pause.
  I speak for all the simple villagers   1705
  Who bear the brunt of this vile injury
  And fear still more harm from these tormentors.
JUAN ROJO   We suffer this misfortune equally;
  Why should we wait until our lives are lost?
  They burn our homes and vineyards down with glee;   1710

Revenge upon such tyrants bears no cost!
[*Enter* LAURENCIA, *disheveled.*]
LAURENCIA   You let me pass, for I've a right
To enter where the men confer.
A woman may not have a vote
But she can make her voice be heard.   1715
Don't you know me?
ESTEBAN   Good God, are you
My daughter?
JUAN ROJO   You don't recognize
Your own Laurencia?
LAURENCIA   I'm afraid
I must appear a dreadful sight
For you to doubt it's I you see.   1720
ESTEBAN   My child!
LAURENCIA   Don't dare call me your child
Again.
ESTEBAN   Why not, my dearest heart,
Why not?
LAURENCIA   I've reasons of all kinds,
But let the first among them be
Allowing tyrants, unavenged,   1725
To snatch me from my family's grasp
Without you seeking due revenge.
I'm not Frondoso's wife yet, so
You cannot claim reprisal's weight
Devolves upon a husband's lot   1730
When such revenge is yours to take.
Until the wedding night has passed,
Our codes prescribe that you'd assume
This obligation stands among
A father's duties, not a groom's.   1735
For even if I buy a jewel,
Until it isn't brought to me,
It's not my place to fret about
Who's guarding it or who's a thief.
You watched Fernán Gómez abduct   1740
A maid and didn't lift a hand
Like coward shepherds who allow
The wolf to carry off the lamb.
How many daggers at my heart
And lewd advances I endured!   1745
How many threats and foul misdeeds
From one who'd be my paramour
And yearned to see my chastity
Surrendered to his appetites!
Look at my hair for evidence   1750
Of how I fought him through the night
And see the blood spilt by his blows.
Have you no honor left as men?

Have I no kinsmen here, no sire?
How has my sorry plight not left   1755
Your likes contorted with the pain
Of seeing me so cruelly pained?
You're lambs, the sheep from which our town's
Old sheep well takes its timid name![1]
Give me your weapons, then, if you'd   1760
Stand useless there like stones, bronze shards
Or jasper blocks. Brute tigers! No,
Not tigers. While these creatures are
Unfeeling, they hunt down and kill
The beasts that rob them of their cubs.   1765
Not even waves can harbor those
That venture to attack their young.
You cowards were born craven hares,
Not Spaniards but barbarians,
Frail chickens—hens!—whose women are   1770
Abandoned to their captors' whims!
Wear distaffs[2] on your belts, not swords!
Why even gird those rapiers on?
By God above, I'll see to it
That only womenfolk respond   1775
To tyrants who'd leave honor stained
By seeking their perfidious blood!
They'll just throw stones at you and laugh,
You spinning women! Sissies! What
Men, cowardly as little girls!   1780
Perhaps, tomorrow you can use
Our headdresses and petticoats
Or make your faces up with rouge!
That cruel Commander, meanwhile, plans
To hang Frondoso for his crime   1785
From high upon a battlement
In secret and without a trial.
He'll do the same to all of us,
You half-men, which is why I yearn
For that day when our town, bereft   1790
Of every woman, will revert
To that illustrious Golden Age
Of Amazons[3] who made men quake.
ESTEBAN   Brave child, I cannot count myself
Among those you would designate   1795
With such dishonorable terms.
I'll go myself now, even if
The whole world stands against my cause.
JUAN ROJO   I, too, however daunted with
The power of this enemy.   1800

1. *Fuente ovejuna,* fount (or well) of sheep (Spanish).
2. Staffs used to hold flax or wool during spinning; a traditional symbol of women's work and of
   women in general.
3. In classical mythology, a fierce race of women warriors.

CUADRADO   We'll die together, then.
BARRILDO   A rag
Tied to a stick is flag enough.
Now let those monsters breathe their last!
JUAN ROJO   What order should we recognize?
MENGO   Kill all of them disorderly!   1805
The village must be of one mind
And all the villagers agreed
The tyrant and his men must die.
ESTEBAN   Then grab your cudgels and your bows,
Your pikes and swords and lances, too!   1810
MENGO   Long live the Catholic Kings, our sole
True lords!
ALL   Long may they live and reign!
MENGO   And death to tyrant traitors! Death!
ALL   Yes, traitorous tyrants, you must die!
                                        [*The men exit.*]
LAURENCIA [*To the village women.*]   The heavens echo your behest,   1815
So forward, women of the town!
March on if you would set about
Regaining your lost honor! March!
     [*Enter* PASCUALA, JACINTA, *and other village women.*]
PASCUALA   What's happening? We heard these shouts.
LAURENCIA   Girls, can't you see the town is off   1820
To kill Fernán Gómez today?
The merest boys have joined the men
To send that devil to his grave.
But why should they alone enjoy
The honor stemming from this feat?   1825
As women we have suffered most
The outrage from his foul misdeeds.
JACINTA   What is it you would have us do?
LAURENCIA   Let's all of us form ordered ranks
And undertake an act so bold   1830
We'll leave the wondering world aghast.
Jacinta, for your suffering,
I name you corporal; you're in charge
Of this brave women's squadron here.
JACINTA   Yet you've endured much worse by far.   1835
LAURENCIA   Pascuala, standard-bearer, right?
PASCUALA   I'll look around here for a pole
So we can hoist a flag on it.
You'll see I'm worthy of the post!
LAURENCIA   We haven't time for that right now   1840
Since fortune presses us to fight
But let us use our headdresses
As pennants we can wave on high.
PASCUALA   We'll have to name a captain, though.
LAURENCIA   Not true.
PASCUALA   How so?
LAURENCIA   Because who needs   1845

A Cid or Rodomonte[4] when
It's I who'll lead with gallantry?

[SCENE: A room in the COMMANDER's residence]

[Enter FRONDOSO *with his hands bound,* FLORES, ORTUÑO,
CIMBRANOS, *and the* COMMANDER.]
COMMANDER   Now take the extra rope you used to bind
His hands and hang him so he's punished more.
FRONDOSO   You're leaving a black legacy behind.   1850
COMMANDER   This battlement should serve us on that score.
FRONDOSO   But sir, it never even crossed my mind
To seek your death!
FLORES   What's all the ruckus for?
[*Loud noise is heard offstage.*]
COMMANDER   What ruckus?
FLORES   Would the peasants in this town
Obstruct our justice?
ORTUÑO   Sir, the doors are down!   1855
[*The noise grows louder.*]
COMMANDER   How dare they when they know this is the seat
Of our command?
FLORES   Together they rebel!
JUAN ROJO [*Offstage.*]   Now burn and raze the place! We'll not retreat!
ORTUÑO   These popular revolts are hard to quell.
COMMANDER   They rise against their lord?
FLORES   The peasants beat   1860
Your doors down, sir, from grudges that impel
Their fury on.
COMMANDER   Come, set the prisoner free.
Frondoso, calm the magistrate for me.
FRONDOSO   Yes, sir. It's love that made their passion wake.
[*He exits.*]
MENGO [*Offstage.*]   May Ferdinand and Isabel prevail!   1865
But death to traitors!
FLORES   Sir, for your own sake
I urge you, flee!
COMMANDER   It's futile to assail
A garrison one cannot hope to take.
They'll soon turn back.
FLORES   Those wronged on such a scale
Aren't likely to retreat until blood flows   1870
And they've exacted vengeance on their foes.
COMMANDER   We'll make a stand here in this room and fight.
This door's as good as any gate, I gauge.
FRONDOSO [*Offstage.*]   On, Fuenteovejuna!
COMMANDER   Hey, they've quite
A leader there! I say we meet their rage.   1875

---

4. Both great fighters. Rodomonte, a major character in Ludovico Ariosto's Italian romance
Orlando Furioso (1516, 1532), is a fearsome and boastful leader of the Moors; El Cid ("the
Lord," Arabic) is Rodrigo (or Ruy) Díaz de Vivar (ca. 1043–1099), a Spanish military leader
who is the hero of the twelfth-century Castilian epic *The Poem of My Cid.*

FLORES   It's your rage, sir, not theirs that gives me fright.
ESTEBAN   The tyrant and accomplices, I wage.
Fight, Fuenteovejuna! Tyrants, fall!
          [*Enter all.*]
COMMANDER   Wait, men!
ALL   No, vengeance cannot wait at all!
COMMANDER   Then tell me where I've erred. Upon the crown   1880
And as a knight, I'll make it up to you.
ALL   Long live King Ferdinand! Now, onward, town!
Die, wicked Christians and false traitors, too!
COMMANDER   I'm speaking to you and you shout me down?
I am your rightful lord!
ALL   Our sole true lords   1885
Remain the Catholic Kings!
COMMANDER   Men, wait. Stand by!
ALL   On, Fuenteovejuna! Now you die!
          [*The* COMMANDER *and his men flee, pursued by the*
          men of Fuenteovejuna. Enter the village women, armed.]
LAURENCIA   Let's stop a bit and reconnoiter here,
Not women but brave soldiers in my ken!
PASCUALA   For vengefulness, a woman has no peer.   1890
We'll spill his blood right here! If not now, when?
JACINTA   Yes, let's impale his body on a spear.
PASCUALA   We're all agreed. Come on, let's do it then!
ESTEBAN [*Offstage.*]   Now die, Commander traitor!
COMMANDER   Here's my death!
I beg Your mercy, Lord, with my last breath.   1895
BARRILDO [*Offstage.*]   There's Flores!
MENGO   That's the rogue so quick to dole
My lashes out. Lay into him and how!
FRONDOSO [*Offstage.*]   I'll be avenged when I tear out his soul!
LAURENCIA   We need no leave to enter.
PASCUALA   Steady now.
We'll guard the door.
BARRILDO [*Offstage.*]   I've lost all self-control   1900
So, tears, my lordships, we can disallow.
LAURENCIA   I'm going in, Pascuala, for my sword
Must stay unsheathed until my name's restored.
                              [*She exits.*]
BARRILDO [*Offstage.*]   Look, there's Ortuño!
FRONDOSO [*Offstage.*]   Slash his ugly face!
          [FLORES *enters, fleeing, with* MENGO *in pursuit.*]
FLORES   Have mercy, Mengo, please! I'm not to blame!   1905
MENGO   If being his pimp could not secure our case,
Your flogging me would fault you all the same.
PASCUALA   Come, hand him to us women. Where's the race,
Man? Stop your pointless running.
MENGO   Sure, I'm game.
This sounds like punishment enough to me.   1910
PASCUALA   You'll be avenged.
MENGO   That's all I want to see.

JACINTA Die!
FLORES   Being killed by women isn't just.
JACINTA Seems quite a turn of fate.
PASCUALA   What tears are these?
JACINTA Perverse procurer for your master's lust!
PASCUALA Oh, die now, traitor!
FLORES   Mercy, ladies, please!   1915
        [*Enter* ORTUÑO, *fleeing from* LAURENCIA.]
ORTUÑO Look here, I'm not . . .
LAURENCIA   I know you well, I trust!
    Come, let the blood of these vile dogs appease
    Your swords!
PASCUALA   Oh, let me meet death slaughtering!
ALL   On, Fuenteovejuna! Thrive, dear king!
                                        [*Exit all.*]

        [SCENE: A room in the palace of the Catholic Kings]

        [*Enter King* FERDINAND, *Queen* ISABEL, *and* DON MANRIQUE.]
DON MANRIQUE   Our plan of action worked so well   1920
    That all objectives were attained
    And we were met with no sustained
    Resistance as the city fell.
    The opposition, sire, was light
    But, had their side presented more   1925
    To counteract our force at war,
    It surely would have proven slight.
    The Count of Cabra stays behind
    To guard the city from attack
    In case their army doubles back   1930
    To mount a second thrust in kind.
FERDINAND We deem it wise that he remain
    To muster and command our troops,
    Ensuring that our force regroups
    And curbing passage through the plain.   1935
    It ought to be impossible
    For any harm to blight us, then,
    Although Alfonso gathers men
    To join his force in Portugal.
    It's fitting that the city should   1940
    Be left in such reliable hands
    For, where our able Count commands,
    All marvel at his hardihood.
    In this way, he can turn aside
    The danger threatening our realm,   1945
    A loyal guardian at the helm
    Who'll keep our kingdom fortified.
        [*Enter* FLORES, *wounded.*]
FLORES   King Ferdinand, good Catholic sire,
    To whom the heavens did concede
    The crown of proud Castile in light   1950

Of all your noble qualities,
Attend to this account of acts
Unmatched in cruelty by men
Throughout this world, from where the sun
First rises bright to where it sets.   1955
FERDINAND   Come, steady now, man!
FLORES   Sovereign king,
The wounds you see would not consent
To my delaying this report
For this life surely nears its end.
In Fuenteovejuna, sire,   1960
That farming town from which I've fled,
The people with inclement breast
Have put their rightful lord to death.
Fernán Gómez lies murdered there,
A victim of the grievances   1965
Those traitorous vassals claimed to bear,
For those aggrieved scarce need pretext.
Thus, dubbing him tyrannical
By full consensus, these vile plebs
Became emboldened over time   1970
To carry out this treachery.
They stormed through the Commander's home
And, though he was a nobleman,
Did not provide him with the chance
To quit these debts and make amends.   1975
Not only were his pleas ignored
But, spurred by their impulsiveness,
The villagers left him with wounds
That rent the cross worn on his chest
Then hurled him out a window down   1980
Into a furious waiting horde
Of women, who proceeded to
Impale him on their pikes and swords.
They dragged his body to a house
And, each displaying greater rage,   1985
Began to pluck his hair and beard
While cruelly slicing up his face.
So outsized did their fury seem
And fierce their mounting hate appear,
The largest pieces left intact   1990
On the Commander were his ears!
Expunging, next, his coat of arms,
They shouted that they wished, instead,
To march beneath your own because
The former caused them great offense.   1995
Then, lastly, they ransacked his home
As if it were some enemy's
And happily among themselves
Divided up his property.
All this I saw with my two eyes   2000

For, infelicitously, fate
Would not consent that I should die
While lying in my hiding-place,
My wounds fresh, waiting out the day
In hope the dark of night would come   2005
So I could steal away unseen
And tell you what the town had done.
You're merciful and just, good sire,
So see these wanton criminals
Are punished by your code of law   2010
For acts so reprehensible.
Oh, hear his spilt blood crying out
And make them pay harsh recompense!
FERDINAND   Brave fellow, you may rest assured
They won't escape our punishment.   2015
So grievous are these late events
We find ourselves bereft of words
And therefore deem it best a judge
Should verify such deeds occurred
To castigate the culpable   2020
And make examples of their breed.
A captain shall escort him hence
To warrant his security.
Malfeasance such as this deserves
Exemplary punition soon.   2025
But now, look to this soldier here
And be attentive to his wounds.
                                        [Exit all.]

[SCENE: The town square in Fuenteovejuna]

[Enter the VILLAGERS, with the head of Fernán Gómez on a lance.]
MUSICIANS   Oh, many happy years
To you, good Catholic Kings,
And death to tyrants all!   2030
BARRILDO   Frondoso, let's hear your song now.
FRONDOSO   Here goes, however freshly penned.
Let quibblers with my meter mend
The verse the best way they know how.
Long live our lovely Isabel   2035
And Ferdinand of Aragon,
Whose union is a paragon
And who, though two, are one as well!
St. Michael[5] take you both to dwell
In Heaven when you hear God's call.   2040
Long life to you, we wish,
But death to tyrants all!
LAURENCIA   Your turn, Barrildo.

5. The archangel who, in Christian tradition, guides the souls of the faithful to heaven.

BARRILDO Here goes mine.
I put a lot of thought in it.
PASCUALA Recite the poem as you see fit 2045
And it should come out sounding fine.
BARRILDO Oh, many happy years to you,
Famed monarchs, fresh from victory!
From this day forward you shall be
Our lords, who bring us luck anew! 2050
May evil dwarves and giants, too,
Succumb before your battle call
And death to tyrants all!
MUSICIANS *Oh, many happy years*
To you, good Catholic Kings, 2055
And death to tyrants all!
LAURENCIA Now Mengo sing.
FRONDOSO Let's hear your stuff.
MENGO I dabble, so I'll take a whack.
PASCUALA Those hash marks on your belly's back
Are witness you've had whacks enough! 2060
MENGO *'Twas on a lovely Sunday morn*
When I, on orders of this here,
Was whipped until my aching rear
Writhed frightfully, its soft skin torn,
I bearing what hence won't be borne. 2065
Long live our Christian monarchers
And death to all these tyranters!
MUSICIANS *Oh, many happy years!*
ESTEBAN Remove his noggin from that lance.
MENGO His face has all a hanged man's charms. 2070
[*Enter* JUAN ROJO, *bearing an escutcheon with the royal coat*
of arms.]
CUADRADO Look here, the royal coat of arms.
ESTEBAN Let our whole village cast a glance.
JUAN ROJO Where should its splendidness be hung?
CUADRADO Right here, upon our own town hall.
ESTEBAN Shine on, brave shield!
BARRILDO Bring joy to all! 2075
FRONDOSO The warm sun rising here among
These symbols hails a bright new day.
ESTEBAN Long live León! Castile, live on,
And prosper, bars of Aragon,[6]
But death to tyrants and their sway! 2080
Dear Fuenteovejuna, heed
The sage advice of this old man
For none who've marked my counsel can
Affirm I've ventured to mislead.
It won't be long before the crown 2085
Sends someone to investigate

---

6. That is, heraldic bars (see line 1120). León: a province of northwestern Spain.

The goings-on round here of late
And, with the king lodged near our town,
We ought devise, while there's still time,
Some story no one can dismiss.   2090
FRONDOSO Your thoughts?
ESTEBAN   Claim unto death that this
Was Fuenteovejuna's crime
So none be taken off to die.
FRONDOSO By us, then, all must be agreed:
It's Fuenteovejuna's deed.   2095
ESTEBAN Is this how we will answer?
ALL   Aye!
ESTEBAN Why don't I act like I've the task
Of the investigator now
So I might best instruct you how
To face the questions he will ask?   2100
Here, let's have Mengo be the first
Upon the rack.
MENGO   You couldn't choose
A frailer guy?
ESTEBAN   I'll only use
You to rehearse.
MENGO   Then, do your worst!
ESTEBAN Who killed the town's Commander, you?   2105
MENGO All Fuenteovejuna, sir!
ESTEBAN Don't make me torture you, vile cur!
MENGO Kill me and it would still be true!
ESTEBAN Confess, thief!
MENGO   I do as I'm told.
ESTEBAN So?
MENGO   Fuenteovejuna! There!   2110
ESTEBAN Pull tight.
MENGO   It's nothing I can't bear.
ESTEBAN We'll foul up any trial they hold!
    [Enter CUADRADO.]
CUADRADO What are you doing, dallying here?
FRONDOSO Cuadrado, what's so troublesome?
CUADRADO The crown's investigator's come.   2115
ESTEBAN Hide quickly while the coast is clear!
CUADRADO A captain also guards the man.
ESTEBAN The Devil watch his back this day!
We all know what we have to say.
CUADRADO They're seizing everyone they can   2120
As hardly any soul has hid.
ESTEBAN There's no need fear should make us weak.
You, who killed the Commander? Speak!
MENGO Who? Fuenteovejuna did!
                              [Exit all.]

[SCENE: A room in the mansion of the Master of Calatrava]

[*Enter the* MASTER *of Calatrava and a* SOLDIER.]

MASTER   This murderous deed's left me distraught.   2125
That such should be his last reward!
I ought to put you to the sword
As payment for the news you've brought.

SOLDIER   I'm just a message-bearer, sir,
And didn't meant to cause you ire.   2130

MASTER   To have a town turned mob conspire
And wrong me thus may not occur.
I'll take five hundred men with me
And raze the village to the ground.
The lawless names of those still found   2135
There will be struck from memory.

SOLDIER   You might well calm such fury down
As they're now subjects of the king
And surely not for anything
Would one wish to enrage the crown.   2140

MASTER   But they fall under my command
So whence their fealty to Castile?

SOLDIER   These grievances our own courts will
Consider when the time's at hand.

MASTER   Now when did any such assize   2145
Remove possessions from the throne?
They are our sovereign lords, I own,
A truth I duly recognize.
We're all the monarch's vassals now
And, given this, I'll check my ire   2150
Although an audience with my sire
Might serve my case best and allow
A youthful aspect to excuse
Whatever grave offense I've done.
My tender age may well be one   2155
Defense this loyal heart can use.
I'll go to see the king in shame,
Compelled by honor to proceed
With fortitude in pressing need
To clear my honorable name.   2160

[*They exit.*]

[SCENE: The town square in Fuenteovejuna]

[*Enter* LAURENCIA, *alone.*]

LAURENCIA   True love's concern for its beloved's good
Becomes thereafter love's appended pain
For fear harm may befall love is a bane
That brings concern as all new worries would.
Though watchful thought decrease this likelihood,   2165
The mind, perturbed, will readily show strain
As love's well-being, stolen, roils the brain,

A torment nowise easily withstood.
I do adore my husband and this dire
Occasion will condemn me to duress   2170
Should fortune fail to favor him on high.
His happiness is all that I desire;
When he is present, sure is my distress,
When he is absent, just as sure I die.
    [*Enter* FRONDOSO.]
FRONDOSO   Laurencia, love!
LAURENCIA   Sweet husband, here?   2175
This move displays a steely nerve!
FRONDOSO   Does such solicitude deserve
This cold reception from you, dear?
LAURENCIA   I beg you, darling mine, beware,
For here you'll meet a ghastly end.   2180
FRONDOSO   Laurencia, may the skies forfend
That my well-being should cause you care.
LAURENCIA   Aren't you afraid to view the throes
Your townsmen face in their ordeal
Or the investigator's zeal   2185
In hastening to inflict their woes?
Stay out of harm's way while you can
And flee before they capture you.
FRONDOSO   What? How could you expect me to
Do deeds unworthy of a man?   2190
Would it be proper to betray
The others in this circumstance
Or not see you when I've the chance?
Don't order me to go away.
What reason would there be for me   2195
To save myself, untouched and whole,
But not acknowledge my own soul
When facing such calamity?
    [*Cries are heard offstage.*]
If I can trust my ears, it seems
The noise I'm hearing are the cries   2200
Some tortured wretch hurls toward the skies.
Come listen closely to his screams.
    [*The* JUDGE *is heard interrogating* VILLAGERS *offstage.*]
JUDGE   The truth and you'll be freed, kind gent.
FRONDOSO   They torture an old man to make
Him speak.
LAURENCIA   He's too strong-willed to break.   2205
ESTEBAN   Pray, loose the ropes a bit.
JUDGE   Relent.
Now say, who killed Fernán, good man?
ESTEBAN   Give Fuenteovejuna blame.
LAURENCIA   Brave father, may God praise your name!
FRONDOSO   What courage!
JUDGE   Grab that boy there. Wretch!   2210
Lay on! Still tighter! Cur! Yes, I'm

Convinced you know. Who did this crime?
No answer? Stretch him, drunkard, stretch!
BOY   Sir, Fuenteovejuna did!
JUDGE   Dumb clods, by all the king commands,   2215
I'll strangle you with my own hands!
Who murdered the Commander, kid?
FRONDOSO   To think a tender lad could face
Such torment and resist so long!
LAURENCIA   Brave villagers!
FRONDOSO   Yes, brave and strong!   2220
JUDGE   You, seize that woman there and place
Her body next upon the rack.
Now it will be the maiden's turn.
LAURENCIA   His anger's causing him to burn.
JUDGE   You'll tell me or I'll kill the pack   2225
Of you right here if he's not caught.
Which one's the guilty villager?
PASCUALA   It's Fuenteovejuna, sir!
JUDGE   Still tighter!
FRONDOSO   This is all for naught.
LAURENCIA   Pascuala hasn't said a thing.   2230
FRONDOSO   The children, either. What's to fear?
JUDGE   Have you bewitched the townsfolk here?
Pull!
PASCUALA   Heaven ease my suffering!
JUDGE   What are you, deaf? I told you, pull!
PASCUALA   Still Fuenteovejuna, yes!   2235
JUDGE   That fat oaf clad in tattered dress
Is next, the one whose paunch looks full.
LAURENCIA   Poor Mengo! Who else could it be?
FRONDOSO   Though no one's broken yet, he might.
MENGO   Ow, ow!
JUDGE   Just slowly stretch him tight.   2240
MENGO   Ow!
JUDGE   This should jog your memory.
MENGO   Ow, ow!
JUDGE   Come, bumpkin, out with it:
Who laid the town's Commander low?
MENGO   Please stop! I'll tell you all I know!
JUDGE   You, let up on the ropes a bit.   2245
FRONDOSO   He's breaking.
JUDGE   Use your back until
The lever halts.
MENGO   I'll tell you when
You stop!
JUDGE   All right, who slew him, then?
MENGO   Old Fuenteovejunaville!
JUDGE   I've never seen such villainy!   2250
They make a mockery of pain!
The one I thought could least refrain
From talking held up valiantly.

I'm weary. Come, let us depart.
FRONDOSO   Good Mengo, may God keep you near!   2255
Your courage has dispelled the fear
I felt for us both in my heart.
        [*Enter* MENGO, BARRILDO, *and* CUADRADO.]
BARRILDO   Three cheers there, Mengo!
CUADRADO   Yes, my word!
BARRILDO   And one cheer more!
FRONDOSO   That was some feat!
MENGO   Ooh!
BARRILDO   Here, friend, have a bit to eat   2260
And drink.
MENGO   What is it?
BARRILDO   Lemon curd.
MENGO   Ooh!
FRONDOSO   There you go, man, drain the cup!
BARRILDO   I knew you could.
FRONDOSO   He's swilling, so it must be good.
LAURENCIA   More food here while he's drinking up.   2265
MENGO   Ooh, ooh!
BARRILDO   This round is my treat, too.
LAURENCIA   He's stately as he knocks them back.
FRONDOSO   It's easy once you're off the rack.
BARRILDO   More?
MENGO   Ooh! As long as it's on you . . .
FRONDOSO   Drink up, old friend. Lord knows you've grounds.   2270
LAURENCIA   This makes one quaff per turn, all told.
FRONDOSO   Bring him some clothes, he must be cold.
BARRILDO   More still?
MENGO   Uh, maybe three more rounds.
Ooh, ooh!
FRONDOSO   Yooh . . . want the wine you've earned?
BARRILDO   Yooh dooh? Here's more to slake your thirst.   2275
Home brew should fill resisters first.
What's wrong?
MENGO   I think this wine has turned.
Let's go before I catch a chill.
FRONDOSO   This jug, you'll see, holds better wine,
But who killed the Commander, swine?   2280
MENGO   Old Fuenteovejunaville!
                [*Exit all except* FRONDOSO *and* LAURENCIA.]
FRONDOSO   He's honored by our show of love
But could you please inform me, wife,
Who took the town Commander's life?
LAURENCIA   Who? Fuenteovejuna, dove.   2285
FRONDOSO   Who killed him?
LAURENCIA   Stop, you're scaring me!
Sure, Fuenteovejuna, churl!
FRONDOSO   And how did I slay you, sweet girl?
LAURENCIA   By loving me so tenderly.
                    [*Exit* FRONDOSO *and* LAURENCIA.]

[SCENE: The Queen's chamber]

[*Enter* FERDINAND *and* ISABEL.]
ISABEL   Your presence here is a surprise,   2290
My lord. Good fortune smiles on me.
FERDINAND   You are a glorious sight to see,
My queen, a comfort to these eyes.
We make for Portugal and seize
This chance to stop en route and rest.   2295
ISABEL   Your Majesty knows when it's best
To change his course and take his ease.
FERDINAND   How did you leave our dear Castile?
ISABEL   In peace, sire, quiet and serene.
FERDINAND   We wonder not when such a queen   2300
Imparts tranquility at will.
     [*Enter* DON MANRIQUE.]
DON MANRIQUE   Sire, Calatrava is now just
Arrived and seeks an audience
With you in humble reverence
To pledge his troth and ask your trust.   2305
ISABEL   It's been my hope to meet the lad.
DON MANRIQUE   My lady, though he may look young,
I promise you he ranks among
The finest soldiers we have had.
     [*The* MASTER *of Calatrava enters as* DON MANRIQUE *exits.*]
MASTER   I'm Rodrigo Téllez Girón,   2310
Your servant, sire, and Master of
The Calatravan ranks whose love
Entreats forgiveness from the throne.
I here confess I've been deceived
Into transgressing noble laws   2315
Established by Castile because
Of faulty counsel I'd received
From cruel Fernán, who led me down
A road of false self-interest, true
But faithless. As you now construe,   2320
I beg forgiveness of the crown
And, should Your Highness grant to me
This mercy, which I scarce deserve,
I promise this day forth to serve
The royal cause stoutheartedly   2325
In, say, your long campaign, my lord,
Against Granada, where you ride
And where you will observe with pride
The valor latent in my sword
Whose unsheathed steel will bravely vie   2330
With foes who'll suffer crushing loss
So I might drape my Order's cross
O'er Moorish battlements on high.
For this, I'll send five hundred men
To fight beside your own troops now   2335

And hereby give my solemn vow,
Sire, never to displease again.
FERDINAND   Rise, Master, off this bended knee,
For we two hold your presence dear
And you are always welcome here.   2340
MASTER   These favors are grief's remedy.
ISABEL   Your words are equally as fine
As your brave feats and gallant air.
MASTER   You are, dear queen, an Esther fair
And you a Xerxes,[7] sire, divine!   2345
     [*Enter* DON MANRIQUE.]
DON MANRIQUE   Your Majesty, the judge is back
From Fuenteovejuna, whence
He comes with news of the events
There that occasioned the attack.
FERDINAND   You judge the rogues who cut him down.   2350
MASTER   I'd show them, were you not here, sire,
What doom awaits those who conspire
To kill Commanders of the crown.
FERDINAND   Their punishment rests with the throne.
ISABEL   I do confess, I'd love to see   2355
My lord wield this authority
Should it please God this power be shown.
     [*Enter the* JUDGE.]
JUDGE   I rode, sire, with due diligence
To Fuenteovejuna where,
Attending to my charge with care,   2360
I acted with expedience,
Investigating how this crime
Was carried out before I'd come
But bear no signed confession from
A soul there after all this time.   2365
The townsfolk spoke as one with stout
Conviction for their common good
And when I'd ask, "Who did this?," would
Shout "Fuenteovejuna" out!
Three hundred villagers there swore   2370
That they knew nothing through their pain
And I despair we'll ever gain
More information on that score.
We even lashed lads ten years old
Upon the rack who held their peace   2375
Despite our promises to cease
And other such things they were told.
In short, I've started so to frown
On finding someone to condemn
That either you must pardon them   2380
Or else eradicate the town.

---

7. The Greek name of the king of Persia (r. 486–465 B.C.E.), whom the Bible calls Ahasuerus. The Book of Esther recounts how he made Esther his queen, not knowing that she was Jewish, and how she prevented a massacre of her people.

To back these findings I've made known,
All journeyed hence to make their case
And tell you more of this disgrace.
FERDINAND   Then let them come before the throne.   2385
[*Enter* ESTEBAN, ALONSO, FRONDOSO, LAURENCIA, *the*
village women, and as many other VILLAGERS *as are needed.*]
LAURENCIA   Are those the monarchs over there?
FRONDOSO   Castile's own might, however far.
LAURENCIA   My God, what handsome beings they are!
St. Anthony[8] exalt the pair!
ISABEL   Are these the murderers you mean?   2390
ESTEBAN   Amassed before you at a stroke
Stand Fuenteovejuna's folk
Who humbly wish to serve their queen.
It was the tyranny and cursed
Insistence on purveying dread   2395
Of that Commander who's now dead—
But not before he'd done his worst—
That was behind our vengeful role.
He had our scant possessions seized
And raped our women when he pleased,   2400
All mercy alien to his soul.
FRONDOSO   So much so that when finally
This lovely lass the heavens sent
To make my heart on earth content
And me as happy as can be   2405
Agreed to take me as her spouse,
He acted as if he'd been wived
And, when our wedding night arrived,
Had her abducted to his house!
Were that pure girl not prone to fend   2410
Off the advances he'd begun,
I think it's clear to everyone
Her virtue would have met its end.
MENGO   Is it not time I said a word?
If, by your leave, I may say so,   2415
You'll all be scandalized to know
How bruised I was by what occurred
For rushing straight to the defense
Of one of our poor village girls
As she was being snatched by churls   2420
To undergo some vile offense.
My sorry derriere still aches
From that perverted Nero's[9] lash
And darn it if they didn't thrash
My backside pink as salmon steaks!   2425
Three men administered the belts

8. St. Anthony of Padua (1195–1231), a Franciscan missionary who was born in Lisbon.
9. The notoriously dissolute Roman emperor (r. 54–68 C.E.) who, according to Roman historians, played his lyre and sang during a fire that devastated Rome in 64.

So utterly unsparingly
That I'm convinced you still can see
The stripes they left beneath the welts.
All told, the ointment and the salve   2430
Concocted from the myrtle shrub
Which I use as a soothing rub
Are worth more than the farm I have!

ESTEBAN   In short, sire, we do gladly serve
As humble vassals of the crown   2435
And have long since hung in our town
Your coat of arms, which all observe.
We ask, my lord, that you respond
With clement mercy in this case.
To recompense this act of grace,   2440
We pledge our innocence as bond.

FERDINAND   As it appears that at no time
There'll be confessions signed in ink,
Though murder is most foul, we think
To grant forgiveness for this crime.   2445
It's well the village should repair
To the protection of Castile
And may depend on us until
We send a new Commander there.

FRONDOSO   This speech, Your Majesty, commends   2450
The measure of your providence
So with these words, wise audience,
Here *Fuenteovejuna* ends.

                                    [*Exit all.*]

FÉLIX LOPE DE VEGA Y CARPIO

The Dog in the Manger†
(*El perro del hortelano*)

CHARACTERS

DIANA, Countess of Belflor
TEODORO, her secretary
OCTAVIO, her elderly steward
FABIO, her servant
MARCELA ⎫
DOROTEA ⎬ her ladies-in-waiting
ANARDA ⎭
TRISTAN, Teodoro's servant
RICARDO, a marquis
CELIO, his servant
FEDERICO, a count
LEONIDO, his servant
LUDOVICO, an elderly count
CAMILO, his servant
ANTONELO ⎫
FURIO ⎬ footmen
LIRANO ⎭
PAGE

The action takes place in and around the house of the Countess of Belflor in Naples.

Act I

> [TEODORO, *his face concealed by a dashing cloak, enters, fleeing with his servant* TRISTAN.]

TEODORO   Quick, Tristan! This way! Follow me!

TRISTAN   This horrid scheme was ill-advised.

TEODORO   You gather we were recognized?

TRISTAN   I can't be sure, but possibly.

> [TEODORO *and* TRISTAN *exit.* DIANA, *Countess of Belflor,
> enters in pursuit.*]

† Translated by G. J. Racz for this Norton Critical Edition.

115

DIANA   Who are you, sir? Don't run away!   5
You heard me: stop! Is it correct
To show a countess disrespect?
Come back here! Look, do as I say!
Hello there, drowsing servants, rise!
Hello! Is no one at his post?   10
I'm sure I didn't see a ghost
Or dream what passed before my eyes.
What, sound asleep amid this row?
    [FABIO, *a servant, enters.*]
FABIO   My lady, did I hear you call?
DIANA   Phlegmatic[1] indolence is all   15
I need to cool my anger now.
Dash off before it's too late, fool—
What other name do you deserve?—
And hurry back if you observe
Who exited the vestibule.   20
FABIO   The vestibule?
DIANA   Move with some speed
And let those feet reply for you.
FABIO   I'm going.
DIANA [*As* FABIO *exits.*]   Rush and find out who
Committed treason by this deed.
    [OCTAVIO *enters.*]
OCTAVIO   I thought I heard you call despite   25
The hour, Your Ladyship, but could
Not fathom why your person would
Need servants at this time of night.
DIANA   You're like St. Elmo's fire,[2] in place
When storms have passed. Sleep seals your eyes   30
So early, yet you're late to rise.
You're moving at so slow a pace!
Strange men still wandering through these halls
Came so near to my chamber door
"It's me," I thought, "they're looking for."   35
Their brazen impudence appalls
All notion of propriety.
Is this the way, Sir Squire-Be-Late,
To aid me in my dire strait
And rectify this injury?   40
OCTAVIO   I thought I heard you call despite
The hour, Your Ladyship, but could
Not fathom why your person would
Need servants at this time of night.
DIANA   Go back to bed. It wasn't me.   45
You'll just feel ill from all this talk.

---

1. Phlegm, one of the four humors in Hippocratic medicine, was believed to make people apathetic.
2. An electric phenomenon that creates a bright glow above the masts of a ship during thunderstorms, long regarded by sailors as a sign of divine intervention.

OCTAVIO Good night.
    [FABIO *enters.*]
FABIO   He flew off like a hawk,
  A truly stunning sight to see!
DIANA You had no closer glimpse?
FABIO   A glimpse?
DIANA Did he not wear a cloak with bright   50
  Gold trim?
FABIO   While running down a flight
  Of stairs?
DIANA   What men! The more each primps,
  The less he's style in his bones.
FABIO I couldn't see. He tossed his hat,
  Put out the lamp, and that was that.   55
  Escaping over lightless stones,
  He paused so he could draw his sword
  When at the gates, then fled again.
DIANA Aren't you the little fighting hen!
FABIO What would you have me do?
DIANA   Good lord!   60
  Cross blades with him and run him through!
OCTAVIO But were he noble, such a feat
  Would throw your name into the street
  Where gossip would dishonor you.
DIANA What would a man of rank want here?   65
OCTAVIO Well, which of all the smitten swains
  In Naples wouldn't take the pains
  To glimpse his ladylove so near?
  A thousand nobles seek your hand,
  All blind to love's infirmities.   70
  Our fugitive is one of these.
  Did you not deem his wardrobe grand
  And Fabio see him try to hide
  His face by putting out a flame?
DIANA You're right—this was a man of name   75
  Who came to woo me at my side
  But only once he'd bribed my men.
  And what an honest lot they are,
  Octavio! Each one virtue's star!
  He won't remain beyond my ken: 80
  The culprit's hat had plumes on it
  And may have fallen when he took
  Those steps to flee.
FABIO   Should I go look?
DIANA That's what I mean, you idiot!
  He hardly would have broken stride   85
  And probably left it on a stair.
FABIO I'll fetch a lamp and see what's there.
DIANA Then, once the man's identified,
  I'll have his helper banished from
  My house.

OCTAVIO   It is most dutiful   90
Of you to hold accountable
These agents of opprobrium
But don't think my words meaningless—
For I don't wish to cause ill will
Or make my lady angrier still—   95
It's your capricious stubbornness
In spurning all who come to woo
That pushes men to such extremes,
Compelling them to hatch up schemes
So they can pitch their suits to you.   100
DIANA   Octavio, do you know something?
OCTAVIO   I know one thing—the city has
Become resigned and sees you as
Unweddable, if ravishing.
So many people suffer care   105
About the county of Belflor.
          [FABIO enters.]
FABIO   I found the hat you sent me for
And looking quite the worse for wear.
DIANA   Produce it. What's this?
FABIO   I don't know,
But that's the hat our wooer threw.   110
DIANA   You're sure?
OCTAVIO   I never thought I'd view
A thing so filthy.
FABIO   That's it, though.
DIANA   You found it on the staircase?
FABIO   Would
I ever lie to you?
OCTAVIO   The plumes
Are nice.
FABIO   A thief, say, robbing rooms?   115
OCTAVIO   No doubt to take what pelf he could.
DIANA   You two will make me lose my mind!
FABIO   Still, that's the hat, thrown while he fled.
DIANA   When last I glimpsed it on his head,
The plumes looked overly refined.   120
Could it have been mishandled so?
FABIO   What fire wouldn't leave its stamp
On any hat that's struck a lamp
And burn the feathers up like tow?
Did Icarus,[3] too, not fly so near   125
The sun his wings burned by degrees
Until he plunged into the seas
Below? Well, that's what happened here:
The lamp, in this case, was the sun

---

3. In Greek mythology, Icarus and his father, Daedalus, escaped from King Minos's labyrinth on
the island of Crete by using wings made with wax; but ignoring his father's warning, Icarus
flew too close to the sun, the wax melted, and he plunged to his death in the sea.

And Icarus, the fallen hat   130
With singed plumes which, when tossed off, sat
Forlorn upon the stairs, undone.
DIANA   You turn my mood to jest this way.
We've much to do to solve this crime.
OCTAVIO   The truth will out in all due time,   135
My lady.
DIANA   When will that be, pray?
OCTAVIO   Let's sleep on it, for all will be
Discovered with the morning light.
DIANA   I'll not return to bed this night,
Upon my life, until I'm free   140
Of doubt regarding what's occurred.
Go summon all my ladies here.
OCTAVIO   You much abuse the night, I fear.
DIANA   Octavio, sleep must be deferred
While I'm still burdened with this care.   145
An interloper lurks about.
OCTAVIO   Were it not wiser that we out
The knave behind this dread affair
Through quiet future inquiry?
DIANA   Discretion's grand, but going to bed   150
With someone's secret in my head
Is too discreet a feat for me.
        [ANARDA, DOROTEA, *and* MARCELA *enter.*]
FABIO   The principals among your train
Are present, as the others will
Know nothing and are dozing still,   155
Surrendered up to sleep's domain.
These ladies of your chamber were
The only ones still left awake.
ANARDA [*Aside.*]   The surges wait till night to break
When angry seas grow choppier.   160
FABIO   Would you prefer we left?
DIANA   Yes, do,
So I might see what there's to find.
FABIO [*To* OCTAVIO.]   She'll quiz them now!
OCTAVIO   She's lost her mind.
FABIO   And thinks me somehow guilty, too!
                        [OCTAVIO *and* FABIO *exit.*]
DIANA   Now, Dorotea first. Come near.   165
DOROTEA   Your Ladyship, is something wrong?
DIANA   Which men are wont to walk along
The street in front of my house here?
DOROTEA   It's Marquis Ricardo I see
Out there—Count Paris, too—as they   170
Stroll by.
DIANA   Take care that all you say
Is truthful when you answer me
Now, if you know what's good for you.
DOROTEA   Your Ladyship, I've never lied!

DIANA   With whom do they confer inside?   175
DOROTEA   Dear countess, even if you threw
   This clay in fire, I'd still profess
   I'd never witnessed either man
   In conversation other than
   With you, in hopes you'd acquiesce.   180
DIANA   They never slipped you any note?
   No page sneaked into here somehow?
DOROTEA   Not once, I swear.
DIANA   That's all for now
MARCELA [To ANARDA.]   Some inquisition, this!
ANARDA   Cutthroat.
DIANA   Anarda.
ANARDA   May I be of aid?   185
DIANA   Who was that man who ran out from . . .
ANARDA   A man?
DIANA   . . . our ladies' chambers? Come,
   I know you're part of this charade.
   Which one of you brought him to me?
   Whom did he choose to blandish thus?   190
ANARDA   You don't think any one of us
   Could manage such audacity?
   What, bring a man to see you here?
   No maid could ever be so bold
   To watch her treachery unfold   195
   Against you, as our troth is clear,
   So cast this error from your mind.
DIANA   Wait. Step aside. As I reflect
   Upon your answer, I suspect—
   Unless this story was designed   200
   To fool—our breacher came to meet
   The maid with whom he trysts inside.
ANARDA   To judge your ire so justified,
   My lady, at this plain deceit,
   I'll chance to say what's going on   205
   And tell all, which may in the end
   Be detrimental to my friend
   Marcela, whom I dote upon.
   The girl's been smitten at the sight
   Of one who fancies her the same,   210
   Though I don't know him or his name.
DIANA   Suppressing this would scarce be right,
   But since there's no more you can say
   To hurt her, why hold back the rest?
ANARDA   You cruelly torment me to test   215
   My secret-keeping in this way,
   Aware that I'm a woman, too.
   You now know all there is to know:
   The man came for Marcela, so
   Do set your mind at ease: it's true   220
   The two are only chatting yet,

Their fresh acquaintance just begun.
DIANA   What shamelessness! I'll be undone,
For wagging tongues all pose a threat
To maiden reputations here.   225
I swear upon my father's grave,
I'll have this stopped at once!
ANARDA   I gave
The wrong impression if you fear
Our lover comes from out these walls
To court Marcela once within.   230
He needn't place his fond self in
Such constant peril when he calls.
DIANA   He's one of my own serving men?
ANARDA   Yes.
DIANA   Who, then?
ANARDA   Teodoro. There.
DIANA   My secretary?
ANARDA   I'm aware   235
They speak, but don't know where or when.
DIANA   That's all, Anarda. You may be.
ANARDA   Show prudence, though you're much aggrieved.
DIANA   In honesty, I'm quite relieved
To learn he didn't come for me.   240
Marcela!
MARCELA   Countess.
DIANA   Come attend.
MARCELA   Your servant, [aside] trembling and distraught.
DIANA   Have I not always trusted you
To guard my honor and my thoughts?
MARCELA   Are people slandering me here?   245
I've demonstrated nothing but
The loyalty you so deserve.
DIANA   You? Loyalty?
MARCELA   What have I done?
DIANA   Do you suppose it no offense
To have your paramour pay suit   250
Inside my private chamber, then?
MARCELA   Well, Teodoro's such a fool
For love, no matter where we are
He'll coo two dozen blandishments.
DIANA   Two dozen, did you say? Well, well,   255
It's quite the year for love, I guess!
They're cheaper by the dozen, too!
MARCELA   Um, what I mean, Your Ladyship,
Is, on his goings in or out,
He translates feelings to his lips.   260
DIANA   He translates! There's a curious word!
What does he say?
MARCELA   Oh, I don't know.
I can't remember now.
DIANA   Try hard.

MARCELA Sometimes he'll say, "I'd trade my soul
 To gaze on end into your eyes,"   265
 Or else, "I live to look on them
 And haven't slept a wink all night
 Just thinking of your loveliness
 And my desires." Another time
 He asked me for a lock of hair,   270
 A keepsake he could use to bind
 His restless thoughts against love's cares.
 But why do you inquire about
 Such silly things?
DIANA   You don't seem vexed
 At all by them.
MARCELA   Why would I be?   275
 I know that Teodoro meant
 These sweet endearments with the most
 Respectable of all intents
 In mind, the holy marriage bond.
DIANA You're so correct, for weddedness 280
 Is love's pure-hearted, chaste result.
 I'll plan the wedding, if you like.
MARCELA You couldn't make me happier!
 My lady, now that I devise
 A tender heart amid your rage   285
 And noble nature in your breast,
 Let me assure you I adore
 The man for having such good sense
 As well as for his being the most
 Discerning, prudent, passionate   290
 And thoughtful suitor county-wide.
DIANA Indeed, this flair is evident
 As he performs his services.
MARCELA His style in a letter penned
 To prove your common ancestry   295
 With, say, a pair of noblemen
 Cannot compare to hearing him
 Beside you whispering words of love
 In sweet tones meant for you alone.
DIANA Marcela, though my mind's made up 300
 To see you married in due course
 Once all arrangements are disposed,
 In simple fact I can't forget
 My noble rank or that I owe
 Far greater reverence to my name.   305
 Allowing this affair to bide
 Beneath my roof would scarce be meet.
 I'll thus indulge my rage a while
 So it be known to everyone.
 You, in the interim, might pursue   310
 Your courtship more judiciously
 Until such time that I should rule

It apt to proffer you my aid,
For Teodoro's sensible—
The man was brought up in my house—   315
And I'm disposed to favor all
Who serve me well, Marcela, not
The least for our familial ties.
MARCELA   The girl you taught is at your feet . . .
DIANA   Go.
MARCELA   . . . kissing them a thousand times.   320
DIANA   Please leave, maids.
ANARDA [*To* MARCELA.]   How did she respond?
MARCELA   Her anger came to favor me.
DOROTEA [*To* MARCELA.]   So then, she's found your secret out?
MARCELA   She has, but knows my heart is clean.
          [ANARDA, DOROTEA, *and* MARCELA *curtsy before exiting.*]
DIANA   So oft on me have Teodoro's grace,   325
    Discernment and fair aspect worked their charm
    That, if his low-born state posed mine no harm,
    I'd hardly find his mind or bearing base.
    Lest love, though general to all, disarm,
    My name comes first, commanding pride of place.   330
    There's no obeisance that I don't embrace
    And such a union would cause rank alarm.
    While jealousy might always lie in store
    From envying what other souls possess,
    I must do nothing I'd be sorry for.   335
    In wishing him my equal, I'd need press
    For Teodoro to be somehow more
    And I, to be his equal, somehow less.
          [DIANA *exits.* TEODORO *enters with* TRISTAN.]
TEODORO   I can't rest while we're on the run!
TRISTAN   And there's good reason for it, too.   340
    If she finds out that it was you,
    Your tenure here is all but done!
    I told you—let the countess just
    Retire—but you could not be stayed.
TEODORO   Love calls and has to be obeyed.   345
TRISTAN   If you'd but parry as you thrust!
TEODORO   Deft swordsmen do things my way, though.
TRISTAN   And were you one, you might begin
    To sense the danger that you're in.
TEODORO   She recognized me?
TRISTAN   Yes and no: 350
    While she may not have seen your face,
    Suspicion has to plague her mind.
TEODORO   When I saw Fabio right behind
    Us on the stairs, what but God's grace
    Kept me from cutting down that pest?   355
TRISTAN   My sure aim when I flipped my lid
    And snuffed the flame out there.
TEODORO   That did

Deter the nuisance from his quest.
Had he pursued the chase in spite
Of this, I would have stopped him dead.   360
TRISTAN · I told the lamplight as we fled:
"Just say we don't live here, all right?"
But when it answered, "That's a lie!"
I let my hat set matters straight.
Am I avenged, then?
TEODORO   I await   365
Cruel death.
TRISTAN   All lovers magnify
Their troubles at the slightest sign
That tender plans have gone askew.
TEODORO   So, what's a soul supposed to do,
Then, Tristan, in a spot like mine?   370
TRISTAN   Stop doting on Marcela, sir!
You know the countess is the sort
Of woman who might well resort
To firing you for wooing her,
Unmoved by these fond escapades.   375
TEODORO   Must I forget her and move on?
TRISTAN   Allow me to hold forth upon
The many ways in which love fades.
TEODORO   Is this more of your folderol?
TRISTAN   All know-how conquers love in turn.   380
Just listen, on your life, and learn
Some simple ways to reach this goal:
Now, firstly, see to it your heart
Forgets about the girl you sought
And banish any foolish thought   385
You have of love till death you part,
For even if you're half inclined
To see these ties renewed, what good
Would your forgetting her be should
You harbor hopes to change your mind?   390
Why, do you think, a man will not
Forget a woman while he lives?
The thought of reuniting gives
A sort of pleasure to his lot.
We men must always take great pains   395
To guard against this consequence
And, if it is in evidence,
To halt its movement through our brains.
You ever see a clock whose screws
Need tightening? Well, its wheels don't move   400
Though nothing's wrong with any groove.
A man with no screws loose can't lose
In life if he'd but act like this,
Dispelling hope despite the urge.
TEODORO   Yet don't sweet memories still emerge   405
To keep alive the former bliss,

Awakening before it dies
The amorous joy that used to be?
TRISTAN   Yep, memory's the enemy
With which the rational mind vies,   410
Just like that Spanish poet said
In lyrics that we know so well.
It's no mean feat at all to quell
Imagination in one's head.
TEODORO   But how?
TRISTAN   By thinking of her flaws   415
And not her charms. Bad memories
Of defects, not good qualities,
Should give a sharp guy's brain some pause.
Don't see her in your mind's eye dressed
All elegant in finery   420
Or leaning on a balcony
In high heels and her Sunday best.
That's just fake scaffolding unfurled
On her exterior, you know,
For it's to tailors that we owe   425
One half the beauty in this world.
So once the thought of her begins,
Imagine her a penitent,
For it should damp your sentiment
To see her sack-clad for her sins.   430
Now, try to bring about this end
And stop envisioning her in skirts
But blemished, so the image hurts.
That's what the doctor ordered, friend,
Like how recalling from the past   435
Some foul, repulsive thing you've chewed
Can serve to put you off your food
And send you on a month-long fast.
A lady's imperfections, too—
When they're expediently recalled—   440
Can leave warm thoughts of her forestalled
And keep old love from plaguing you.
TEODORO   The crude physician hawks his brands!
A rustic cure for each disease!
These panacea "remedies"   445
Are as ham-fisted as your hands.
It sounds like there's a quack on call—
You never studied medicine!
I don't conceive of women in
The way you render them at all.   450
I view them more as crystalline,
Like glass that you can see right through.
TRISTAN   I'm sure you'd feel their edges, too,
When they break up and make a scene.
If you won't weigh the defects of   455
A lady, let me volunteer,

Since I've no longer any fear
That you'll forget the one you love.
I once was smitten, truth be told—
When I was still a handsome wag—   460
With one big lying saddlebag,
A waif-like fifty summers old.
Of all the flaws defining her,
The maid's pot belly was the worst,
For it could hold—and still not burst—   465
Besides a set of furniture,
A stack of papers just the force
Of which would make a desktop creak,
Or any quantity of Greek
Combatants, like a Trojan Horse.[4]   470
You've heard about that walnut tree
Whose trunk had so much room to spare
An office clerk resided there
With his entire family
And never wanted for more space?   475
This woman's gut did so protrude,
A weaver with his wife and brood
Could well have lived inside that place!
I needed to forget that bit
(My own best interests were at heart),   480
Yet, memory only seemed to start
Up flights of fancy that would flit
From lilies pure to jasmines pert,
To marble, silver, falling snow
And finally to huge curtains, though   485
These actually were the woman's skirt!
This left attempts to purge her stalled
Until I sought a sharper strain
Of thought that led me, now more sane,
To picture things her flab recalled,   490
Like baskets full of squash or rags
In hampers piled high in stacks
Or over-stuffed mail-carrier sacks,
Straw mattresses or sleeping bags.
Thus, love and hope became again   495
One vile contempt I could indulge
And I forgot about her bulge
Forever and anon—amen!
Considering what that belly holds,
Forgetting it was some neat trick,   500
As anyone could doubtless stick
Four pestles in its fleshy folds!
TEODORO   But as Marcela's graces show
No sign of defect I can see,
I'll hold her in my memory.   505

4. The Greeks built a giant wooden horse and hid their soldiers within it before offering it to the
Trojans. The trick allowed them to enter and conquer Troy.

TRISTAN   Your stubbornness will cause you woe.
Persist and bad times may ensue.
TEODORO   But grace itself is what she is!
TRISTAN   Remember that the countess's
Good graces are worth being in, too.   510
[DIANA *enters.*]
DIANA   Oh, Teodoro . . .
TEODORO   [*Aside.*] Now what more?
DIANA   A word with you.
TEODORO   At your command.
TRISTAN [*Aside.*]   Her pointed inquiry will land
The girl and us, too, out the door!
DIANA   A certain lady friend of mine,   515
Possessing little confidence,
Asked me to pen the sentiments
This love letter contains. Our fine
Rapport compelled me, though I know
Not how admirers couch romance   520
And come to ask that you enhance
My phrasing, Teodoro, so
Do read it.
TEODORO   Lady, if I tried
Improving what your hand has wrought,
My efforts would be all for naught,   525
A useless show of foolish pride.
I've no need to review your turn
Of phrase. Please give it to your friend.
DIANA   No, read these lines!
TEODORO   Should I amend,
You'll feel deceived. It's I who'll learn   530
High style from a quill so true.
I never wrote of love before.
DIANA   What, never ever?
TEODORO   I foreswore
Love, as my flaws convinced me to.
I just can't see why I'd be prized.   535
DIANA   This seemingly must be the case,
For why else would you hide your face
And run about these halls disguised?
TEODORO   My lady, I? Who said that? When?
DIANA   My people. Last night. They tell me   540
You shrouded your identity
And my own steward saw you then.
TEODORO   You know how Fabio and I play
Our silly games, each pulling stunts
To make the other seem a dunce?   545
DIANA   Here, read.
TEODORO   I'm thinking someone may
Be jealous of my household post.
DIANA   True, envy may have played a part.
Now, read it.

TEODORO   I've no doubt your art
And eloquence will strike me most.   550
[*Reading.*] It's envy but to love because one sees
Another love, though feeling this before
Love is a wondrous trick Love holds in store,
Perhaps the most impossible of these.
Yes, love sprang from my jealousy's unease;   555
Though fairer, I'm chagrined I hadn't more
Good luck in love to merit by that store
The joys that what I envy most decrees.
I've no cause for such diffidence and yearn
Unloved in jealousy that won't desist.   560
I must needs love, though, to be loved in turn,
Declining to surrender or resist.
No words can let these feelings show. Discern
My lot who will. I know how I exist.
DIANA   Your thoughts?
TEODORO   Well, if this letter says   565
Exactly what the lady means,
I've never read a finer one,
But must confess I don't quite see
How love can then be envy's child
When almost everyone contends   570
That envy is the fruit of love.
DIANA   Well, I suspect my lady friend
Delighted in the sight of him
While never feeling passion's rage
Until she saw her swain involved   575
With someone else, at which she came
To love through envy and desire.
Could that be true?
TEODORO   By some accounts,
My lady, though this jealousy
Springs forth from yet another fount,   580
No less a source than love itself,
As cause cannot rise from effects
But these effects from some first cause.
DIANA   Still, Teodoro, I expect
That this is what occurred with her.   585
She did tell me she only felt
A slight attraction to the man
But, once she saw him love, beheld
The highwaymen of her desires
Assailing her on honor's road   590
And found her very soul stripped bare
Of that decorum she had hoped
To live her life by all her days.
TEODORO   My lines would be so poor compared
To yours, so how could I presume?   595
DIANA   Go in and try.
TEODORO   I wouldn't dare.

DIANA   I do beseech it, on my soul.
TEODORO   I see Your Ladyship but wants
  To prove my ignorance by this.
DIANA   I'm waiting. Find me when you're done.   600
TEODORO   My lady.
                                    [TEODORO *exits.*]
DIANA   Tristan, come attend.
TRISTAN   To serve you, madame, though abashed
  That you should see my breeches' state,
  A sign my master's strapped for cash—
  And he your secretary, too!   605
  Now you'll agree an honest man's
  Remiss to leave his footman frayed.
  A servant is his looking glass,
  Reflecting shield and harbinger
  So can't be shabbily attired.   610
  A man of wit once quipped we serve
  As human ladders to our sires,
  For gazes scale our bodies first
  To reach their faces once they mount.
  It's all that he can do, I guess.   615
DIANA   He gambles, then?
TRISTAN   If only! Zounds,
  The gamblers I know never seem
  To lack for money night or day.
  Now, even kings in olden times
  Would undertake to learn a trade   620
  In case they lost their crowns or realms
  In battle or upon the seas
  And had to earn a livelihood.
  Yes, happy those whose faculty
  For betting starts while they're still young!   625
  Whenever they're a little short,
  A wager is as good a play
  As any to recoup their stores.
  An expert painter, doing all
  To turn a lifelike portrait out,   630
  Will use each last bit of his skill,
  Yet any half-wit can pronounce
  The striking likeness valueless.
  But when a gambler calls his bet
  And ends up with the winning hand,   635
  The money's all his—every cent!
DIANA   No gambling, then?
TRISTAN   He plays things safe.
DIANA   I'm led to understand he's quite
  The lover.
TRISTAN   What, him have affairs?
  Oh, that's a beaut! The guy's like ice!   640
DIANA   You mean to say that handsome, trim,
  Discreet and courteous young gent

Cannot at present claim to have
A single, harmless dalliance?
TRISTAN I deal in hay and horses, ma'am,   645
Not love letters or valentines.
He works for you all day here so
I get the sense he's occupied.
DIANA But doesn't he go out at night?
TRISTAN I don't accompany him now   650
Because I have this broken hip.
DIANA What happened, Tristan?
TRISTAN   How about
I answer like a battered wife
Who tells someone who sees the bumps
And bruises on the pretty face   655
Her jealous husband roundly thumped:
"I took a tumble down the stairs."
DIANA You fell?
TRISTAN   And even rolled a stretch!
My ribcage kept a count of each
Stone step.
DIANA   Well, what did you expect   660
Would happen, Tristan, when you threw
Your hat and put out all the lights?
TRISTAN [Aside.]   Confound the rotten luck! By God,
She's onto us about last night!
DIANA What's that you say?
TRISTAN   Wait, let me think . . .   665
Lights . . . hat . . . yes, I remember now!
Some bats had made their way inside
And, hoping I could bring them down,
I tossed my hat up where they flew.
When one of them passed near the lamp,   670
I tried to kill it, snuffing out
The flame instead and, in a flash,
Went headlong down the flight of stairs,
My legs no longer under me.
DIANA That's really a compelling tale!   675
A book of remedies I read
Prescribes blood as an agent for
Removing excess body hair—
I speak, of course, of blood from bats—
So let's have bloodletting while there's   680
The chance to pull some hair and rid
This house of batty escapades.
TRISTAN [Aside.]   She smells a bat! Or worse, a thief!
Should I end up a galley slave[5]
'Cause he's a slave to some fine gal?   685
DIANA [Aside.]   Oh, what am I supposed to think?
        [FABIO enters.]

5. Criminals were often sentenced to row in the king's galleys (a type of ship).

FABIO   The marquis Ricardo is here.
DIANA   Bring chairs at once, so we can sit.
              [RICARDO *enters.* FABIO *and* TRISTAN *exit.*]
RICARDO   With that same care that love, Diana, sets
    Upon a heart pursuing passion's goal   690
    As it ignores all obstacles and threats,
    I come here smitten to adore you whole.
    I plead my cause as rivals place cruel bets
    That I can't win what you alone control
    And think themselves far likelier of success,   695
    Though it's self-pride, not love, that they profess.
    Your Ladyship is such a lovely sight,
    I know she's in fine fettle at a glance.
    With women—wise men own that this is right—
    Fair looks announce their wellness in advance,   700
    So when one's charming, elegant and bright,
    It's daft and should be looked upon askance
    To ask about her health and thereby pose
    A question whose clear answer each man knows.
    Quite sure that you are well, Diana, by   705
    This radiant beauty that exudes good cheer—
    If this does not reverse the cause I ply—
    I dare to ask you how I'm doing here.
DIANA   By viewing beauty so, you qualify
    This trait as what Italians far and near   710
    Call "grazia."[6] I would say these thoughts reflect
    Quite well on your good taste and intellect.
    Don't ask me how you're doing, though, for I'm
    Not mistress of your soul enough to know.
RICARDO   Still, it's a favor you on my sublime   715
    And honorable love might well bestow.
    Your kinsmen are convinced that it's now time
    For carrying out what's been proposed, although
    The only thing we lack is your assent.
    Let fond hope not devolve into lament.   720
    I'm master, as you know, of vast demesnes
    That I've been heir to in my noble line,
    But if these stretched from burning southern plains
    To where Dawn's rosy northern mantles shine;
    And if I owned what gold the world contains   725
    Or heaven's frozen teardrops were all mine—
    Those western pearls—or diamonds from the east,
    In search of which sea crossings haven't ceased,
    I'd offer you this opulence as well.
    My lady, you may rest assured I'd tread   730
    The darkest climes where sunlight barely fell
    If doing so would serve you in good stead
    Or stamp salt fields with feet of my pine shell[7]

6. Poise, gallantry, grace.
7. I.e., his ship.

On transatlantic voyages that led
To those most distant beaches I could find,   735
Beyond the farthest reaches of mankind.
DIANA I'm certain, marquis, that your love is true
And, as it flows from your nobility,
Will pledge to give your gallantry its due
Though this irk Federico endlessly.   740
RICARDO The count is sharp and needs a trick or two
To show that he's superior to me.
I trust the honest pressing of my cause
Will blind you to his wiles and give you pause.
     [TEODORO *enters*.]
TEODORO I've done as you requested.
RICARDO   I impede   745
Your Ladyship, which I do much deplore.
I won't require more time of you.
DIANA   No need
For haste. I write to Rome.
RICARDO   What vexes more
Than guests on letter-writing day who heed
No hint to leave?
DIANA   So wise.
RICARDO   Your servitor.   750
     [*To* CELIO.] So, Celio, what say you?
CELIO   When my heart speaks,
It hopes your heart will win the love it seeks
                    [RICARDO *and* CELIO *exit*.]
DIANA Did you rewrite my note?
TEODORO   I did
As ordered, not convinced it's good,
Refashioning it best I could.   755
DIANA Let's see.
TEODORO   Here, read it.
DIANA   As you bid.
     [*Reading*.] To love one who is loved might envy be
Would this love not have blossomed all the same.
A lover loves in all sincerity
And will not make of love a jealous game.   760
When Love perceives another's ecstasy
To be its own true heart, Love stakes its claim
With words that tumble out confusedly
As modest blushes color cheeks in shame.
I say no more, not wanting to offend   765
From out below a cherished one above
Or rob myself of so desired an end.
Here's all I understand about true love:
What I don't merit, I can't comprehend,
But won't imply it's aught I'm worthy of.   770
You've done well to preserve the tone.
TEODORO You mock me.
DIANA   Would that it were true!

TEODORO   What do you mean?
DIANA   That of the two,
   I must say I prefer your own.
TEODORO   This worries me, for masters hate   775
   When obvious inferiors
   Know more than their superiors.
   Now I dread suffering this fate!
   You've heard the story of the king
   Who told his minister at court   780
   He feared his writing came up short
   And wished to have this courtier bring
   Some brio to the lines he'd spun,
   Requesting he rewrite a note?
   Well, reading what his favorite wrote,   785
   The king deemed his own work outdone.
   So, witnessing the king decree
   His words a wonder to behold,
   This minister ran home and told
   His son, the eldest of his three: 790
   "We need to flee the realm at once!
   My life's in danger if we stay."
   The youth, in obvious dismay,
   Then asked his father what affronts
   Had caused their woe. "The sovereign's learned,"   795
   He said, "that I know more than he."
   Now I fear your detesting me
   Because my talent's been discerned.
DIANA   Good Teodoro, if I deem
   Your version better, don't you fret.   800
   The phrasing is most pleasant, yet
   Still mirrors nicely my own theme.
   So I beseech you, don't assume
   This praising of your eloquence
   Implies I've lost all confidence   805
   In words that flow from my own plume.
   Besides that, I'm a woman prone
   To making errors in what I write
   And not the cleverest one in sight,
   As anyone might easily own.   810
   Here love "from out below," you say,
   Can leave the one above aggrieved,
   But on this point you are deceived,
   For love does not play out that way
   And no one loving thus offends.   815
   Offense springs only, as I rate,
   From not extending love, but hate.
TEODORO   So Nature's cosmic plan contends.
   Still, artists painting Phaëthon[8] show

---

8. Like Icarus, a figure for hubris: Phaëthon, son of the sun god Helios, attempted to drive his father's chariot across the sky, but was unable to control the horses and came too close to the earth, setting it ablaze.

A sun-drenched charioteer whose dream   820
Was brought low when his gilded team
Plunged fast onto the peaks below.
All scenes of Icarus, too, are done
With sunbeams melting waxy wings
To cause his fall.
DIANA   Who'd view such things,   825
Though, if a woman were the sun?
Serve well that mistress high above
Your precedence and don't lose heart,
For romance is a stubborn art
And ladies aren't immune to love.   830
I'll keep your version in my care,
Desirous to reflect on each
Word here.
TEODORO   It's full of faulty speech.
DIANA   Well, I see no faults anywhere.
TEODORO   You flatter me, my lady. Here,   835
I brought yours back.
DIANA   Hold onto it,
Though you may deem my note more fit
To be torn up.
TEODORO   Torn up?
DIANA   Oh dear,
Why fear this loss when there may be
A greater loss we still may face?   840
                                   [DIANA *exits*.]
TEODORO   She's gone. Whoever thought the grace
And pride of her nobility
Would let the countess bare her soul
To have these sentiments be known?
But then again, it could be shown   845
I fool myself to seek this goal.
I can't recall a single case
In which she'd said such things to me.
"Don't fear this loss when there may be
A greater loss we still may face"?   850
"A greater loss" could mean the love
That caused her lady friend unease.
No, this is stuff and nonsense: she's
That lady she had spoken of.
Or not—the countess's quick wit,   855
Along with her mercurial strain,
Makes all this seem against the grain,
At least as I've imagined it.
Choice nobles here in Naples plot
To wed her, men I'd scarce deserve   860
Now even as a slave to serve.
I'm scared and in a dangerous spot.
She knows Marcela has my heart
And, learning of our sympathy,

Has sought to make a fool of me, 865
And yet these lingering doubts depart
When I remember that a trace
Of shyness made her cheek turn red
Or that her voice broke when she said
"A greater loss we still may face." 870
What rose that greets the crying dawn,
Dew turning petals into eyes,
Has ever smiled so to prize
Dawn's tears as she did now to fawn
On me, which I so clearly viewed, 875
As red-tinged blushes overflowed?
What pallid apple ever glowed
So radiantly crimson-hued?
If I'm not mad, then all she spoke
And all I heard I'll judge as too 880
Succinct to serve as any clue
But far too much to be a joke.
Vain thoughts, be careful where you fly!
The titled rank that you pursue
Is gilded by those fair looks, too. 885
One glance at her proves I don't lie.
Diana is just beautiful.
Her understanding has no peer.
        [MARCELA *enters.*]
MARCELA   Can we speak?
TEODORO   Just our being here
Means nothing is impossible, 890
Marcela dear. For love so true,
I'd happily succumb to death.
MARCELA   And I would breathe my final breath
Two thousand times to be with you.
I sat awake the whole night through, 895
A little bird, my conscience fraught,
Until I saw that Dawn had roused
Apollo[9] out from where he housed
In darkness. Then I brightly thought
"I'll see my own Apollo, drowsed." 900
But how the night's events progressed!
The countess made things look so dire
And proved unwilling to retire
Until she'd put her cares to rest.
Those jealous friends with whom I'm blessed 905
Informed the countess of our bond,
To which I only can respond
That friendships of which servants boast,
Though honest-seeming, at the most
Are of the kind more feigned than fond. 910

---

9. In Greek and Roman mythology, the god of poetry, music, the sun, healing, and more; also associated with idealized male beauty and athleticism.

In short, the countess knows our minds.
She's named Diana,[1] like the moon
Who, coming out a tad too soon,
Stops cold what amorousness she finds.
Still, Teodoro, all these binds   915
Will work out for the best, I swear.
I spoke with her, and she's aware
That you've behaved most gallantly,
Declaring that you'll marry me,
While I've declared how much I care.   920
I also praised those traits I prize—
Your grace, gentility and style—
And watched the countess deign to smile,
Relieved to learn I'd set my eyes
On one so honorable and wise.   925
Forgetting, then, her discontent,
She promised me that she'd consent
To seeing us wed as but she could,
Though only once she'd understood
Your heart's troth and what last night meant.   930
I thought for sure she'd be enraged,
The order of her home dissolved
With punishment for all involved,
The two of us then disengaged.
Her noble blood, though, was assuaged   935
As that judicious character
And mind, to which I here refer,
Were seized with your intrinsic worth.
Oh, blessed are those on God's green earth
Who serve a mistress such as her!   940
TEODORO   The countess pledged to see us wed,
    You tell me?
MARCELA   Do you doubt her plans
    To oversee our marriage banns?
TEODORO [*Aside.*]   I've let myself be much misled.
    How did I get it in my head   945
    That she could think of me that way?
    The very thought brings me dismay.
    Which highborn lady ever stooped
    So low or lofty falcon swooped
    So low to catch such humble prey?   950
MARCELA   What are you muttering over there?
TEODORO   She spoke with me, Marcela, yet
    Not once did that coy lady let
    Me know that she'd become aware
    The muffled man in this affair   955
    Who ran these halls last night was I.
MARCELA   How shrewd of her to act so sly!
    The ploy allowed her to withhold

1. The virgin Roman goddess of wild animals and the hunt, associated also with the moon.

Your punishment for being bold,
Which marrying us will rectify   960
As there's no sweeter penalty
For two who love each other well
Than marriage.
TEODORO   So true! I can tell
That it's the noblest remedy.
MARCELA   We'll wed?
TEODORO   How happy I would be!   965
MARCELA   Then prove it!
TEODORO   Take this fond embrace,
For arms in love, like quills, can trace
Round o's on paper or in air.
What other flourish says "I care"
More than this one my arms encase?   970
          [DIANA enters.]
DIANA   It looks like things are settled here.
I have to say, it makes me smile,
For when one issues stern rebukes,
It's grand to see things reconciled.
Now, don't you fret on my account.   975
TEODORO   I just informed Marcela how
Distressed I was last night to think,
My lady, after I'd run out,
That you might misconstrue my flight—
Which caused your household great offense—   980
As something more indicative
Of mischief than of pure intent.
I'd die to cause my dear one shame,
So when she told me that you'd shown
Great mercy toward us and agreed   985
To see the two of us betrothed,
I couldn't keep from hugging her.
I wouldn't lie to you on this,
Though I might well invent some ruse,
For nothing in the world enlists   990
A highborn person's favor more
Than speaking plainly, I'm convinced.
DIANA   Your lack of loyalty toward me
And disrespect for this chaste house
Would justify harsh punishment   995
Now, Teodoro, but the proud
Forbearance I've displayed with you
Should not be viewed as licensing
This brazen absence of restraint.
When love becomes a shameful thing,   1000
No privilege on earth can stay
The castigation it deserves.
Until such time as you are wed,
Marcela would be better served
Confined to one of my own rooms   1005

Lest all the other maids who wait
Observe the two of you cavort
And take for normal such displays.
I have to see them wed as well!
Where's Dorotea? Come attend.   1010
  [DOROTEA *enters*.]
DOROTEA   My lady.
DIANA   Dorotea, take
  This key and leave Marcela pent
  Inside my chambers a few days,
  As she's some needlework to do.
  I think this best. It's not from spite.   1015
DOROTEA   What's this, Marcela?
MARCELA [*To* DOROTEA.]   Just the cruel
  Contrivance of a dictator
  Beneath my inauspicious star!
  She locks me up because of him.
DOROTEA   Those doors are hardly iron bars.   1020
  When jealousies occasion jail,
  True love retains the master key.
                          [MARCELA *and* DOROTEA *exit*.]
DIANA   So, Teodoro, it's your wish
  To marry?
TEODORO   Only if this meets
  With pleasure on my lady's part.   1025
  You must believe my conduct caused
  Not nearly the offense that's claimed,
  For you know well how Envy's drawn
  Provisioned with a scorpion's tongue.
  Had Ovid ever served before,   1030
  His House of Envy[2] wouldn't sit
  On barren wilds' rustic bournes
  Amid the sunless mountains there,
  For here is where it dwells and thrives.
DIANA   So then it isn't true you love   1035
  Marcela?
TEODORO   I'm sure I'd survive
  Without her absolutely fine.
DIANA   She tells me that you've lost your wits
  For her.
TEODORO   I hadn't much to lose
  There, stopping now to think of it!   1040
  But do believe me, ladyship:
  Although Marcela merits such
  Effusive courtesies from me,
  I haven't served that many up.
DIANA   You must have used some honeyed words   1045
  In wooing her that might beguile
  A lady of a higher rank?

2. The Roman poet Ovid (43 B.C.E.–17 C.E.) describes in his *Metamorphoses* how the goddess
  Minerva (Athena) called upon the house of Envy, in a melancholy and inaccessible place.

TEODORO   Men use cheap words to suit their wiles.
DIANA   Oh, tell me what you told her, pray!
   Come, Teodoro, how do men   1050
   Woo women with their flowery speech?
TEODORO   Well, when you love, you have to beg,
   And wrap a thousand lies around
   The truth, should this be voiced or not.
DIANA   I'd like to hear your blandishments.   1055
TEODORO   I find the way you press me odd,
   My lady, but all right. I said:
   "Those starry orbs that are your eyes
   Provide mine with the light they need,"
   And: "Coral's not as pearly white   1060
   As teeth in your celestial mouth."
DIANA   Celestial?
TEODORO   Well, a pitch like this
   Is standard fare, my lady, when
   A suitor's feeling passionate.
DIANA   Your taste in women is quite poor!   1065
   Don't be surprised if I lose faith
   In your discriminating powers,
   For I know that Marcela's grace
   Rates lower than her blemishes,
   Which seem more glaring over time.   1070
   These, coupled with hygienic flaws,
   Occasion me no end of strife
   With her . . . But I don't wish to set
   Your mind against the maid you love.
   Still, I could say a thing or two   1075
   About . . . no matter. Let's keep mum
   As to her charms or lack thereof.
   I'm pleased to learn of your romance
   And wish to wed you happily.
   But since you're such a lady's man,   1080
   How, Teodoro, can I help
   That lovelorn friend of mine to feel
   As joyous as Marcela does?
   She mopes about with heart unhealed
   For love of one beneath her rank.   1085
   Pursuing such a passion strips
   Her title of authority
   While swearing off desire for him
   Just leaves her mad with jealousy.
   Still unaware, the commoner,   1090
   A mindful man, has nonetheless
   Remained for now restrained toward her.
TEODORO   So I'm the expert, then, on love?
   I wouldn't have the faintest clue
   What to advise.
DIANA   But surely your   1095
   Beloved Marcela's heard your suit?

What sweet words do you use with her?
The walls have ears. If they could speak,
What would they say?

TEODORO   Walls don't have ears
And there's no gossip to repeat.   1100

DIANA   You're blushing, Teodoro. Look!
The color in your cheeks is proof
Of sentiments your tongue denies.

TEODORO   Marcela is a little fool!
One day—just once—I took her hand   1105
But after that I put it down
And gave it back to her again.
I don't know what she's on about!

DIANA   Some hands, as in the Church's pax,[3]
Our Catholic sign of holy peace,   1110
Are kissed before they're let loose of.

TEODORO   The woman's harebrained, as you see.
It's true I dared to kiss her hand,
A peck I bashfully bestowed.
I thought to cool my lips upon   1115
Its lily whiteness, pure as snow.

DIANA   The snow and lilies intermixed?
So that's the poultice you'd apply
To remedy an aching heart?
You surely have more sage advice.   1120

TEODORO   Well, if my lady's friend desires
A man beneath her lofty state
And loving him would signify
Dishonoring her noble name,
Then let her come up with some ruse   1125
By which she'd, say, in some disguise,
Delight in him.

DIANA   Still, there's a chance
The lady would be recognized.
Were it not best to have him killed?

TEODORO   Marcus Aurelius, men claimed,   1130
Dispelled his wife Faustina's itch—
Her gladiator lover slain—
By giving her his blood to drink.[4]
But Roman remedies are frowned
Upon today in Christian lands.   1135

DIANA   So true. We've no Lucretias now.
Our age has no Torquatus or
Virginius while Faustina cruised
Old Rome with Messalinas and

---

3. The pax, kiss of peace, or holy kiss was an ancient greeting among Christians, incorporated into liturgical practice.
4. Faustina was the wife of the Roman emperor Marcus Aurelius (r. 161–180 C.E.). Although she is described in many sources as sexually promiscuous, the emperor honored her in life and deified her at her death. The *Historia Augusta* relates the story of her passion for a gladiator, supposedly cured by forcing her to bathe in his blood.

Poppeas,[5] Teodoro, too.   1140
Now, write another note for me
To my advantage and my friend's.
God keep you, sir. Oh, God! My God!
   [DIANA *falls.*]
I've fallen! Don't just stare! Come lend
A hand.
TEODORO   I hesitate out of   1145
Respect for your exalted rank.
   [TEODORO *covers his hand with his cloak and helps* DIANA *to*
   her feet.]
DIANA   How crude of you to offer it
Enveloped in your cloak like that.
TEODORO   It's how Octavio gives you his,
Escorting you to mass.
DIANA   That's not   1150
A hand I ever asked for, though.
It must be aged now, by my troth,
Some seventy years, so near death
It comes pre-shrouded and half still.
A person in distress can't wait   1155
For rescuers to dress in silk.
What good is strapping armor on
To aid a friend who's been attacked?
While you're still fussing, he'll be killed.
In any case, the simple act   1160
Of lending an uncovered hand,
Although a breach of protocol,
Is proper, like a face unveiled,
When virtuous features need no palls.
TEODORO   I thank you for these compliments,   1165
My lady.
DIANA   Well, when you're my old
Retainer, you can keep your hand
Inside the lining of your cloak.
But you're my secretary now,
So listen to this sound advice: 1170
I'd guard the secret of my fall
If ever it's your hope to rise.
                          [DIANA *exits.*]
TEODORO   Should I believe these words are true? I might,
Though fair Diana is a woman, too.
She bade me give my hand when a pink hue   1175
Suffused her cheeks and put pale fear to flight.
She quivered. I could feel it. Here's my plight:

---

5. Lucretia was the virtuous Roman matron who committed suicide after being raped. Torquatus and Virginius are models of Roman male virtue: the former was a consul who had his own son put to death for leaving his military post; the latter killed his daughter Virginia rather than consent to her violation. The stories of Lucretia and Virginia are both associated with the triumph of the Roman Republic. Messalina and Poppea, like Faustina, were empresses of Rome and are associated with the immorality and sexual excesses of the Empire.

Is this a happy chance I should pursue?
Its outcome seems in doubt, so if I do,
I'll have to steel my nerves and banish fright.   1180
Abandoning Marcela isn't fair,
For women don't deserve the bitter pill
Of being left by men who swear they care.
Should women leave men, though, as they do still,
To follow some new pleasure or affair,   1185
Then let them die from love, too, as men will.

Act II

[*Count* FEDERICO *enters with his servant* LEONIDO.]
FEDERICO   You saw her here?
LEONIDO   She shimmered by
Like dawn suffusing meadows green
Embroidered under her light's sheen
With flowers beneath the morning sky.   1190
I have a feeling piety
Will not detain the countess long.
This chaplain's mass, if I'm not wrong,
Is shorter than it ought to be.
FEDERICO   If only I could speak with her!   1195
LEONIDO   You're cousins and can talk alone
Without a meddling chaperone.
FEDERICO   My fond hopes, Leonido, blur
These family ties to make them seem
Convenient and, thus, suspect now.   1200
Before I sought this wedding vow,
I never lacked for self-esteem.
I mean, a gentleman can pay
A lady visits, be he kin
Or intimate, without chagrin   1205
Till marriage plans come into play.
But once these longings start to stir,
Though hidden, he grows far less bold,
Calls not as often as of old
And hardly speaks a word to her.   1210
I'd hoped to hold the countess near
Through love and revel in my gain,
But loving her has brought the pain
Of losing what I held most dear:
The freedom I enjoyed to see   1215
My cousin, free as I saw fit.
[*Marquis* RICARDO *enters with his servant* CELIO.]
CELIO   She came on foot, I'm sure of it,
With others in her company.
RICARDO   She must have thought, the church close by
And she just radiant with her suite,   1220

That walking here would grace the street.
CELIO   You know how in the eastern sky,
    When peaceful morning first breaks through,
    The rays of sun shine forth in full
    And bathe in golden light the bull   1225
    Agraze in pastures damp with dew?
    That's how a versemaker of yore
    Described the blush of dawn full-blown
    And how, too, fair Diana shone,
    Our stunning Countess of Belflor,   1230
    A comely, perfect sight pristine
    With those bright orbs she calls her eyes.
RICARDO   My love moves you to see the skies
    And paint the morning so serene!
    You're right to picture her a sun   1235
    That lights her suitors up and shines
    Upon them, zodiacal signs,
    In making her diurnal run.
    Look! Federico stands outside
    To catch her golden rays in full.   1240
CELIO   So, which of you will be the bull
    Or Taurus, then, and risk your hide?[1]
RICARDO   His ardor's left him first in line
    For those warm beams that are her morn's.
    I'll wait, then, and forgo the horns   1245
    As Leo here, the lion's sign.
FEDERICO   Is that Ricardo?
LEONIDO   That is he.
FEDERICO   I shouldn't be surprised, I guess,
    To see him in such dapper dress.
LEONIDO   The marquis steps out stylishly.   1250
FEDERICO   Your mentioning such strategies
    Makes you sound like the jealous one.
LEONIDO   You're jealous?
FEDERICO   Now that you've begun
    To praise my rival's qualities!
LEONIDO   But if Diana loves no man,   1255
    Just what is it you're jealous of?
FEDERICO   That, being a woman, she might love
    Some other man someday.
LEONIDO   She can
    Be so contemptuous, proud and vain,
    All swains are equally denied.   1260
FEDERICO   Her beauty prompts this haughty pride.
LEONIDO   I see no beauty in disdain.
CELIO   My lord, Diana's coming out.
RICARDO   And so my night turns into day!
CELIO   You'll speak to her?

---

1. Taurus is the astrological sign of the bull. Bulls were sacrificed in the Roman feast of the *tau-robolium*. Bulls also suggest the horns of cuckoldry.

RICARDO   I'll have my say   1265
If Federico's not about.
    [OCTAVIO, FABIO, TEODORO, *and* DIANA *enter, followed by*
    MARCELA *and* ANARDA, *the ladies wearing cloaks.*
    FEDERICO *approaches from one side.*]
FEDERICO   My lady, I had hoped to see you here.
DIANA   Good count, you are a welcome sight, indeed.
RICARDO   I, too, your humble servant, countess, have
Been waiting here to walk with you a bit.   1270
DIANA   Good marquis, fortune shines on me this day!
What gallantry!
RICARDO   It's born of my esteem
For you, Your Ladyship.
FEDERICO [*To* LEONIDO.]   She doesn't seem
To favor me from what I can deduce.
LEONIDO   Keep talking.
FEDERICO   Leonido, what's the use?   1275
I'd rather hold my tongue and not be heard
When no one wants to hear me say a word.
    [*All exit through the far door except* TEODORO.]
TEODORO   Don't flee me, fancy, brave new thought
Upon imagination's wind!
You're crazy and undisciplined!   1280
I laugh at what my folly's sought
But fear my mind is overwrought,
So slow down while I press your speed.
If my intent is daft, indeed,
I see but what my mind espies: 1285
To come away with such a prize,
A little daring's what I'll need.
Fond thought, if now you would dispel
Hopes that, for being too large, are vain,
Let's first together ascertain   1290
The basis for your rationale:
Do you love whom you serve as well?
You might say this gives me the chance,
If I see straight and not askance,
So I'll not deem the whole affair   1295
Another castle in the air
And this a misjudged circumstance.
Still, should these lofty dreams come bust,
I'll see that you receive the blame,
Though our ambition was the same   1300
And faulting you would be unjust.
Yet, if you lay aside mistrust,
Wild thought, and let me elevate
Your being to that higher state
Where I feel fear, so great love's height,   1305
You might just thank me for the sight
Our lowly selves could contemplate.
If an offended man should side

With his offender, everyone
Will think it right the wrong was done.   1310
In this case, though, I'm gratified
Your boldness steeped my soul in pride.
Should it turn out we both be lost,
The one excuse we can exhaust
Is that you sank because of me   1315
While I pursued you willingly,
Unmindful of this fancy's cost.
Go, wayward thought in peace, then, though
A thousand deaths from boldness loom,
For one who's lost well can't assume   1320
The name of "lost" for losing so.
While others make a thankful show
For what they've found, I'm more inclined
Toward gratitude for this grand kind
Of losing, for to lose so will   1325
Occasion envy of the ill
That's brought me to this state of mind.
[TRISTAN enters.]
TRISTAN This note intrudes on your laments.
It's from Marcela, sent here straight
In hopes that you'll commiserate   1330
With her confinement's discontents.
No need to tip me for my pains;
When men or women serve no need,
It's common not to pay them heed,
As palace custom long ordains.   1335
And yet, how many visitors
Annoy a man of high estate—
And you impersonate one great!—
By coming as petitioners.
While one whose fortune is more vague   1340
And family wealth a bit unsure
Will find that others shun his door
As if he suffered from the plague!
I'll disinfect this plaint she wrote—
Her sour whine—with vinegar.   1345
TEODORO If your hands took the thing from her,
It's bound to be a winy note!
I'm sure your pickled fingers add
A touch of grape to all, you souse!
(Reading.) To Teodoro, my dear spouse.   1350
Spouse? Oh, that stupid girl! I'm mad.
How silly of her!
TRISTAN   Silly, aye!
TEODORO Go ask my fortunes flying higher
Why someone like me would desire
A flitting little butterfly?   1355
TRISTAN Keep reading, though a perch awaits
Your Lordship in divine domains.

Wine breeds small gnats[2] but still refrains
From scorning what it generates.
Now, if my recollection's clear,   1360
That butterfly you'd leave behind
Was once an eagle in your mind.

TEODORO   Now when my thoughts amid that sphere,
Wherein the sun's bright golden rays
Appear, look down on one so small,   1365
The wonder is she's seen at all.

TRISTAN   I like that fancy turn of phrase,
But what's your answer to this chit?

TEODORO   Watch.

TRISTAN   What, you ripped it up?

TEODORO   Just so.

TRISTAN   Why do that, sir?

TEODORO   Because there's no   1370
More speedy a response to it.

TRISTAN   You treat Marcela callously.

TEODORO   Well, I'm a changed man now by far.

TRISTAN   Enough with that. You lovers are
A lot like pharmacists, I see.   1375
They write prescriptions as you do
These letters, counseling curatives.
The drug for grief cruel envy gives?
Blue violet extract in a brew.
Prescription for a rare disdain?   1380
A flash in the pan—borage oil
To bring the blood down off its boil
And thereby *templicate*[3] the pain.
The balm for absence can be found
In mustard plasters for the chest,   1385
Although this fragrant cure works best
With civic-minded folks around.
The purge for wedded enmity
For couples married ten days straight
Allow them to evacuate   1390
In *homeo-antipathy*.
The remedy for Capricorns[4]
Is pure forbearance or *la mort*,
For cuckolds will still have to sport
Resented, zodiacal horns.   1395
The science for an empty purse
Pursuant to a spending spree
Is *restitutiology*,
Whose antidotes can reimburse.

2. Midges or gnats often appeared in fermenting wine. See Matthew 23.24 in the King James
   Bible: "Ye blind guides, which strain at [out] a gnat, and swallow a camel."
3. Borage or starflower is widely used in herbal medicine. In Spanish, the expression *"quedar en
   agua de borrajas"* (to result in borage water) refers to dashed expectations—something like "a
   flash in the pan" in English. "Templicate" is the first of a number of nonsense words in this passage, as Tristan attempts to sound learned and latinate.
4. The astrological sign of Capricorn (the goat), also alluding to the horns of cuckoldry.

And thus the pharmacist supplies   1400
Prescriptions for each human ill
Until the patient pays the bill—
No matter that he lives or dies—
At which point all his files are shred.
You closed Marcela's case this way   1405
And tore up what she had to say
Before her letter could be read.
TEODORO That's nonsense! Why don't you curtail
Your winebibbing before you come?
TRISTAN Me? You're the one who's giddy from   1410
Those heights that you presume to scale.
TEODORO Look, Tristan, every person born
Fulfills some private destiny.
Not knowing what this fate may be
Means living out a life forsworn.   1415
I'll be the count of all Belflor
Or die before my aim's forestalled.
TRISTAN Sir, "Cesare" I think they called
That duke, a Borgia, whose shield bore
The phrase "Caesar or Nothing" where   1420
No person could mistake his goal.[5]
Once grisly death had freed his soul
And put an end to this affair,
A fearsome wit penned this rebuke:
"'Caesar or Nothing,' you did say,   1425
But you were both these, Cesare—
Caesar *and* nothing, haughty duke."
TEODORO I'll take the motto for my own,
Then, Tristan, and let Fortune run
Her fickle course.
         [MARCELA *and* DOROTEA *enter.*]
DOROTEA   If anyone   1430
Is dispositioned to bemoan
The surfeit of your discontent,
Of all Diana's train, it's I.
MARCELA Well, no one else has so stood by
Me since the countess had me pent.   1435
Oh Dorotea, I will feel
Eternally obliged to you!
Marcela knows no friend as true
As you've been during this ordeal.
Anarda thinks I'm unaware   1440
That she's in love with Fabio,
Yet she's the cause of all my woe,
The one who roused Diana's care
Regarding Teodoro's love.

---

5. The Italian cardinal and duke Cesare Borgia (1475–1507) adopted as his motto "*Aut Caesar aut nihil*" and had it engraved on his sword. He died in an ambush in Navarre. His famous epitaph reflected on his hubris, although it did not include the lines Lope gives here.

DOROTEA He's right there!
MARCELA   Teodoro, dear!   1445
TEODORO Marcela, stop a moment here.
MARCELA Where would I hurry to, my dove,
  With you before my smitten eyes?
TEODORO Be careful what you do or say,
  For palace tapestries betray   1450
  More confidences than court spies.
  Why else would weavers shape their thread
  As human figures for our ken
  If not to warn us that live men
  Behind these forms hear what we've said?   1455
  A mute prince, seeing his sire about
  To be slain, screamed, no longer mum.
  Though you may deem these figures dumb,
  They'd just as certainly cry out.
MARCELA So, have you read my plaintive note?   1460
TEODORO I ripped it up without a glance.
  I've learned my lesson from romance.
  Our love's in shreds with what you wrote.
MARCELA Are those the pieces on the floor?
TEODORO Yes, that's your letter.
MARCELA   And our bliss,   1465
  Just scraps?
TEODORO   Marcela, wouldn't this
  Be better for us both before
  We cause ourselves unwonted grief?
  If you, as I, can be prepared
  To put aside the love we shared,   1470
  Our present woes will find relief.
MARCELA What can you mean?
TEODORO   I'm not disposed
  To cause the countess more duress
  Than I now have.
MARCELA   I must confess,
  I fear that lately I've supposed   1475
  You've had a change of heart toward me.
TEODORO Marcela, God be with you, friend.
  The love we had is at an end,
  But not our bond of amity.
MARCELA Is this how Teodoro deems   1480
  Marcela now?
TEODORO   It's only just,
  For as a friend of calm, I must
  Restore decorum where late schemes
  Of mine have compromised the house
  In which I've thrived.
MARCELA   I'll have my say!   1485
TEODORO Just leave now.
MARCELA   Is this any way
  To treat me?

TEODORO   You're a fool to grouse!

[TEODORO *exits*.]

MARCELA   Oh, Tristan, Tristan!
TRISTAN   Speak your mind.
MARCELA   What's happening?
TRISTAN   Well, this change of heart
Lets Teodoro act the part   1490
Of certain women.
MARCELA   But what kind?
TRISTAN   The I'm-as-sweet-as-sugar sort.
MARCELA   Pray, tell him . . .
TRISTAN   I won't be implored,
As I'm the scabbard for his sword,
His signet sealing notes at court,   1495
The cadence of his swings and sways,
The hatbox for his plumed chapeau,
A cloak for when he's on the go,
His February's count of days,
His shadow and his silent mime,   1500
A post horse on his courier trail,
His speedy comet's blazing tail,
A rainstorm in his summertime.
I form a part of him, as does
The nail that crowns a fingertip.   1505
If cut, our severed comradeship
Would leave me wondering who I was.

[TRISTAN *exits*.]

MARCELA   What think you of this?
DOROTEA   I'm surprised
But dare not say a thing.
MARCELA   So don't.
Let me speak for you.
DOROTEA   Then I won't.   1510
MARCELA   I will.
DOROTEA   Marcela, be advised:
Here, Teodoro's right about
These gossipy old tapestries.
MARCELA   When love's besieged by jealousies,
What fear could ever blot it out?   1515
If I didn't know how proud and vain
The countess was, I'd speculate
He hopes to rise above his state.
These inklings that I've had explain
The recent favor he's received.   1520
DOROTEA   You're mad, so not another word!
MARCELA   My vengeance will not be deterred.
I'll see him sorrowfully aggrieved!
I'm not so dumb I won't know how.

[FABIO *enters*.]

FABIO   Pray, is the secretary here?   1525
MARCELA   Go right ahead, feel free to jeer!

FABIO   Lord, no! The countess sent me now
   To bring the man to speak with her.
MARCELA   Sure, Fabio, but in any case,
   Ask Dorotea what took place   1530
   And what my insults of him were.
   I called the secretary "dumb"—
   He really is an idiot.
FABIO   Oh, it's a prank, then, isn't it?
   Would either of you give me some   1535
   Idea of what this game's about?
   Your gibing strikes me as untoward.
MARCELA   Our gibing? That's a good one!
FABIO   Lord,
   I seem to be the odd man out.
MARCELA   Look, Fabio, this is it. I'm through   1540
   With Teodoro's tug of war
   And realize now that I adore
   A man who looks a lot like you.
FABIO   Like me?
MARCELA   Well, don't you sport a mild
   Resemblance to yourself?
FABIO   Who, me?   1545
MARCELA   I'll need to put this prudently:
   If I say that you drive me wild,
   That I'm attracted by your air
   Or that I'm yours and these be lies,
   May blighted love speed my demise,   1550
   The cruelest fate a soul can bear.
FABIO   You take a page from guile's own book:
   By dying you'd leave me forlorn,
   My heart in pieces as I mourn,
   And give back broken what you took.   1555
   If this is not a game you play,
   To where is all this leading, then?
DOROTEA   You won't see such a chance again.
   Be daring, man, and seize the day!
   Marcela will—and needs to—love   1560
   Her Fabio.
FABIO   Her will, indeed,
   May seal this love, but not her need.
DOROTEA   As Teodoro soars above
   Her head of late, she looks to you.
FABIO   That said, I must resume my quest.   1565
   To one who's but your second best,
   You send a curious billet-doux
   Addressed "To Teodoro, thence
   To Fabio, should the first decline,"
   Which I forgive, although the line   1570
   Does give propriety offense.
   Yours truly, madame, come what may.

We'll speak of this another time.
                                        [FABIO *exits.*]
DOROTEA   What have you done?
MARCELA   I don't know. I'm
   Not feeling like myself today.   1575
   Anarda's fond of Fabio, right?
DOROTEA   She is.
MARCELA   Then I'll inject cruel strains
   In their romance, for love here reigns
   As God of Jealousy and Slight.
        [DIANA *and* ANARDA *enter.*]
DIANA   But I've already told you why!   1580
   What's all this importuning for?
ANARDA   The more I hear you speak, the more
   Your reasons fail to satisfy.
   Marcela's savoring a talk
   With Dorotea over there.   1585
DIANA   She'd have to be the one I care
   To see the least while on my walk.
   Marcela, leave us here to stroll.
MARCELA   Come, Dorotea. Let's retire.
   It's evident I still inspire   1590
   Alarm or hatred in her soul.
                        [MARCELA *and* DOROTEA *exit.*]
ANARDA   May I be frank?
DIANA   You may, indeed.
ANARDA   Two men come, not enamored of
   Your Ladyship but blind with love
   While your demurrals far exceed   1595
   Cold Anaxerete's[6] disdain,
   Lucretia's icy chastity
   And other classic priggery.
DIANA   I'm weary of this old refrain.
ANARDA   Who is it that you plan to wed?   1600
   You mean to say Ricardo's not
   As rich and dashing as that lot
   Of lords who'd woo you in his stead?
   They pale by the marquis's side.
   Likewise, could not a lady from   1605
   The noblest royal line become
   Your cousin Federico's bride?
   Why turn the two away with such
   Contempt, though, that the act seems odd?
DIANA   Why? One's a dolt and one's a clod.   1610
   Since you don't understand as much,
   Anarda, you're more fool than they.

---

6. In Greek mythology, a maiden who remained unmoved by the shepherd Iphis's love for her, even after he killed himself at her door. The goddess Aphrodite (Venus) turned her into stone to punish her.

I cannot love them for I love
Another man with no hope of
Our future union.
ANARDA   You don't say!   1615
You love?
DIANA   Does not a woman yearn?
ANARDA   But you've been like a block of ice!
The sun's own rays would scarce suffice
To melt you when they ought to burn.
DIANA   My icy heart, Anarda, is   1620
An abject puddle lying at
A commoner's sweet feet.
ANARDA   Who's that?
DIANA   The shame I'd feel revealing his
Identity is yet a sign
Of family pride. I won't say who.   1625
It's quite enough that you construe
The harm that this may do my line.
ANARDA   If Pasiphae, though, loved a bull
As Semiramis[7] did a horse—
I'll guard their honor, not be coarse   1630
And skip beasts more contemptible—
How could your love for any man,
Whoever he is, bring you ill?
DIANA   Although a woman love, her will
Can make her hate, and hate I can.   1635
It all seems for the best; I do
Not want to want.
ANARDA   Can you?
DIANA   I vow
I loved when I so wished, but now,
I trust I won't, not wishing to.
        [*Music is heard offstage.*]
Who's singing?
ANARDA   Clara and Fabio.   1640
DIANA   Perhaps these strains will ease my mind.
ANARDA   How love and music thrive combined!
List! Let's hear how the lyrics go.
        [*Singing is heard offstage.*]
Who can make do with love, then do without?
Oh, who can fall in love and then fall out?   1645
No one makes do with love, then does without,
And no one falls in love and then falls out.
ANARDA   You hear the message in that song?
It contradicts what you maintain.
DIANA   The lyrics' gist is rather plain   1650

---

7. In Greek mythology, Pasiphaë, wife of King Minos of Crete, was cursed with lust for one of her husband's bulls, with whom she conceived the Minotaur. Semiramis was a queen of ancient Assyria in the ninth century B.C.E., famed for her political skill. Some traditions present her as lusting for a horse.

But my determination's strong
And I know that I'm in control
Of whether I need love or hate.
ANARDA   This mastery seems to abrogate
The very powers of the soul.   1655
    [TEODORO *enters.*]
TEODORO   My lady, Fabio says you bade
Him fetch me for an audience.
DIANA   I've been desiring you for hours.
TEODORO   I'm here, and most obedient.
Forgive this bothersome delay.   1660
DIANA   You've had a look at both the men
Who hope to take me for their wife?
TEODORO   I have.
DIANA   They're very handsome gents,
Is that not so?
TEODORO   Exceedingly.
DIANA   I balk at making up my mind   1665
Without your counsel. Which of them,
You think, should have me for his bride?
TEODORO   I don't see how advice from me
Could possibly affect a choice
So personal and intimate.   1670
Whichever suitor you anoint
My lord will be the better one.
DIANA   My faith that you'd advise me right,
Good Teodoro, on so great
A question has been undermined.   1675
TEODORO   There must be elder statesmen here
More expert at these royal affairs.
Your steward, old Octavio, might
Bring much experience to bear
On pressing matters of this kind.   1680
DIANA   I want the nobleman you'll serve
To be a person that you'll like.
Who's better looking—say the word—
The marquis, right?
TEODORO   Indeed, he is.
DIANA   I'll wed Ricardo, then. Go break   1685
The news to him. He'll tip you well.
                          [DIANA *exits with* ANARDA.]
TEODORO   Who ever suffered such a fate?
Have all my hopes unraveled now?
Is this the end to everything?
Could I have really planned to wed   1690
A noblewoman? Sun, come singe
These wings I used to soar too high,
For only your corrective rays
Could purge presumption's feathered pride,
Which sought angelic beauty's grace!   1695

Diana's realized her mistake.
How stupid could I've been to trust
In blandishments and honeyed words!
How rare it is, indeed, for love
To bloom between unequal blood!   1700
Is it so odd a pair of eyes
This utterly enravishing
Should lead to thoughts so ill-advised
When they'd have fooled Ulysses,[8] too?
No one's to blame for such a loss   1705
But me, although it's still not clear
Exactly what it is I've lost.
I'll just convince myself I lived
Through some horrendous accident
And, during my recovery,   1710
Fought hard against incompetence
And that will be the end of it.
Forget that dream you figured forth
Of being count and start to guide
Your rowboat safely back to shore.   1715
We'll love once dear Marcela, then.
Yes, poor Marcela will do fine.
Let ladies seek their gentlemen
And love remain by class aligned.
As you were fashioned out of air,   1720
Fond thought, to air be you recalled,
For those who seek to rise above
Their station, lacking merit, fall.
            [FABIO *enters.*]
FABIO   So, did you ever speak with her?
TEODORO   Indeed,
I did just now, good Fabio, and delight   1725
To say our lady finally has agreed
To undergo the Church's holy rite.
You saw two suitors hoping she would cede,
But her mind's chosen one love to requite—
Ricardo's.
FABIO   What discernment she can use!   1730
TEODORO   The countess asked me to convey this news
Myself to him, but since we're close, I'll send
You in my stead for this reward. Go net
What coins the marquis has to give.
FABIO   My friend!
You'll not be poor while I'm still in your debt!   1735
Back soon—I fly!—the better to attend,
So pleased am I with you and this more yet!
Ricardo should be praised, it's only meet,
For vanquishing Diana's no mean feat.
                        [FABIO *exits.* TRISTAN *enters.*]

8. The Greek hero Odysseus (Ulysses) was famed for his cunning and guile.

TRISTAN   I came as quickly as I could.   1740
Can what they're telling me be true?
TEODORO   Yes, Tristan, if you mean how I've
Been consummately disabused.
TRISTAN   I saw the two of them in turn,
Each sitting by Diana's side   1745
Just hammering away at her,
Although I'm yet to be apprised
Of who the lucky fellow is.
TEODORO   Ah, Tristan, but a while ago
That fickle sunflower came by,   1750
That weather vane, that mirrored pose,
That transient river by the sea
Reversing course like none has flowed.
Diana was just here, that hex,
That woman, that fleet phase of moon,   1755
That monster of inconstancy
So pleased to rub salt in my wound
And countenance my vanquished pride.
She practically bade me select
The suitor I'd prefer as lord,   1760
Assuring me she couldn't wed
Without my helping her decide.
Words failed me I was so nonplussed!
That I refrained from crazy talk
Just goes to show how crazed I was!   1765
Next, she informed me that she liked
The marquis and that I myself
Should go impart her choice to him.
TRISTAN   She's picked a husband, then, pray tell?
TEODORO   Ricardo.
TRISTAN   If I didn't know   1770
That you were so dejected now
Or that it's terribly unjust
To kick a fellow when he's down,
I might well mock your arrogance.
Come on now—who are you to think   1775
You might aspire to be a count?
TEODORO   Aspire? I expire, I'm convinced.
TRISTAN   You only have yourself to blame.
TEODORO   I won't deny it—I was quick
To trust in what a woman's eyes   1780
Revealed.
TRISTAN   Well, let me tell you this:
No poison in this world abides
More toxic to man's reasoning
Than venom in a woman's eyes,
My poor man.
TEODORO   I feel such chagrin   1785
Now, Tristan, that I swear to you
I scarce can keep my own eyes raised.

The past is passed, though, and the cure
Means laying in oblivion's grave
That love and this whole episode.   1790
TRISTAN   You'll be contrite and penitent
When next Marcela hears you woo.
TEODORO   I'm sure we'll all be friends again.
[MARCELA *enters.*]
MARCELA   It's hard to feign a love one doesn't feel
Or to forget a love a whole year shared.   1795
The more I thought I could, the more I've erred
As I recalled a love that felt so real.
But if I must, and still my honor seal,
Let love's own disillusion be repaired
By this invented love I've just declared,   1800
No little cure for so great an ordeal.
Why strike a second love up when one's still
In love with someone else and thereby cause
Oneself new troubles while avenging nil?
I won't be used, but take this chance to pause,   1805
For through such remedies to treat the ill,
Love not so much grows icier as thaws.
TEODORO   Marcela.
MARCELA   Why, who's that?
TEODORO   It's me.
You can't have cast me from your mind.
MARCELA   You're so struck from my memory   1810
I'd be a different maid to find
A thought of you there running free.
If I were still that girl you knew,
I'd spend all day engrossed with you.
To think no more of you would mean   1815
My soul would have to flee the scene
Forgetting, though not wanting to.
How can you even say my name?
How could that mouth of yours dare speak
So unabashed?
TEODORO   It was my aim   1820
To test a constancy so weak
In love it barely staked a claim.
I understand what's come to pass
Is that it didn't take you long
To find a proxy from our class.   1825
MARCELA   A wise man doesn't test how strong
A woman is, or how firm glass,
So don't pretend this was your way
Of seeing whether I would stray.
I know your thoughts a thousandfold: 1830
You hoped to live awash in gold
And that great folly ruled the day.
So how's it going? Has it been
The romp you thought your life would be?

Were you paid back what you put in?   1835
What? There are pleasures you can see
Of which she's not the origin?
What is it, man? Is something wrong?
What happened to your happy song?
Did fair winds turn into a squall?   1840
You come to pay your own a call,
But will you stay or move along?
You've plunged me in this dark abyss,
Though I'm still hopeful you'll restore
The light that was my former bliss.   1845
TEODORO   If it's revenge you're looking for,
What crueler sort is there than this?
Marcela, look, true love is born
Of noble blood the heart bestows.
Don't treat this penitent with scorn.   1850
Revenge ill suits a victor's pose;
It's untoward and must be forsworn.
You won, see? I've come back on cue.
The dream my mind thought would come true
Did not turn out as we had planned.   1855
I beg of you to understand
If there's an ounce of love in you.
I'm not here now because I learned
That I could never rise in life,
Although that would have left you spurned.   1860
I'm here because, mid all that strife,
Fond memories of you returned.
I own that you're victorious.
Let these, then, prompt you to recall
A love more meritorious.   1865
MARCELA   Well, God forbid that I forestall
Your chance for something glorious!
No, don't give up—you're doing fine.
If you desert the countess now,
She'll think her suitor lacks a spine.   1870
Pursue your joy as you know how;
I'm certainly pursuing mine.
My love for Fabio's no sin
But just a sage response to that
Predicament you left me in.   1875
He may not rate to hold your hat,
Yet, I'll have my revenge therein.
God keep you. All this talk today
Has wearied me. It mustn't be
That Fabio should pass by this way.   1880
He's practically half-wed to me.
TEODORO [To TRISTAN.]   She's going, Tristan! Make her stay!
TRISTAN   My lady, when a suitor leaves,
It's hardly certain he deceives
Or that the love he proffered ends.   1885

By coming back, he makes amends
As much as the offense aggrieves.
Marcela, please, lend me your ear!
MARCELA   What is it, Tristan?
TRISTAN   Kindly wait.
[DIANA *enters with* ANARDA.]
DIANA   Marcela . . . Teodoro . . . here?   1890
ANARDA   You seem to fly into a state
Whenever these two talk so near.
DIANA   Let's hide behind that tapestry
So we don't make our presence known.
Love's always roused by jealousy.   1895
MARCELA [*To* TRISTAN.]   For heaven's sake, leave me alone!
ANARDA   He's reconciling them, you see?
They probably just had a fight.
DIANA   The lackey's pandering prevents
My rational mind from thinking right.   1900
TRISTAN   A lightning bolt that stunned his sense
Went by no faster in its flight
Than his infatuation for
That silly beauty eyeing him.
Bedazzled by her wealth no more,   1905
He knows far greater treasures brim
In one so fair, whom he'll adore.
That comet passed by in a blur,
Marcela. Teodoro, show
You're sorry.
DIANA   Well, some messenger   1910
The fellow is!
TEODORO   If Fabio
Already is engaged to her,
And she's been so swept off her feet,
Why fetch me when their plans are set?
TRISTAN   Now you're miffed, too?
TEODORO   It's only meet   1915
The two should wed without regret.
TRISTAN   How can you be so indiscreet?
Come over here—your love's at stake!
Extend your hand for her to take
And make peace while your tempers cool.   1920
TEODORO   You think you'll change my mind, you fool?
TRISTAN   This one time, lady, for my sake,
Won't you, too, give this man your hand?
TEODORO   I never told her that I planned
To love another in her place   1925
But she said . . .
TRISTAN   That was all a stand
To reap revenge while saving face.
MARCELA   It's not a stand! It's really true.
TRISTAN   Be quiet, goose! Come here, you two.
You're both behaving stupidly.   1930

TEODORO   I begged her to come back to me
But won't again, I swear. We're through!
MARCELA   God strike me dead if I go back!
TRISTAN   Such language!
MARCELA [*To* TRISTAN.]   Now I'm feeling faint
But need to stay on the attack.   1935
TRISTAN   Be strong!
DIANA   The knave allays their plaint
So skillfully! He has a knack.
MARCELA   I've things to do now, Tristan, let
Me go!
TEODORO   Yes, send her on her way.
TRISTAN   Be off, then.
TEODORO   Hold her back!
MARCELA   My pet,   1940
I'm coming!
TRISTAN   No one makes them stay,
So why is it they're both here yet?
MARCELA   My everything, how can I leave?
TEODORO   Stones sunk in ocean floors don't cleave
As firmly there as I to you.   1945
MARCELA   This warm embrace will prove me true.
TEODORO   Which other would I fain receive?
TRISTAN   It doesn't look like you need me,
Although you really wore me out.
ANARDA   You find this droll?
DIANA   I want to see   1950
How much there is to learn about
A man and woman's perfidy.
TEODORO   You sure hurled insults at me, dear.
TRISTAN   A middle man who's played no part
In bringing two young people near   1955
Should feel small for his lack of art,
Admit defeat and disappear.
MARCELA   I wouldn't trade you, darling mine,
For Fabio or all earth's pelf.
If I swear falsely, may divine   1960
Wrath strike me dead.
TEODORO   Then I myself
Will reaffirm my heart's design:
God grant that, with my dying gasp,
I see you smile in Fabio's clasp
If ever I forsake your troth.   1965
MARCELA   Would you undo what made me wroth?
TEODORO   Why, anything that's in my grasp.
MARCELA   Say every woman that you know
Is ugly.
TEODORO   Yes, compared to you.
That can't be what you're asking, though.   1970
MARCELA   There's still one thing I'm working through
About this whole imbroglio

And since we're friends again, Tristan
May hear.
TRISTAN   Speak plainly as you can,
No matter how insidious.   1975
MARCELA   Say that Diana's hideous.
TEODORO   She's uglier than the devil's clan.
MARCELA   And foolish.
TEODORO   ⸗ She'll just never learn!
MARCELA   A windbag.
TEODORO   Yes, a total bore.
DIANA   I'll stop their speaking out of turn   1980
Before they mock me anymore.
Though ice runs through my veins, I burn.
ANARDA   Don't let them see you while they sneer.
TRISTAN   If anyone still wants to hear
Bad things about the countess, I   1985
Know some.
DIANA   Should I sit idly by
And listen to that rascal jeer?
TRISTAN   First, there's . . .
DIANA   If I afford the knave
The pleasure of a second one,
The more fool I.
          [DIANA *and* ANARDA *emerge from behind the tapestry.*]
MARCELA   I must go now.   1990
                    [MARCELA *exits with a curtsy.*]
TRISTAN   The countess!
TEODORO   Countess, we were just . . .
DIANA   Well, Teodoro . . .
TEODORO   Lady, I . . .
TRISTAN   That's thunder pealing overhead;
I won't await the lightning bolts!
                                        [TRISTAN *exits.*]
DIANA   Anarda, bring a writing desk   1995
So Teodoro might compose
A letter for me in his hand
That I will dictate to him now.
TEODORO [*Aside.*]   My heart has never beat so fast.
Could she have overheard our talk?   2000
DIANA [*Aside.*]   Love opens half-closed eyes the best
When jealousy reveals the truth.
That he should love Marcela yet
And claim I lack the qualities
To make me worthy of a swain—   2005
I can't believe they'd mock me so!
TEODORO [*Aside.*]   How quietly she voices plaints!
I'm right to say it's wise at court
To learn one's lesson keeping mum,
For hanging tapestries have ears   2010
And walls look silent, but have tongues.
          [ANARDA *enters with a small desk and writing materials.*]

ANARDA   I brought the smaller one and your
Own writing set.
DIANA   Come take the quill,
Good Teodoro, and pay heed.
TEODORO [*Aside.*]   She'll banish me or have me killed.   2015
DIANA   Write this.
TEODORO   I'm listening.
DIANA   You don't
Look comfortable on bended knee.
Anarda, fetch a cushion here.
TEODORO   I'm fine.
DIANA   Fool, put it underneath!
TEODORO [*Aside.*]   I'm wary of this favor since   2020
Her rage may soon be uncontrolled,
For why should knees be honored when
It's possible that heads might roll?
Let's see what comes next.
DIANA   Take this down.
TEODORO [*Aside.*]   What help would crossing myself yield?   2025
    [DIANA *sits in a tall chair, dictating while* TEODORO *writes.*]
DIANA   "When a lady of rank declares her love for a commoner, it is
    most vile of him to speak to another woman. Let a man who
    does not esteem his own good fortune forever remain a fool."
TEODORO   That's it?
DIANA   What more is there to say?
Yes, Teodoro, you may seal.
ANARDA [*To* DIANA.]   My lady, what's this all about?
DIANA   Mere trifles that relate to love.
ANARDA   What love is it that you've declared?   2030
DIANA   How is it you don't know, dim one?
The very stones that shape this house
Are murmuring his name no less!
TEODORO   The letter has been closed and sealed.
It only needs to be addressed.   2035
DIANA   Well, put your own name on it, then,
But keep it from Marcela's eyes.
You'll better understand its sense
While reading it at quiet times.
                    [DIANA *exits.* MARCELA *enters, unnoticed.*]
TEODORO   I can't discern what's happening here.   2040
The woman loves at intervals
The way a surgeon bleeds a man.[9]
Whoever thought that passion's pulse
Would beat like this in fits and starts?
    [MARCELA *approaches* TEODORO.]
MARCELA   I couldn't hear Diana's speech,   2045
My love, as I hid quivering
With nerves behind that tapestry.

---

9. Blood-letting was an ancient medical practice, still in use in the early modern era, thought to
    help rid the body of excess blood and find the right balance of humors (see p. 66, n. 2).

TEODORO   She told me her intention was
To see you wed to Fabio.
This dispatch penned on her behalf   2050
Will fly to her estate by post
To seek the dowry you deserve.
MARCELA   What's that you say?
TEODORO   Marcela, let
It all be for the best, but once
You're wed, don't speak my name again   2055
In deadly earnest or in jest.
MARCELA   But, love . . .
TEODORO   It's too late now for plaints.
                                          [TEODORO *exits.*]
MARCELA   If Teodoro's cooled on me,
This isn't how he would behave.
That madwoman's attentions are   2060
The reason he blows cold like this,
A bucket on her waterwheel:
When low, she fills him to the brim
With waters of her favor, but
Then empties him when he'd rise up.   2065
You ingrate, Teodoro! Ooh!
No sooner does her blue blood touch
Your soul than you forget I live!
She woos you and you leave me sad;
She leaves you sad and I am wooed.   2070
How much more patience can I have?
          [RICARDO *enters with* FABIO.]
RICARDO   I couldn't stop a second, Fabio.
I'll kiss her hands for all she's given me!
FABIO   Marcela, hurry, let our mistress know
The marquis calls on her.
MARCELA [*Aside.*]   Cruel jealousy,   2075
How could you strike another ruthless blow
While I'm still reeling in fond reverie?
FABIO   Be off with you!
MARCELA   I'm going.
FABIO   Say our new
Lord has arrived—her future husband, too!
                                          [MARCELA *exits.*]
RICARDO   Tomorrow at my lodgings you'll collect   2080
A thousand gold escudos[1] and a horse,
Purebred and Naples-born, to ride unchecked.
FABIO   That's more than I deserve for this, of course.
RICARDO   It's just the start of what you can expect.
Though you but serve Diana, you're a source   2085
Of comradeship to me.
FABIO   I kiss your feet.

---

1. This is a huge sum of money. For reference, a poor man in 1620 might spend no more than thirty *escudos* in a year.

RICARDO   For all I owe you, this would scarce be meet.
    [DIANA *enters.*]
DIANA   Your Lordship, here?
RICARDO   How could I stay behind
  When Fabio's brought me such delightful news?
  I suffered thinking you were disinclined   2090
  To marry and my suit would be refused.
  Give me your feet, then. Savoring in my mind
  Our love's most happy state, I'm so bemused
  I fear now for the working of my brain,
  Contented all the same to go insane.   2095
  Who thought this soul could so deserve your eye
  Or that my passion could be more than dream?
DIANA   I'm at a loss to give you a reply.
  I sent no word—is this some humorous scheme?
RICARDO   Well, Fabio?
FABIO   You don't think I'd just drop by   2100
  Much less invent a message so extreme
  Unless it were in Teodoro's name?
DIANA   It seems my secretary is to blame.
  I praised you over Federico and,
  Although my cousin's wealthy and highborn,   2105
  My servant just assumed I'd pledged my hand
  To you, though no like promise has been sworn.
  Your Lordship, pardon these two fools. They planned
  No such deceit.
RICARDO   Fair lady, then I scorn
  To proffer Fabio forgiveness where   2110
  The favor of your image grants this prayer.
  I kiss your feet and hope you're not immune
  To these attempts I make to press my claim.
                                [RICARDO *exits.*]
DIANA   So, are you happy now, you big buffoon?
FABIO   Why does Your Ladyship think I'm to blame?   2115
DIANA   Fetch Teodoro here. [*Aside.*] How very soon
  Upon my woes that tiresome suitor came
  With all my jealous yearnings still in force!
FABIO [*Aside.*]   There go my gold escudos and my horse!
                                  [FABIO *exits.*]
DIANA   I've banished Teodoro from my mind,   2120
  So tell me, Love, what more will you from me?
  You'll say what's causing me such misery
  Is not you but your shadow there behind.
  Cruel jealousy! The bane of all mankind!
  You counsel women detrimentally,   2125
  For should they do as you advise, you'd see
  The honor they so cherish much maligned.
  I must remember, though my love's immense,
  That I'm the sea and he a humble craft.
  Majestic waters drowning makes no sense.   2130
  Adrift, my soul is battered fore and aft

While honor pulls Love's string till it's so tense
The bow will break ere it can launch its shaft.
    [TEODORO *and* FABIO *enter.*]
FABIO   The marquis would have murdered me
   But, now that I've been spared, truth is,   2135
   It felt much worse to lose the coins!
TEODORO   May I suggest to you something?
FABIO   What's that?
TEODORO   Count Federico went
   Half mad when told the countess chose
   To wed the marquis and not him.   2140
   Now that the wedding's off, make known
   This news, as he might just produce
   Those gold escudos you so crave.
FABIO   I'll race there in a flash!
TEODORO   Be off!
                                 [FABIO *exits.*]
   [*To* DIANA.] You summoned me?
DIANA   The scatterbrain   2145
   Did well to leave us just in time.
TEODORO   I've spent this last hour, lady, lost
   In contemplation of the lines
   That capture wonderfully your thoughts
   And realize now my cowardice   2150
   Is born of my respect for you.
   Now that I've rightly been reproved
   For such obeisance like a fool
   Uncertain of encouragement,
   I have resolved here to confess   2155
   I love you, though it must be said
   I love you with all due respect.
   I'm trembling—don't you be afraid.
DIANA   My Teodoro, I know that.
   Why wouldn't you feel love for me,   2160
   Your Ladyship, to whom you have
   Forever pledged your solemn troth?
   I reckon you my favorite
   Of all my house's servants here.
TEODORO   So tell me, pray, what is your gist?   2165
DIANA   What more is there to understand?
   Be very careful not to let
   Your feelings cross a tragic line.
   I'd keep such vain desires in check
   For there's so little that commends   2170
   You to a lady's high estate.
   Poor Teodoro, I suspect
   That any favor I would deign
   Bestow on you should dignify
   Your life and gladden all your years.   2175
TEODORO   At times, it seems Your Ladyship—
   I don't mean to be forward here—

Has many lucid intervals
In which her judgment stays intact
But less her doubtful frame of mind.   2180
What good could it have done, I ask,
For you to proffer me false hopes
That left me in such fervid states?
I took to bed, as you well know,
Enfeebled by my joy's sheer weight,   2185
For almost an entire month
Since first this coquetry transpired.
You see my passion waxing cool,
Then burn hot like a raging fire;
Should I, though, generate the heat,   2190
You curl up in an icy ball.
Why not leave me Marcela, then?
This moral tale about the dog
That guards the manger comes to mind.
Consumed with envy, you obstruct   2195
My asking for Marcela's hand,
But once you see me out of love,
You reappear to drive me mad
And rouse me from all fitful sleep.
So eat, then, or let others eat!   2200
I can't subsist on this regime
Of disappointment and despair.
Should you decline to, I'll return
To one who treats my love in kind.
DIANA   No, Teodoro. Not to her.   2205
Marcela will not be for you.
You may wed any other maid
Your eyes alight upon, but this
Cannot be changed.
TEODORO   Cannot be changed?
Are you suggesting, ladyship,   2210
Though I love her and she loves me,
That I look elsewhere for a wife?
You mean that I'm supposed to seek
Attachment where I've no regard
Or claim affection where there's none?   2215
Marcela worships me as I
Do her, and I declare our love
Most virtuous.
DIANA   You shameless rogue!
I'll have you slain for this offense!
TEODORO   What are you doing, ladyship?   2220
DIANA   I'll slap your face, you impudent
And filthy knave!
          [FEDERICO *enters with* FABIO *just as* DIANA *is slapping* TEODORO.]
FABIO   Let's wait out here.
FEDERICO   Perhaps, you're right. We won't go in.
And yet, I cannot bide the time.

Good heavens, countess! What's all this?   2225
DIANA   A mistress's annoyance when
A servant fails to hold his tongue.
FEDERICO   If I can be of any aid
To you . . .
DIANA   Not here. I would discuss
Some private matters with you, count.   2230
FEDERICO   Then I'll come back another time
When we can speak at greater ease.
DIANA   I'm at ease now. Let's go inside.
I've finished with this trifling thing.
I'd like to tell you my intent   2235
In reference to Ricardo's suit.

                     [DIANA *exits.*]

FEDERICO   So, Fabio?
FABIO   Yes, sir?
FEDERICO   I suspect
That hidden feelings lie behind
This angry outburst she's displayed.
FABIO   God only knows what happened here.   2240
I must say, though, I was amazed
To see good Teodoro cuffed
And openly reviled thus.
My lady's never acted so.
FEDERICO   His handkerchief is drenched with blood!   2245

            [FEDERICO *and* FABIO *exit.*]

TEODORO   If all this isn't love, then by what name,
Love, would you call such lunatic events?
If ladies love this way, from this day hence
I'll call them "Furies," as they've earned the fame.
But as nobility knows love's the same   2250
Regardless of its acolytes' descents,
Why be so cruel, dear foe, as to dispense
With one you love and die? Is that your aim?
That murderous palm divests itself of charm
Though I will kiss you yet, bewitching hand,   2255
Accustomed as I am to your sweet harm.
By now I'd hoped to find your heart more bland.
To take these slaps for love pats does disarm,
Though how they pleased you, I can't understand.
    [TRISTAN *enters.*]
TRISTAN   It seems I'm fated to arrive   2260
Once all the action's over with
Like some fainthearted swordsman, sir.
TEODORO   Oh, Tristan!
TRISTAN   Good my lord, what's this?
A bloodied handkerchief?
TEODORO   Love thinks
That jealousy can best be taught   2265
When blood is drawn.

TRISTAN   Such foolishness!
Whatever could have been the cause?
TEODORO   Don't be so shocked. The countess reels
From true desire that, in her eyes,
If acted on, would prompt a loss   2270
Of honor to her noble line.
She'd just as soon deform my face,
Which serves her as a looking glass
Where honor contemplated stares
Back uglier than in the past.   2275
TRISTAN   If ever in a fit of pique
Lucía, say, or Juana broke
Her sentimental ties with me
And left deep scratches on my throat
Or pulled my hair while booting me—   2280
This just because I played around
And one had happened on the truth—
So what? They're wenches from the town
In worsted stockings and, worse still,
Those clunky shoes poor friars wear.   2285
But when so grand a lady leaves
Her lack of self-respect so bared,
The conduct is most base, indeed.
TEODORO   It drives me crazy, Tristan, when
One moment she's adoring me   2290
And then abhorring me the next.
She doesn't want me to be hers
Much less Marcela's. If I cease
To cast a glance at her, she finds
Some pretext forcing us to speak.   2295
So have no doubt—by nature she's
The dog in the manger, whose dish
Is hunger, letting no one feast,
And standing neither out nor in.
TRISTAN   A wise professor, I've been told,   2300
Exalted in his field, engaged
A housekeeper and serving boy
Who quarreled all the livelong day.
They quarreled at lunch, at supper, too,
And fought so much they shook   2305
His slumber with their nightly rows.
This left no quiet time for books
Until one day, mid-lecture, when
The learned doctor felt some cause
To rush home to that fractious house   2310
And, entering unannounced there, gawked
At finding this duet in bed,
Just cooing gladly at their ease,
At which he said: "May God be praised
To see you like this, both at peace!"   2315

That's how I hope to find you two
One day when all this quarrelling's done.
    [DIANA *enters*.]
DIANA [*To* TEODORO.]   Hello.
TEODORO   Your Ladyship.
TRISTAN [*Aside*.]   She has
    To be a sprite!
DIANA   I've only come
    To check on whether you need aid.   2320
TEODORO   See for yourself.
DIANA   Are you all right?
TEODORO   I'm fine.
DIANA   Why is it you don't add
    "And at your service"?
TEODORO   How can I
    Be in your service anymore
    If you're to treat me this way hence?   2325
DIANA   You know so little.
TEODORO   Just enough
    To sense but not to comprehend:
    For I don't understand your words
    But sense your actions on my face.
    When I don't love you, you grow mad,   2330
    But when I do, you grow irate.
    You call me when I don't attend,
    But act offended when I do.
    You'd have me fathom your desires,
    But later treat me like a fool.   2335
    Just kill me, then, or give me life,
    But end this limbo that I'm in.
DIANA   Did I cause you to bleed?
TEODORO   Well . . . no.
DIANA   Where did you put your handkerchief?
TEODORO   It's here.
DIANA   Come, give me it.
TEODORO   What for?   2340
DIANA   So I can keep dear blood near me.
    Go find Octavio, now. I've asked
    The man to see that you receive
    Two thousand gold escudo coins.
TEODORO   What for?
DIANA   Why, for new handkerchiefs.   2345
                        [DIANA *exits*.]

TEODORO   I've never heard such crazy things!
TRISTAN   I swear that woman is bewitched!
TEODORO   I'm thousands of escudos rich!
TRISTAN   If that's the price she pays per hit,
    You might survive another few.   2350
TEODORO   She said they're for more handkerchiefs
    And took my bloodied one away.

TRISTAN Don't rue that virgin nose she slapped;
Deflowering it has cost her dear.
TEODORO Say, I don't think this dog's half bad;   2355
It bites, but later licks the wound.
TRISTAN Remember how the housekeeper
Who worked for that professor changed?
It's heading that way.
TEODORO   God be served!

Act III

[FEDERICO *and* RICARDO *enter.*]
RICARDO You saw it?
FEDERICO   With my own two eyes.   2360
RICARDO The countess slapped him in the face?
FEDERICO We've all put servants in their place,
But discipline was just a guise,
For when a gentlewoman awes
Her peers by sullying her hand   2365
On some man's face, all understand
There has to be some other cause.
He looks like an aristocrat,
Which cannot have escaped your ken.
RICARDO Her servant at her service, then?   2370
FEDERICO He'll bring about his ruin like that.
RICARDO Some similarities of note
Between them and two pots arise
In one old fable that a wise
Philosopher of morals wrote.   2375
Although one pot was made of clay
And one of copper or of steel,
They both endured the same ordeal
Of coursing down a waterway.
The copper near, the clay pot sought   2380
To stay some distance off, agasp
It might be cracked. I fully grasp
This patent elemental thought
About the sexes in this clash
Of clay and copper. Have no fear—   2385
Should either of these pairs draw near,
There's one in each that's sure to smash.
FEDERICO Diana's show of noble pride
And passion was a shock to me.
Perhaps I didn't really see   2390
Precisely what I thought I'd spied,
But seeing Teodoro served
By footmen and with horses nigh—
These new wings have him flying high!
He never would have been observed   2395

Adorned in all this finery
Had there not been some change of late.
RICARDO   Before all Naples starts to prate
About this base indignity
And your good name's dragged through the mud—   2400
If true, if false, it's all the same—
The man must die.
FEDERICO   Yes, it's a shame,
But she'll know I defend our blood.
Can this be done?
RICARDO   Of course it can.
Our very city limits hold   2405
A crew that, in exchange for gold,
Would happily dispatch the man.
We'll find a murderer for hire
And solve this problem presently.
FEDERICO   It couldn't be too soon for me.   2410
RICARDO   His brazenness will meet a dire
Response this day in consequence.
FEDERICO   Are these assassins here?
RICARDO   No doubt.
FEDERICO   Oh, Providence itself turns out
To aid you, sharing your offense.   2415
          [*The footmen* FURIO, ANTONELO, *and* LIRANO *enter with*
          TRISTAN, *who is wearing elegant clothing.*]
FURIO   The wine's on you today, my friend, since you've
The windfall of this dazzling attire.
ANTONELO   I'm certain Tristan knows it's only right.
TRISTAN   There's nothing that would give me more delight.
LIRANO   You do, in truth, look dapper!
TRISTAN   What you see,   2420
Dear gents, is frippery and child's play
In contrast to the profits I've in store.
If Fortune doesn't change the rules mid-game,
I'll soon be secretary and he, count.
LIRANO   Your master really has received a lot   2425
Of favors from the countess.
TRISTAN   Yes, for now
He's serving as her trusted right-hand man
And portal to her patronage.
ANTONELO   Forget
This idle talk of fortunes and let's drink!
FURIO   This tavernacle[1] here should serve divine   2430
Lachrymae Christi . . . or malmsey, at least.
TRISTAN   Let's try some Greek wine, too, which I'll consume
Until my banter sounds like Greek to you!
RICARDO [*To* FEDERICO.]   That dark-haired fellow with the pallid face
Must be the leader of the pack since he   2435

---

1. Tristan puns on *tavern* and *tabernacle*—the box in which the bread and wine for communion are kept, in a Catholic church. Lachrymae Christi (tears of Christ) is a famous type of Neapolitan wine. Malmsey is a sweet Madeira wine.

Commands the most attention and respect.
Here, Celio.
CELIO   My lord?
RICARDO   I'll have a word
With that pale blowhard there.
CELIO   Excuse me, sir.
Before you grace this holy hermitage,
The marquis here would like to speak with you.   2440
TRISTAN   My friends, I'm being summoned by a prince
And must attend to matters near at hand.
Go on and have yourselves ten flasks of wine
And don't forget to sample the fromage.
Just let me see what this is all about.   2445
ANTONELO   Come quickly, will you?
TRISTAN   Faster than a flash!
          [FURIO, ANTONELO, *and* LIRANO *exit.*]
What is it that Your Lordship would discuss?
RICARDO   Our seeing you amid so many toughs
Has spurred Count Federico here and me
To wonder whether you'd be man enough   2450
To kill another man.
TRISTAN [*Aside.*]   Good heavens, are
My lady's suitors asking this? There must
Be some base plot afoot. I'll play along.
FEDERICO   Have you no answer?
TRISTAN   Sir, I press myself
To fathom whether you are making sport   2455
Of our pure way of life, for by the soul
Of he who portions potency to men,
No sword in all of Naples fails to quake
At just the mention of my valiant name.
Have you not heard of Hector, then? Beside   2460
My furious arm, that other Hector pales.
The Trojan fellow.[2] I'm from Italy.
FEDERICO [*To* RICARDO.]   This man here, marquis, might be just
     the one.
Upon our souls, we're not here poking fun.
If, as you say, you share your namesake's fire   2465
And would commit a homicide for hire,
Just state your price and we'll remit the sum.
TRISTAN   I'll kill the devil for two hundred gold
Escudos, sir.
RICARDO   You'll have three hundred, man,
But do the deed this very night.
TRISTAN   I'll need   2470
The victim's name, then, and some money down.
RICARDO   You know the Countess of Belflor, the fair
Diana?
TRISTAN   I've some friends who work for her.

---

2. In Homer's *Iliad*, Prince Hector was the great champion of the Trojans.

RICARDO   Would you dispatch one of her manservants?
TRISTAN   Her manservants, her handmaidens—indeed,   2475
  I'd kill her Frisian carriage horses, too!
RICARDO   It's Teodoro we would see you slay.
TRISTAN   I'll have to come up with some other plan,
  Then, as the secretary, I have learned,
  Is loath to venture out at night, afraid   2480
  He might have caused Your Lordships some offense,
  Though I've been asked to serve him and protect.
  Let me accept the post and, one night soon,
  I'll slit the ruffian's throat from ear to ear.
  He'll *requiescat*, then, *in pace*[3] while   2485
  I, free of all suspicion, rest in peace.
  So, gentlemen, are we agreed?
FEDERICO   There's not
  Another soul in Naples we'd so trust
  To bring the candidate in question low.
  Go serve him, then, and when he least expects   2490
  The blow, dispose of him and come to us.
TRISTAN   I'll take a hundred of those coins for now.
RICARDO   I've only fifty in my purse, but once
  I see you settled in Diana's house,
  You'll have a hundred—and then hundreds more!   2495
TRISTAN   It isn't hundreds that I'm looking for!
  It's time Your Lordships went your merry way;
  I wouldn't want for my associates
  El Grande, Pug Face, Contractor, the Claw
  Or Wall Buster to figure out our game.   2500
RICARDO   You're right. Farewell, then.
FEDERICO   What a stroke of luck!
RICARDO   Now Teodoro is as good as dead.
FEDERICO   The clever scoundrel really does look tough.
      [FEDERICO, RICARDO, *and* CELIO *exit.*]
TRISTAN   I'll have to warn my master right away.
  My friends and that Greek wine will have to wait   2505
  And home is still a little distance off.
  Hold on—this looks like Teodoro here!
    [TEODORO *enters.*]
  Where are you headed to?
TEODORO   I wish I knew
  Where I was going, Tristan, but I'm caught
  Without direction on this course I run,   2510
  Alone and soulless, driven by the thought
  That I should set my sights upon the sun.
  All yesterday we spoke; now I'm distraught
  To see her act as though all's come undone.
  You'd swear it was her ploy to mock this swain   2515
  And let Marcela revel in my pain.

---

3. (May he) rest in peace (Latin).

TRISTAN   Let's hurry home. It's vital that we not
  Be seen together now.
TEODORO   What do you mean?
TRISTAN   I'll spell out as we go the murderous plot
  In which I've been compelled to intervene.   2520
TEODORO   What? Murder? Me? Why?
TRISTAN   You'll escape this spot.
  Speak softly, though, and let me set the scene:
  The marquis and the count in one cruel breath
  Contracted me to bring about your death.
TEODORO   They want me dead?
TRISTAN   Considering the blows   2525
  Our lady gave you signs of love foretold,
  And wrongly thinking I was one of those
  Assassins who kill citizens for gold,
  They offered me a fortune to dispose
  Of you, and money down to make me bold.   2530
  I told them I'd an offer from a friend
  To serve you at her home, where I could end
  Your life with ease while others would discern
  My feigned attempts to guard you from this fate.
TEODORO   If only God above saw how I yearn   2535
  To die and end thereby this death-like state!
TRISTAN   You sound unhinged.
TEODORO   You mean I shouldn't burn,
  However sweet my plight? Accommodate
  Diana with some way to lift this threat
  Of honor lost, and we'll be married yet.   2540
  Till then, though, fearing for her name, the more
  She burns, the more I'm coldly spurned.
TRISTAN   Now what
  If I took care of that?
TEODORO   I'd swear you bore
  More wiles in you than old Ulysses!
TRISTAN   But
  What would you say if I brought to your door   2545
  A "father" with descent that's so clear cut
  You'd be our lady's peer in noble rank?
  You'd have your wish and only me to thank.
TEODORO   That's doubtless true.
TRISTAN   Some twenty years ago,
  The elderly Count Ludovico sent   2550
  To Malta's isle a son who shared your name,
  The nephew of the Knight Grand Master there,
  But he fell captive to Bizerte's Moors[4]

---

4. The island of Malta was home to the military and religious Christian Order of the Knights Hospitallers after 1530. The Knights carried out attacks on Ottoman and North Africans ships, while North African corsairs (pirates) attacked Christians. Both sides took captives, who were enslaved and/or redeemed for ransom. Bizerte, the northernmost city in Tunisia, was a haven for corsairs, who were generally, though not exclusively, Muslim.

And no one ever heard from him again.
This count will be your sire and you, his son.   2555
Leave everything to me.
TEODORO   This crazy scheme
    You're hatching, Tristan, might have dire results
    That cost us both our honor and our lives.
TRISTAN   We're home. God keep you till we meet again.
    I swear, before the chimes of midday sound,   2560
    You and Diana will be newly wed.
                                              [TRISTAN *exits.*]
TEODORO   The sole cure for this illness I've foreseen
    Is quite the opposite, as lovers know
    That keeping love alive can boast no foe
    More feared than parting ground put in between.   2565
    By going far away from her, I mean
    Through absence, Love, to flee this mortal blow;
    No lightning bolt, however bright its glow,
    Can pierce great distances through earth's dense green.
    For only by creating ample space   2570
    Between us will this love cease coming round.
    A great remove removes love's lasting trace.
    The reason we forget is scarce profound:
    Love perishes amid that barren place
    And its remains are laid beneath that ground.   2575
        [DIANA *enters.*]
DIANA   How does our Teodoro fare?
    Is he still stinging from our blows?
TEODORO   If adoration brings me woes,
    How could I not but cherish care?
    What would I do if you removed   2580
    This malady I suffer from?
    I'd only end up feeling glum
    To think my state might be improved,
    For passionate infirmities
    Are sweet pain to the patient's eyes,   2585
    Afflictions he will no less prize
    Should his own death result from these.
    It grieves me that my care impels
    This servant in his present state
    To take the burden of its weight   2590
    Away from where his mistress dwells.
DIANA   Away? From here? Whatever for?
TEODORO   Men seek to kill me.
DIANA   They may yet.
TEODORO   They're jealous of the woes I've met,
    Which sprang from happiness's store.   2595
    And so I've come to ask your leave
    That I might flee to Spain tonight.
DIANA   I see two things this noble flight
    By one so knowing may achieve:
    The situation you abhorred   2600

That caused this strife now disappears
And, though I'll shed my share of tears,
I'll see my honored name restored.
The count, who has not been assuaged
Since I first slapped you, gives no pause   2605
To jealous rage and seeks some cause
For me to have you disengaged.
Yes, go to Spain—I'll have them mete
Six thousand gold escudos out.
TEODORO   With me abroad, your foes won't spout   2610
Such idle talk. I kiss your feet.
DIANA   Go, Teodoro. Though you see
Your countess, I'm a woman, too.
TEODORO [*Aside.*]   She's crying. What am I to do?
DIANA   You mean, you're really leaving me?   2615
TEODORO   I am, my lady.
DIANA   Stay. No, go!
   Wait!
TEODORO   What's your pleasure?
DIANA   Not a thing.
   Leave now.
TEODORO   Goodbye.
DIANA [*Aside.*]   I'm floundering!
What turbulence at sea is so
Unsettling as a passion's storm?   2620
Are you still here?
TEODORO   My parting bow,
   Fair lady.
                                    [TEODORO *exits.*]
DIANA   Here's a fine state now!
Oh, curse you, honor! You transform
The simplest pleasures into pain!
A rash invention you were, too.   2625
Just who on earth came up with you?
And yet, you make our kind refrain
From acts beneath our dignity.
             [TEODORO *enters.*]
TEODORO   Confirming but that I may leave
   Now.
DIANA   I don't know. You can't conceive   2630
How hurtful witnessing you flee
Feels, Teodoro! Yes, it's clear
You'd not come back here if you knew.
TEODORO   I seek the soul I left with you,
For where else could it be but here?   2635
Before I go, I mean to pack
My whole self up, so please return
My being to me.
DIANA   If this concern
For wholeness is what brings you back,
Why ask for your release at all?   2640

Be off, for now my love contends
With family honor's nobler ends
And you would just provoke a fall.
Go, Teodoro. Please depart
And don't come back here once you're gone,   2645
For though a part of you stays on,
Where'er you bide, you'll have my heart.
TEODORO   God keep Your Ladyship and bless
Your days.

                                          [TEODORO *exits.*]

DIANA   I curse my titled name
For not allowing me to claim   2650
The one my fond soul would possess.
Some state this, having said good-bye,
My eyes, to light I so adored.
Now rue this plight to be deplored.
You've looked awry, now you must cry.   2655
Since our forbidden bond became
First visible through your low glance,
You'll pay the price for this mischance,
As I cannot accept the blame.
Eyes, do not weep. Tears mollify   2660
The very ills for which they're stored.
Now rue this plight to be deplored.
You've looked awry, now you must cry.
Because you couldn't look away,
Excuses served to dull the hurt.   2665
"The sun looks down," you'd say, "on dirt,
Yet sullies not a single ray."
So stop your crying now and dry
These tears before they seem untoward.
Yes, rue this plight to be deplored.   2670
You've looked awry, now you must cry.
          [MARCELA *enters.*]
MARCELA   If any trust you've placed in me
For serving years at your behest
Permits my making one request
You'd grant me as a courtesy,   2675
Your chance to aid me is at hand:
As I have caused you grave offense,
You'll never need to see me hence
If I left for a distant land.
DIANA   I aid you, dear Marcela? Speak.   2680
Inform me what this chance entails.
MARCELA   They say that Teodoro sails
For Spain this day so he might seek
Safe harbor there. Pray, send me as
His wife and best resolve this plight   2685
Removing me so from your sight.
DIANA   You're sure this is the wish he has ?

MARCELA   I hardly would have made the plea
  I did, requesting your consent,
  Were I not sure of his intent.   2690
DIANA   You spoke with him?
MARCELA   And he with me.
  I've come now to enlist your aid.
DIANA [*Aside.*]   Must I be forced to hear about
  Their joy so soon?
MARCELA   We've talked things out
  Together and have finally made   2695
  A plan for leaving here that seems
  The best of all we've yet discussed.
DIANA [*Aside.*]   Oh, foolish honor! Though it's just
  That you don't pardon my extremes,
  What good is it to castigate   2700
  When you afford me no relief
  For fond desire that brings such grief?
MARCELA   What causes you to hesitate?
DIANA   Marcela, dear, I couldn't do
  Without you. These fond pleadings wound   2705
  My love and also have impugned
  Our Fabio, who worships you.
  I'll see you marry him, instead.
  Now just let Teodoro part.
MARCELA   I can't stand Fabio! My whole heart   2710
  Is Teodoro's!
DIANA [*Aside.*]   To be led
  To voice my love is most unkind!
  I mustn't say whom I adore.
  Yes, Fabio will befit you more.
MARCELA   But, lady . . .
DIANA   I've made up my mind.   2715
                                          [DIANA *exits.*]
MARCELA   How would it change my fortunes to allow
  My feelings to contend with such great might?
  When jealous fury braces for a fight,
  What mad extremes would it not disavow?
  Oh, wayward steps, turn back your progress now!   2720
  Your hurried pace has only sped my plight,
  For what's a tree but love succumbed to blight
  When frost first withers blossoms on the bough?
  My soul was gladdened by its buds' array
  Now by her tyrant mourning clothes obscured;   2725
  By freezing passions, love keeps them at bay
  And though the wait for blooms is long endured,
  What matter flowers in their fair display
  If they be lost before their fruit's matured?
    [MARCELA *exits. The aged Count* LUDOVICO *enters with* CAMILO.]
CAMILO   If you would still produce an heir,   2730
  What other option have you left?

LUDOVICO   My many years find me bereft,
　　Fierce foes that led me to despair,
　　For though I may be justified
　　To seek remarriage at my age,   2735
　　Let caution be my judge and gauge
　　If I should really need a bride.
　　So, what if I remarry, then,
　　But give no son the breath of life?
　　I'd just be saddled with a wife!   2740
　　Young women cling to aged men
　　Like ivy twirls around an oak.
　　They clasp their trunks as if to please
　　Yet end up putting on the squeeze
　　And prosper while their husbands choke!   2745
　　But all this talk of wedding bells
　　Just conjures up my tragic past,
　　Camilo. Memories hold fast,
　　Invoking all my private hells
　　As I hope, lacking inner peace,   2750
　　That Teodoro reappears.
　　I've grieved the boy these twenty years.
　　　　[A PAGE enters.]
PAGE   A merchant who has come from Greece
　　Would like a word with you, my lord.
　　　　[TRISTAN enters, dressed like an Armenian with a funny-looking
　　　　turban, accompanied by FURIO, who is also wearing one.]
LUDOVICO   Then show him in.
TRISTAN   Dear count, I kiss   2755
　　Your hands. The skies would be remiss
　　Should their divine strength not afford
　　Your Lordship comfort for his heart's
　　Laments.
LUDOVICO   You are most welcome, sir,
　　But say—what brings a traveler   2760
　　Like you to these quite distant parts?
TRISTAN   I left Constantinople's port
　　For Cyprus first, embarking thence
　　To Venice on a ship that brought
　　Rich Persian fabrics I could vend.   2765
　　My craft docked, I recalled a tale
　　I heard oftimes when I was young
　　And, keen to visit Naples, this
　　Most beauteous city, thought I'd just
　　Pass through it while my servants went   2770
　　Attending to our merchandise
　　And let my eyes see for themselves
　　This lovely place's vast delights,
　　Its comely grandeur and fair scapes.
LUDOVICO   Yes, Naples is quite grand, indeed,   2775
　　And passing fair.

TRISTAN   You speak the truth,
My lord. My father worked in Greece
In trade and profited the most
There from the marketing of slaves.
And so it happened that he bought   2780
In old Azteclias⁵ one day
A strapping lad, the handsomest
Example of a youth on earth
And living testament to how
God's beauty shines through Nature's work.   2785
The boy was being sold by Turks
With other wretches of his class
All captured on a Maltese ship
In Chafalonia by a band
Of pirates that the pasha led.   2790
LUDOVICO [To CAMILO.]   His story agitates my soul!
TRISTAN   My father, smitten, bought the boy
And brought him to Armenia so
The child could be reared beside
My sister and me there.
LUDOVICO   Desist,   2795
My friend, with telling tales that pierce
The heart!
TRISTAN [Aside.]   It cuts him to the quick!
LUDOVICO   But say, what was the young lad's name?
TRISTAN   Why, Teodoro, sir.
LUDOVICO   Oh, dear!
What force the truth contains! Look, tears   2800
Of joy are soaking this old beard.
TRISTAN   So, Serpalitonia and he—
That is, my sister and that youth,
Good-looking to a fault—were raised
With love, which often can induce   2805
A tendency toward cherishment,
And fell in love as well-loved kids
Will do. At sixteen years of age,
With father absent on a trip,
They consummated their desires,   2810
Which left my sister big with child
For all the world to see until
Young Teodoro, terrified,
Absconded from this circumstance,
Deserting her in his distress.   2815
Catiborratos, our fond sire,
Resented less his son's offense
Than this most rash abandonment
And soon died of a broken heart.

---

5. Tristan rounds out his tale with invented (as in this case) as well as actual Mediterranean place
names and with ridiculous names for the persons invented.

We had the newborn baptized then   2820
(For even in those distant parts
They celebrate this sacred rite
Although the church is not the same),
Administering the sacrament.
Terimaconio he was named   2825
And in Tepecas can be found,
For there this striking youth resides.
So, on a stroll through Naples's streets,
Just marveling at its many sights,
I took out notes describing all   2830
Of Teodoro's natural traits
And, when I asked about him, heard
This odd surmise from some Greek slave
In service at my lodging house:
"That wouldn't be," said she, "the count's   2835
Grown son, lost years ago at sea?"
My soul was stirred to find this out
So, taking it upon myself
To seek your home at this report,
I entered accidentally   2840
The lovely Countess of Belflor's,
Where who of all God's creatures should
I see there first?
LUDOVICO   My fond heart is
   A-flutter!
TRISTAN   Teodoro, sir!
LUDOVICO   My Teodoro?
TRISTAN   Try he did   2845
To flee me, but to no avail.
I thought my vision to be skewed
At first for, bearded now, he looked
Quite different from the boy I knew.
When I caught up with him, he spoke   2850
With me, though markedly ashamed,
And begged me, as none guessed his past,
To kindly not divulge his name
For fear his having been a slave
Might harm his reputation there.   2855
I answered that I couldn't see
How past captivity impaired
His standing, as I'd just found out
He was a noble in his land.
At this he scoffed, so I call here   2860
To verify if, by some chance,
The story of your life aligns
With his. Now, if this be the truth
And Teodoro is your son,
Your grandchild should be known to you   2865
Or even, with my sister, brought
To Naples—not to seek redress

Through marriage vows—although you'd find
The woman worthy, I attest—
But so the strapping lad might meet   2870
His estimable grandfather.
LUDOVICO I clasp you in this fond embrace!
I know from how my soul is stirred
And wishes to express its glee
That all things are as they appear.   2875
My dearest, most beloved boy,
Long lost to me these many years,
Alive to cheer my heart again!
Camilo, what do you advise?
Should I go off to meet the lad?   2880
CAMILO Why hesitate? Don't walk now, fly!
You'll gain more life wrapped in his arms;
Lord knows you've borne your share of grief.
LUDOVICO My friend, if you would choose to come
With me, my happiness would be   2885
Complete. Should you prefer to rest
Here, though, until we two return,
My home and everything I own
Remain at your disposal, sir.
I cannot tarry here too long.   2890
TRISTAN En route, quite near, I left a cache
Of diamonds that I must retrieve
But will be here when you come back.
Come, Mercaponios, let's be off.
FURIO I'm ready, sir.
TRISTAN   Ay-thay ook-tay   2895
The ait-bay.
FURIO   Icely-nay un-day!
TRISTAN So, et's-lay am-scray!⁶
                              [TRISTAN and FURIO exit.]
CAMILO   How they prate!
LUDOVICO Come now, Camilo. Follow me.
                         [LUDOVICO exits with CAMILO.]
TRISTAN Psst! Have they gone?
FURIO   The old guy flies!
His coach and footmen lag behind.   2900
TRISTAN It couldn't possibly be right
That Teodoro is his son?
FURIO A lie like that could have a grain
Of truth in it, so don't be shocked.
TRISTAN Here, take this Moorish cloak away.   2905
I'll need to chuck these foreign clothes
Lest someone see through my disguise
And recognize me after all.
FURIO Undress, then—quick!

---

6. The "Greek" exchange is transparent: "They took the bait." "Nicely done!" "So let's scram!"

TRISTAN   I'm quite surprised
At how a father's love endures.   2910
FURIO   Where should I meet you, then?
TRISTAN   Drop in
The old Elm Tavern and wait there.
FURIO   I'll see you soon.
                                              [FURIO *exits*.]
TRISTAN   With all this wit,
Who wants for gold? I folded up
This shift here underneath my shirt   2915
And wore it like a cassock so
It wouldn't look too singular
In case I suddenly were forced
To ditch this whole Armenian hoax
And toss off in some alleyway   2920
This turban and that Grecian coat.
        [RICARDO *and* FEDERICO *enter*.]
FEDERICO   Look, here's that valiant murderer again,
The one who'd cut short Teodoro's days.
RICARDO   My good sir, is this any way for men
Of honor, those who seek the people's praise,   2925
To carry out the vows they made back when?
TRISTAN   No, my lord, no . . .
FEDERICO   What, dupe us with these nays
Like equals?
TRISTAN   Prithee, let me say a word.
You censure me before I can be heard.
I've entered Teodoro's service here   2930
Where, as I said, I'll see the wastrel gored.
I won't offend decorum—never fear!—
There'll be no public bloodying of my sword,
For prudence is a virtue heaven's sphere
Did gift to us, the sole good whose reward   2935
The ancients celebrated. Like I said,
Consider Teodoro good as dead.
He mopes about the mansion's halls by day
And stays secreted in his room at night
As if some singular engrossment lay   2940
Upon his mind that robs him of delight.
Be patient, for I'll take his breath away
With one thrust of my blade run through just right.
No need for haste—we'd better take things slow.
I'll know precisely when to lay him low.   2945
FEDERICO   The man makes sense, so we should wait until
He carries out in service what he's vowed
And strikes our lover dead.
RICARDO   I'm sure he will.
Yes, Teodoro's done for.
FEDERICO   Not so loud!
TRISTAN   Your Lordships, while I'm plotting out the kill,   2950
Don't mind me cadging, as I'm not too proud,

Say, fifty more escudos for a horse—
So I can make a quick escape, of course.
RICARDO   I have it here. Please take it as a sign
That we two, once you've seen the intrigue through,   2955
Will pay in full.
TRISTAN   My life's put on the line
Each day in service of good men like you.
Farewell. I wouldn't wish to undermine
Our plans by speaking here where they might view
Us from the balconies.
FEDERICO   A prudent one!   2960
TRISTAN   Let's hope you think so once the deed is done.
                                                    [TRISTAN *exits.*]
FEDERICO   A daring man!
RICARDO   So crafty he can't fail!
FEDERICO   He'll murder all too well.
RICARDO   Yes, splendidly!
        [CELIO *enters.*]
CELIO   Was ever there a more peculiar tale?
FEDERICO   What's happening, Celio? Come, report to me.   2965
CELIO   A curious incident you might bewail
Has just transpired. Observe the count's place. See
That crowd of people gathering about?
RICARDO   Did Ludovico die?
CELIO   No, hear me out.
They've come in joy to wish the old count well   2970
Now that he's found the son he thought was lost.
RICARDO   But such good news, as far as we can tell,
Ascribes the two of us no hidden cost.
CELIO   It doesn't strike you that these fortunes spell
Bad luck now that your wedding plans are crossed   2975
By Teodoro being the count's lost heir?
Diana's servant!
FEDERICO   Oh, my soul's despair!
RICARDO   He's Ludovico's son? How can this be?
What makes the citizens so sure?
CELIO   Who knows?
The story's long and told so differently   2980
I've neither time nor mind to interpose.
FEDERICO   Who ever lived to bear such misery!
RICARDO   My wedded glories have been turned to woes.
FEDERICO   I'll go see for myself.
CELIO   I'll follow you.
You'll soon learn everything I say is true.   2985
        [RICARDO, FEDERICO, *and* CELIO *exit.* TEODORO *enters,*
                dressed in traveling clothes, with MARCELA.]
MARCELA   You mean, you're really going, then?
TEODORO   And you're the reason I depart.
What good's befallen any heart
That's forced to vie with greater men?
MARCELA   Here come your lying claims again,   2990

As false as your betrayal's been.
You leave because you failed to win
Diana's love while slighting me,
A failure you'd prefer to see
Consigned now to oblivion.   2995
TEODORO   What, me love her?
MARCELA   No, it's too late
For more denials of that crazed
Desire that's left you lost and dazed,
Half bold, half cowardly, I rate:
You lacked the nerve to show but great   3000
Respect for her on lofty heights,
Yet set those low, plebeian sights
On equaling her noble birth.
Mid love and honor on this earth
Rise snow-capped peaks that stall delights.   3005
Avenged of the deceit you've wrought,
I love you still, though vengeance breeds
Forgetting, since cooled passion needs
Revenge to dissipate to naught.
If you should ever give me thought,   3010
Imagine that I pay no mind,
For then you'll love me more, I find,
Because what circumstance can claim
To best rekindle love's spent flame
Than when a man feels he's maligned?   3015
TEODORO   You pined for Fabio, so maintain
This false illusion in your head.
MARCELA   Your scorn will hasten us to wed
As recompense for such disdain.
          [FABIO enters.]
FABIO   Since Teodoro won't remain   3020
Much longer here, I wouldn't thwart
These last goodbyes or dare cut short
Your final moments with the man.
TEODORO   Soon jealousy will have to span
The seas or follow me to port.   3025
FABIO   You're going, then?
TEODORO   I have my things.
FABIO   The countess would a word with you.
          [DIANA enters with DOROTEA and ANARDA.]
DIANA   You're leaving us—it's really true!
TEODORO   I wish my feet could sprout fleet wings
But spurs, at least, would fit the bill.   3030
DIANA   Anarda, have the clothes been packed?
ANARDA   Yes, all is set to sail, in fact.
FABIO [To MARCELA.]   He's going, then?
MARCELA   What, jealous still?
DIANA [To TEODORO.]   Come where we can't be heard.
TEODORO   You know
I serve you ever.

[DIANA *and* TEODORO *speak off to one side.*]
DIANA   You depart,   3035
Fair friend, and carry off my heart.
TEODORO   Your cruel ways prompted me to go.
DIANA   What can I do? You know my plight.
TEODORO   Are those tears?
DIANA   No, there's something in
My eye.
TEODORO   What bides there and what's been   3040
There is your love.
DIANA   Of course, you're right,
Though it lay hidden on the whole
And only now flouts my command.
TEODORO   Though I depart, you understand,
My body goes, but not my soul.   3045
I leave what was a part of me
Behind with one it ever serves,
For beauty such as yours deserves
To have souls serve it faithfully.
Say what your pleasure is. My whole   3050
Being's yours.
DIANA   A tragic day's at hand.
TEODORO   Though I depart, you understand,
My body goes, but not my soul.
DIANA   Are those tears?
TEODORO   No, there's something in
My eye, just like there was in yours.   3055
DIANA   Perhaps, my heartlessness perdures?
TEODORO   I'm sure that's what it must have been.
DIANA   I packed in some trunk over there
Mementos you may think inane.
I'm sorry—I could not refrain—   3060
So when you open it, prepare
To go on boasting of your prize,
Those spoils of war that cost me dear:
"Diana put these keepsakes here
With tears still flowing from her eyes."   3065
ANARDA [*To* DOROTEA.]   They're lost, though neither understands.
DOROTEA   Love comes to light while lovers live.
ANARDA   We'd better stay. Look how they give
Each other tokens holding hands.
DOROTEA   It seems Diana's come to be   3070
The dog in the manger, indeed.
ANARDA   She took his hand with no great speed.
DOROTEA   No other eats, but nor does she.
         [LUDOVICO *enters with* CAMILO.]
LUDOVICO   Illustrious Diana, well might such
Good cheer excuse a man in his old age   3075
For calling on a lady unannounced.
DIANA   What brings you, count?
LUDOVICO   You mean that you alone

Are unaware of what all Naples knows?
The moment all the people heard the news,
I found myself surrounded in the streets   3080
And haven't managed yet to see my son.
DIANA   What son? I don't see what your joy's about.
LUDOVICO   So has my lady never heard the tale
Of how I sent my boy to Malta's isle
Escorted by his uncle twenty years   3085
Ago, and how the Pasha Ali's[7] ships
Enslaved them both?
DIANA   I think I do recall
Once hearing of this woe.
LUDOVICO   Today, madame,
The heavens deemed it meet that I should see
My son again pursuant to these griefs.   3090
DIANA   And right you are, good count, to bring this news
To my glad ears.
LUDOVICO   Now therefore, countess, you're
Obliged, in fair exchange for such good news,
To render me this son now serving you
Incognizant his sire awaits him here.   3095
If only his dear mother were alive!
DIANA   Your son serves me? Is Fabio, then, your child?
LUDOVICO   Not Fabio, but my Teodoro, ma'am.
DIANA   What? Teodoro?
LUDOVICO   Yes.
TEODORO   How can this be?
DIANA   Speak up now if your father is the count.   3100
LUDOVICO   So he's the one?
TEODORO   Your Lordship, noble sir,
See here . . .
LUDOVICO   What more is there to see, my son?
My dearest boy, my long-lost child! I've but
To die now in your arms!
DIANA   How strange this is!
ANARDA   So, Teodoro is a nobleman,   3105
My lady, and of such exalted rank?
TEODORO   My lord, I'm overcome to hear this news.
You're certain I'm your heir?
LUDOVICO   Were I not sure,
The sight of you alone would furnish proof
Beyond dispute. You look just like I did   3110
When I was young.
TEODORO   Oh, prostrate at your feet,
I beg Your Lordship . . .
LUDOVICO   Mercy! Say no more,
For I'm beside myself, my handsome boy!
God bless you, what a noble mien you have!

---

7. Several Ottoman viziers by this name ruled North Africa over the course of the sixteenth
century.

How finely Nature stamped gentility,   3115
Brave Teodoro, on that highborn brow!
Let's leave this place at once so you can take
Possession of my house and all I own.
Come now and see the noblest coat of arms
In all the realm above my manor's door.   3120
TEODORO   My lord, you've caught me on my way to Spain
And so I must . . .
LUDOVICO   But why to Spain? All right,
Then Spain these arms shall be.
DIANA   I beg of you,
Good count, leave Teodoro here until
Such time as he arranges his affairs   3125
And dresses properly to greet his sire.
I'm loath to have him leave the manor's grounds
Amid this throng of onlookers outside.
LUDOVICO   You're wise as only one of rank can be.
I hate to leave the boy a moment here   3130
But will withdraw in order to prevent
More uproar. I do beg Your Ladyship
To send my son to me before night falls.
DIANA   I swear it.
LUDOVICO   Teodoro, until then.
TEODORO   I kiss your feet a thousand times.
LUDOVICO   Now death   3135
May take my soul, Camilo.
CAMILO   He's indeed
A comely youth.
LUDOVICO   If I dwelt more on this
Good fortune, I would certainly go mad.
                    [LUDOVICO *exits with* CAMILO. DOROTEA, ANARDA,
                         MARCELA, *and* FABIO *approach* TEODORO.]
DOROTEA   Give all of us your hands to kiss!
ANARDA   Your rank grants you great wherewithal.   3140
DOROTEA   Dispense your favors on us all!
MARCELA   Yes, nobles who are free like this
Win subjects over, heart and soul.
You might embrace us fondly, too.
DIANA   Here, step aside and let me through.   3145
That's plenty of your folderol.
Lord Teodoro, your hands, sir.
It's your good graces I implore.
TEODORO   I kneel before your grace now, more
My lady than you ever were.   3150
DIANA   Please leave the count and me alone.
I'd speak with him in privacy.
MARCELA [*To* FABIO.]   What think you?
FABIO   It's insanity!
DOROTEA   So, what will happen now?
ANARDA   I own
We'll hardly see the countess play   3155

The dog in the manger much more.
DOROTEA She'll eat, then?
ANARDA   There's much food in store!
DOROTEA Then let her burst with it, I say!

[DOROTEA, ANARDA, MARCELA, *and* FABIO *exit.*]

DIANA Still Spain-bound?
TEODORO   I? Was that my goal?
DIANA Yes, you who said, valise in hand: 3160
  "Though I must go, you understand,
  My body goes, but not my soul."
TEODORO Good fortune favors me and you
  Can only mock.
DIANA   No joy or tears?
TEODORO Let's treat each other hence as peers   3165
  Like noble men and women do
  Since we now know we're both highborn.
DIANA You've changed with rank, it seems.
TEODORO   I sense
  Your own desire is less intense.
  Our equal state's left you forlorn.   3170
  You loved me when subordinate,
  For Love, as is its wont, will choose
  An object of desiring who's
  Beneath it.
DIANA   That's not accurate,
  For as of now you'll be all mine   3175
  And we two will be married this
  Most charmed of nights.
TEODORO   You've no more bliss
  To give me, Fortune!
DIANA   I'll opine
  You'll not find anywhere on earth
  A lady touched by luck this way.   3180
  Now, change out of those clothes.
TEODORO   Today
  I'll learn just what my birthright's worth
  And meet the father I've found, but
  Still couldn't tell you where or how.
DIANA Then go, dear count. Farewell for now.   3185
TEODORO Farewell, dear countess.
DIANA   Listen.
TEODORO   What?
DIANA "What?" When a servant speaks that way,
  It grates upon his lady's ear.
TEODORO From now on, I am master here
  And it's a different game we play.   3190
DIANA My lord, I want no jealousy
  Toward poor Marcela anymore.
  She'll rue this blow like none before.
TEODORO We, born into nobility,
  Aren't wont to cause ourselves such strife   3195

By loving servants.
DIANA   Do attend
More to your speech.
TEODORO   Your words offend.
DIANA   They do? But who am I?
TEODORO   My wife.

                                        [TEODORO *exits*.]

DIANA   What more can I desire? You've no more bliss
To give me, Fortune. What he said was true.   3200
        [FEDERICO *and* RICARDO *enter*.]
RICARDO   May two old friends make bold to ask what all
This joyful clamor is about?
DIANA   Of course
I'm pleased to tell Your Lordships what I know.
FEDERICO   Let's start with how your servant suddenly
Became a nobleman.
DIANA   I thought you'd ask—   3205
Though I must take my leave—about the man
Becoming count and soon my husband, too.

                                        [DIANA *exits*.]

RICARDO   What dreadful news!
FEDERICO   Yes, I can hardly think.
RICARDO   Oh, had that ruffian only done him in!
        [TRISTAN *enters*.]
FEDERICO   Look, here he comes.
TRISTAN [*Aside*.]   All's happening as I've planned!   3210
To think a lackeyonic wit like mine
Could put the whole of Naples in a spin!
RICARDO   Wait, Tristan, or whatever your name is.
TRISTAN   Most people here just call me "Manslayer."
FEDERICO   We sure see why.
TRISTAN   He'd be a corpse by now   3215
Were he a commoner and not a count.
RICARDO   What difference does that make?
TRISTAN   Three hundred was
The price you put on Teodoro's head,
Although the man you paid for me to slay
Was but a servant then and not a lord.   3220
Count Teodoro is a special case
And killing him will cost Your Lordships more,
For it's far trickier to slay a count
Than four to six retainers, hitherto
Half-dead from hunger, dying without hope   3225
Or moribund from envy.
FEDERICO   Name your price,
Just do the deed tonight.
TRISTAN   A thousand, say.
RICARDO   You have my word.
TRISTAN   I'll need more payment, then.
RICARDO   Here, take this chain.
TRISTAN   Start counting out the rest.

FEDERICO   I'll get it.

TRISTAN   So will Teodoro, soon.   3230
   Wait, listen.

RICARDO   What, yet more demands?

TRISTAN   Be still.

   [FEDERICO *and* RICARDO *exit.* TEODORO *enters.*]

TEODORO   From where I stood concealed from view,
   I saw you talking with those thugs.

TRISTAN   You wouldn't find two bigger mugs
   If you combed Naples through and through.   3235
   Besides this chain, they promised me
   A thousand gold escudos should
   I murder you today.

TEODORO   What could
   You have concocted for that fee?
   I'm breaking out into a sweat!   3240

TRISTAN   If you'd but seen me speaking Greek,
   You'd pay me more than I could seek
   From these two crazies, I would bet!
   I swear, it wasn't hard at all
   To don strange garb and Greekalize—   3245
   It's babbling in another guise—
   As I used funny names to call
   Fake beings and towns, which could be a
   Serpelitonia, Xiphanos
   Azteclas, Catiborratos,   3250
   Tecas or Philimoclia.
   Now, doesn't that sound Greek to you?
   Since no one understands a word,
   That's what these people think they've heard.

TEODORO   All kinds of thoughts are coursing through   3255
   My brain that give me cause for dread.
   If anyone should figure out
   Your story's fictive, have no doubt
   You'll see me soon without a head.

TRISTAN   It's too late to reverse these deeds.

TEODORO   I swear you must be Satan's spawn.   3260

TRISTAN   Let Fortune steer the plans I've drawn.
   Just wait and see where all this leads.

TEODORO   Here comes the countess—say no more!

TRISTAN   She won't see hide nor hair of me.
   [TRISTAN *hides before* DIANA *enters.*]

DIANA   Oh, Teodoro! Aren't you off   3265
   To meet your sire?

TEODORO   A kind of grief
   Has held me here and I've returned
   To seek permission yet again
   To carry out my first intent
   And sail to Spain.

DIANA   If this should stem   3270
   From that Marcela's dogged call

To arms, your pretext is absurd.
TEODORO   Marcela? No.
DIANA   What ails you, then?
TEODORO   Oh, I can hardly let the words
Go out my lips and in your ears.   3275
DIANA   Proceed, good Teodoro. Speak
Although it do my honor harm.
TEODORO   That Tristan, then, to whom deceit
Itself might well build monuments
And craftiness write lyric odes   3280
While Crete admires his labyrinths,[8]
Observed my love had little hope
And, knowing Ludovico lost
A son, came up with this unheard-   3285
Of scheme he has me playing out.
Yes, I! The son of Mother Earth,
A man who's known no other sire
Than what I own of wit and pen
And learning. Though the count believes   3290
That I'm his son and we could wed,
Both nobles now, to live out all
Our days in happiness henceforth,
My natural nobility
Forbids imposture of this sort   3295
Since I am by my nature one
Who only can profess the truth.
This said, I would to Spain again
And seek the leave I've asked of you,
For I cannot betray your love,   3300
Descent or radiant qualities.
DIANA   You've been both wise and foolish, then:
Wise in declaring this to me,
As it reveals a noble soul,
But foolish in that you assume   3305
I wouldn't marry you for that,
For now I've just the right excuse
To overlook your humble state
Since pleasure's not in noble parts
But in the mind once it conforms   3310
To what a person's wishes are.
Yes, I will marry you forthwith
And, just to make sure Tristan keeps
Our secret hidden all our days,
Will bid the guards, once he's asleep,   3315
To throw his body in the well
And have him drowned.
TRISTAN [*From his hiding place.*]   Now hold on there!
DIANA   Who's that?

---

8. In Greek myth, the Cretan labyrinth, built by Daedalus to house the Minotaur, was famed for its complexity.

TRISTAN   Why me, Tristan, of course,
Who'd justly have a grievance aired
Against the worst ingratitude   3320
A woman ever has displayed.
I brought about your heart's delight
And now I live to rue the day!
You'd really throw me down a well?
DIANA   You heard me say that?
TRISTAN   Don't feel bad   3325
If you don't ever catch this fish!
DIANA   Come back here.
TRISTAN   No, you don't!
DIANA   Come back.
I promise, then, for all your charm
And banter that you'll find in me
The truest friend you've ever had—   3330
But you will need to keep this scheme
A secret, though it was all yours.
TRISTAN   Why wouldn't I, when I've as much
To lose as both of you?
TEODORO   Hear that?
What's all the shouting and that crush?   3335
          [LUDOVICO, FEDERICO, *and* RICARDO *enter with* CAMILO *and*
          FABIO, *as well as* ANARDA, DOROTEA, *and* MARCELA.]
RICARDO   Together we'll escort your son
Back home.
FEDERICO   Yes, all of Naples pours
Into the street to see him here
And waits as one outside his door.
LUDOVICO [*To* TEODORO.]   Then, with the countess's kind leave,   3340
A carriage waits for you without
Where all the city's noblemen
Will lead you home upon their mounts.
Come with me, son, to your old house.
For far too long you've been away   3345
From where you came into this world.
DIANA   Before he leaves for his estate,
Dear count, I think it well you knew
That I'm his wife.
LUDOVICO   Stop Fortune's wheel
From turning with a golden nail   3350
For all the favors that she yields!
Now I've a daughter, too, although
I only sought a son.
FEDERICO [*To* RICARDO.]   Let's give
Our warm felicitations, friend.
RICARDO   Congratulations! He still lives!   3355
Long life to Teodoro, then,
Though while still jealous of this match
I pledged to that base scoundrel there
One thousand gold escudos—that's

Excluding this luxurious chain—   3360
To have him killed. Fast, apprehend
This swindler and inveterate thief!

TEODORO   No, any person who defends
His master's honor in this way
Commits no crime.

RICARDO   Is that so? Who's   3365
This craven, would-be ruffian, then?

TEODORO   My servant, and to give him due
Reward for his protecting me
While I make good on private debts,
I hereby, with Diana'a leave,   3370
Bid he and Dorotea wed
As Fabio and Marcela have
Been married by Her Ladyship.

RICARDO   I'll gift her dowry.

FEDERICO   I'll give one
To Dorotea, then.

LUDOVICO   I think   3375
My son and his estate will prove
Fit dowry for the countess, too.

TEODORO   And so, dear public, on this note,
I beg you to keep mum this truth
That Teodoro's secret holds.   3380
Now, hereby with your kind consent,
The Dog in the Manger, that most
Renowned of plays, is at an end.

PEDRO CALDERÓN DE LA BARCA

Life Is a Dream[†]
(La vida es sueño)

CHARACTERS

SEGISMUND, the prince, son of Basil
BASIL, King of Poland
ROSAURA, a Russian noblewoman
CLOTALDO, an old nobleman, father of Rosaura
ASTOLF, Duke of Moscow
STELLA, niece of King Basil
CLARION, Rosaura's servant
GUARDS
SERVANTS
SOLDIERS
LADIES-IN-WAITING
COURTIERS
MUSICIANS

The action alternates between a remote mountain prison in Poland and the Polish court, including their environs.

Act I

Scene i

[Enter ROSAURA, *high on a mountainside in Poland, dressed in a man's traveling clothes. Having been thrown from her horse, she descends while addressing the runaway animal.*]

ROSAURA Dash off, wild hippogriff![1]
Why are you charging wind-swift down a cliff
So barren and strewn with stone
You'll only tumble headlong all alone
Into its tangled maze?   5
Dull lightning bolt devoid of fiery rays,

---

† Translated by G. J. Racz for *The Norton Anthology of Drama*, Vol. 1 (2009) and revised for this Norton Critical Edition.
1. A mythical cross between a horse and a griffin, which gives it the wings and head of an eagle and the claws of a lion.

Scaled fish, bird shy of hue,
Where is that horse sense instinct tendered you?
Dwell on these pinnacles
And be a Phaëthon[2] for the animals,   10
While I, forlorn and blind,
Oblivious to the path fate has in mind
For me, descend the brow
Of this imposing, sun-burnt mountain now
And dodge its tangled hair,   15
Emerging I could hardly tell you where.
This welcome, Poland, would
Be more hospitable if strangers could
Sign in with ink, not blood.
I'm hardly here, but bleed hard on your mud.   20
Still, fortune foresees all:
Where does one find compassion for a fall?
    [*Enter* CLARION, *a servant.*]
CLARION   One? Make that two of us
And count me in when you kick up a fuss!
My lady, may I speak?   25
As two, we left our native land to seek
Adventure in the world,
Both saw strange sights, watched miseries unfurled
Before our very eyes
And tumbled down these hills to great surprise.   30
I've shared all your duress,
So tell me now, what's causing you distress?
ROSAURA   I'd hoped to spare your ear
From my complaining, Clarion, out of fear
A servant might be prone   35
To start bemoaning troubles not his own.
There's so much joy to find
In sorrows, one philosopher opined,
That those who've naught to rue
Will seek a share so they can grumble, too.   40
CLARION   Philosopher? Perhaps
A whiskered drunk! I say a hundred slaps
Would leave the rogue well served,
And then I bet he'd whine they weren't deserved!
But what should we do now,   45
My lady, stranded here, you will allow,
At just the worst of times,
Right when the sun is seeking western climes?
ROSAURA   Who ever tread such singular terrain?
If my imagination will refrain   50
From fooling with my sight,
I dare say, by this day's faint-hearted light,
I see a structure rise

---

2. In classical mythology, Phaëthon, son of Helios (the sun), drove his father's chariot but lost control of the horses; to save heaven and earth from destruction, Zeus (Jupiter) killed him with a thunderbolt.

Amid those peaks.
CLARION   Now, either my heart lies
Or hope views what it wills.   55
ROSAURA   A palace born within these barren hills
So rustic and so crude
The sun is loath to look on frames so rude;
An edifice of rough
Construction, fashioned ruggedly enough   60
That, lying at the base
Of rocky crags that touch the sun's warm face
And bask in brilliant lights,
It looks like some huge stone pitched from the heights.
CLARION   Let's wander down a bit   65
Where we can get a better look at it.
If destiny is kind,
The castle-dwellers there might feel inclined
To take us in.
ROSAURA   Its door
Stands open like a gaping mouth mid-roar   70
And night springs from its jowls,
Engendered in the cavern of its bowels.
      [*Chains clank within.*]
CLARION   Good God, do I hear chains?
ROSAURA   I'm frozen stiff, but fire runs through my veins!
CLARION   Just dig my early grave!   75
If that isn't a captive galley slave,
My fear's deceiving me.

                        Scene ii

[SEGISMUND, *within.*]
SEGISMUND   Oh, abject wretch! To bear such misery!
ROSAURA   What voice sounds these laments?
Fresh sorrows and new torments wrack my sense!   80
CLARION   Strange fears besiege my head!
ROSAURA   Come, Clarion.
CLARION   Lady mine!
ROSAURA   It's time we fled
From this enchanted tower.
CLARION   I might have made
A run for it, but I'm just too afraid!
ROSAURA   Do I glimpse from afar   85
The weak and pallid gleam as of a star
Whose feeble, flickering haze,
The emanation of dull heat and rays,
Diffuses through some room
A light so pale it magnifies the gloom?   90
Yes, even standing here
I spy unlighted hollows that appear
To be dark prison cells,
The rank tomb where some live cadaver dwells.

I'm just awed! There within,   95
A squalid man lies clad in animal skin,
Restrained by chains, it seems,
His only company those sickly beams.
Since we've no hope for flight,
Let's listen as he chronicles the plight   100
Of his lost liberty.
        [SEGISMUND *is revealed, chained beneath a faint light and
        dressed in animal pelts.*]
SEGISMUND   Oh, abject wretch! To bear such misery!
I've struggled, heavens, night and morn
To comprehend what horrid crime
Was perpetrated at the time   105
When I, offending you, was born.
At last I grasp why cosmic scorn
Should be my portion after birth:
Your justice may enlist no dearth
Of reasons to be harsh with me   110
As being born, I've come to see,
Is mankind's greatest sin on earth.
But still I venture, stars, to learn,
If only for some peace of mind,
Discounting my dark birth, what kind   115
Of crime could warrant in return
A punishment as fierce and stern
As this I live, a living hell?
Weren't all the others born as well?
If all came in the world this way,   120
What sort of privilege had they
I'll never savor in this cell?
The bird is born with sumptuous hues
And hatches wielding Beauty's power.
In time, this lovely feathered flower,   125
A winged bouquet of shades, will choose
To soar the sky's blue avenues
As swift as anything flies free,
Forsaking the sure sympathy
And peaceful quiet of its nest.   130
As I've more soul within my breast,
Should I enjoy less liberty?
The beast is born, and on its fur
Fair markings leave their bold design.
In time, this horoscope-like sign   135
Drawn by the master picturer
Will learn, when human cravings stir
In cruel self-interest, not to flee
But act as cruel as man can be,
Like some dread monster in a maze.   140
As worthier of higher praise,
Should I enjoy less liberty?
The fish is born not breathing air,

Expelled amid sea slime and grass.
In time, this scaly ship will pass   145
Unfettered through the waves, aware
It's free to swim the hydrosphere[3]
And, measuring the watery
Expanses of the open sea,
Conceive of greater spaces still.   150
As I possess the freer will,
Should I enjoy less liberty?
The stream is born, a snake that wends
Its way where wildflowers bide.
In time, this silvery fresh will glide   155
Along green banks as it extends
A song of gratitude that sends
Its thanks up toward the canopy
For granting it the majesty
Of open fields in which to flow.   160
As I've more life within me, though,
Should I enjoy less liberty?
In suffering that's known no ease,
I smolder like Mount Etna,[4] whose
Release comes only when it spews   165
Its heart out of its vortices.
Which edicts, laws, codes or decrees
Deny a man who's sepulchered
That sweetest privilege proffered,
The natural prerogative   170
Just God above would freely give
To beast and stream, to fish and bird?
ROSAURA   His words evoke in me a fear
And sympathy that cloud my sense.
SEGISMUND   Who's overheard my soul's laments?   175
Clotaldo?
CLARION   Answer, "Yes, I'm here!"
ROSAURA   None but this sad heart drawing near
Who, stumbling on your cell, has braved
The melancholy it's encaved.
          [SEGISMUND *seizes her.*]
SEGISMUND   I've no choice but to kill you so   180
You'll never live to know I know
You know how craven I've behaved.
My honor dictates that I stretch
These arms about your neck and wring
The life from you for eavesdropping.   185
CLARION   I'm hard of hearing, and didn't catch
A word you said!
ROSAURA   Were you, poor wretch,
Born human, I would surely meet

---

3. Bodies of water (literally, both the bodies of water and the aqueous vapor surrounding the earth).
4. A volcano in Sicily.

With mercy, prostrate at your feet.
SEGISMUND   Your voice could cause my heart to melt,   190
Your presence challenge all I've felt,
Your guise make my disquiet complete.
Who are you? Pent inside these walls,
I've known so little of the world—
My cradle and my grave unfurled   195
Before me in this tower's palls—
That from my birth my mind recalls—
If birth it was—no other place
Than these backwoods of barren space
Where I endure in wretched strife,   200
A living skeleton stripped of life,
A dead man only live by grace.
In all my days, I've spoken to
One man and one alone. He knows
The grievous nature of my woes   205
And taught me all I hold most true
About the earth and heavens. You
Appear now, shocked that I could be
The monstrous human rarity
You spy mid ghosts and wraiths, so feast   210
Your eyes: I'm a man of a beast
And a beast of a man, you'll see.
Yet, while I've paid misfortune's price,
I've versed myself in politics,
Observing how the wild brutes mix   215
And listening to the birds' advice.
My measurements have been precise
When I map starry paths in space.
But you alone possess the grace
To cause my anger to subside,   220
My eyes to doubt what they've descried,
My ears to trust all they embrace.
And every time I fix my gaze
On you, I feel fresh wonder soar.
The more I look at you, the more   225
I want to see you all my days.
It's dropsy[5] making my eyes glaze
And brim with water now, I think,
For knowing it's sure death to drink,
They drink you in still more like wells.   230
Still, seeing that my seeing spells
My death, I'll look unto death's brink.
Yes, let me look on you and die!
For all I know, come my last breath,
If seeing you will mean my death,   235
What will not seeing you imply?
Much worse than death would signify—

5. An excessive accumulation of fluid.

Dread fury, rage, and wracking pain.
At least in death my teeming brain
Will grasp life's harsh finality: 240
Why grant life to a wretch like me
When happy mortals can be slain?
ROSAURA I'm awed by you, yet filled with dread.
Still marveling at your tender speech,
I find it difficult to reach   245
Conclusions that remain unsaid.
I'll only say the heavens led
Me here to this sequestered site
To help console me in my plight,
If by "consoling" what is meant   250
Is happening on a wretch who's pent
And makes one's own distress seem slight.
A learned man down on his luck,
The story goes, became dirt poor
But soon surmised he would endure   255
By feeding on the herbs he'd pluck.
"Who else," he asked, "could be so struck
By worldly cares and yet abide?"
At this, he turned around and spied
His answer straightway, noticing   260
Another wise man gathering
The wild herbs he'd cast aside.
I've sighed my fate could be no worse;
Mere living seemed a daunting task.
So when it came my turn to ask,   265
"Who else could suffer through the curse
Of luck so ill-starred and adverse?"
You answered me with sympathy
Because of which I now can see
How all you've said was but a ploy   270
To turn my sorrows into joy
And thereby ease my pain for me.
So if this sharing of my woes
Can soothe your pain to some extent,
Take all you wish by listening,   275
I'll still possess no end of them.
My name is . . .

Scene iii

[CLOTALDO, *within.*]
CLOTALDO   Tower guards! Are you
Asleep or simply faint of heart?
Your negligence let travelers
Intrude where outsiders are barred!   280
ROSAURA I don't know what to think or feel!
SEGISMUND My jail keeper Clotaldo's men!
When will my sorrows ever end?

CLOTALDO [*Offstage.*]   Look lively and be vigilant!
They must be seized, alive or dead!   285
Be careful now, they may be armed.
    [*The sound of* GUARDS *offstage.*]
Oh, treason!
CLARION   Tower guards—yes, you
Who've kindly let us come this far—
As long as there's a choice involved,
We're easier to take alive!   290
    [*Enter* CLOTALDO *with a pistol, and* SOLDIERS, *all with their
    faces hidden.*]
CLOTALDO   Make sure your faces are concealed
As this precaution's been devised
To keep whoever happens by
From recognizing all of you.
CLARION   I love a jolly masquerade!   295
CLOTALDO   Oh, ignorant, misguided fools!
By trespassing upon a site
Off limits to all wayfarers,
You violate the king's decree
That stipulates no sojourner   300
Should ever set his curious eyes
Upon the wonder mid these crags.
Surrender and give up your swords
Or else this firearm, an asp
Recast in metal molds, will spew   305
A venom forth that penetrates
Your skin, two bullets with enough
Foul smoke and noise to grieve the air.
SEGISMUND   Say, tyrant master, what you will,
But do these wanderers no harm.   310
I'll hold my bleak existence cheap
And rot here chained among your guards—
Where, by God's name, I'm left no choice
But to dismember this bound flesh
With my own hands or teeth—before   315
I'll stand for their unhappiness
Or end up, mid these lonely crests,
Lamenting more of your abuse.
CLOTALDO   If, Segismund, you know full well
How large your own misfortunes loom,   320
Enough for heaven to have sealed
Your doom before your birth; if you
Know that this prison serves to keep
In check your haughty fits of rage,
A bridle for your furious starts   325
To harness them in lieu of reins,
Why must you go on raving? Guards,
Make fast these prison doors and keep
This man again from sight.
    [*They bolt the door.* SEGISMUND's *voice is heard within.*]

SEGISMUND   How right
  You've been, cruel skies, to wrest from me   330
  My liberty! I'd only rise
  Against you like a giant who,
  To smash the crystallinity
  The sun displays upon its route,
  Would pile jasper mountains high   335
  Atop a base of solid stone.[6]
CLOTALDO   Perhaps, preventing such an act
  Explains why you must suffer so.

Scene iv

ROSAURA   As I've observed how arrogance
  Offends your grave propriety,   340
  It would be senseless not to beg
  You for this life prone at your feet.
  May you be moved to pity me
  And be not unrelenting should
  Humility or arrogance   345
  Make sympathy impossible.
CLARION   Humility or Arrogance
  Should work. As stock protagonists
  They move the plots bad playwrights use
  In far too many sacred skits.[7]   350
  But if they don't, then mid extremes,
  Not over humble or too proud,
  I beg you, somewhere in between,
  Do what you can to help us out!
CLOTALDO   Guards! Guards!
SOLDIERS   My lord!
CLOTALDO   Disarm these two   355
  And blindfold them at once! These men
  Must never be allowed to leave
  These confines or retrace their steps.
ROSAURA   My sword, sir. Duty and respect
  Oblige me to surrender this   360
  To you alone, the principal
  Among us here, and not permit
  Its cession to a lesser power.
CLARION   My own is such the worse for wear
  That anyone could take it. Here.   365
ROSAURA   I yield it, should I not be spared,
  To mark the pity I've been shown,
  A token worthy of regard
  Because of one who wore it girt
  In days gone by. Indulge my charge   370

---

6. An allusion to the giants of classical mythology, who piled up two mountains (Pelion on Ossa) in an unsuccessful effort to overthrow the gods on Mount Olympus.
7. A dismissive reference to *autos sacramentales*—short sacred plays, comparable to morality plays in medieval England, that often feature allegorical characters.

And hold it dear, for I know not
What muted secret it enfolds,
Except to say this gilded sword
Contains great mysteries untold
And, having sworn on it a pledge,   375
I've come to Poland to avenge
A grave wrong done me.
CLOTALDO   Stars above!
Can this be? All my old suspense
And sorrow, my remorse and grief
Conspire to cause me still more pain.   380
Who gave you this?
ROSAURA   A woman did.
CLOTALDO   What was the lady called?
ROSAURA   Her name
May not be spoken.
CLOTALDO   Is this your
Assumption or do you avow
That there's some secret in this sword?   385
ROSAURA   She who bestowed it said, "Set out
For Poland, using all the charm
And artful cunning you possess
To make the noblemen you meet
Bear witness to this testament.   390
I'm certain one among them there
Will show you favor in your quest,"
Though she declined to give his name
In case the man she meant was dead.
CLOTALDO   God help me! What assails my ears?   395
Now, how will I contrive to prove
That what has just transpired here
Is no illusion, but the truth?
This is the sword I left behind
With fair Viola as a pledge   400
That whosoever wore it girt
Upon his thigh within my ken
Would find himself a much-loved son
And me a sympathetic sire.
But now, alas, what can I do?   405
Chaotic thoughts run through my mind
For he who brings this sword in grace
Brings with it unawares his death,
Condemned before he ever fell
On bended knee. This senselessness   410
Confounds me! What a ruinous fate
And tragic destiny are mine!
This is my son; all markers point
To these corroborating signs
Within my heart, now pulsing at   415
The portals of my breast. Its wings
Still flutter there, incapable

Of forcing back the bolts, akin
To one who's locked inside a room
And, hearing noises in the street,   420
Peers through a window eagerly.
Like him, my heart cannot conceive
What's happening and, mid such noise,
Looks through the eyes to catch a view,
As eyes are windows of the soul   425
Where hearts pour out in teary dews.
What choice have I? God help me now!
What choice have I? To lead this man
Before the king—how harsh the blow!—
Would mean his certain death. I can't   430
Conceal him, though, and thus infringe
Upon my sworn obedience.
I'm torn between these deeply felt
Emotions and the duteousness
I owe my liege. Why vacillate?   435
Pledged loyalty, and not our lives
Or loves, must needs take precedence.
Just so, let loyalty abide!
I seem now to recall a claim
He made of having solely come   440
To right a wrong, yet well I know
How wronged men can be villainous.
He's not my son, he's not my son!
He does not share my noble blood!
But if some threat to his good name   445
Indeed occurred—a plight no one
Escapes, as honor is composed
Of such infirm material
The slightest touch can shred its weft
And whispered rumor stain its woof—   450
What else would any nobleman
Essay for honor's sake, what else
But seek the satisfaction owed,
However plenteous the peril?
He is my son! He shares my blood!   455
We've witnessed his courageous mien
And as I stand here, wracked with doubt,
One saving recourse comes to me:
I'll go myself to tell the king
That he's my son, but must be killed.   460
If honorable piety
Won't stay his hand, then nothing will.
Now, should I warrant him his life,
I'll join his quest to seek amends
For wrongs endured. But if the king   465
Is overly intransigent
And puts my son to death, he'll die
Not ever knowing I'm his sire.

Come, strangers, we're to journey now,
But rest assured that I'll provide   470
Good company in misery
For, mired in our present doubts,
Unsure which here will live or die,
Whose wretchedness is paramount?

                                        [*Exit all.*]

Scene v

[*Enter* ASTOLF, *escorted by soldiers, and* STELLA, *accompanied by ladies-in-waiting. Music is playing.*]

ASTOLF Bedazzled by the shimmering rays   475
Your eyes shoot forth like comet tails,
The drums and trumpets fire off praise
In salvos seldom heard in vales,
Where birds and brooks trill other lays.
This equal musical delight,   480
Performed by instruments in thrall
To one so heavenly a sight,
Lets feathered clarions sound their call
And metal birds put notes to flight.
Their strains, fair lady, honor you   485
Like cannonades salute the queen,
The birds Aurora's rosy hue,
The trumpets Pallas the Athene,
The flowers Flora damp with dew.[8]
You've banished black night's sunlessness   490
By making light of day, for you're
Aurora, this earth's happiness,
Its Flora, peace, its Pallas, war,
And my heart's queen in loveliness.
STELLA Such honeyed discourse flows sincere   495
And in accord with how men act,
But one mistake you make, I fear,
Is that fine words can't counteract
A soldier's garb and martial gear.
These militate against you while   500
My being fights your aspect so
Intensely I can't reconcile
The flattery I'm hearing flow
With all the rigor of your style.
For it is vile and indiscreet,   505
Unworthy of the basest brute,
The seed of treachery and deceit,
To trade on wiles to win one's suit
Or guile to speed a maid's defeat.

---

8. A comparison to three classical goddesses: Aurora, the Roman goddess of the dawn; Pallas Athena, the Greek goddess of wisdom, the useful arts, and war; Flora, the Roman goddess of flowers and spring.

ASTOLF   You misconstrue my plain intent   510
In voicing all this errant doubt
Concerning what these words have meant.
Here, Stella, with your kind consent,
Is what this cause has been about:
The death of King Eustorge the Third,[9]   515
Proud Poland's monarch, left his son
Prince Basil sovereign afterward.
One sister was my mother, one
Yours. Not to bore you with absurd
Recitals of each king and queen,   520
I'll make this brief. Fair Clorilene,
Your mother—and to me, Her Grace,
Who now rules in a better place
Beneath the starry damascene[1]—
Was elder, with no progeny   525
But you. Her younger sister was
Your aunt, but mother unto me,
Fair Recisunda, whom God does
Hold likewise dear in memory.
In Moscow, where I came of age,   530
She'd married. Here, I must forgo
Strict sequence and turn back a page:
King Basil, lady, as you know,
Has lost the war all mortals wage
Against Time. Ever with a mind   535
To study, he was disinclined
To woo. His childless queen now dead,
Our bloodlines stand us in good stead
To be the heirs he'll leave behind.
You hold a strong claim to the throne—   540
His elder sister's daughter would—
But I, a male, the fully grown
Son of his younger sister, should
Be favored to ascend alone.
We sought our uncle, then, impelled   545
To plead the justness of each case.
His reconciling us compelled
The naming of this time and place
So that our meeting could be held.
Such was my aim in setting out   550
From Moscow's distant, lovely land.
I've come for Poland's crown without
A fight, but found this fight on hand,
Though I've declined to press the bout.
Oh, may the people, God of Love,[2]   555

---

9. A fictional Polish monarch; his lineage includes Basil and his sisters, Clorilene and Recisunda,
below, as well as Basil's deceased wife, also named Clorilene (see line 660).
1. That is, the heavens; damascene work is metal ornamented by having patterns incised into its
surface and then filled with silver or gold.
2. Eros, in Greek mythology; Cupid in Roman.

Precise astrologers they are,
Be wise like you and think well of
Our union! Let them thank the star
That designates you queen above,
For you're the queen I choose! Be shown   560
The honors you deserve! So please
It that our uncle yield his throne,
Your virtue bring you victories
And my love make this realm your own.
STELLA   I trust my own heart shares the aim   565
You've set forth in your dashing speech.
I only wish that I could claim
The throne now sits within my reach
So you could rule with lasting fame.
Still, I confess you must convince   570
Me that your faith will pass the test
Of quelling my suspicions since
The portrait pendant on your chest
Belies these fine words from a . . . prince.
ASTOLF   I'd hoped to give you a complete   575
Account of this, but know not how
As trumpets noisily entreat
Attendance on the king, who now
Approaches with his royal suite.

Scene vi

[*Trumpets blare. Enter the aged King* BASIL *with retinue.*]
STELLA   Wise Thales!
ASTOLF   Learned Euclid,[3] hail!   580
STELLA   You rule today . . .
ASTOLF   Today you dwell . . .
STELLA   Mid starry signs . . .
ASTOLF   Mid starry trail . . .
STELLA   And calculate . . .
ASTOLF   And measure well . . .
STELLA   Each orbit's path . . .
ASTOLF   Each sphere's true scale.
STELLA   Oh, let me twirl like ivy round . . .   585
ASTOLF   Oh, let me lie down duty bound . . .
STELLA   Your trunk, as fitting and discreet.
ASTOLF   Here prostrate at your royal feet.
BASIL   Dear niece and nephew, my profound
Embrace! As loyal from the start   590
To my most sentimental plans,
You come with such a show of heart
That I pronounce you, by these banns,
True equals, each a part to part.

---

3. Two Greek thinkers: Thales (sixth century B.C.E.), a philosopher and mathematician, was viewed
   as the founder of physical science, and Euclid (active ca. 300 B.C.E.) was a mathematician
   renowned as the father of geometry.

I ask, though, since my person nears   595
Exhaustion from the weight of years,
That you respectfully refrain
From speaking, as it will be plain
My speech will soon amaze your ears.
For well you know—now mind my words,   600
Beloved nephew, dearest niece,
Grand nobles of the Polish court,
Good subjects, kin, friends I esteem—
For well you know, men have bestowed
On me the epithet of "wise"   605
To honor my enlightenment.
Against Oblivion and Time,
Timanthes in his portraits and
Lysippus[4] in his sculptures grand
Proclaim me "Basil Rex,[5] the Great"   610
And so I'm called throughout these lands.
For well you know, the sciences
Are what I've loved and cherished most,
Fine mathematic formulae
By which I've robbed Time of its role,   615
Foreseeing what the future holds,
The only source of its renown,
And presaged more events each day.
For when my charts reveal accounts
Of incidents set to occur   620
In centuries still unbegun,
The dupe is dull chronology
As I glimpse first what's yet to come.
Those circular, snow-colored spheres
In glassy canopies that move[6]   625
Illuminated by the sun
But rent by cycles of the moon;
Those gleaming, diamantine orbs
And planets crystalline in space
Where incandescent stars shine bright   630
And zodiacal creatures graze,
Remain the major inquiry
Of my declining years, the books
In which the heavens list all fates,
Benign or far less merciful,   635
On paper strewn with diamond dust
In sapphire ledgers finely lined
With patterned bars of glittering gold,
Inscribed with multitudes of signs.
I study these celestial tomes   640

---

4. Two Greek artists: Timanthes (late fifth century B.C.E.), a painter, and Lysippus (active ca. 320 B.C.E.), a sculptor.
5. King (Latin).
6. According to the cosmology of the Greek mathematician and astronomer Ptolemy (active 127–148 C.E.), still dominant in the Renaissance, the planets, sun, moon, and stars all circle the earth in vast crystalline spheres.

And let my spirit wander free
In fast pursuit of starry trails
Wherever their swift paths should lead.
Wise heavens, if you'd only stopped
This active mind before it filled   645
Their margins with its commentaries
Or indexed every page at will!
If only you'd conceived my life
As but the first of casualties
Exacted by their wrath, this might   650
Have been my only tragedy.
But those who are misfortune-prone
Feel merit slice them like a knife,
For whomsoever knowledge harms
Is nothing but a suicide!   655
Though I be late in voicing this,
Events tell better tales than speech
And so, to leave this congress awed,
I ask again that you not speak.
My late wife, your Queen Clorilene,   660
Bore me a male child so ill-starred
The wary skies announced his birth
With wonders patently bizarre.
Before her womb, that sepulcher
Predating life, gave living light   665
Unto the boy—for being born
And dying are indeed alike—
His mother had seen countless times,
Amid the strange delirium
Of dream, a monstrous form not quite   670
A human, but resembling one,
Which disemboweled her from within.
Once covered with her body's blood,
The brute would kill her, then emerge
Half mortal man, half viper slough.   675
Now, come the day the child was born,
These omens proved to be correct,
For dire portents never lie
And strictly see how things will end.
Spheres inauspiciously aligned   680
Provoked the scarlet-blooded sun
To challenge the cold moon to duel
And turned the heavens rubicund.
With all the earth their battleground,
These two celestial lanterns gleamed   685
In savage combat perched on high,
Both beaming bright as they could beam.
The longest and most horrible
Eclipse that ever did transpire—
Besides the one that dimmed the globe   690

The day Our Lord was crucified[7]—
Occurred next. As the planet sensed
Itself engulfed in living flames,
It must have thought the throes of death
Were making its foundations shake.   695
Then, suddenly, the skies grew black
And sturdy buildings lurched and spun.
The clouds rained stones upon the land
And rivers coursed along like blood.
This fatal confluence of stars   700
Or planetary pull prevailed
At Segismund's birth, presaging
The foulness of his soul that day.
For life, he gave his mother death,
And by such savagery affirmed: 705
"I am a man who will not cease
To menace all mankind in turn."
Recurring to the sciences
For guidance, I divined dire plans
For Segismund. I learned my heir   710
Would be the most rebellious man
The world could know, the cruelest prince
And even most ungodly king
Whose reckless rule would leave the realm
Divided and in open rift,   715
A fractious School for Treachery
And roiled Academy of Vice.
These signs revealed one so possessed
Of furious rage and violent crime
I even saw him set his heels   720
Upon me as I lay beneath—
This causes me distress to say—
The brute soles of his conquering feet!
The silver hairs that grace this crown
Were but a carpet for his steps.   725
Who'd not put credence in such doom
Precisely when such doom is read
Secure in one's own study where
Self-interest plies its influence?
So, putting credence in the fates   730
As prophets given to dispense
Bleak auguries of promised harm
Through omens and foretokened signs,
I ordered that the newborn brute
Be everlastingly confined   735
To find out whether an old sage
Might thwart the dictates of the stars.

---

7. According to Matthew 27.45, Mark 15.33, and Luke 23.44, darkness lasting three hours fell over all the land when Jesus was crucified.

The false news of his stillborn birth
Was propagated near and far
While I, forewarned, ordained a tower   740
Be built between the craggy peaks
Of two remote, secluded hills
Where light could scarcely hope to reach
So that these rustic obelisks
Might seal off entry to the place.   745
The strict laws and harsh penalties
For breaking them were then displayed,
Declaring a forbidden zone
Off limits to all sojourners
Who'd think to pass, the grave result   750
Of these events I've just referred.
There Segismund, my son, dwells yet,
Imprisoned, wretched, and forlorn,
Attended by Clotaldo, still
His only company of sorts,   755
Who tutored him in sciences
And catechized him in beliefs
Of Christian faith, the only man
Who's seen him in captivity.
Three issues guide me here: the first,   760
As I hold Poland in such high
Esteem, my lasting wish has been
To free her from the heinous plight
Of serving tyrant kings. Indeed,
A sovereign who would so imperil   765
The native soil that is his realm
Cannot be said to govern well.
The second bears upon the charge
That, by my actions, I've removed
The right to reign from its true line—   770
Of which no codex[8] would approve—
Through lack of Christian charity
As no existing law permits
A man who'd keep another man
From tyranny and insolence   775
To take on those same qualities.
For if my son's a tyrant, then
How may I perpetrate vile crimes
To keep him from committing them?
The third and final point entails   780
Determining to what extent
A person errs too readily
By trusting in foretold events,
For though my heir may be disposed
To outbursts and impetuous acts,   785
This bent is but a tendency.

8. A compilation of laws.

The direst fate, we know for fact,
Much like the rashest temperament
Or strongest planetary pull,
May boast some influence on free will   790
But cannot make man bad or good.
Engrossed, then, in these quandaries
And hesitant with self-debate,
I hit upon a remedy
That's sure to leave your senses dazed.   795
Tomorrow, I will have enthroned—
Without him knowing he's my son
Or your next king—the man who bears
The fateful name of Segismund.
Beneath the royal canopy   800
And seated in my august place,
He'll have his chance to reign at last
As all my subjects congregate
To pledge their humble fealty.
In doing so, it is my hope   805
To solve three matters that relate
To questions you have heard me pose.
One, should my heir display a mien
Deemed prudent, temperate, and benign
And thus belie what heartless fate   810
Forebode in all it prophesied,
The realm will see its natural line
Restored, as till this hour the prince
Has held court only in those hills,
A neighbor but to woodland things.   815
Two, should my son reveal himself
Rebellious, reckless, arrogant
And cruel, inclined to give free rein
To vice that typifies his bent,
I will have acted piously,   820
Complicit with time-honored codes,
And shine like an unvanquished king
When I depose him from the throne,
Returning him to prison not
In cruelty, but punishment.   825
Three, should the heir apparent
Show the qualities that I suspect,
My love for Poland's subjects will
Provide you with a king and queen
More worthy of this sceptered crown,   830
To wit, my nephew and my niece.
The individual right to reign
Comes wedded in these two, conferred
By dint of their intended bond,
And both will have what both deserve.   835
For this is my command as king;
The nation's father bids it so.

I urge it as a learned sage;
This wise old man is thus disposed.
If Spanish Seneca[9] believed   840
The king is but a humble slave
Within his own republic's land,
Then I beseech you as the same.
ASTOLF   If, as the man whose future gains
Are most affected by these plans,   845
I have your leave to answer first,
I'll speak for all the court at hand
And say, let Segismund appear!
It's quite sufficient he's your son.
ALL   Restore the royal line! Yes, let   850
Our long-lost prince rule over us!
BASIL   Good subjects, my sincerest thanks
For this outpouring of support.
Escort the kingdom's Atlases[1]
To their respective chamber doors.   855
You'll have your prince upon the morn.
ALL   Long live our great King Basil! Hail!

      [*All exit except* BASIL, *who is detained by the*
      entrance of CLOTALDO, ROSAURA, *and* CLARION.]

Scene vii

CLOTALDO   A word with you, sire?
BASIL   My good friend
Clotaldo! Welcome here today.
CLOTALDO   I might, indeed, have been most pleased   860
To come, sire, at some other time
But now it seems a tragic turn
Must for the moment override
The privilege our law confers
And courtesy our ways demand.   865
BASIL   What's happened?
CLOTALDO   A calamity
That in another circumstance
Might not have proved so dire a blow
But been a cause for jubilance.
BASIL   Go on.
CLOTALDO   This handsome youth you see,   870
Through derring-do or recklessness,
Gained entrance to the tower grounds
And saw the prince there pent in chains.
He is . . .
BASIL   Clotaldo, have no fear.
Had this occurred some other day,   875

---

9. Lucius Annaeus Seneca (4 B.C.E.–65 C.E.), Roman philosopher, statesman, and playwright
born in what is now Spain. A constant theme in his writings is that virtue (and thus happiness)
lies in the individual, independent of always uncertain fortune.
1. That is, those who support the kingdom, just as in classical mythology the Titan Atlas bears
the heavens on his head and hands.

He would have felt my royal wrath,
But as I've just divulged this news,
It matters little that he knows,
As I've today confirmed the truth.
Come see me by and by. I've such   880
A many wonders to relate
And you so much to do for me.
You'll learn soon of the role you'll play
In carrying out the most sublime
Event this world has countenanced.   885
As for these prisoners—I'm loath
To punish you for negligence
And thus, with mercy, pardon them.
                                        [*Exit* BASIL.]
CLOTALDO   Oh, may you rule a thousand years!

                    Scene viii

CLOTALDO   The heavens have restored my luck!   890
I've no need for professing here
That he's my son, as he's been spared.
Strange pilgrims, seek your wonted route,
You're free to go.
ROSAURA   I kiss your feet
A thousand times.
CLARION   I'll . . . *miss* them, too.   895
So what's one letter more or less
Between friends who have come to terms?
ROSAURA   You've given me my life back, sire;
It's thanks to you I walk this earth.
Consider me eternally   900
Your grateful slave.
CLOTALDO   A life is more
Than I can give you in your plight.
No gentleman that's nobly born
Can live as long as he's aggrieved.
For if it's certain that you come,   905
According to your very words,
To right a wrong that you've been done,
I can't have given your life back;
You didn't have one when you came.
A life defamed is not a life.   910
[*Aside.*] I hope my words leave him inflamed!
ROSAURA   I don't possess one, I confess,
Though I accept what you've bestowed
And, after I'm avenged, I'll boast
True honor so pristine and whole   915
The life I claim as mine that day
Will turn aside all future threats
And seem the gift it is at last.
CLOTALDO   Take back this burnished blade you've pledged

To bear. I realize your revenge   920
Won't be complete until it shines
Bright with your adversary's blood.
Of course, a sword I once called mine—
I mean, just as I held it now,
Possessing it to some extent—   925
Would know how to avenge.
ROSAURA   I wear
It in your name and once again
Do swear on it I'll be avenged
Despite my able enemy's
Superior force.
CLOTALDO   Is it so great?   930
ROSAURA   So great I must forswear my speech
And not because I feel I can't
Confide in you far greater things
But so you'll not withdraw from me
The sympathetic ministering   935
You've shown.
CLOTALDO   I'd sooner join your cause
If you would but disclose his name.
This knowledge also might forestall
My rendering him unmindful aid.
[*Aside.*] Who is this mortal enemy?   940
ROSAURA   Good sir, so you'll not think I hold
Our newfound trust in low esteem,
Know that my honor's bitter foe
Is no one less than Astolf, Duke
Of Moscow.
CLOTALDO [*Aside.*]   What a stunning blow   945
To all these plans! His cause appears
More grave than even I'd supposed.
I'll delve more deeply into this.
If you were born a Muscovite,
Then he who is your natural lord   950
Could hardly be accused of slights.
Return to your ancestral land
And try to quell this ardent zeal
That hurls you madly forth.
ROSAURA   The wrong,
My lord, that left me so aggrieved   955
Was anything but slight.
CLOTALDO   Perhaps,
A slighting slap that stung too hard,
Offending—heavens!—that dear cheek?
ROSAURA   The injury was worse by far.
CLOTALDO   What was it, then? I've seen so much   960
Of late it scarce could cause alarm.
ROSAURA   I'll tell you, though I know not how,
Considering the deep respect
And veneration that I feel

For you and all this represents.   965
How can I venture to explain
The riddle these deceptive clothes
Conceal? They don't belong to whom
You'd guess. Judge wisely what this shows:
I'm not who I appear to be   970
While Astolf's plan has been to come
Wed Stella. Think, how might I feel
Insulted? Now I've said too much!
                    [*Exit* ROSAURA *and* CLARION.]
CLOTALDO   Beware! Pay heed! Keep up your guard!
This is a puzzling labyrinth   975
Where even reason toils to find
The thread laid down to exit it.²
My honor is the one aggrieved,
Its foe by all accounts quite strong,
A vassal I, a woman she.   980
May heaven steer my hand from wrongs,
Though I'm not certain that it can.
The earth is one confused abyss;
The skies above more ominous
And all the world a wonderment.   985

Act II

Scene i

[*Enter King* BASIL *and* CLOTALDO.]
CLOTALDO   Your orders have been carried out
With due dispatch.
BASIL   Then he is come,
Clotaldo? Tell me what transpired.
CLOTALDO   Sire, this is how the deed was done:
I plied him with the calming drink   990
You wished distilled, a most superb
Confection of ingredients
That blent the might of sundry herbs.
The tyrant strength of such a mix,
Its secret potency concealed,   995
Deprives a man outright of sense
And robs him of the power of speech
While rendering him a living corpse.
The violence of its attributes
So dulls the mind and saps the force   1000
That those benumbed by it lie mute.
Stale arguments repeatedly

---

2. Theseus, hero of Greek myth, was able to escape the Cretan labyrinth after he killed the Minotaur (half man, half bull) with the assistance of Ariadne, who had fallen in love with him.

Ask whether this is possible,
But time-honored experience
With scientific principles   1005
Has shown this ever to be true.
For Nature's secrets find a home
In Medicine and there exists
No single creature, plant, or stone
That cannot boast of properties   1010
Unique to it. If base intent
First prompted man to catalogue
The thousand poisons causing death,
How little more had he to search
When classifying qualities   1015
Of every venom known to kill
To find those that would bring on sleep?
Let's lay aside, then, any doubts
Concerning whether this be true,
As reason backed by evidence   1020
Provides us with conclusive proof.
So, bearing that peculiar brew
Of opium and henbane[1] held
Together by the poppy's charms,
I slipped down to the narrow cell   1025
Where Segismund dwelt. There, we spoke
A while of the philosophies
And disciplines he'd mastered, each
From voiceless Nature when she speaks
In mute guise of the hills and skies,   1030
For years at so divine a school
Had trained him in the rhetoric
Of every bird and beast he knew.
Attempting, then, to animate
His spirit and to sound his mind   1035
Before the task at hand, I turned
The topic to the speedy flight
A mighty eagle flaunted high
Above us, scornful of the wind's
Low-lying sphere and soaring like   1040
Some feathery bolt amid the rings
Of fire in the canopy,
A comet blazing on the heights.
I praised the creature's lofty sweep
By saying, "Now I see how right   1045
You are, grand queen who rules all birds,
To feel that you outshine the rest."
Well, that one reference in my speech
To majesty caused such duress
In him, he gave vent to bold thoughts,   1050
His proud ambition summoned up.

---

1. A narcotic derived from the poisonous plant of the same name.

The pure blood coursing through his veins
Incites and instigates him thus
To eye great feats, and he exclaimed:
"Then even from the raucous realm   1055
Of birds a leader must emerge
To claim the fealty he compels!
My lessons in misfortune should
Console me with the argument
That only the superior strength   1060
Of jailors keeps my spirits pent,
For I would never willingly
Submit to any man alive."
Thus, seeing him enraged by talk
Of subjects that exemplified   1065
His present pain, I offered him
The potent brew. No sooner had
This potion passed from cup to lip
Than all his willful rage collapsed
In heavy sleep. An icy sweat   1070
Coursed through his veins, and every limb
Perspired to such macabre effect
That had I not been warned that this
Was no true death, I would have thought
He'd breathed his last. At just this time,   1075
The men you'd charged to carry out
This bold experiment arrived
And, placing him inside a coach,
Conveyed him to your chambers where
Accommodations following   1080
Strict protocol had been prepared
To lodge him with due majesty.
They laid him sleeping in your bed
And, when the potion's numbing force
Wears off and his deep slumber ends,   1085
They'll serve him as you've ordered, sire,
As if he were the king himself.
So should my fast obeisance
Incline you to reward me well
For all these efforts, lord, my sole   1090
Wish is to learn a puzzling truth.
Pray, pardon me this liberty:
What purpose lies behind this move
Of Segismund unto the court?
BASIL   Clotaldo, well might you voice doubts   1095
About my plan, and these I will
Allay if you'll but hear me out:
As Segismund, my only son,
Was born beneath a baleful star
That, well you know, predestined him   1100
To sorrows, tragedy, and harm,
I'd hoped to probe the heavens now,

As they're incapable of lies
And never ceased revealing signs
Of what that cruelty may be like   1105
Still lodged within his brutal soul.
I'll fathom, then, if stars reprieve
Their harshest edicts or, when moved
By man's restraint and bravery,
Reverse dire omens, for we know   1110
Each person rules his stars and fate.
As this is what I wish to probe,
I've had him brought inside these gates
To tell him he's my son and put
His inclinations to the test,   1115
For should he prove magnanimous,
He'll reign. But if his temperament
Should rage tyrannical and cruel,
He'll be constrained forthwith by chains.
Why is it, you do well to ask,   1120
That this experiment you aid
Could only have been brought to pass
Once deathlike sleep had been induced?
My sole wish is to satisfy
Your every query with the truth.   1125
Should my son learn he's prince today
But on the morrow come to see
His strange existence once again
Subjected to jail's miseries,
Mere contemplation of this state   1130
Would doubtless lead him to despair,
For once he's found out who he is,
What could console him in his pain?
It's therefore been my plan to leave
The door to pretext open wide   1135
So I may claim that all he saw
Was dreamt and so, by this design,
Determine two essential things:
His natural condition first,
According to which he'll proceed   1140
To bare his soul in deeds and words,
And second, whether such a ruse
Can furnish solace to a wretch
Who, presently obeyed by all,
Might soon return to prison depths   1145
To understand that he had dreamt.
This he'd do wisely to believe
Because, Clotaldo, in this world
All think they live who only dream.
CLOTALDO   How readily could I present   1150
Sound refutations of this plan!
But these would serve no purpose now
As I am led to understand

The prince has wakened from his sleep
And, at this moment, comes our way.   1155
BASIL   My thought is to withdraw from sight
While you, as tutor, extricate
Your pupil from what lingering doubt
And puzzlement still plague his mind.
The prince will learn the truth at last.   1160
CLOTALDO   Then I have your permission, sire,
To make these acts known?
BASIL   Tell him all,
For once he sees his perilous
Position, he'll more likely seek
To quell the drives inside of him.   1165

> [*Exit* BASIL. *Enter* CLARION.]

Scene ii

CLARION   A halberdier[2] whose reddish hair
And whiskers matched his uniform
Just whacked me good and hard four times
As I ran here to stay informed
Of court events as they unfold.   1170
What window offers finer views—
Not counting those in front-row seats
That ticket vendors hold for you—
Than man's own eyeballs in his head?
For, with or without sense or cent,   1175
Whenever there's a show to see,
He'll sneak a peek with impudence.
CLOTALDO   Ah, faithful Clarion, servant once
To her—sweet skies above!—yes, she
Who, trading in misfortune, brought   1180
To Poland with her my misdeed.
Good Clarion, have you news?
CLARION   Word is,
My lord, that your benevolence
In stating this intent to right
Rosaura's wrong has her convinced   1185
She should again wear women's clothes.
CLOTALDO   It's for the best, lest she be deemed
Too frivolous.
CLARION   Word is, she's changed
Her name to boot and, cleverly
Rechristening herself your niece,   1190
Has watched her reputation surge
At palace where she now attends
Fair Lady Stella, singular
In beauty.

---

2. A soldier armed with a halberd, a weapon common in the fifteenth century that combined a steel spike and an axelike blade mounted on a long shaft.

CLOTALDO   Then, I've helped the child
Gain part of her lost honor back.   1195
CLARION   Word is, she's biding time until
The moment you return to act,
Restoring her good name in full.
CLOTALDO   No surer thing to bide exists,
For only Time as it transpires   1200
Can put an end to all of this.
CLARION   And word is, too, that she's regaled
With treatment fit a queen at court
By falsely posing as your niece
While I, who served her night and morn,   1205
Am left to die from hunger's want,
Forgotten and ignored by all,
Although a Clarion nonetheless.
For if I ever did sound off
To Astolf, Stella, or the king,   1210
They might be shocked by what they heard.
Both manservants and clarions toot
Like trumpets in this noisy world
And just don't harbor secrets well.
The moment that her fingers lift   1215
This veil of silence from my lips
The song I sing might well be this:
No clarion blaring at first light
Did ever sound more right.
CLOTALDO   Your grievance is well taken, man,   1220
But I can help address this plaint.
For now, attend me in her stead.
CLARION   Look! Segismund, and unrestrained!

Scene iii

[*Enter* MUSICIANS, *singing, and* SERVANTS *attiring* SEGISMUND,
who appears amazed.]
SEGISMUND   God save me! What's this I perceive?
God help me grasp what I've seen here!   1225
I'm awed and not untouched by fear
But can't be sure what to believe.
Do I stand at the court today
Mid sumptuous fabrics, lush brocades,
Lithe footmen and fair chambermaids   1230
Who serve me in their fine array?
Did I awake from sleep to be
Found lying in some stately bed
Surrounded, like one highly bred,
With valets to attire me?   1235
To claim I dream would be a ruse
When I know full well I'm awake.
I'm Segismund, for heaven's sake!
Oh fair skies, won't you disabuse

My fancy's flight and make it clear   1240
What wondrous circumstances might
Have troubled it thus in the night
To leave me so convinced I'm here?
Whatever turns out to be true,
Who could dispute what I've observed?   1245
I'll let myself be richly served
Here, come what may, in this milieu.
2ND SERVANT   There's melancholy on his brow.
1ST SERVANT   Could anyone who's led a life
  So drear not bear such signs of strife?   1250
CLARION   Yes, me.
2ND SERVANT   Go there and ask him now.
1ST SERVANT   Another round of singing?
SEGISMUND   Why,
  Not now. I don't care to hear more.
2ND SERVANT   You looked so wonder-struck before,
  I thought songs might amuse you.
SEGISMUND   My   1255
  Ordeal would be as burdensome
Without these choruses of cheer.
I only truly wish to hear
The martial strains of fife and drum.
CLOTALDO   Your Royal Highness! Majesty!   1260
  Oh, let me be the first to kiss
Your hand lest I appear remiss
In pledging you my fealty.
SEGISMUND   Is this Clotaldo toadying?
  He used me ill when I was jailed—   1265
Why would he wish me so regaled?
Oh, what on earth is happening?
CLOTALDO   The great confusion that you find
  This new condition brings about
Has raised in you some lingering doubt   1270
That clouds your reason and your mind.
I've come to help you be less prone
To things that cause undue concern
Because today my lord will learn
He's heir apparent to the throne   1275
Of Poland. If till now you've dwelt
Sequestered vilely far afield,
It's all because your fate was sealed
By cards intemperate fate had dealt,
Portending bane that would allow   1280
Our empire here to come to grief
The moment that the laurel leaf
Would come to grace your august brow.³
But trusting in your better will

---

3. Roman emperors were frequently represented wearing a crown of laurel, symbolic of victory
(and specifically, in Rome, of military triumph).

To prove the stars erroneous—   1285
For men who are magnanimous
Find ways to overrule them still—
They've brought you to the palace from
The tower where they kept your cell,
Your senses dulled by sleep's deep spell   1290
And all your forces rendered numb.
The king, your sire and my liege lord,
Will come soon, Segismund, to call,
At which time he will tell you all.

SEGISMUND   Vile traitor, odious and abhorred!   1295
What could remain for me to know
When knowing my identity
From this day forward leaves me free
To flaunt my power and cause men woe?
How could you bring this treasonous act   1300
Against your land, to jail your prince
And strip him of all honors, since
No right or reason could retract
A crown, blood pledged?

CLOTALDO   Is this my plight?

SEGISMUND   You've long betrayed our country's laws,   1305
Fawned on the king to aid your cause
And treated me with cruel delight.
For this, the king, the law, and I,
In light of crimes we three condemn,
Now sentence you to die for them   1310
At my own hands.

2ND SERVANT   My lord!

SEGISMUND   Don't try
To thwart me or impede my plan;
I won't be hindered. By the cross,
Dare step between us and I'll toss
You headfirst through that window, man!   1315

1ST SERVANT   Clotaldo, flee!

CLOTALDO   Oh, woebegone,
To manifest such reckless pride
Not conscious you've dreamt all you spied!

                                        [*Exit* CLOTALDO.]

2ND SERVANT   Be mindful that . . .

SEGISMUND   You'd best move on.

2ND SERVANT   He looked but to obey his king.   1320

SEGISMUND   When unjust laws are duly weighed,
The king, too, may be disobeyed.
They owed their true prince everything.

2ND SERVANT   His charge was not to reason why
The king's will isn't sovereign.   1325

SEGISMUND   You must care little for your skin
To make me constantly reply.

CLARION   Correct, sire! Right the prince is, too!
It seems like you're the one remiss.

2ND SERVANT   What gives you leave to speak like this?   1330
CLARION   I took the leave myself, man.
SEGISMUND   Who
   On earth are you?
CLARION   A meddling drone
   And chief among that nosy group,
   The best example of a snoop
   Our great wide world has ever known.   1335
SEGISMUND   In this strange realm, I've yet to greet
   A man who's pleased me more.
CLARION   Kind lord,
   I aim to please and am adored
   By every Segismund I meet.

Scene iv

[*Enter* ASTOLF.]
ASTOLF   Oh, ever happy dawns the day   1340
   When you, the son of Poland, show
   Your face resplendent and aglow
   In joyfulness and bright array!
   You tinge the earth's horizons red;
   Your crimson mantle hues the skies,   1345
   For like the morning sun you rise
   Out some secluded mountain bed.
   Ascend, however late! Defer
   No more the crowning of this brow
   With leaves that grace the laurel's bough   1350
   And shall not fade.
SEGISMUND   God keep you, sir.
ASTOLF   You might have earned a stern rebuke
   For having failed to see in time
   That rank deserves more reverence.[4] I'm
   The titled Astolf, highborn Duke   1355
   Of Moscow, cousin to your line.
   We're equals, each a noble peer.
SEGISMUND   So, when I say "God keep you" here,
   What does that greeting undermine?
   Prone as you are to boastful rot   1360
   About your name and to complaint,
   I'll say without the least restraint
   When next we meet, "God keep you not."
2ND SERVANT   Such brusqueness, Highness, still occurs
   Throughout his speech and can cause chills,   1365
   But then, they raised him in the hills.
   The noble Astolf far prefers . . .
SEGISMUND   His smug complacency and strut
   Annoyed me greatly. Then to doff
   His hat and fail to keep it off . . .   1370

4. That is, a duke should not be addressed merely as "sir" (line 1351).

2ND SERVANT   He's royal.
SEGISMUND   But a royal what?
2ND SERVANT   That said, it's fitting there should be
  More mutual respect from two
  Who aren't mere noblemen.
SEGISMUND   Pray, who
  Dispatched you here to torment me?   1375

Scene v

  [*Enter* STELLA.]
STELLA   Your Royal Highness, may the throne
  Beneath this canopy extend
  A welcome that shall never end
  To one it proudly claims its own.
  And may you reign here free from fears   1380
  Of intrigue as our monarch who'll
  Augustly and serenely rule
  For centuries, not merely years.
SEGISMUND   Oh tell me, who is that discreet
  And sovereign beauty standing there?   1385
  What human goddess passing fair
  At whose divine, celestial feet
  The skies cast down their crimson light?
  What lovely maid do I admire?
CLARION   Your cousin, Lady Stella, sire.   1390
SEGISMUND   Say "sun" and you'd be no less right.
  How fine of you to wish me well
  With fine-wrought words in this strange place.
  Since first I saw that fine-shaped face,
  Your well-wishing has worked its spell   1395
  And as I've come to feel such fine
  Remarks unearned, though gladly heard,
  I'm grateful for the gracious word.
  Sweet Stella, you who rise and shine
  To light the mornings with your rays   1400
  And cheer the radiant orb's bright run,
  What function do you leave the sun
  By rising at the break of days?
  Oh, let me kiss that gorgeous hand,
  A snow-white chalice where the breeze   1405
  Imbibes quintessence at its ease.
STELLA   My lord, be courteous in your stand.
ASTOLF   If she succumbs to this, then I
  Am lost!
2ND SERVANT   I sense good Astolf's pain
  But can I make the prince refrain?   1410
  My lord, I'm sure you fathom why
  Such blunt words are indecorous
  With Astolf present . . .

SEGISMUND   Didn't we
   Agree you'd stop opposing me?
2ND SERVANT   I only say what's right.
SEGISMUND   All this   1415
   Has greatly angered me today!
   Thwart any outcome I expect
   And I will deem that incorrect.
2ND SERVANT   But sire, I even heard you say
   That service and obeyance both   1420
   Are acts correct beyond compare.
SEGISMUND   I think you also heard me swear
   I'd throw a nuisance, on my oath,
   From off this balcony to die.
2ND SERVANT   You can't treat men like me with so   1425
   Much disregard and scorn.
SEGISMUND   Oh, no?
   Why don't I just give this a try?
      [*He grabs the* 2ND SERVANT *and exits, followed by all.*
        SEGISMUND, ASTOLF, STELLA, *and* CLARION *return.*]
ASTOLF   I can't believe what I've just seen!
STELLA   Come quick with aid you can bestow!
                    [*She exits.*]
SEGISMUND   He plunged into the sea below   1430
   And God let no one intervene!
ASTOLF   I'd look to moderate these sorts
   Of reckless acts and rash pursuits;
   Men are no farther from base brutes
   Than mountains are from palace courts.   1435
SEGISMUND   Keep talking like some paragon
   Of virtue as you lecture me
   And, sooner than you think, you'll see
   You've naught to place your hat upon.
           [*Exit* ASTOLF. *Enter* BASIL.]

Scene vi

BASIL   What's going on here?
SEGISMUND   Not a thing.   1440
   I stopped a knave from pestering me
   And tossed him off the balcony.
CLARION   Take care, you're talking to the king.
BASIL   Not one day at the palace, yet
   Already human life's been lost.   1445
SEGISMUND   He claimed I couldn't, and it cost
   Him dear. Looks like I won that bet.
BASIL   It grieves me greatly that our late
   Reunion be so villainized.
   I'd thought that, having been apprised   1450
   Of how the stars have steered your fate,
   You might supplant this rage with tact.
   And yet, to what do you resort

On first appearing at the court?
A savage, homicidal act.   1455
What kind of fatherly embrace
Could you expect these arms to give
When I could only hope to live
To breathe the air by God's good grace
Far from your murderous grasp? Who could   1460
Behold a naked dagger glow
Before it struck a mortal blow
And fail to shrink in fear? Who would
Bear witness to the blood-red pall
That lingered where a man was killed   1465
And not be moved? The strongest willed
Among us would heed instinct's call.
As I perceive the grievous harms
That issue from your cruel embrace
And contemplate this bloodied place,   1470
I'll keep safe distance from those arms.
So though I'd planned, my love revealed,
To fling these arms about your neck,
I hold these sentiments in check,
Fear-stricken by the might you wield.   1475
SEGISMUND I've lived outside their fold till now
And don't see what I stand to lose.
A father who would so abuse
Authority to disavow
His own son's birthright merits scorn.   1480
Entombed as if I were deceased,
Raised wild like a savage beast
And treated like some monster born
To forfeit life by your decree,
I hold that clasp for which you yearn   1485
Of no emotional concern—
You robbed me of humanity.
BASIL By heaven's just omnipotence,
I rue the day I gave you life
To countenance this fiery strife   1490
And tolerate such insolence.
SEGISMUND Had you not sired me willfully,
I'd have no basis for complaint,
But since you did, what need restraint?
You took my life away from me.   1495
And while no act is nobler than
To give, whatever that gift's worth,
No baser act exists on earth
Than taking back that gift again.
BASIL Are these the thanks that lay in store   1500
For turning a poor prisoner
Into a prince?
SEGISMUND   I can't infer
What I've to be so thankful for,

You tyrant to my will! Malign,
Decrepit despot! You'll soon breathe   1505
Your last! What gift do you bequeath
But that which rightfully is mine?
Since you're my father and my king,
The grandeur and nobility
That Nature's law bestowed on me   1510
Were mine for the inheriting.
So in my new exalted state
And in no way obliged to you,
I say your day of reckoning's due
For all the years you'd abrogate   1515
My honor, life, and liberty.
You should be thanking me, you know,
For not collecting what you owe,
As you, sir, are in debt to me.
BASIL   Impulsive, wild and barbarous!   1520
All heaven augured has come true.
Look down, skies, on his rage and view
Him utterly vainglorious!
Although my ultimate behest
Disclosed your true identity   1525
And palace graces guarantee
The prince be prized above the rest,
Attend these words for your soul's sake:
Be humble, man, and less extreme,
For all you see might be a dream,   1530
Though you may think you're wide awake.
                                          [*He exits.*]
SEGISMUND   What could he mean? I, dreaming, when
All this is patent to my eyes?
I touch, I feel, and can devise
What I am now and was back then.   1535
You may well rue your choices, yet
They're not acts you can disavow,
For I know who I am and now,
Despite your sighs of deep regret,
You still can never strip away   1540
The prince and heir apparent's crown.
Though your first sight of me was down
In that dank prison where I lay,
My fast self-knowledge has increased
And now that I've seen through the sham   1545
Of what I was, I know I am
Some mongrel mix of man and beast.

                         Scene vii

        [*Enter* ROSAURA, *dressed as a lady-in-waiting.*]
ROSAURA   Dame Stella wants me near,
    Though I'm afraid of meeting Astolf here.

Clotaldo thinks it wise   1550
He not know who I am nor lay his eyes
On me until my honor is restored.
I trust his goodwill toward
My present cause, in debt to one who came
And rescued both my life and precious name.   1555
CLARION [*To* SEGISMUND.]   So, which among the host
Of things you've seen today has pleased you most?
SEGISMUND   I wasn't much surprised
By anything. All was as I'd surmised.
But since you have inquired,   1560
The thing on earth that's most to be admired
Is woman's beauty. Mind
Me now: I'd read, while odiously confined,
That out of all the creatures in His plan,
God spent most time on that small cosmos, man.   1565
But this cannot be true,
For woman is a slice of heaven, too,
And lovelier by far,
As distant from male clay as earth from star,
Like her I now behold.   1570
ROSAURA   The prince! I must withdraw and be less bold.
SEGISMUND   I beg you, woman, stay.
Don't make the sun set at the break of day
By leaving on the run.
You'll blend the dawn and twilight into one,   1575
Cold dark with sunbeams bright,
And cut too short the shining of the light.
Wait! What's this I perceive?
ROSAURA   I can't trust my own eyes, yet must believe.
SEGISMUND   I've seen this loveliness   1580
Before.
ROSAURA   I've seen this grandeur once with less
Immoderacy when
It lay in chains.
SEGISMUND   I've found my life again!
Speak, woman—yes, I use
The most endearing term a man can choose—   1585
Who are you? Have we met?
No matter; you owe me allegiance, yet
Some strange bond links us more.
I'm certain that I've seen your face before.
Who are you, woman fair?   1590
ROSAURA [*Aside.*]   I must pretend. [*To* SEGISMUND.] A lady
   wrought with care
Who serves in Stella's train.
SEGISMUND   No, say you are the sun, in whose domain
Of fire the stellar bides,
For Stella basks in rays your light provides.   1595
In all the fragrant realm
Of flowers, there's but one goddess at the helm,

The rose, whom others call
Their empress, being loveliest of all.
I've seen the finest stones   1600
Extracted from the earth's profoundest zones
Revere the diamond's shine,
Their emperor as brightest in the mine.
At lush courts in the sky
Where stars from teetering republics vie,   1605
I've seen fair Venus[5] reign
As queen of all that vast and starred demesne.
Mid perfect spheres I've seen
The sun rule lesser orbs, which he'd convene
At court, where he holds sway,   1610
Presiding as the oracle of day.
How could a case arise,
Then, where the planets, stones, and flowers prize
Great beauty, yet yours serves
A lady far less fair? Your charm deserves   1615
More praise than hers bestows,
Oh bright sun, Venus, diamond, star, and rose!

Scene viii

[*Enter* CLOTALDO.]
CLOTALDO   Persuading Segismund must fall to me,
    As he was once my ward. What's this I see?
ROSAURA   I'm flattered by your praise,   1620
    Though silence plies a lofty turn of phrase,
    For when a person's judgment seems most blurred,
    The best response is not to say a word.
SEGISMUND   You mustn't go yet. Stay!
    You wouldn't leave me in the dark this way?   1625
    That can't be your desire.
ROSAURA   I beg permission, Highness, to retire.
SEGISMUND   Brusque exits can aggrieve;
    You don't so much request as take your leave.
ROSAURA   What choice have I when you won't let me pass?   1630
SEGISMUND   I'm civil now, but might become more crass
    Soon, for resistance strains
    My patience like a poison in my veins!
ROSAURA   Not even poison laced
    With fury so intensive it effaced   1635
    This patience you declare
    Could ever stain my honor, nor would dare.
SEGISMUND   You're trying hard, I see,
    To make yourself appear less fair to me.
    You'll always find me game   1640
    To take on the impossible. The claim
    Some knave made that I couldn't cause his death

---

5. The Roman goddess of love.

Was breathed with his last breath,
So if I dared to probe all I could do,
I'd throw your honor out the window, too!   1645
CLOTALDO   His rage will not relent.
What should I do, dear heavens, with him bent
Upon this lustful crime,
Imperiling my name a second time?
ROSAURA   The fateful prophecy   1650
That warned this kingdom of your tyranny
Foresaw the crimes you'd bear,
The scandal, murder, treason, and despair.
Still, who could stoop to blame
A human being who's just a man in name,   1655
Cruel, reckless, inhumane,
A barbarous tyrant no one can restrain,
Reared like some savage beast?
SEGISMUND   I'd thought my wooing at the very least
Would spare me this display   1660
And hoped to win your favor in this way.
But since my suit occasions such alarm,
See what you think of me without the charm!
Leave us, the lot of you, and bolt the door.
See no one enters here.
                                        [*Exit* CLARION.]
ROSAURA   I die for sure!   1665
Wait . . .
SEGISMUND   Fleeing my embrace
Will hardly put this tyrant in his place.
CLOTALDO   Again he kindles strife!
I hope this meddling won't cost me my life.
Desist, sire! Let her be.   1670
SEGISMUND   This is the second time you've angered me,
You doddering old dunce.
Have you no fear you'll pay for these affronts?
How did you slip in here?
CLOTALDO   I entered, summoned by these tones of fear,   1675
To urge you to restrain
Such impulse if you ever wish to reign.
You're not king yet, so temper this extreme
Behavior. All you see may be a dream.
SEGISMUND   You know I grow irate   1680
When you use fantasy to set me straight.
Would it be dream to slay
You or quite real?
          [*As* SEGISMUND *draws his sword,* CLOTALDO *grabs hold of it*
          and kneels before him.]
CLOTALDO   I know no other way
To save my life, my lord!
SEGISMUND   How dare you place your hands upon my sword?   1685
CLOTALDO   I won't release this blade
Until a body comes to give me aid

And calm your rage.
ROSAURA   My God!
SEGISMUND   Let go, I said,
  You senile fool, or you're as good as dead!
  If you continue so, [*they struggle*]   1690
  I'll crush you in my arms, detested foe!
ROSAURA Who'll help us? Anyone!
  Clotaldo's being killed!
              [*She exits.* ASTOLF *enters,* CLOTALDO *falls at his feet,*
                  and ASTOLF *steps between* CLOTALDO *and* SEGISMUND.]

Scene ix

ASTOLF   What have you done
  To him, good-hearted lord?
  Cold blood should never blight so brave a sword   1695
  With stains of infamy.
  Resheathe your blade and let the old man be.
SEGISMUND I will when his depraved
  Blood tinges it bright red.
ASTOLF   His life is saved—
  He's sued for sanctuary at my feet   1700
  And not to spare him, sire, would scarce be meet.
SEGISMUND Allow me, then, to spear your life as well
  So I might have revenge for what befell
  Me earlier at your hands.
ASTOLF   No self-defense
  Could cause judicious majesty offense.   1705

Scene x

    [ASTOLF *and* SEGISMUND *draw their swords. Enter King*
      BASIL *and* STELLA.]
CLOTALDO Don't injure him!
BASIL   What, drawn before the king?
STELLA It's Astolf, furious and battling!
BASIL Just what is happening here?
ASTOLF Sire, not a thing now that Your Grace is near.
        [ASTOLF *and* SEGISMUND *sheathe their swords.*]
SEGISMUND A great deal, sire, be you near or not.   1710
  I'd just begun to murder this old sot.
BASIL Why, was no reverence shown
  For these gray hairs?
CLOTALDO   My liege, they're mine alone
  And little matter.
SEGISMUND   Nothing you could say
  Would force me to respect that hoary gray   1715
  And all its vile deceit.
  I'll see it some day, too, beneath my feet,
  Which may at last avenge
  My stolen life and bring me sweet revenge.
                                              [*He exits.*]

BASIL   Before you see these things,   1720
   You'll sleep again and learn these happenings
   At court that couldn't seem
   More real to you were but the stuff of dream.
                           [*Exit* BASIL *and* CLOTALDO.]

                          Scene xi

ASTOLF   The stars above so rarely lie
   When they predict catastrophes.   1725
   They forecast ills with acumen
   But blessings hesitatingly.
   How famous an astrologer
   Would that man be who only spied
   Disasters for, without a doubt,   1730
   These always manage to transpire!
   My life and Segismund's attest
   To this contrivance of the stars,
   Which presaged for the two of us
   Divergent fortunes from the start.   1735
   For him, they foresaw misery,
   Misfortune, insolence, and death.
   As all these have been evident,
   The stars have since been proved correct.
   For me, though, lady, once I'd gazed   1740
   Upon your eyes' unrivaled beams—
   Beside which sunshine looks like shade
   And light from heaven epicene[6]—
   They seemed to foretell gladdened times
   Of triumph, comfort, and acclaim,   1745
   Which proved to be both true and false
   Because stars only forecast fates
   With accuracy when they turn
   The joy they bode to wretchedness.
STELLA   I've no doubt that these gallant words   1750
   Are spoken with the best intent
   But you must mean them for the maid
   Whose painted likeness hung about
   Your neck, good Astolf, first you came
   To visit me and seek the crown.   1755
   As this is so, these sentiments
   Belong to her, and her alone.
   Go seek sweet recompense from her
   Because, as promissory notes,
   The courtly grace and oaths of faith   1760
   You use as currency to serve
   For other maids and other kings
   Are worthless in love's constant world.

----

6. That is, delicate, lacking vigor.

Scene xii

[*Enter* ROSAURA.]

ROSAURA [*Aside.*]   Thank heavens my calamitous
   Adversity has reached its end!   1765
   Whoever's seen what I've seen should
   Have nothing more to fear again!
ASTOLF   I'll take her portrait from my chest
   And lovingly hang in its place
   The image of your loveliness.   1770
   For where fair Stella shines, no shade
   Can fall, no lowly star besmirch
   The sun's bright realm! I'll fetch it now.
   Oh, fair Rosaura, pardon this
   Transgression, but you aren't around.   1775
   When men and women are apart,
   Their troth is worth no more than this.
                                     [*He exits.*]
ROSAURA   Because I feared I might be seen,
   I hid and couldn't hear a thing.
STELLA   Astrea![7]
ROSAURA   Yes, fair lady mine.   1780
STELLA   How very much my heart's consoled
   To find you here of all my train,
   For I could think to bare my soul
   To no one else.
ROSAURA   You honor one
   Whose only wish has been to please.   1785
STELLA   Astrea, I can scarcely claim
   I know you, yet you hold the key
   To opening my inmost heart.
   Because of all you clearly are,
   I'll risk confiding to you what   1790
   I've long been keeping in the dark
   From my own self.
ROSAURA   I'm here to serve.
STELLA   Then, let me keep the story brief.
   My cousin Astolf—cousin, sure!
   Why say he's so much more to me   1795
   When some things are as good as said
   In thought, where wishes are fulfilled?—
   Yes, Astolf and I are to wed
   If it should be the heavens' will
   To undo countless miseries   1800
   By granting us this happiness.
   A lady's portrait that he wore
   About his neck when we first met
   So saddened me, I gently pressed
   To know the maid's identity.   1805

---

7. The name Rosaura has assumed (see line 1891), derived from the Greek word for *star* (as Stella
  is from the Latin).

A gallant man, he loves me well
And has withdrawn now to retrieve
The likeness. Modesty forbids
My being here on his return,
So wait for him and, when he comes,   1810
Request he leave the miniature
With you. For now, I'll say no more.
Your beauty and discretion show
That you'll soon know what love is, too.

                                        [*She exits.*]

                    Scene xiii

ROSAURA   I wish to God I'd never known!   1815
Just heavens, help me now! Is there
A woman anywhere alive
Whose artfulness could find a means
To rescue her from such a bind?
Have those inclement skies above   1820
Oppressed a lady so before,
Assailing her with ceaseless grief
Until she's wretched and forlorn?
My delicate predicament
Makes it impossible for me   1825
To be consoled by arguments
Or counseled on my miseries,
As ever since that first mischance
Befell me, not one incident's
Occurred that hasn't brought me grief.   1830
This sad succession of events,
All heirs apparent of themselves,
Arise like phoenixes from ash
As each, newborn, begets the next.[8]
They come to life mid smoldering death,   1835
The cinders of this renaissance
Their sepulcher and birthing bed.
"Our cares are cowards, and poltroons,"[9]
A certain sage was wont to say,
"Stalk humans cravenly in packs."   1840
But I declare misfortunes brave
For always forging nobly on
And never beating weak retreats.
Whoever has experienced
The strain of care may face life free   1845
Of worries or the nagging fear
That cares will ever leave his side.
I know this far too well from all

---

8. The phoenix was a mythical bird that immolated itself on a self-built pyre and was reborn from its own ashes.
9. A Spanish expression akin to "cares come in threes," with the added suggestion that misfortunes are too cowardly to bully people individually.

The woes inflicted on my life
And can't recall a time when cares   1850
Were absent. They'll refuse to rest
Till I succumb, a casualty
Of fate, into the arms of death.
What choice would any woman have
If she were in my place?   1855
Disclosing my identity
Might cause Clotaldo great offense,
For he's vouchsafed my refuge, life,
And honor under great duress.
By keeping silence, he believes,   1860
I'll see my honored name restored,
But if I don't say who I am
When Astolf spies me here at court,
How will I feign not knowing him?
For even if my voice and eyes   1865
Unite to fake their ignorance,
My soul would give them all the lie.
So what am I to do? Why plan
Contrivances when it's so plain
To see that, notwithstanding all   1870
The thought I'd given to prepare
For my encountering him again,
This heartache will respond the way
It pleases? Who among us boasts
Dominion over all his pain?   1875
So with a soul too timorous
To dare determine what my course
Should be, oh, may my heartache end
Today, may all the pains I've borne
Desist, and may I leave behind   1880
Both semblances that once deceived
And lingering doubt. But until then,
Sweet heavens, stand guard over me!

Scene xiv

[*Enter* ASTOLF *with the portrait.*]
ASTOLF   Fair lady, here's the portrait you . . .
    My God, what's this?
ROSAURA   My lord appears   1885
    Amazed. What causes his surprise?
ASTOLF   Beholding you, Rosaura, here.
ROSAURA   Rosaura? Why, Your Lordship is
    Confused and certainly mistakes
    Me for another maid. I'm called   1890
    Astrea, and my humble state
    Could scarcely captivate a duke
    Or bring such rapture to my life.

ASTOLF   Rosaura, let this pretense end.
You know the soul can never lie;   1895
Though I may see Astrea here,
I'll love her like Rosaura yet.
ROSAURA   I comprehend you not, my lord,
Hence my replies are hesitant.
I'll only say that I was bid   1900
By Stella, Venus's star here,
To tarry in this place until
Such time as you, my lord, appeared
To ask from you on her behalf
The portrait causing her such hurt—   1905
An understandable demand—
Which I would then remit to her.
My lady's pleasure wills it so;
However small the pleas she makes,
Though they be to my detriment,   1910
Are Stella's still, and I obey.
ASTOLF   Say what you will, Rosaura, though
You're terrible at subterfuge.
Go tell that music in your eyes
To play in concert with the tune   1915
Your voice sings so their melody
Might temper this discordant clash
And harmonize their instrument,
Adjusting measures in the dance
Of all the falsehoods that you speak   1920
And that one verity you feel.
ROSAURA   Let me repeat, I wait but for
The portrait.
ASTOLF   Very well. I see
You won't forsake this pretense, so
I'll answer, then, with one my own.   1925
Astrea, given my esteem
For Stella, let the lady know
That my obliging her request
To fetch this pendant seems a poor
Example of gentility.   1930
Hence, as she is so well adored,
I send her the original,
Which you may bear her in the flesh,
Revealing the extent to which
You and the likeness are enmeshed.   1935
ROSAURA   A man who sets out bold and brave
To bring back something on his word
And then returns not with this prize
But with some thing of greater worth
Conceded him, still thinks himself   1940
A slighted fool whose mission failed.
I'd hoped to take my portrait back
Though the original won't pale

In force beside it. Still, I can't
Return so slighted. Come, my lord,   1945
You'll hand the portrait over now—
Without it I must shun the court.
ASTOLF   And if I don't relinquish this,
What then?
ROSAURA   I'll muster all my strength—
Let go of it!
ASTOLF   You strike in vain.   1950
ROSAURA   The portrait mustn't ever end
Up in another woman's hands.
ASTOLF   You're spirited!
ROSAURA   False-hearted cheat!
ASTOLF   That's quite enough, Rosaura mine.
ROSAURA   I yours, you scoundrel? You're deceived!   1955

Scene xv

[*Enter* STELLA.]
STELLA   Astrea! Astolf! What's all this?
ASTOLF   Now Lady Stella's come.
ROSAURA [*Aside.*]   Oh, Love,
Grant me the prowess to retrieve
My portrait! Lady, if you want
To know why we are quarreling,   1960
I'll tell you.
ASTOLF   What's the point of this?
ROSAURA   You bade me, lady, tarry here
For Astolf so he might remit
To me the portrait you desired.
Well, once I found myself alone—   1965
The mind can traipse so easily
Through scores of subjects, as you know—
This talk of portraits drifted back
To jog my memory, as it would,
Till I recalled my sleeve bore one   1970
Of me, and thought I'd take a look—
For when no one's around, we must
Amuse ourselves with what is near—
But then I dropped the thing just as
Duke Astolf presently appeared   1975
To bring the other portrait by.
He picked mine up, but so resists
Complying with the charge he's borne
That now he says he'll harbor it
Along with yours. Despite my pleas,   1980
He won't consent to hand mine back.
Your Ladyship came just in time
To see me in the frenzied act
Of repossessing it by force.
The portrait dangling in his grasp   1985

Is mine, which you could verify,
My lady, with a simple glance.
STELLA   You may return her miniature.
          [*She takes it from him.*]
ASTOLF   My lady . . .
STELLA   Yes, I must allow
It almost does you justice, maid.   1990
ROSAURA   You see it's mine, then?
STELLA   I've no doubt.
ROSAURA   Now ask him for the other one.
STELLA   Please take your portrait and retire.
ROSAURA [*Aside.*]   Why should I care what happens next
As long as I've reclaimed what's mine?   1995
                                              [*She exits.*]

Scene xvi

STELLA   I'd like the portrait that I asked
You for. I'll never lay my eyes
On you or speak to you again.
Still, knowing it remains your prized
Possession pains me to no end,   2000
Not least because I fondly did
Petition it.
ASTOLF [*Aside.*]   What's there to say
In such confused predicaments?
[*To* STELLA.] Fair Stella, I'm your servant still
In every possible regard.   2005
It's just not in my power now
To grant your wish because . . .
STELLA   You are
A faithless lover and a lout!
Forget I asked for it at all;
Why should I want her portrait when   2010
The very sight of it recalls
My having had to plead for it?
                                              [*She exits.*]
ASTOLF   Don't go! Please listen! Give me time,
Rosaura! Dear Lord, grant me strength!
Just how, from where, for what and why   2015
Did you turn up in Poland now
To seek your ruin as well as mine?
                                              [*He exits.*]

Scene xvii

[SEGISMUND *appears as he did at the play's start, wearing animal
pelts and in chains, asleep on the ground. Enter* CLOTALDO,
CLARION, *and two* SERVANTS.]
CLOTALDO   Just leave him drowsing on the ground.
Today his overweening pride

Will end where it began.
1ST SERVANT   I've tried   2020
To chain him as he'd once been bound.
CLARION   Why rush to wake and be decrowned
When sleeping, Segismund, will save
Yourself the sight of fortune's knave?
The glory you've enjoyed is fled   2025
And you'll endure, alive but dead,
A specter from beyond the grave.
CLOTALDO   An orator with this much flair
Will also need a cloistered space,
Some quiet, isolated place   2030
Where he might discourse free of care.
Go seize that speechifier there
And lock him in his tower retreat.
CLARION   Why me?
CLOTALDO   Because it's understood
That clarions left unmuffled could   2035
Sound off and noisily repeat
Our palace secrets in the street.
CLARION   Do I, perchance, plot endlessly
To murder my own father? No!
Was I the one who dared to throw   2040
That sorry Icarus in the sea?[1]
Am I reborn or still just me?
Is this a bad dream? Why this plan
To jail me?
CLOTALDO   Your name's Clarion, man.
CLARION   Then during my imprisonment   2045
I'll be a viler instrument,
The cornet, and stay mute a span.
                    [*The* SERVANTS *take* CLARION *away.*]

                    Scene xviii

          [*Enter King* BASIL, *disguised.*]
BASIL   Clotaldo.
CLOTALDO   Sire! Does this disguise
Befit your Royal Majesty?
BASIL   The foolish curiosity   2050
To view the prince with my own eyes
And see the state in which he lies
Has led me to his cell today.
CLOTALDO   Just look at him there, brought to bay
In chains, dejected and forlorn.   2055
BASIL   The star beneath which you were born
Determined it would be this way.
Go wake him. So much for my schemes.

---

1. In Greek mythology, Icarus and his father, Daedalus, escaped from King Minos's labyrinth on the island of Crete by using wings made with wax; but ignoring his father's warning, Icarus flew too close to the sun, the wax melted, and he plunged to his death in the sea.

The drink you brewed has run its course
And all its herbs have lost their force.   2060
CLOTALDO   His sleep is restless, yet he seems
To speak.
BASIL   What manner of strange dreams
Could visit Segismund alone?
SEGISMUND [*In his world of dream.*]   A pious prince is one
who's known
For purging tyrants from his lands.   2065
Clotaldo dies by these two hands
While Basil, prostrate, yields his throne.
CLOTALDO   My dying makes the plot complete.
BASIL   He joins effrontery with threat.
CLOTALDO   He'll see me foully murdered yet.   2070
BASIL   And vanquish me beneath his feet.
SEGISMUND [*Still dreaming.*]   Parade your valor in the street,
The world's great theater, onstage where
Its size will loom beyond compare.
Avenging my base sire's neglect   2075
Will only have the right effect
If Segismund's triumphant there.
[*He awakens.*] What's this about? Where can I be?
BASIL   He's not to learn that I'm here, too.
Now do what you've been charged to do   2080
As I retire where I can see.
      [*He withdraws from view.*]
SEGISMUND   What's happened? Is this really me
In chains again amid this blight,
A horrid and pathetic sight?
And is that you, my living tomb,   2085
Old tower? God help me meet this doom!
But, what strange things I dreamt tonight!
CLOTALDO   The ruse must be maintained, and I'm
To do it, take what it may take.
Is it not time for you to wake?   2090
SEGISMUND   Yes, it's well past my waking time.
CLOTALDO   Do you intend to spend the prime
Of day asleep? Can it be right
That, ever since we tracked the flight
Of that grand eagle heaven bound,   2095
You've lain here drowsing on the ground
And never once awakened?
SEGISMUND   Quite,
And haven't yet, as I'd conceived.
As far as I can ascertain,
I sleepwalk still through dream's domain   2100
And would not feel at all deceived
If everything that I'd believed
Took place would dissipate anew
Or if what I saw now weren't true.
For one in chains, it's no great leap   2105

To understand, though fast asleep,
That one can dream while waking, too.
CLOTALDO   What did you dream while so confined?
SEGISMUND   Supposing that it was a dream,
   Clotaldo! Here is what I deem   2110
   Occurred, and not just in my mind:
   I wakened yesterday to find
   Myself—this taunts me!—lounging in
   A bed so bright it might have been
   The flowery cot by which the Spring   2115
   Adorns the earth with coloring
   From all the hues contained therein.
   A thousand nobles bowed before
   My vaunted feet and, once they'd hailed
   Me as their prince, I was regaled   2120
   With banquets, jewels, robes, and more.
   You purged what calm my senses bore
   By naming me, to my delight,
   King Basil's heir by natural right
   And though my fortune's fallen since,   2125
   I briefly reigned as Poland's prince.
CLOTALDO   What great reward had I in sight?
SEGISMUND   Accusing you of treachery,
   My heart made bold with power and vice,
   I tried disposing of you twice.   2130
CLOTALDO   But why were you so cruel to me?
SEGISMUND   I'd thought to rule with tyranny
   And match the evil I'd been done.
   I loved none but one woman—one—
   The only real thing to transcend,   2135
   As I believe, my dreaming's end,
   An endless need that's just begun.
                                 [BASIL *exits.*]
CLOTALDO [*Aside.*]   The king was moved by what he heard
   And fled affected from the tower.
   Our talk in your last waking hour   2140
   About that eagle must have spurred
   These dreams of empire afterward.
   Still, Segismund, you really ought
   To honor one who reared and taught
   You, even in the realm of dream.   2145
   For doing good is man's supreme
   Imperative and not for naught.
                                 [*He exits.*]

Scene xix

SEGISMUND   How very true! Then let's suppress
   The fury of our savage state,
   The vile ambition and the hate,   2150
   So when we dream we won't transgress.

For dream we will, though we possess
No sense of where it is we thrive
And dreaming just means being alive.
The insight life's experience gives   2155
Is that, until man wakes, he lives
A life that only dreams contrive.
The king dreams he is king and reigns
Deluded in his full command,
Imposing order in his land.   2160
The borrowed plaudits he obtains
Blow scattered through the wind's domains
As death—man's life is so unjust!—
Transmutes them into ash and dust.
Oh, who on earth could wish to wield   2165
Such might when waking means to yield
It all to death's dream, as we must?
The rich man dreams his riches great,
Which makes his wealth more burdensome.
The poor man dreams that he'll succumb   2170
To misery in his beggared state.
He also dreams who prospers late.
The striver and aspirer do,
The mocker and offender, too.
In fact, all mortal souls on earth   2175
Dream their conditions from their birth,
Though no one knows this to be true.
I'm dreaming now that darker days
Await me, chained, in this dark cell
As I'd dreamt I'd been treated well   2180
Of late in some strange coddled phase.
What's life? A frenzied, blurry haze.
What's life? Not anything it seems.
A shadow. Fiction filling reams.
All we possess on earth means nil,   2185
For life's a dream, think what you will,
And even all our dreams are dreams.

Act III

Scene i

[Enter CLARION.]
CLARION   I lodge in this enchanted tower
A captive, for I know the truth,
But if my knowledge means sure death,   2190
What will my ignorance lead to?
That such a hungry, hungry man
Should perish like a living corpse!
I'm feeling sorry for myself,
So go ahead, say, "That's for sure,"   2195

For surely, that's not hard to see.
This silence, too, is pretty rough,
But when your name is Clarion, well,
There's just no way to hold your tongue.
My sole companions in this place—   2200
And this would be a wild guess—
Are mice and spiders lurking here.
Who needs a goldfinch for a pet?
My teeming brain is still awhirl
With everything I dreamt last night: 2205
The sound of trumpet blares and shawms[1]
Came mingled with deceptive sights
Like one of flagellants that marched
In some procession of the cross,
First rising, then descending, then   2210
Succumbing once they saw the lost
Blood flowing down their fellows' backs.
These bouts with hunger here of late
May cause the swoons in me as well,
For, while I'm left to starve by day,   2215
An empty Plato[2] offers no
Consolement of philosophy,
While each night I, awaiting board
Within this room, don't ever eat.
So if this new Church calendar   2220
Considers quiet "blessed" now,
Let Secret be my patron saint—
I'll fast for him and break no vows.
I haven't breathed a word yet, so
My punishment seems well deserved: 2225
What greater sacrilege is there
Than silence in one hired to serve?

Scene ii

[*The sound of drums and* SOLDIERS' *voices offstage.*]
1ST SOLDIER   They're holding him inside this tower.
Here, batter down these bolted doors
And storm the cell!
CLARION   Good heavens, have   2230
They come for me? I'm pretty sure,
Since they seem pretty sure I'm here.
Whatever could they want?
1ST SOLDIER   Charge in!
2ND SOLDIER   He's here!
CLARION   Oh, no he's not!
SOLDIERS [*To* CLARION.]   My lord!
CLARION   They must be drunkards on a binge!   2235

---

1. A double-reed Renaissance woodwind, forerunner of the modern oboe.
2. Greek philosopher (ca. 427–ca. 347 B.C.E.); though here invoked to play on the word "plate,"
   Plato is a particularly appropriate choice, given his concern with the nature of reality.

2ND SOLDIER   All hail, our prince and rightful liege!
  To you alone do we submit
  Our forces, natural-born heir,
  And not to any foreign prince.
  To prove our troth, we kiss your feet.   2240
SOLDIERS   Long live the prince, whom we love well!
CLARION   Good God, can this be happening?
  Is it the custom in this realm
  To seize a body every day
  And make a prince of him before   2245
  He's thrown back in the tower? Must be,
  Since each day there's a different lord.
  Looks like I'll have to play the part.
SOLDIERS   Give us your feet!
CLARION   I can't because
  I need to use them for myself   2250
  And it would be a tragic flaw
  To govern as a soleless prince.
2ND SOLDIER   We've seen your father and declared
  Our will to him: it's you alone
  We recognize as Poland's heir,   2255
  And not the Muscovite.
CLARION   You told
  My father? Have you no respect,
  You lousy bunch of so-and-so's?
1ST SOLDIER   One can't keep loyal hearts in check.
CLARION   Well, loyalty I can excuse.   2260
2ND SOLDIER   Restore the kingdom to your line.
  Long live Prince Segismund!
SOLDIERS   Long life!
CLARION   Ah, they said "Segismund." All right,
  So Segismund's the word they use
  To mean a prince is counterfeit.   2265

Scene iii

[*Enter* SEGISMUND.]
SEGISMUND   Is someone calling out my name?
CLARION   Am I a has-been as a prince?
2ND SOLDIER   Who here is Segismund?
SEGISMUND   I am.
2ND SOLDIER   You reckless fool! Impersonate
  The heir apparent to the throne?   2270
CLARION   Now that's a game I'd never play.
  Besides, it was the lot of you
  That segismundized me and so
  The only foolish recklessness
  Put on display here was your own.   2275
1ST SOLDIER   Great prince, brave Segismund! Although
  The standards that we bear are yours,
  It's solemn faith alone compels

Our number to proclaim you lord.
Your father Basil, our great king,   2280
Has lived in terror of the skies
Fulfilling their dread prophecy
That presaged you would see him lie
Subdued beneath your feet. For this,
He'd planned to yield your titled claim   2285
And highborn right to Astolf, Duke
Of Moscow, and eclipse your reign.
King Basil had convened the court
When Poland learned an heir survived
And wished him to succeed the king,   2290
Reluctant that a foreign line
Should govern them on native soil.
So, holding the inclemency
Of starry fate in noble scorn,
They sought your cell to see you freed   2295
From these cruel chains. All live in hope
The rightful heir will leave these grounds
And, buttressed by their arms, reclaim
For them the scepter and the crown
Out that usurping tyrant's grip!   2300
Come forth! Amid this barren land
An army, sizable and strong
Of rebels and plebeian bands,
Acclaims you. Longed-for liberty
Awaits you, hear its beckoning call!   2305
VOICES [*Offstage.*]   Long live Prince Segismund! All hail!
SEGISMUND   What's this? Must I be held enthralled
Again, cruel skies, to fleeting dreams
Of grandeur Time will surely mock?
Must I again be forced to glimpse   2310
Amid the shadows and the fog
The majesty and faded pomp
That waft inconstant on the wind?
Must I again be left to face
Life's disillusion or the risks   2315
To which man's limits are exposed
From birth and never truly end?
This cannot be. It cannot be.
Behold me here, a slave again
To fortune's whims. As I have learned   2320
That life is really just a dream,
I say to you, false shadows, Go!
My deadened senses know your schemes,
To feign a body and a voice
When voice and body both are shams.   2325
I've no desire for majesty
That's phony or for pompous flam,
Illusions of sheer fantasy
That can't withstand the slightest breeze

And dissipate entirely like   2330
The blossoms on an almond tree
That bloom too early in the spring
Without a hint to anyone.
The beauty, light, and ornament
Reflecting from their rosy buds   2335
Fade all too soon; these wilt and fall
When but the gentlest gusts blow by.
I know you all too well, I do,
To fancy you'd act otherwise
Toward other souls who likewise sleep.   2340
So let this vain pretending cease;
I'm disabused of all I thought
And know now life is but a dream.
2ND SOLDIER   We have not come here to deceive.
Just cast your eyes upon the lair   2345
Of haughty hills that ring this tower
And see the host of men prepared
To follow and obey you.
SEGISMUND   Once
I saw the same approving crowd
Appear before me as distinct   2350
And clear as I perceive things now,
But I was dreaming.
2ND SOLDIER   Great events
Are oft preceded, good my lord,
By portents, which is what occurred
When you did dream these things before.   2355
SEGISMUND   A portent. Yes, you must be right.
If all is truly as you've deemed
And man's life, sadly, is so short,
Then let us dream, my soul, let's dream
Again! But this time we will face   2360
Full recognition of the fact
That we may waken from this sleep
At any hour and be brought back.
Still, knowing such things in advance
Should temper disappointment's stings;   2365
To put the cure before the harm
Does much to mock the injuring.
In short, as all have been forewarned
That, even when man's sway seems sure,
Our power is borrowed on this earth   2370
And harks back always to its source,
What can we lose by venturing?
I thank you, vassals, for this show
Of loyalty. With all my skill
And bravery I'll smash this yoke   2375
Of foreign slavery you fear!
Come, sound the call to arms. This sword
Will vouch my courage is no lie.

It's my intent to levy war
Against my father, proving thus   2380
That heaven prophesied the truth.
I'll see him prone beneath my feet—
Unless I wake before I do,
In which case it might just be best
To say no more about these plans.   2385
ALL   All hail to you, Prince Segismund!

Scene iv

[Enter CLOTALDO.]
CLOTALDO   Good heavens, what's this uproar, man?
SEGISMUND   Clotaldo.
CLOTALDO   Sire. [Aside.] He's sure to vent
His rage upon me now.
CLARION   I bet
He throws the codger off this cliff.   2390
                                        [He exits.]
CLOTALDO   I bow to you, though I expect
To die here at your feet.
SEGISMUND   Pray stand,
Good father. Rise up from the ground,
My polestar and sole guiding light!
You coaxed my better nature out   2395
And well I know the debt you're owed
For rearing me so faithfully.
Let me embrace you.
CLOTALDO   How is that?
SEGISMUND   I'm dreaming now, but in my dream
I'm striving to do good. No chance   2400
To do kind deeds should be ignored.
CLOTALDO   My lord, since you profess these acts
Of grace as your new creed, I'm sure
You'll take no great offense with me
For likewise cleaving to these views.   2405
Wage war against your father? Then
I simply cannot counsel you
And aid the downfall of my king.
So slay me, humbled still upon
This ground you tread.
SEGISMUND   Oh, traitor! Vile,   2410
Ungrateful wretch! Almighty God!
Some self-command might serve me well
Until it's certain that I wake.
I envy your stouthearted show,
Clotaldo. Thank you for this faith.   2415
Go, then, and serve the king you love;
We'll meet upon the battle lines.
All others, sound the call to arms!
CLOTALDO   I kiss your feet a thousand times.

SEGISMUND   Come, Fortune! Off we go to reign,   2420
  So dare not wake me if I sleep
  Nor let me sleep should this be true,
  For whether this be truth or dream
  It's vital still that man do good
  In dream or sleep for good's own sake,   2425
  At least to win himself some friends
  For when he ultimately wakes.
                     [*All exit as the call to arms sounds.*]

Scene v

        [*Enter King* BASIL *and* ASTOLF.]
BASIL   Good Astolf, who can stop a bolting horse
  And still its rage into serenity?
  Or check a surging river's headlong course   2430
  Before its waters flow into the sea?
  Or halt a falling boulder gathering force
  While hurtling down a mountain fast and free?
  Yet, these are easier to turn aside
  Than willful masses spurred to act by pride.   2435
  Divulge by edict any news from court
  And all at once you'll hear the echoes sound
  Throughout the hills, as anguished cries exhort
  "Hail Astolf" while "Hail Segismunds" resound.
  The throne room has been turned into a sort   2440
  Of second stage where horrid plays abound,
  A baneful theater where fate flaunts her will
  And only tragedy is on the bill.
ASTOLF   Then, sire, I will assuredly delay this cause
  For celebration proffered by your hand   2445
  And shun both flattery and loud applause,
  For Poland, where I'd looked to rule as planned,
  Resists my reign today and flouts your laws
  So I might prove my worth to lead the land.
  Bring me a steed whose spirit knows no like;   2450
  You've heard me thunder, now watch lightning strike!
                        [*He exits.*]
BASIL   No one escapes the inescapable
  Or any danger omens have in store.
  Resisting fortune is impossible;
  Ignoring forecasts just makes them more sure.   2455
  In my case, this harsh law looms terrible
  As fleeing danger brings one to its door.
  Base ruin now appears my secret's cost,
  For I'm alone to blame now Poland's lost.

Scene vi

[*Enter* STELLA.]

STELLA   If your wise presence, sire, can't stop the spread   2460
Of opposition forces gaining ground
While ever more combative factions head
Throughout our streets and plazas, palace bound,
You'll see the realm awash in waves of red,
Your subjects bathing in the blood now found   2465
But in their crimson veins. What tragic gloom
Surrounds our kingdom's decadence and doom!
To sense the downfall of your rule so near
Amid the savage violence of this plot
Astounds the eye and terrifies the ear.   2470
The wind grows still, the sun turns to a blot;
Each rock will be a headstone to revere,
Each flower the marker on a fresh grave's spot,
Each edifice a lofty house of death,
Each soldier but a skeleton with breath.   2475

Scene vii

[*Enter* CLOTALDO.]

CLOTALDO   I've made it here alive, for God is kind.
BASIL   Clotaldo, have you news about my son?
CLOTALDO   The masses, sire, a monster rash and blind,
Besieged the tower and, seeing it overrun,
Freed Segismund. No sooner did he find   2480
A second time this second honor won
Than out he burst emboldened and uncouth,
Resolved to prove the heavens spoke the truth.
BASIL   Bring me a steed, for as your king I must
Defeat this ingrate out of royal pride.   2485
But this time in my crown's defense I'll trust
Cold steel where once my hapless science vied.
                                                    [*He exits.*]
STELLA   Bright sun, I'll be Bellona[3] at your side
And join my name to one far more august.
On outstretched wings I'll soar above the frays   2490
And rival Pallas in my warlike ways.
                [*She exits as the call to arms is sounded.*]

Scene viii

[*Enter* ROSAURA, *who stops* CLOTALDO.]

ROSAURA   I know the seething valor pent
Within your breast attends the call
To arms, but hear me now, for all
Can see that war is imminent.   2495
When I arrived in Poland just
A poor, humiliated maid,

---

3. The Roman goddess of war.

Your valor was my only aid
And you the sole man I could trust
To pity me. Then you procured   2500
That I'd reside—oh, heart!—disguised
At palace, where I was advised
To keep my jealousy obscured
And my good self from Astolf's sight.
He spied me, though, and now insists   2505
On mocking me with garden trysts
He holds with Stella every night.
But I hold this, the garden's key,
Which you could use for entering
The place unseen, and thereby bring   2510
An end to all my cares for me.
So might my honor be restored
By one who's strong, brave, and resolved
To see this problem duly solved
By winning vengeance with the sword.   2515
CLOTALDO   It's true I've been disposed to act
On your behalf since first we met,
Rosaura, and collect that debt—
Your tears bore witness to this fact—
By all the powers I possess.   2520
That's why I urged you to acquire
More proper feminine attire
So you'd be clad in seemly dress
When Astolf sighted you at court.
It couldn't, then, occur to him   2525
Your clothes were but a flighty whim
To turn lost honor into sport.
At just that time I moved to find
Some way to make the rogue repent
His insult, even if this meant—   2530
For honor so engaged my mind!—
Contriving Astolf's death. See where
The ravings of an old man lead?
He's not my king, and thus the deed
Should cause not wonder or despair.   2535
I'd plotted murder when the same
Urge struck Prince Segismund, who tried
Dispatching me! Good Astolf spied
This wrong and, self-neglecting, came
To my defense stoutheartedly.   2540
His noble showing of largesse
Bore all the marks of recklessness
And far surpassed mere bravery.
Now, as mine is a grateful soul,
How could I ever cause the death   2545
Of one whose heart left me with breath
And handed me my life back whole?
My care and my affection stand

Divided now between you two:
As I gave back a life to you   2550
But then received one from his hand,
To which of you do I owe more?
Which action claims priority?
Receiving now obliges me
As much as giving did before   2555
And so fulfillment of my plan,
Which once seemed certain, now does not.
I'd suffer compassing the plot
And wrongly kill a worthy man.

ROSAURA   It's not my place here, I believe,   2560
To sway one so superlative
But, noble as it is to give,
It's just as vile to receive.
So, following this principle,
You owe that man no gratitude,   2565
For anyone would now conclude
That, though he made life possible
For you and you for me, it's clear
He basely undermined your fame
And compromised your noble name   2570
While I've made you look cavalier.
He, therefore, causes you offense.
I, therefore, merit your first thought
As what you've given me is naught
But what he gave in impudence.   2575
You, therefore, ought to strive to save
A reputation thus disgraced
And favor my claim, not his, based
On what you both received and gave.

CLOTALDO   A mark of true nobility   2580
Entails this giving with free hands,
But showing gratitude demands
That one receive as graciously.
The reputation that's pursued
My person holds me generous   2585
And honored by the populace,
So add to these marks gratitude,
Which I'd assume should I but live
As thankful as I'm liberal,
For honor is as notable   2590
When men receive as when they give.

ROSAURA   You gave this damaged life to me
And I recall well how you pled.
When I accepted it, you said
A life lived with indignity   2595
Was no true life and so the thought
That I've received one is absurd.
The life your giving hand conferred
On me was not a life, but naught.

If you'd be liberal before   2600
You're grateful, following your fame,
As I have heard you just proclaim,
My hope is that you'll soon restore
The life you thought you'd given. Why,
If giving makes one seem sublime,   2605
Be liberal first and you'll have time
For feeling grateful by and by.
CLOTALDO   Then liberal first I'll be, for these
Persuasive arguments declare
Your fitness to be named my heir.   2610
Take my bequest and seek the ease
A convent grants,[4] for in your case
This recourse makes the greatest sense:
Exchange this fleeing from offense
For refuge in a holy place.   2615
The kingdom presently is torn
By factional extremity
And such affliction mustn't be
Made worse by one who's nobly born.
Through this solution, I'll be viewed   2620
Both loyal to my country's fight
And generous to your suffered slight
While showing Astolf gratitude.
This remedy resolves things best;
What else might you have settled for?   2625
God knows I couldn't help you more
Were I your father in this quest.
ROSAURA   Were you my sire out to avenge
This wrong, I'd suffer it as mine.
But as you aren't, I must decline.   2630
CLOTALDO   How, then, will you exact revenge?
ROSAURA   I'll kill the duke.
CLOTALDO   What's this? The same
Poor maid who grew up fatherless
Displaying such courageousness?
ROSAURA   That's right.
CLOTALDO   What moves you?
ROSAURA   My good name.   2635
CLOTALDO   Soon Astolf will claim reverence . . .
ROSAURA   He stole all honor from my life.
CLOTALDO   As king, and Stella as his wife.
ROSAURA   An outrage God won't countenance!
CLOTALDO   It's madness, child.
ROSAURA   I'm sure you're right.   2640
CLOTALDO   Control these urges.
ROSAURA   So you say.
CLOTALDO   You'll lose your life . . .
ROSAURA   It's true, I may.

---

4. Women were expected to pay a dowry to the religious order when they entered a convent.

CLOTALDO   And honor, too.
ROSAURA   How well I might.
CLOTALDO   What will this mean?
ROSAURA   My death.
CLOTALDO   Don't wage
  War out of spite.
ROSAURA   My honor calls.   2645
CLOTALDO   That's folly!
ROSAURA   Valor never palls.
CLOTALDO   Sheer lunacy!
ROSAURA   Or wrath and rage.
CLOTALDO   Can't this blind fury be allayed
  In any other way?
ROSAURA   No, none.
CLOTALDO   But who will second you?
ROSAURA   No one.   2650
CLOTALDO   You won't be swayed?
ROSAURA   I won't be swayed.
CLOTALDO   The deed brings with it quite a cost.
ROSAURA   I would be lost at any rate.
CLOTALDO   If that's the case, my child, then wait—
  Together let us both be lost.   2655
                                    [*They exit.*]

Scene ix

[*Trumpets blare as* SOLDIERS *march onstage with* CLARION
and SEGISMUND, *who is dressed in animal pelts.*]
SEGISMUND   If proud Rome's Golden Age
  Could view my entrance on this martial stage,
  How loudly would it voice
  Delight at this strange triumph and rejoice
  Amazed to understand   2660
  A beast had armies under his command!
  With such unbridled might,
  The heavens could be mine without a fight!
  But spirit, help me quell
  These arrogant displays and not dispel   2665
  This lingering applause;
  I'd grieve to wake without it now because
  To lose what dreams contain
  Would surely bring me pain.
  The less I hold things dear,   2670
  The less I'll suffer when they disappear.
      [*A clarion sounds offstage.*]
CLARION   Look there! A wingèd horse—
  I'm sorry, but my stories pack more force
  When I hyperbolize—
  Four elements incarnate in its guise:[5]   2675

---

5. According to the theory of matter dominant from classical Greece through the Renaissance,
  all matter is made up of four elements: earth, air, fire, and water.

Its body mass the earth,
Its soul the fire ablaze beneath its girth,
Its froth the water and its breath the air.
I relish chaos and confusion where
The soul, froth, breath, and body all can be   2680
A monster made of fire, wind, land, and sea,
Though dapple-gray of hue
And patchy, straddled by a horseman who
Digs spurs into its side
To fly upon his ride.   2685
But, this is a refined
And jaunty dame!
SEGISMUND   Her radiance leaves me blind.
CLARION   Lord, it's Rosaura! See?
                                            [He exits.]
SEGISMUND   The heavens have restored this sight to me.

Scene x

[Enter ROSAURA, dressed in a loose-fitting skirt, with a
    dagger and sword.]
ROSAURA   Magnanimous Prince Segismund!   2690
Your lordly heroism shines
Upon this day of noble feats
From out the shades of darkest night!
For as the brightest-gleaming orb
Among the stars displays its power   2695
In Dawn's embrace, restoring light
To roses and to blooming flowers,
Emerging crowned with fulgent rays
Above the mountains and the seas,
Dispersing beams, dispensing glow,   2700
Illuming froth and bathing peaks,
So may you rise atop the world,
Proud Poland's shining sun! Avail
A woman fraught with wretchedness
Who, prostrate at your feet today,   2705
A woman first and then a wretch,
Trusts you'll comply—as either one
Of these conditions should suffice—
Since each is more than I could want
To obligate a gentleman   2710
Who boasts of gallantry to act.
Three times already have you looked
On me with wonder, blind to facts
About my life, as all three times
My clothes displayed a different self: 2715
On the occasion we first met
Inside a cell so dank I held
My grieved existence charmed beside
Your own, you took me for a man.

When next you gazed on me, at court,   2720
You saw a woman mid your sham
Of majesty, which wasn't more
Than specter, shade, or dream.
The third time here, your eyes behold
This monstrous and unnatural freak   2725
Attired in female finery
Yet bravely bearing manly arms.
As you'll be more disposed to aid
My cause once pity moves your heart,
I'll tell now of the tragic blows   2730
That fate's compelled me to absorb.
I was of woman nobly born
In Moscow at the royal court.
My mother had to have been fair,
For she was not a happy maid.   2735
A vile deceiver laid his eyes
On her, a traitor who remains
Both nameless and unknown to me.
His valor, though, has given rise
To mine, and being the result   2740
Of his desires, I now repine
Not being born a pagan child
So I half-madly might feel pleased
To think this man was like those gods
Whose cunning metamorphoses   2745
Into a swan, gold shower, or bull
Left Leda ravished, Danaë duped,
And fair Europa raped.[6] I thought
I was digressing, but these lewd
Accounts of perfidy provide   2750
An overview to this sad tale.
My mother, far more lovely still
Than any woman, fell betrayed
By her seducer's gallant words
And thus, like many, was undone.   2755
The old trick of a marriage pledge
Imparted by a honeyed tongue
Beguiled her so, that to this day
Its memory dispels her joys.
In fact, the tyrant so recalled   2760
Aeneas[7] in his flight from Troy
He even left his sword behind.
We'll leave its blade ensheathed for now
But have no doubt I'll draw this steel
Before I end my sad account.   2765

---

6. All the transformations listed were of a single Greek god, Zeus (Jupiter), undertaken in sexual
   pursuit of the women named, and all were retold in the *Metamorphoses* (ca. 10 c.e.) by the
   Roman poet Ovid.
7. The mythical Trojan hero and progenitor of the Roman people, whose story is told in Virgil's
   Aeneid (19 b.c.e.); as Aeneas fled with his family from the Greek sack of Troy, his wife (though
   not his sword) was inadvertently left behind.

So, from their bond, a loose-tied knot
That neither ties one down nor binds,
Not quite a marriage or a crime—
It's all the same now to my mind—
I issued forth, my mother's twin   2770
And living picture when it came
Not to her comely countenance
But all her sorrows and travails.
As heiress to the vast estate
Of love's misfortune she bequeathed,   2775
I hardly feel the need to say
I've come into her destiny.
The most I'll say about myself
Is that the thief who dared despoil
The trophy of my honor's claim   2780
And left my maiden virtue soiled
Is Astolf! Heavens, how my heart
Beats quick with rage when I pronounce
His name, a natural response
To hearing enemies announced.   2785
Duke Astolf, disremembering
The joys he'd so ungratefully found—
Yes, memories of love gone by
Are just that quickly blotted out—
Arrived in Poland, called away   2790
From this great conquest, having come
To claim fair Stella as his bride,
A torch beside my setting sun.
Now who would think so stellar-made
A union, sanctioned by the stars,   2795
Could come unraveled just because
Maid Stella came between our hearts?
I, then, dishonored and deceived,
Remained forlorn, remained half-crazed,
Remained a corpse, remained myself,   2800
Which is to say, too much remained
Of that infernal turmoil lodged
Within the Babylon⁸ of my mind.
I swore myself to silence, then,
As there are trials and pains in life   2805
Authentic feeling can convey
Far better than the mouth could hope,
And voiced my grief by keeping mute.
One day, though, as I sat alone,
My mother, Violante, stormed   2810
The fortress where these miseries lay
And out they poured like prisoners

---

8. Literally the capital of Babylonia, a powerful state in southern Mesopotamia and in the Old
Testament a place of exile for the Jews in the sixth century B.C.E.; metaphorically associated
with the confusion of tongues (as in the story of the Tower of Babel, Genesis 11.1–9) and, in
the New Testament's Book of Revelation, the symbol for evil.

Colliding all in unleashed haste.
I felt no shame confessing them,
For when a person shares her griefs   2815
With one she knows has likewise felt
Her share of them from being weak,
The sorrow starts to dissipate
And spreads a balm upon the hurt.
A bad example, after all,   2820
Can be of use. In short, she heard
My plaints with sympathy and tried
Consoling me with her own woes—
A judge who's been delinquent finds
Forgiveness easy to bestow!   2825
So, as she'd learned that honor wronged
Could never hope to be set right
By whiling idle hours away
Or simply watching time go by,
She set me on a different course.   2830
Her sage advice? That I pursue
And hold my tempter liable for
The loss his blandishments produced,
Obliging him with courtly ways.
Now, to ensure this quest would pose   2835
Small risk to me, fate intervened
To outfit me in manly clothes.
My mother took an old sword down,
The one I've girded round my waist,
And so the time has come at last,   2840
As I have pledged, to bare its blade.
Convinced this sword would be a sign,
She said, "Set out for Poland's fields
And let her grandest noblemen
Be certain to observe the steel   2845
Now gracing you. In one of them
Your luckless fortune may well find
A sympathetic ear, and all
Your sorrows solace in due time."
I came, indeed, to Poland, where—   2850
Let's skip a bit, for why repeat
What everyone already knows?—
A bolting brute, half-horse, half-beast,
Unsaddled me outside that cave
Where you first spied my loveliness.   2855
Now skip to where Clotaldo takes
A special interest in my quest
And begs the king to spare my life,
A favor Basil deigns to grant.
On learning my identity,   2860
He urges me, dressed like a man,
To put on lady's clothes and serve
Maid Stella on the palace grounds

Where I've used all my craft to thwart
Duke Astolf's love and Stella's vows.   2865
Let's also skip where seeing me
Confounded you that time at court
As I, then wearing female garb,
Appeared in yet another form,
And speak of what Clotaldo's done.   2870
Self-servingly, he now ascribes
Great weight to Astolf being king
With Stella reigning as his bride
And, to my honor's detriment,
Has bid me suffer this offense.   2875
Brave Segismund, how clear it dawns
On all this day that sweet revenge
Belongs to you! The heavens smile
On your felicitous release
From out so crude a prison cell   2880
Where you had grown resigned to be
A rock against all suffering
And beast unmoved by sentiment.
Now, as you take up arms to fight
Your native land and sovereign,   2885
I come to pledge my aid, bedecked
In chaste Diana's[9] flowing robes
Atop a suit of Pallas's
Own armor. Draped in clashing clothes
Of genteel fabric and cold steel,   2890
I join your forces dually dressed.
To battle, then, bold general!
For it's in both our interests
To stop these banns from going forth
And set this royal bond aside: 2895
For me, so that the man I call
My husband takes no other wife;
For you, so that no gain in strength
Resulting from their allied states
Will threaten our great victory   2900
Once you've returned as prince to reign.
I come, a woman, urging you
To join the cause to which I'm bound;
But as a man, I come to press
This late reclaiming of your crown.   2905
I come, a woman, at your feet
To move you to commiserate;
But as a man, I come to serve
Beside you in your people's aid.
I come, a woman, so you might   2910
Assuage my sorrows and my pain;

9. The Roman virgin goddess of wild animals and the hunt, associated also with the moon.

But as a man, I come with sword
And person ready to assail.
So, should you find yourself inclined
To woo me as a woman, rest   2915
Assured that, as a man, I'd be
Compelled to kill you in defense
Of honor, honorably, because
In this campaign of love you've planned,
I'll play the woman with my plaints,   2920
But fight with honor like a man.

SEGISMUND   Just heavens! If it's really true
I dream, suspend my memory!
It isn't possible for all
I've seen to fit into a dream!   2925
If God would but reveal to me
How I might blot these troubles out
And give them not another thought!
What mortal ever faced such doubts?
If I had only dreamt I dwelt   2930
Amid such luxury, how could
This woman have recounted what
I saw and seemed so plausible?
It was true, then. That was no dream.
If this is so, which by all rights   2935
Should leave me more confused, not less,
Who is it that could call my life
A dream? Do this world's glories so
Resemble dreams in what they vaunt
That even the most genuine   2940
Are destined to be reckoned false
As fake ones are considered true?
Have these so little difference
That every man must ask himself
Now whether all he relishes   2945
Around him is a lie or truth?
Why must the copy counterfeit
The true original so well
That none dare hazard which is which?
If such be life's design, and all   2950
Our splendid pageantry and strength,
Our solemn pomp and majesty,
Must vanish into shadow's depths,
Let's seize the time that's given us
And reap what pleasures may be reaped,   2955
For all we now enjoy on earth
Is but what we enjoy in dreams.
I hold Rosaura in my power;
Her beauty captivates my soul.
So let me profit from this chance   2960
To let love set aside the codes

Of valor, trust, and chivalry
That she's invoked in her request.
As this is but another dream,
Let's all dream happy things on end   2965
And rue them only once we wake!
Be careful or your logic might
Convince you this is fact again!
A dream may reach vainglorious heights,
But who'd pass heaven's glories up   2970
For human ones, had he the choice?
What happy turns of fate weren't dreams?
What man has felt tremendous joy
And not then asked himself in time,
Once memory had reviewed the scene: 2975
"Weren't all these things I witnessed but
A dream?" If knowledge like this means
Great disappointment—for I've learned
That pleasure is a lovely flame
The merest breath of air blows out   2980
So only wafting ash remains—
Let's look toward the eternal, then,
And seek renown that never dies
Where joy will not succumb to sleep
Or splendor ever napping lie!   2985
Rosaura's honor lingers lost
And it's incumbent on a prince
To see that honor be restored.
I swear by God above I'll win
Her honor back before my crown   2990
And save her name from future harm!
It's best I flee temptation so
Enticing. Sound the call to arms!
I'll wage war on my foes this day
Before the night's encroaching shade   2995
Can shroud the sunlight's golden rays
In somber black and dark-green waves.
ROSAURA   Sire, why do you withdraw from me?
I would have hoped that soothing words
Were due my sorrows at the least   3000
As balm for salving heartfelt hurt.
How is it possible, then, lord,
That I should go unseen, unheard?
Why won't you even look this way?
SEGISMUND   Rosaura, only honor's call   3005
Could prompt this seeming cruelty
In serving kinder mercy's cause.
My voice declines to answer you
To let my honor give reply.
I hold my speech so that my deeds   3010
Will speak for me in their own right

And shield my gaze from you because
No man in such dire straits can pledge
To aid a woman's honor when
She looks the sight of loveliness.   3015
                      [*Exit* SEGISMUND *and* SOLDIERS.]
ROSAURA   Why does he speak in riddles, skies?
He knows my suffering has been great,
So how could he equivocate
By giving such abstruse replies?

Scene xi

        [*Enter* CLARION.]
CLARION   My lady, when you've time to spare . . .   3020
ROSAURA   Why, Clarion! Man, where have you been?
CLARION   Just trying to read my fortune in
A deck of cards, confined up there—
They slay me . . . no, they slay me not—
A face card would ensure a brush   3025
With death, but trumped, would leave me flush
With life again. That parlous spot
All but convinced me I would bust.
ROSAURA   Whatever from?
CLARION   From finding out
The secret of your past. No doubt   3030
        [*Drumbeats sound offstage.*]
Clotaldo . . . What's that sound I just
Heard?
ROSAURA   Beating drums and battle whoops?
CLARION   Armed soldiers sortie from the court
To end the palace siege. To thwart
Prince Segismund's unruly troops,   3035
They'll make a stand for all they're worth!
ROSAURA   It's cowardly to be allied
With him and not fight at his side,
A scandalous wonder on this earth,
Where cruel acts flourish and survive   3040
In anarchy despite man's laws.
                                            [*She exits.*]

Scene xii

SOME VOICES [*Offstage.*]   Long live our king's triumphant cause!
OTHER VOICES [*Offstage.*]   Long may our freedom live and thrive!
CLARION   Long live their freedom and their king!
I wish the both of them the best,   3045
But nothing leaves me more distressed
Than being forced to choose one thing.
Instead of risking life and limb,
I'll step aside, avoid distress,

And act like Nero[1] through this mess—   3050
He never let things get to him!
It's up to me now to decide
What else should worry me but me.
I'll just make sure that I can see
The party rage from where I hide.   3055
Ah, this is where I'll catch my breath,
Secluded in this rocky sheer.
No, death will never find me here
And I don't give two figs for death.
        [*He hides.*]

Scene xiii

[*With the sound of arms clashing, King* BASIL, CLOTALDO, *and*
ASTOLF *enter, fleeing.*]
BASIL   What king has ever felt defeat   3060
    Or father harassment so dire?
CLOTALDO   Your army has been routed, sire,
    And scatters in confused retreat.
ASTOLF   None but the treacherous victors stride
    The field.
BASIL   When battle's course is run,   3065
    The loyal force is those who've won
    And traitors are the losing side.
    Let's flee my tyrant son and his
    Inhuman rage, Clotaldo, flee
    His savage wrath and cruelty!   3070
        [*Shots are heard offstage, and* CLARION *falls wounded
        from his hiding-place.*]
CLARION   Sweet heavens, help me now!
ASTOLF   Who is
    This soldier of misfortune here
    That wallows at our feet in mud,
    His body soaked and stained with blood?
CLARION   A hapless piece of man, I fear,   3075
    Who vainly sought to turn his face
    From death, but met it anyhow,
    Whose final dodge did not allow
    Him final shrift.[2] There's just no place
    To hide from death and not be found,   3080
    From which a man might well assume
    The more he tries to spurn the tomb,
    The sooner he'll lie underground.
    Go, then, rejoin your vast brigades
    And charge into the bloody breach   3085
    Where you'll be farthest from harm's reach,
    Mid clashing swords and cannonades,

---

1. The notoriously dissolute Roman emperor (r. 54–68 c.e.) who, according to Roman historians, played his lyre and sang during a fire that devastated Rome in 64.
2. That is, a final confession to a priest.

More safe than hiding in the hills,
Which offer no security
Against the tide of destiny   3090
Or what inclement fortune wills.
Think you by fleeing you'll be fine
And cheat death in this way again?
You'll die precisely where and when
Your deaths fulfill God's grand design.   3095

                              [*He collapses offstage.*]

BASIL   You'll die precisely where and when
Your deaths fulfill God's grand design!
Almighty heavens, truer words
Than these man never spoke before!
They lead me toward a greater truth   3100
Imparted by this talking corpse
Whose wound is but a second mouth
From which that trickling liquid drips
Like wisdom off a bloody tongue
To teach how man's initiatives   3105
All come to naught when they presume
To counteract the powers on high.
My own attempts to rid this land
Of treachery and homicide
Has ended in its capture by   3110
The forces I had most opposed.
CLOTALDO   Though it is common knowledge, sire,
That fate's familiar with all roads
And hunts down even those who think
Themselves hid mid these stones, it still   3115
Is hardly Christian sentiment
To say one can't escape its ills.
A prudent man might easily
Emerge victorious over fate.
I beg you, sire, if you stand fair   3120
To common wretchedness and pain,
Seek refuge where it might be had.
ASTOLF   Your Majesty, Clotaldo may
Advise you as a prudent man
Who's reached a wise, mature old age,   3125
But I'll speak as a daring youth:
You'll find a horse concealed within
The tangled thickets of these hills,
A fleet abortion of the wind.
Ride hard until you're safe; I'll guard   3130
The rear to safeguard your escape.
BASIL   If death fulfills God's grand design
Or otherwise should lie in wait
For me today, I'll stand my ground
And meet it face to face at last.   3135

Scene xiv

[*The call to arms sounds, and* SEGISMUND *enters with his entire
company, including* STELLA *and* ROSAURA.]

SOLDIER   Here! Somewhere mid these bosky hills
In thickets off the beaten path
The king is hiding.
SEGISMUND   After him!
Look under every living plant!
I'll see this dusky forest combed   3140
First trunk by trunk, then branch by branch!
CLOTALDO   Flee, sire!
BASIL   What purpose would it serve?
ASTOLF   What now, then?
BASIL   Astolf, step aside.
CLOTALDO   What is your wish, my lord?
BASIL   There's but
One recourse left me at this time.   3145
If it is I you look for, prince,
Then look no further than your feet
Where I now lay this carpet wove
Of white hairs from my snowy peak.
Come, tread upon my neck and trounce   3150
My crown, humiliate me, drag
My dignity and reverence down,
Take vengeance on my honor fast
And use me as your captive slave.
For what has my precaution served?   3155
Let fate receive its proper due:
The heavens stayed true to their word.
SEGISMUND   Proud worthies of the Polish court,
Attend your true and rightful prince
And I'll make sense of what these strange   3160
Events you've witnessed have evinced.
What heaven has decreed shall come
To pass is writ in God's own script
Upon this drawing board of blue,
Where shining print and twinkling signs   3165
Embellish these celestial sheets
Like gilded letters hand-inscribed.
Not once have stars deceived or lied,
Though one soul does lie and deceive:
That man who'd read this coded script   3170
To hazard wildly what stars mean.
My father, humbled at my feet,
Believing he could shun the rage
Portended for me, had his son,
Born human, made a beast and caged.   3175
His action thus ensured, despite
My natural nobility,
My pure aristocratic blood

And all my gallant qualities—
For I was born a docile soul   3180
And gentle child—that so deprived
An upbringing and inhumane,
Debasing, brutish way of life
Would father in me beast-like ways.
Now, how was this confounding fate?   3185
For say some stranger should predict
One day: "An animal shall slay
You by and by." What strategy
For thwarting such a fate would force
A man to rouse brutes from their sleep?   3190
Or if that stranger warned, "The sword
You gird upon your thigh shall be
The one to cause your death," how vain
All efforts to eschew this end
Should seem if one then bared the blade   3195
And left it pointing at his chest!
Or if he bode, "The silvery spumes
That cap the sea shall some day serve
As gravestones on your watery tomb,"
How prudent would it be to brave   3200
The ocean deep precisely as
Its cresting waves and snow-capped peaks
Arose like mountains of clear glass?
To act so heedlessly tempts fate,
As he who wakes a sleeping beast   3205
Discovers once he's sensed its threat;
As he who fears a sword's cold steel
Learns while unsheathing it; as he
Who swims in stormy seas construes.
For even if—now hear me out—   3210
My fury were a sleeping brute,
My savagery a tempered sword,
And all my raging tranquil seas,
Harsh treatment and blind vengefulness
Would not reverse man's destiny,   3215
But hasten that it come to pass.
That mortal who, by hopeful acts,
Would influence the turns of fate
Must seek a more judicious path.
Foreseeing future harm does not   3220
Ensure the victim will be spared
Its ravages, for while it's true
That man may save himself some care
Through sheer humility—that's clear—
This happens only once the harm   3225
Presents itself, as there is just
No chance that fate will be disarmed.
Let this amazing spectacle,
These strange events, this horror show

And wondrous pageant play serve as   3230
A lesson to us all. Who knows
A more exemplary case? Despite
Divining heaven's secret plans,
A father lies at his son's heels,
A king who's forfeited command.   3235
The skies had willed this to occur
And, intrigue as he might to stave
Off fate, he failed. What chance could I
Then hope to have—a man less gray,
Less brave, less erudite than he—   3240
To alter fortune's ways? Rise, sire.
Give me your hand. Since heaven has
Exposed the ruses you contrived
As yet more futile ploys to change
Their plotted course, I humbly bare   3245
My neck to you, beneath your heels,
So you might settle these affairs.
BASIL   My noble son, this virtuous
Display has fathered you again
In my own heart. You'll reign as prince.   3250
The laurel leaf and palm are meant
For you as victor on this day.
Let gallant actions be your crown.
ALL   Long live Prince Segismund! All hail!
SEGISMUND   Now that it seems my valor's bound   3255
To win me yet more victories,
I'll start with my most dogged foe
And quell myself. Come, Astolf, take
Rosaura's hand and be betrothed.
Thus will your debt of honor be   3260
Repaid, and I'll vouchsafe for this.
ASTOLF   Correct though you may be about
Such satisfaction, lord, admit
The lady cannot claim descent
And that I'd stain my family name   3265
By marrying a woman who . . .
CLOTALDO   Before you say more, Astolf, wait.
Rosaura's blood is noble as
Your own, and gladly would I duel
The man who'd gainsay this, for she's   3270
My child. That should suffice for you.
ASTOLF   How's that?
CLOTALDO   I thought it best to keep
The secret hid till she could be
Both honorably and nobly wed.
The story is quite long, indeed,   3275
But in the end, she is my child.
ASTOLF   If this is true, I will uphold
My pledge.

SEGISMUND   We've only Stella now
To turn our thoughts to and console.
Considering her sudden loss   3280
Of so renowned and brave a prince,
I place in my own hands the charge
Of finding one who rivals him,
If not superior in worth
And riches, then at least his peer.   3285
Fair Stella, take my hand.
STELLA   I've no
Right to the happiness I feel.
SEGISMUND   Clotaldo, loyal servitor
Of my good sire, these arms now stretch
Forth to embrace you, promising   3290
To render all you may request.
1ST SOLDIER   This man has never served your cause
And yet is honored so? What lies
Ahead for me, then, as the font
Of all this turmoil and the might   3295
That freed you from your tower jail?
SEGISMUND   That selfsame tower. And to ensure
You'll not set foot from there alive,
We'll station guards at all the doors.
Of what use is the traitor once   3300
The treason has been carried out?
BASIL   Your wisdom awes this gathering.
ASTOLF   He seems a different person now.
ROSAURA   A prudent and judicious prince!
SEGISMUND   But why should you feel awe or fear?   3305
The dream that was my schoolmaster
Will grieve me if it reappears
And I awake to find myself
Imprisoned once again, locked up
In my rank cell. But should it not,   3310
To dream this would be quite enough!
For on this earth, I've come to see
That all of human happiness
Must reach an end, just like a dream.
So in what little time is left,   3315
I'll seize this opportunity
To ask forgiveness for our flaws,
As noble souls like yours are wont
To pardon others for their faults.

SOR JUANA INÉS DE LA CRUZ
Trials of a Noble House†
(*Los empeños de una casa*)

Loa
(Prologue in the form of a Laud)

CHARACTERS

HAPPINESS
FORTUNE
DILIGENCE
MERIT
CHANCE
MUSIC

[MUSIC enters.]
MUSIC A voice invites you all to hie
To this most artful of events,
Wherein we'll seek to ascertain
Which happiness on earth is best.
Attend its clarion call!   5
Your silence, please! Attention, one and all!
At issue is to what joy may
Be readily attributed:
Does Fortune's favor tender it
Or is it born of Merit's sweat?   10
Come one, come all! Attend this clarion call!
A clever question can't fail to enthrall!
So, silence, please! Attention, one and all!
[MERIT *and* DILIGENCE *enter from one side,* FORTUNE *and* CHANCE
from the other.]
MERIT Your convocation drew me here
Though I'm afraid the question's moot.   15
FORTUNE I've come to triumph, not to fight,
Convinced I'm too correct to lose.
CHANCE Same here, as I can well ascribe
It to my own self by default.

† Translated by G. J. Racz for this Norton Critical Edition.

271

MUSIC   Come one, come all! Attend this clarion call!   20
My clever question can't fail to enthrall!
Your silence, please! Attention, one and all!
MERIT   Melodious voice, well might you bring
This sonorous summons to an end,
For if the question that you pose   25
Here seeks life's greatest happiness
And, that determined, who or what
Is most responsible for it,
This pressing matter has been long
Resolved by natural reasoning,   30
Which, ruling on the issue, found
In Merit's favor in this case
(Most aptly, too). So why put forth
A settled question for debate?
DILIGENCE   Well spoken, friend! Though you are who   35
You are and I your staunch ally
(For Diligence will always be
Discovered close by Merit's side),
You may well "merit" this award—
Your name's enough to warrant it—   40
Though if we went our separate ways,
It's scarce a contest you would win,
For Merit, when he's left devoid
Of Diligence's company,
Though hungry for this accolade,   45
Would not obtain the prize he seeks.
However, given that we find
Ourselves together once again—
You being Merit after all
And I, your partner, Diligence—   50
We won't have anything to fear
From Fortune now.
FORTUNE   Oh, is that so?
Would you presume to circumscribe
My jurisdiction's sweeping scope
When I'm accompanied by Chance,   55
With whom I form a potent team?
MERIT   You think that Fortune ever could
Trump Merit in contesting me?
FORTUNE   I do—when hasn't Fortune vied
With Merit to his detriment?   60
DILIGENCE   Let me repeat: when Diligence
Stands by his side.
CHANCE   You're incorrect,
For when has Diligence sufficed
Against the onslaught of bad luck?
DILIGENCE   A host of instances have shown   65
A little foresight quite enough
To counteract the harm he does.
CHANCE   Still, careful calculations teach

That Chance is likely to have struck
Before precaution intervenes.   70
MERIT   No, Fortune, I just can't stand by
And see your faulty logic hailed
With glory, which your triumphing
In such a challenge would entail.
Come now: who do you think you are,   75
Contending with my inner worth,
You, some old goddess conjured up
By undeserving posturers?
Deprived of honor in my court
Where I preside by my ideals,   80
Unworthy persons crawl to you,
Rearguing cases on appeal.
What are you but a tyrant so
Malign you'd undertake no less
Than proffering unearned rewards   85
While punishing the innocent?
What are you, favor's surrogate,
Who also lets self-interest thrive,
A rationale for carrying on
Irrationally all the time?   90
Perhaps, you're chaos's own clock,
Refusing to obey hard rules,
Prepared to chime with twenty bells
When it's but early afternoon?
Or, yet again, the horrible   95
Destruction of your acolytes,
Those dupes you elevate by day
If only to bring low by night?
Or are you . . .
FORTUNE   Merit, hold your tongue!
You think you're quite the orator   100
But never could contend with me.
This bluster's nothing more than words,
So how can insults serve your cause?
While you're so busy venting rage
In envy of the joy I bring,   105
I revel in what I create.
You know that every time you vie
With me for any sort of prize
You end up slinking off with plaints
While I declare the trophies mine,   110
So why must you go on like this?
Instead of trying to rival me,
Sir, wouldn't it behoove you more
To render homage at my feet?
Consider these examples drawn   115
From ancient history: when did
We ever meet upon a field
Of battle where I didn't win?

What good was it to Darius
In Persia that sweet victory   120
By rights was his, once I'd resolved
To champion Alexander's Greeks?[1]
Did being master of the world
Protect the Macedonian, then,
From any of my rancor once   125
I fancied looking down on him?
In aiding rustic Tamerlane[2]
To oust the sultan he deposed,
Did I not turn a royal nape
Into a shepherd's stepping stone?   130
When Caesar at Pharsalus won
With Fortune favoring the brave,
What use were reasoned strategies
Or moral rightness to Pompey?[3]
The finest prodigies on earth,   135
Its paragons of virtue, stand
Quite far beyond staid Merit's reach,
Yet still surrender fighting Chance.
Who furnished Theseus with thread
And left Troy desolate and burnt?[4]   140
Who gave Odysseus the arms
That Ajax rightfully deserved?[5]
Am I not arbiter supreme
Of all things tied to peace and war
Since I determine through my will   145
When there'll be conflict or accord?
DILIGENCE   Don't waste your time with arguing—
The very voice that called us talks
And, serving now as oracle,
Will set us right and put a halt   150
To our suspense.
CHANCE   It's not by Chance
You'll hear again this clarion call:
MUSIC   Your silence, please! Attention, one and all!
MERIT   You summon us but don't make clear
Just who among such opposites   155
The title "joy's purveyor" fits,
Thus importuning all.

1. Darius, king of Persia, was unexpectedly defeated by the invading armies of Alexander III, king of Macedon, in 331 B.C.E. Alexander the Great, as he is generally known, would die at age 32, possibly from poisoning.
2. The great Turco-Mongol conqueror Tamerlane, founder of the Timurid empire in Central Asia and Persia, was said to have been a shepherd. He famously defeated the Ottoman sultan Bayezid in 1402 and humbled him in captivity.
3. In the crucial battle of Pharsalia in the Roman Civil War (48 B.C.E.), Julius Caesar defeated Pompey despite having a much smaller army.
4. Theseus, hero of Greek myth, was able to escape the Cretan labyrinth after he killed the Minotaur (half man, half bull) with the assistance of Ariadne, who had fallen in love with him. The Greeks conquered Troy after years of besieging it by tricking the Trojans with a giant wooden horse filled with warriors.
5. During the Trojan War, Odysseus vied with Ajax for the weapons of the dead Achilles and managed to receive them despite Ajax's greater valor.

MUSIC   One here . . .
FORTUNE   Of which pair, if they're not akin?
MUSIC   Will win.
DILIGENCE   But which? See, taking the stage floor . . .   160
MUSIC   You four.
CHANCE   What are you hiding in the wings?
MUSIC   Mere things.
FORTUNE   We grapple with these echoings
    Full faint of heart, for all we hear   165
    Is this, resounding soft but clear:
MUSIC   One here will win, you four mere things.
MERIT   Who'll end this squabbling to deploy . . .
MUSIC   . . . Such joy?
FORTUNE   And have these honors proudly done . . .   170
MUSIC   . . . To one?
MERIT   Yes, one to whom the glory's news . . .
MUSIC   . . . By rights ensues?
DILIGENCE [*To* MERIT.]   It's yours, a prize you cannot lose,
    For Music's dulcet tones accord   175
    The trophy, Merit's due reward.
MUSIC   Such joy to one by rights ensues.
CHANCE   Without the slightest look askance . . .
MUSIC   . . . It goes to Chance.
CHANCE   So, who will feel this consequence?   180
MUSIC   Then, Diligence.
CHANCE   Which stalwart will this leave most vexed?
MUSIC   Well, Merit next.
CHANCE   Will these three take a rosy view?
MUSIC   And Fortune, too.   185
CHANCE   But surely only one must do,
    So granting this pre-eminence . . .
MUSIC   It goes to Chance, then Diligence,
    Well, Merit next and Fortune, too.
MERIT   The winner can't be all of us—   190
    It isn't possible. She speaks
    In cryptic clauses that unite
    With ours and garble what we mean.
    But if we piece together all
    These echoes of her vague replies,   195
    We might obtain a better sense
    Of what she means once they're combined.
FORTUNE   An excellent idea! Perhaps,
    This will provide us with a glimpse
    Inside her opaque mind.
CHANCE   And thus   200
    Allow us to perceive the gist
    Of her impenetrable words.
DILIGENCE   Let's sing them now with musical
    Accompaniment so they won't seem
    So recondite and difficult.   205
ALL with MUSIC   One here will win, you four mere things.

Such joy to one by rights ensues.
It goes to Chance, then Diligence,
Well, Merit next and Fortune, too.
MERIT   We have our answer, as she'll say   210
No more than what we know for now—
That one of us is bound to win—
And with this truth, leave all in doubt,
Declining to divulge a name.
FORTUNE   No doubt she'd like the victor found   215
Through argument and skilled debate.
CHANCE   No, doubtlessly she means that Chance
Should bring this question to an end.
DILIGENCE   No, there's no doubting Music can't
Resolve this absent Diligence.   220
MERIT   All this conjecturing is vain,
For Merit's first among you here.
FORTUNE   Without proof, though, our doubt remains.
MERIT   A happy soul may well be one
Who finds his joy is meritless,   225
Which drives this very happiness
To pain him once he's overrun
With shame to know he hasn't done
A thing to warrant this glad state
And sees his glee evaporate   230
Before he ever feels it whole.
Hence, only a deserving soul
Can merit happiness that's great.
MUSIC   Pure happiness entails far more
Than owning what's deserved.   235
If joy possessed is not joy felt,
Whom does such gladness serve?
FORTUNE   This line of reasoning makes no sense.
Your faulty argument implies
That happiness, in Merit's eyes,   240
Is not due luck but recompense.
What joy not born of accidents
Could proffer genuine delight
When it had always been in sight?
What happiness is earned by man?   245
It stands to reason no one can
Feel more than he who lacked all right.
MUSIC   The only happiness on earth
That may be judged complete
Is not one souls anticipate,   250
But joy that's unforeseen.
CHANCE   We'd be remiss to disregard
That adage touting Chance that shows
How much he can assuage our woes
Or make experience more ill-starred.   255
The evidence for this is hard,
For, chances are, none would advance

Without a life that's touched by Chance.
Ignore him at your peril—it's
Far wiser giving what befits   260
Chance than to look at him askance.
MUSIC   It's much more common, after all,
For life's felicities
To spring from Chance's accidents
Than from man's industry.   265
DILIGENCE   I must protest—that's not the case!
Real happiness, I understand,
Must come from work by one's own hand
And not from other people's grace.
Industrious persons need not face   270
The risk of chance or accidents.
A well-known proverb's eloquence
Depicts this joy as more secure
In stating what is no doubt sure:
Good luck is born of Diligence.   275
MUSIC   No soul on earth should ever fear
The loss of gladness, then,
If he or she can forge new joys
Through pure assiduousness.
MERIT   It may at first glance look as though   280
Each being here (or so it seems)
Deserves the crown of Happiness,
But how appearances deceive!
The laurels should be Merit's, earned
By sheer endeavor's just decree.   285
MUSIC   Can't be!
MERIT   You'll see!
FORTUNE   Can't be! This time it's Fortune's prize.
My haughty arrogance high-flown,
The cosmos's machinery
Lies humbled at its feet below.   290
MUSIC   Not so!
FORTUNE   It's so!
DILIGENCE   Not so! The prize is rightfully mine.
If Fortune over there pursues
This trophy as a mercy, then
It's something that I'm surely due.   295
MUSIC   Not true!
DILIGENCE   It's true!
CHANCE   It's not true! Chance effectively
Remains the cause of earthly bliss,
So Chance deserves these accolades.
For siring joy, the prize is his.   300
MUSIC   It is?
CHANCE   Yes, 'tis!
MERIT   That's quite enough! We seem entrenched
And there's an impasse to resolve.
For all our remonstrations here,

We can't claim anything's been solved.   305
It might be best to change our tack.
FORTUNE   And do what?
MERIT   Call on Happiness
Herself to grace this house, the joy
Already here appearing less
Earthborn and more divine. She should   310
Be able as a deity
To tell us who's responsible
For bringing her within man's reach.
FORTUNE   Then I'll defer my claim until
Such time as Happiness decides.   315
But how are we to summon her?
Where does she dwell?
DILIGENCE   Amid delights
Of those Elysian Fields,[6] the sole
Demesne where Happiness is safe.
But how are we to summon her?   320
CHANCE   We'll add our voices to the same
Harmonious choir singing here.
DILIGENCE   So, gathered at this joyous fête,
We strike our invocation up,
Imbued with fondness and respect.   325
        [MERIT, FORTUNE, DILIGENCE, *and* CHANCE *begin singing and
        gesturing.*]
MERIT   Elysian queen, be crowned in glory's rays!
FORTUNE   Oh sceptered empress, grand beyond all praise!
DILIGENCE   Desired end of all man would devise!
CHANCE   The goal of every mortal enterprise!
MERIT   Great treasure, absent which all wealth is poor!   330
FORTUNE   True beauty, which all others pale before!
MERIT   Without you, Love falls short of its delights!
FORTUNE   Without you, Power could scarce attain its heights!
DILIGENCE   The greatest good without you turns to grief . . .
CHANCE   . . . You soothe our woes and bring our ills relief!   335
MERIT   No troubles bide in your imperium!
FORTUNE   In short, come,
CHANCE   Happiness!
DILIGENCE   Yes, come!
MERIT   Do come!
ALL   Yes, answer our collective call,
Sweet Happiness, since you
Alone can clarify this point   340
For all with certitude.
        [*A clarion sounds offstage.*]
MUSIC   Hurray! Let all rejoice!
ALL   What cause is there for glee?
MUSIC   Soon Happiness will join
Your number, brought by pleas   345

6. In Greek mythology, paradise.

Both heartfelt and loud-voiced.
Hurray! Let all rejoice!
[*Two curtains are drawn, and* HAPPINESS *appears with a crown and scepter.*]
MERIT   What semblance shines forth more divine?
FORTUNE   How singularly beautiful!
DILIGENCE   Such grace bespeaks a miracle!   350
CHANCE   Now, when has Happiness not looked
So marvelous?
MERIT   All joys are fair,
But none can hold its ground beside
This highest one. Come, let's attend
Her words and hear how she decides.   355
HAPPINESS   As I've been summoned to appear
To give this reckoning of myself,
I'll act as final arbiter
Until you see your every doubt dispelled.
The question is: to which of you,   360
For all the reasons here alleged,
May Happiness's origin
Most accurately be attributed?
Now, Merit makes his argument
For something he alone deserves,   365
As if his toils in any way
Were on a par with my almighty worth.
Yet Diligence claims I'm obliged
To choose her since she gives me chase,
As if my holy precincts could   370
Be reached by feet so utterly mundane.
Next, Fortune, blind as ever, seeks
This same distinction as she hopes
To work some influence inside
That sacred inner sanctum I call home.   375
And lastly, Chance, maliciously
Or, what's more likely, absent sense,
Presumes that Providence be led
And governed by his rule of accident.
To answer each of you in turn,   380
I wish you first to be informed—
And this with all due diligence—
That joy I am, but not the vulgar sort.
While Diligence might breed that ilk
And Merit likewise win this kind—   385
It's fine that Chance and Fortune, too,
Might light on gladness of the common stripe—
Just know I'm blessed Happiness,
So far superior to those
That such entitlement or hap   390
Could never hope to reach my lofty throne.
To think of me as Fortune's gift
Misprizes what's at my command;

The precious treasures I bestow
Are bounties that can't issue from blind hands.   395
Nor do these come from Merit's sweat,
For while it's possible at times
To draw the odd divine caress,
They're dealt unearned and can't be claimed as rights.
So, which true Happiness stands here?   400
I'm certain not to be believed,
As people just don't trust their eyes
To view a Happiness that's so extreme:
The joyous coming of the great
María, grand in every sense,   405
And Marquis Cerda, our viceroy.[7]
Long may they live in endless happiness!
Now tell me whether Diligence
Or Fortune, Chance or Merit could
In any manner offer you   410
A happiness remotely comparable?
So, if you'd have me designate
The source of gladness this day shared,
It only can be credited
To joy incarnate in this royal pair   415
And their most noble son, José,[8]
The flower of their highborn line,
Whose sure succession guarantees
Still greater triumphs for their house sublime.
Now that you understand how hope   420
Itself could scarce expect to scale
This happiness's sacred heights
Or fame divulge to man what it entails,
Be thankful first of all before
You let sheer jubilance ensue.   425
Your glee, though hardly recompense,
Should serve at least to show your gratitude.
MERIT   Well spoken! Then, let's celebrate
This happiness that sits among
Our company, so grand it seems   430
Three separate joys rolled into one!
Let's lift our voices, then,
Before great joy like this:
Oh, sacred Happiness!
Be welcome in our midst,   435
For Happiness like you
Is dear and would be missed!
MUSIC   Oh, sacred Happiness,
You're welcome in our midst!

---

7. Sor Juana was commissioned to write *Trials of a Noble House* and all the short pieces that
accompany it to celebrate the arrival in Mexico of the new Spanish viceroy, Tomás Antonio de
la Cerda, Marquis of Laguna, and the vicereine, María Luisa Manrique de Lara, Countess of
Paredes. They ruled from 1680 to 1686.
8. José, son of the viceroyal couple, was born in Mexico in 1683.

FORTUNE   Sublime María, may   440
  You, too, be well received—
  Still Europe's goddess, now
  Our New World's deity!
CHANCE   And welcome, Cerda, who'll
  Subdue an arrogant   445
  America's proud napes
  Beneath his feet forthwith.
MUSIC   Most sacred Happiness,
  Be welcome in our midst!
MERIT   May beauty in José   450
  Leave all its stamp on him,
  For greater loveliness
  Can't be exhibited!
MUSIC   Yes, sacred Happiness,
  You're welcome in our midst!   455
FORTUNE   This Anteros should have
  A Cupid[9] to share in
  His older brother's glow
  Without decreasing it.
HAPPINESS   So may this heir to both   460
  Your noble houses shine,
  Exemplar of a par
  With your most gentle lines!
FORTUNE   Now let the viceroys so
  Move Fortune she submits   465
  To their good sense and leaves
  Off blindly giving gifts.
MUSIC   Oh, sacred Happiness,
  Be welcome in our midst!
MERIT   As Merit shares their blood   470
  And worthy parentage,
  I'll tarry by their side
  To mutual benefit.
MUSIC   Most sacred Happiness,
  You're welcome in our midst!   475
DILIGENCE   Let Diligence assure
  Her tending will persist,
  Augmenting the renown
  That comes to all by it.
MUSIC   Most sacred Happiness,   480
  You're welcome in our midst!
CHANCE   Chance, too, will strive to serve
  Your noble house with this:
  I'll bring more certain joys
  And minimize my risks.   485
MUSIC   Oh, sacred Happiness,
  Be welcome in our midst!

---

9. In Greek mythology, Anteros was given as a playmate to his brother Eros (Cupid). They were
   the sons of Aphrodite (Venus), goddess of love, and Ares (Mars), god of war.

FORTUNE   Their lovely womenfolk
  Decked out in fancy trim
  Leave Venus[1] envious   490
  And Flora coveting.
MUSIC   Oh, sacred Happiness,
  You're welcome in our midst!
MERIT   Three suns light up this house
  With all refulgent rays   495
  As smiling Dawn appears
  To usher in the day.
CHANCE   How can this dwelling laud
  The Happiness it holds
  Except to show the debt   500
  Of gratitude it owes?
DILIGENCE   Which, truth to tell, is so
  Immense it far exceeds
  What anyone could pay,
  Regardless of his means.   505
FORTUNE   We haven't any way
  To thank them for this gift
  But to accept their joy
  With love, which we can give.
MERIT   For when the gods decide   510
  To honor one on earth,
  High Merit ranks among
  The honors they confer.
CHANCE   Let these festivities
  Wind down, then, with this hymn,   515
  Which we here happily
  Intone in unison:
MUSIC   Oh, sacred Happiness!
  Be welcome in our midst!
  You're always welcome here,   520
  Most blessed Happiness!
HAPPINESS   Bide ever in their house
  So it may always thrive
  As Happiness joins true
  Nobility inside!   525
FORTUNE   Let's all be thankful, then,
  That joy has come like this
  And make our voices one:
ALL   Oh, most revered archbishop! With
  Your Grace here we are jubilant   530
  For, by your presence in our midst,
  This eve your happy coming marks
  The coming of our Happiness!
MUSIC   This eve their happy coming's marked
  The coming of our Happiness!   535

---

1. Roman name for Aphrodite, goddess of love. Flora: Roman goddess of flowers and the springtime.

Song

Celestial Lysi,[1] welcome these
Our timid, though heartfelt, respects.
While scarcely worthy of your praise,
They humbly seek your heart's content.
It's no tremendous sacrifice   5
To lie before your altars sprawled;
This paltry offering of love
Is hardly sacrifice at all.
It couldn't hope to gladden you;
Its vanity's not so extreme   10
As ever to presume its words
Could satisfy you in the least.
Just one amid a multitude,
A trifling tribute's what it is,
Aspiring neither to be grand   15
Nor, for that matter, to exist.
It's only right the purity
Your altars boast should not be stained
With blood that mars its holy slabs
Instead of warming mortal veins.   20
The victims strewn before your throne
Are by the mind's own workings sired,
Each brought low by its own distinct
Conceptual sickle of desire.
They've no fear of provoking scowls;   25
What greater happiness have they
In witnessing you grow irate
Than feeling they've earned your disdain?
Assured of grief, love labors on
In knowledge that no chastisement   30
Is crueler to an acolyte
Than wanting of its punishments.

---

1. The vicereine, María Luisa. Here and elsewhere, Sor Juana addresses her by a fanciful name, as was the convention in lyric poetry and pastoral romance.

Trials of a Noble House

CHARACTERS

DON CARLOS
DON JUAN
DOÑA ANA
DON PEDRO
DOÑA LEONOR
DON RODRIGO
CELIA
CHESTNUT
HERNANDO
Two CLOAKED MEN
Two musical CHORUSES
(consisting of MUSIC and five VOICES)

Act I

[DOÑA ANA *enters with* CELIA.]
DOÑA ANA   We'll both wait up, then, Celia, till
My brother makes it home tonight.
CELIA   Yes, up till dawn! You've got that right!
The man claims one or two is still
An early hour and, if I may,   5
Though he be idling, master is
Not lying, for he'll see that his
Return is at the break of day.
What's prompting this abrupt concern
About his being, may I inquire?   10
At other times, you just retire
And have me wait for his return.
DOÑA ANA   Good Celia, such are his affairs
That, guided by the certainty
I love him dear, he's rendered me   15
The confidant of all his cares.
Two years before this episode,
As you well know, he quit Madrid
To sojourn in Toledo, bid
To claim some debts that he was owed.   20
He thought he'd come home soon, though, where

285

He'd left me far too long alone
Without a proper chaperone.
Thus, I could see and be seen there.
I saw Don Juan and he saw me.   25
He started, then, to pay me suit
Which I was glad to see to boot
As I was taken equally.
My brother, meanwhile, was detained.
It seems the legal actions brought   30
Progressed more slowly than he'd thought.
Well, either that or he's remained,
I've learned since, for a lady there
Of such perfection, people claim
No quill pen could commend to Fame   35
A woman so beyond compare.
His ardor for the maid unmet
By similar feelings she might show,
He bides here in Toledo, so
In love, with hopes he'll win her yet.   40
My brother, thinking I'd been left
Too long unguarded at the court
Or that my coming might cut short
His feeling utterly bereft,
Arranged things so that I might dwell   45
With him as these affairs dragged on.
Well, off I went to tell Don Juan,
Who followed on my heels pell-mell,
A gallantry I'd thought I'd find
A flattering and dashing act   50
Were it, alas, not for the fact
That second thoughts had plagued my mind.
A base and vile love, you know,
Will take offense at gallantries,
Unused to noble deeds like these.   55
To get back to my brother, though:
Through dogged inquiry, he tried
Repeatedly to ascertain
The reason for his love's disdain
And why his courtship was denied.   60
He learned another had her heart—
Though I don't know the gallant's name—
And seethed more at this suitor's claim
Than at rejection on her part.
Despairing of this kind ensures   65
That envy's bane will work its curse,
Which makes a rival's pleasure worse
Than any pain the self endures.
My brother bribed the lady's maid—
A vile act! Is Love so blind   70
That, leaving reasoning behind,

It pays to have more woe displayed?
The servant had her lady's trust
And, called on to investigate
The shape of this romance's state   75
As well as where the passion must
Be headed, told him faithlessly
That she had come to understand
The lady she was serving planned
That very night, unseen, to flee   80
Her home, the suitor by her side.
At this, my brother's fury flared.
What jealous man was ever scared
Of danger's scenes like these provide?
To see his ardent breast appeased,   85
He had his friends pose as the law
(The malice should occasion awe!)
And this night had her lover seized.
Her true beau now in custody,
They'll bring her by our domicile   90
To find safe haven for a while,
Entrusted, as it were, to me.
Once clear her person's here to stay
And they've all left our residence,
The "law men" will feign negligence   95
And let her suitor get away.
No, he won't miss his chance to skip—
Intent on thwarting his arrest,
He'll use his feet as he knows best
And give these fake police the slip.   100
This way, my brother can steer clear
Of censure for the scheme he's wrought
And, ducking danger, will have brought
His ladylove to live right here,
Where he can pay his court unchecked,   105
The better, then, to fan love's flame
Without suspicion, fear or blame
At home, where she could scarce object.
But if she ever came to know
The scope of his deceptive plan,   110
She'd surely come to hate the man
For having scotched her passions so.
Thus, Celia, as this dread affair
Plays out with who knows what ahead,
How could I just go off to bed   115
When my whole mind is fraught with care?
CELIA   My lady, this is no surprise,
For when in matters of the heart
Have men not used a little art
To dress up truth in flowery lies?   120
And who would honestly be shocked

In like affairs to hear news of
A woman's reckless acts for love
Or diehard schemes their beaus concoct
Or vile betrayals by false maids?   125
Don't such things happen everywhere?
In this house, though, if I may dare,
These high jinks come to pass in spades!
Of all this you've reported on,
I marvel only at one fact: 130
That lately it appears you've lacked
Romantic interest in Don Juan.
You've had no cause to have begun
This trading of beneficence
For undeserved indifference,   135
Nor did he ever give you one.
DOÑA ANA He never gave me cause, it's true,
But that I haven't one's a lie.
CELIA How so?
DOÑA ANA   You find this startling? Why?
The will is blind to who loves who.   140
Don Juan, a courteous man, pursued
His gallant courting of me till
Such sheer refinement tried my will
As I withdrew the more he wooed!
I mean, to what could I aspire   145
Once it was clear he loved but me?
And, being mine so thoroughly,
What was there left me to desire?
That's not the only reason why
His flame's extinguished in my breast.   150
Another burns there unsuppressed
That's likelier to purify.
Each day along this street I view
The handsomest of men stroll by.
If he's not Phoebus[1] from on high,   155
Then who he is I've not a clue.
Toward this man, Celia, my heart's sprung
From sheer attraction or pure whim . . .
Look how I blab regarding him!
I really ought to hold my tongue!   160
CELIA Are those tears?
DOÑA ANA   Naturally they are!
Whatever will become of me?
I've gone adrift and can't quite see
How I can stop, I've erred so far.
CELIA [Aside.] Now here's a fine mess! Troubles loom   165
And this can only turn out bad.
Before I'd heard all this, I had

---

1. Phoebus is another name for the Greco-Roman god Apollo, associated with the sun and with
male beauty.

That Don Juan hidden in her room!
For some time he'd been noticing
Cold treatment from her run its course.   170
Like Tarquin,[2] then, he'd thought to force
His love and ruin everything.
Who is this newfound paramour,
My lady?
DOÑA ANA   Though it's just begun,
Don Carlos de Olmedo's won   175
My heart.
          [Knocks are heard offstage.]
                    But someone's at the door.
See who it is. When we've more ease,
I'll tell you all.
CELIA   Hello? Who's there?
CLOAKED MAN [Offstage.]   Police!
DOÑA ANA   The lady's with that pair.
Admit them all—go!
CELIA   Come in, please.   180
          [Two CLOAKED MEN enter with DOÑA LEONOR.]
CLOAKED MAN   Good madame, as I know full well
The reverence that's due this house,
I trust our presence here will bring
More honor yet and not arouse
Suspicions. I entreat you, thus,   185
To take this lady off our hands
And keep her here until such time
As our patrolmen understand
The reason why her travelling
Companion killed another man.   190
Forgive me now, but duty calls
And I'll return once I've the chance
To make all inquiries.
                    [The two CLOAKED MEN exit.]
DOÑA ANA   How's that?
Run, Celia! Tell them to come back
And take this woman from my home!   195
I'll have you know that I'm abashed
To hear of such shenanigans!
CELIA [Aside.]   How well the lady goes about
Pretending she's not wanted here!
DOÑA LEONOR   Madame, my heart is in my mouth!   200
I'm not expressing myself well:
Should you feel any sympathy
At all for me to view these tears,
I beg of you, upon my knees,
To take no pity on my life   205
But only on my precious name.

---

2. Son of the last king of Rome; his rape of the virtuous Lucretia was traditionally considered to
have precipitated the end of the monarchy and led to the Roman Republic.

As I lodge safe with you here now,
Don't let these unknown agents take
My person to some other place
Where, unprotected, I might lose   210
My honor. If I were unchaste,
As I suspect you must assume,
I'd not be pleading with you thus
Nor suffering from inquietude.

DOÑA ANA   Your beauty and these present woes   215
Have moved my heart to pity you.
[*Aside to* CELIA.] My brother sure described her right!

CELIA [*Aside to* DOÑA ANA.]   Her splendor's otherworldly. Could
She be so fine on stormy seas,
Imagine her fair-weather looks!   220

DOÑA ANA   Stand up, please—there's no cause to kneel.
Forgive me if I failed to act
Attentive to your needs. I was
Upset and all occurred so fast
I fear I've lacked for courtesy   225
Not knowing who you are, of course,
And acting so aloof. But now
I see the way that you comport
Yourself reveals a gentle blood
And so I pledge wholeheartedly   230
To serve you while you bide with us.

DOÑA LEONOR   Oh, let me kiss those gracious feet,
Fair goddess, you whose temple home,
High altars, sacred rites and shrines
Grant sanctuary to a wretch   235
Whom fortune so disfavors.

DOÑA ANA   Rise
And tell me what events conspired
To cause this sudden wretchedness,
Though ladies lovely as you are
Might well expect their share of it.   240

CELIA [*Aside.*]   My mistress seethes with jealousy—
Who'd want to be in her shoes now?

DOÑA LEONOR   Embarrassment and shame might well
Affix a muzzle to my mouth
And keep this tale from being told,   245
But why would one who so succumbed
To such a sorry state of things
Then choose to hush the matter up?
I'd do myself a favor here
Responding frankly, as you urge,   250
For every indicator seems
To fault me for what's just occurred
Although the reasons for my woes
Are far more decent than they look.
Do hear me out.

DOÑA ANA   Let silence be   255
  My answer.
CELIA   Unbelievable!
  Confessions made by candlelight—
  At midnight, too? This can't be good!
DOÑA LEONOR   The tragic series of events
  Behind this present circumstance   260
  That's left me with so many cares
  Will move you once you understand
  Why I'm now here. If my account
  Provokes a smile as it unfolds,
  At least my worries will have brought   265
  Some pleasure to another soul
  So I may feel relief as well
  To lift these sorrows from my chest
  And thus alleviate my pain
  Unburdening myself of them.   270
  Now, I was born of noble blood,
  The first step in an ill-starred life,
  And it's no small misfortune when
  A wretch descends from noble lines.
  While high birth is a precious gem   275
  Whose value can't be evidenced,
  For someone who's so miserable
  It's only an impediment.
  Base fortune and descent repel
  Each other, as they're opposites,   280
  And common troubles of my kind
  Conflict with rank's imperatives.
  I don't suppose I need to say
  That I was born a lovely girl,
  As you can see that for yourself   285
  With all the troubles it's unfurled.
  I'll only tell you—and I wish
  I didn't have to be the one,
  Since no doubt I'll be criticized
  For voicing this or keeping mum—   290
  That if you heard from my own lips
  How I was celebrated for
  My wondrous mind, I'd seem a fool
  Just saying something of the sort.
  Yet, if I didn't, I could scarce   295
  Explain my present state to you
  And, hushing up the truth like this,
  Appear to be the greater fool.
  Some background, then, about my life
  Might make plain my experience,   300
  As once again my modesty
  Must yield to sheer embarrassment.
  To comprehend what's just transpired,

One fact's incontrovertible:
My learning brought about my harm—   305
Mine's been a downfall by the book.
Inclined from a most tender age
To intellectual pursuits,
Oft reading late into the night
In tireless questing for the truth,   310
I studied so intensively
That, in the briefest span of time,
I used my brain to turn scant years
Into a lifetime of the mind.
Before we knew it, I'd become   315
The center of attraction—me!—
As people deemed my wisdom proof
Of natural abilities
Instead of what it really was:
The laurels reaped of diligence.   320
And so, my homeland's great esteem
In light of this acquirement
Came pouring in from everyone,
Whose acclamations cheered me on.
Whatever statements I would make   325
(That's whether these were smart or not)
Seemed wise, as I'd a pretty face
And elegance to back them up.
The public's superstition rose
To such great heights that, in its clutch,   330
They hailed me as a goddess—me!—
The only idol they'd beheld,
As overtalkative Fame flew
And word spread through the neighboring realms,
Where distance takes a grain of truth   335
And sees that it's hyperbolized.
My gifts were viewed through spectacles
Whose lenses magnified their size
And made my humble faculties
Look disproportionately large.   340
These sacrificial victims all,
Devoutly prostrate, laid their hearts
Upon my sacred altar's slabs
With such devotion to my cult
That worship there, which earlier   345
Had only been volitional,
Turned into rites so formalized
And mandatory in due course,
This veneration soon became
A kind of festival at court.   350
Whoever was at variance,
Through reasoned choice or stubbornness,
Declined to make these feelings known
For fear the crowds would see dissent

As something strangely deviant   355
And thus presume so odd a stance
Indecent, given my renown,
Or censure it as balderdash.
I heard the public's loud applause
Though, foundering amid the storm   360
Of adoration I received,
Still failed to find a sheltering port,
Much less a gentleman to love,
Beloved by all souls though I was.
I rallied to my own defense   365
At these events, as maidens must,
And was, to danger's detriment,
Triumphant over harm itself.
I aired a friendly modesty
Toward every stranger that I met   370
So people wouldn't speculate
That there was any I preferred.
My parents, who became convinced
Their child was a measured girl,
Began to chaperone me less,   375
A rash decision on their part,
For why remove the locks from gates
Or send away the standing guards
When these kept warring forces pent
Inside me, desperate to emerge?   380
In short, they gave me such free rein,
The march of time could scarce deter
That tempter, risk, from finding me
Where caution once had stood its post.
And so, among the crowds who came   385
To marvel at my fame up close
And win some of my own applause
For insights vainly volunteered,
A certain youth—cruel heavens! How
Unkind of you to let appear   390
By chance, from out the blue like this,
The love I've always waited for—
Don Carlos de Olmedo, yes,
A stranger here, but nobly born
And from so notable a line   395
That, though the people where he'd lodge
May not be quite aware of who
He is, ignore him they cannot.
With your indulgence, then, I'll take
A chance describing him to you,   400
Which may excuse my waywardness
Or help to see my worries soothed
In fond hopes you might comprehend
The wild extremes my love entails
And not be shocked by any act   405

You take to be beyond the pale.
Contrasting qualities conjoin
In that enigma of a face,
Where comeliness and bravery
Are most auspiciously embraced. 410
His masculine proportions lack
All traces of the feminine
And I saw this perfection best
In what his features didn't miss.
A manly anguish has so marred 415
His looks, this truly virile cast
Prevented Beauty's chance to claim
Dominion there or plant her flag.
So far is he from vain regard
And distant from false gossip's praise, 420
He doesn't think enough of looks
To deem them worthy of disdain,
For beauty, surplus on a man,
Is like the icing on a cake:
Delightful to enjoy, though less 425
So when it's boastfully displayed.
That sleek physique is his alone.
Had Nature ever thought to give
Such sterling grace and elegance
To any other one but him, 430
They would have suited that man ill,
For these match only my love's soul.
How provident creation was
In this one detail, placing so
Genteel a human form and such 435
A dashing spirit hand in hand!
His wisdom and intelligence,
Extremely subtle and advanced,
Reveal an intellectual age
That much belies his callow years. 440
Of all his charms, an affable
Insouciance makes others clear,
Not least a bearing debonair,
His keen aristocratic tastes,
A winning shyness—no, reserve— 445
Besides a wealth of pleasant ways
That, even when he doesn't shine,
As shining qualities, shine through.
He is, in fact, so kind to all,
So generous in attitude, 450
Refined in how he makes his points
And in the manner he comports
Himself—in short, then, so ideal
That, being the gentlemanly sort,
He's disinclined to flaunt his spoils 455
When prizes can be humbly won.

Long-suffering of Fortune's slings,
Not letting favor make him smug,
He stands firm in the face of risk,
Though cautiously when trouble calls.   460
Now tell me, with the traits he has—
And I can scarcely list them all—
If even the most even-keeled
Of maids could manage to stay chaste.
In short, I fell in love with him,   465
Though hate to weary you so late
With every detail relevant
To all the trials I underwent,
As trials of the heart, you know,
Are what all souls experience.   470
For courtships tend to start off well,
With lovers free and at their ease,
Though quarrels soon ensue until
They end in tragedy and grief.
In any case, the love we shared   475
Grew stronger and we coveted
Our happy union, unexplored
As yet in any marriage bed.
We sought its sanction through the bond
That Hymen[3] blesses couples with.   480
My father's interference loomed—
Already he'd begun his bid
To see me properly espoused
By judging some prospective beaus,
Though this review distracted him   485
Before he caused us any woe.
So we made up our minds this night
To have me flee, thus trampling on
A father's natural love for me
And my own reputation's stock.   490
I took my first few shaky steps
Outside, so cowed was I by nerves
And in so vulnerable a state
That I had scarcely gripped my skirt
In one hand as I modestly   495
Made sure the other held my veil
Before two strange cloaked men approached
From out the dark of night and hailed
Our startled selves with "Who goes there?"
Now, as they'd caught me out of breath   500
And unaware of my own acts
(For often, when one most would hedge
To keep the truth concealed, this stealth
Reveals the facts one wanted hid),
"Oh, Carlos, we are ruined" I cried.   505

---

3. Greek god of marriage.

These anguished words had passed my lips
For but a moment when the men
Unsheathed their swords, at which one said
To his companion, fully drawn:
"Dispatch him! Do him unto death!   510
The tyrant lady he abducts
Is Leonor de Castro, my
Own cousin." Well, my lover drew
His steel at this and, thus inspired,
Did plunge the blade's tip through the chest   515
Of his assailant, who exclaimed
A piteous "Ah, me!" as he fell.
His comrade, witnessing the fray,
Unleashed a call to arms so loud
More men appeared forthwith to help   520
And, even though my Carlos could
Have made a run and saved himself,
He wouldn't leave me there at risk
And, ergo, didn't make so bold.
Next, officers of the police,   525
Who happened to be on patrol,
Approached us, then, a second time
And Carlos, who declined to flee,
Again drew steel in self-defense
Until, persuaded by the tears   530
That now accompanied my pleas,
Surrendered up his sword to them.
Detaining him and seizing me
For causing their companion's death,
They saw the slain patrolman was   535
None other than Don Diego de
Castro, my cousin, lady, so
They left my person and my plaints
Where we'd be safe, in your grand house.
Thus, all at once I find myself   540
Bereft of honor, my good name,
Consolement, sweet repose or rest,
Quite breathless and without relief,
Until the moment comes around
For my own execution, when   545
My Carlos's is carried out.
DOÑA ANA [*Aside.*]   Good heavens! What did I just hear?
The very man I idolize
Is also loved by Leonor!
Oh Juan, Love took so little time   550
Exacting your revenge. Poor me!
I feel your cares as anyone
Would, my good lady. Celia, take
The maid to my room. I'll wait up,
In turn, until my brother comes.   555
CELIA   My lady.

DOÑA LEONOR   Yes, do lead the way.
If following should be my fate,
Then destiny must be obeyed.

[DOÑA LEONOR *exits with* CELIA.]

DOÑA ANA   If Carlos's physique and gallantry
Could put me into such a state alone,   560
How will they look in envy's torrid zone
When they've already burned so bright for me?
I wished him mine, but not on bended knee,
Though knowing now he claims her as his own
Makes parting them no triumph I condone   565
Nor ousting his first love a victory.
Forgive me, Don Juan! I all but forgot
This love I'd once requite, but here demur.
How can I, now that jealousy has shot
Such poison in me all my longings stir?   570
Sure, Carlos is more fair, but were he not,
He'd seem so, now that he belongs to her.

[DON CARLOS *enters, his sword drawn, with* CHESTNUT.]

DON CARLOS   Good lady, if misfortunes find
A sympathetic refuge here,
May your abode house all of mine   575
And thus rank first among its peers.
Now no less than the law itself
Pursues me as a fugitive
And, given that my getaway
Is nobly sanctioned cowardice,   580
I prostrate myself, out of breath,
And seek asylum at your feet
Although, now that I've lost my soul,
Of what good is my life to me?

CHESTNUT   My life does me a world of good   585
So, lady, if you're not averse,
I'm not afraid of asking you:
May I hide underneath your skirt?

DON CARLOS   Be quiet, fool!

CHESTNUT   It wouldn't be
The first time in our troubled age   590
That one who didn't turn to priests[4]
Tried skirting justice in this way!

DOÑA ANA [*Aside.*]   It's Carlos! Here's a stroke of luck!
How chance conspires to aid my love
While passions still burn hot. I'll win   595
His favor yet through acts he'll judge
Beneficent, preserving all
The outward trappings of respect.
In sheltering him where generous hands
Can furnish many a caress,   600

---

4. Churches provided sanctuary to criminals avoiding the law. The original has a joke on *sacristán*, which means both the person who assists the priest and a farthingale (hoop for skirts).

I'll manage coyly to present
Desire in compassion's guise.
With no harm to my virtuous name
Or insult to my family pride,
I'll move him to surrender here   605
So I won't seem the one to yield.
I know he loves fair Leonor—
Still, what great ardor do men feel
That keeps them true to just one maid
If they should see the time and place   610
For other opportunities?
But stop there, Love! Why hesitate
When my own circumstances show
How fickle those in love can be?
Good sir, misfortunes are the fruit   615
Of that high standing blood decrees
And fodder for sweet solacing.
So, if yours find deliverance
In me, then take your refuge here
Where you can safely catch your breath.   620
But duck into that storeroom there,
Which overlooks the garden plot,
For, should my brother come home now,
He'd think this were a liaison
And seeing me alone with you   625
Would only put you more at risk.
DON CARLOS   My lady, I'd be mortified
If this kind offer to assist
My person brought you any harm.
CHESTNUT   You're kidding! That's your main concern?   630
Well, by the wench that gave me birth!
DOÑA ANA   I'm not so easily deterred.
Just hurry. Slip into that room.
My brother won't set foot in there
As it's a pantry where I store   635
Our nicer things for visits: chairs
And carpets—you know—finer ware
For when like gentlepeople call
On their obligatory rounds.
A garden lies beyond those walls   640
Should any need arise to flee.
Here, let me show you what I mean
So you can put your mind at ease.
Before you enter there, I'll need
Take one precaution here and bolt   645
The door so, when my brother knocks,
I'll be forewarned of his return.
CHESTNUT [*Aside to* DON CARLOS.]   Wow, what a swanky
    place to lodge
And what a comely woman, too!
Sir, here's what eats me up inside—   650

(It's either that or hunger pangs—
I didn't get the chance to dine!):
Why couldn't you make this gal fall
In love with you—she's pretty rich—
Instead of Leonor, whose claims   655
Are nil besides her show of wit?
DON CARLOS   For God's sake, knave!
DOÑA ANA   Come on, let's go.
[*Aside.*] Now that you've dangled happiness
Before me, Love, you must allow
This joy to be experienced.   660
              [DOÑA ANA *exits, followed by* DON CARLOS *and* CHESTNUT.
                        DON RODRIGO *enters with* HERNANDO.]
DON RODRIGO   How's that, Hernando?
HERNANDO   It's what happened, sir:
Your daughter fled your household in a whir.
DON RODRIGO   And you don't know with whom?
HERNANDO   How could I say?
You saw how many gallants came this way
To join Toledo's trains   665
In marveling at her beauty and her brains.
With all those men, I couldn't sort out who
Was there to praise from who was pitching woo!
You let that endless stream flow on so long,
I can't but think such laxity was wrong.   670
Despite her being modest and demure,
Your daughter's chance to stray became more sure
As it grew ever likelier she'd meet
A suitor who would charm her off her feet.
DON RODRIGO   You try my patience with your lecturing!   675
Is this a time for disquisitioning?
Oh, vixen! Who'd have known,
With all that cool hypocrisy you've shown
In coming off so cautious and reserved,
That such a fickle nature could be served   680
By so untrue a heart?
Oh, women, with your venomed monster's art!
What man could ever trust
These half insane, half fearless packs of lust
Who all may well succumb   685
No matter whether they're profound or dumb?
Oh, wicked child! I thought your dazzling looks
Along with that propensity for books
Would, in our penury,
Be all the dowry that you'd need from me   690
But, seeing as you've fled,
I've come to view these charms as banes instead.
So now the fame that made it possible
To fête you as the latest miracle
Will only harm my own   695
By making this misfortune widely known.

Still, why this sudden impulse to complain
When vengeance would serve better in the main?
Now, how can I effectuate a plot,
The crime being known, the perpetrator not?   700
Insulted thus, I surely might presume
To see myself avenged, but then of whom?
HERNANDO   My lord, although I've not the slightest proof
Of just who snatched the girl beneath your roof,
The rumors that I've heard   705
All finger the same culprit, and the word
Is that Don Pedro de
Arellano led Leonor astray.
DON RODRIGO   Well, if it was that lad,
What difficulty would the boy have had   710
Requesting of me that she be his wife?
Why bring this shame on us and cause such strife?
HERNANDO   My lord, so many sought your daughter's hand
With ardent hopes, I'm sure you'll understand
That, even had he told you his intent,   715
You still might not have given your consent.
Young men in love are terrified they'll lose
The objects of affection that they choose,
So you won't hear me scoff
At what he felt, just how he brought things off.   720
When faced with losing her, his greatest fear,
He thought it best to cut and run from here.
So, if you're asking me, do what's required;
You're on in years and tired.
Don Pedro is a young, rich, worthy son   725
And all the damage is already done.
Just keep your calm with him—why should you not?—
And offer him what he's already got.
Say: "Bring my daughter back from where you've fled
And I'll see that the two of you are wed."   730
Believe me, he'll accede. No man foreswears
An honorable solution to his cares.
Do this and soon you'll note
The venom's turned into its antidote.
DON RODRIGO   Oh, good Hernando! What's of more worth than   735
A faithful friend or loyal serving man?
I'll end this insult sticking in my craw
And make my enemy my son-in-law.
HERNANDO   Well, just administer the cure before
Your sad affliction enters common lore.   740
          [DON RODRIGO *exits with* HERNANDO. *The stage now dark,*
                    DOÑA LEONOR *enters, fighting off* DON JUAN.]
DON JUAN   No, wait, cruel murderess of my heart!
I mean no harm—don't run away!
If this is how you treat your love,
What lies in store for those you hate?

Oh, can't you see this flight holds cheap   745
The very victories you boast?
You've triumphed, so why turn your back
On one whom passion's vanquished so?
Your running off from me like this
Presents a contradictory scene: 750
You flee a soul that holds you dear
While I chase one that's killing me.
DOÑA LEONOR   Good sir, if I may call you that,
I've only just found refuge here
And haven't even met the man   755
Who owns this house where I've appeared,
So how could I attend your pleas
When such endearments give me pause?
I only understand my great
Astonishment about it all.   760
Besides, I fear that you mistake
My person for a different maid
And thus are passion's fool in this.
Collect yourself and ascertain
I'm not the gentlewoman, sir,   765
That you'd pursue.
DON JUAN   Oh, this is all I need,
Ungrateful heart, for you to act,
Ignoring all my pleas,
As though my love's nobility
Weren't high enough to suit your line.   770
How would attending to my plaints
Bring injury to your family pride?
My darling, at the very least
Our past experience in love
Might well have proved to you my worth.   775
You've watched my passion's waves succumb
Repeatedly upon your shores,
That beachhead where each roiling surge
Of ardor, never mind how great,
Would gently break while I still yearned   780
There at the limits of your strand
Upon the sea of my fond hopes.
DOÑA LEONOR   I've told you, sir, I'm not the maid
You seek. Now, that's enough. Please go
Or I'll be forced to call someone   785
Who'll listen to your present cause
And grant your wishes, if it's true,
But castigate you, be it false.
DON JUAN   Pray, heed me.
DOÑA LEONOR   I've no reason to.
DON JUAN   Look, tyrant, either you'll relent   790
And heed me of your own free will
Or I will force you to attend.

Won't listen while I'm courteous?
Try hearing me when I'm uncouth!
      [DON JUAN *grabs* DOÑA LEONOR *by the arm.*]
DOÑA LEONOR   What are you doing? Heaven, help!   795
DON JUAN   The skies will hardly succor you.
   It's meet that pity not be shown
   To one who shows no sympathy!
DOÑA LEONOR   Ah, me! Won't anyone defend
   My innocence?
      [DON CARLOS *enters with* DOÑA ANA *struggling to hold
      him back.*]
DOÑA ANA   I beg you, please—   800
   Let me see what these noises are!
   It's dangerous for you to go
   If it's my brother who's arrived.
DON CARLOS   Forgive me, but those piercing tones
   Did cut me, lady, to the quick.   805
DOÑA ANA [*Aside.*]   I saw to it the door was barred
   And so my brother can't be home,
   Although I'm still a bit alarmed
   That Carlos might yet chance upon
   His lady here at any time.   810
   Still, if she's safely in my rooms,
   Brought there with Celia at her side,
   I wonder what produced those sounds.
   The room's pitch black and I can't see
   A thing. Who's there?
DON CARLOS   My lady, I—   815
   But why ask?
DON JUAN   Doña Ana, dear,
   My lady and my life! Why does
   Your treatment of me here diverge
   From all those happy promises
   And gentle, love-inspiring words   820
   You whispered to me in Madrid,
   From which I thought my hopes embraced?
   I've catered to your every whim,
   A salamander mid your rays[5]
   And sunflower, like Clytia,   825
   Who basked in Phoebus's warm beams;
   I left the comfort of my home
   To serve you as my heart's own queen,
   Thus forfeiting my father's love
   And my birth province's respect.   830
   If not exactly amorous,
   You acted kindly with noblesse
   And, seeming tacitly content,
   Gave reason for my soul to think

---

5. The mythical salamander could only live in the presence of fire. The lover as salamander, existing in the fire of love, is a common metaphor in the Petrarchan tradition of love poetry. Clytia:
   nymph loved by the sun god Phoebus, associated with the heliotrope or sunflower.

Its hopes for a romantic bond   835
Might be a welcome offering
Accepted as a sacrifice
Upon your altar's holy slabs.
So why all this remoteness now
And sudden urge to brush me back?   840
DOÑA ANA [*Aside.*]   Good heavens, what did I just hear,
Don Juan de Vargas's pained voice
Condemning my ingratitude
While praising his flirtatious ploys?
Who ever could have brought him here?   845
DON CARLOS   My lady, please!
      [DON CARLOS *moves within reach of* DOÑA LEONOR.]
DOÑA LEONOR   Good sir, desist!
I'm asking you to leave me be!
DON CARLOS   Oh, lovely Doña Ana! It's
Don Carlos, that poor gentleman
You sheltered in his time of need.   850
DOÑA LEONOR [*Aside.*]   Don Carlos, did he say? My word!
I swear that, from the way he speaks,
That's my Don Carlos, but I must
Be wrong. He's so much in my thoughts,
I sense his person everywhere,   855
A precious jewel I've sorely lost,
Though I know well he sits in jail.
DON CARLOS   Dear lady!
DOÑA LEONOR   Leave me be, I said!
My pleas should put an end to this!
DON CARLOS   If chance would have it you're upset   860
To find that I've pursued you here,
Forgive this trespass on my part;
I thought my presence might succeed
In keeping you from undue harm.
DOÑA LEONOR [*Aside.*]   Good heavens, but that sounds a lot   865
Like Carlos!
DON JUAN   My ungrateful love!
Why must you be so cold to me?
      [CELIA *enters with a light.*]
CELIA   I wonder, has my mistress come?
I'll need to relocate Don Juan,
Whom I've kept hidden in her rooms.   870
But look—what's this before my eyes?
DOÑA LEONOR [*Aside.*]   What's this I see here? By God's wounds!
Is that not Carlos I espy?
DON CARLOS [*Aside.*]   Have my nerves got the best of me
Or is that Leonor?
DOÑA ANA [*Aside.*]   Don Juan?   875
In this house? I can hardly breathe!
DON JUAN [*Aside.*]   Don Carlos de Olmedo, here?
He's Doña Ana's lover! All
Signs point to it and that's why she—

Perfidious, inconstant, false—   880
Feels free to treat me with disdain.
DOÑA LEONOR [*Aside.*]   How can it be that Carlos dwells
  Among our number, heavens, when
  I've wept to think him in a cell?
  Concealed, instead, inside these rooms,   885
  He now makes amorous assaults
  On me, whom he deems someone else!
  So he's that lady's lover! All
  Signs point to it. But can it be?
  (Am I imagining these things   890
  I see?) The man was taken off
  To jail and I lodged here within.
  My life's one cruel abyss of grief
  And pain!
DON JUAN   Oh, easily enticed!
  Is this the reason for your scorn?   895
  You hid another man inside
  Your house while I've been miserable!
  Well, that explains your cold disdain!
  Betrayer! As an age-old creed
  Forbids the venting of my rage   900
  Upon a lady for revenge,
  This stringent and despotic code
  Excusing women from the wrath
  Of retribution thus condones
  My taking vengeance on your love!   905
DOÑA ANA   Don Juan, desist! Put this aside!
DON CARLOS [*Aside.*]   So many warring sentiments
  Contend in my embattled mind
  That, in this crush of clashing thoughts,
  I'd comment, but my speech grows thick.   910
  I'm trying hard to grasp this scene
  But can't make heads or tails of it.
  And heavens, Leonor's here? How?
DOÑA ANA   Desist, I said!
DON JUAN   Cruel heart, be warned!
  It's time I put your love to death!   915
      [*Knocking is heard.*]
CELIA   My lady, master's at the door.
DOÑA ANA   What say you, Celia? Now I'm doomed!
  Kind sirs, if you'd be moved to guard
  A lady's name in this tight spot,
  Remember that I had no part   920
  In letting any of you in.
  Go hide inside for now. I swear
  That I'll reveal upon the morn
  The cause behind these strange affairs
  That plague your once clear minds with doubt,   925
  For if my brother finds you here,

My life and honor may be harmed.
DON CARLOS   My lady, you may lay these fears
   To rest as far as I'm concerned
   Since I should lie before the feet   930
   Of one who sheltered me from harm.
DON JUAN   I, too, ungrateful wretch, accede,
   Although you do me great offense.
   I'll do, of course, as you command,
   For I can't see you less in debt   935
   To me than to another man.
DOÑA ANA   I'm grateful for this gesture, sir.
   Now hurry, Celia. Stash these two
   In separate rooms, for there's no doubt
   They'll need to stay beneath this roof   940
   Till dawn, when they can slip away.
CELIA   It won't be long before first light.
   Don Juan, sir, you may come with me.
   As for that specter, you decide,
   My lady, what to do with him.   945
                          [DON JUAN *exits with* CELIA.]
DOÑA ANA   Good sir, you may accommodate
   Yourself in that room there.
DON CARLOS   I fly
   And hope to God I find a way
   To break free of this messy bind!
                                      [DON CARLOS *exits.*]
DOÑA ANA   You'd also do well to retire   950
   Now, Leonor.
DOÑA LEONOR   I will at once,
   Though were it, lady, not required
   By you, my shame would keep me hid.
                                   [DOÑA LEONOR *exits.*]
DOÑA ANA   Who ever's seen confusion like
   The kind I'm witnessing tonight   955
   Transpire within a few hours' time?
   I'm practically beside myself!
        [CELIA *enters.*]
CELIA   He's in my chambers, lady, fit
   And safe. What else, then, might I do?
DOÑA ANA   Go down and let my brother in.   960
   For now, that should be all, I think.
CELIA [*Aside.*]   Just look at her, so gripped by fears
   She quite forgot to ask me how
   Don Juan contrived to enter here.
   Now that she's out of danger, though,   965
   I'll come up with some pale excuse,
   Attributing the blame for it
   To some dishonest servant's ruse.
   When many maids work side by side,
   A lot of them you just can't trust,   970

For they'll protect their kind with lies
Or else make accusations up.

[CELIA *exits.*]

DOÑA ANA   Sweet Lord, the trials I've endured
Since fair Don Carlos stole my love!
Don Juan pursues me to no end,   975
My rival lodges in my house,
The servants threaten my good name
And now my brother prowls about!
He's here—I'll put a good face on.

[DON PEDRO *enters.*]

DON PEDRO   Dear sister! Up? Your fond regard   980
For me is everywhere on view
When you repay this loving heart
Awake and dressed to greet the sun
And me at just the crack of dawn.
Where did you stash my Leonor?   985
DOÑA ANA   I asked the lady to withdraw
To my own chambers till such time
As you, dear brother, should return—
But, goodness, what kept you so long?
DON PEDRO   A pesky kinsman noticed her   990
As we were making our escape
And Carlos nearly did him in
With one thrust when the two crossed swords.
Well, seeing what an uproar this
Had caused, though no one spied her face   995
Or knew with whom the lady fled,
To make sure all that ruckus posed
My plotted getaway no threat,
I bade a couple serving men
Pick up her wounded relative   1000
And see the wretch transported home,
Thus feigning that I pitied him.
With Carlos taken prisoner,
The others seized my Leonor
So she could be brought here to you.   1005
Until I saw the calm restored,
I didn't dare to leave the scene.
DOÑA ANA   Well, I commend your vigilance,
For this delay returning home
Protected many souls from risk.   1010
DON PEDRO   You show sound judgment on all things.
So, I'm assuming you would urge
That I leave Leonor alone
For now to rest here undisturbed
As she is, after all, our guest?   1015
I'll let my protestations wait,
As time's march favors me in this.
That suitor isn't worth his name
Who'd put his own desires before

The wellbeing of his ladylove.   1020
Besides, I think you need some rest,
As you've experienced enough
Excitement lately thanks to me
And would do well to get some sleep.
DOÑA ANA   To serve you, brother, I'd delight   1025
In facing perils worse than these,
For our two hearts so beat as one,
Your sorrows register as mine
And it occurs to me right now
As I rehearse them in my mind   1030
That your affliction and my own
Are born of similar concerns.
DON PEDRO   I well believe all that you say.
DOÑA ANA [Aside.]   If you but understood these words . . .
DON PEDRO   Come on, then, let us each to bed,   1035
If any lover finds repose.
DOÑA ANA [Aside.]   Let I, who also love, find rest,
As if repose soothed lovers' souls.
DON PEDRO [Aside.]   Oh Love, if you encourage schemes,
Inspire hopes to bolster me.   1040
DOÑA ANA [Aside.]   Oh Love, if you are care itself,
Then help my careful acts succeed!

                          [DON PEDRO and DOÑA ANA exit.]

Song

María,[1] you're so beautiful
That lesser sun ascendant here
Conceals the essence of his rays
When radiance such as yours appears!
With eyes like sky-blue orbs that cast   5
Celestial beams upon all men,
You rule as arbiter of light
By opening or closing them.
To prove they share the properties
That every dazzling sun can boast,   10
They've mined the minerals in your hair
And turned them into shining gold
As in King Solomon's Ophir,[2]
So that the wind's capricious force,
Whipped up in tempests rarely seen,   15
Produces gusts of gilded storms
Without a glimpse of black in sight.
It's just as well that duskier shades
Don't sit atop so fair a head
And leave their shadowy tincts in place;   20

1. This song is addressed to the vicereine, María Luisa Manrique de Lara.
2. Ophir is a gold-producing region described in the Book of Kings and Chronicles in the Old
   Testament. King Solomon's fleet brought gold and other riches back from the region.

More common beauties should be left
With hues that glimmer black, like jet,
As if recurring so to charms
Employed by beggar goddesses.
Those flaxen tresses on your brow   25
Adorn it like a crown of locks,
Bright golden gleams of light streaked red
Upon a diamond mountaintop
Like drifts of snow that give your skin
So niveous a natural tint   30
That they confirm how fair you are
In awe of one so delicate.[3]
Celestial Lysi, in the end
Forgive these lines if they're inept:
My bark, launched on your perfect sea,   35
Proved fragile and beyond its depth.
Yet who among us has the skill
To leave your qualities well served?
Extol yourself, as you alone
Can voice the reverence you deserve.   40

First Interlude at the Palace

CHARACTERS

MAGISTRATE
LOVE
FLATTERY
RESPECT
COURTLINESS
HOPE

[The MAGISTRATE enters, singing.]
MAGISTRATE   As Magistrate where suitors woo,
    It's my intention at the court
    To make the palace figures found
    Here into figures of pure thought.
    For metaphysics rules the day   5
    As these conceits materialize.
    Onstage the finest beings are those
    Of metaphysical design.
    So let them all be seen in turn
    Because, though concepts can't be glimpsed,   10
    They will seem real here, never mind
    That Plato be displeased with this![1]

---

3. Sor Juana emphasizes conventional European ideals of beauty that privileged fairness and blond hair. This is particularly striking in a Mexican context, where there was an increasing mix of peoples and ethnicities over the course of the seventeenth century.
1. The Greek philosopher Plato insisted on the immaterial essence of things and the inability of the senses to grasp them.

Ambassador of ladies' scorn
Am I, yet I could scarce be called
The master of their favor since   15
No favor thrives mid palace halls.
Thus scorn remains the prize today,
Vain laurels only sweat can earn,
Though such an accolade is won
Precisely when it's least deserved.   20
So enter, Beings, and show yourselves
Before it grows too late!
Impatience flourishes
At court, where no one waits.
          [LOVE *enters, hooded.*]
LOVE   I enter first, Sir Magistrate,   25
To see if I deserve to win.
MAGISTRATE   Who are you, then?
LOVE   My name is Love.
MAGISTRATE   But why come with your face half hid?
LOVE   Because, though oft at court, I'm quite
Delinquent.
MAGISTRATE   Well, if that's the truth,   30
Why come around the court at all?
LOVE   It's something that I have to do
Despite the blame I get for it
To exculpate a greater fault.
MAGISTRATE   How's that?
LOVE   Whoever doesn't love   35
At court appears a vulgar sort.
The lesser of two evils, then,
Compels this frequency of calls.
MAGISTRATE   For that you think you merit such
A prize?
LOVE   I do.
MAGISTRATE   Then you're a dunce!   40
Who said scorn should be wasted on
As meritless a thing as Love?
[*Singing.*] So off the stage with you!
You claimed to have aspired
To ladies' scorn, although   45
It's favor you desire!
                              [LOVE *exits and* FLATTERY *enters.*]
FLATTERY   My dear Sir Magistrate, I trust
The same could not be said of me.
MAGISTRATE   And you are . . . ?
FLATTERY   Flattery, of course,
Required of all those men who'd seek   50
To woo a lady at the court.
MAGISTRATE   All well and good, but why compete
For this award when you're required?
Now, there's a way to go for broke!
It sounds like you're in debt to us   55

But still believe it's you we owe!
(*Singing.*) So off the stage with you!
How ladies all behave!
They love incurring costs
Their suitors have to pay!   60

[FLATTERY *exits and* RESPECT *enters.*]

RESPECT   I come next, honorable sir,
The most esteemed of beings you've met,
To claim the prize that you'd confer.
MAGISTRATE   And who might you be?
RESPECT   I'm Respect.
MAGISTRATE   I couldn't give it to you, then.   65
RESPECT   Why not?
MAGISTRATE   Because awarding it
Would mean your downfall at the court.
RESPECT   How so?
MAGISTRATE   What gods would freely give
To mortal men may never be
Solicited. You can't contend   70
For such a prize and not display
A shameful disrespect for them.
(*Singing.*) So off the stage with you!
What good's elicited
To have Respect fall short   75
In several respects?

[RESPECT *exits and* COURTLINESS *enters.*]

COURTLINESS   Of all pretenders, only I
Deserve to claim this prize, good sir.
MAGISTRATE   And your name would be . . . ?
COURTLINESS   Courtliness.
You'll see things are as I've affirmed.   80
MAGISTRATE   What basis have you for this claim?
COURTLINESS   Well, I'm attentive and refined,
Both humble and obsequious,
Watch over friends with eagle eyes
And love but for sweet love's own sake.   85
MAGISTRATE   You lie with what you've just put forth,
For if you only loved for love,
The outcome being ladies' scorn,
You wouldn't seek this dubious crown
Because it's deemed an accolade.   90
Now that I know you well enough,
As far as I can ascertain,
You really can't be Courtliness.
COURTLINESS   What makes you see things otherwise?
MAGISTRATE   Come here. Did you yourself not say   95
That you were Courtliness?
COURTLINESS   That's right.
MAGISTRATE   And you don't see why this can't be?
COURTLINESS   How is it evident to you?
MAGISTRATE   Your very words belie your cause.

Were you a genuine lover, you'd   100
Revere your ladylove and hold
Her person in such high esteem,
It wouldn't cross your mind to think
Your love for her could ever be
Remotely worthy of her charms.   105
However great this passion was,
You'd be compelled to certify
The object greater than the love,
Admitting that, for all one does,
Love cannot truly be repaid.   110
Thus, acting courtly and refined
Means loving absent gauche displays.
[*Singing.*] So off the stage with you!
Let Courtliness be known
By quiet gallantry   115
And not through flashy shows.
                    [COURTLINESS *exits and* HOPE *enters, veiled.*]
HOPE   Sir Magistrate, just having learned
That there's a competition on
To see who merits ladies' scorn,
I'm keen to seek the victor's palm.   120
MAGISTRATE   Say who you are and I'll be judge
Of what you might deserve.
HOPE   I can't—
My banishment would come forthwith
If you discovered who I am.
MAGISTRATE   But how could I confer this win   125
If you stay unidentified?
HOPE   Why, isn't it enough to hear
That no one's worthier of this prize?
MAGISTRATE   If you won't tell me who you are
And I don't have the slightest clue,   130
How could your vaunted victory
Be warranted when I've no proof?
So shed the fear that grips you now
Of exile from these palace halls.
I pardon you for all past crimes,   135
No matter if they're thousands strong.
Unveil yourself, then.
HOPE   Now you see—
I'm Hope.
MAGISTRATE   I can't believe my eyes!
But you're a commoner, low-born!
HOPE   I don't know why you're so surprised;   140
I've always frequented the court,
Where I go by an alias.
MAGISTRATE   What name do you assume?
HOPE   Distrust,
I'm called, by the intelligent,
And that's true on the outside, though   145

       I'm all Hope when you peer within.
       So, hearing this event announced,
       I've come to see my victory clinched,
       For let's be honest, Hope alone
       Deserves a heap of palace scorn.   150
MAGISTRATE   That isn't true, for scorn acquires
       A kind of substance at the court
       In emanating from the mouths
       Of ladies, lingering on their lips
       Before resounding in the air   155
       As echoes prone to vanishing.
       Yes, this makes cool disdain a prize
       That each contestant seeks to win
       And one especially apt for those
       Quick-witted, clever and well-schooled.   160
       It isn't meet that ladies waste
       Disdainful commentary on fools.
       [*Singing.*] So off the stage with you,
       Impostor with two names!
       For all your faking, Hope   165
       Remains a low-born dame.
       Thus ends this cavalcade
       Of figures marching by
       Without a one that rates
       To carry off this prize.   170
       So all should know disdain
       From ladies may at turns
       Be readily attained,
       Though never truly earned.
       Let all five enter, then,   175
       So each may here admit
       That none who seeks this prize
       Can ever look to win.
          [LOVE, FLATTERY, RESPECT, COURTLINESS, *and* HOPE *enter.*
          Each sings a brief song.]
LOVE   Yes, everything you say is right,
       For even though Love rules,   180
       True Love, indeed, is Flattery
       And not what contracts move.
FLATTERY   No, neither is it Flattery
       Since serving at the court
       As much as one's allowed to do   185
       Becomes its own reward.
RESPECT   Respect has nothing coming, then,
       For anything it's shown
       Since no one in this life is paid
       Exactly what he's owed.   190
COURTLINESS   That goes for Courtliness as well,
       For when you think of it,
       Refinement can't be chanced upon
       Where it's imperative.

HOPE I'm Hope, though being who I am   195
Entitles me to nil.
From this day on, I'll change my name
To "Hopeless" like my ilk.
MAGISTRATE So hear ye all who would attend
At palace seeking scorn: 200
Disdain is near impossible
To merit at the court.

Act II

[DON CARLOS *enters with* CHESTNUT.]
DON CARLOS Oh, I'm beside myself with care!
CHESTNUT While I, who've always followed you,
Slept self-contained the whole night through,   1045
Just drowsing by my own self there.
DON CARLOS You haven't heard what came about?
It must have been a dream I had.
CHESTNUT I'm sure it was, though I might add
I, too, dreamt as I slept, knocked out   1050
Like some grand dame till morning's light.
Those clothes that Leonor gave me
Before she fled turned out to be
My pillow and my bed last night.
DON CARLOS You mean, as we were set to skip,   1055
She left you with her finest dress?
CHESTNUT It's not just me, I must confess,
To whom your lady gave the slip!
DON CARLOS Where are these garments?
CHESTNUT   Over there.
I'm trying hard to break them in.   1060
I've borne their weight and now they've been
Here bearing mine—it's only fair!
DON CARLOS I've seen her, so I know full well
She's here, unless I've got loose screws.
CHESTNUT Well, you know what they say, sir: lose   1065
A cow, you think you hear its bell.
It's clear the night's reversals shook
Your mind, for losing Leonor
And wanting all you had before,
You see her everywhere you look.   1070
But, who's the new gal? What's the whole
Idea behind this escapade?
May God take pity on the maid
The way she pitied this poor soul!
The moment that I came to see   1075
That you both had begun to chat,
I tried to fall asleep so that
You'd have a little privacy.
DON CARLOS Don't speak as if she'd ill repute.

As nothing that I'd planned went right,   1080
She harbored both of us last night
With those police in hot pursuit.
Thus ministering to me, she gave
Her promise I'd be free of care
And hid me in her chambers, where   1085
I learned her brother was the brave
Don Pedro. There I'd rest serene,
Pledged Doña Ana on her name,
And even if her brother came,
Assured me I'd remain unseen.   1090
With all these shows of courtesy
And plights of faith that she'd confess,
Her stunning beauty still seemed less
Immense than her gentility.
Discreet but flattering, she began   1095
To praise me in a certain guise
That I'd have taken otherwise
Were I a different sort of man.
But these are thoughts that whims impart
To striplings who, in arrogance,   1100
Take kindness as an inference
Of each maid's acquiescent heart.
With errant malice so misplaced,
The self-complacent take as proof
That any girl who's not aloof   1105
Conversely has to be unchaste.
So, subject to this bitter pill
Of fancy rash men take for fact,
No wonder women never act
So well as when they're treated ill!   1110
Attention of this nature can't befit
Presumptuous men and may evince
Real harm to the conceited since
They have no rightful claim on it.
See? Getting back to last night, though: 1115
Once I'd received her guarantee,
She looked on me most favorably,
Old Chestnut—almost too much so!
She lent a sympathetic ear
To all I'd been through, promising   1120
That she would look to everything
Provided that I sheltered here.
Discreetly, thus, she saw it meet
To seek my safety best she could
And cited dangers to me should   1125
I venture out into the street.
The thought of leaving her abode
Appeared impossible just then
Until things changed, as you'll learn when
You hear the following episode: 1130

Conditions being as I'd made known,
We of a sudden heard, it seems,
Another woman's frantic screams
From some room just outside our own.
Though Doña Ana tried, of course,   1135
To block my wandering about,
Through sheer persistence I won out
And overtook her pleas by force.
A maid who'd heard the same uproar
Came running with a candle's light   1140
Whose gleams afforded me a sight
Of Leonor.
CHESTNUT   Who?
DON CARLOS   Leonor.
CHESTNUT   Which Leonor? What, in a dream?
Who ever heard such silly rot?
I knew you were half bats, but not   1145
Delusional to this extreme!
Sir, now you're scaring me real bad!
Why don't we take things nice and slow?
It's all right to be daft, you know,
But Jesus, not stark-raving mad!   1150
You're acting like some moonstruck pup—
And once a month to be a loon
Is fine, since howling at the moon
Can get a young man's gander up—
But this derangement's unrestrained!   1155
If neighbors heard you talk this way,
They'd watch your movements night and day,
Assuming you were addle-brained.
DON CARLOS   Were I not where I am, you cur,
I'd . . .
CHESTNUT   Easy! There's no cause for war.   1160
I've also seen your Leonor.
DON CARLOS   You have? Where?
CHESTNUT   In your pocket, sir,
A lady painted,[1] so to speak,
Whose likeness looked to be alive
As if my looking could contrive   1165
To bring those blushes to her cheek.
I wavered, having only glanced
Upon her face, but soon inferred
That, as your love said not a word,
She'd been cosmetically enhanced!   1170
DON CARLOS   What bunk!
CHESTNUT   Don't fly into a huff
Because she looked alive to me:
I've been around enough to see
Live painted ladies strut their stuff.

---

1. Portrait miniatures were often exchanged and carried by lovers.

DON CARLOS   Her beauty rivals our sun's, right,   1175
   So why need makeup, do you think?
CHESTNUT   Perhaps so, but a touch of pink
   Could only make her shine more bright.
   Still, if you did spy Leonor,
   What is it you would plan to do?   1180
DON CARLOS   I guess I'd wait until I knew
   What factors brought her to this door.
   It might have been my lucky star
   That led her to this stopping place
   And, if that is indeed the case,   1185
   We might as well stay where we are.
   I think it would be better, then,
   To watch how incidents proceed
   And find out whether I've a need
   To carry off my love again.   1190
CHESTNUT   How right you are, sir! Now look front
   And center: heading straight our way
   Is—so it seems by light of day—
   The house's maid.
DON CARLOS   What could she want?
   [CELIA enters.]
CELIA   I pray you, sir, my mistress sends   1195
   Word urging you to step outside
   Into our garden plot and bide
   There some, as master now intends
   To pass through chambers on this floor
   And seeing you would mean your doom.   1200
   [Aside.] Her real fear is that, from this room,
   Don Carlos might spy Leonor.
DON CARLOS   Then let her in all confidence
   Know I obey.
                                        [DON CARLOS exits.]
CELIA   My work's done here.
CHESTNUT   Now hear, good lady, be a dear . . .   1205
CELIA   What's there to hear?
CHESTNUT   My penitence.
CELIA   The rascal's pretty good at woo;
   You don't hear that from many men.
CHESTNUT   Is it not a confession when
   I start recounting sins to you?   1210
CELIA   Don't toy with my affections, cad.
   I never asked to hear the lot!
CHESTNUT   Ah, let's strike while the iron's hot
   And have fun while it may be had!
CELIA   I told you—I'm not interested!   1215
CHESTNUT   Why all this fierce resistance, dove?
   With two of us, cooped up, in love,
   My options here are limited.
   Why would a servant act so vain?

CELIA   Hey, who's a servant, you dish rag?   1220
CHESTNUT   Oh, hush! I'm only being a wag
Because you're acting so inane.
CELIA   I have to go but, in a bit
I may be back, if that's your game.
                                                    [CELIA exits.]
CHESTNUT   A game it is, my jaunty dame,   1225
So you know two can play at it.
                [CHESTNUT exits. DOÑA LEONOR and DOÑA ANA enter.]
DOÑA ANA   Ah, Leonor! Did you sleep well
Last night?
DOÑA LEONOR   My lady, would that you'd
Not asked this very thing of me,
In truth.
DOÑA ANA   But why not? [Aside.] Oh, the cruel   1230
Requirements of courtesy
Toward one who rivals me in love!
DOÑA LEONOR   Your asking this demands I give
An answer you can only judge
A flattering "yes" or thankless "no."   1235
In either case, I'll likely find
Both fail me in this circumstance
Because your honor and my plight
Are so inexorably at odds
That an affirmative reply   1240
Would doubtless sound obsequious,
A negative one, impolite.
DOÑA ANA   Your wisdom and your loveliness
Strike me as incompatible.
Yes, it's a pity one so wise   1245
Should also be this beautiful.
DOÑA LEONOR   Since your fair features, lady, have
Instilled in you the confidence
To think yourself the prettiest
Of all, of course you're generous   1250
In praising women you don't see
Competing with you on those grounds.
DOÑA ANA   How are you faring, given all
Your recent cares?
DOÑA LEONOR   I flail about
Amid this storm, a sailor poised   1255
To view his vessel wrecked—
One minute keel hits ocean floor;
My stern juts in the air the next.
[Aside.] How ever could I find the words—
My heart is fluttering, I'm so faint!—   1260
To ask why Carlos should be here?
What's left for me to be afraid
Of when I choke on jealousy's
Cruel poison after all my woes?

DOÑA ANA   Please do speak freely, Leonor.   1265
DOÑA LEONOR   Forgive me, but I need to know—
As I've confessed my love to you,
It would be ludicrously coy
Of me to feign insouciance
About the one thing at this point   1270
You're well aware I must be told.
And so I'll ask you, lady, straight—
As you know Carlos owns my heart
And last night we became engaged—
What circumstances led him here?   1275
DOÑA ANA   I'd much prefer not answering such
A pressing question at this time.
DOÑA LEONOR   Why not?
DOÑA ANA   Because right now I trust
That listening to some singing might
Divert you.
DOÑA LEONOR   On the contrary: 1280
My pain will only be assuaged
When I hear the reply I seek,
So if you will . . .
DOÑA ANA   I'll only say
For now the whole affair transpired
By chance. Shhh! Let's be mum. Here comes   1285
My brother.
DOÑA LEONOR   Maybe I should hide
Somewhere again.
DOÑA ANA   There's no need to:
I've told him of the bind you're in,
Presuming he'd divine a way
To end this strange predicament,   1290
For somehow men prove more adept
At dealing with these challenges
Than we.
DOÑA LEONOR   I'm certain you're correct,
So what's still causing me distress?
          [DON PEDRO *enters.*]
Good heavens, what's this I behold?   1295
This man can't be your brother, right?
DON PEDRO   Yes, lovely Leonor, I'm he.
You look surprised.
DOÑA LEONOR [*Aside.*]   I'm frozen like
A statue! Fortune, you are cruel
To pile woes on me for sport   1300
And lead me to Don Pedro's house.
I'm lost!
DON PEDRO   My lovely Leonor,
You're absolutely safe with me.
You'll leave here with your honor whole,
However sizable the cost—   1305

A thousand human lives, nay, souls!—
Secure from slander's idle threat.
DOÑA LEONOR   For this attention to my pains,
Don Pedro, you've my gratitude.
DON PEDRO   Dear lady, though the angry waves   1310
Of your disfavoring fortune hurled
You unattended on these shores,
Let no man claim than no man sought
To see your happiness restored.
I've shown you my devotion all   1315
These days, which met with cold disdain
That's served no other purpose than
To purify these acts of grace,
Though courtliness at any cost
Makes one seem graciously aloof.   1320
You're sheltered now at my estate,
Where catering to your every mood,
Desire and need is our intent
Until you feel you own these halls.
Good sister, look to Leonor.   1325
DOÑA ANA   Where's Celia?
    [CELIA enters.]
CELIA   Lady, did you call?
DOÑA ANA   Have Clori sing with Laura, then.
    [Aside.] And once you've looked to that, it seems
The time would never be more ripe
For carrying out a brilliant scheme   1330
I've improvised: you'll deftly lead
Don Carlos to that grating there
So he can see us talk, but not
Hear every word we will have aired.
We'll wait to see, then, whether this   1335
Design achieves its goal and sows
A seed of jealousy in him,
For though this green-eyed monster boasts
A knack for fanning flames of love,
It doesn't operate alike   1340
With women who are being wooed
And those who are already wives:
With wives, suspicion leads to rage;
With sweethearts, doubt leaves men bewitched.
Now tell the girls we'll have that song.   1345
CELIA   That first, and then the other thing.
                                [CELIA exits.]

DON PEDRO   Oh, lovely Leonor! Indulge
This supplicant and let me break
A vow of silence keeping me
From voicing amorous complaints,   1350
For what man tormented by love
Will not cry out in agony?

What defect in my passion prompts
This constant scorn with which you greet
My suing? Has this decorous   1355
Attention caused you some offense?
If falling for you is a crime,
How is it all the other men
Transgressing with the same misdeed
Receive a lighter punishment?   1360
If scorn's the justice those fair looks
Dispense with cool indifference,
Why must my sentence be so harsh
When other judgments are more slight?
How is it that you find his love   1365
So much more favorable than mine
And show such mercy toward his pain
When love is all the same in us?
You look upon my own as sin
While his shines meritorious!   1370
If he seemed far superior
Is there no chance devotion could
Prevail and my regard for you
Make up for what I lack in looks?
This very quality I own,   1375
A gentleman's polite reserve,
May be to blame, for happiness
Bides often where it's least deserved.
But since I'm fated to adore
You, mistress, till the end of time,   1380
Well might you keep this prize withheld
As long as you would recognize
The courtly way I pressed my love
While you held mercy for me back.
DOÑA LEONOR   Don Pedro, while you heap this flight   1385
Of honors on me, may I ask,
In light of your exalted name,
For still another greater yet?
As you've observed how Fate's conspired
To bring my fortunes low, I beg   1390
Of you, don't add now to these woes:
The shame I feel of ill repute
And all the cares I bear are far
Worse penalties than any noose.
My good name sorely compromised   1395
And all these pressing griefs at hand,
It hardly seems appropriate
To dally in this circumstance—
Not your sweet wooing of my heart
Nor my attending here to it.   1400
I'm pleading with you—pray, be mum
Unless your love has plotted this
To seek revenge on my disdain,

In which case, bring it to an end.
These sorrows that I feel of late   1405
Have in themselves seen you avenged.
    [DON PEDRO *and* DOÑA LEONOR *continue talking to one*
    side while DON CARLOS, CELIA, *and* CHESTNUT *enter at*
    the grating.]
CELIA   Stop! You can only come this far,
For even though my lady said
You ought to stay inside, I thought
I'd grant this harmless favor, gents,   1410
By letting you, behind this grille,
Catch soothing strains my master's meant
To entertain a certain maid
He so adores his head spins round
Just thinking of her. Listen here.   1415
CHESTNUT   Hear me out first.
CELIA   I can't right now.
    [CELIA *exits, then re-enters on the other side of the stage.*]
CHESTNUT   She's gone and locked the door on us
Like nuns eavesdropping at a grate!
Now all we need's a prioress
To overhear the things we say!   1420
    [CHESTNUT *moves closer and peers through the bars.*]
Good lord, now I'm the one who's nuts!
Your virulent insanity
Must be contagious. I just caught
Your madness, sir!
DON CARLOS   By which you mean . . .
CHESTNUT   Not only do I hear the bell,   1425
I think I even see the horns!
Looks like the cows are coming home!
    [DON CARLOS, *too, moves closer to the bars.*]
DON CARLOS   What's this? Love, don't leave me forlorn!
Don Pedro, Doña Ana, and . . .
And Leonor? Now she's appeared   1430
Two times, so this can't be a ghost.
CHESTNUT   And you're not angry that she's here?
DON CARLOS   No, not until I find out why.
I've taken refuge here myself
Through no fault of my own, so how   1435
Could I assume that sin compelled
Her stopping at this house and not
Good Fortune's merciful resolve
To see us reunited thus?
CHESTNUT   Most lovers wouldn't be so calm   1440
And I've seen you less rational.
What if Don Pedro seized the day
And, grabbing this bull by the horns,
Grabbed Leonor some other ways?
Huh? How would you react to that?   1445
DON CARLOS   Look, Chestnut, why don't you shut up?

It's vile for a gentleman
To intimate he might distrust
A lady whom he much adores,
Thus causing her undue offense.   1450
Should he commit so base an act,
It serves him right that she offends.
But list! They tune their instruments.
DOÑA ANA   Let's hear that song!
CELIA   Some music, then!
MUSIC   Of all the woes in Love's domain,   1455
Which causes hearts the sharpest pain?
1ST VOICE   Not basking in a lover's glow
Is still the gravest ill I know.
That has to be Love's greatest grief.
1ST CHORUS   Not true.
1ST VOICE   That's my belief.   1460
2ND CHORUS   Don't you agree?
2ND VOICE   The jealous flights
That oft occasion sleepless nights
Can boast no rival for distress.
2ND CHORUS   You think so?
2ND VOICE   I do, yes.
1ST CHORUS   Don't you concur?
3RD VOICE   The restless urge   1465
That absence forces to emerge
Can waken fatal lethargies.
1ST VOICE   It's not that.
3RD VOICE   As you please.
2ND CHORUS   You don't agree?
4TH VOICE   The constant cares
Incited by these love affairs   1470
Make happiness a futile aim.
2ND CHORUS   Not so.
4TH CHORUS   Still, that's my claim.
1ST CHORUS   Do you dissent?
5TH VOICE   Should Love begrudge
A worthy suitor, let all judge
This cruelest of all passion's woes.   1475
1ST CHORUS   Untrue.
5TH VOICE   No, this voice knows.
2ND CHORUS   Of all who gave responses here
About Love's griefs, it would appear
That only you know Love's worst bane.
1ST CHORUS   Of all the woes in Love's domain,   1480
Which causes hearts the sharpest pain?
DON PEDRO   The answer that first singer gave
Among the ones who sang just now
Still resonates with me somehow.
The harshest pain a man must brave   1485
In love will always be more grave
Than any other one he'll know:

Not basking in his lover's glow,
Which may lead to eternal night.
DOÑA LEONOR   You're wrong.
DON PEDRO   I'm sure I'm right.   1490
DOÑA ANA   Good brother, I think differently
About these things for, in the end,
The pain with which hearts most contend
Is born of their own jealousy.
Despite the abject misery   1495
A lack of favor can instill,
Green envy is a greater ill
And may inflict a mortal blow.
DOÑA LEONOR   That's not true.
DOÑA ANA   Yes, it's so.
DOÑA LEONOR   Though this conceit seem far off track,   1500
The worst I feel that could befall
A lover is to taste the gall
Of his or her beloved's lack
For, wanting this lost lover back
And all the love their bonds bestow   1505
Does naught but make the passion grow,
Which leaves the lover more distraught.
DOÑA ANA   Not so.
DOÑA LEONOR   Well, that's my thought.
DON CARLOS   Oh, Chestnut! Here I would have said
Love's bane is just those jealous flights   1510
And what comes with them—sleepless nights—
If I'd dared heap them on my head.
As Love would rather see me dead,
Though, let me die from fear of these
Instead of from their maladies,   1515
For that would be too much to bear.
CHESTNUT   That so?
DON CARLOS   It is, I swear.
CHESTNUT   Sir, Love can make guys throw a fit
Or hurt a working man's morale.
If I should spy some servant gal   1520
But have no money to permit
My courting her a little bit,
What other state could so abash
A lover than a lack of cash,
Which thwarts a blossoming romance?   1525
MUSIC   That's not correct.
CHESTNUT   Fat chance.
CELIA   I say the greatest discontent
That Love could proffer comes about
When not one footman takes me out
Or shows me any lavishment.   1530
That's why my hunger won't relent!
I'm fed up having to behave
Like some poor seamstress left to crave

A thimble that would comfort me.
MUSIC   Indeed!
CELIA   Just wait and see.   1535
DOÑA ANA   Dear Leonor, if music fails
To soothe you now, let's sit outside
Awhile. Our garden's sure to bring
Your soul some peace.
DOÑA LEONOR   What hopes have I
For solace when my sole relief   1540
Is furnished by these bitter tears?
DON PEDRO   Oh, come now, my celestial dream.
DOÑA ANA [*Aside to* CELIA.]   Do everything I've ordered here
And soon I'll order you a dress
If everything we've planned out works.   1545
              [DON PEDRO, DOÑA ANA, *and* DOÑA LEONOR *exit.*]
CELIA [*Aside.*]   That's how to order things in style,
Although when masters say the words
"I order you," you can't be sure
It's something that they'll recollect,
As they're more used to barking out   1550
Commands than making promises.
They craft excuses for themselves,
Explaining to their hirelings
That they were giving orders when
Their servants thought they'd ordered gifts!   1555
So here's more stagecraft for you now:
I'll let those two back in again,
As it would seem the spurned Don Juan,
Who was my biggest headache, let
His own self out—and wisely, too—   1560
Not leaving so much as a trace
Behind him as he slipped off, key
In hand, and tiptoed through the gate
That opens to the garden spot.
My mistress took my words for truth   1565
When I explained some other maid
Had basely let him in her rooms.
So, thanks to my hypocrisy
And all the perjured oaths I swore
To back my fabrication up—   1570
Convincingly, not overboard—
She's reconfirmed her faith in me
And bid that I return to work
Advancing this entangled plot,
Which I'll do now. Don Carlos, sir?   1575
DON CARLOS   What is it, Celia? I'm forlorn.
CELIA   You heard the music playing, then?
It was a fine performance.
DON CARLOS   Yes,
And thank you for your thoughtfulness.

But tell me now—Don Pedro sat   1580
Alongside Doña Ana with
Another maid. Why was she here?
CELIA [*Aside.*] The fish bites! Watch me reel him in!
That lady, sir? You mean the one . . .
I'm not at liberty to say   1585
Unless I have your solemn word
You won't repeat what I relate.
DON CARLOS I promise you. Now, why'd she come?
CELIA I fear that gossiping about
What other people do's a sin,   1590
But as you've left me with no doubts
That the particular you'd know
Is just what I ought not divulge,
Here goes—you didn't hear this news
From me: that maid, a miracle   1595
Of beauty, finds herself of late
The object of my master's woo.
Last night—don't ask me how or why—
She slipped into Don Pedro's rooms.
He courts her now with blandishments   1600
To what end, I don't understand,
Nor could I in good conscience say
That anything he's done is bad.
Perhaps, his longing to become
A discalced friar explains this need.   1605
I'm sorry I can't be more help
In answering your inquiries.
I think we'd both be better off
If you'd heard this from other lips.
                              [CELIA *exits.*]
DON CARLOS Oh, Chestnut! Did you catch all that? 1610
The insult cuts me to the quick!
CHESTNUT Wait, what was there for me to catch?
She didn't tell the half of it!
DON CARLOS Just skies! Can what I've heard be true?
Is this a trance? Am I bewitched?   1615
What's happened to my reasoning?
Who am I? Where have I been borne?
Was it not I who idolized
The loveliness of Leonor,
Attending her with such gay charm   1620
And serving her with so much grace
That she looked favorably on me,
Rewarding my indulgent ways
Until I felt assured I'd won
Her hand of alabaster white,   1625
The only happy man in all
That wretched lot she'd left behind?
Did she not flee with me last night,

Abandoning her sire and home,
And thus confer the happiness   1630
So many sought on me alone?
Was she not captured by the law?
Oh, how is it I find her now
So well accommodated here
In Pedro Arellano's house?   1635
The man pursues her for his wife
While I . . . No, better I should burn
My lips off than so fruitlessly
Recite the ways that I've been hurt.
But heavens! Couldn't Leonor   1640
Have made it to this house by chance
And therefore not share any blame
For being with another man
Since she could scarce forestall events?
And can't Don Pedro, knowing well   1645
He has at last this paragon
Of beauty now to his own self
Alone here, sheltered in his house—
He's quite a strapping lad—yes, can't
He take advantage of the luck   1650
That Fortune's placed into his hands
Without my steadfast Leonor
Succumbing as he turns more bold?
I'm certain this could be the case.
Am I upholding honor's code,   1655
Though, letting my sworn rival woo
The woman I would make my wife
With Time's slow march a favoring crawl
That keeps him at my loved one's side?
And could I really be so base   1660
To stand by idly thus and watch
As Pedro plies her with his suit
While I do naught to see it stopped?
Good heavens, no! This can't persist!
Come, Chestnut, it's high time we went   1665
To rescue Leonor in spite
Of Lord knows just how many men
Who'll rally round Don Pedro's cause.
CHESTNUT   Sir, are you nuts, for crying out loud?
Or haven't you discerned the troop   1670
Of footmen waiting in this house
Who'll give us, clear of prying eyes,
Lord knows how many painful whacks
And be commended for their pains
As loyal servitors? You're mad!   1675
DON CARLOS   What, coward? Answer me like that?
Let thunder make the heavens roar
And angry skies hurl down their wrath!

Let hell below spew terrors forth,
Yet I will free sweet Leonor!   1680
CHESTNUT   If that's your plan, then our first step
Must be to find her. Traipsing toward
The gallows surely is our next.
    [DON RODRIGO *and* DON JUAN *enter.*]
DON RODRIGO   As you're Don Pedro's friend, Don Juan,
Do what you can to change his mind.   1685
My bringing you was thus designed
So he could be prevailed upon.
You've witnessed how these goings-on
With Leonor aroused alarm
And brought my family honor harm.   1690
Now you alone can speak with him
To make him see my plight is grim—
But use soft words so they'll disarm.
I've told you the particulars;
It's best, when men negotiate,   1695
To have third parties mediate
And not those whom a grievance spurs.
An insult to such nobles stirs
A passion in their highborn breasts
That, fight it as they try to, tests   1700
Their mettle, which they come to see
As shame, not insult's remedy,
The reason why the insult rests.
DON JUAN   Good Don Rodrigo, I in strict
Compliance with chivalric law   1705
Assure you that Don Pedro will
Be brought around to your just cause.
I know him to be reasonable,
So wouldn't wish you to infer
His change of heart were due to me   1710
And not the due your self deserves.
Lest he decline to speak with us,
It might be best if we appeared
Unheralded. [*Aside.*] But wait! Who's that?
Don Carlos de Olmedo, here?   1715
I only fought with him last night!
That ingrate, Doña Ana! What
A basilisk!²
    [CELIA *enters.*]
CELIA   Oh, Jesus Christ!
Don Juan de Vargas comes with some
Old man, sir, and they've spotted you!   1720
DON CARLOS   No matter—nothing gives me fright.
DON RODRIGO   Look, it's Don Carlos! Just our luck!
His presence here will compromise

---

2. Mythical creature, generally depicted as a snake, which could kill its victims with just a glance.

The very business we've at hand.
CHESTNUT   Start saying the Apostle's Creed,[3]   1725
For something tells me, now they're here,
That both of us might be dead meat.
They've finally realized you're the one
Who wounded Leonor's blood kin
And took her from her father's home.   1730
DON CARLOS   No matter, Chestnut, I submit,
Resigned to what may come my way.
We'd best go in now. Follow me.
DON RODRIGO   Don Carlos, young Don Juan and I
Are visiting on business we've   1735
An urgent need to carry out
With our Don Pedro at this time.
If it's no inconvenience, sir,
You'd be most kind to set aside
Your own with him and pardon us   1740
This liberty, for older men
Who deal with noble youths like you
Believe it age's privilege
To ask such things, the more so when
You're courteous and mild.
DON CARLOS [*Aside.*]   Good God!   1745
Could Don Rodrigo still not know
That I'm to answer for his lot?
DON JUAN [*Aside.*]   Good God! I don't know how I keep
My rage in check! Just setting eyes
On that Don Carlos drives me mad!   1750
CELIA [*Aside to* DON CARLOS.]   Don Carlos, think how
        compromised
You leave your love when out like this!
What if her brother sees you here?
I beg you—go inside and hide!
DON CARLOS [*Aside.*]   Good God, she's quite right, it appears!   1755
For if he does see me about,
His sister's life will be at risk
And I'll look like a cad in light
Of how she's helped me through all this.
So what's a man like me to do?   1760
As Doña Ana's honor must
Rank first, what choice have I now but
To hide here while her brother comes?
I'll take revenge soon for the wrongs
He did and envy he inflamed.   1765
CELIA [*Aside to* DON CARLOS.]   For God's sake, will you hurry up
Before Don Pedro shows his face!
DON CARLOS   Wise Don Rodrigo, you'll forgive
A roving youth's embarrassment—
The gray hairs on your snowy peak   1770

---

3. A statement of Christian belief that is part of the Mass; here, a prayer at death's door.

Instill in me profound respect—
But I pass through Don Pedro's house
Without his knowledge, so do pray
You'll understand I must abscond
Before he comes. A lady's name   1775
Requires it and gentlemen
Oblige.
DON JUAN [*Aside.*]   I, countenancing this?
He need have made it no more plain
That Doña Ana, basilisk
From hell itself, conveyed him here!   1780
Why don't I just dispatch the wretch
And bring my suffering to an end?
No, first I'll carry out my pledge
To Don Rodrigo, as I vowed
I'd serve him as a go-between.   1785
I'll just return here afterwards,
As I still have with me the key
For entering through the garden gate.
Yes, that's when I'll take my revenge!
DON RODRIGO   I'm not surprised one bit, my boy! 1790
I'm old, but had a youth well spent.
It's obvious a strapping lad
Like you will sow his wild oats,
So go about your business, then,
And find a hideout from your host   1795
If that's what need necessitates.
It's not my habit to intrude
In matters outside my concern.
DON CARLOS   God keep you, then.
DON RODRIGO   And heaven, you.
CELIA   Come on, already! [*Aside.*] Thank the Lord   1800
We rode out that predicament!
Please wait here, sir, while I inform
My master you require him.
DON CARLOS [*Aside.*]   An Etna rumbles in my soul![4]
DON JUAN [*Aside.*]   What hot volcano roils my heart?   1805
                [DON CARLOS *exits with* CELIA *and* CHESTNUT.]
DON RODRIGO   See what the world is like, my son?
Don Pedro does me grievous harm;
Don Carlos thereon injures him
While some third party hereabouts
Will doubtless do Don Carlos wrong.   1810
And all these ills the skies allow
In castigation of our sins,
Disposing that we bear the brunt
Of all such evils we endure
In just exchange for those we've done.   1815

---

4. Mount Etna, on Sicily, is the largest active volcano in Europe.

DON JUAN [*Aside.*]   Oh, I'm beside myself with rage
To have this insult trumpeted
Before my eyes! However will
I quell this lava-spewing chest
In time for me to intervene with calm   1820
And settle Don Rodrigo's case?
A man who slights his own affairs
Can hardly set another's straight.
        [DON CARLOS *enters at the grating.*]
DON CARLOS   Now that I've had to find a place
To lay low out of sheer respect   1825
For Doña Ana, whose largess
In sheltering me has saved my neck,
I'll watch here where I can't be seen
And eavesdrop on this heart-to-heart
To learn why Don Rodrigo's come,   1830
For something's sounding an alarm
In that astrologer, my soul,
Foretelling me my life's at risk.
        [DON PEDRO *enters.*]
DON PEDRO   Brave Don Rodrigo! Sir, you grace
This house! Whatever business brings   1835
Your good self here forever claims
A debt of gratitude from me
For all the honor it bestows.
DON RODRIGO   Don Pedro, these I fain receive
From you, for soon you'll be informed   1840
Of how this day lost honor's led
My steps unto your noble door.
DON PEDRO   Nor is it news, Don Juan my friend,
That you do honor us as well.
Be seated, please, so I may learn   1845
The reason you come visiting.
DON JUAN   To render you a service, sir,
And since our cause permits us no
Delay, I won't be diffident:
Don Pedro, you're aware, no doubt,   1850
That, as a proper gentleman,
You've obligations to uphold
If you would be perceived as one.
This said, our Don Rodrigo feels
Aggrieved by you, wherefore he comes   1855
To seek redress.
DON PEDRO   By me, Don Juan?
Do tell me how I've hurt your pride.
[*Aside.*] God help me! What could I have done?
DON RODRIGO   Don Pedro, this is not the time
To play the wounded innocent,   1860
Though if the wonder you've expressed
Is just your way of showing me
Due deference and kind respects,

Let gratitude for this display
Absolve you of the need for it.   1865
You acted on your own to woo
My Leonor and didn't think
To seek my aid—I, who gladly would
Have proffered it—removing her
By vile means from where she dwelt,   1870
A wrong . . . But no sense for harsh words
Right now to castigate a crime
That stole what scarce can be restored.
Why treat you with severity
When it's your mercy I implore?   1875
For if the worst can be repaired,
I'll overlook the smaller blows.
You doubtless know, as it's a fact,
The city of Toledo boasts
No nobler bloodline than my own.   1880
As this is recognized by all,
What possible objection could
You have to being my son-in-law?
If it's, perchance, because I'm poor
While you're rich, I'll remind you, sir,   1885
That I was not the one whose big
Idea it was to have the girl
Run off with you, who chose her first
And sought this of your own accord.
Now, as a gentleman, you've no   1890
Choice but to marry Leonor
As, after all, I'm not to blame
For so impetuous a flight.
I know she's somewhere in this house
And, as her father, won't abide   1895
Her staying here one moment more
Without the benefit and bond
Of matrimony.
DON PEDRO [*Aside.*]   Help me, Lord!
In this position, what response
Could counter Don Rodrigo's words?   1900
If I deny his daughter's here,
He'll easily belie the claim,
But if the truth should reach his ears
About Don Carlos taking her,
Then she'll be his and I forlorn,   1905
For losing her, I lose my life.
Yet, if I marry Leonor,
It may turn out she'll snub me
As my wife, so how now can I feign
Some way of stalling my reply?   1910
DON JUAN   What causes you to hesitate,
My friend, when this proposal lends
More honor to your noble line?

Good Don Rodrigo comes himself,
Discreet and calm as he is wise,   1915
To offer you the happiness
His daughter's beauty will confer
Upon one man to call his own.
DON PEDRO   To answer, let me just say first,
My gentle Don Rodrigo, I've   1920
Revered my fair love's beauty so
That, while you're well aware I wooed
The maid insistently, I hope
You realize that the foolish heart
Still beating in this gallant chest   1925
Could scarce bring me to look on her
Or speak to her with base intent.
My only wish of wedded bliss
Prevailing yet, be here apprized
That last night Leonor found out   1930
(I'm really bad at telling lies!)
My sister had just taken ill
And, as your daughter's high esteem
For Doña Ana won the day,
She came alone in the belief,   1935
Sir, that you'd likely be delayed
By the distraction cards provide.
Once night had fallen, though, she feared
She wouldn't make it home in time
Since she'd gone off without your leave.   1940
To ascertain, then, who'd be first
To reach your door, we hastily
Dispatched a footman, who returned
Soon to inform us all that you,
Indeed, were in your house and, vexed   1945
At finding Leonor not there,
Reacted as one might expect
And left to look for her, aggrieved,
All news sufficient to deter
Her coming back to face her sire.   1950
In brief, sirs, that is what occurred.
I neither snatched fair Leonor
From you nor could, my fond intent
Remaining that we two be wed.
To fail so as a gentleman   1955
Would mean my gazing on a face
Forever sullied in my glass.
And just so you won't take these words
As tactics to delay our banns
Which I've just artfully contrived,   1960
You have, good sir, my solemn pledge
That I will marry Leonor
The moment she's to give consent.

With this assurance, nothing more
Should stand between desire and deed   1965
Unless my own unworthiness
Prevent our being family.
DON CARLOS   God, Chestnut, did you hear that speech?
I've lost my mind and now my life!
CHESTNUT   The stuff about your life is new,   1970
But not that part about your mind.
DON RODRIGO   Don Pedro, far be it for me
To doubt your version of events
Or hint it isn't possible
They happened as you narrate them.   1975
The fact is, though, as all now know
About this courtship you've pursued,
Aware that Leonor is gone
And that I seek her; knowing, too,
I found her hidden in your house,   1980
My honor cannot be restored
Until you take her for your wife.
Your worries that my Leonor
Might not be so inclined to wed
Won't keep your wish from being fulfilled,   1985
For as my daughter she can have
No pleasure but her father's will.
Go call her now. You'll see how fast
I'll set this matter straight.
DON PEDRO   I pray,
Sir, that you give the girl some time   1990
So that she won't be so afraid.
Why don't we let my sister break
The news to her? It's obvious
I'm keen to be espoused at once
And thus assume my happiness,   1995
So why can't we put off the banns
Until the morn so as to give
Your future son-in-law the chance
To see his friends and relatives
Invited to this sacrament   2000
And us occasion in the next
Few hours to take your daughter home,
Where we two finally can be wed?
DON RODRIGO   Your idea makes much sense. So it's
Agreed: tomorrow you'll be joined   2005
To Leonor, your fiancée.
DON PEDRO   To hear this from you is pure joy!
DON RODRIGO   Until the morrow, then, my son.
I, too, must undertake my share
Of preparations.
DON PEDRO   Sire, I'll go   2010
With you to aid in these affairs.

DON RODRIGO   No need to, lad, just tarry here.
You've things to do and it grows late.
DON PEDRO   But really, I should come and help.
DON RODRIGO   You stay right here.
DON PEDRO   Then, I obey.   2015
DON JUAN   Don Pedro, God be with you, sir.
DON PEDRO   And He with you, Don Juan.

          [DON RODRIGO *and* DON JUAN *exit.*]
                             My mind
Is reeling so, I can't be sure
If what I'm feeling is a sign
Of great distress or happiness,   2020
Of sheer good fortune or tough luck.
The old man offers Leonor
To me, so marriage seems locked up.
These plans, though, have advanced so far
So fast that I could ill afford   2025
To make excuses now, though I've
Still fears concerning Leonor
And how she might refuse my hand.
It's possible, however, she'll
Take stock of things, amenable   2030
To seeing her father's wish fulfilled,
And be my wife. Now I'll head off.
Love, make that hard heart tenderer!

       [DON PEDRO *exits.* DON CARLOS *enters with* CHESTNUT.]
DON CARLOS   I can't believe I'm standing here
And didn't die to hear those words!   2035
Since Don Rodrigo wrongly thinks
Don Pedro snatched his Leonor,
He's gone and offered her to him!
The flattering rogue was in fine form,
Just all too glad to marry her   2040
Without it troubling him a mite
That she'd fled with another man.
CHESTNUT   Well, what did you expect? The guy's
As marriageable as the next
And doesn't pussyfoot around.   2045
He saw this lovely bird fly high
And aimed to bring the quarry down.
Now that she's left the nest, it seems
She's in the bag—just not with you!
DON CARLOS   I'm so beside myself from all   2050
This, Chestnut, I can scarce regroup
My thoughts or reckon what to do.
CHESTNUT   Sir, I've a foolproof remedy
By which you'll see yourself avenged:
This Doña Ana's rich and seems   2055
Just bursting to become a bride.
Go woo her till she falls in love

And reap revenge a thousand times
By having that inveterate dunce
Not out-lawed from, but in-lawed midst 2060
Hell's precincts *in aeternum*,⁵ see?
DON CARLOS A fine comeuppance that, you twit!
CHESTNUT Don't underestimate this scheme,
For by the sounds of it, you don't
Know how infernal in-laws are! 2065
Plus stepmothers, plus notaries,
Pack mules—I know this list by heart—
Aunts, innkeepers, executors . . .
Look, if you scrutinized the rolls
Of miscreants in hell, you'd find 2070
No soul in torment that could hold
A candle to their evil ways.
DON CARLOS I'm wretched, Chestnut, yet what ruse
Can I concoct to stay these banns?
Oh, Leonor, if I lose you, 2075
I'll lose my very life as well!
CHESTNUT Your life? You won't be one hair shy
If we could reach her now and have
This case that you're appealing tried
Before her privy court. Perhaps, 2080
We'll see the judgment soon reversed.
DON CARLOS And if her father forces her?
CHESTNUT What, force her now? The old man's turn
As Tarquin must be ages past.
Let's find her. Here now, don't despair, 2085
For even should her "no" sound odd,
She and Don Pedro won't be paired.
DON CARLOS You're right about this. Yes, let's go.
CHESTNUT Then come, and cut your moping short.
This whole thing will just drag on if 2090
We hang around here anymore.

Song

You, beauteous and tender bud,
Reduce the meadow's vivid blooms
To drabness as the canopy's
Refulgence pales beside your hues.
For anyone who gazes on 5
Your cherub face can plainly see
A rose's perfume blended there
With radiance from the starlight's gleam.
All-powerful Cupid, you who shoot
The sweetest arrows known to man 10

5. For all eternity (Latin).

That whistle by and wound the wind,
Which crackles to be pierced like that;
You, beautiful celestial orb,
Who'd scarcely spread your infant rays
Before our hearts were overcome   15
With joy for warmth you'd sent our way;
Oh, loving hinge, uniting blood
That erstwhile flowed in separate hearts
Which marriage bonds joined confident
They'd never have to beat apart;   20
You, eastern sky of pinkish cast,
Whose plump and rosy cheeks have wrought
A rising sun more radiant
Than that accompanying Dawn;
Oh, Mars and Venus's own son,   25
Inherit both their finest traits
So that your father's strength enfolds
You and your mother's sweet embrace!
Resplendent and beloved José,[1]
You're winning over everyone   30
In common fondness for your charms,
Uncommon in a child so young.
A nascent daystar, you reverse
That other sun's habitual flight,
Your cradle blazing in the West,   35
This new world where your rival dies.
Accept our courtly song of praise
Despite its flaws in style and form.
Why turn away this reverence
Because its eloquence falls short?   40

Second Interlude

Characters:

ARIAS
MUÑIZ
ACEVEDO
1ST COMPANION
2ND COMPANION

[MUÑIZ *and* ARIAS *enter.*]
ARIAS   So, while our fellow thespians relax
From starring in two acts
That almost took to play
The time mail takes to travel in a day,
The threat this piece will be restaged just means   5

---

1. This song is addressed to José, son of the viceregal couple, born in Mexico in 1683. He would
have been three months old when the play was first presented.

We'll all end up soon in the Philippines—
Spain's penitentiary since olden times
Where labor, too, was forced, not just these rhymes[1]—
Let's sit awhile, Muñiz my friend, and smirk
At all the imperfections of this work.   10
MUÑIZ   The idea's impudence leaves me intrigued,
But you must be fatigued
Now, Arias. Me, I've got no more to give—
I'm ground to dust, so sift me through a sieve!
Too tuckered out to lie,   15
I'm feeling pulverized and left so dry
By those two lengthy scenes you'd ridicule,
It's like I've ridden on a rented mule!
Why can't we hit the sack
And let the others go on the attack?   20
Right now, I'm rather partial to some rest.
ARIAS   Of all ways to unwind, pal, sniping's best.
I find the process leaves me fortified,
For when I keep my venom pent inside,
The poison starts to swell   25
Until I take my jabs and all is well.
MUÑIZ   You're right, I guess, although
What playwright could fool Deza[2] with a show
So plodding and contrived—
And in his home, no less?   30
ARIAS   Is that what's causing you so much distress?
A novice, Don Andrés,
Some fledgling writer, authored this disgrace.
Such youthful verse bespeaks
The fluffy down that dots his callow cheeks.   35
MUÑIZ   Well, were I barber to the hapless knave,
I'd give his clumsy lines a thorough shave,
For they'd be better borne
Once all their needless fuzziness were shorn.
To fête the viceroy here, if I may say,   40
Why didn't he just calmly choose a play
By Rojas, Calderón
Or that Moreto,[3] who are fully grown?
When viewers see their names,
On this you have my word,   45
There's not a jeer or catcall to be heard.
ARIAS   This piece was never staged
Before.
MUÑIZ   It might have aged
Some more.

---

1. The port of Cavite, in the Philippines, was the site of a prison to which convicts were sent from both Spain and New Spain. A forced verse (*verso de pie forzado*) was one for which the end-rhyme was predetermined, so that the poet had to compose the rest of the text around it.
2. The official Fernando de Deza, who commissioned the play from Sor Juana. The play was first performed in his house on October 4, 1683.
3. Francisco de Rojas (1607–1648), Pedro Calderón de la Barca (1600–1681), and Agustín Moreto (1618–1669) were three of the best-known Spanish dramatists of the time.

ARIAS   Well, that's what makes me want to jeer.
Why not perform the *Celestina*[4] here,
The second one in which you played the bawd   50
So well you left me awed
And struggling to suppose
You weren't a sorceress in manly clothes.
MUÑIZ   Of course, that play would please!   55
They're better when they come from overseas.
The ones from Spain not only are the best,
But easiest to digest.
They're light, unlike those plays that don't traverse
That waters, so are heavier and worse.   60
The *Celestina* you deem unsurpassed
In wit is more half-caste,
A patchwork quilt crocheted,
Which has its charms, but isn't quite well made,
Like sugar mills here grind,   65
Still sweet, but hardly thoroughly refined,
Though some parts that are great
Can compensate for lines that just don't rate.
Still, that's another bill. As for tonight's,
I can't abide what Acevedo[5] writes.   70
ARIAS   He penned the piece?
MUÑIZ   They say the play's by him,
The devil take the whim
From which these interludes and dramas flow!
I can't believe it, even if it's true.
ARIAS   God grant him life—but one that's dreadful, too!   75
MUÑIZ   What way to stop this nonsense can there be
So we won't have to suffer through Act Three?
ARIAS   Look here, I've got a slick
Plan up my sleeve that's sure to do the trick.
MUÑIZ   What's that?
ARIAS   We'll both pretend   80
We're groundlings[6] and, by whistling, bring an end
To this lame piece of . . . hack work, if you please.
That ought to shut down these festivities!
The players won't expect to hear us hiss
But, realizing that something is amiss,   85
Will run onstage, where they'll
Be told by us they heard the groundlings rail.
MUÑIZ   Wow, that's a clever plan! There's just one hitch:
I don't know how to hiss.

---

4. *La segunda Celestina* was an unfinished play by the Spanish playwright Agustín de Salazar. Although it was published in 1694 with an ending by Salazar's friend Juan de Vera Tassis, Sor Juana also composed an ending for the play, which remained unpublished. The reference to the "half-caste" (*mestiza*) play in this scene is evidence for her authorship.
5. Francisco de Acevedo, a contemporary of Sor Juana's, was a Mexican humanist and author of a religious play presented a year after *Trials*.
6. The groundlings (*mosqueteros*) stood in the theater courtyard instead of paying for a seat. They were the rowdiest portion of the audience and often interrupted plays as they made their dissatisfaction known.

ARIAS   Boy, there's a glitch!
But why is it so hard?
MUÑIZ   I have to say,   90
I can't pronounce the "s" the Spanish way.[7]
ARIAS   All right, then—you don't have to make a peep:
Like Sylvan in Arcadia,[8] I'll tend sheep
And whistle for us both. Now don't protest—
I only hiss for two at your behest.   95
MUÑIZ   Well said, my friend! Let's go.
ARIAS   Some brio here!
        [ARIAS hisses.]
MUÑIZ   Hey, look at me—I'm whistling loud and clear!
This drama leaves me cold for a premiere!
        [Others hiss offstage.]
Yes, gentlemen, I'm whistling loud and clear.
So let the hissing fly!   100
        [The hissing continues offstage.]
ARIAS   It's my turn. Now I'm whistling loud and clear!
        [ARIAS hisses. ACEVEDO enters with his COMPANIONS.]
ACEVEDO   What's this horrendous hissing hereabouts?
MUÑIZ   You know that poem: "The whistles and the shouts . . ."?
ACEVEDO   The groundlings whistling? Oh, they wouldn't dare!
ARIAS   Sounds like they'd take their whistling anywhere.   105
ACEVEDO   Poor whistled me! My efforts won't be missed!
To think, an Acevedo drama, hissed!
It's curtains for the play! My death is set.
ARIAS   Come on, man, don't die yet.
ACEVEDO   I'll hang myself right now.   110
MUÑIZ   Well, there's a good, stiff way to take a bow!
ACEVEDO   I'm looking for a rope.
ARIAS   There's lots to hang yourself with here, I hope.
ACEVEDO   I'll take a noose and, tightening its knot,
Extract myself from yet a tighter spot.   115
        [Each sings his quatrain in turn.]
MUÑIZ   So now that you've been roundly hissed,
Don't hang yourself, fond friend.
The whistling that I heard out there
Is specially made for men.
ACEVEDO   You sibilant devils hissed until   120
My grief was terminal.
The whistling that you heard out there
Was not for men, but bulls.
1ST COMPANION   If you're intent on suicide,
Go on and take the rope.   125
Their stringing you along like this
Does more than they had hoped.

7. Through line 136, the interlocutors poke fun at the difference between the Spanish pronoun-
   ciation of the letter "s," sometimes described as a hissing or whistling sound, and the softer
   Mexican version of the same.
8. "Sylvan" (i.e., rural, of the woods) is a conventional name for a shepherd in pastoral
   romance. Arcadia is the idealized countryside that provides the setting for the genre.

ACEVEDO   Don't hiss at me, you devil's spawn,
My mind can't process this.
As empty-headed as I am,   130
Your disapproval stings.
ARIAS   Then let the hissing fly anew
And whistle loud, my friends!
For hisses long reverberate
Inside a hollow head.   135
    [*All hiss.*]
ACEVEDO   They're Sh-paniardsh by the sh-oundsh of it,
And off the boat at that.
They'll bring the theater down unless
They stop this vile attack.
MUÑIZ   So let the hissing fly again   140
And whistle loud, my friends,
For hisses do reverberate
Inside a hollow head.
2ND COMPANION   Let poetasters everywhere
Learn this from what they hear: 145
If cheering's what you're looking for,
These whistles are your cheers.
    [*All sing.*]
Yes, let the hissing fly once more
And whistle loud, my friends!
Your hisses will reverberate   150
Inside a hollow head.
    [*They hiss.*]
ACEVEDO   Enough already with the jeers
And spare the lash, I beg!
You have my word, I'll never stage
Another play again!   155
MUÑIZ   This penalty you self-impose
Seems altogether light.
It's obvious the punishment
Just doesn't fit the crime.
    [*All sing.*]
So let the hissing fly encore!   160
Sure, whistle loud, my friends,
For hisses do reverberate
Inside a hollow head.
    [*They hiss.*]
ACEVEDO   What retribution would you deem,
Then, fitting and correct?   165
As long as you don't hiss my work,
Come garrote me to death.
ARIAS   You asked us, so I'll answer you:
The sentence you deserve
Is writing out your plays again   170
From word to painful word.
ACEVEDO   Oh please, not that! No penalty
On earth's more sure and swift!

I'd rather perish here onstage
While thunderously hissed!   175
MUÑIZ   He asked us to, so answer him
By whistling loud, my friends!
For hisses will reverberate
Inside a hollow head.

Act III

[DOÑA LEONOR *enters with* CELIA.]
DOÑA LEONOR   If you don't let me leave right now
Or lift this spell, then I'll be forced
To perish here a suicide.
CELIA   Grab hold of yourself, Leonor—   2095
Your reputation's on the line.
DOÑA LEONOR   What will it matter if I'm viewed
As virtuous, Celia, after I've
Just heard such devastating news?
Can my own sire remain so duped   2100
As to believe Don Pedro swiped
Me last night from our house and thus
Demand I be this person's wife?
And all this now, oh God, on top
Of learning that my Carlos—talk   2105
About your faithless lovers!—woos
Fair Doña Ana mid these halls
In hopes that someday they'll be wed
When only he, as my betrothed,
Can free me from the wretchedness   2110
A marriage forced upon me holds.
You see, in this predicament,
My sorrow finds no place to call
Its refuge and my life's ordeals
No champion who'll take up their cause.   2115
CELIA [*Aside.*]   It's true she heard it all from me.
Don Carlos, equally confused
By what my mistress had me say,
Is also victim of this ruse
To make poor Leonor's despair   2120
Dispatch her to Don Pedro's arms
So Doña Ana might espouse
Don Carlos. I can see her heart
Is set on this and, coveting
That dress, invent these phantom ploys.   2125
My lady, as you know you aren't
That ingrate Carlos's first choice
And, as my master worships you,
Your sire's disposed to give your hand
In marriage to him soon. You know   2130
As well that, as this whole thing stands,

If you decline to marry him,
You'll lose a fine match and your name.
So wouldn't it best to take
A breath so you can better gauge　　　　　　2135
How splendid such a bond would be
And what an abject shame to miss?
Once you've gone through with it, you'll glean
Three thousand happy benefits,
Among these, all in one fell swoop,　　　　2140
Your line's propriety restored,
A father pleased to be obeyed,
Kin heartened by the ties you've forged,
A doting husband overjoyed
And base Don Carlos paid in kind.　　　　　2145
DOÑA LEONOR　What are you saying, Celia? First,
Before I'd be Don Pedro's wife,
You'll see the stars in heaven bolt
Their sempiternal canopy
And waters from the salty seas　　　　　　2150
Cast off perpetual routines
Whereby the beach's sands restrain
Their billows' unrelenting force.
You'll witness first that fiery heart
Amid our microcosm's orbs　　　　　　　2155
Disturb the order here on earth
And leave our lives in disarray.
You'll watch as nature's hierarchies
Become haphazardly arranged
With fire breeding flakes of snow　　　　　2160
And sparks erupting forth from ice.
Before abandoning the thought
Of wedding Carlos, though he slight
These pure affections, first I'll be
My scourge and executioner.　　　　　　2165
Before I'll stop my loving him,
I'll first . . .
CELIA　　　Why don't you stop these "firsts"
And start to chart a second course?
If this refusal's resolute,
I'll leave off giving you advice　　　　　2170
And ask what you've a mind to do.
DOÑA LEONOR　My mind, my friend—for so you've been
As confidant to all my woes—
Is hopeful you'll provide for me
A chance to slip outside this home　　　　2175
So that my sire, on his return,
Won't make me wed against my will.
I'll seek a cell once I've escaped
In some secluded cloister, built
So I might live the buried life,　　　　　2180
And cry about the tragic state

These ills have left me to lament
For what remains to me of days.
Perhaps there my unlucky star
Will have no further thoughts of me.   2185
CELIA   Yours might forget you, true, but mine
Will hound me if I let you leave,
For if my master found me out,
He'd let me have it no holds barred.
You might not be the star-gazer,   2190
But I'll be surely seeing stars!
DOÑA LEONOR   Dear friend, do this good turn for me
And I'll be your eternal slave!
I've never asked for anything
Before.
CELIA   Well, that may be the case,   2195
But what you think a favor may
Be one I pay for seven times!
DOÑA LEONOR   Then have it your way, enemy!
If you won't help arrange my flight,
I'll kill you first and then myself!   2200
CELIA [*Aside.*]   Look out, the gal is hopping mad!
Sweet Jesus, could her rage be so
Extreme she'd go on the attack?
If I keep Leonor pent here,
She may be lady of the house   2205
Some day and make me pay but dear
For hindering her from slipping out!
But let the maiden flee the place
And I'll incur my master's wrath.
It sounds like I'd be better off   2210
All round if I could just distract
Her now and fill Don Pedro in
On what his wayward lover plans,
For, knowing she would flee his arms,
He'd surely stop her in her tracks.   2215
If I could just pull off this scheme,
I'll be in both their graces. Then,
She won't feel I've offended her
And he'll owe me a lasting debt!
My lady, as you're so resolved   2220
To see this action run its course,
Go fetch the coat that's in your room
While I wait here and guard the door.
DOÑA LEONOR   You've given me my life back whole!
CELIA   Well, I've a tender heart myself!   2225
When I see some poor woman cry,
I turn to butter and just melt!
DOÑA LEONOR   I'll dash in, then, and grab my cloak.
                                [DOÑA LEONOR *exits.*]
CELIA   Rush off and hurry back to boot!
I'll be right here when you return   2230

To barricade the door on you
And let good King Marsilius know
His Melisendra's[1] on the loose.

                    [CELIA *exits.* DON JUAN *enters.*]

DON JUAN   Instead of savoring these delights
That Celia's garden key holds out,   2235
I find myself beside this green
Investigating nagging doubts.
No, not "investigate"—the word's
Misused in cases where hard proof
Is all but wholly verified.   2240
Oh God, if it were only true
My envy and these wrongs were mere
Suspicions with which I've been plagued!
How dare I not pursue revenge,
Though, when not doing so would make   2245
The shame in this offense against
My honor certain and my own?
For if suspicion in itself
Offends, how could my honor hope
That doubts about my injury   2250
Will not be deemed real evidence
When insult to nobility,
In cases where it's evident,
At best makes certainty that's false
Become a doubt that's all too true?   2255
If vile suspicion on its own
Can leave one's honor so abused
That judging truth unsure does all
But certify the injury,
How could it even cross my mind   2260
That any action might be seen
As detrimental to my name
If I don't validate the slight?
I'll wait here hidden, then, until
That rival I abhor arrives,   2265
For, seeing his love requited so,
Who'd doubt our suitor, thus repaid,
Will pass again through here tonight
When now he comes and goes all day?
I'll enter, then, and wait for him.   2270
May honor lead my vengeance forth!

                    [DON JUAN *exits.* DON CARLOS *enters with*
                    CHESTNUT, *who is carrying a bundle of clothes.*]

DON CARLOS   I've searched through this entire house
And still can't find my Leonor.
I've never been so desperate!

---

1. Medieval Spanish ballads tell the story of Melisendra, who was captured by the Moorish king
Marsilius and rescued by her husband, Gaiferos.

CHESTNUT   Sir, tell me that it isn't true   2275
    You haven't noticed that they've barred
    The doorways leading to that room
    Because of Doña Ana's dread
    Her brother might discern you here
    Or you'd lay eyes on Leonor   2280
    And that this plot was engineered
    To keep the two of us locked in
    So Ana could become your bride?
DON CARLOS   That's it, then. Don Rodrigo must
    Be told at once that it was I   2285
    Who snatched his daughter from his house
    And I who wish to marry her.
    He gives her to Don Pedro, sure
    The rogue abducted his dear girl,
    So I've no doubt he'd promise her   2290
    To me if he'd but understand
    That I'm the one she ran off with.
CHESTNUT   Oh, great! Now there's a brilliant plan!
    You think you'd ever reach the street
    With Doña Ana standing guard?   2295
    She won't be in the hay asleep!
DON CARLOS   Don't worry, Chestnut. Leave that part
    About outwitting her to me.
    You know I'm not the type to act
    So overcautious and restrained   2300
    When cares like these would set me back.
    My only reservation, though,
    Is strong enough to disincline
    My heart from fleeing, as I'd have
    To leave poor Leonor behind   2305
    Where any unforeseen event
    May make my presence here required.
    So, I've been thinking—you should go!
    They'll take less notice of a squire
    In service going on the lam   2310
    When they still hold his gentleman.
    You'll take this letter, which explains
    My delicate predicament,
    To Don Rodrigo, so he'll learn
    The truth at last.
CHESTNUT   Saint Thecla,[2] help!   2315
    How could it even cross your mind
    To send me when you know full well
    I'd be arrested by the law
    As your accomplice in that clash
    That left Don Diego stabbed? As it   2320

---

2. Popular martyr saint, particularly associated with female piety; she was the cross-dressing and itinerant companion of Saint Paul the Apostle.

Was you who perpetrated that
And I was merely present there,
Why should I pay *in solidum*?[3]

DON CARLOS   Still, Chestnut, this is what I will.

CHESTNUT   And this is what I will not do!   2325

DON CARLOS   You're going, as God lives—that's that!

CHESTNUT   Sir, what's the rationale behind
An oath that says I'm going as
God lives when I'll most surely die?

DON CARLOS   Is this a time for idle jests?   2330

CHESTNUT   If I was joking, now I'm not!

DON CARLOS   Cur! Bandy words with me! You try
My patience with these constant prods!
Go now, as God lives, or I'll kill
You right here!

CHESTNUT   Then you may unhand   2335
Me, sir. Now things seem cut and dry:
By fleeing, I've a better chance.
The letter, then, so I may go.

DON CARLOS   Yes, go . . . and make sure you return
At once to free me from this spot   2340
I'm in.

CHESTNUT   If you'll permit me, sir,
I'd like to tell a story I'm
Reminded of by what you said,
Exactly what the doctor would
Have ordered. (We may need one yet!)   2345
A fledgling bullfighter expressed
A wish to borrow his friend's horse.
This pal, foreseeing sure remorse
But bound to honor said request
Though promptly paralyzed with dread   2350
To think his steed might meet its end,
Whipped off a letter to his friend
To take care of this thoroughbred
As it was worth a barrelful
Of cash, at which his friend observed   2355
With calm: "Man, you'd be better served
To send that message to the bull!"
You're like the friend here who'd contrive
To cast me out to face sure wrath,
Not knowing whether there's a path   2360
At hand to lead me back alive.
What's causing me this laugh attack
Is, while I'm fraught with all this care
With all my fortunes in the air,
You're telling me to hurry back!   2365
I'm like the matador, then, see?

3. Joint liability (Latin); i.e., the obligation each liable party has to make good on the entire liability shared.

You really should communicate
This message that you've written straight
To Don Rodrigo, sir, not me!
  [CELIA *enters*.]
CELIA Don Carlos, sir, my mistress seeks   2370
A word with you. If you would just
Repair unto the garden, she's
A pressing matter to discuss
That obligates your presence there.
DON CARLOS She need but speak to be obeyed. 2375
I fly. [*To* CHESTNUT.] Now, do as I command.
     [DON CARLOS *exits with* CELIA.]
CHESTNUT I'm wondering if there's any way
That I can weasel out of this
Without Don Carlos learning of my plans . . .
What artful dodge will let me place   2380
This note in Don Rodrigo's hands
Without my being recognized
By him or anyone at that?
I sure could use a trickster like
That Garatuza,[4] once so apt   2385
At working miracles throughout
The Indies, which, that being my place
Of birth, left me revering him
As if he were a local saint.
Oh guiding spirit, be you one   2390
Who wields a fan to cool herself
Or girds cool steel upon his thigh,
Whoever you are—I need help!
Supply me with some cunning plot
That's worthy of old Calderón   2395
And let me leave these trials behind!
But hold on! My own wits propose
The stratagem I'm looking for:
While set on playing Helen to
My master's artless Paris,[5] his   2400
Poor Leonor gave me her jewels
To carry bundled with some skirts.
Her clothes are here and served last night
As comfy padding for my bed.
Were I to wear this dress outside,   2405
Would even one veiled lady here
In vast Toledo look as chic?
My mind's made up. It's time I changed.
These rags are going in the street!
  [CHESTNUT *removes his cloak, sword, and hat.*]
So, first things first: I'll pen these locks 2410

---

4. Martín de Villavicencio y Salazar, a famous rogue who traveled across New Spain pretending
  to be a priest.
5. In Homer's *Iliad*, Helen, Queen of Sparta and wife of Menelaus, elopes with Paris, son of King
  Priam of Troy, thereby setting in motion the conflict that would lead to the Trojan War.

With bobby pins and keep them pent,
As such a carefree, windblown look
Would doubtless slay too many men.
Then, there's the question of which cloth
To use to wrap around my brow: 2415
By angling the adornment right,
I'll profit from it all around.
Skirts enter the equation next:
Just look at these materials!
This shade of blue could only make   2420
My stunning self more beautiful
As I lean toward a dusky hue.
You want jewels? Come and gawk at these!
Perhaps, I'll wear them later when
I don a bit more finery.   2425
And lucky me! I've even found a shawl
Inside the bag of clothes she left.
I have to try it on! Let's hope
This bodice covers up my breasts!
What's missing? Some foundation. Yes!   2430
I hope to God that I can find
A little in here and a brush
To see it's properly applied.
Oh no, the thing's not functioning
And now I've smeared it on my face!   2435
Some rouge, perhaps? Nah, who needs paint?
I'm sure this little masquerade
Will bring the color to my cheeks—
Once all dolled up, I'll blush for shame.
Hey ladies, take a look at this: 2440
My collar's truly lovely lace.
The frames that give hoop skirts their shape
Could hardly make it sit so high.
I really am a pretty gal.
God save me, what a stunning sight!   2445
Well, everything looks good on me—
What wouldn't with this figure, eh?
And now these final touches should
Put sheer perfection on parade.
These gloves should keep my hands from view   2450
As well as add a touch of charm,
For how can I boast Jacob's limbs
When I've got Esau's[6] hairy arms?
This veil should be the topper, though,
And screen my face from sight a bit.   2455
This little piece of silk sure does
The trick! Lord, has there ever been
A gaping chasm more obscured

---

6. The Book of Genesis relates the story of how Jacob wore goatskin in order to pretend to be his
   much hairier brother Esau and deceived his father into giving him the blessing intended for Esau.

Or thief more muffled in the night;
A rampart offering more defense   2460
Or page boy telling bigger lies;
A gypsy who deceived as much
Or profiteer with greater scams?
And finally, then, to complement
My grace and beauty here—this fan,   2465
So like me with the wind it breaks
And all the hot air that it blows!
Perhaps, some lady watching this
Will whisper to a friend, "You know,
The clown depicts Tapado,[7] that   2470
Impostor who fooled Mexico,"
Though what you're watching's not real life
But just some play as it unfolds,
So don't think all these twists of plot
Are products of this servant's wit—   2475
I wouldn't dupe your ladyships
Or wish Your Excellency tricked.
There now, I'm armed and dangerous.
No doubt four thousand pretty boys
Will follow me in hot pursuit,   2480
The sort that are just overjoyed
To woo whoever passes by
And tend to fall in love *en masse*
If not with beauty, with ideals
Their fond imaginations hatch.   2485
So here's some ladyness for you:
A dainty walk with mincing steps;
The back straight, posture proper; charm
Exuding graceful airs; the head
Cocked—tilted—no, inclined a bit   2490
To one side; hand in cloak as such;
My one seductive eye on view,
The other coyly covered up . . .
But all these looks are wasted where
They can't be strutted and adored.   2495
I fear I'll break some hearts, but what's
A gal to do?
          [CHESTNUT *attempts to exit, but bumps into* DON PEDRO.]
DON PEDRO   Fair Leonor,
Why are you veiled this time of night?
(*Aside.*) Oh, Celia told me she'd forsake
Love for a convent and it's true!   2500
Where are you off to in such haste?
CHESTNUT [*Aside.*]   Good God, he thinks I'm Leonor!
My precious scheme will come undone
The second that he lifts this veil!

---

7. Don Antonio de Benavides, who passed himself off as a marquis and arrived in Mexico with falsified papers to claim an official position. He was discovered and eventually executed in 1684.

DON PEDRO   Sweet Leonor, pray, why so mum?   2505
    Where are you headed, Leonor?
CHESTNUT [Aside.]   He's really Le-annoying me!
    But since he's taken me for her,
    I'll juggle two identities
    And raise my voice's pitch a bit   2510
    To keep this ruse from being discerned.
DON PEDRO   Dear lady, why do you not speak?
    Does this deep love I feel deserve
    Your mute reply? Why so intent
    On flight? Is my adoring you   2515
    In such a courtly way a crime
    Or living with a love so pure
    That, even knowing you do love
    Another, my attentions are
    So duteous to your family name,   2520
    Pledged obligations and sweet charms
    That I'm resolved to marry you—
    To hell with danger, come what may?
    For, in your present circumstance,
    I've no doubt that you'll put more faith   2525
    In noble duty, tried and true,
    Than any dictate of your stars.
    How is it that the noble blood
    Still coursing through the doting heart
    Of one so just and affluent   2530
    Can't prompt a treatment less severe?
    Do I deserve such cold disdain?
    If this is so, as I have feared,
    Then ministrations such as these
    Do but ensure that I'll be spurned.   2535
    Just think about it for a while:
    Do you allege you'd not prefer
    A suitor who adores you plain
    To one who scorns you with finesse?
CHESTNUT [Aside.]   It's quite a thrill to be pursued!   2540
    I'll never be surprised again
    To see gals vaunting haughty pride.
    There's nothing in the world like woo
    To swell one's head with vain conceit.
    It's time I made this lovesick fool's   2545
    Own head spin round from cockiness.
    Don Pedro, I have done my best
    To hide the reasons for this flight
    But fear now that I must confess
    I flee because your stingy board   2550
    Is killing me with hunger pangs,
    For you're a milquetoast sir, it's true:
    Your sister is a battle-ax,
    Your serving wenches maiden aunts,
    Your footmen worse than animals   2555

And I, at last, distraught and vexed
From want, am setting off to look
For cream puffs at the first bake shop
I find.
DON PEDRO [*Aside.*]   What unbecoming words,   2560
So much unlike the genteel wit
And lovely looks we've all observed
In Doña Leonor! Dear lady, as
A gentleman I find it strange
To hear you voice complaints about
My kin and household in this way.   2565
If your plan's to discredit my
Good standing, seek another mode.
Such common talk hurts not so much
My reputation as your own.
CHESTNUT   You're killing me with hunger, sir.   2570
Does what I'm saying sound like Greek?
DON PEDRO   It doesn't, though I'm sorely pressed
To recognize you by such speech.
CHESTNUT   Well, understand my gist or not,
My exit, too, should leave you sore.   2575
[CHESTNUT *tries to exit.*]
DON PEDRO   Wait—you can't go! I won't consent
To such a thing, as I've informed
Your father that you're in my home
And I'd be able to account
For your wellbeing and whereabouts   2580
At any time, as I've avowed.
Since you're opposed to marrying me,
The least that I can do is hand
You back to him as I have pledged,
As everyone now understands   2585
Resistance to our wedding comes
Entirely from you, not me.
CHESTNUT   Don Pedro, you're a silly fool
And take unlicensed liberties
Like this of standing in the way   2590
Of ladies of distinction when
They only look to get some chow.
DON PEDRO [*Aside.*]   Fair skies, it's hard to comprehend
How such talk can be Leonor's!
I sense the maid is playing dumb   2595
To drive me to despair in hopes
Of cooling off this ardent love
So I won't look to marry her.
Good heavens, does she hate me so?
Her little ruse has backfired, then;   2600
My burning passion for her knows
No bounds and thus won't be deterred.
Fair Leonor, what good resides
In acting like a little fool

When I know all too well you're wise?   2605
If anything, this clever scheme
Has only made me love you more.
Your grace and wit in playing dumb
Have struck me as a *tour de force*.
CHESTNUT [*Aside.*]   I'm really in a pickle now!   2610
He'll have his way with me, I think,
If I don't change my tune and fast!
Let's see if this will do the trick.
Don Pedro, as a woman knows
Which side her bread is buttered on,   2615
I've watched impressed as you've displayed
Sheer gallantry in your response
To my unending string of snubs.
I think I'll change my course, then, now,
Cross over to the other side   2620
And acquiesce to be your spouse
This very evening.
DON PEDRO   What say you,
Dear soul?
CHESTNUT   That I'll be yours tonight
As sure as two plus two make four.
DON PEDRO   Don't blurt such news out! Take your time   2625
So I don't die of happiness,
As sorrow's failed to do me in.
CHESTNUT   Sir, for the love of God, don't die
Before you've left me one great gift:
A son who will inherit this   2630
Genteel estate your family owns.
DON PEDRO   Is that what worries you when all
That I possess is yours alone?
CHESTNUT   Hell's bells! I know of what I speak.
Perhaps, a token of your love . . .   2635
DON PEDRO   No gesture would delight me more!
Can I take what you say on trust
Or are you toying with my heart?
CHESNTUT   What, I some actress mouthing words?
You have my word I'll wed, but have   2640
I yours for better or for worse?
DON PEDRO   You wound me, lady, doubting mine.
CHESTNUT   How much you wanna bet cold feet
Will make you ditch this blushing bride?
DON PEDRO   You leave my honor much aggrieved.   2645
CHESTNUT   I want your solemn pledge and vow
That, if you do have second thoughts
About our union, I'll remain
Unharmed.
DON PEDRO   I can't see how that ought
To matter, given the complete   2650
Impossibility my love

For you could ever ebb or wane.
Now may I, lady, since you've come
Around to giving your consent,
Request that dainty hand to kiss?   2655
CHESTNUT [*Aside.*]   It's not like Jacob had a choice.
Here, take a look at all of it.
DON PEDRO   But why present it to me gloved?
CHESTNUT   I'm sad to say it isn't well.
DON PEDRO   Pray, what's the matter with your hands?   2660
CHESTNUT   The two were injured when I held
Them out to visitors one day
And all the ointments doctors have
Prescribed and all their soaps have failed
To bring their pristine whiteness back.   2665
      [DON JUAN *is heard offstage.*]
DON JUAN   Vile traitor, die here at my hands!
DON PEDRO   Whose voice is that I hear inside?
      [DON CARLOS *is heard offstage.*]
DON CARLOS   These hands will bring about your death
Since this is how you choose to die!
DON PEDRO   By God, this ruckus in my house!   2670
CHESTNUT   It may be coming closer yet!
      [DON CARLOS *and* DON JUAN *enter fighting, with* DOÑA ANA *attempt-
      ing to deter them.*]
DOÑA ANA   Stop, gentlemen! I beg you, please!
My brother, no less! Now I'm dead!
CHESTNUT   Is this the way they'd celebrate
My beauty, trading fatal blows?   2675
DON PEDRO   Two men who'd run each other through
At this late hour and in my home?
They bring dishonor to my name!
I'll see this base affront avenged
By killing both, especially   2680
As it's Don Carlos who offends.
DOÑA ANA [*Aside.*]   Who could have thought my brother would
Appear so suddenly? I'm lost!
DON CARLOS [*Aside.*]   Don Pedro's here, and normally
That wouldn't trouble me at all,   2685
But Doña Ana seems at risk
And I'm concerned on her account.
CHESTNUT   Is this the battle of Oran?[8]
I'd better snuff this candle out,
As that'll be my only chance   2690
To slip unnoticed through this door,
Since that's my only worry now.
      [CHESTNUT *blows out the candle and everyone fights.*]
DON PEDRO   Oh, kill the lights, eh? That won't thwart
This steel from carving out its wrath.

---

8. Spanish troops conquered the North African city of Oran in 1509, in a tremendous rout.

What difference does it make? You'll meet   2695
Your deaths in darkness all the same!
DON CARLOS   Here's just the opportunity
I need to free my love from harm.
Her zeal in aiding me appears
To have endangered her wellbeing.   2700
   [DOÑA LEONOR *enters with a cloak covering her face.*]
DOÑA LEONOR   Good heavens! I left Celia here
And now my ears pick up the clash
Of swords while everything's gone dark.
What's going on? Oh, help me, Lord!
Whatever these strange happenings are,   2705
The only thing that matters now
Is whether I can find the door.
   [DOÑA LEONOR *bumps into* DON CARLOS.]
DON CARLOS   Here's Doña Ana, to be sure.
Dear lady, hurry and be borne
At once from out this dangerous spot.   2710
DOÑA LEONOR   A strange man carrying me off?
Well, I'd be glad to leave this place
With anybody by default,
Though taken for another maid.
He'll see his error in the street   2715
Where I'll at least be left outside
And he can aid the one he seeks.
DOÑA ANA   I'm not pained that my brother spied
This altercation, as he saw
It was Don Carlos in the fray   2720
And I can say his sword was drawn
In bold defense of Leonor.
I'm only discomposed to think
That he's at peril in my house.
If only I could chance on him   2725
And hide the poor man once again!
DON PEDRO   He who offends my honor dies!
CHESTNUT   This fight's disoriented me
And I can't find my way outside.
The door's around here somewhere. Ouch!   2730
What's this? Oh God, a cabinet
I've just collided with face first
And broken into pieces tens
Of dozens of their cups and flasks.
Carafes don't vie with lovely forms,   2735
So looked to have this beaker snubbed!
DOÑA ANA   I hear commotion at the door—
For sure that's Don Juan slipping out
So no one sees him in the house
Or, worse, my brother spies his face.   2740
But two still settle their accounts,
So which could brave Don Carlos be?
   [DOÑA ANA *makes her way toward* DON JUAN.]

DON CARLOS   I found it! This must be the door!
    Come, lady! Let's make our escape!
                    [DON CARLOS *exits with* DOÑA LEONOR.]
DON PEDRO   Now taste my wrath and meet the Lord!   2745
DOÑA ANA   Yes, that's my brother. This one must
    Be Carlos, then. I still have time.
    Oh, hurry and I'll hide you, sir!
DON JUAN   It's Doña Ana, who contrives
    To hide me from her brother's view.   2750
    I've no choice but to follow her.
                    [DOÑA ANA *exits with* DON JUAN.]
DON PEDRO   So, cowering in the dark to dodge
    My righteous sword, you treacherous curs?
    Some idle servant, bring a light!
        [CELIA *enters with a light.*]
CELIA   What's all the ruckus going on?   2755
DON PEDRO   Why don't we see? [*Aside.*] Good Lord, what's this?
    They must have found the door unlocked
    And fled. Don Carlos surely slipped
    In here that way as well. But why
    Should I be vexed by this as long   2760
    As Leonor remains inside?
    It might be wise to ascertain
    How he came in, though. Leonor,
    Retire to your rooms. I'll have
    Your father brought here and informed   2765
    I wish to have our nuptials set
    This very evening in my home.
CHESTNUT   The only thing I'm wishing for
    Is someone who can set my nose.
                [CHESTNUT *exits and* DON PEDRO *locks the door.*]
DON PEDRO   I'll lock up Leonor in case   2770
    Expedience was couched behind
    Her sudden claim to favor me
    And bolt the door shut from outside
    So, if it does turn out she feigns
    Her love, the joke will be on her.   2775
    For now, though, I'll try finding out
    Which one among our servitors
    Allowed my foe inside this house
    And what it was that could have caused
    That masked man to fight Carlos here.   2780
    Arriving first, my sister saw
    Far more than I and even left
    With them, so I'll need know just how
    It was she happed to be right there
    Precisely when the fight broke out.   2785
            [DON PEDRO *exits.* DON RODRIGO *enters with* HERNANDO.]
DON RODRIGO   Hernando, here's what I've heard tell:
    Our kinsman, Don Diego, fell
    A victim to my daughter's kidnapper,

Who stabbed him as he fled with her
Since Don Diego recognized her plight   2790
And, as her blood, felt forced to fight
In her defense. And thus the fray began
Until my Leonor's abductor ran
Him through, which might have done the poor wretch in
Had he not of a sudden been   2795
Conveyed home by some men out in the road.
No sooner back in his abode,
Don Diego, thought half-dead, came to,
At which he recognized the crew
Whose kind compassion gave him life again   2800
To be none other than Don Pedro's men
Who'd deemed this recourse so much more discreet
Than causing a commotion in the street.
This all aligns with what Don Pedro said—
That Leonor had rushed beside the bed   2805
Of his dear sister, whom she feared was ill—
And with his wish that I should wait until
Today to learn if she would give her hand.
But now I finally understand
He holds his marriage oath at bay   2810
By using suchlike tactics of delay
And so, to see this matter solved,
I've come here once again, resolved
He wed my daughter and comply
Thus with our gentlemanly code or die.   2815
HERNANDO   How right you are, sir, for when honor ails,
A rapid remedy alone prevails.
That fool who'd only wish his illness gone
Can count on ailing ever and anon.
          [DON CARLOS *enters with* DOÑA LEONOR, *who is still veiled.*]
DON CARLOS   See, lovely Doña Ana, there's   2820
No danger here to make you shrink.
DOÑA LEONOR [*Aside.*]   Good heavens, the deceiving rogue!
So Carlos whisks me off, convinced
I'm Doña Ana? She's his love—
What clearer indication need   2825
I seek?
DON CARLOS [*Aside.*]   This is a trial, skies
Above! What have I done? To free
Kind Doña Ana from that fray,
I've left behind my Leonor!
Where can I safely leave this one   2830
In tow before reversing course
And rescuing my future wife?
But look—some man's approaching me.
Who's there?
DON RODRIGO   Don Carlos?
DON CARLOS   Who inquires?
[*Aside.*] It's Don Rodrigo! What a piece   2835

Of luck! Whom could I better trust
To safeguard Doña Ana's life
And virtuous name till I return?
Being old and wise, he'll satisfy
Her brother's doubts about what caused   2840
This venturing forth and leave me thus
Unburdened to retrace my steps
Post haste so I might save my love
Through my own bravery. Good Don
Rodrigo, I'm in dire straits   2845
And only you can help resolve
My plight.
DON RODRIGO   How may I be of aid,
Don Carlos?
DON CARLOS   Sir, this lady is
Don Pedro's sister, whom a host
Of unforeseeable events   2850
Compelled to exit her abode
With no choice but my company
Because her honor was at risk.
I know it's not correct for me
To be alone with her, so bid   2855
You please escort her to your home
While I set to a task at hand.
DON RODRIGO   Don Carlos, she'll be safe with me.
You're right that all would look askance
Were you to keep her. I'll be sure   2860
To set her brother's mind at ease.
DON CARLOS   You do me a great favor, sir.
Now, by your leave.
                                    [DON CARLOS *exits.*]
DOÑA LEONOR [*Aside.*]   What, can it be
I've been remanded to my sire?
DON RODRIGO   Hernando, hah! It just occurred   2865
To me to see Don Pedro since
Don Carlos also snatched a girl—
This time, his sister—from her house
And, as I've picked up other cues
That he's in love with her as well,   2870
Prevail upon the qualmish youth
To marry Leonor at once.
He's practically my son-in-law
And, as such, I should guard his name
While he'd do well to thwart a cause   2875
That might bring his own honor harm
And, in so doing, buttress mine.
HERNANDO   How right you are! One way to hold
The upper hand until such time
As he fulfills his promises   2880
And marries Leonor would be
To hold his sister under watch.

don rodrigo   Come with me, lady, as I need
To enter here. Be not afraid
Of any danger, as I've pledged   2885
My troth to guard you best I can.
doña leonor [*Aside*.]   My father ushers me again
Into my enemy's abode!
I've no choice but to follow him—
I can't unveil myself just yet.   2890
don rodrigo   Look, that's Don Pedro, isn't it?
Good lady, bide a short time here
With stout Hernando while I chat
With your dear brother man to man.
doña leonor [*Aside*.]   Unholy heavens, either cast   2895
These blows aside or give me death,
For any horrid end that comes
Would be less agonizing far
Than so prolonged a martyrdom!
don rodrigo   I'd better catch him while I may.   2900
    [don pedro *enters*.]
don pedro [*Aside*.]   To think I'm yet to figure out
Which servant gave my enemy
Untrammeled access to my house
Or where my faithful sister is!
I'll need to search the garden plot   2905
Where there's the possibility
That, scared by all this brouhaha,
She's scurried off to seek some peace.
I'll make my way there now, but here
Is Don Rodrigo—good thing, too!—   2910
Since Leonor just volunteered
Her willingness to be my wife.
Accept my warmest welcome, sir,
For, had you not come visiting,
I would have set on a search   2915
For you this very minute then.
don rodrigo   I thank you, sir, for your concern.
Come, let's sit down, for we have much
To talk about.
don pedro [*Aside*.]   I gather what
He's here for likely may redound   2920
To some advantage for my love.
don rodrigo   You doubtless will have guessed by now,
Don Pedro, what affair directs
My steps unto your door again:
It's honor, sir, and I have kept   2925
My faith that you would keep your word.
Though you're a gentleman, until
You wed you place your name at risk
With this one promise unfulfilled,
For honor is a precious jewel,   2930
You know, about which noble hearts

Like yours can scarce be cavalier,
For even crystal so rock-hard
It fails to break apart when struck
Can be besmirched by breath of mouth.   2935
This must have crossed your mind and you'd
Be right, sir, to have figured out
That honor brings me here, although
It's not the foremost reason why
I call on you. I come with all   2940
Due signs of courtesy in mind
To let you know not only is
My honor's interest at stake,
But the integrity that marks
My noble house's honored name.   2945
So gallantly do I now come
To treat this matter with you, sir,
That I'm prepared to shunt aside
My honor and to place yours first,
Perhaps availing you more yet.   2950
Still, I concede this present cause
Exudes self-interest from a man
Who'd wish his future son-in-law
To boast the high regard of all,
For thus I benefit myself.   2955
You see how watchful I remain
Of my own honor and how well
I fare preserving it when I'm
Likewise engaged preserving yours.
To wit, good sir: I'm sure you know   2960
Don Carlos de Olmedo, pure
Of blood and highborn gentleman,
The scion of a noble house . . .
DON PEDRO [*Aside.*]   Why mention Carlos to me here?
Just where could this be leading now   2965
Without a word about my banns?
He's learned Don Carlos carried off
His daughter from their home last night.
My life and honor both are lost!
DON RODRIGO   Your face is drained of color, though   2970
I'm not surprised, for hearing talk
Extolling honor's qualities,
Your noble cast would be at fault—
Your honor, too—had you not blanched
In recognition of your breach.   2975
As you, therefore, are living proof
That love may motivate misdeeds,
Your own transgression might absolve
Don Carlos on this selfsame front.
You shouldn't be at all surprised   2980
To hear he's done what you have done.
    [DOÑA ANA *enters, hiding behind the rear curtain.*]

DOÑA ANA   I'll try my best, concealed, to learn
　　　What business Don Rodrigo brings
　　　In calling on my brother here.
　　　Though I still keep Don Carlos hid,　　　　　　　　2985
　　　My brother did lay eyes on him
　　　And what may come has left me tense.
DON RODRIGO   So, I'm not saying anything
　　　You haven't heard to some extent:
　　　Don Carlos pays your sister suit　　　　　　　　2990
　　　And all in the most proper way.
　　　These feelings are requited, too,
　　　So why should you be jarred? The same
　　　Occurred with you and Leonor.
DON PEDRO   Good God! Am I to understand　　　　　　2995
　　　That Carlos loves my sister? No!
DOÑA ANA   I wonder how it is this man
　　　Has caught wind of our liaison?
DON RODRIGO   Dear sir, it's hardly my intent
　　　To waste your time with facts you know　　　　　3000
　　　But, faced with that predicament
　　　Your own good self experienced
　　　And being on poor terms with you,
　　　He snatched your sister from your home.
DON PEDRO   What's this you're saying?
DON RODRIGO　　　　　　　　　　　　That he used,　　3005
　　　As surely you're aware, the base
　　　Stunt you employed, committing thus
　　　The same offense against your line
　　　As you've brought unto mine. So what's
　　　This act, now that I've calmly come　　　　　　3010
　　　To talk things over? Don't you see
　　　The skies bring down upon our heads
　　　Reflections of our own misdeeds?
　　　Why such a shocked expression, then?
　　　Dear boy, pay heed to my advice:　　　　　　　3015
　　　In instances where honor ails,
　　　It's hardly fit that one prescribe
　　　Strong medicine to treat one's ills
　　　When palliatives may bring relief.
　　　Harsh physics do more harm than good.　　　　　3020
　　　Encountering a limb diseased,
　　　An expert surgeon doesn't just
　　　Subject his patient to the knife
　　　And hack off what was causing pain,
　　　But will initially apply　　　　　　　　　　3025
　　　Some balsam on the arm or leg.
　　　He opts for amputation when
　　　It's recognized that surgery's
　　　The only drastic measure left.
　　　So let's act as wise doctors do:　　　　　　　3030
　　　Don Carlos has discussed with me

How Doña Ana went with him
And now I have her in my keep.
As they're resolved to wed at once
Without your blessing, wouldn't it   3035
Be better just to give consent
And prudently convert a grim
Necessity into a choice?
The cleverest of minds conspire
To outfit each compulsory act   3040
In clothes that make it seem desired.
At least, that's how I look at things.
I trust you'll think this through and see
That, given where your honor stands,
It's much the best way to proceed.   3045
As far as these affairs pertain
To me, be cognizant I call
Resolved to see you wed this night,
For there's no cause to put things off,
Especially as I've lately learned   3050
That it was you who left the kind
Don Diego, my poor nephew, stabbed
For recognizing you mid-flight
As you were snatching Leonor.
Your claim not to have taken her   3055
Squares badly with the news I'm told.
It's time this pretense was adjourned.
In short, I won't be satisfied
Until you take her for your wife.
DOÑA ANA   I tremble while my brother looks   3060
To ready his response, but find
No explanation as to what
Could prompt him to invent these ploys
For Don Rodrigo's benefit.
DON PEDRO   Sir,
Addressing the concerns you've voiced: 3065
First, I admit I lied about
Not taking Leonor, but both
Your reputation and my name
Compelled me to maintain this hoax.
Since you allege the only way   3070
To set things straight is wedding her,
Know this adjacent room conceals
The beauty that's your stolen girl
And, in your presence here today,
I'll give my hand to her as lord   3075
And master, although none of this
Espousing will take place before
You yield me Doña Ana, so
That, in accord with your advice,
The maid can wed Don Carlos here   3080
And now. [Aside.] My sister for a bride!

If that won't pacify my foe,
I know no other wile that can.
DON RODRIGO   Your talents and nobility
Are patent at the merest glance!   3085
I'm thankful for this shift in course
And part to fetch your sister now.
          [DOÑA ANA *enters.*]
DOÑA ANA   I'm here, good Don Rodrigo, much
Obliged to one who, duty bound,
Did keep me safe. You have my thanks   3090
While you, dear brother, I beseech,
Though well you might be cross, to look
Inside your ardent soul and see
The ravages love leaves behind
So you'll excuse my fervent heart's   3095
Transgressions by recalling yours,
If that's what fond affections are.
DON PEDRO   Rise, Ana—you've no cause to kneel.
You would have made it easier
For me to see you married off   3100
Had you not brazenly recurred
To such indecencies.
DON RODRIGO   Let's save
Recriminations for a more
Propitious time while you dispatch
A loyal footman to transport   3105
Don Carlos to your home at once.
DOÑA ANA   There won't be any need for that.
I have him hidden in my rooms—
You did just promise him my hand!
DON PEDRO   Procure him on the instant, then.   3110
DOÑA ANA   I'm very happy to obey!
My firm persistence in pursuit
Of love has finally been repaid!
                              [DOÑA ANA *exits.*]
DON PEDRO   Where's Celia?
          [CELIA *enters.*]
CELIA   You called, master?
DON PEDRO   Take
This key to Doña Ana's room   3115
And summon Doña Leonor.
                    [CELIA *takes the key and exits.*]
Oh Love, you've made my dreams come true,
Enabling these, my amorous
Designs, to finally be attained!
          [DOÑA LEONOR *enters unseen.*]
DOÑA LEONOR [*Aside.*]   They think I'm Doña Ana, so   3120
I'll take this chance to slip away
Now from my father, which is still
My most immediate concern.
I'll come up with some other plan

Ere long to leave Don Pedro spurned,   3125
But one thing at a time for now.
What's this? A man is walking up
The stairs! I wonder who it is.
   [DON CARLOS *enters*.]
DON CARLOS [*Aside*.]   I'm here, resolved no matter what,
To liberate my Leonor   3130
From this ignoble custody.
As Doña Ana finds herself
Beyond familial peril's reach,
My valor has no cause to hide
Its face, so hear me out, dread skies: 3135
I'll pry the woman from this house
Myself or not leave here alive!
   [DON CARLOS *walks by* DOÑA LEONOR.]
DOÑA LEONOR   May God have mercy on my soul!
It's Carlos and, so blind with rage,
He didn't even notice me.   3140
I wonder why it is he came,
As he's already whisked me off
Assuming I was Ana. Why,
Dear heavens, would you have me bear
Such ignominy in my life!   3145
Now, could it be amid these trials
He left his ladylove behind
And has returned here to redeem
Her? I'll move closer, then, and try
To catch what these two have to say.   3150
DON CARLOS   Don Pedro, as an enemy
Compelled to set foot in your house,
I'll spare you empty niceties.
Now here I am, sir. But who is
This, Don Rodrigo?
DON RODRIGO   Steady there,   3155
Don Carlos, now control yourself.
I've come to say that all affairs
Are settled in your favor, thanks
To good Don Pedro's continence.
You owe the man your gratitude   3160
And are forever in his debt.
Sincere congratulations, son,
For very shortly you'll possess
This beauty that you so adore.
Yours be eternal happiness!   3165
DON CARLOS [*Aside*.]   How's that? It sounds like he's aware
Of what transpired in his home,
As Chestnut must have given him
The note. Now Don Rodrigo knows
For sure that it was I who led   3170
His daughter off and is astute
Enough to give me Leonor.

Don Pedro, who's been disabused
Of any chance to marry her,
Desists at last in laying siege.   3175
Sir, I can hardly answer you,
So dumbstruck am I by your speech.
Let such unbridled joy excuse
This once my silly loss for words.
If unexpected happiness,   3180
The likes of which I don't deserve,
Did not drive me the least bit mad,
Then I could hardly claim I'm sane.
DON RODRIGO   There, see what I was telling you?
He loves her more than I can say!   3185
DOÑA LEONOR [*Aside.*]   Good heavens, did I grasp this right?
Congratulations blithely served
Don Carlos? What's this happiness?
DON PEDRO   It would have been more proper, sir,
Had you discussed affairs with me,   3190
But as these nuptials were desired
So much by Don Rodrigo, whose
Gray hairs I prize as my own sire's,
I'll reckon myself fortunate
So honorable and nobly born   3195
A gentleman should grace my home.
DOÑA LEONOR [*Aside.*]   I can't abide this anymore.
I'll see the traitor doesn't wed!
        [DOÑA LEONOR *comes forward, still veiled.*]
DON RODRIGO   You've picked a perfect time to make
Your way hence, lady, but is there   3200
A reason why you hide your face?
The man you'd marry stands right here.
Don Carlos, stop this resolute
Politeness now and give your hand
To Doña Ana.
DON CARLOS   Wait, to whom?   3205
DON RODRIGO   To Doña Ana, your new wife.
Why, what's wrong, man?
DON CARLOS   Good heavens, I've
Been much beguiled and betrayed!
I, marry Ana?
DOÑA LEONOR [*Aside.*]   Thank you, skies.
He holds the lady in disdain.   3210
DON PEDRO   Say, Don Rodrigo, what's all this?
Did you not call here to arrange
A marriage at Don Carlos's
Behest to my dear sister?
DON RODRIGO   Yes,
But only since Don Carlos left   3215
The lady here with me, as he'd
Removed her from your home, he said,

Alone, in just his company,
Because her life was under threat.
My lady, isn't that correct?   3220
DOÑA LEONOR   It is, sir. I hereby confess
To being Carlos's betrothed
And wait but for your kind consent.
DON CARLOS   It wasn't wise to have exposed
Yourself like this to public scorn,   3225
Fond Doña Ana, but I fear
You leave me with no other course.
The present circumstance has forced
My hand and I must use plain speech—
A person who'd pursue me so   3230
Can suffer my discourtesy.
You, more than anyone here, ought
To know that nothing in the end
Could make me forsake Leonor.
DON RODRIGO   What, Leonor? Sir, come again?   3235
Which Leonor?
DON CARLOS   Your daughter, sir.
DON RODRIGO   My daughter? Why, the thought's absurd!
She's pledged to be Don Pedro's wife.
DON CARLOS   If he should even draw near her,
I'll slay the villain on the spot!   3240
DON PEDRO   That's it! I won't stand idly by
While this insulting popinjay
Makes bold at one and the same time
To snub my sister in this way
And claim the woman that I love!   3245
        [DON PEDRO and DON CARLOS *draw their swords.* DOÑA ANA *and*
        DON JUAN *enter, holding hands.* CELIA *enters by the other door*
        with CHESTNUT *still dressed in woman's clothing.*]
DOÑA ANA   Dear brother, at your feet, the man
I wish to wed and I do . . . [*Aside.*] What,
Do I lead Don Juan by the hand?
His cape concealed his face till now,
So how could he be recognized?   3250
DON PEDRO   But Ana, what's this all about?
CELIA   Don Pedro, here's sweet Leonor.
DON PEDRO   Oh, mistress lovely and divine!
CHESTNUT [*Aside.*]   You're struck to see your comely maid
While I'm here frozen stiff with fright!   3255
At least my master's back in view,
Which shouldn't leave me any cause
For fear, as he'll rush to my aid.
DON RODRIGO   I can't believe what I just saw!
Don Carlos, are you saying now   3260
The woman you entrusted me
And whom you wish to marry is
Not Doña Ana?

DON CARLOS   Sir, I schemed
    To paint things so, for Leonor's
    The only object of my love.   3265
DOÑA ANA [*Aside.*]   I'll use my wits to end all this
    Confusion, for I've seen enough.
    Now that my marrying Don Juan
    Appears as good as done, I'll do
    My best to make him think it's what   3270
    I want, since he'll soon be my groom.
    Wise Don Rodrigo, Carlos who?
    I fail to grasp your vexed response.
    I only know that, ever since
    We both lived in Madrid, Don Juan   3275
    Has owned my heart and claimed complete
    Dominion over all my thoughts.
DON JUAN   Don Pedro, I kneel supplicant
    Before you.
DON PEDRO   I'm the one who ought
    To cheer, as he who was my friend   3280
    Will by and by become my kin.
    So, to assure our marriages
    Will come to pass in unison,
    Give Doña Ana here your hand
    While I give Leonor my own.   3285
        [DON PEDRO *approaches* CHESTNUT.]
DON CARLOS   You'll die a thousand times before!
CHESTNUT [*Aside.*]   I must be something to behold
    If they'd do battle over me.
DON PEDRO   Give me your hand, my sovereign queen!
    Oh, conqueror of my vanquished will,   3290
    I'm yours!
CHESTNUT   In order to increase
    Its softness, I've preserved the thing
    A year inside this dogskin glove.
DON CARLOS   I won't permit this on my life!
        [DOÑA LEONOR *removes her veil.*]
DOÑA LEONOR   Hold on a second, Carlos! What   3295
    Am I, invisible? I'll be
    Your loving wife despite the scorn
    You've heaped on me, for I'm disposed
    To love you for it even more.
DON CARLOS   Was that you all this time, dear jewel?   3300
DON PEDRO   Could I be dreaming and see two
    Sweet Leonors where there was one?
CHESTNUT   You mean you've never heard that tune,
    "Just when you think you know a girl . . ."?
DON PEDRO   Then who's this portent that I thought   3305
    To be a mirror of my love?
        [CHESTNUT *removes his veil.*]
CHESTNUT   Alas, none other than the dog
    Who gave his life to make these gloves.

CELIA   If I laugh anymore, I'll bust!
I can't believe you pulled this off!   3310
DON PEDRO   Your life is over, Chestnut! Done!
CHESTNUT   But why, sir? When I gave my word
Of honor that we'd soon be wed—
A promise that I'd still fulfill—
You tendered me your solemn pledge   3315
That, if you ever changed your mind,
I'd not be harmed. So as the groom
Is breaking the engagement off—
Though I'm prepared to follow through—
Be sure that you uphold your vow,   3320
As I was set to discharge mine.
DON CARLOS   But Chestnut, why are you decked out
In women's clothes?
CHESTNUT   I'll tell you why:
So, once you'd given me the note—
Which I've still on me, by the way—   3325
For Don Rodrigo's eyes alone,
The one purporting to explain
What caused that uproar in the street
And how you'd taken Leonor,
I donned this skirt in case the Law   3330
Was out to capture us in force.
Don Pedro took a shine to me
And, quickly falling in a swoon
About my looks, grace, style and charm,
Had me sequestered in these rooms!   3335
DON CARLOS   Wise Don Rodrigo, wouldn't you
Agree that Leonor is mine
And that this beauteous lady should
Be given to me as my wife?
DON RODRIGO   As long as Leonor is wed   3340
And honor's none the worse for it,
I don't care who her husband is!
Don Carlos, welcome, then, to this
Proud family. I have gained a son.
DON PEDRO [Aside.]   Good heavens! I can hardly speak   3345
I'm so embarrassed by what just
Transpired for everyone to see!
In any case, I'd best conceal
My deep chagrin, as it's too late
To change things now. Yes, I'll concede   3350
This was a funny trick you played
Provided that my sister weds
Don Juan.
DOÑA ANA   I offer you my hand
And with it my entire soul.
DON JUAN   Sweet lady, I accept and can   3355
With confidence attest you'll find
Your love requited equally.

DON CARLOS   Now, Leonor, it's time you gave
Your hand to me.
DOÑA LEONOR   This day and each
Day, Carlos—it's been ever yours.   3360
CHESTNUT   Talk sweet to Chestnut, Celia dove,
And there may be another hand
On hand.
CELIA   I doubt that very much,
As I save mine for kitchen work,
But would a finger be enough?   3365
CHESTNUT   As long as you're attached to it,
I'll take a finger, if I must!
On that note, blessed audience,
Attentive gentlepersons all,
These *Trials of a Noble House*   3370
Are finished. Please forgive our faults.

Dance of the Four Nations

*(Being the Spaniards, the Negroes, the Italians,
and the Mexicans)*

[*The Spaniards enter.*]
1ST CHORUS   Love orders us to wage a war
Whose joys cannot be bound:
The martial drums resound,
The bugler blares his horn
2ND CHORUS   And fifes are piping all around,   5
The contest heralded in chords!
Mid tuneful signs
That we should charge their battle lines,
3RD CHORUS   We shout: "Love sallies forth on conflict's field
Triumphant, where her enemies will yield   10
And she expects full victory to be sealed!"
1ST CHORUS   Her foe is Duty in this fight,
Who plans to win as well
Because, to hear him tell
His side of things, he's right   15
2ND CHORUS   And so it is he'll sell
His cause with zealous skill and might.
At his sortie,
Assailing his fond enemy,
3RD CHORUS   "Beat war drums all you like," his army cries,   20
"My laurel crown will signal your demise,
As I alone am worthy of this prize!"
1ST CHORUS   While Love prefers the comely shine
María's[1] charms reflect,

1. This last piece of the celebration returns to the praise of the vicereine, María Luisa Manrique
de Lara, and the viceroy, Tomás Antonio de la Cerda, mentioned in line 52.

Obedient Respect   25
Thinks people should incline
2ND CHORUS   Their minds toward missions that direct
Their thoughts to praise his shrine.
So Love, you see,
That far superior deity,   30
3RD CHORUS   Will thus emerge victorious from the start,
For winners win by powers of the heart,
Which outweigh any reason can impart.
Oh, victory, victory, victory!
May yours the winner's palm and glory be,   35
Unvanquished champion of the battlefield!
Yes, long live Love, whose forces never yield!
1ST CHORUS   Watch rightful Duty vie
This day with Love, engaged
In courteous dispute   40
The two will nobly brave.
2ND CHORUS   At times, they see themselves
As siblings who've stayed close;
At others they concede
Their projects are opposed.   45
1ST CHORUS   Here triumph, then, is held
To be its opposite,
As only through a loss
Can one secure a win.
2ND CHORUS   The question is: which one   50
Of these deserves to kiss
Illustrious Cerda's feet?
He reigns victorious!
1ST CHORUS   Or those of his fair wife,
Whose fragrances perfume   55
The air far more than all
Of flowery April's blooms?
2ND CHORUS   Well might the jasmines learn
What whiteness is when set
Against her lovely hues   60
Or pale carnations, red.
1ST CHORUS   A humbled Venus yields
Her apple in defeat
And Pallas the Athene[2]
Her victor's laurel leaf.   65
2ND CHORUS   And don't forget their sprout,
That good-looking José,
As tiny grandees grow
Far grander still with age.
      [*The Negroes enter.*]
1ST CHORUS   On this date, when translucent rays   70
From these two daystars, lustrous suns

---

2. Pallas Athena (Minerva), Greek goddess of wisdom and courage.

Upon poor planet Earth, eclipse
The lamp of heaven's blazing run;
When, Venus- and Adonis-like,[3]
Their handsomeness a thing sublime,   75
They outshine the inhabitants
Of Cyprus's[4] enchanted isle;

2ND CHORUS   When Jupiter and Juno[5] lay
Their majesty aside for now
And leave, for humbler residence,   80
Their crystal palace in the clouds;
Vertumnus and Pomona[6] will
No longer tend the garden spots
Their fertilizing feet sustained
By treading on each seeded plot.   85

1ST CHORUS   Today, in short, when noble souls,
The viceroy and his peerless spouse
(Whose famous family names alone
Should bear this testimony out,
For all the fabled kings of yore,   90
However greatly mythified,
Remain in shadow's mystery
While these are manifest in light),

2ND CHORUS   A wife and husband so in love
The pleasure of their marriage bed   95
Makes union of their equal parts,
One soul where once was separateness,
So much so, were María gone,
Tomás could find no other mate.
María, too, without Tomás,   100
Would want no one to take his place.

1ST CHORUS   So, as they've put aside the pomp
Their wonted grandeur once conferred,
These rays of light conform themselves
To simpler dwellings in our world.   105
Let's raise our voices in their praise
And not let silence mar a day
On which the humblest effort lets
Our whole assembly celebrate!

2ND CHORUS   So, let our lips bring forth a sign   110
Of this regard that fills our hearts
To explain or, at least, make plain
What putting into words is hard.
Though it may be impossible
For us to show our gratitude,   115
Let no one say we didn't strive
To muster all that we could do.
     [The Italians enter.]

3. The beautiful youth Adonis was the lover of the goddess Venus (Aphrodite).
4. The island of Cyprus was considered the birthplace of Venus (Aphrodite).
5. In Roman mythology, king and queen of the gods.
6. In Roman mythology, the god of gardens and the goddess of orchards.

1ST CHORUS   On this enjoyable and festive day
    When godly beauty takes on human form
    In fair María while brave Cerda strides   120
    In glory—may he triumph evermore!—
    Today, when comely Cupids shoot those suns
    Their heavenly, resplendent quivers hold,
    Bright arrows of laudation they retrieve
    To launch again, the better to extol;   125
    When honeyed swarms of putti in the spring
    Surround awhir the rosebush's pink buds,
    So buzzing with desire for the blooms
    They'd dare to love but venture not to touch;
    Yes, on a day when this most happy home   130
    Can warrant kissing soles of noble feet
    Whose deep impressions from this briefest stay
    Will bring it joy for all eternity;
    When cuddlesome José, that tender shoot
    Of royal provenance and gentle birth,   135
    A new son nestling in the Dawn's own arms,
    Diffuses his own light to greet the birds;
    On this day when society's belles dames,
    Like glowing Nereids[7] out the sacred sea,
    Eclipse fair Venus in their comeliness   140
    And vie with Thetis in sublimities;
    Let's all in humble subjugation come
    To render homage, sacrificing whole
    The ready victims we now offer up,
    Pure hearts upon the altar of our souls.   145
    Excessive glory clothes your votaries,
    Who fervently pay tribute at your shrine.
    Let incense be exuded from our breasts
    And love perfume now aromatic minds!
    No blood or fire stains your marble slabs;   150
    This sacrifice flows free from loving hearts,
    So let our fiery will stand in their stead,
    For willing victims all is what we are
    And, thus, we ask you, prostrate at your feet
    In one submissive show of our esteem,   155
    Accept our heartfelt offerings, aware
    These praises, though most ardent, are too brief.
        [The Mexicans enter.]
2ND CHORUS   Come forth, proud Mexicans,
    Rejoicing as you come,
    And see a thousand suns   160
    Resplendent here in one.
    For if America,
    Once pagan and untamed,
    Believes its god should be
    The blazing orb of day,   165

---

7. Sea nymphs, of which Thetis, mother of the great warrior Achilles, was the best known.

Then look upon this sun
Incarnate here and laud
How she illuminates
The heights of heaven's vault;
A sun that mid snow-white   170
And carmine clouds sends forth
A gleam from eyes that shine
Like radiant sapphire orbs;
A sun whose glorious light
Immerses all earth's spheres   175
In yellow beams that vie
With rays from gold Ophir:
María, matchless queen!
You teach the skies how stars
Should glint and show the Spring   180
What April flowers are.
Your blushing cheeks
Together place on view
The pale carnation's white
Beside more crimson hues.   185
Praise her unvanquished spouse
As well, who's bravely earned
The laurels he's attained,
All richly well-deserved.
Then there's that fair-skinned pink,   190
That purple jasmine bud,
The fruit that noble vines
Produced conjoined in love:
That sweet José, in whom
His fatherland should find   195
More treasure than remains
In Potosí's[8] rich mines.
So let's surrender, then,
You proud Americans,
To these three godlike souls,   200
Rejoicing in their midst.
        [*The four nations come together, playing instruments
        and singing a song.*]
3RD CHORUS   In happy competition thus
Do Love and Duty gamely vie.
As friends, each aids the other's cause,
Though each competes to take the prize,   205
For it's the victor's laurel crown
And public's loud applause they seek
In rendering all the deference
Due Cerda at his noble feet.
So Duty, first, would have it known   210
It's unbecoming and inapt

8. Known as the Cerro Rico or Cerro de Plata (rich mountain or mountain of silver), Potosí was
   the site of the largest Spanish silver mining operation in the Americas.

To take what one's obliged to do
And make it seem a gracious act.
More courtly than her counterpart,
Love answers that, were this the case,   215
She'd voluntarily allot
The homage Duty obligates.
Then Duty proffers this insight:
It's crucial that we understand
The reason it's called "tribute" is   220
It's paid, not gifted with free hands.
But Love more logically responds
That, though the show of honor's one,
Affection in its offering
Can turn a duty into love.   225
And so Love wins, with Duty left
Confessing that a victory
By such a cherished foe has eased
His ignominious defeat.
In concert joyously as one,   230
These former adversaries now
Pay tribute they'd both gladly give,
And give as though not duty-bound.
    [A turdión⁹ *is played and all dance.*]
4TH CHORUS   To Cerda, glorious and invincible,
In pious reverence of whose sacred cult   235
Love yields her arrow's quivers, Mars his crowns
Of laurel and great Jove his lightning bolts;
And to that Venus fair, for whom the Sea
Erects in crystal temples thrones of snow,
The Sky ethereal altars in the clouds   240
And solid Earth substantial altar stones;
That Mantuan goddess, radiant and divine,
Whose shrine boasts offerings once bestowed as gifts
To Venus, such as apples and seashells,
Or pure Diana, such as bows and skins;¹   245
And to the nobly born José, stout branch
Of royal trunks still flowering all this time,
The offspring that unites Laguna's house
Forever with the grand Paredes line;
Make, all of you, a fitting sacrifice   250
That properly reflects your loving thoughts
Of so illustrious a viceroyalty
And bring unto their altars all you ought.
May these, then, by accepting such poor gifts,
Acknowledge our intentions are the best,   255
For our conception of this offering
Exceeded what resources we possess.

---

9. A lively dance, similar to a galliard, with quick steps and turns.
1. María was related to the Dukes of Mantua through her father's line. As the Mantuan goddess,
   she exhibits as spoils on her altar the offerings once made to other deities.

As gods we praise are incorporeal,
They far prefer the sacrifice that comes
From out their fervent devotees' pure hearts   260
To any spilling of a beast's warm blood.
We beg your pardon for this humble fare,
Assuaged you look more favorably upon
Sincere attempts to honor you that fail
Than smug self-satisfaction from your flock.   265
So may the master of this happy house
Now cast this sovereign homage we impart
In living monuments that honor him
Whose number will be counted out in stars.
    [A jácara[2] *is played and all dance.*]
3RD CHORUS   Now that these shows of gratitude   270
Evincing our desire to please
Have proven all to be so small
The grander they've aspired to be;
And now, illustrious Cerda, that
The voices we proposed to raise   275
In manifesting love for you
Emerged as echoes far too faint;
And now, divine María, that
No laud has reached your heaven's spheres,
As songs have proved unsuitable,   280
Reducing us to silence here;
And now, most nobly born José,
That these collective throats have sung
Their adoration in salute
Of your first rising, like a sun;   285
And now, fair ladies gathered here,
That Love has made fond overtures
To this assembly, all the while
Ensuring due Respect's observed;
And now that, estimating just   290
How great a favor you, sir, have
Conferred upon us, Duty will
Need all of Time to pay it back,
May your benign indulgence bear
The insufficient praise brought forth.   295
Your grandeur all but guaranteed
Our humble efforts would fall short.
But as this homage is your own,
It can't help but be adequate,
For all things yours are bounteous,   300
Your reverence being what it is.

---

2. The *jácara* was a short ballad form sung and danced in between sections of a longer play.

BACKGROUNDS AND CONTEXTS

Theater New and Old

FÉLIX LOPE DE VEGA Y CARPIO

The playwright presented his tongue-in-cheek treatise to the Madrid Academy, a literary society, in 1609. In this early version of the long-standing European quarrel between the ancients and the moderns, Lope displays his considerable knowledge of the classics while claiming to eschew them as models. His new art of playwriting focuses on pleasing the audience that pays for the plays rather than on following Aristotelian rules of propriety and form. Although Lope continued to rely heavily on classical allusions, his manifesto provides clear evidence that he saw himself breaking with tradition to create a new art form, one uniquely attuned to the demands of its audience. To judge from Lope's phenomenal success as a playwright—hundreds of his plays survive today—he more than fulfilled those demands.

The New Art of Writing Plays[†]

You ask me, noble spirits flower of Spain—
Whose famed Academy will surely reign
Supreme, ere long, not only over those
Italian assemblies which rose
5　By Lake Avernes under Cicero,[1]
But those Athenian gatherings also,
At the Lyceum[2] owing their renown
To philosophic conclaves like your own—
To tell you what in plays is now allowed
10　For those whose wish it is to please the crowd.

The subject seems an easy one, it's true,
And easy it would be for those of you
Who've written little, but who've studied more
The art of writing and of all such lore.
15　For what condemns my efforts at the start
Is that I've always written without art.

Not, thank God, that I didn't know the rules.
I did my course of Grammar in the schools,

---

†　From Félix Lope de Vega y Carpio, "The New Art of Writing Plays," in *Theatre/Theory/Theatre: The Major Critical Texts from Aristotle and Zeami to Soyinka and Havel*, trans. Marvin Carlson, ed. Daniel Gerould (New York: Applause Books, 2000), pp. 136–45. Reprinted by permission of the translator. Notes are by the editor of this Norton Critical Edition.
1. The Roman philosopher and orator Cicero (106–43 B.C.E.) had a villa near Lake Avernus in Campania, Italy.
2. Athenian site used for assemblies, teaching, and study; associated with Aristotle's school of philosophy.

Casting my eye on every useful source
20 Before the sun had ten times run its course,
Leaving the Ram and coming to the Fishes,[3]
Only to find, contrary to my wishes,
That plays today in Spain are not devised
The way that their inventors all advised,
25 But barbarously our poets their talents waste
Confirming vulgar patrons in their taste.

Playwriting here began in such a way
That he who would artistic rules obey
Will perish without glory or resource,
30 For custom is more powerful a force
Than reason or coercion. It is true
That I have sometimes written like those few
Who follow art, but then my eye is caught
By monstrous works, with painted settings fraught,
35 Where flock the crowds and ladies canonize
By their support such sorry exercise.

So when I have a comedy to write
I lock up with six keys out of my sight
Plautus and Terence,[4] and their precepts too
40 For fear their cries will even reach me through
Dumb books, for I know truth insists on speaking.
And then I write, for inspiration seeking
Those whose sole aim was winning vulgar[5] praise.
Since after all it is the crowd who pays
45 Why not consider them when writing plays?

True comedy must its own end embrace
Like every sort of poetry, in this case
To imitate men's action and display
A portrait of the customs of the day.
50 Poetic imitation all must be
Composed of elements that number three:
Discourse, and pleasant verse, and harmony.
All three of these are also to be found
In tragedy, but comedy is bound
55 To deal with humble and plebeian themes
While tragedy seeks royal and high extremes.
Now see if in our plays the flaws are great.

They were called *actos*, since they imitate
The actions and the doings of the crowd.
60 Lope de Rueda[6] was in Spain endowed
With skill in writing *actos* and one may

---

3. I.e., a full astronomical year, as the sun moves from Aries to Pisces.
4. Comic Roman playwrights; here, classical models for playwriting in the Renaissance.
5. *Vulgo* and *vulgar* in Spanish simply mean "people/of the people."
6. Early Spanish dramatist and dramatic impresario (c. 1505–1565).

See still in print his comedies today,
In prose so low in style as to display
Mechanics rude, and stories dealing with
65 Love coming to the daughter of a smith.

And so the custom holds in many places
To keep the ancient name of *entremeses*[7]
For these old plays where art was still allowed
That show a single action of the crowd
70 And never place a sovereign on show.
Twas thus the art, because its style was low,
Came to be scorned, and comedies ere long
Added in kings to please the ignorant throng.

In his *Poetics*[8] Aristotle shows,
75 Though sketchily, how comedy arose,
With Athens and Megara[9] in contention
Which was the first to sponsor this invention.
For Magnetes Athenians made their claim
While Epicarmus[1] Megara would name.
80 The origins, according to Donatus,
Were ancient sacrifices, and he taught us
As Horace did, to say that Thespis brought us
The first true tragedies, while comedies
Were started off by Aristophanes.[2]

85 Twas comedy that Homer imitated
Within his *Odyssey*, but he created
The *Iliad* with tragedy in mind,
In imitation of which I defined
My own *Jerusalem*[3] by epic's name
90 But added tragic, doing much the same
As all those people who call comedy
The celebrated Dante's trilogy
As Prologist Manetti recognizes.[4]

Now comedy, everyone realizes,
95 Was silenced for a time, under suspicion.
Twas then that satire first came to fruition.

---

7. Interludes.
8. Aristotle's treatise on poetry, from the fourth century B.C.E., and rediscovered in Europe in the sixteenth century.
9. Ancient Greek cities.
1. Magnes (Magnetes) was an Athenian comic poet of the fifth century B.C.E.; Epicarmus (generally spelled Epicharmus in English) was a Greek dramatist and philosopher based in Sicily, also associated with comedy.
2. Aelius Donatus was a Roman grammarian and rhetorician in the fourth century C.E. Horace (65–8 B.C.E.) was a Roman poet and satirist in the age of Augustus; Thespis was a Greek poet traditionally associated with tragedy and variously credited with inventing the prologue, roles for a single actor, and masks. Aristophanes was a comic playwright in ancient Athens, many of whose plays survive today.
3. Lope's epic poem *Jerusalén conquistada* (1609), which he called a "tragic epic."
4. Dante's three-part poem, the *Divine Comedy*, completed in 1320; humanist Gianozzo Manetti wrote a biography of Dante in the early fifteenth century.

Its cruelty soon brought it to an end,
And the New Comedy[5] became the favored trend.
First came the chorus, then it was decided
100 How many characters could be provided.
Although Menander, Terence's descendant,
Despised the chorus as an idle pendant,
Terence observed the precepts with more care.
The style of comedy he'd never dare
105 Give tragic grandeur, a mistake pernicious.
Which many see in Plautus' works as vicious.
Terence was much more cautious of the laws.

From history the tragic author draws.
Through fictions comic authors seek applause.
110 Humble in origin, comedy was known
As flat of foot, its actors could be shown
Without cothurni[6] or the tragic scene.
Many comedic genres there have been—
Atellan farces, mimes, and the togatas,
115 Also the tavern plays, and palliatas—[7]
Which then as now were various in approach.

Poets with Attic[8] elegance would reproach
In comedy both vice and evil living,
And the Athenians were always giving
120 Prizes alike for comic poets and planners.
Thus Tully[9] called these plays mirrors of manners,
And also living images of truth,
The very highest accolade, in sooth.
So comedy matched history in renown.
125 See then if it deserves so rich a crown!
But I perceive, by all your weary looks,
That this is merely translating old books
And boring you with scholarly distraction.
Believe me, I had reason for my action.
130 I must recall this ancient lore again
In order to be able to explain
The art of writing plays today in Spain.
Here everything is done in art's despite
And if I were to tell you how to write
135 Today, my own experience must season
My discourse, not the ancient laws or reason
And certainly not art, which truth reflects—
A truth the ignorant multitude rejects.

---

5. Greek comedy c. 350–320 B.C.E., characterized by gentle satire of private individuals and domestic life. Menander (c. 342–292 B.C.E.) was its greatest exponent.
6. Cothurni: thick-soled buskins or boots worn by actors of tragedies.
7. Atellan farces: early Roman farces, originally improvised, relying on slapstick; fabula palliata, or "play in Greek dress" (from the Latin pallium, for a Greek cloak), was the name given to Roman translations or adaptations of Greek New Comedy, eventually replaced by the fabula togata (i.e., in Roman clothes, or togas).
8. Athenian.
9. I.e., Cicero.

If, my wise friends, it is for art you're zealous,
140 Read Udine's learned doctor, Robortellus[1]
On Aristotle and especially
In what he writes concerning comedy,
For writings have appeared in such profusion
That everything today is in confusion.
145 If you wish my opinion on the plays
Most popular today and on the ways
The crowd and laws it fosters now support
Vile chimeras and monsters of that sort—
I must obey, forgive but understand me,
150 Whoever has the power to command me.
Gilding the errors of the public taste
I'll tell you in what mode I'd have them placed,
The only path for art today it seems
Is that midway between the two extremes.

155 Select your subject and don't be dismayed—
Forgive these rules—if kings must be portrayed.
Though as for that I understand our lord
Philip the Prudent,[2] King of Spain, deplored
Seeing a king in them, either because
160 He thought it went against artistic laws
Or did not want authority on show
Before an audience so mean and low.
This but repeats Old Comedy's depictions.
Plautus brought even gods into his fictions
165 As Jupiter in his *Amphitrion*.[3]
God knows I don't approve such goings-on
Since Plutarch, as Menander he discussed
Showed for Old Comedy no small disgust.
But since so far from art our era strays
170 Betraying it in Spain a thousand ways
Let learned doctors here avert their gaze.
Tragedy mixed throughout with comedy
Terence with Seneca—although this be
Another minotaur or Pasiphaë,[4]
175 One section serious, another slight,
Such varied mixtures lead to much delight.
For this let nature our example be
Gaining much beauty in variety.

Be sure that in your fable you've employed
180 One single action, by all means avoid

---

1. Humanist critic and commentator Francesco Robortello (1516–1557), born in the Italian city of Udine, wrote an influential early commentary on Aristotle's *Poetics* (1548).
2. I.e., Philip II.
3. One of Plautus's most famous comedies, which placed mythological characters in farcical situations.
4. Seneca was a famous Roman tragedian; Lope is arguing here for tragicomedy, even if, as a mixed genre, it might resemble the monstrous Minotaur (half man, half bull) of Greek myth, born of Pasiphaë's love for a bull.

The episodic, that is, draw the line
At all those things outside the main design.
And yet be sure that nothing you delete
That is required to make the whole complete.
185 No use advising that your action run,
As Aristotle wished, within one sun,
But our respect for him we surely lose
When tragedy's sententious style we fuse
With meaner comedy's more humble fable.

190 Take up as little time as you are able
Unless to history you have aspired
In which some years of time may be required.
If you require a character to take
A lengthy journey, utilize the break
195 Between the acts. If this offend,
Those who do not approve should not attend.
Oh, many in these days gain satisfaction
Seeing in one fictitious day an action
Requiring years, although they realize
200 No actual day could see such enterprise.
But since we can expect a Spaniard's rage
If in two hours' traffic on the stage
He's not presented everything in mumming
From Genesis until the Second Coming
205 I think it best to recognize his need,
And offer him whatever will succeed.

The subject chosen, write in prose, dividing
The story into three acts, coinciding
If possible, with real unbroken days.
210 That clever author, Captain Virués,[5]
Made comedies in three acts, that before
Had crawled, as babies do, upon four,
Since comedies were also infants then.
And I myself, when I was twelve or ten
215 Scrawled on four sheets of paper four-act plays,
An act on every page, and in those days
An *entremés* filled each entre'acte.
Now there may be but one, and that in fact
A dance, for dance to comedy is fitted
220 As even Aristotle has admitted.
And Athenaeus, Plato, Xenophon[6]
Speak of it, though the latter frown upon
Indecorous dancing, like those parodies
Of ancient choruses by Callipedes.[7]

5. Cristóbal de Virués (1550–1614) was one of several early Spanish dramatists credited with
reducing four acts to three.
6. Athenaeus: Greek rhetorician, third century B.C.E.; Plato: perhaps the most influential of the
Athenian philosophers (428–348 B.C.E.); Xenophon: Greek historian (c. 430–350 B.C.E.).
7. Greek tragic actor.

225 The matter being split into two parts,
Be sure to carry through from where it starts
Until the action end, and don't untie
Your plot until the final scene is nigh.
Hold back your ending. If the crowd expects it
230 They'll turn their backs, while heading for the exit,
On what they watched for hours when they feel
That you have nothing further to reveal.
Silence on stage should rarely be allowed,
For when no one is speaking, then the crowd
235 Grows restless and the story slows its pace.
Avoiding this defect adds art and grace.

Begin then, in plain language phrase your matter,
Avoiding odd conceits or clever patter
On family doings, which is what the chatter
240 Of your few characters will represent.
But if you have a character who's meant
To give advice, persuade, or turn aside,
Then rhetoric and wit may be applied.
Here truth is given its due, for we depart
245 From common speech and utilize more art
In seeking to condemn or to persuade.
Aristides[8] the rhetorician, laid
A charge on comic language to be
Pure, clear, and flexible, adding that we
250 Find this in common speech, which differs quite
From that found in society polite,
Where sonorous discourse is cultivated
And language is adorned and elevated.

Do not drag in quotations nor offend
255 With words flamboyant, for if you intend
To imitate real speech, don't put before us
The discourse of Pancaya or Metaurus,[9]
Or hippogriffs, or centaurs, or the like.
Whenever kings are speaking, try to strike
260 A note of royal gravity, for the sage,
Sententious modesty befitting age.
Describe young lovers with those passions proved
So those who listen will be deeply moved.
Soliloquies should be, for he who writes them
265 A way to transform whoever recites them,
And changing him change everyone who came.
He may pose questions, answering the same,
And in his plaints, let him invite no blame
By giving women less than due respect.

8. Greek rhetorician.
9. Panchaea (Pancaya) is an imaginary island paradise; Metaurus is a river in Italy, scene of a
famous Roman victory against the Carthaginians in 207 B.C.E.

270 The ladies naturally we would expect
    To be in character. If they change their dress,
    Let it be seemly done, for I confess,
    The crowd is always pleased by male disguise.

    Impossibilities avoid, your duty lies
275 Only in seeking truthful imitation.
    Don't let your lackey speak above his station
    Nor, as we've seen in certain foreign plays,
    Express conceits. Whatever someone says
    He should not contradict what he has spoken,
280 I mean forget. Sophocles, by this token
    Erred when Oedipus doesn't understand
    That Laius[1] was destroyed by his own hand.
    Each scene with wit and epigram conclude,
    Expressed in verse, with elegance imbued,
285 So that the one entrusted with the ending
    Will not arouse disgust in those attending.

    In your first act set forth your matter, leaving
    Until the second act the interweaving
    Of deeds, so by the middle of the third
290 The end of all may still not be inferred.
    Deceive anticipation, thus you may
    Let understanding follow when you stray
    Quite far from what was promised at the start.
    Use prudence, never let your verse depart
295 From what will suit your subject matter best.
    Complaints should be in *décimas* expressed.
    Sonnets are good for those in expectation,
    Romances are best suited for relation
    Of actions, though *octavas* have more lustre.
300 For grave events, the tercets you should muster
    And *redondillas*[2] for the heart's concerns.
    Figures of rhetoric one never spurns
    Such as repeating or anadiplosis
    And, at the start of lines this figure closes,
305 Anaphora in various permutations,
    Ironies and such-like manifestations,
    Apostrophies, queries, and exclamations.

    To make your public by the truth deceived
    Is a device that has been well received.
310 It's always found in Miguel Sánchez'[3] plays,
    An innovation meriting high praise.

1. Sophocles (496–406 B.C.E.) is one of the three great tragedians of classical Athens whose plays survive; Oedipus and Laius are characters in his *Oedipus the King*.
2. Lope explains which metrical structures are best suited to each kind of content. *Décimas* are ten-line stanzas with verses of eight syllables; *romances* are popular ballads in eight-syllable verses; *octavas* are eight-line stanzas with verses of eleven syllables; *redondillas* are four-line stanzas with verses of eight syllables.
3. Minor dramatist of Lope's time.

Equivocation and uncertainty
Arising from the ambiguous will be
Forever popular, since crowds delight
315 In thinking only they perceive aright.
Best are those plots where honor has a part,
These stir profoundly every hearer's heart.
Also show virtuous action, for tis known
That everyone loves virtue to be shown.

320 Thus if an actor should the role attempt
Of traitor, he arouses such contempt
No one will sell him what he wants to buy,
And everywhere he goes, the people fly,
But he who's loyal is honored and invited,
325 Not even by the highest is he slighted.
They seek him, to regale and to acclaim.

Four pages for each act should be your aim,
For twelve best suit the patience and also
The time of those who come to see the show.
330 Don't be too clear in satire, for you know
Greek and Italian dramas were forbidden
In which the satire was not sagely hidden.
Don't prick too deep, if anyone you blame,
For this will garner neither praise nor fame.
335 Some precepts, though by ancient art neglected,
As aphorisms yet should be respected,
Though we have little space to treat them now.
Vitruvius tells stage directors how
Three kinds of scenes are managed, Maximus,
340 Horace in his epistles, Crinitus,[4]
And others give details on such things as these—
Backdrops, false marble, houses, huts, and trees.
On costume Julius Pollux[5] is the source
For all we need to know, although of course
345 In Spain today there are presented plays
Containing the most barbarous displays—
Turks wearing Christian collars, Roman knights
Dressed in tight breeches—these are common sights.

Not one of these should any designate
350 More barbarous than myself, who dares to state
Precepts in art's defense, even while knowing
I don't resist the vulgar current's flowing.
For this England and France call me untaught.
What can I do, for I have now begot
355 Four hundred eighty-three dramatic pieces,

---

4. Vitruvius: Roman architect of the first century B.C.E., author of the famous treatise *De Architectura*, in which he discusses Roman theaters. Maximus: Roman historian and author of moral anecdotes; Crinitus: Pietro Riccio, fifteenth-century Florentine humanist.
5. Greek rhetorician of the second century B.C.E., with a particular interest in theater.

A sum this week's new offering increases,
And all of these but six, I must admit,
The gravest sins against the art commit.
And yet, at last, I must defend my plays
360 While knowing they are flawed in many ways

Because their vogue depended on these flaws
For sometimes something charms the taste because
It is in fact contrary to the laws.

Humanae cur sit speculum comoedia vitae
365 *Quaeve ferat inveni commoda, quaeve seni*
Quid praeter lepidosque sales, excultaque verba,
Et genus eloquii purius inde petas,
Quae gravia in mediis ocurrant lusibus, et quae
Iucundis passim seria mexta iocis,
370 *Quam sint fallaces serui, quam improba semper,*
Fraudeque et omnigenis foemina plena dolis,
Quam miser, infelix, stultus, et ineptus amator,
*Quam vix succedant, quae bene coepta putes.**

Then listen carefully and do not fear
375 For art, since comedy is of that sphere
That, when one listens, everything comes clear.

* *Here is an approximate translation of the Latin passage:*
How comedy reflects our human state
How well both young and old she represents
What else can matter with such grace relate
With cultivated words and eloquence
How charmingly she mixes matters light
With grave concerns, the serious with jest,
How traitors are exposed and put to flight
And scheming women's strategies confessed.
How silly courses simple lovers run
And how things may end ill, though well begun.

MIGUEL DE CERVANTES SAAVEDRA

Although far better known for his *Don Quixote* (1605, 1615), Miguel de Cervantes was also a playwright, though he did not find great success in his own time. In the "Prologue" to his published plays and interludes (1615), he reminisces about the development of Spanish theater during his lifetime. Cervantes saw the theater evolve from a simple form with basic texts, costumes, and scenery in the time of Lope de Rueda (1505–1565) to the more elaborate plays and productions of Lope de Vega and his time. Describing his own long history as a playwright, Cervantes rues his failure to sell plays to acting companies in the new era, and explains his decision to publish them instead.

[Writing for the Theater]†

I recall having seen the great Lope de Rueda[1] in a play, that famous man of the theater and of understanding. He was from Seville, and a gold beater, which are those who make gold leaf; he was notable for his pastoral poetry, and none then or since has surpassed him in that mode. Although I was a boy then, and could not really judge the quality of his verse with any certainty, when I revisit those lines that remain in my memory from these, my mature years, I find that what I have said is true. * * *

In the time of this famous Spaniard, all the appurtenances of the company's manager fit in one sack, as they were no more than four white shepherd's jackets embossed with gilt leather, four beards, wigs, and shepherd's crooks, and little else. The plays were dialogues, much like eclogues, between two or three shepherds and a shepherdess, enlivened and spaced out by two or three interludes, of either a black woman, a villain, a fool, or a Biscayan.[2] * * * There were no stage machines, nor fights between Moors and Christians, on foot or on horseback; no figure appeared or seemed to appear from the center of the earth through the space beneath the stage, which was made of four benches arranged in a square with four or six planks on top, so that it was raised about four handspans from the floor; nor were there clouds full of angels or souls that descended from the heavens. The theater was adorned with an old blanket, pulled from one side to the other with two strings, to make the dressing room. Behind it were the musicians, singing some old ballad with no guitar to accompany them. * * *

After Lope de Rueda came Navarro,[3] from Toledo, who was famous for playing a cowardly ruffian. He made plays somewhat more elaborate, moving the costumes to chests and trunks. He moved the music out from behind the blanket, where it had been sung before, onto the stage. He removed the actors' beards, for until then no one had acted without a false one, and made them all play their parts barefaced, except for those who were to play old men or other characters who required a change in appearance. He invented machines, clouds, thunder and lightning, challenges and battles, yet none of this reached the lofty pinnacle it occupies today.

And truly no one can contradict me on this—and this is where I must be less modest—for the theaters of Madrid then showed *The Traffic of Algiers*, which I composed, *The Siege of Numantia,* and *The Naval Battle,* in which I dared to reduce plays to three acts, from the five they had previously.[4] I showed, or better yet, I was the first to represent the imaginations and hidden thoughts of the soul through allegorical figures on the stage, to the great and general delight of the audience. I composed in this period almost twenty or thirty plays, all of which were performed without meriting an offering of cucumbers or other projectiles—they had their run with no

† From "Prologue," in *Ocho comedias y ocho entremeses nuevos* (*Eight New Plays and Eight New Interludes*) (1615). Translated by the editor for this Norton Critical Edition.
1. Early dramatist and dramatic impresario (c. 1505–1565) whose company traveled through Spain.
2. Basque, from the region of Biscaya in Northern Spain. Biscayans were often stereotyped and mocked for their linguistic difference and supposed irascible nature. Cervantes wrote an interlude entitled "The False Biscayan."
3. This figure has not been conclusively identified.
4. Critics agree that this was not in fact Cervantes' innovation. *Numantia* in fact has four acts. *The Naval Battle* has not survived.

whistling, shouts, or hubbub. Yet other matters claimed my attention, and I abandoned my quill and the theater. Then came that prodigy of nature, the great Lope de Vega, and stole the crown of playwriting. He overwhelmed all actors and placed them under his rule; he filled the world with his own pleasing and well-made plays—so many, in fact, that he's written over ten thousand pages—and, most remarkably, has seen them all performed or at least heard that they were performed, and although some—for there are many—have wanted to share in the glory of his work, all of their writing together does not amount to half of Lope's alone.

Some years ago I returned to my old leisure, and, under the impression that the times would still ring with my praises, I composed some plays again. But those birds had flown: there were now no actor-managers to request them of me, although they knew I had them, and so I stashed them in a chest, dedicating and condemning them to perpetual silence. One publisher told me he would have bought them from me, had not one of the licensed managers told him that while much could be expected from my prose, little could be expected of my verse. To tell the truth, I was chagrined to hear it, and I said to myself, "Either I am no longer myself, or the times have much improved, even though generally the reverse is true, and we praise all times past." I took another look at my plays and at some interludes that were stashed away with them, and I saw that they were not so bad that they did not merit emerging from the fog of that one manager's understanding to the light of other, less fussy and more discerning ones. Yet I lost interest and sold them to the publisher, who has printed them here as he offers them to you. He paid me reasonably; I took my money easily, with no outstanding deals or debts to actors. I hope that they're the best in the world, or at least reasonably good; you shall see, dear reader, and if you find anything good in them, when you run across my naysaying manager, tell him to change his ways, for I offend no one, and that he should note that they contain no obvious non-sense, and that the verse is that which plays require, of the lowest of the three styles, and that the language of the interludes corresponds to the characters introduced therein.

AGUSTÍN DE ROJAS VILLANDRANDO

The dramatist and actor Agustín de Rojas Villandrando specialized in the short pieces known as *loas*, which were performed at the start of plays to engage the audience. His *El viaje entretenido* (*The Pleasant Voyage*) (1603)—a collection of dialogues and *loas* about the world of the theater—includes a detailed history of Spanish theater in verse form. Rojas Villandrando expresses great pride in the Spanish tradition, closely connecting theatrical greatness to Spain's military feats and imperial expansion, from the defeat of Muslim Granada, to the conquest of the New World, to Spanish triumphs in Italy. Literary achievements, Rojas Villandrando stresses, go hand in hand with national victories as both chart the apotheosis of Spain. This *loa* thus captures another meaning of the term—song of praise—to offer a triumpha-list history of Golden Age drama.

[A Brief History of Theater in Spain]†

And yet, where drama's quality
progressed the most in excellence
turns out to be the latest place
where it's become more prominent,
35 none other than our mother Spain,
for it was in those happy times
when our two glorious Catholic Kings
(whose names should be immortalized),
brave Ferdinand and Isabel,
40 enthroned now in the realm of saints,
expelled that remnant of the Moors
still dwelling in the south of Spain
within Granada's emirate,
establishing from that year forth
45 the Holy Inquisition, just
as theater in our land was born.[1]
Then Juan de la Encina[2] wrote,
a vaunted literary man
who started our tradition off
50 and left three eclogues by his hand,
which he himself performed before
the Duchess and the Admiral
of Infantado and Castille,
the first to pen what others would.
55 So, to his greater glory, then,
and to our nation's stage as well,
around the time Columbus had
discovered founts of untold wealth
throughout the Indies and New World
60 while that Great Captain,[3] who began
the vanquishing of Naples, took
to subjugating all its lands,
a kind of native theater saw
a similar discovery,
65 which spurred the Spanish populace
to undertake the same good deeds,
heroic feats and noble acts
they viewed upon the public stage,
theatrical performances
70 of valiant gestes and epic aims

---

† From *Loa* VIII, in *El viaje entretenido* (*The Pleasant Voyage*) (1603). Translated by G. J. Racz for this Norton Critical Edition.

1. Ferdinand of Aragon (1452–1516) and Isabel of Castile (1451–1504), often known as the Catholic Monarchs, united their kingdoms through their marriage (1469) and conquered the Nasrid kingdom of Granada (1492) to consolidate Spain. The Spanish Inquisition was established in 1478 to ensure the orthodoxy of converts to Catholicism.

2. Early Spanish playwright and composer (1468–1529) who specialized in short pastoral plays known as eclogues.

3. Gonzalo Fernández de Córdoba (1453–1515), Spanish commander renowned for his role in Spain's conquest of Naples at the turn of the sixteenth century.

evinced in men distinguished both
in letters and the art of war.
Here, one of two scenarios
plays out on stage: the first shows forth
75 some estimable gentleman's
descent and his nobility,
the second, some cruel prince's base
deportment and rank cruelties
so spectators might emulate
80 the one and deem the other vile.
This shows how drama inculcates
the highest virtues known in life,
a voyage of discovery
discovered in these new milieus,
85 a new world in its special way
desired by the multitudes,
for honor, treasure, benefit
and pleasure bide within this gift,
as comedy was nothing less
90 to playgoers than all these things.
It's been thus since the dawn of man,
invented, written and performed
not only by the ancient Greeks
and Romans, but by many more.

          ✳   ✳   ✳

95 I wouldn't dare presume to write
on any foreign dramatist
so, speaking but of Spanish ones,
our Lope de Rueda[4] begins
promoting Spanish comedy
100 and giving order to its lines.
This actor of great comic skill
and major poet of his time
divided dramas into acts
and authored prologues for each piece
105 called "loas," which are songs of praise.
Another feature took the themes,
confusions, intrigues and affairs
transpiring in the play at large
and interspersed these comically
110 between the acts to mirror parts
of that main work, and so was born
the entr'acte or the *entremés*,
wry interludes composed in prose
more humorous than circumspect.
115 Musicians strummed a cheap guitar
offstage beyond the public's view
to fill longueurs between the scenes

---

4. Early dramatist and dramatic impresario (c. 1505–1565) whose company traveled through Spain.

discordantly and out of tune.
That's when the clown would start his dance
120   and stun the crowds by sticking out
his tongue so frequently this rare
delight left everybody wowed.
In time, these practices were left
behind as Spain's supply of wits
125   declined to such a great extent
that poets took to spilling ink
to turn out in disordered prose
ungainly pastoral laments
in comic plays where shepherds spoke
130   for six acts, as they did back then,
their only props a coarse hide coat,
some old vihuela⁵ or a lute
and rustic's beard without a bit
of gold or silk for them to use.
135   Eventually our dramatists
left both the coats and beards behind
and started introducing themes
of love into their storylines,
in which a lady played a role—
140   the object of her sire's concerns—
a suitor, too, whom she disdained
and still another loved by her,
an older gentleman who'd scold,
a fool who'd spy on love's retreats,
145   a townsman who would wed the pair
and one who'd plan their marriage feast.
That's when the fathers wore long coats,
had beards, of course, and long white hair.
Though you might see a woman's dress,
150   real women on the boards were scarce,
their parts performed by boys. This, too,
fell out of use as actors wore
the costumery and tunics fit
for Christian characters and Moors,
155   with Berrio⁶ starting up this trend.
Thus others, following with these themes,
placed figures of more gravitas
upon the boards, like kings and queens.
The first, Juan de la Cueva,⁷ was
160   the playwright who, you may have heard,
composed *The Tyrant Father*, then
divided this into two works.
Cervantes wrote *The Commerce of
Algiers*, Commander Vega booked

---

5. Stringed musical instrument, somewhat like a large guitar.
6. Most likely Gonzalo Mateo de Berrio (1554–1628?), Granadan dramatist mentioned by several contemporaries; none of his plays have survived.
7. Early dramatist (1550–c. 1610) renowned for introducing Spanish history as a theatrical subject.

165   his *Lauras*, Don Francisco de
la Cueva[8] his *The Beautiful
Adonis*, then Loyola[9] that
Audalla, which were all quite fine.
A use of songs and ballads marked
170   dramatic output at this time.
Two blind men native to these forms
habitually intoned this verse
and plays like these contained four acts
with interludes in every work,
175   which ended with a little dance
that rendered audiences glad.
This style passed, another came:
now characters were higher class
with Spanish theater much improved.
180   That's when Artieda hit the scene
by writing *Merlin's Spells*. Meanwhile,
Lupercio penned his tragedies
as *Semiramis*, brave in war
and peace, appeared from Virués,
185   Morales wrote *The Crazy Count*
and there were less patrician plays.[1]
These dramatists wrote high-flown verse
while actors donned lush tunics sewn
from satin and fine velvet cloth
190   and wore silk stockings for their hose.
These plays unfolded in three acts,
presenting challenges and threats
as players sang in twos and threes
and, finally, there were actresses.
195   Then plays with stage machinery
and other genres plied the boards,
some touching on religious themes,
with others comedies of war.
In those days, Pero Díaz wrote
200   his *Rosary* with striking skills;
Alonso Díaz penned his play
Saint Anthony[2] and all Seville
could scarce produce a dramatist
who'd hatched no play about a saint.
205   Now actors sang in threes or fours
and actresses lit up the stage
decked out, at times, in male attire,
the height of elegance unfurled,
and made grand entrances adorned

---

8. Francisco de la Cueva (c. 1550–c. 1625), author of tragedies.
9. Juan Bautista de Loyola, sixteenth-century Toledan dramatist; his plays have not survived.
1. Valencian dramatist Andrés Rey de Artieda (1544–1613), whose Merlin play has not survived.
   Lupercio Leonardo de Argensola (1559–1613) was a tragedian who also wrote attacks on the *comedia* ("Against the Theater," in this volume). Cristóbal de Virués (1550–c. 1609), Valencian tragedian. Dramatist Alonso, or possibly Pedro, de Morales was active in the later sixteenth-century.
2. These plays have not survived.

210 with necklaces of gold and pearls.
Then even horses tread the boards,
a showing of magnificence
that none had ever seen before
and hardly was the least of them.
215 This kind of theater also passed
and gave way to our own, which might
by rights be called the Golden Age,
incorporating at one time
adept performers, splendid plays,
220 great intrigues, lessons and conceits,
inventive plots, light interludes,
sweet music, lyrics, novelties,
displays of genius, dances, masks,
fine clothing, pomp, rich spectacles,
225 engagements, tournaments and jousts,
all features joint and several
combined to such supreme effect
that we today can scarce believe
how any theater yet to come
230 could say more than the plays we've seen.
Now, what will those who follow do
that theater hasn't done before?
And what will they invent that no
one's seen before? One thing's for sure:
235 our drama, in the end, has reached
such heights of excellence it's plain
to see we're losing sight of it.
God grant it doesn't lose its way!
Today, that reigning sun of Spain,
240 Lope de Vega, our bright light
(a rising Phoenix and ideal
Apollo for all poets) writes
his comedies day in, day out,
and all of these exceptional.
245 I couldn't count them if I tried
nor anyone record them all.

*   *   *

Who doesn't know these dramatists?
Which hasn't merited his fame?
Who isn't stunned to hear their wit
250 and eloquence pervade these plays?
Our present situation thus,
forgive me then if I presume
to ask from you on their behalf
a show of reverence that's due
255 their theater, for in light of all
the efforts they expend to make
these works, you should forgive the faults
of those who act them on the stage.

MIGUEL DE CERVANTES SAAVEDRA

The second act of Cervantes' play *The Lucky Scoundrel* (1615) opens with a dialogue between the allegorical figures Curiosity and Drama (Comedia). Curiosity wants to know how it is that Drama has changed so radically—what has happened to the classical hallmarks of theater, to the older, five-act structure, to the Aristotelian unities of time and place? Drama's answer describes the changes that characterize Lope de Vega's new art. It also links the mobility of the theater to the expanded geographical and imperial horizons of the time: plays can jump "[t]o Germany from Guinea" in a world that has become far larger in the wake of European exploration and conquest.

[Drama and Curiosity]†

* * *

CURIOSITY Oh, Drama . . .
DRAMA   Curiosity,
  What is it you would know?
CURIOSITY   Just why   1210
  You've parted with the costumery
  By which you'd been identified:
  The buskins of high tragedy
  And wooden clogs of rustic stock
  Or toga, when more classical   1215
  Varieties displayed their pomp?
  And how is it that you've reduced
  To three the five acts you'll attest
  Have served so well in making you
  August, enjoyed and serious?[1]   1220
  A drama's action now transpires
  Here *and* in Flanders, side by side,
  With scarce a word to note a shift
  In theater, interval or clime.
  I hardly know you anymore.   1225
  Some news might help me understand
  These ways so we'll be friends again—
  I've always been your biggest fan.
DRAMA Time changes almost everything
  And, in this way, perfects the arts   1230
  As years ring innovations in
  On their inevitable march.
  For I was good in days gone by
  And, if you'll notice, not half bad
  In these, although I'm hardly fond   1235
  Of theater precepts that demand

---

† From Act II of *El rufián dichoso* (*The Lucky Scoundrel*) as it appeared in *Ocho comedias y ocho entremeses nuevos* (*Eight New Plays and Eight New Interludes*) (1615). Translated by G. J. Racz for this Norton Critical Edition.
1. Curiosity comments on the transformation of Spanish *comedia* from the older structure that characterized earlier tragedies to the more agile three acts that Lope de Vega championed.

The unities of time and space
Bequeathed by Seneca's old tomes
Or Plautus's or Terence's[2]
Or ancient Greek works that you know.   1240
I put aside a part of these,
But also chose to keep a few
Because, no matter what art will,
In practice these aren't all in use.
Encompassing a thousand things,   1245
My whole plot's acted out on stage
And not related, as before,
So therefore moves from place to place.
Today, these actions all transpire
In many different sites at once.   1250
I have to go where they occur—
Forgive me if you think that's dumb.
Thus, drama can appear a map
With but a finger's span between
Eternal Rome and London town   1255
Or Ghent and Spain's Valladolid.
The theatergoer hardly cares
To see the action shift about
To Germany from Guinea, say,
Though in the very same playhouse.   1260
Ephemeral thought can travel light
And readily can follow all
These actions to their various sites
Without becoming tired or lost.

FÉLIX LOPE DE VEGA Y CARPIO

The opening of Lope's tragic masterpiece, *Punishment without Revenge* (1631), invokes contemporary theatrical practice and reflects on what audiences find in drama. While the debauched Duke of Ferrara is out for the evening, he overhears an actress rehearsing her role. Lope identifies her as a historical figure: "Andrelina," the internationally famous Isabella Andreini (1562–1604), who had toured Italy and France with her troupe, the Gelosi. Her lines, full of denial and regret, make an impression on the Duke, who cannot bring himself to listen to more. Instead he decides to go to bed uncharacteristically early, but not before explaining that theater offers its own kind of lesson by holding up a mirror to the human comedy. As in Hamlet's directive to the players, to let their play "hold as 'twere the mirror up to nature" (*Hamlet* 3.2), the Duke here reiterates the Renaissance idea that theater, by reflecting life, provides access to the truth.

---

2. The unities of time and space, precepts derived from Aristotle's *Poetics*, held that the action of a play should take place in one location and over the course of one day. Born in Cordoba, in what is now Spain, Seneca was a Roman author who wrote on rhetoric. Plautus and Terence were the great Roman comic dramatists of the third and second century B.C.E., respectively.

[The Mirror of Life]†

* * *

RICARDO   If entertainment's what you seek,   175
  Come rest your ear against this door.
DUKE   They're singing?
RICARDO   Listen!
DUKE   Who might dwell
  Within?
RICARDO   An actor-manager,
  My lord.
PHOEBUS   The best, I dare aver,
  From Italy.
DUKE   They do sing well,   180
  But are his plays good?
RICARDO   Fights still rage
  Between two camps for just this cause:
  Friends favor them with loud applause
  Each time his dramas grace the stage
  While foes pronounce them pitiful.   185
PHOEBUS   To be fair, they can't all be great.
DUKE   When I wed, Phoebus, decorate
  The best rooms we've available
  And book the best plays theater knows.
  So if it happens you should find   190
  Some lowbrow, pay those works no mind.
PHOEBUS   The only ones we'll take are those
  That men of breeding have approved.
DUKE   Are they rehearsing?
RICARDO   A maid pines.
DUKE   It's Andrelina¹ reading lines.   195
  That's acting! Ah, I'm really moved!
      [A WOMAN'S VOICE is heard offstage.]
WOMAN'S VOICE   Fly, thought! Don't make me reel!
  No more, cruel memory—fade!
  You've watched past glories made
  A tortuous ordeal   200
  And all I've come to feel
  I'd rather not recall now but efface—
  My prior state of grace.
  Though you may think a cure lies in your powers,
  What place have tragic words in happy hours?   205
DUKE   She's wonderful.
PHOEBUS   Unmatched, I'd say.
DUKE   I'd hear more, but not feeling quite
  Myself, will off to bed tonight.

---

† From *Castigo sin venganza* (*Punishment without Revenge*) (1631). Translated by G. J. Racz for this Norton Critical Edition.
1. Isabella Andreini (1562–1604), internationally renowned leading lady of *commedia dell'arte*.

RICARDO At ten?
DUKE   Life vexes me today.
RICARDO The lady is decidedly   210
  Unique.
DUKE   I fear her speech is fraught
  With some grave lesson to be taught.
RICARDO To you, my lord? How could that be?
DUKE   Ricardo, you know how a play
  On stage is like a looking glass   215
  Such that the oldster, youth and ass,
  The he-man, brave and popinjay,
  The pure maid and the lusty wife,
  Yes, even governor and king
  Can see in it a mirroring   220
  Of codes of honor, love and life—
  The human comedy in brief—
  Where customs harsh and light play out,
  A mix of fiction, fact and doubt
  With stark displays of wit and grief?   225
  I listened as this actress poured
  Her heart out in that tragic role
  As though she spoke about my soul.
  Her message to me struck a chord.
  Would you persuade me now to hear   230
  A second speech read? Don't forget
  That noble lords have never yet
  Preferred to see the truth so clear.

Class, Gender, and the Performance of Identity

FRANCISCO DE QUEVEDO

The poet and satirist Francisco de Quevedo (1580–1645) was known for his punishing wit. In this biting poem, he charts the negative effects on Spanish society of the immense wealth that flooded into Spain from the Americas. Gold is born in the New World, Quevedo quips, and then lives in Spain, but it goes to die in Genoa, where it must pay off the bankers who issued loans to the Spanish crown. Beyond international politics, however, gold presents a challenge to the very structure of society. Lineage and blood become unimportant in the face of "Sir Money," who can transcend all obstacles and erase all distinctions. Quevedo's poem thus charts the increasing role of new money in determining social roles, and illuminates the theater's probing of the increasingly fractured relationship among birth, virtue, and position.

Sir Money Is a Mighty Lord[†]

Oh, mother, I'm in thrall to gold,
my lover and beloved most true,
forever yellowish of hue
like all who squirm in Love's sure hold.
5 Doubloon or small change, he makes bold
to do what strikes my fancy's chord.
Sir Money is a mighty lord—
see all he can afford!

His noble New World birth has spurred
10 the crowds to follow in his train
and, though his life is spent in Spain,
he lies in Genoa interred.[1]
When has his presence not conferred
quick glamour on a savage horde?
15 *Sir Money is a mighty lord—*
see all he can afford!

He's gallant, yes, but on that score
still wan like any coin of his.
A man of means is what he is,

---

† "Poderoso caballero es Don Dinero" ("Sir Money Is a Mighty Lord") (1603). Translated by G. J. Racz for this Norton Critical Edition.
1. The Genoese loaned large sums to the Spanish Crown.

20   as much a Christian as a Moor.
Decorum? Coarseness? Either or.
Man's laws exist to be ignored.
Sir Money is a mighty lord—
see all he can afford!

25   His parents being high-born, too,
this personage can claim descent
for, in veins from the Orient,[2]
all bloodlines run to royal blue.
Both duke and cowherd, by his due,
30   are treated with the same accord.
Sir Money is a mighty lord—
see all he can afford!

Who doesn't feel a certain thrill
to see the lowest of his line
35   still bask in glory from his shine—
I mean, Dame Penny of Castille?
He seats the lowly where he will
and makes the coward wield a sword.
Sir Money is a mighty lord—
40   *see all he can afford!*

With noble coats of arms like these,
among the purest ones you'll find,
he funds arms of another kind,
a commerce born of family trees:
45   the sturdy oaks that plough the seas
are envious of his miner's hoard.
Sir Money is a mighty lord—
see all he can afford!

To back his contracts at a stroke
50   and lend his counsel consequence,
he transacts with establishments
where brokers watch his foes go broke.
He nullifies all things bespoke
while bribing judges in his ward.
55   *Sir Money is a mighty lord—*
see all he can afford!

He can't deny his majesty
(though power entails its share of woe)
or, even drawn and quartered, show
60   a lessening of authority.[3]
He grants both beggar and grandee

---

2. Quevedo puns on veins as layers of rock in a mine and conduits for noble blood, to suggest that gold trumps any Spanish concern for religious or ethnic genealogies.
3. Quevedo puns on coins "quartered" into units of lesser value, as well as on the common practice, both official and unofficial, of clipping coins to reduce the amount of precious metal in each unit.

what only riches can award.
Sir Money is a mighty lord—
see all he can afford!

65 I've never seen the dames adverse
to being favored by his gaze.
The face a bright doubloon displays
prompts them to paint their faces worse.
Coins still inside his leather purse
70 induce their seeking this reward.
Sir Money is a mighty lord—
see all he can afford!

His coats of arms are worth far more
(I'm right to note their sums' increase)
75 when wealth props up a shaky peace
than bucklers rate in times of war.
The poor have but the grave in store
while strangers find themselves adored.
Sir Money is a mighty lord—
80 *see all he can afford!*

FRAY LUIS DE LEÓN

Fray Luis de León wrote his 1583 treatise on the proper behavior of a wife, based on Proverbs 31 in the Old Testament, for his newly married niece. The section on makeup contextualizes the anxieties that theater evoked in its early modern critics, especially in relation to women as actresses or audiences, who were a particular target for antitheatrical prejudice. León sets out to convince women that "they should want to appear as they are," and should avoid the artifice of makeup, that "deceitful trickster." He privileges the natural, dismissing women's efforts to beautify themselves as not only sinful but ineffective: everyone, he claims, can see through the simulation of makeup. León concludes by connecting makeup more broadly to pretense, and suggesting that husbands who allow their wives to wear makeup are inviting deception.

[On the Dangers of Makeup]†

[God intends that] good women should not wear anything that could not just as well be placed on an altar; that is, all their dress and adornments should be holy, both in the intention with which they wear them and in the restraint they use. And He says to them, that their body should not be clothed with light thoughts but rather with the good order of reason; and that from the private composure of the mind should be born fitting dress on the outside, and this dress should not be cut to fit any whims, or reprehensible and worldly customs, but instead according to what is required for the sake of honesty[1] and decency. God specifies a holy form of dress, in

† From *La perfecta casada* (*The Perfect Wife*) (1583). Translated by Laura Muñoz and Barbara Fuchs for this Norton Critical Edition.
1. In the period, "honesty" meant "chastity" when applied to women.

order to condemn the profane. He says purple and fine linen, but says nothing of the embroideries that are now fashionable, nor the needlework, nor the finely spun gold thread. He says dress, but not diamonds or rubies; He refers to what can be sewn and made at home, rather than pearls from the deepest ocean. He allows clothes, but neither curls, nor crimped hair, nor cosmetics. The body should be clothed, but the hair should be neither disheveled nor crimped as in anticipation of great misery. And since there is great excess in this, most notably in the makeup of the face, even among women who are honest in all other ways, and also because this is the proper place to speak of it, we shall now say something about this matter.

Although, to tell the truth, I confess to your grace that the very excess that draws me to address this matter makes it somewhat daunting. For who would not be afraid to oppose something so established? And who might dare convince women that they should want to appear as they are? What reason might counter the poison of mercury?[2]

* * *

And if [women] love those who, acquiescing to their pleasures, allow them to be revolting and ugly, does it not follow that they should at least not detest me, but rather listen to me with equanimity and attention? For what I wish to tell them about this will be only to teach them how to be beautiful, which is their principal desire.

I do not want to tell them about the sin which some ascribe to makeup; instead I only want to make them aware of it, showing them that it is a deceitful trickster who does the opposite of what it promises them, for, just as in a game children play, it announces to women that it adorns them but actually tricks them and blackens them. Once they know it for what it is they can bring it to justice and shame it publicly with all its little pots around its neck.

* * *

All you women who are corrupted by this, heed my advice! Make masks of beautiful faces and put them on; paint varnish on canvas rather than skin, and you will benefit greatly. First, since you enjoy being false beauties, this way at least you will remain clean. Second, you will have no fear of being unmasked by the sun, the dust, or the air. And lastly, with this artifice you will be able to hide not only dark skin but also bad features. For it is clear that beauty is not so much about a certain coloring but rather about each feature being well modeled in its own right, and the right proportions between them.

And it is clear that makeup, although it may correct skin color, cannot correct the features, for it cannot broaden a narrow forehead, nor enlarge small eyes, nor fix a crooked mouth. Yet they say that good coloring is worth much. To which I ask, in whose eyes? For good features, even if they are dark-skinned, are beautiful, and perhaps even more beautiful than those which are fair; and ugly features, though they become white as snow, remain ugly after all. Some might say they are at least rendered less ugly, but I say they are more so, because before the paint they were ugly but clean, while it leaves them ugly and dirty, which is the most detestable ugliness of all.

---

2. Mercury was frequently used in cosmetics in the period.

Good color is worth something, if it is truly that. But this is neither a good color nor even close to it, but rather a fake color through which everyone can see, a pretense that at times falls off, a grossness that disgusts everyone, a trick that promises one thing and gives another, and which disfigures and tarnishes. What madness is it to call good that which is bad, to seek their own harm, and to deliberately torment themselves just to be despised, which is what they hate most? To what end do they adorn and care for their faces, if not to look good and please those who look upon them? But who is so lacking in good taste as to find pleasure in these concoctions? Who is there who will not condemn them? Who is so foolish as to wish to be tricked, or so dim-witted as to not see through this deceit? Who so lacks reason as to judge as beautiful what clearly does not belong to the face at all, but rather is applied on top, added and extraneous?

I would like to know whether these beauties begging for attention would consider beautiful a hand which had six fingers. Would they not hide it from sight? Would they not invent some kind of glove to hide the extra digit? And so, if they consider ugly a hand with one finger too many, how can they believe that paint three fingers thick on their face makes them beautiful? All things have a natural proportion and measure, and the good disposition and appearance of these depends on their just dimension—either lack or excess makes for ugliness and coarseness. Thus these women we are discussing, who add embellishments and exceed what is natural, even if they were beautiful, are made ugly by their own hands.

* * *

And what shall we say about the evil that comes from deceit and pretense, and the way in which they practice this and become accustomed to it? This is not so much to convince women that it is bad to use cosmetics, but rather to impress upon husbands how important it is that they not permit their wives to do so. For they should understand that with this women begin to show themselves otherwise than as they are and to conceal the truth from their husbands. Thus they gradually probe their husbands' natures and accustom them to being deceived so that, when they find them amenable, they may go on to greater deceits. Aristotle is right when he says on this matter that "as in her life and her habits a wife must be forthright with her husband, so in her face and adornments she must be pure and without cosmetics."[3] A good wife must not deceive the one with whom she lives on any front, if she wants to preserve their love, for that is based on goodwill and truth and the absence of deceit between those who love each other. For, just as it is not possible to combine two fragrant waters while they are each in their own phials, so, too, as long as a wife closes off her spirit under the cover of pretense, and hides her face beneath adornments and cosmetics, there can be no true mingling in love between her and her husband. For should the husband love her in that guise, it is clearly not her he loves but rather the painted mask that she sports, as though in a play he loved the one who plays a beautiful maiden. And she, for her part, being loved in this way, does not love him either, but

---

3. Book III of the *Economics*, a text that has survived only in Latin translation and which is attributed to the Greek philosopher Aristotle (384–322 b.c.e.) or one of his students, includes a section on the qualities and appropriate behavior of the good wife.

rather begins to hold him in low esteem, and in her heart she laughs at him and looks down on him, and as she learns how easy it is to trick him, in the end deceives him and burdens him.

LUPERCIO LEONARDO DE ARGENSOLA

Theater produced strong reactions in early modern Spain. For every ardent lover of the *comedia*, there was a moralist convinced that theater would be the downfall of society. In 1598, Philip II, alarmed by the moralists' arguments, prohibited all performances in Madrid by traveling companies. Although he was himself a tragedian in the older, Aristotelian mode, Argensola was convinced that the new theater presented a real moral threat. He was particularly exercised by the effect that actresses seemed to have on their admirers, including the noblemen who adored them. He also deplored the impropriety of actresses of dubious virtue playing holy figures such as the Virgin Mary. Argensola's recommendation to Philip II against allowing the theaters to reopen in Madrid was part of an ongoing debate. Defenders argued for theater's importance as a mirror for virtues, and for the necessity of funding the hospitals with the money generated, while antitheatrical critics such as Argensola sounded the moral alarm.

[Against the Theater][†]

A nobleman of this realm became so entangled in the love of some silly little actress, that not only did he spend his wealth on her, he also publicly and scandalously kept a house for her, complete with silver dishes, where the servants embroidered dresses for her and served and respected her as though she were his legitimate wife, while his actual wife experienced much unpleasantness because of this. This gentleman stooped so low that he endured vile rivals of that same profession, or rather vice, who also dealt with this woman, simply to keep her happy, with all other manner of situations that I may not properly describe to Your Majesty, among them the fact that the very husband of this wretch was instrumental and the means to all this harm.

Another such person, of equal quality and also a nobleman, spent some years as a player, living with another of these women of the stage, following her blindly across various kingdoms. When her husband (who, like the other, tolerated the adultery) fell ill, a faithful servant who knew well of his lord's disgrace nursed the man back to health, fearing that if he were to die his master would marry the actress. And regarding this case also there are many lewd and scandalous matters that may not be recounted to Your Majesty.

Another nobleman succumbed to one of these women to such an extent that he neglected his own wife though he had no children, and did not live with her. The woman's husband, who, as in the previous cases (and as is true for all of this profession) acquiesced, he kept busy with a post in the public jurisdiction, even though he was not legally entitled to it.

[†] From a letter to King Philip II of Spain (1598). Translated by Laura Muñoz and Barbara Fuchs for this Norton Critical Edition.

Another nobleman was also most scandalously involved with another of these women, while the husband put up with it and flaunted the riches that this arrangement brought him, walking around with gold chains and buttons, and displaying the many *escudos*[1] his wife had earned.

Other actors have loaned out their wives and sisters, who pursue this occupation, and have been rewarded for these abominations with money, clothes, and other valuables.

Some gentlemen of high standing have nearly killed each other for jealousy in competing for these fallen women, and Your Majesty has imprisoned and condemned a few of them for crimes committed for this reason.

Many other similar cases could be mentioned here, which I keep quiet in order not to offend your Majesty's ears. Defenders of *comedias* respond to this harm by stating that those who have sinned thus would find some other way to sin. This response is unworthy of intelligent people, for aside from the fact that sinning is of less concern when it is secret and without scandal, it is not for Your Majesty, as some have claimed it is, to allow this public fault. For the truth is that if these women were not practicing this trade, they would not be sought after and coveted, and in not being so would also not be bad; and if they were, it would not be with such notable persons and with such scandal. And so, the lure that the devil uses with these men and women has been the singing and dancing, the dances and fine costumes, and the variety of roles they play every day, dressing up as queens, goddesses, shepherdesses, or men. And what one can hardly bear to say or even to write is that the costume and role of the purest Queen of the Angels has been profaned by these women and by these low instruments of lewdness. So true is this, that in a *comedia* performed in this court about the life of Our Lady, the actor who played the person of Saint Joseph was living with the woman who represented the person of of Our Lady, and this was so well-known that it shocked and caused great laughter among the audience when they heard the words that the most holy Virgin said to the angel: *Quo modo fiet istud*, etc.[2] And in this same *comedia*, when it came time for the mystery of the Birth of Our Savior, this same actor who played Joseph was scolding the woman under his breath because it seemed to him that she was looking at a man of whom he was jealous, calling her the worst name that can be given to loose women. Such things are unworthy, my lord, of Your Majesty's ears, but they are even more unworthy of being done, and they are done because no one has stopped them.

It is with this kind of people and in this manner that the feast of the Sacrament[3] is celebrated, which is one of the reasons, they say, that Your Majesty should order the return of the *comedias*, and yet certainly even if Your Majesty did so, the representation of holy figures and matters should be completely forbidden. [The actors] in their costume drink, swear, blaspheme and gamble, all in the habit and outward form of saints, angels, Our Virgin Lady, and even God himself. And then they go out in public

---

1. Gold coins worth 340 *maravedís* each.
2. "How shall this be, seeing I know not a man?" (Luke 1:34, King James Bible). Mary speaks these words to the angel Gabriel, who announces her conception and the future birth of Christ.
3. The Feast of the Sacrament (Corpus Christi) was celebrated in Spain with solemn processions and allegorical theatrical representations known as *autos sacramentales*.

pretending to be moved to tears and playing at what should always be true, and only discussed by upstanding people. Even a mortal man, because he was king, thought that not just any painter should dare to paint his portrait. And surely Your Majesty would not allow a player to mimic your form on the stage. And yet, to think that, having justly forbidden these people from representing the knights of the military Orders, placing their insignia on their costumes as they used to do, they should now, on the feast they call Corpus [Christi] as on other days when they put on these *comedias*, wear priestly robes and, worst of all, paint the stigmata of our Savior on hands that have just been playing cards or the guitar!

The report in favor of the players[4] states that *comedias* teach the ignorant many stories, as if this were an advantage and not a disadvantage of the plays. For not to know the causes of things and simply to see their effects creates confusion in their minds, and a faith which is very contrary to the truth. For plays in some respects either pretend metaphorically certain things that the uneducated then believe to be true histories, so that they absorb false doctrine, in holy matters as in profane ones. Sometimes this occurs because those who write *comedias* are largely unlearned, and in order to vary their fare according to the tastes of the people, they add most inappropriate things to histories, and even indecent and rude ones, not to mention their divine *comedias*, in which a great deal of nonsense has been heard. In one [play] which was performed a few days ago about the marriage of His Serene Highness King Don Juan, father of King Ferdinand the Catholic,[5] they added actions and events that contravened not only the truth, but the very dignity of his person. To Her Highness the queen, his wife, they attributed such lewdness as would be reprehensible even in a person of much lower standing. The freedom with which these *comedias* satirize people of all different states and nations will surely lead to hatred against the Spanish, especially since they will assume that Your Majesty accepts this since they are performed in your court. What is more, the sacred words and even the prayers of the Ave Maria and the Kyrie eleison,[6] which the Church utters with so much respect, are mixed into indecent songs in the theaters. How could this be allowed to proceed unchecked?

The vermin bred by the *comedia* are men living in sin, gluttons, thieves, pimps for their wives—and with all this they are so favored and protected that for them there is no law or prohibition. To prove this with individual examples: in Spain today there are players who are murderers and have not suffered for it, but instead were allowed to go free and clear. They immediately bring to bear on their case the intercessions of the many whom they fool with their jests, so that there is no rope or whip for them. And they are so proud of this that they demand that their profession be among not only those allowed, but those considered to bring honor to the republic, as being lawful and ordinary. And doubtless it will be considered as such if after this ban it is allowed again, or if at the very least the penalties of public disgrace and others implemented by the law are not renewed. For even though this prohibition was considered, ignorant people (and the players spread this opinion) will believe that no such laws ever existed or that they

4. An earlier, pro-*comedia* recommendation to the king, against which Argensola argues.
5. Juan II of Aragon (1398–1479) was the father of Ferdinand II of Aragon (1452–1516), who married Isabel of Castile and united Spain into its modern configuration.
6. Christian prayers usually translated as "Hail Mary" and "God have mercy."

were repealed, as they believed before, when this corruption became the common opinion. There were parents who, without being actors themselves, taught this profession to their sons and daughters, wrote their contracts, and handed them over to the players, so that we used to see four-year-old girls on stage dancing a sarabande[7] in an immodest fashion. And Your Majesty is well aware of this, since one of these girls was brought to you so that you could observe her talents, and you, in most holy fashion, refused to see her and instead sent her to be confined at Santa Isabel.[8]

The recommendation to Your Majesty also states that lawmakers fear the introduction of novelties in their republics and that this would easily be the case if the *comedias* were prohibited. They do not consider that the very novelties the lawmakers fear are the ones being defended in this recommendation. Verses and songs and new performances are the very things that Plato prohibits in his *Republic*.[9] Moreover, this excessive use of *comedias* is new in Spain, since thirty years ago there were hardly any and they were then very moderate, in their topic as in their costume and characters; they were rarely seen and then in private homes. And so the great novelty is that we have them now, and the way they were spreading. In Venice and in other places they do not have them and they live and bear it.

All the particular cases related here are true, and much uglier, and in order to relate them truthfully they have first been investigated. And if it were possible they would include the names of the people and places involved, although in some cases the events have been so public that few are unaware of them.

And since Your Majesty's rule extends to the smallest things (such is your concern for the public good), it is not unworthy of your greatness to lower yourself to these issues and remove the harmful traps that the devil has set in *comedias* for the bodies and souls of Your Majesty's subjects.

SOR JUANA INÉS DE LA CRUZ

In what is perhaps her most famous poem, the Mexican nun Sor Juana Inés de la Cruz (1651–1695), whose *Trials of a Noble House* is included in this anthology, examines the hypocrisy of a society that blames women for giving in to the men who seduce them. Sor Juana exposes the problems with a gender system that holds women to higher standards, encouraging them in a social performance of honor and chastity while men pursue them.

Men Who Chide Women[†]

The poet posits the contradictions of pleasure and censure in men who denounce women for the behavior they themselves have brought about.

---

7. A lively and popular dance in the period, widely considered scandalous for its suggestiveness.
8. A school for orphans founded by Philip II in 1592.
9. The ancient Greek philosopher Plato, in Book III of his treatise on the ideal city, the *Republic*, suggests that a city would do well to banish a visiting actor from its midst. Although Plato qualifies his claim by specifying that certain poets or storytellers might be beneficial, Renaissance moralists often chose to focus on the first recommendation.
† Redondilla 92 in *Castalian Inundation* (1689). Translated by G. J. Racz for this Norton Critical Edition.

Oh, silly men, who falsely chide
the women whom you bring to shame,
incognizant that you're to blame
for what you cause but can't abide,

5 If you do so intensely crave
that they endure the scorn they should,
how can you wish them to be good
while prompting them to misbehave?

You break their wills and, when you're done,
10 employing solemn turns of phrase,
impute to their inconstant ways
what powers of persuasion won.

This reckless daring really ought
to show how daft you all appear,
15 like little boys who come to fear
the bugbears their own minds have wrought.

Your foolish pride won't leave you glad
until you've found what you pursue:
a Thaïs, while you pitch your woo,
20 but a Lucretia, once had.[1]

What frame of mind, which knows no peer
and seeks no counsel, presses men
to fog a mirror up and then
complain what's cloudy isn't clear?

25 Both favor and disdain dispel
all hopes of earning your good will
as you cry treatment you deem ill
then mock us when you're treated well.

Due continence wins no regard,
30 for, if the chastest should demur,
"ungrateful wretch" you men call her
and "fickle" she who fights less hard.

Forever silly, you exclude
all sense from your unsound complaint:
35 now one's to blame for firm restraint,
now one for moral turpitude!

How could the woman you pursue
display the temperance she intends

---

1. Thaïs was a Greek courtesan admired by Alexander the Great; her name was routinely used for courtesans in Greek and Roman comedy. Conversely, Lucretia, the virtuous Roman matron who killed herself after being raped, was considered the exemplar of female chastity.

40 when, deemed ungrateful, she offends
    but, judged immodest, angers you?

    Amid these fits of choler spent—
    as you recount of your amours—
    luck favors her your love abjures,
    so grumble to your hearts' content!

45 Your grievous pleas, once they've begun,
    provide her liberties with wings,
    yet once a woman's done such things,
    how can you wish these acts undone?

    Who bears more culpability
50 for passion mired in ill repute:
    the woman, fallen per your suit,
    or he who sued on bended knee?

    Who's more at fault for wrong wherein
    all souls involved transgress some way:
55 poor women who will sin for pay
    or scheming men who pay for sin?

    Why feel so scared you won't confront
    the blame you own but can't condemn?
    Want what your plotting makes of them
60 or make them into what you want.

    Bid these seductions fond adieu
    and soon you might pick up the signs
    of one who has her own designs
    and sets her honest eyes on you.

65 I've watched your cache of weapons mesh
    in service of your haughty need,
    for men, in promise and in deed,
    embody devil, world and flesh.

Stages, Actors, and Audiences

ALONSO LÓPEZ PINCIANO

Alonso López Pinciano, one of the most distinguished humanist critics of sixteenth-century Spain, wrote an extensive poetic treatise largely in dialogue form, *Philosophía antigua poética* (1596), in which he attempted to clarify and illustrate Aristotle's rules for literature. Pinciano's classicism with respect to drama is widely regarded as a counter to the new theater of Lope de Vega. Despite its emphasis on classical rules, however, the excerpt below conveys a powerful sense of what the theater meant for educated audiences in Pinciano's time. Three friends discuss what they will see and where, as well as what they value in theatrical performances and productions. With as much of a focus on the practical and the actual as on the theoretical, they apply Aristotelian principles—verisimilitude, measure, and so forth—to costumes, scenery, and the actors' performances. Along the way, they tell us much about how actors created their roles and how those roles were received.

[Theory and Practice of Theatergoing][†]

I.

After dinner, Pinciano received a message from Fadrique that Hugo had arrived, that the two of them had decided to go that afternoon to a performance, and that they would be pleased if he would come along as a third.

Pinciano did not respond, but instead took up his cape and went to his companions, to whom he said: "Indeed, gentlemen, given how most people mispend their time—at least I do—there are worse ways to pass it, for theater teaches us many things that we ignore, and as it is done aloud it makes more of an impression than if we read them at home."

"That is so," answered Fadrique, "for if the plays are as they should be, they can and should be heard by any man; yet a wicked nature gradually alters them, so that what was once honest becomes indecent."

Then he asked, "Where shall we go? At the Cruz they are performing *Iphigenia* and at the Príncipe[1] a comedy."

Hugo said, "I am very partial to tragedy."

Pinciano: "And I to comedy."

And Fadrique: "Then flip a coin to see where we shall go; I'm happy to see anything."

---

† From *Philosophía antigua poética* (1596). Translated by Laura Muñoz and Barbara Fuchs for this Norton Critical Edition.
1. The Corral de la Cruz (1579) and the Corral del Príncipe (1582) were the two first *corrales* (open-air theaters) in Madrid. *Iphigenia*: this early version of a tragedy based on the *Iliad* has been lost, if it ever existed; the seventeenth-century play by the same title postdates López Pinciano.

"No, you should choose," said Pinciano to Fadrique, and Hugo said the same.

Fadrique said, "Then let's go to the one which is the closest."

At this point they were near the Monastery of the Holy Trinity, for they had gone down Urosas street and up Relatores.[2]

Pinciano said, "We are closer to the tragedy."

So they went off to Cruz Street, and once they had taken their seats in the theater, Fadrique, suddenly and apparently à propos of nothing, said: "Truly Poetry is like Medicine, for in theory it is most noble, but in practice it loses much of its grandeur. What greater pursuit is there than to scrutinize the secrets of nature? For the medical sciences not only study the natural philosophy of man, but for the sake of man they consider all medicinal matter, as they call it, including animals, plants, herbs, fruits, and flowers; they look deep into the core of the earth, from which they take the properties of metals; they dive into the waters and examine the fish; and, not content with this, they fly into the air, climb into the heavens and, to benefit man, take the best parts of astrological learning, the movement of the skies, the rising and setting of the most important stars. In short, Medicine is an archive, no, rather, it is a crucible where the purest and finest natural philosophy is purified. This all comes from observation, which is the flower of medical theory, yet its practice is rubbish, as Sr. Hugo can attest."

Hugo laughed and said, "We won't hold that cutting remark against you. I know I learned an art that is more difficult than I would have wished, and less valued than it should be. But what has been the point of this harangue?"

Fadrique: "I'll get to that, I'm not finished yet. All of this applies equally to Poetry, for although theory is such an important part of it as it relates to the supernatural, which we call primary Philosophy or Metaphysics, its practice is held in low regard."

Pinciano says: "Sr. Fadrique makes a good point, for these days practical poets are so little esteemed that there is hardly a man who takes pleasure in being called one. Instead, like criminals, they meet secretly so as not to lose their authority."[3]

Fadrique said, "Not even you, Sr. Pinciano, have understood me. What I am saying is that Poetry is a principal and noble art; yet its action in theater is not at all noble."

"Look at what news Mr. Fadrique brings us!" said Pinciano, "There are those who say that actors are so immoral that they should not be given the Holy Sacrament,[4] as is decreed and ordered by the Sacred Scriptures— that is what I heard from a preacher."

Fadrique laughed heartily and then said: "That Preacher had a better will than his understanding, and in his error he managed to hit the mark. It's true that a certain type of player is vile and immoral. Much as the dancers of the sarabande[5] do now, players used to encourage vulgarity and indecency with vulgar and indecent movements. These the Romans called

2. These are actual streets in central Madrid (Urosas is now named for the playwright Luis Vélez de Guevara).
3. This is likely a reference to the literary societies, based on Italian models, that flourished in Madrid and other cities in the period.
4. I.e., they should not be allowed to take communion.
5. A dance in triple meter that originated in the the Spanish colonies of the sixteenth century before making its way to Spain. It was immensely popular even after being banned.

"histrionics", and they are said to be forbidden from receiving the Holy Sacrament of the Eucharist. But why should the players whom the Romans called "actors," such as the tragedians and the comedians, be considered immoral? What reason can there be for such foolishness? For if medicine is an acceptable art and justice is necessary, how could the apothecary and the constable, who are the practitioners of medicine and law, be considered immoral? Not even the executioner is vile, for he follows a royal mandate. Therefore if Poetry is as we have said, honest and useful work in the world, why should the one who puts it into practice be vile and immoral? Can't you see that this is nonsense? I'm not saying that acting is a profession as acceptable as others (for it has something of the servile and obsequious), but I do say that it is neither vile nor immoral, but rather in a certain sense necessary. Consider, for instance, our Holy Mother the Church, which says in an Antiphony to Our Lady: "Before this Virgin there should be great rejoicing with songs and performances."[6]

Pinciano then said, "Church songs and performances are very good and useful."

And then Fadrique, "Did I say that all those in a theater are bad and harmful? Let actors do what poets have told them to and they shall be very useful to the republic."

"If everyone agreed with you, Sr. Fadrique," said Hugo, "there would be even more actors than there are now, and they would be lazier than they should by rights be."

Fadrique responded, "Moderation in this, too, would be good. And what I am going to say is not to criticize the Republic, but rather to offer advice for the principal actors of the companies, who go about broke and hopeless because they lack sense and needlessly have in their companies an army of careless spenders. With seven or eight people even the best comedy or tragedy in the world can easily be represented, and yet they have in each company fourteen or sixteen, who consume everything produced by the sweat of their brow, when the principal actors might be earning more."

Hugo said, "And so there might be fewer men involved in that department, who might be profitably employed elsewhere, for although acting may not be a bad trade, if four men are enough why should eight do it?"

Pinciano said then, "It would also help those who put on the *comedias*, for it would lower their costs."

"That is the least of it," said Fadrique, "More important is Sr. Hugo's point."

And then Pinciano: "I agree with reducing the number of players, but then how will they form two armies in the theater with only seven or eight people?"

Fadrique laughed and said: "For something like that, they might take a dozen or two of those who are closest among the audience."

And Hugo said to Pinciano, "Do you not recall that we condemned as unsuitable those plays that act out battles in front of the people, and that we said those were heroic subjects rather than tragic ones?"

"I remember," replied Pinciano, "And yet the poets write them this way!"

---

6. Antiphonies are short liturgical songs.

Fadrique responded, "Then the actors should reject them, and so they will benefit themselves and teach the foolish poets a thing or two."

II.

The friends were silent for a while. Then Fadrique said, "The audience comes in very slowly today for such a new play, and one that has never been performed at Court."

Pinciano explained, "It's not without reason, for the Acrobat[7] has invited all to see his somersaults, which are clearly possible, as they can be seen in plain sight, yet hardly to be believed, given the difficulty of the things he does."

Fadrique said, "He must be recently arrived, for I have not heard news of him. I wonder, what is it that he does?"

Pinciano replied, "I cannot describe it all, but I can tell you part of it. He walks along a tightrope, and there's more: sometimes he walks on platform shoes, other times on stilts over a foot high. I am not doing it justice: he dances on the rope, and does what they call somersaults in the air, then lands back on his feet on the rope, as if it were a level and spacious hall."

"Even all that Pinciano has told us," said Hugo, "cannot justify anyone going off to see those performances over the delightful and beneficial ones of the theater, for in the end plays entertain for longer and a man can always take away some counsel for his own affairs."

"Both cost money," said Pinciano, "and if I were given the choice, I know exactly what I would choose."

"You would choose very badly," said Hugo.

Fadrique intervened, saying: "I would like to judge this case now, especially since I know that this matter has already been considered by some who have seen the one and the other. All things in the world are subject to the man of reason, for by the use of reason man surpasses all other earthly things. From which can be seen clearly that any work of the mind is more perfect than one of the body."

Pinciano said, "There is no action taken by man that is not effected by one or the other, for man is a union of body and soul, and actions (as the Philosopher says)[8] are made from the foundations or combinations of matter and form."

"I see now," responded Fadrique, "that the soul does not go about, nor does it eat, drink, reason, inquire, or choose, but that man does so, that is, the union of body and soul together eats, drinks, reasons, questions, and chooses. However, because some of these actions are much more spiritual and others corporeal, we call some of these works of the spiritual faculty and others of the bodily faculty, and that is simple enough, as it is to say that the operations of the soul are higher and nobler than those of the body. This being the case, I say that the dramatic actions of players are much more subtle and spiritual than those of tumblers. And on this point in particular, the performances of the former are more brilliant and skillful than those of the latter. However, a corporeal act could through its excellence equal and surpass certain of the spiritual ones,

---

7. The name in Spanish, Buratín, is another word for acrobat.
8. Aristotle argues in the *Poetics* that actors give form to the matter of the poet.

which are low and common and have nothing rare or new about them. You understand me; let's move on."

It seemed to Fadrique that Pinciano had not quite grasped the matter fully, because he remained thoughtful, and so he continued, "What I am saying is that the performances of actors and players are in general nobler in terms of their effect, because they are more intellectual, but those of these particular tumblers are greater in terms of the excellence they achieve with their bodies, just as the feats of an individual soldier, were they excellent, could be more notable and worthy than the efforts of an ordinary captain. And so the exceptional and extreme nature of a performance, so to speak, albeit it be base and corporeal, can make it quickly transcend a spiritual one. And what I take from this discussion is that tumblers can outdo and surpass common and ordinary actors by the greatness of their performances, but that acting is itself more subtle, fruitful, and honorable, for the reasons argued before."

"That would be so," said Pinciano, "if the tambourine always rang true, and if the actors always performed with their understanding. But I see them perform with their bodies, and often without good judgment, or even against good judgment."

"That may be," replied Hugo, "when they are presenting some madman, yet in that case they are performing with their understanding, for such a role may require even more skill than others."

"That is not what I mean," said Pinciano, "but rather when they act as buffoons, and wish to delight the theater with lewd and indecent movements and words."

Hugo replied, "Any who do that should be drummed out of town and sent to sea, or at least be denied their homeland."

"I agree," replied Pinciano, and then he added: "If I had any authority to administer the Republic, I would appoint an inspector to watch every play before it could be performed in public, and to scrutinize its morals."[9]

They were silent for some time, after which Fadrique said, "The inspector you propose would be useful for other more important things (although what you describe certainly is that), for many times I have heard plays that offend good policy, and instead of teaching anything they corrupt the audience and poison it."

Pinciano said, "Oh, how suitable Sr. Fadrique would be for a post like that! Beyond the fact that he has written on politics, he knows much about economics, and he would know very well how to discriminate among kinds of dramatic poetry."

Hugo smiled, saying, "It would be better to assign such a person to more important things than those we are discussing."

Fadrique added these arguments to those of the other two: "I know that we men are born not only for ourselves but also for the Republic and for our friends; and so you will find me ready to do anything for which you need me, for I know you would never order me to do anything that might dishonor me."

"Just so," Hugo was saying, when they began tuning the instruments inside, and one of the actors stuck his head and part of his shoulders

---

9. Official censors were gradually introduced: a 1615 decree specified that the censor should review scripts before they were distributed to actors.

out to the theater from between some curtains. He was dressed as a shepherd, in a sheepskin jacket with golden bands, a gallant cap, and large collar with a very stiff ruff that must have had a pound of starch.

Pinciano saw him and said, "What does a shepherd have to do with tragedy?"

Fadrique said, "The tale might well require shepherds and even fishermen: it was shepherds (in a very serious matter, epic in nature) who brought Sinon before King Priam."[1]

"And another thing," said Hugo. "There is more to say about this man. I mean his costume, with that elegant sheepskin, and a cap unlike anything shepherds wear and which seems a poor imitation, and more than anything it is ruined by that collar, wide as a sieve, with each ruffle as large as the hand of the muddler who made it or the fool who wears it."

"Those are flaws," said Fadrique, "and the last of them the worst, for it is unreasonable and hardly verisimilar that a shepherd should wear something like that. But they are incidental and, as long as they do not affect the main actors and the most important one, they can be ignored and tolerated."

"What!" said Pinciano, "Is ornament incidental to the actor and the performance?"

"That is not what I am saying," said Fadrique, "but rather that while ornament is essential these flaws in the ornament are not. For a shepherd might be elegantly dressed for a feast day, or some wedding; ornament, I insist, both in the theater and in everyday life is essential, almost as much as the movement and gestures which the Romans call "vultus" and "gestus."[2]

Pinciano said, "What's all this about vultus, gestus, and expression?"

Fadrique replied, laughing, "I'll tell you: once the sick man is dead, the physician has no more to do."

Hugo said, "That's a good one."

"No," said Fadrique, "it's true. For then he hands him off to the priests so they can do their job. Just so, once the poet brings the poem to life, he hands it over to the actors so they can do their job. Just as when the sick man dies the doctor's job is over and the priest's begins, so once the poem is brought to life the job of the poet ends and that of the actor begins. This can be divided into the two parts already spoken of: the ornament, and the movements and gestures. Listen, if you still do not understand: ornament refers to the adornment of the theater and the actor; and gestures are those movements the actor makes with his body, feet, arms, eyes and mouth, when he talks and sometimes even when he is quiet."

"Well that is good to know," said Pinciano, "for although it is not about poetry, it is about something related to it, and it is not a bad idea for a physician to know something of apothecary."

Fadrique said, "What you mean to say is that since in the last few days we have given you a few lessons on Poetics, we should now continue to performance and acting. So be it! Let Sr. Hugo say what he knows, and I will do the same."

---

1. In the account of the fall of Troy in Virgil's *Aeneid*, Sinon is a Greek soldier who pretends to have been abandoned by his compatriots and convinces the Trojans to receive as an offering to Athena the hollow wooden horse in which Greek soldiers lie hidden.
2. The Roman orator Cicero, in his *Rhetorica ad Herennium*, notes that effective delivery requires the speaker gracefully to regulate voice, countenance (*vultus*), and gesture (*gestus*).

Hugo said, "What I know can be stated briefly: with regard to the action, ornament should consider the character, time, and place (gender and sex go without saying). With regard to the characters, after taking into account their status, their age should be considered, for clearly a Prince requires a different ornament and attire or dress than a servant, and a young man than an old one. The second consideration—of time—is very important, for Spain now calls for very different ornament and attire than that of one thousand years ago. For this reason it is key to consult carefully those histories that might bring to light the costumes of different times; and similarly one should learn about different regions, for each tends to have a different costume. An actor must do this diligence meticulously, for the poet almost never pays attention to this, as one who writes poetry to be read rather than to be acted, and omits the parts that pertain to the performance of an actor, whose job it is to act. From this we can assume that a good actor, and especially a head actor, should know much of myths and history so that he might dress the persons in his play according to their different periods and situations."

"Ornament is also necessary and beneficial for the theater itself and the requisite effects, which should be according to the kind of poem: if pastoral there should be forests; if urban, houses, and so on according to the different types of ornament; the stage effects should be most carefully chosen, for there are some that are better suited for one miracle, and others for another; they also vary according to the character, so that an angel should appear to fly and a saint to walk on air, although they both descend from above, and a devil should seem to come up from below."

Here Pinciano said, "And if it's one of those suspended in the air, he should be depicted not on his way up, but on his way down."

Hugo laughed and Fadrique said, smiling, "That's right, and I know what I'm talking about, for in speaking of devils I mean the principal one, who is in the deepest place."

He continued, "In short, the actor should study the types of machines and devices that make either an earthly person, through magic, or a divine one, without it, appear quickly and as if by miracle. And this in brief is what pertains to ornament."

"Music is also part of the ornament, and especially for tragedies it should never stray far from the subject matter, but rather consist of songs on the same, so as to underscore the action."

Pinciano said, "But isn't that up to the poet? I mean, the songs to be sung?"

Fadrique said, "It is most common now for the music to be introduced by the actor, and not to be the work of the poet; it wasn't always thus; but everyone, actors and playwrights, should avoid adding little songs extraneous to the plot, as Aristotle admonished in his *Poetics* with very good reason, for they remove any verisimilitude and sometimes even the moral of the story. This occurred with Agathon,[3] who began to include these songs, or extraneous singing in his plots. Let the actor maintain verisimilitude in his performance when he may, for there is little point in the poet's work if the actor ruins the good things he writes; and the poet could say as Plautus did: "If

---

3. Greek tragedian (c. 445–c. 400 B.C.E.), considered the first to add choral parts unrelated to the main plot to his plays.

Pelion performs my comedy *Epidicus*, which is my favorite, it will seem bad to me." As though to say, Pelion ruins all plays. And this is what I have to say about ornament."[4]

III.

[Fadrique continues] "I speak now of gestures and movements, those things which are for an actor more intrinsic and essential the more they show the essence of the poem."

So saying he continued, "The life of the poem is in the hands of the actor, so that many bad plays are made good by a good actor, and many good ones are made bad by a bad actor. This is what the epigrammatic poet meant when he said:

> *The book you are reading now, Fidentinus,*
> *You read and understand in such a way*
> *That it ceases to be mine and becomes yours.*[5]

And if you want to examine a dramatic poem, analyze it outside of the performance; for a good actor will make a bad play good, and on the contrary a bad actor will make a good one bad. It is advisable, then, that the actor consider the person he is to imitate and so transform himself into that person, so that it will seem to everyone not an imitation but rather the appropriate action. For if he laughs while imitating a person who is tragic and serious, he will not be fulfilling the poet's purpose, which is to move [the audience], and far from moving them to tears, he will move them to laughter instead."

"Well," said Pinciano, "that's not a bad exchange, if instead of tears he gives us pleasure."

Hugo replied, "That laughter is sardonic, like that of the rabbit, which when it is being roasted bares its teeth as though laughing. The audience is angry at what the actor has done, and their laughter is not a sign then of the pleasure they get from the play, but rather of the ridicule and mockery they shower on the actor. As we said before, he must first move himself if he wants to move others."

Here Pinciano said, "Hold on, for I have a doubt. I have heard that he who remains aloof, without being moved one bit, is best at moving others to laughter with a sharp and witty word. So it would seem to be good for the tragic actor to move others to tears without crying himself."

"Your reasoning is strong," Fadrique said, "and I will not counter it, except to say that your point only applies to comic actors. And although there is another answer for this, it is very metaphysical and will not be well understood, because I will not be able to explain myself very well. Hugo has expounded very well on what actors should do."

Hugo continued, "I could now bring in, to a different end, the story of that ancient mime who pranced and danced before Caesar in the Roman theater. This mime, after dancing very well, was ordered to leave the stage to make room for other planned celebrations. He paid no attention and instead began to dance madly, imitating a madman; the audience took

4. *Epidicus* is a comedy by the Roman dramatist Plautus (c. 254–184 B.C.E.).
5. These lines are by Martial (c. 40–c. 103), a Roman poet from Hispania who wrote humorous epigrams.

pleasure in his cheek as though he were truly mad while he, from his position, kept slapping those nearest him, so that the madness which he imitated seemed to everyone very real."

Fadrique laughed, saying, "Perhaps he truly was mad, for a mime is never more than a step away from madness, especially given how excited he was from all that movement. Perhaps you praise as skill what was actually vice."

Hugo said, "Be that as it may, whether sane or mad, he performed it beautifully, prancing and giving the audience much to laugh at, except those he managed to hit. Let this stand as a general example of how important it is that actors practice their craft with true skill, for truly they take our money and make us wait two hours, and so it is not too much to ask that they truly perform their parts. This was how the Greeks and the Romans used to do it, and ancient orators learned from them, so that, when it came time to give their public speeches, they could move emotions and expressions with the movement of their body, legs, arms, eyes, mouth, and head, because, depending on the emotion one wants to achieve, there are different movements which come from habit and nature. And, in short, just as the poet portrays things with concepts, and concepts with words, the actor, with the movement of his body, should declare and show and give life to the words of the poet."

Pinciano said, "What you say seems very reasonable, and I would like to see some rules for this."

Fadrique replied, "There is no rule other than to follow the nature of the man being imitated, for we see that each man moves his feet, hands, mouth, eyes, and head in a different way, according to the passion he feels. The timid man shuffles his feet while the daring man charges forward; the one who trips advances against his will. So in thinking through the different persons, ages, and regions you will find great differences in the movement of the feet, which the theater should imitate, for tragic and serious characters move slowly, common and comic characters move more quickly, older ones more heavily, young men less so, and children cannot keep still. And there are also great differences among the provinces, for Northerners are sluggish, the French are too quick, and the Spanish and Italians moderate. And these I offer as examples of the movement of feet."

"As for the hands, one should also note the nimbleness and slowness of different ages and regions, and moreover the variety of affects, which determine whether to move one hand or both; if one, it should be the right, for the left will imitate well, for most men are right-handed, or almost all of them are, and so the left-handed actor should be right-handed in the theater."

"In general the actor should consider the character he is going to imitate; if he is serious, the actor can play his hand,[6] depending on the subject matter, for if he is dispassionate he can move his hand softly, now raising it, now lowering it, now moving it from side to side. If he is angry he will move it more haphazardly, separating his index from the other fingers, like one who is threatening. If he is teaching or narrating, he can join that same finger to his thumb and middle finger, which he will occasionally separate and rejoin. The index alone stretched out and the rest of the fingers gathered into a fist, raised towards the right shoulder, is a sign of assertion

---

6. The Spanish has an untranslatable pun here: *jugar de mano* means "to play first," as in a game of cards.

and conviction of a certain thing. The movement of the hand is done modestly and according to nature, beginning from the left and moving it downwards, then moving it upwards toward the right side. And when we chastise ourselves over something that we have done, we put our hollow hand over our heart. But any actor who acts before an older one should not use his hands to reason before him, because that is poor manners. He can do so if he is impassioned, because passion blinds reason. And in this we might look to and consider the common nature of man, as with everything else. Both hands are sometimes yoked together for certain emotions, for when we abhor something, we place the back of the right hand in the palm of the left, then disdainfully move them away from us. We beg and worship with our hands clasped and raised. Crossed arms demonstrate humility."

"One who is impassioned with anger bites his lip; one who is happy allows his lips to part from each other ever so slightly."

"The eye offers marvelous movements: although it is such a small part of the body only it can signal anger, hatred, vengeance, love, fear, sadness, joy, harshness, and tenderness; and just as the eye follows the emotions, the eyelids and brows follow the eye. A downturned brow makes for a sad eye, a raised one for a happy one. Eyes wide open and unmoving signal derangement, or an ecstasy of rage."

"The head as a whole, too, has its own movements, such as moving it left to right to deny and inclining it to affirm, and keeping it lowered to indicate shame."

"I say again that these are only a few examples of the many to be considered in this matter, which are practically infinite. To briefly wrap this matter up: the actor should be meticulous in his observation of movements, for men use the parts of their bodies to make conversation and for the give-and-take and passions of the soul. And so he will imitate nature, which all art follows and this more than any other—I mean poetry, which actors execute."

IV.

Fadrique was silent after this and Hugo said, "There is much to be said about the actor's duty to be who he should be, and also much to criticize in certain careless ones, but Sr. Fadrique has explained his doctrine generally so as not to tire himself out."

Pinciano said, "Had you not spoken this way, I would have said that any conversation that grants respite to the tired cannot be tiresome. What is tiresome is waiting so long for these actors to come out."

Hugo said, "There's no argument here, for the best entertainment of all is Sr. Fadrique's conversation. But leaving that aside, this is not a bad way to spend the time, for here we can enjoy many different kinds of things: seeing people gathered, seeing a handkerchief make its way from top to bottom, into the patio I mean, with a small knot, seeing the fruit vendor, or the pastry vendor, undo the small knot of coin and make a larger one with the fruit that they ask of him, and throw it up high, perhaps to strike one on the mouth who unwittingly bites the fruit through the handkerchief. The scuffles over 'this bench is mine,' and 'this seat was placed here by my servant,' and the proof and testimony relating to this, and when one crosses the theater to find his seat, how they make a graduate of him with a thousand 'heys!' And what about when in their section the ladies start fighting for seats, or sometimes for jealousy? And what of the times when they rain on those below them, without a cloud in the sky?"

Fadrique said, "All those things you mention are certainly very entertaining, but best of all is when a man spends his time to his liking, and there are some who do not enjoy the things you mention." He continued, "In the time of the Romans, in many places and best of all in Rome, there was a theater so spacious that all the people could fit in it, and each person, according to his station, had an assigned seat, in such a manner that they came and went from that place at any hour as they pleased. And if the current theater were like this many would leave the entertainments you describe and would instead be enjoying other things outside the theater, and then they would arrive later, at the right time."

So Fadrique was saying when the musical chorus entered, singing a ballad appropriate to what was to come, which was Euripides' tragedy with new scenes. The music offered a few examples of the power and fickleness of Fortune. And with this the singers left the stage and on it appeared the character of Fortune, a lady with two wheels instead of feet and wings on her hands, who recited the prologue.

When she exited, Pinciano said, "The plot has been well explained, and the one who played Fortune represented her well."

Hugo said, "What plot? That was the tragic Prologue, which just explains what has happened before and which we need in order to understand what is to come. The plot relates both the past and what is to come, and so contains, in short, all of the action."

"It is true," said Fadrique, "that poets do not usually write the plots of poems; others who want to interpret them later on do so in order to show off, and so the poet should write his works so clearly that there can be no need to explain them. If possible, it would be good to do away with the Prologue completely, as it only tells what came before."

"That does not seem very difficult to me," said Pinciano, "for I have seen many plays without these so-called narrative prologues."

Fadrique said, "Most poems have prologues, but they are disguised, especially in tragic works, in which the characters provide the prologue through their very actions. For that is how the ancient poets always used to do it, as we said when we were speaking of as the prologue."

"And even epic plays have a disguised prologue," said Hugo.

Fadrique added, "The epic prologue is the same thing as the proposition, as has been declared and validated by the Philosopher.[7] It tells not of the past but rather, in a way, of the future, with the poet anticipating what he will sing in the future. Of all this we have spoken already, let us not linger on things already explained. There are other, more important considerations here, and one is the character who performed this. It makes the action less verisimilar, less familiar to common use, or should I say the abuse of introducing such spectacles. For, considering reason above all, to introduce inanimate characters into the action, especially in an acted poem, is unreasonable, and such is Fortune, who has just spoken the Prologue."

---

7. Here and elsewhere in his oeuvre, López Pinciano invokes Aristotle's *Poetics* to equate these two terms ("prologue" and "proposition").

Then Hugo said, "The matter certainly deserves some consideration. In a typical epic, which has less need of verisimilitude, it may be permitted, and these false characters may even be fitting. But in poems which are acted out before our eyes, it is not allowed. Even then, some comic poets have used them; Plautus in the *Trinummus* brings in Lust to speak to her daughter Poverty; in the *Aulularia*, he brings out the genie Lar to the Guardian Angel; in the *Cistellaria* he has Help, and in *Rudens* the star Arcturus. In his *Plutus* Aristophanes[8] has Wealth and Poverty."

Fadrique: "That may be so. But those characters are outside of the play proper because they are in the comedic Prologue, and this explains those in Plautus. I especially allow Aristophanes, for although his false characters, Wealth and Poverty, appear in the middle of the play, among the ancients Wealth was considered a god."

Pinciano: "I would appreciate it if, just as you have given me examples of this for comedies, you could do the same for tragedies such as the one that is being acted at present."

Fadrique: "I can't remember any. In my opinion, as long as the story is well constructed, none of this should prevent it from being approved and praised, for, as Horace says, when something is mostly good I am not troubled by a few flaws.[9] In fact, they should not even be considered flaws, just because they depart from the ordinary, for art often departs thus in lovely ways, and just as histories do not reflect all the precepts of statecraft and politics, so not all those of Poetics are experienced in plays. Thus it is not enough to condemn a play by saying, 'This was not done by Homer, nor by Virgil, nor by Euripides, nor by Sophocles . . .'"[1]

As he was saying this, Clytemnestra entered the theater with her daughter Iphigenia, as if she had just landed in Aulis. Mother and daughter entered with great pomp, with the daughter riding behind her mother on a horse, and headed towards where Agamemnon[2] stood on the stage.

Seeing this, Hugo said: "What was the reason for the six hundred mules in *Clytemnestra*?"

Fadrique replied, "And why Clytemnestra on six hundred mules?"

They both laughed heartily; only Pinciano did not laugh, because he did not understand. He wanted to ask for an explanation, but so as to not disturb the performance he left it alone with the intention of picking it up at a later time. The play ended, and the ending did not seem at all bad, although it was not tragic, and Pinciano was left with no small doubt about the end of the tragedy: whether or not it was necessary that it be tragic and sad, or whether it could be happy and pleasant, as was the case with this tragedy. The play was over at a late hour because it was long, and the three companions, wishing to attend to their obligations, went their separate ways.

Pinciano wishes to meet them again to know more about these mules and Clytemnestra, and, God willing, he will seek them out and be free of

8. The great Roman comic dramatist Plautus (c. 254–184 B.C.E.) wrote around 130 plays. The ones cited by Hugo are among those that have survived in their entirety. Aristophanes (c. 448–380 B.C.E.), Greek comic dramatist; his comedy *Plutus* [Wealth] has not survived.
9. In his *Art of Poetry* (19 B.C.E.), the great Roman lyric poet Horace (65–8 B.C.E.) argued that minor flaws need not ruin a great poem.
1. To exemplify excellence, Fadrique lists the great Greek and Roman epic poets—Homer and Virgil—and the great Greek tragedians, Euripides and Sophocles.
2. In Greek mythology, Agamemnon, king of Argos, was the brother of Menelaus and husband of Clytemnestra. He led the Greek forces against Troy and sacrificed his daughter Iphigenia to the goddess Artemis at the port of Aulis in order to secure favorable winds for his fleet.

his doubts as soon as possible. And he will let you all know of this, as he always does and should do. Dated four days before the September Calends.[3] The end.

MIGUEL DE CERVANTES SAAVEDRA

Cervantes' novella *The Dialogue of the Dogs* (1613) is a canine picaresque in which two highly articulate mutts marvel at their newfound ability to speak. The dog Berganza tells of his adventures with masters of various social classes. In this passage, he relates how he spent some time with a struggling poet who tried to sell his plays to an acting company. Berganza highlights the tensions between the poet's grand vision for his play, including costly costumes, and the reality of the company's limited resources for putting it on. The actors show their displeasure with the play by trying to toss the poet in a blanket; his response is to claim they have no taste.

[My Time with the Actors][†]

Every morning at dawn there would appear seated below a pomegranate tree, one of many in the orchard, a young man who looked like a student, dressed in woolen cloth, which rather than black and fleecy was dun and worn. He was busy writing in a notebook, and from time to time he would strike his brow and bite his nails, gazing up at the sky. At other times he was so caught up in his thoughts that he would not move a muscle, not even his eyelashes, so engrossed was he. Once I got close to him without his seeing me and heard him muttering to himself, and after a long while he shouted, "By God, this is the best octave that I have written in all my days!" And writing quickly in his notebook he seemed hugely pleased, all of which told me that the poor wretch was a poet.

I approached him with my usual caresses so that he would know I was tame, and lay down at his feet. Reassured, he continued with his thoughts and scratched his head again, as he returned to his absorption, and to writing down what he had thought up. As he was doing so there came into the orchard another young man, handsome and well dressed, with some papers in his hand that he turned to from time to time. He went up to the first young man and asked, "Have you finished the first act?"

"Just now," answered the poet, "and as splendidly as can be imagined."

"In what fashion?" asked the second.

"In the following:" answered the first, "his Holiness the Pope comes out in his pontifical robes, with twelve cardinals, all dressed in purple, because the events that my play relates took place at the time of *mutatio caparum*,[1] when cardinals wear purple instead of red, and so it is only fitting, for the sake of propriety, that my cardinals come out wearing purple. This is a very important matter for the play—not that others would get it right, given that they make a thousand mistakes and commit follies at every

---

3. I.e., the first of September.
† From *El coloquio de los perros* (*The Dialogue of the Dogs*) (1613). Translated by Barbara Fuchs for this Norton Critical Edition.
1. Latin, the changing of the capes. A showy ceremony in which cardinals changed their robes from red to purple or vice-versa at specific moments in the liturgical calendar.

step! There is no way I could have gotten this wrong, because I read the whole Roman manual of ceremonies just to get these vestments right."

"And where on earth do you think my manager will find purple vestments for twelve cardinals?" countered the other.

"Well, if he tries to take out even one of them," answered the poet, "I'll sprout wings and fly before I let him have my play. By God! And shall we lose such a magnificent sight? Imagine how a Pope with twelve grave cardinals and all those ministers that must necessarily accompany them would look in a theater. By heaven, it would be one of the finest and greatest spectacles ever seen on stage, even with *Daraja's Bouquet!*"[2]

At this I realized that one of them was a poet and the other an actor. The actor recommended that the poet pare back his cardinals, if he did not want to make it impossible for any manager to stage the play. To which the poet answered that they should be grateful that he had not put in the entire conclave present at the memorable occasion that he was trying to memorialize with his wonderful play. The actor laughed, and left him to his task while he went to attend to his, which was to study his lines in a new play. The poet, after having written some verses of his magnificent play, leisurely took from his bag some crusts of bread and about twenty raisins, which I could have counted, although I doubt there were even that many, as they were mixed in with the breadcrumbs. He blew the crumbs off and ate both the raisins and the stems, for I saw him throw none away, and then he chased them with the crusts of bread. The lint from his bag made them look moldy, and they were so stale that although he tried to soften them several times in his mouth, he could never get them to relent. All this was to my advantage, for he threw them to me . . .

Between one thing and another, we ended up at the house of a manager who, if I remember correctly, was named Angulo the Bad, to distinguish him from another Angulo, who was not a manager but an actor, the finest one the theater has ever seen, then or now. The whole company came together to listen to my master's play (for so I considered him now), yet by the middle of the first act they gradually walked out, one by one or two by two, except the manager and me, who were then the sole audience. This play was such that even I, who am an ass where poetry is concerned, thought it must have been written by Satan himself, for the total ruin and perdition of the poet, who was swallowing hard at the sight of an audience that had forsaken him.

His prophetic soul was just warning him of the danger that threatened him when all the actors, of whom there were more than twelve, came back. Without a word, they took hold of my poet, and had the manager not intervened, with all his authority, pleas and shouts, they would doubtless have tossed him in a blanket. I was astounded, the manager disgusted, the actors merry, and the poet depressed. Patiently, though with a pained expression on his face, he took his play, stuffed it in his shirt, and muttered, "It is no use casting pearls before swine."

2. A lost play on Moorish themes.

JUAN DE ZABALETA

The dramatist and chronicler Juan de Zabaleta's *El día de fiesta por la tarde* (*Holiday Afternoons*) (1659) describes what early modern Spaniards did with their days off. Although Zabaleta ostensibly writes in disapproval of such pursuits as parties, gardens, pleasure reading, and plays, he nonetheless offers a remarkably lively portrait of an afternoon at the *corral de comedias*. Before the play even begins, a comedy of sorts has played out in the theater, as patrons fight over seats and flirt with each other. As the play finally gets under way, Zabaleta expresses his pity for the actors, barely audible above the noise, who are heckled if they delay and mocked if they blunder. Zabaleta's account reminds us that the text of a play cannot offer a full sense of the performance or of the experience of going to the theater.

[The Audience Settles In][†]

Anyone who intends to spend the afternoon at the theater bolts his food on a holiday. The desire to get a good seat prevents any lingering at the table. Once at the door of the theater, the first order of business is to try to get in without paying. This is the greatest misfortune of players: to work very hard yet have only a few pay. For twenty people to pay only three *cuartos*[1] would not do much harm, if it did not lead others to do the same. When one person does not pay, countless others follow his example. Everyone wants to imitate the privileged one and so appear worthy of the privilege themselves. They so desire this that they will brawl for it, and by brawling they achieve it. It is rare for someone who has brawled once in order not to pay, not to get in for free thereafter. A fine reason to fight, to profit from the exertions of those who, in order to entertain, work themselves to exhaustion! And then, on top of paying nothing, they forgive nothing! If the actor wears a poor costume, there are complaints and hisses. I'd like to know how this man who paid nothing and those who imitate him expect the actor to dress in fine clothes, since they refuse to pay him his due. Do they not know that actors are poor, and that God will take offense at being denied the stipend that the kingdom has designated for Him?[2] If God is displeased when we do not aid the poor with what is ours, how much more displeased will He be when we keep what is theirs?

Our idler then moves into the theater and approaches the man who assigns places on the benches. He asks for one and is told there are none, but that it seems that a certain place previously set aside may remain empty, and advises our man to wait until the guitars come out, and if the seat is still empty he may sit. Having agreed to this, the man goes off to the dressing room to pass the time. There he finds women taking off their everyday clothes to dress up as actresses. Some wear so little that it's as if

---

† From *El día de fiesta por la tarde* (*Holiday Afternoons*) (1659). Translated by Laura Muñoz and Barbara Fuchs for this Norton Critical Edition.
1. The *cuarto* was second smallest coin in circulation, worth 4 *maravedís*. Three *cuartos* is not the full price of entrance, which would have ranged from 14 to 24 *maravedís*, but rather what was paid by those who cheated the players.
2. As noted in the Introduction to this volume, theaters raised funds for religious charities and particularly hospitals.

they were going to bed. He stands in front of one who, having walked to the theater, is having her maid put on her stockings and shoes. This cannot be done without sacrificing modesty. The poor woman suffers this indignity, but does not dare protest—since these are all votes of confidence she does not wish to offend anyone. Any hiss, no matter how unjustified, discredits her, for where someone else's reputation is concerned, everyone believes that the accusers have more discerning taste than they do themselves. The woman continues to dress, and patiently endures being watched. The most immodest woman on stage is nonetheless modest in the dressing-room, for here immodesty is a vice while on stage it is her profession. The man never takes his eyes off her. These things can never be looked upon without placing the soul at great risk. The moth approaches the flame quite naturally, and yet it burns. However natural it might be for a man to turn his attention to these things, only a miracle will save him from burning. Whoever thinks this is the point of such entertainment, should know he does so at great risk of harm.

Our man looks through the curtains, to check if the place he might get is empty and sees that it is. He assumes its owner will not come, and goes and sits in it. Scarcely has he taken his seat, when in comes the owner and defends his claim. The seated man resists and a fight breaks out. Did this man not go out to amuse himself? What does quarreling have to do with amusement? Can there be such barbarous people in the world, who turn amusement into unpleasantness? If he could not find a place to sit he should have stood, for it is less cumbersome to stand for three hours than to quarrel for an instant, and having sat down he should have gotten right back up when the owner of that place came in, for sitting there doesn't mean he has the right to the place. If it seems embarrassing to have to leave his place with everyone watching because another person demands it, how much more shameful to have others see him try to take possession of another's claim! If he insists on keeping it so as to signal to everyone watching that he is not afraid to fight, then he does wrong, because there is no shame in capitulating to reason. If he sat down in error, believing that the owner of the place would not come to claim it, the fault does not lie with the owner, and to insist on staying would be to seek a reward for his mistake. Whoever is at fault should pay the penalty. If he retains the seat because all who have sat in a place that is not theirs do the same, then he is mad, for error sets a bad example. Best to go one's own way when common practice is flawed.* * *

The disturbance is settled. The one who had paid for the seat yields it and sits in the one offered to him by those who settled the argument. The commotion is over as quickly as it had begun, and our man turns his attention to the women's gallery (known in Madrid as the stewpot).[3] He examines the faces, falling for one that strikes his fancy and then guardedly signaling to her. It is not the stewpot that you have come to see, my good man, but the play. Already four misdeeds and the entertainment has yet to begin. That is not a good way to observe the solemnity of God's day.

---

3. I.e., the *cazuela*.

Our man turns this way and that, when he feels someone tugging at his cape from behind. He twists around to see who it is and finds a fruit-seller who, leaning forward between two men, whispers to him how that woman there, tapping her knee with her fan, says that she much admired the boldness he showed in the earlier argument, and in return he should buy her a dozen oranges. The man looks towards the stewpot and sees that it is the same woman who had caught his eye. He hands over the money and sends word that she may ask for anything she likes. Oh, that fruit stinks of the devil! As the fruit-seller moves away, the man begins to plan how he will wait for the woman at end of the play and to feel that the play is taking forever to get started. He complains loudly and bitterly about the delay, leading the men standing below him to rush the players along with insulting words.

Now that I have gotten to this matter, I cannot continue without discussing it further. Why do these men insult the players? Because they do not enter as soon as they sit down? Because they take up the time that could be spent on other vices? Why is having to wait such an annoyance? No one who goes to a play does so without knowing that waiting is in store, and to pretend that this is unexpected is to have lost either one's memory or one's mind. If the players were still asleep at their lodgings, the hecklers might have a point, but they are always dressed and ready long before it is time to start. If they delay it is either because there are not enough people to underwrite the cost of a day's work, or because they await someone so important that, in order not to displease that person, they risk annoying those whom they most need to please, that is, the common people.

How is it that those who insult dare to do so? They take cover in the noise. They know the entire audience appears as one and under the cover of confusion they voice their insults. None of those who unjustly shout insults would say as much in the street without great risk of retaliation from those they insult, or from the law. Not only is it senseless and cowardly to treat the players badly, it is inhuman ingratitude, for they more than any other profession in the republic wish to please and entertain those they serve. Such is the thoroughness with which they rehearse a play that they undergo this torment for many days. The day they debut any one of them would give up a whole year's worth of food in exchange for putting on a good show. When they go on the stage, what weariness and trouble they hide in order to play their roles well! If they must take a fall, they throw themselves as if from a mountain, as though they were suicidal—yet they have human bodies just like anyone else, and blows hurt them as much as they would any other. If the play calls for someone to die, the player it falls to rolls about the stage frothing at the mouth, though the floor be covered in dirt and bristling with rusty nails and splinters, without a thought to his costume, as though it were embossed leather, when more often than not it is very fine. If the play calls for someone to flee across the stage, in order to do so correctly, they move with such speed that their collar—surely not cheap—gets caught on a nail, leaving a huge tear in what must have been a very expensive costume. I once saw a well-known actress (she died not long ago) who, while acting out a fit of rage, tore the handkerchief in her hands to shreds in order to effectively convey the scene, even though that cloth was worth twice as much as the actress made. And yet she did more than this, for the scene was such a success that she tore a different handkerchief to shreds every night that the play was put on. Actors go to such extremes to fulfill their obligation to entertain everyone that, having spent a few days in the dressing room when there were few patrons, I heard them tell each other that those were the times when they must act with greatest care, so as to avoid being disheartened by the lack of an audience, for it is not the fault of those who have shown up that there are so few of them there. The players ignore the fact that they are working for nothing, and work themselves to exhaustion to give great entertainment to the very few who are there to see them. All of this should be greatly appreciated by each audience member, as a representative of the group that was thus indulged. If nothing else, the ingratitude of doing otherwise would be a great fault.

The guitars come out, the play starts and our listener pays attention to what he should perhaps ignore. When women play love scenes, the desire to be convincing leads moderation to break its bounds, so that they perform much too vividly. These scenes would be a good time to look away, but he does not do so. Physiognomists say that elongated eyes are a sign of bad habits.[4] They infer this from the humor that is said to cause this elongation. I do not know how much truth there is to this belief. What I do know is that those who are long in the eye, that is, those who look without restraint, have no good features to their soul. Those who are free with their looks are free in their desires. Anyone who has no trouble looking is highly unlikely to have any trouble desiring.

Now then, I want teach those who attend plays how to listen to them, so as not to leave the theater with more sins than when they arrived. One must make sure to understand the plot on which the play is based, which will ensure its enjoyment. See whether the playwright has created his characters skillfully and whether he manages them gracefully, for this, if done correctly, gives great pleasure. Pay attention to whether the verses are well composed, clean and grave, for if composed thus they may both entertain and instruct—there are many who pay little attention and so miss the instruction and the pleasure. Note if the scenes are new and verisimilar,[5] for if they are, you will find the novelty amusing while the verisimilitude will provide the great pleasure of lies with the whole air of truth to them. If all these fail to provide what you seek, there is always the pleasure of criticizing them instead.

Everyone enjoys those moments when a player leans over too far, slips, and falls into the crowd. Yet a few flaws do not make a play bad. If everything in a work of art were equally good, the whole would not be good. There must be some weak parts in order for the whole work to be admirable. In music the bass parts do not have the same pleasing quality as the higher pitches, yet without them music would not offer such agreeable sounds. In painting, shadows may be a weakness, but without them the highlights would be muted. If a work of art had no flaws because of

---

4. The supposed science of physiognomy attempted to link facial features to character traits.
5. Verisimilitude—the quality of seeming real or possible—was highly prized by literary theorists during the Renaissance. Verisimilitude offers a possible truth, thereby elevating poetry, which deals with universals, over the specific and limited truth of history.

human imperfection, then it would require flaws by design. Nature has made sure that, as no man would have the courage to try less hard in creating works worthy of note, some things are imperfect by their very nature. It is Heaven's will that not all great minds should find themselves equal to the task when creating a great work of art. No one should be faulted for this, as it is Heaven's wish. Strength always appears stronger in the presence of weakness. If one's attention could never flag during the plainer parts, it would lack the energy to engage with the high speeches.

That covers what one might say about the written play. Let us now turn to what one should focus on in the acting. Our audience member should pay great attention to the suitability of the costumes, for there are some players who are very skillful in dressing for their role. The laces of their shoes are often tied so naturally that it is admirable to behold. Let him note whether the actions are in line with the words being spoken, and the actions will be as more words. Let him observe whether the players' eyes help convey what they say, for if so the eyes will lead the way. He should pay no mind to the dances, for he will lose himself in them. Beyond the action on stage, he should look around at the people clapping at nonsense and he will have much to keep him occupied. If he spends his time like this for the duration of the play, it is sure to have been time well spent. This being so, I would be glad to have him pass the time in such calm and beneficial pursuits.

Women also attend plays, and women, too, have a soul, so that it would be good to give them some sound advice on these matters. On Sunday men go to the theater after eating, and women before they eat. The woman who goes to the theater on Sunday usually makes a full day of it. She makes arrangements with some neighbor or another, and they lunch on whatever is available, saving the usual midday meal for the night. They go to mass, and afterwards go from there straight to the stewpot, in order to find a good seat. There is no one to take their money at the door yet. They go inside and find it spottily occupied, as if with the pox, by other women as crazed as they are. They do not take the front row, because that is for the women who want to see and be seen. They find modest seats in the center, where there is plenty of room. They are very glad to have such a good spot. They will see later. They look around for something to entertain them while they wait and find nothing, but after hurrying all morning to get to the theater simply resting in their seats is enough. More women arrive, and the cheekiest of them sit on the parapet of the stewpot, so that those sitting in the middle are buried as in a cave. Now idleness begins to do its mischief.

The guitars come out and everyone settles down. The lady who is closest to the entrance to the stewpot hears the players but does not see them. The one who sits in the last row sees them but does not hear them, and so neither truly sees the play, for plays cannot be heard without seeing nor can they be seen without hearing. The action tells a great deal of the story, and if the words cannot be heard the actions are mute.

428

JUAN MARTÍ

In this unauthorized 1602 sequel to Mateo Alemán's hugely popular picaresque novel *Guzmán de Alfarache* (1599), the protagonist joins an acting
company on their way to Valencia. He dabbles in literary theory, reviewing
various kinds of comic theater, from the clever to the bitingly satiric, and foregrounds the figure of the fool as a Spanish improvement on Greek and Roman
models. He then recounts how a hopeful poet attempts to sell his plays to the
cynical manager, Heredia. Despite the acting company's very real need for
material, they cannot help but laugh at the poet's sorry efforts, so he complains
that Lope de Vega has ruined them for any other plays.

[Fools and Poets]†

There are many ways that plays produce laughter. Both the works and the
words are the more urbane and clever when they move to laughter without harming anyone, and this type can be presented before kings and
princes. Conversely, those born of mordant wit, malicious gossip, ugliness, and indecency are bad, and so the player must beware of them, for
kings, princes, and great lords naturally abhor all ugliness. Using a fool, as
they do in Spain, is good and harmless, for he produces laughter by beginning many pronouncements and ending none of them, making a thousand
funny observations. He is a character whom the common people love best
of all the ones who appear in plays, for he holds within him both ignorance and cleverness, as well as a rustic and coarse lechery, which are
your ridiculous types. Because all ugliness suits him (I mean insofar as it
produces laughter), he is the most fitting character for a play. With this
invention, Spaniards have outdone Greeks and Romans, who used servants
in their plays to be funny, but whose characters were missing some types of
absurdity, for they had only a mordant wit or lechery, or at most both, and
they lacked the pretense of simple ignorance, which always makes for great
laughs. * * *
A poet in a long flannel coat, like a Portuguese, was asking for the manager. Those who were there recognized him and, as they knew his ways,
suspected he must bring with him some blasted play, as was in fact the
case. They told the manager he should not miss the chance to take a look,
as he would die laughing, and that he should have the piece read in front
of everyone. Heredia came out and said to him, "And what would your
grace have us do for you? I am the manager, and if your grace brings
poetry—for we know you are a famous poet—you would grace us with it,
for there is a lack of good plays, and especially for a place with such tastes
as Valencia, which makes any manager tremble."
The good man was very pleased at such a welcome, and said, "Your grace
should not worry about plays, for I will provide you with any you might
need. I have two underway and this one I've got here, whose very title will
tell you what it is."

† From *Segunda parte de la vida de Guzmán de Alfarache, atalaya de la vida humana* (*Second Part of the Life of Guzmán de Alfarache, Watch Tower of Humanity*) (1604). Translated by Barbara Fuchs for this Norton Critical Edition.

"And what title have you given it?" said Heredia, "Good titles are very important."

"One could give it any number of titles," said the poet, "but I think *The False Captive* suits it best."

"Excellent," said Heredia, "And now if your grace would be so kind as to read it, for here is Mr. Guzmán, who is a man of good taste, and I will entrust this business to him. I will abide by what he says, though I am sure it will be a fine play, since it comes from your hand."

"What do you mean, a good one?" said the poet, "It will speak for itself, for I intended to give it to no other than Porras,[1] who has offered me a thousand *reales* for each play."

"Read it," said Heredia, "and if it's as we expect, you'll have no need to weep for Porras."

The sad poet took out his bundle, though he never should have, and began with some verses that he must have found in some old fabric shop, so badly measured were they. He lifted his eyes at each line and looked intently at the audience as though he were reciting miracles. We were all besides ourselves with laughter, so that there was no way to pretend otherwise, until he finally realized it and said in a huff, "I think that your graces are much too used to a diet of Lope de Vega,[2] and nothing else seems good to you."

1. Gaspar de Porras (or Porres, as his name is sometimes rendered) was a theatrical manager who had a long and prestigious career in Madrid in the late sixteenth and early seventeenth centuries. He commissioned plays from Cervantes (although he seems never to have received them) and both produced and published the plays of Lope de Vega.
2. The offended poet invokes the outsize reputation of Lope de Vega in the period. Lope was so widely regarded as the gold standard for theater and poetry that the expression "*es de Lope*" ("it's by Lope") was used to indicate that something was excellent.

CRITICISM

General Studies

JOSÉ ANTONIO MARAVALL
The Social Role of Artifice[†]

The taste for the difficult occupied a preferential position in baroque[1] mentality; in judging any work whatsoever, it gave a prominent role to the qualities of novelty, rarity, outlandishness, the breaking of norms. All these traits (as present in the conceptions of seventeenth-century individuals) were connected in that they each derived from a longing for novelty, just as this longing in turn originated from the tendency to seek out difficulty.

   *   *   *

The role of novelty underwent profound change from the sixteenth to the seventeenth century. During the Renaissance century it gave impetus to social life in numerous aspects, and although it was only found in certain strata of the urban population (never among the rural population, nor in many sectors of the cities), it came to be a vital principle that stimulated the ascendant social groups. When monarchical absolutism firmly closed its ranks in defense of a privileged social order, it saw itself threatened with collapse by the changes coming in the wake of the sixteenth-century spirit and its economic and demographic boom. That provoked, in this second phase we are indicating, a serious distrust vis-à-vis novelty. It was excluded from all manifestations of collective life that might affect the fundamental order and was confined to those areas judged to be innocuous or at least of no consequence for the political order. That practice came to be adopted by all regimes of force occupying the government of peoples (as we have occasion to see even nowadays). Perhaps one has to view this reaction as indicative of the state of anxiety in the face of change that threatened to break up the traditionally organized social life, an anxiety awakened at the time by a general feeling of crisis. A rejection of the new that was threatening everywhere emerged in those who feared possible damage to their privileged positions. "Everything is calm," Pellicer warned his readers (8 March 1644), "and time is very much pregnant with novelties that they say will soon be born."[2] In his gazetteer tone, Barrionuevo translated what we have just described with the following words: "Monstrosities are seen and heard

---

† From *Culture of the Baroque: Analysis of a Historical Structure*, trans. Terry Cochran (Minneapolis: University of Minnesota Press, 1986), pp. 225–40, 309–13. Reprinted by permission of the University of Minnesota Press and Editorial Ariel.
1. For Maravall, the historical period extending roughly from 1600 to 1675 [editor's note].
2. José Pellicer, *Avisos*, ed. Semanario Erudito, 33, p. 150 (8 March 1644).

every day in Madrid";[3] at the very least, his news sheets on the whole indicated overwhelming confusion, both when it occurred and when it was corrected.

Thus the seventeenth-century individual, and particularly the Spaniard, did not expect anything favorable (I refer, of course, to those integrated in the system). Consequently, for them it was a matter of blocking the way to all novelty (in politics, religion, philosophy, and morality) precisely because of the fact that, even though undesirable, it appeared by virtue of the disorder of the times. "In politics there are novelties every day," commented a letter of the Jesuits (2 March 1638),[4] and Barrionuevo informed his public that "in this place we see new things every day" (19 August 1654).[5] Therefore, this was what the sector of those integrated into the system, who mounted the "propaganda campaign" in its baroque rendition, wanted to avoid or at least to neutralize in terms of its possibilities for revolt. But since, after the Renaissance experience and after hearing how much had been said in its favor for more than a century, the public spirit would not so easily reject the attraction of the new, free rein was now given to those areas where the accompanying threat to the order would not be serious or would turn out to be so remote that there would be no problem in stifling its excesses in time. Art, literature, and poetry continued exalting novelty, and certain social groups' taste for the new could be siphoned off by these activities. (However, if a ten-line ballad or any minimal stanza contained a suspicious allusion to the dealings of any minister, it would suffice for the author to be jailed without charge for years; such was the case of Adam de la Parra.)[6]

The baroque proclaimed, cultivated and exalted novelty. It recommended it: "According to this it will be good for us to follow another path abounding with novelty, so that benefit might be gained."[7] There was the desire to maintain it as a universally valid principle: "everything in this world is novelty," said Fernández de Ribera, although in universalizing it in such a way he obviously made it lose all of its virulence.[8] Baroque declarations in favor of the new were no less fervent than those of the sixteenth century, but to the extent that they were permitted they were limited to poetic game playing, literary outlandishness, and trick effects machinated on stage, which evoked wonder in and suspended the depressed psyche of the seventeenth-century urban inhabitant. Nothing of novelty, let me repeat, so far as the sociopolitical order was concerned; but, on the other hand, there was an outspoken utilization of the new in secondary, external aspects (and, with respect to the order of power, nontransferable ones) that allowed for a curious interplay: the appearance of a daring novelty that enveloped the creation on the outside concealed

3. Jerónimo de Barrionuevo, *Avisos*, BAE [Biblioteca de Autores Españoles], 222, p. 187 (29 May 1658).
4. *Cartas de jesuitas*, MHE (Memorial Histórico Español), 14, p. 339 (2 March 1638).
5. Barrionuevo, *Avisos*, BAE, 221, p. 46 (19 August 1654).
6. See the great number of similar cases cited in the first chapter [not included here]. Concerning Adam de la Parra, see J. de Entrambasaguas's preface to de la Parra's *Conspiración herético-cristianísima*, translated by A. Roda (Madrid, 1943).
7. Cristobal Suárez de Figueroa, *El pasagero*, p. 361.
8. Rodrigo Fernández de Ribera, *El mesón del mundo*, edited by Carlos Petit Caro (Seville, 1946), p. 68.

a doctrine—here the word *ideology* would not be out of hand—that was inflexibly anti-innovation, conservative. A force reconstitutive of traditional interests was smuggled in by means of the novelty that one was attracted to for enjoyment. Because of this, the baroque writer was very interested in novelty. It was a way to provide for the smooth ingestion ("pleasing," according to the norm of the sempiternal Horacian precept) of an entire system reinforcing the monarchical seignorial tradition. Because in the baroque the pedagogy and all modes of directing human behavior endeavored to reach the individuals' extrarational levels and from there to move them and integrate them into the supporting groups of the prevailing social system, one of the most important means was attracting attention through the *suspense* of novelty whenever no risk was involved. The new pleased, the never-before-seen attracted, the invention making its debut fascinated; but this would only be permitted in apparent challenges that would not affect the underlying foundation of beliefs holding up the absolute monarchy's social framework. On the contrary, in making use of these novelties as a vehicle, the persuasive propaganda in favor of the established order was more easily introduced.

We already know that the baroque placed little trust in strictly intellectual arguments, in Scholastic[9] thought shaped by traditional society, which criticism had eroded in many spheres during the preceding three hundred years. It preferred to appeal to extrarational means that moved the will. And novelty is a very forceful means: it charms one's taste and will into following it. "Novelty draws one's eyes and they, one's will," said Céspedes y Meneses.[1]

Thus preceptists and practitioners of different arts were in agreement about seeking novelty in one fashion or another because without obtaining it nothing would be successful (with the understanding that it was a question of arts that were in themselves inoffensive). Carballo requested that the poet make an effort to invent "rarer and more amazing" things.[2] When an author's work was praised, as Setanti did with that of J. Merola. its positive quality resulted from "its rarer invention,"[3] and the author himself very inappropriately boasted about it. A theoretician of history, Jerónimo de San José, would admiringly inform us about "the grace of innovation which is rarity."[4] Even in those arts characterized not by verisimilitude but by truth (above all, history), where the truth was always demanded of whoever practiced it, we now find that this advice to follow truth was curiously nuanced. In effect, Cabrera de Córdoba clearly recommended the baroque writer's subordination to the demands of the new: "The truth must be about what is noteworthy, to teach and delight because of its singularity and strangeness."[5]

9. Relating to medieval theology and philosophy, with a strong basis in religious dogma [editor's note].
1. Céspedes y Meneses, *El español Gerardo*, p. 193.
2. Luis Alfonso de Carballo, *Cisne de Apolo*, edited by A. Porqueras (Madrid, 1958), vol. 1, p. 74.
3. Jerónimo Merola, *República original sacada del cuerpo humano* (Barcelona, 1597), the first unnumbered pages.
4. Jerónimo de San José, *Genio de la historia*, edited by Higinio de Santa Teresa (Vitoria, 1957), p. 331.
5. Luis Cabrera de Córdoba, *De historia, para entenderla y escribirla*, edited by S. Montero Díaz (Madrid, 1948), p. 42.

This path toward captivating the will, toward making use of the new, thus gave force to the unique, to what remained outside of the norm. It related to the tendency toward a greater freedom from precepts, a freedom characterizing authors and the public in baroque society; at the same time, this society saw the reinforcement of the absolute power with which the prince could impose his mandate on collective life. All the authority withdrawn from Aristotle was given in manifold to the absolute king.[6] When Lope proposed a disavowal of the laws of classical poetics (never mind that he, without saying so, came to set up another system of precepts), it was to assure that whatever the king wanted was law and that if everybody could make the literary norm an object of personal judgment and rejection, on the other hand nobody had the capacity to examine critically the royal mandate before which nothing was possible but blind obedience.

To the extent that the area of novelty, of the extraordinary and the strange, was so severely curtailed, thereby restricting the area accessible to personal examination and taste, and to the extent that in other spheres personal evaluation remained subject to an indisputable authority, the free energies accompanying the desire for the new were unleashed more forcefully in the realm allotted to them. Whatever this culture had of a gesticulating or capricious quality emerged from this interplay of harsh constriction and permitted expansion, depending on which realm one was dealing with, a duality that we find at the base of baroque society. This led to the out-of-the-ordinary and free enthusiasm for outlandishness, a final and unhealthy manifestation in the exercise of freedom that, for the individuals of the seventeenth century, remained possible in one sector of existence.

Even those who would seek other paths, for reasons of personal preference, displayed a tendency to give themselves over to outlandish novelties. The seventeenth-century writer had to recognize (as López de Vega noted, although not without a certain personal ill humor) that "given the general corruption of our century the realm of the outlandish still retains a greater appearance of virtue than blame."[7] Therefore, he confessed that "being determined to introduce something new into the light of the public, I made a unique selection of paradoxes." To secure a "good sale" [buen despacho] for what was printed, it was necessary "to

6. Here I will raise a question that G. M. Foster's (New York, 1962) interesting suggestion poses for us:

> In general, the positive attraction of the new and novel seems to be associated with industrial societies. Whether peoples with the most interest in novelty became the first industrialists because of this interest, or whether an industrial system produced these values, we cannot be sure. I suspect the latter—that aspirations are developed through the opportunity to satisfy them. In any event, the relationship between a productive economy and a tradition for change is so close that it cannot be thought of as being due to chance (*Traditional Cultures and the Impact of Technological Change*, p. 65).

I believe that in Spain the connection would follow the second direction indicated by Foster: the industrial stagnation of the seventeenth century would produce the limitation or diversion, accordingly, of the taste for novelty, although it would never succeed in suffocating it, and both phenomena depend on the triumph of conservative interests in the seventeenth- and eighteenth-century monarchy.

7. Antonio López de Vega, *Paradoxas racionales*. Although the work's permission to be printed dated from 1655, it nevertheless remained unpublished; it was published, with a preliminary study by E. Buceta, in Madrid, 1935 (the quote appears on p. 30).

attract the readers' attention with something outlandish."[8] But there were those who not only recognized that taste for the outlandish was widespread in the public, but also admitted it in the system of precepts, although with certain requisites. In effect, one of the defenders of the new theater (that is, of baroque theater proper), González de Salas, admitted the outlandish in extraordinary cases as a manifestation of superior genius—"the novelty, the outlandishness and even the temerity that the genius can be permitted."[9]

*   *   *

Despite the mechanisms of repression that were set in place (sentences from Inquisition tribunals, deaths from torture, civil executions by royal order and without a trial), it was unavoidable that the passion for the unknown, for the new and extraordinary, and, finally, for its corruption in the outlandish would go to such extremes, already beyond the permitted limits—limits that would also be broken by mystics and heretics on the one hand (recall Miguel de Molinos) and those rebelling against political authority on the other (the movements of revolt and of separatism in Andalusia). The case of Quevedo is exemplary: not being satisfied with his "rarities," with his novelties or freedoms on the literary plane, he ultimately tried to use his freedom to criticize the government. This attempt was already a step outside of what was permitted, and as a consequence he had to undergo a long imprisonment.[1]

*   *   *

At times novelty, which was liable to outlandishness by dint of being pursued by the seventeenth-century public, turned into the most banal caprice. To that would correspond the introduction of exotic and ephemeral vogues in men's and women's clothes and in their personal appearance: beards and long hair for men, uncommonly high shoes for women, and many other novelties in their dress—even extending to the capricious taste for lap dogs, which around that time were introduced in feminine circles, something criticized by Francisco Santos.[2]

This widespread expansion of the expedients that baroque culture utilized to reach vast strata of the population, including the lower social levels, is further confirmation of the mass urban character (appealing to the numerous common people of the city was normal) in the culture's products. Jerónimo de San José's reference is very clear: "It is something to be considered that the strangeness or outlandishness of style that used to be of interest to odd persons and scholars, is today not as interesting for them as for the multitude at large and the ignorant common people."[3]

8. Ibid., pp. 5, 7.
9. Jusepe Antonio González de Salas, *Nueva idea de la tragedia antigua* (Madrid, 1633), pp. 193ff. Concerning González de Salas, it is interesting to consult the pages that A. Vilanova dedicated to him in *Historia de las literaturas hispánicas*, vol. 3.
1. From the sociohistorical point of view, B. W. Wardropper proposed a differentiation between *tragedy* and *comedy* in Spanish baroque theater. According to this distinction, comedy "gives free rein to the antisocial and anarchic impulses of individuals rebelling against society"; "the message of comedy is that individuals have rights to exceed the rights of society. This message was and is revolutionary" (see his study *La comedia española del Siglo de Oro*, published following E. Olson's *Teoría de la comedia* [Barcelona, 1978]); the quotes appear on pp. 231, 235). It seems a suggestive point of view, but one that is difficult to prove.
2. Francisco Santos, *Día y noche de Madrid*, BAE, 33, p. 435.
3. San José, *Genio de la historia*, p. 300.

Let us not forget that in reference to the theater, Racine would say, without excluding his own exquisite tragedies, that it was written for the "vile populace."[4] There is no doubt that utilization of such expedients would have to be found in close congruence with the conditions of baroque society.

Interest in novelty translated into genuine—although superficial—enthusiasm for invention. The baroque individual, who always preferred nature transformed by art to simple nature, would agree with the words Martínez de Mata used to close his *Discurso VIII*: "Nature never produces anything for the benefit of man that is not in need of his art and ingenuity to perfect it."[5] Martínez de Mata was an economist who exalted manufacturing and foresaw an age when industry would predominate, something that almost none of the Spanish writers imagined. But whether giving the expression a serious or banal meaning, all of them were nevertheless inclined to prefer the products of art or technique—that is, the work of human invention. The appearance of a new product of human invention enthused many people, and when nothing better could be obtained, this enthusiasm was placed in the banal invention of, for example, a new stanza form. León Pinelo tells us that in public fiestas, other "inventions" were seen together with *comedias*, costumes, and dances.[6]

* * *

In any case, the Spanish mentality of the baroque epoch had the general quality of deriving satisfaction from all artifice, from whatever ingenious invention of human art that appeared, in terms of the novelty it offered. What Céspedes y Meneses said about his able character could be said about anybody capable of such achievement: "His skill and artifice suspended them and evoked their wonder," a sentence in which novelty and suspension once again appear intertwined.[7] The same author gives us a curious example of how a construction of this type amazed: "Thus this awesome and secret artifice was endowed with such rare ingenuity, with so much subtlety, that no one without particular knowledge of it would fathom its working; it was a scheme from a German engineer."[8]

One of the reasons for the theater being a seventeenth-century spectacle was its artifice, and as such it was specifically adaptable to the baroque's objectives. References to theatrical activities that could be cited in this connection are practically inexhaustible in the collections of writings that circulated during the epoch. As much in the *Cartas de jesuitas* as in the sheets of the *avisos*,[9] one can find mention of comedies staged to celebrate all sorts of events, because the theater offered multiple

---

4. Jean Racine, *Principes de la tragédie*, edited by E. Vinaver (Paris, 1951), p. 37.
5. Francisco Martínez de Mata, *Memoriales y discursos*, edited by G. Anes, p. 285 (they are the work's last words).
6. León Pinelo, *Anales de Madrid*, edited by Fernández Martín (Madrid, 1971), pp. 290, 310, 311.
7. Gonzalo de Céspedes y Meneses, "El desdén del Alameda," in *Historias peregrinas y ejemplares*, edited by Y. R. Fonquerne (Madrid, 1970), p. 115.
8. "Pachecos y Palomeques," ibid., p. 269.
9. Collection of Jesuit letters from 1634–48; proto-journalistic letters by the Madrid writer Jerónimo de Barrionuevo to a cleric in Zaragoza, in which he relates the news of the court, covering the years 1654–58 [editor's note].

possibilities for obtaining the expected effects in accordance with the varied nature of the events. Its role in seventeenth-century society could not be any greater. Almansa provides us with a curious fact: among the numerous properties that Rodrigo Calderón possessed at the moment of his fall (titles, public offices, honors, jewels, and money) it was recorded that "he had a lifetime theater box in Valladolid's houses of comedy, and another in the open-air theater of the Cruz de Madrid."[1] Premieres were announced, texts were sent back and forth; the "mounting" of a comedy (as it was then called) always awaited great fiestas, much talked about events (Carnival, Shrovetide, the Night of St. John, Corpus Christi, visits of great personages to Madrid), the days for celebrating saints and birthdays of royal persons, or other days of special significance. "Two great comedies of majestic ostentation" were given for the king's birthday (1622); in hopes that the queen would rapidly recover her health, a comedy about the fable of Perseus[2] was presented (1653) in the Buen Retiro.[3] Barrionuevo tells us (24 November 1655) that the marquis de Heliche had twenty-two new comedies prepared and divided them among eight companies to celebrate when the queen gave birth.[4] "They are already putting the stage machinery in order for a grand and festive comedy that is ordered for when the Queen gives birth," announced the same Barrionuevo on a later occasion (the reader was informed about this one on 28 November 1657) for the arrival of the Prince of Wales, the duchess of Mantua, and the duchess of la Chevreuse.[5] The Jesuits spoke about *comedias* in the palace, in the Buen Retiro, and about the new theaters being constructed. Comedies were also performed in the houses of seigniors; according to a Jesuit, the cardinal of Borja offered one in his palace, and León Pinelo mentioned one that was performed in honor of an aristocrat's anniversary. They were also put on in convents and schools, such as the comedies that the Jesuits organized in the fiestas commemorating the founding of the Society, which the king attended.[6]

Every year during the days of Shrovetide there was much theatrical activity, as in the year 1632 when León Pinelo related that there were three comedies repeated every day at the palace.[7] The Night of St. John was another propitious occasion: in reference to 1640, the writer tells us that he himself prepared "a comedy presented on the large pond, with machines, stage props, canopies and lights, all resting on boats."[8] Plays were also put on in Madrid, Barcelona, Valencia, Bilbao, and Seville.[9] There was ultimately no more visible or influential way to take a greater part in baroque social principles than in theatrical representations. There was no better way to emphasize the grandeur, the splendor, and the power,

1. Andrés Almansa y Mendoza, *Cartas de Andrés Almansa y Mendoza. Novedades de esta Corte y avisos recibidos de otras partes (1621–1626)*, printed in *Libros raros y curiosos* (Madrid, 1886), Letter 6 (22 October 1621), p. 103.
2. Greek hero who vanquished the Gorgon Medusa.
3. Pinelo, *Anales de Madrid*, pp. 241, 351. [The Buen Ratio is a seventeenth-century royal palace in Madrid, designed for recreation—editor's note.]
4. Barrionuevo, *Avisos*, BAE, 221 (24 November 1655), p. 222.
5. Pinelo, *Anales de Madrid*, pp. 247, 300, 312.
6. *Cartas de jesuitas*, MHE, 16, pp. 19 and 21 (2 October 1640). Other Jesuits' references to the comedy and fiesta of Cardinal Borja, in MHE, 15, p. 383.
7. Pinelo, *Anales de Madrid*, pp. 247, 300, 312.
8. Ibid., p. 318. The wind, however, was responsible for spoiling the production.
9. R. Froldi, *Il teatro valenziano e le origine della commedia barocca* (Pisa, 1962).

and this was already an expedient of effective psychological action on the multitude. Therefore, this effect was the essential aim of the use of the theater, and the fact that on consecutive days the people were allowed to enter royal locations to attend comedies did not correspond to democratic inclinations of the Austrian monarchs.[1] In a way, the performances were done for the purpose of their attending. When a Jesuit tells us that "stage machinations and comedies of the Retiro communicated freely with the people because of the generosity of His Majesty," it indicates the major objective of this animated stage life.[2]

Díez Borque has studied the structure of theater locales—that is, of the permanent theaters at the beginning of the seventeenth century—with their highly differentiated range of tickets and prices. The mass character of the spectacle becomes obvious in his study; in considering how inexpensive tickets were for people of the lower class, while those destined for the elite public remained high, he wrote: "Keeping this price was undoubtedly a concern so as to make the theater accessible for the great majority, in accordance with its function as a mass spectacle destined not for reflection but to dissesminate ideals that were intended as collective ideals."[3] Barrionuevo offered a curious news item: "Every day the comedy has been put on it has earned one thousand ducats . . . and every day the comedy was put on in the Retiro the king earned five thousand reales, the coliseum or pantheon being filled by five o'clock in the morning."[4] In this way it helped allay the expenses, sometimes nonsensical, entailed by the stage set, expenses whose total corresponded to the dominant principle of ostentation typical of baroque society: as one approached majesty, it was necessary to raise expenses to totals worthy of all the people's admiration. Barrionuevo (23 January 1655) recounted that the comedy under preparation in the theater for the king would cost fifty thousand ducats; two years later (23 January 1657) he wrote about another comedy in La Zarzuela[5] at a cost of sixteen thousand ducats. On 26 December 1657, he said that the grand comedy of the Retiro, prepared in honor of the queen's giving birth (which in his news sheets had been announced for months), would cost, with all its complements, 600,000 ducats. The political plan behind the theater campaign counted on the fact that these things would be said, without a doubt; but in the midst of baroque society such a plan also had to assume that some, like Barrionuevo himself, would make further comments: "All this comes about very purposely designed for the present misfortunes and calamities."[6]

Probably one must consider that this unrestrained activity in stage representations (the commentators never spoke of their literary value but of their magnitude, cost, the almost insuperable difficulty of setting them up, and so on) was not developed to satisfy the tastes or personal

1. I.e., the Habsburgs [editor's note].
2. *Cartas de jesuitas* (22 June 1639), MHE, 15, p. 270. Barrionuevo, BAE, 221, p. 148 (16 June 1655).
3. In his [José María Díez Borque's] edition of [Lope de Vega's] *El mejor alcalde, el rey* (Madrid, 1973), p. 67.
4. Barrionuevo, *Avisos*, BAE, 222, p. 199 (19 June 1658).
5. Royal hunting lodge near Madrid [editor's note].
6. Barrionuevo, *Avisos*, BAE, 222, p. 165 (20 February 1658). Similar comments were frequently repeated.

frivolities of kings and rulers, but to stun and attract the public mass. Barrionuevo again tells us that because of some serious political difficulties to be overcome, "there has been put together a grand comedy of San Gaetano, using all of the Court's best ingenuities, with trick stage machinery and devices." Given the circumstances, and full of suspicion about what might be said in such a comedy, the Inquisition requested it for review and retained it until finally, because of the queen's support, it was staged in an amended version. Hence on this occasion the gazetteer commented: "the assembly of the people is a day of judgment and there were so many people who went to see it at the prince's open-air theater that as they left one man was caught underfoot and smothered to death."[7] In response to the announcement about a comedy's public opening in the Retiro, so that everybody might see it in the following days, Barrionuevo predicted that the "uproar of people going will be infinite."[8]

Aubrun has written something in this regard that we must take into account. According to him, "when someone from Madrid crosses the threshold of an open-air theater, he or she loses his or her qualification in society as a merchant, servant, son or daughter, adventuress or picaro; they are transformed into a spectator with the same title as their neighbors and along with them share the same demands, the same mentality, the same *morality* of the theater."[9] One must add, however, that such procedure would serve precisely to ensure that on leaving each one would feel more in one's own social status, judging oneself to be in agreement with nature and thus able to function with confidence. We might also ask whether this "estatist promiscuity" elevated the laborer or downgraded royalty, as we might assume by some of the crude diversions to which royalty devoted itself.[1]

One of the things having the greatest influence on this development of dramatic art (unprecedented perhaps since ancient Greece) is the fact that—apart from other motivations—the stage setting of theater allowed recourse to the use of surprising artifices. At the end of the baroque's experience of theater, Bances Candamo admired the stage poem or comedy for its "manufacture," its "interior artifice," for the "ingenious machine of its contexture":[2] the theater satisfied the quotidian and banal taste for invention. In a short and packed study, Alewyn

---

7. Barrionuevo, *Avisos*, BAE, 221, pp. 212, 214.
8. Ibid., p. 148.
9. See the article [by Ch. V. Aubrun, "Nouveau public, nouvelle comédie à Madrid au XVIIe siècle] cited in *Dramaturgie et société*, 1968, p. 7.
1. There were also manifestations of the theater adapting itself to the cruder aspects of baroque sensibility. Pellicer tells us that (31, p. 139 [14 February 1640]) that the queen liked to hear hissing at the plays she attended, whether they were good or bad; she was also entertained by women fighting in the galleries and by the fact that mice were let loose. Many years later, Barrionuevo gave a similar report:

> His majesty has ordered that tomorrow only single women without hoopskirts go to the comedy because more will fit that way, and it is said that he and the queen want to view it without being seen and that there are cages with more than a hundred fattened mice ready to be released at the high point of the fiesta; when it happens there will be much to see and much entertainment for their Majesties.

Ultimately such a royally repugnant plan was not carried out (27 February 1656; BAE, 221, p. 250).

2. Bances Candamo, *Theatro de los theatros de los passados y presentes siglos*, edited by D. W. Moir (London, 1970), p. 78.

showed how the stage representation of baroque theater was based on the broadest utilization of sensible expedients: "the arts of the mimic, the painter, the musician, the set designer, and the machinist are joined here to assault all the senses simultaneously, so that the public cannot escape." The development of means of lighting, allowing stage representations to abandon the day for the night, added the effects of illumination to the repertory of theatrical representation, thereby multiplying its possibilities.[3]

Here occurred a seeming historical contradiction of the baroque. In one aspect there was an apparent instance of medievalization, even in the theater that had the pretense of being one of its most modern creations (and baroque individuals presumed themselves to be modern). Like the theater of the Middle Ages, the baroque theater again incorporated the upper parts of the scenic space; it unfolded in a vertical sense, trying to take over that part of the world that is nearest to heaven. But although this continued to give them cause to exalt their feelings about the otherworld, the individuals of the seventeenth century used such means to demonstrate a domination of nature whereby these effects of wonder are achieved. The technical difficulty of artifice was alien to the medieval human being, whereas its appreciation was decisive for the baroque: whoever manifested this type of domination succeeded in persuading, attracting with regard to what was proposed. By virtue of technical resources, such as the more skillful and calculated use of pulleys, the seventeenth-century individual was successful in having the public see actors representing divine persons, saints, the kings and their allegories, and superior beings who colonized the upper spaces;[4] in the eyes of the public, this artifice produced a sensible verification of their superiority.

The lighting effects were of great importance for achieving surprise and collective reaction, that is, for moving the public extrarationally, which was their purpose; without them, the other expedients could not have been manipulated, at least could not have attained the force they were acknowledged to have. The light itself, with all of its changes, frequently performed the action. Barrionuevo commented on a comedy using stage machinery that was presented before the king and queen: "The apparatus is superb, even the lights are exquisite."[5] The light medium expressed what the artist predominantly made use of in the epoch. The successes of artifice were probably greater in this realm (correlative to the development of the science of optics, despite the great distance separating the artist or stage designer from a knowledge of optics). The effects that one can attain with light when it is ingeniously manipulated were taken into account, including its entire technical basis, in the theater. A similar development took place in painting, and—metaphorically at least—in poetry; I would even add, allegorically, in politics, around the image of majesty. Caravaggio praised Jusepe Martínez[6] for being a "great

3. Richard Alewyn, L'univers du baroque, French translation (Paris, 1964), p. 71.
4. This final observation is from Alewyn (p. 76), who did not place it in relation with the historical changes but who acutely manifests why it is of interest.
5. Barrionuevo, Avisos, BAE, 221, p. 247.
6. Caravaggio: Italian painter (1571–1610) famed for his use of theatrical lighting (chiaroscuro); Martínez: Aragonese painter and critic (1602–1682). Maravall's translator has inverted the relationship: Martínez writes on Caravaggio, not the other way around [editor's note].

naturalist" (that is, for dominating the effects of nature); in his paintings "the figures received a fierce light of great rigor."[7] With a light such as this in so many of the epoch's paintings, in many theatrical representations that were put together, the illuminated object came to be a pretext or support for the resplendent and dazzling effects of illumination itself.

Lighting, along with so many other expedients acting upon the senses, activated the changing and wondrous play of effects in the theater and, to a different extent, in painting and the other figurative arts, whose relation with baroque theater has been pointed out by Tintelnot.[8] The idea of a similar play of effects combined with the basic aspects of the baroque world view. In a changing, varied, reformable world, the taste for changes and for the metamorphoses was satisfied in stage effects and the enthusiastic interest in artifice by recourse to stage machinations.[9] There was a genuine development of stage engineering; admiration for it is reflected in many pamphlets dedicated to describing the dazzling effects of certain representations that became famous.

From the first decades of the seventeenth century, the English public sought ingenious productions in the theater. The role of the *metteur en scène* took on great importance, as demonstrated by the preserving of an infinity of drawings and projects, and the important artist Inigo Jones made drawings for sets during the second period of Shakespeare. There were Shakespearean works, such as *The Winter's Tale*, in which surprising set effects played a great role from the time of its first presentations: when the protagonist, turned into a statue, suddenly appears before the spectators, she begins to come to life, impressing them with the "trick theatricality" of the stage director.[1] In Spain it has been observed that Lope was against the use of artifice in the theater;[2] but, despite some irony on his part, it is certain that *artifice, inventions, appearances*, or (according to the new word that began to be used at that time) *tramoyas* [stage machinery] were acquiring an always greater portion of the stage and having greater importance in the presentations.[3] There is information about the great engineering apparatus used in staging Lope's *La selva sin amor* and also about the performance of the great "machinist" Cosme Loti in the theater established on the royal site of the Buen Retiro.[4] Let us observe that references to stage effects in the margins of manuscripts began to multiply and become more complicated. A large study now underway will

7. Jusepe Martínez, *Diálogos practicables del nobilísimo arte de la pintura*, edited by Valentín Carderera (Madrid, 1866), p. 123.
8. Hans Tintelnot, "Annotazioni sull'importanza della festa teatrale per la vita artistica e dinastica nel barocco," in *Retorica e barocco*, edited by Enrico Castelli (Rome, 1955) p. 235.
9. L. P. Thomas, "Les jeux de scène et l'architecture des idées dans le théâtre allégorique de Calderón," in *Homenage a Menéndez Pidal* (Madrid, 1925), 2, pp. 501ff.
1. P. Quennell, *Shakespeare et son temps* (Paris, 1964), p. 363.
2. See K. Vossler, *Lope de Vega y su tiempo*, translated by Ramón de la Serna, 2d ed. (Madrid, 1940), p. 222. It is possible that the elements to be manipulated in the scenography of the time were not numerous, as J. Gállego maintained (*Visión y símbolos en la pintura española del Siglo de Oro* [Madrid, 1972], p. 137); yet one need not gauge this merely in terms of real practice, but must also bear in mind the epoch's considerations and reflections. After Lope's death, scenographic means certainly increased greatly, and references—not literary but merely in news items or private or public references—constantly emphasized the great role played by stage machinery.
3. See Hugh A. Rennert, *The Spanish Stage in the Time of Lope de Vega* (New York, 1909; recently republished, n.d.).
4. Rennert, Ibid., pp. 241–42.

undoubtedly reveal the great wealth of set inventions in the Spanish theater of the seventeenth century.[5] Certainly, from Cervantes's *La Numancia* to so many works of Calderón (citing no more than the chronological extremes of interest), stage machinations reached a great sophistication, with instances of mechanical apparitions, strange illuminations, rocks that opened up, palaces that were contemplated in vast overviews, transformed landscapes, meteors, and serious accidents of nature that were imitated to the astonishment of the spectator—not to mention the ships, horses, and wild animals that move on stage, all showing the complex development of theatrical techniques. * * *

But for us it is of interest to confirm the consciousness of the role of technical artifice in the theater, of its importance and extent, which gave rise to the linguistic phenomenon that the words *comedia* and *tramoya* were frequently used together; in many cases, the second term served to express the idea of the first. We have read the reference to *tramoyas* and *comedias* in a passage from León Pinelo and in the paragraph cited earlier from one of the Jesuit letters. In taking note of a comedy in the Teatro Nuevo del Retiro, another Jesuit letter related: "They say that the stage machines [*tramoyas*] it has are huge." Both are references to the years 1639 and 1640. Around the same time, Pellicer also informed his public about comedies in the Retiro, commenting about them only that they had "many stage machines."[6] In later years, Barrionuevo included items that were roughly equivalent: "a comedy of stage machines" in the Retiro; days later he gives this curious reference yet again: "It is all stage machinery"; and still later: "It is said that the apparatus of the Retiro comedy is huge and exquisite." "The industry can do anything,"[7] he commented, as if it were a matter of some of those industrial inventions that were appearing, above all in England—those that were going to revolutionize the world and, along with it, its distribution of power. Let us notice that in the way of "literary" comments there is not even a word on this, nor on hundreds of other examples. The Jesuits and, later, Barrionuevo continued to give accounts of works having stage machinery and apparatuses.[8] Barrionuevo tells us that the marquis de Heliche, who was very familiar with the subject, dealt with such machinery and was assisted by a person called "Bacho the 'tramoyista.'"[9] Let us recall that passage from Fontenelle where the philosopher explains to the marquise, his interlocutor, why Phaeton in the theater rises to the upper reaches of the stage set. If a scholastic, he says, were to treat the matter, he would maintain that it is

5. J. B. Trend ("Escenografía madrileña en el siglo XVII," *RBAM* [*Revista de la Biblioteca, Archivo y Museo de Madrid*], 3, 1926, pp. 269–91) gave some interesting information about the representations of comedies organized in honor of Prince Charles (later Charles I of England) in his surprise visit to Madrid. Trend observed a curious correspondence between the development of the theatrical locales in London at the end of the sixteenth and beginning of the seventeenth century and the development taking place in Madrid during the same epoch. And he gave an interesting scenographic sketch of Philip IV's Salón de Comedias that could not be more instructive about what I have called the epoch's "perspectivism."
6. Pellicer, *Avisos*, ed. *Semanario erudito*, 31, p. 142. The Jesuits also prepared them "with awe-inspiring stage machines" (ibid., 30, 219).
7. Barrionuevo, *Avisos*, BAE, 221, pp. 106, 121, 141.
8. *Cartas de jesuitas*, MHE, 15, p. 414; Barrionuevo, *Avisos*, BAE, 221, pp. 267, 153; Barrionuevo, *Avisos*, BAE, 221, pp. 53, 119, 120, 131, 165.
9. Barrionuevo, *Avisos*, BAE, 221, p. 237.

because the end of occupying the upper regions of space belongs to Phaeton's essence; but a modern, Cartesian physicist knows that if Phaeton is
ascending on stage it is because behind the backdrop some weights are
falling. Thus although the marquis de Heliche was not a profound Cartesian physicist but only a baroque engineer of stage machinery, he was
acquainted with the secret and knew how to make clouds, horses, or
saints ascend and descend: Barrionuevo said that to prepare his work "the
Marquis de Heliche summoned Diego Felipe de Quadros, a lead contractor, and requested 300 hundredweights for the machinery's counter-
weight."[1] Here is one more instance of the "rationalization" of the baroque
mind.

✳ ✳ ✳

To accentuate these effects before a public of courtiers and even on
occasion a broader public, the royal persons themselves or persons of high
status participated in the theater—no longer for the enjoyment of confusing illusion and reality, but to attract to human grandeur all the possibilities of admiration and captivation at the disposal of artistic effects. These
stage diversions of the grandees are well known. Rennert has related data
about them, even regarding the participation of the king himself.[2] Deleyto
mentioned theatrical representations, first in chambers in the royal palace
designed for effect, then around 1630 in the palace of the Buen Retiro in
rooms constructed precisely for the interplay of machines and stage
machinations, where such "tramoyistas" as the Italian Cosme Loti, the
Valencian Candi, and others stood out.[3] Tintelnot collected similar information about Versailles, Vienna, and the Polish court.[4] The presentation of Bocángel's El nuevo Olimpo—one instance among many (and
more could be drawn from the French court)—reveals their utilization
to deify the grandees. In the play, which was performed to celebrate the
queen's birthday, the infanta was given the role of the Mind of Jupiter
presiding over the fiesta that was presented on stage, and all the other
roles were distributed among persons of the nobility (the work was published in 1649). Let us recall that Tirso boasted that "the greatest powers of Castile" themselves liked to play the role of the principal character
of El vergonzoso en Palacio.[5] All of this came to create, on the level of
reality, the amazing effects that the theater's mechanical, verbal, and
optical resources unfolded before the suspended attention of the
spectator.[6]

✳ ✳ ✳

1. Ibid., p. 242.
2. Rennert, The Spanish Stage, pp. 232–33.
3. José Deleyto Piñuela, El rey se divierte, 3rd ed. (Madrid, 1964), pp. 149–50.
4. Hans Tintelnot, Die Barocke Freskomalerei in Deutschland (Munich, 1951).
5. Tirso de Molina, Cigarrales, p. 118.
6. The social interpretation of the theater's own technical aspects has to be related to the sociohistorical interpretation that some of us have attempted to carry out and that is being developed in younger writers with interesting results. In relation to Lope de Vega, I have cited Díez
Borque's study that precedes his edition of El mejor alcalde, el rey. Let us recall M. Sauvage's
study, Calderón: Essai (Paris, 1973), in which he brought out the dramatic tension and ultimate
conformity between morality and order on the level of social responsibility within a mentality
proper to estatist society (which characterized seventeenth-century society in all areas).

MARGARET R. GREER AND
ANDREA JUNGUITO

Economies of the Early Modern Spanish Stage[†]

* * *

Study of the *Comedia* has, in overwhelming proportions, focused on expli-cating the arterial connections between its dramas and the spiritual, political, or ideological "heart" of early modern Spain. In teaching drama, professors often spend a bit of the first class discussing the structures of the *corrales*, the range of ticket prices, the socio-economic breadth of the audience, etc. However, the "blood" that kept that theatrical heart pump-ing, nourishing it and the social organism it served, was money—the cash to buy scripts from playwrights, pay actors, buy costumes, and pay the theatre lease. Furthermore, it was the revenue that the *corrales* pro-vided for the support of the hospitals that safeguarded the theatres time and again from reformers' attempts to close them. It is not, therefore, sufficient to pay lip service to the relationship between economics, aes-thetics and ideology in the Spanish classical theatre and then have done with it.

The thesis we will seek to demonstrate is that the economics of the the-atre community in large part replicated the ideological structure and the political economy of the Catholic monarchy. We will concentrate on three areas: 1) the centrality of the Corpus Christi *autos sacramentales*, 2) the balance between the paying "vulgo"[1] Lope de Vega evokes in his *Arte nuevo*[2] and income from royal and aristocratic patronage of the theatre and major dramatists; and 3) the role played by centralization of theatre life in Madrid. We will then illustrate our thesis by following the fate of on-stage merchants as the centre of theatrical life shifted to court-centered Madrid. Various economies of exchange dramatized on Spanish stages—the exchange of women in marriage, class or caste relationships, Church and State alliance, for example—were necessarily played out within and conditioned by this fundamental theatrical economy. The increasing popularity of cultural studies has encouraged more scholars to study the economies of sexual, racial, or caste/class exchange dramatized overtly or covertly in the *Comedia*, a development we applaud; but to do this sort of study effectively, we need to be aware of the larger theatrical economy on which the *corral* stages were built. We do not pretend that this is a novel approach; we happily acknowledge an important debt to cultural materialist studies of English drama published in the last two decades by Jonathan Dollimore, Alan Sinfield. Jean Howard and others, and to Walter Cohen's major comparative contribution, *Drama of a Nation: Public Theater in Renaissance England and Spain,* which highlights parallel development between the two theatrical traditions. However, too little further work on the Spanish *Comedia* has followed the path blazed

† From *Revista Canadiense de Estudios Hispánicos*, Vol. 29, Issue 1 (October 2004): 32–37. Reprinted by permission of the publisher.
1. The common people [editor's note].
2. New Art. See pages 377–86 in this volume [editor's note].

by Cohen, and he deliberately omitted a crucial segment of the Spanish theatrical picture that distinguishes its history from that of English theatre: the Corpus Christi celebrations and the part played by organized religion—economically as well as ideologically.

Such study is also needed, we believe, to complement and balance the influential work of José Antonio Maravall and the picture he paints of the Baroque *Comedia* as an early form of mass culture, a propaganda tool with which a resilient aristocracy secured broad acceptance of its conservative value system. While recognizing the major contributions he has made in *Teatro y literatura en la sociedad barroca* and *La cultura del barroco*,[3] we believe that the picture he paints is too monolithic and too "top-down" in its characterization of cultural interchange. Juan Oleza, from his Valencian base, describes the process as involving, at least initially, a more reciprocal exchange between classes. He suggests that the aristocracy, previously absorbed in its own private theatre and courtly celebrations, became aware in the latter sixteenth century of the growth and potential import of popular theatre and, on the one hand, developed a taste for aspects of its repertoire, and on the other, sought to control and reorient it ideologically as a powerful instrument for forging social hegemony. Yet this is still a broad description. The question we want to ask is, just how did this "play" out? Through what specific institutions and agents did such a reorientation process operate, and can we trace it textually, in surviving play scripts, and through historical documentation? As Marx said, men (and women) make history, but not in conditions of their own choosing (Dollimore 3). To focus, therefore, on the contributions of individual theatrical entrepreneurs and dramatists is not, in this case, a reversion to an idealist conception of a free subject, but a "close reading" of the process by which socio-economic conditions activate the human agents who effect the modification of cultural discourses in one particular case.

By an overwhelming majority, scholarly attention to early modern Spanish theatre has centered on "secular" theatre, that written and performed for the public theatres, because it is more appealing and more intellectually accessible for a modern or postmodern public.[4] However, the lynchpin of the theatrical economy was, virtually throughout the sixteenth and seventeenth centuries, the religious theatre performed for the annual Corpus Christi festivities in cities and towns across the peninsula. Competition between cities to present the most impressive celebration with the most lavish costuming and best actors is documented as early as 1532 for Seville. Initially, the *autos* performed for that celebration were organized, financed and performed by the local guilds, who also competed to outdo each other. To accomplish this required regular practice and more opportunities for performance by the actors—guild members who, performing as a side-line to their trade, had demonstrated particular histrionic gifts. Scattered references to actors indicate that small local companies organized and performed at least sporadically by

---

3. For Maravall, see pages 433–45 in this volume [editor's note].
4. "Secular" in this instance can include plays with religious themes written in the three-act form of the *Comedia* and performed in the *corrales*, such as Lope's *Lo fingido verdadero* or *La buena guarda* or Calderón's *La devoción de la cruz*.

the decade of the 1530s, as early as those in Italy that would later travel to Spain (Sanz Ayán and García García 18–22). One of those companies was that of Lope de Rueda, who was probably acting in the 1530's; documents he signed for the Corpus performances in Seville show that he had his own company by 1542–1543. He and his fellow actors were artisans turned actors: he was a gold-beater by trade and others were listed as a silk-spinner, a "dancer and drummer," a stocking-maker and a carpenter. Rueda's company also played in palaces and toured towns and cities around Spain. He later signed a long-term contract to write and perform Corpus *autos* in Valladolid, and was planning to equip a theatre there when he died. His career thus illustrates the symbiotic relationship between religious performances and popular secular theatre; to insure the presence of the best itinerant company to perform Corpus *autos*, municipalities allowed more frequent performances, beyond those on holidays, for a paying public whose growing taste for theatre those performances fed. A similar symbiosis with Corpus performances would facilitate the establishment of public theatres in Lima and Mexico at the end of the sixteenth century.

As the elaborateness of the Corpus Christi performances increased, the cost of producing them outgrew the resources of the guilds, and administration and finance of the Corpus festivities (including the theatrical performances) passed from the Church and the guilds to the municipal government in all Spanish cities. In Seville, for which early theatre is well documented, the transfer from the guilds to the town council took place in 1544 (McKendrick 240–41). The brilliance of the Corpus celebration became a point of local pride, one in which Madrid acquired a special advantage after Felipe II made it his capital and it became the principal hub of theatrical activity. The symbiosis was not altered, however, as being named to perform the Corpus Christi *autos sacramentales*[5] was central to the financial viability of the theatrical companies chosen to represent them. Apart from the basic payment for the *auto* performances, companies competed for the *joya*, a prize for the best performance; the companies' actors and actresses renewed or upgraded their wardrobes with rich new costumes, which were a major part of the "capital" they possessed; and the companies earned additional income performing the *autos* in nearby towns and villages after the Madrid performances (witness the *Carro de la muerte* episode in *Don Quixote* or Calderón's *Mojiganga de las visiones de la muerte*).[6] The Madrid Council also used its economic and sometimes legal power to insure the presence of the best actors and actresses for Corpus performances. Companies that had been performing in the *corrales* were not allowed to leave Madrid at the end of the theatrical season to go on tour until the companies for the Corpus performances had been constituted, and authorities sometimes jailed actors or impounded their goods to prevent them from leaving. Furthermore, contracts for exclusive rights to performance in the two Madrid *corrales* between Easter

---

5. One-act religious allegorical plays, generally in praise of the Eucharist [editor's note].
6. Cart of death; comic short play on "Visions of Death" [editor's note].

and Corpus were awarded with an eye to insuring the services of the best companies for Corpus performances (McKendrick 240–43).

The contribution of Jesuit theatre also deserves recognition, although its support of the theatrical economy was indirect, consisting in broadening familiarity with theatrical performance. Jesuit schools, from the first established in Messina and Salamanca in 1548, rapidly multiplied across Spain as they did across Europe. By the end of the sixteenth century, the number in Spain alone had reached 62, and when the order was suppressed in 1773, the order was operating more than 800 educational institutions (Menéndez Peláez 31–32; O'Malley 15–16). These schools regularly used drama in Latin, and sometimes in the vernacular, to teach grammar, rhetoric, and moral doctrine. The schools were at the centre of the towns and cities where they were located and their dramatic performances regularly drew large and distinguished audiences of townspeople. Hence, their use of drama cultivated a wider familiarity with theatre and integrated it into community life.

Given the importance of such religious institutions in the development of theatre companies and audiences for theatre, we can see that the impact of the Church on early modern Spanish theatre was "bottom-up" and economic, as well as top-down and ideological, as exercised by ecclesiastical or Inquisition censorship. Furthermore, it appears that censorship of Spanish theatrical texts, in comparison to the cases of England and France, paid relatively little attention to political censorship, concentrating more on questions of Catholic doctrine or perceived lack of respect for religious authorities.

The second force in the theatrical economy that requires attention is balancing the input of the *vulgo* versus that of wealthy aristocratic and royal patrons. We all know well Lope's self-justification in the *Arte nuevo* for ignoring classical precepts: "Y escribo por el arte que inuentaron / Los que el vulgar aplauso pretendieron, / Porque, como las paga el vulgo, es justo / Hablarle en necio para darle gusto" (286).[7] Prices paid by patrons who occupied the hierarchically-ordered viewing spaces in the *corrales* might suggest that the wealthy occupants of the *aposentos* and *ventanas* would weigh heavily. But the data published by John J. Allen gives a sense that, as far as dramatists and *autores de comedias*[8] were concerned, it was largely the *vulgo* who paid, who provided their support. Most if not all of the entrance fee paid by men who stood in the *patio* and women who sat in the *cazuela* went straight to the *autor*, as did the entry fee of those who, after paying a second fee, occupied the lateral raked seating. Although arrangements and proportions varied over time, the extra fee paid for a bench or *banco* on the raked seating went to the *arrendador* and to the hospitals supported by the *cofradía*[9] that sponsored the *corral*. Only a small portion of the income of

---

7. "And then I write, for inspiration seeking / Those whose sole aim was winning vulgar praise. / Since after all it is the crowd who pays / Why not consider them when writing plays?" Lope, trans. Carlson, p. 378 [editor's note].
8. *Aposentos* and *ventanas*: reserved seating areas for upper-class spectators. *Autores de comedias*: acting company managers [editor's note].
9. *Patio*: courtyard; the least expensive area of the *corral*. *Cazuela*: area reserved for lower-class women. *Arrendador*: renter; i.e., the intermediary who handled the financial arrangements for hiring the companies that performed in the *corral*. *Cofradía*: the religious brotherhood that managed the *corral* [editor's note].

the *autor* would have come from the *aposentos*. Most of the boxes were leased by the year, or were controlled by the owners of neighboring houses who paid only an annual fee for *vistas*[1] and were apparently not reliable about paying that fee. Since the *autor* purchased playscripts, and the favour or disfavour of the paying public for that script directly affected his daily receipts, the distribution of *corral* receipts would encourage him to select texts that pleased the *vulgo* who provided his daily bread.

Just what socio-economic groups constituted this "vulgo," however? Despite the widely accepted idea that people of all social classes in Spain could frequent the *corrales*, Jane Albrecht, in *The Playgoing Public of Madrid in the Time of Tirso de Molina*, rejects the viability of a truly popular and democratic theatre, given prevailing economic conditions. Albrecht's analysis of the "poor" in Spain led her to conclude that this term applied to a broad base of the social spectrum, which included a large portion of the laboring class, a group she describes as the "working poor." The results of her investigation, based on real wages, cost of living (food and housing) and data developed by consumption economists, allow her to conclude that only a few unmarried working people could afford to attend the theatre sporadically given the fact that most of them would have spent all their income on fulfilling primary needs and not on theatre tickets.

Similarly, she explores the audience of *corrales* to identify the type of patron who had both the economic means and the time to attend these events. Besides acknowledging the well-documented presence of noblemen and clergy, Albrecht focuses on identifying the audience in the *patio* area and the *cazuela*. According to her, the presence of non-noble women was limited and depended upon their husbands and masters. Much of the *patio* audience consisted of members of the domestic service and other individuals who lived in noble residences (servants, tutors, accountants, secretaries, pages, *escuderos*, *hidalgos*,[2] and poor gentlemen), who did not necessarily pay their own entrance fee. The President of the *Consejo de Castilla*, for example, reserved a bench in the *patio* for his servants (Albrecht 76–77). Some prosperous artisans and merchants probably constituted part of the audience, particularly on Sundays and holidays. Regarding the *vulgo* that attended the *patio*, Albrecht persuasively argues that it has been wrongly linked to people of low income and that its pejorative sense is not related to the economic situation of the people but is rather associated with its lack of taste, and its limited education and intellectual formation. In synthesis, analysis of the economic situation of the country led Albrecht to conclude that the working class was not well represented in the *corrales* and that the audience was mostly made up of "noble, new and old, *caballeros*, simple *hidalgos* and their wives, sisters and hangers-on, the clergy, students and well-off artisans and merchants who aspired to nobility" (100).

If we look at the economic situation of playwrights, Lope claimed to be the first to live by the fruits of his pen and compared his plays to "paños de Segovia,"[3] merchandise for exchange (Wright 19–20). He also appears to have been the first author to claim rights of intellectual property and to

1. Views [editor's note].
2. *Escuderos*: squires. *Hidalgos*: lowest level of the nobility; gentlemen [editor's note].
3. Famed cloth from the city of Segovia in central Spain [editor's note].

attempt to block publication of others' works under his name (Roger Chartier quoted in Wright 77). On the other hand, he regularly supplemented his earnings by serving as secretary to the duke of Sessa, courted other aristocratic patrons, and assiduously sought a position at court, which was, as Elizabeth Wright puts it, "the ultimate social capital" (81). Attempting to associate himself with a leisured and lettered aristocracy, in his trial for libel in 1588, he denied having received payment for those "paños de Segovia," his plays, claiming that he wrote them for his own entertainment (Wright 22). Other dramatists, less prolific than Lope, would have been even less able to live solely by the pen. Some were priests, others supported themselves as lawyers, military officers, and/or served a noble mæcenas. Successful dramatists therefore necessarily wrote for a double public, those members of the public who voted with their feet, voices, whistles, and sometimes more solid projectiles; and an aristocratic elite that exercised its control through the Council of Castile and the municipal councils, the *cofradías,* and other forms of institutional or personal patronage (Ruano and Allen 184–97).

The third major factor in the evolving theatrical economy was its centralization in Madrid. Seville and Valencia were important centres for the early development of popular theatre within Spain. As merchant cities that prospered from trade with the Americas and the Mediterranean, respectively, they were open to new social and cultural developments. Hence it is not surprising that it was an artisan turned actor from Seville, Lope de Rueda, who according to Cervantes, "sacó [las comedias] de mantillas y las puso en toldo y vistió de gala y apariencia" (179).[4] Nor that another *sevillano,* Juan de la Cueva, from a distinguished Seville family and formed in Juan de Mal Lara's humanist circle, tried to bridge classical models and erudite Renaissance forms with popular traditions and introduced Spanish history and legend in several of his plays. In Valencia, Juan de Timoneda composed his dramatic texts to suit the tastes of his Valencian bourgeois class as well as the needs of new itinerant companies, particularly in *Las tres comedias* (1559), adapting Italian erudite prose comedies to Spanish tastes.

The influence of the aristocratic public was much increased once Madrid was made the capital and gradually became the principal hub of theatrical activity. That fact is immediately visible in the price of *corral* seats during the five years (1601–1606) in which the court moved to Valladolid. While the basic entry fee of 12 *maravedís* that went to the *autor* stayed the same, the supplemental fee charged by the *cofradía* for the *Hospital General* was halved, as was the price for the raked seating, rental of benches, and the boxes (Ruano and Allen 190–91). The earlier price structure was restored as soon as the court returned. The influence of that court environment is evident in the classic *Comedia* formula that came to prevail with the ascendancy of Lope and his contemporaries—aristocratic love intrigues, concern for honour, loyalty, and masculine friendship, and court political intrigue. The continuing importance of the *vulgo,* however, made its presence felt in plots played out on two tiers, with servants functioning as foil and comic relief to the dilemmas of their masters, a structure that also provides space for critique of the established order, as did popular

---

4. "brought [Spanish plays] out of the nursery, to exalt them and dress them in fine attire" [editor's note].

Elizabethan theatre. That classic *Comedia* formula generally masked raw economic interests and largely ignored the existence of merchants and artisans, who were present in earlier texts from Seville and Valencia.

* * *

WORKS CITED

Albrecht, Jane White. *The Playgoing Public of Madrid in the Time of Tirso de Molina.* New Orleans: UP of the South, 2001.

Cervantes Saavedra, Miguel de. *Obras completas.* Ed. Ángel Valbuena Prat. Madrid: Aguilar, 1956.

Cohen, Walter. *Drama of a Nation. Public Theater in Renaissance England and Spain.* Ithaca: Cornell UP, 1985.

Dollimore, Jonathan, and Alan Sinfield. *Political Shakespeare. New Essays in Cultural Materialism.* Ithaca: Cornell UP, 1985.

Maravall, José Antonio. *La cultura del barroco.* Barcelona: Ariel, 1980.

———. *Teatro y literatura en la sociedad barroca.* Madrid: Seminarios y Ediciones, 1972.

McKendrick, Melveena. *Theatre in Spain, 1490–1700.* London: Cambridge UP, 1989.

Menéndez Peláez, Jesús. *Los jesuitas y el teatro en el Siglo de Oro.* Universidad de Oviedo, 1995.

Oleza Simo, Juan, *et al.* "Hipótesis sobre la génesis de la comedia barroca y la historia teatral del xvi." *Teatro y prácticas escénicas, II: la comedia.* Ed. Ana Giordano Gromegna *et al.* London: Támesis; Institución Alfonso el Magnánimo, 1986. 9–42.

O'Malley, John W. *The First Jesuits.* Cambridge: Harvard UP, 1995.

Ruano de La Haza, José María, and John J. Allen. *Los teatros comerciales del siglo XVII y la escenificación de la comedia.* Madrid: Castalia, 1994.

Sanz Ayán, Carmen, and Bernardo J. García García. *Teatros y comediantes en el Madrid de Felipe II.* Madrid: Complutense, 2000.

Vega y Carpio, Félix Lope de. *El arte nuevo de hacer comedias en este tiempo.* Ed. Juana de José Prades. Madrid: Consejo Superior de Investigaciones Científicas, 1971.

Wright, Elizabeth. *Pilgrimage to Patronage. Lope de Vega and the Court of Philip III, 1598–1621.* Lewisburg: Bucknell UP, 2001.

JODI CAMPBELL

Plays and Politics[†]

Of the thousands of plays that enacted stories on Spanish stages throughout the seventeenth century, a significant proportion included kings as principal characters. Some of these plays featured well-known stories about historical figures, such as Pedro I of Castile, Alexander the

† From *Monarchy, Political Culture, and Drama in Seventeenth-Century Madrid: Theater of Negotiation* (Hampshire: Ashgate, 2006), pp. 1–23. Copyright © 2006 Ashgate. Reprinted by permission of Taylor & Francis Books UK. Quotations in Spanish have beeen translated by G. J. Racz.

Great, or Edward III of England. Many featured mythical kings from ancient Greek and Roman legends, while others simply invented fictional rulers from long ago and far away. These plays belonged to a new genre, the three-act *comedia*, which appeared in Spain in the late sixteenth century. Although dramatists since the early Renaissance had been careful to follow the guidelines set by classical Greek and Latin playwrights, the writers of the Spanish *comedia* began to bend the rules. According to classical dramatic precepts, which drew strict divisions between comedies and tragedies, kings did not appear in comedies. Aristotle established that a tragedy was characterized by the rise and fall of a powerful figure, whether god, prince, or noble, while a comedy placed an ordinary man in an unpleasant or absurd situation; the two were not meant to share the stage. One of the principal innovations of the *comedia* was to blend the comic and the tragic into a single dramatic form.[1] An important consequence of this mixture of classical forms was that kings and ordinary people for the first time began to appear in the same stories. This brought the figure of the king down from his Greek association with divinity and heroism, set above other men, to the position of an ordinary mortal, having to deal with the conflicts, passions, and obstacles of life on earth. Placing kings in *comedias* emphasized their human side.

In the realm of political theory, although theories of divine right and the sacredness of royal authority were common in the sixteenth and seventeenth centuries, writers began to draw kings down to the human level as well. Thomas Hobbes' study of the political system as a mechanical apparatus left no room for divine right as an element of kingly rule: kings were ordinary men chosen by their subjects, who then conferred sovereign power upon them.[2] The "mirror of princes" genre of political literature, popular in the sixteenth and seventeenth centuries, taught as one of its principal lessons that kings needed to dominate their personal weaknesses as men in order to fulfill well their duties as monarchs. The progression of these ideas of the monarch as a man limited by obligations, responsibilities, and constitutional restrictions, as opposed to a ruler governing as the direct representative of God, had its most extreme consequences in England in 1649 when King Charles I (who believed in divine right) was deposed and executed by his subjects (who did not). When these issues appeared in the Spanish *comedia*, and they frequently did, it was often the overlapping presence of the king and his subjects in the same story that occasioned the dramatic conflict. Either the interests of the king were in conflict with the goals of other characters, or the king himself was torn between his desires as a man and his responsibility to act in the best interests of his people. In either case, a stage occupied by

---

1. The Aristotelian categories of literature were lyric, epic, tragedy, and comedy, but by 1617 the Spanish theorist Francisco Cascales had limited these categories to three: lyric, epic, and drama. Although Cascales himself did not approve of the "monstrous" new blend, in 1635 the writer and chronicler José Pellicer de Tovar defended its quality to the Academia de Madrid, saying that it combined the best elements of the other styles, and by this time it had become the standard pattern for Spanish dramatists. Cascales, *Tablas poéticas* (Murcia, 1617) and Pellicer, *Idea de la comedia de Castilla*, reproduced in Federico Sánchez Escribano and Alberto Porqueras Mayo (eds.), *Preceptiva dramática española del Renacimiemo y el barroco* (Madrid, 1965), pp. 217–27.

2. Thomas Hobbes, *Leviathan* (1651), chapter XVIII.

both king and commoner was a possibility that proved very attractive to seventeenth-century playwrights.[3]

* * *

Drama, and particularly the *comedia*, can function as a source that lets us look beneath the surface of traditional political history to understand how ordinary Spaniards may have experienced and perceived the political changes of the seventeenth century. This was the "Golden Age" of Spanish literature, and the *comedia*, a three-act play whose structure was standardized by the great playwright Lope de Vega in the first years of the seventeenth century, was the most popular and widespread genre.[4] Thousands of people crowded into the public theaters every week to see the stories of kings, saints, fools, adventurers, lovers, and heroes from myth and legend played out before them. Over the course of the seventeenth century, these plays formed a principal element of Spanish popular entertainment. The two principal theaters of Madrid were packed with spectators year-round, *comedias* were part of court functions and local festivals, and well-known poets and playwrights vied for attention from their audiences. Those who chronicled the activities of the city always noted when a *comedia* was performed at a particular event or when one was performed to such acclaim that people were heard singing snatches of its music or reciting its most moving speeches on the streets in the days following a performance.

Another feature of this new genre was its goal of representing matters and customs relevant to contemporary Spanish life. Nearly all seventeenth-century dramatic theorists at some point employed the metaphor of the *comedia* as a mirror held up to the world, reflecting an image that was meant to instruct. Their arguments for its didactic value suggest that the *comedia* was meant to communicate useful and viable ideas.[5] Playwrights, in turn, acknowledged the powerful influence of the spectators in the form of their approval or rejection of plays and their economic support of the theater, and strove to satisfy their audiences' expectations. The fact that so many plays involved conflicts between kings and their subjects suggests that dramatists—and their public—found these stories appealing and understood them to be lessons about how to resolve or avoid these conflicts.

The format of the *comedia* allowed it to tell a brief but complete story with its conflict and resolution, which playwrights used to approach problematic situations and explore the variety of possible resolutions. When the plots involved political situations, especially those examining the relationship between a king and his subjects, the solutions they offered can reveal a great deal about the political awareness and expectations of the audience. This audience, in turn, was significant because it was far

---

3. Ricardo de Turia, *Apologético de las comedias españolas* (Valencia, 1616) and Cristóbal Suárez de Figueroa. *El pasajero* (Madrid, 1617) both commented on the advantage of mixing tragedy and comedy to be able to present both great and humble figures on the same stage.

4. For a more extensive definition of the characteristics and subcategories of the *comedia*, see A. Robert Lauer, "The Comedia and Its Modes," *Hispanic Review*, 63/2 (1995): 157–78.

5. The *comedia*, according to Luis Alfonso de Carvallo, was "an imitation of life, a mirror of customs, an image of truth" (*Cisne de Apolo*, 1602); Micer Andrés Rey de Artieda called it "a mirror of life, its goal to reveal vices and virtues" (*Discursos, epístolas y epigramas de Artemidoro*, 1605); and Lope de Vega referred to it simply as "a mirror of human life" (*Arte nuevo de hacer comedias en este tiempo*, 1609).

broader than that reached by any other form of literature and represented all levels of Spanish society. The king occasionally made appearances in the two principal public theaters, the wealthy had their boxes, the local authorities had benches in each theater, and the prices for admission to the open patio were low enough for the most humble subject to attend as well. The physical construction of the theaters divided the audience into social groups that reflected the actual position of these groups in society, but regardless of this physical division, all of these groups had some sort of space in the theaters, and the experience of the drama was shared by king and commoner alike.[6]

This was also a time when Spanish philosophy and theology favored the metaphor of the world as a stage, and life as a dream. As life was a kind of testing ground for people, to see how well they could play their social roles and obey the precepts of Christianity, so the theater was a testing ground for society. Questions of honor, justice, love, and loyalty could be examined and tested in the form of endlessly variable fictional situations. Golden Age dramatists dealt with the question of kingly authority as much as political writers did, although their experiments took a different form: they could portray trustworthy kings and tyrannical kings, ideal situations and insoluble problems. It is as if the theater were a kind of laboratory in which different ideas could be tested and the outcome judged. Since the decades of the *comedia*'s greatest popularity coincided with the decades of Spain's greatest political crises, the ways in which Spaniards experimented with fictional kingship on stage revealed their concerns and expectations about their own kings.[7] How these situations were resolved reflects the way the society saw itself, what it regarded as ideal, and what it condemned as impermissible.

The fictional experiments of the *comedia* took place against a backdrop of political change, as the seventeenth century was a time when the structure and perception of monarchy were being redefined, not only in Spain, but all over Europe.[8] Historians have argued for generations over the exact meaning and nature of absolutism, but a general sketch reveals two concurrent processes.[9] One was an increasing concentration of power in the person of the king, "an ever widening supremacy and competence inherent in the ruler's personal will and decision," supported by an understanding that the monarch's authority and legitimacy were derived directly from God.[1] This included a change in the perception of kingship, often fostered by campaigns to enhance the image of royal figures through costume, art, and architecture designed to promote a sense of awe and

6. Ricardo García Cárcel, *Las culturas del Siglo de Oro* (Madrid, 1999), pp. 46–7, argues that Golden Age theater is a good example of the difficulty of distinguishing between "elite" and "popular" culture because it appealed so widely to everyone.
7. For the purposes of this study, when referring to the wide variety of rulers who were characters in the *comedia*, I have used the term "king" as a synonym of "monarch," signifying any ruler who is sovereign in a particular territory, such as the dukes of the Italian city-states or the emperors of Rome. These characters exemplify features of the relationship between sovereigns and vassals, whether or not they specifically hold the title of king.
8. One of the best recent works on this process is Paul Monod, *The Power of Kings: Monarchy and Religion in Europe, 1589–1715* (New Haven, 1999).
9. An overview of competing definitions of absolutism is given by Michael S. Kimmel, *Absolutism and Its Discontents: State and Society in Seventeenth-Century France and England* (Oxford, 1988), pp. 9–13. See an excellent criticism of the term in Ruth Mackay, *Limits of Royal Authority: Resistance and Obedience in Seventeenth-Century Castile* (New York, 1999), pp. 1–4.
1. Pérez Zagorin, *Rebels and Rulers, 1500–1660*, vol. 1, *Society, States, and Early Modern Revolution* (New York, 1982), p. 90.

majesty. By enhancing the individual power of the king, absolutism also strove to enhance the king's ability to make laws, wage war, and impose taxes without the consent of his subjects. The basis of the relationship between ruler and subject, according to the ideals of absolutism, "was the unlimited fidelity owed to the king as a personal suzerain whose authority was unchallengeable."[2]

While this process focused on the individual, enhancing the power and majesty of the king, the second was a more bureaucratic one in which the monarchy sought to increase its practical control over systems of justice, law, and commerce, as well as over provincial and municipal affairs. This involved a process of administrative centralization and political integration, a challenge for many early modern states in which long-standing social, regional, and institutional centers of authority (nobles, representative assemblies, the church) strove to protect their privileges and liberties. In the case of Spain, the Habsburg monarchy faced a particular challenge in that it ruled one of the most diverse and far-flung states of Europe. This "composite monarchy" was a collection of regions with distinct identities: not only did the Spanish Habsburgs govern territories in the Netherlands, Italy, and the Americas, but the Iberian peninsula alone contained the territories of Castile, León, Navarre, and Aragon (and, between 1580 and 1640, the kingdom of Portugal), along with the territories of Catalonia and Valencia. United only by the person of the king, these regions frequently had different customs, languages, and representative institutions, along with strong constitutional traditions that preserved their regional uniqueness and limited the powers of the monarch. In the seventeenth century, these traditions increasingly were perceived by the Castilian-based monarchy as obstacles to effective government, and Spanish rulers and their ministers struggled against them in their efforts to maximize their resources through uniformity of taxation and legal systems in the various provinces.[3]

The general outlines of absolutism are clear, and most historians agree that this process of overriding traditional liberties and privileges was one of the crucial steps towards the creation of the modern nation-state. Beyond that, there has been much discussion in recent decades about the actual practice and dimensions of absolutism: whether it perpetuated or ended feudalism, worked for or against the interests of the aristocracy, functioned with or without the support of the bourgeoisie, or was perhaps only an elaborate illusion of smoke and mirrors.[4] In any case, what is clear

2. Bob Scribner, "Understanding Early Modern Europe," *The Historical Journal*, 30:3 (1987), pp. 752–3. Rather than being viewed as an unjust imposition, this process in many cases was favored by subjects dismayed by the religious and political chaos of the sixteenth century who were willing to surrender some of their rights to a powerful central authority in the interest of order and stability. See Julian H. Franklin, *Jean Bodin and the Rise of Absolutist Theory* (Cambridge, 1973), introduction and chapters 2 and 3, Guemer Lewy, *Constitutionalism and Statecraft during the Golden Age of Spain* (Geneva, 1960), p. 17, and Glenn Richardson, *Renaissance Monarchy: The Reigns of Henry VIII, Francis I, and Charles V* (New York, 2002), p. 32.
3. A good survey of this aspect of early modern government is J. H. Elliott, "A Europe of Composite Monarchies," *Past & Present*, 137 (November 1992): pp. 48–71. See also Christian Hermann (ed.), *Le premier âge de l'état en Espagne (1450–1700)* (Paris, 2001).
4. Hillay Zmora, among others, suspects that the spectacle of absolutism "has dazzled and overawed modern historians more than it did contemporary nobles." *Monarchy, Aristocracy, and the State in Europe 1300–1800* (New York, 2001), p. 89. The richest debates about early modern absolutism have been in the field of French history: see especially the work of William Beik, James Russell-Major, Roland Mousnier, Sarah Hanley, Sharon Kettering, Roger Mettam, and James Collins.

is that absolutism was far more complex and nuanced than the stark tenet that kings had the executive agency and divine authority to do as they pleased. It may have rested on a shared assumption of the king's theoretical ability to override the privileges of regions and social groups without any form of consent, but monarchs were generally wise enough not to attempt this in practice. They possessed absolute power only as long as everyone agreed that they possessed absolute power, and this agreement could be maintained only as long as kings did not make excessive use of that power against the interests of their subjects.

As historical studies have shifted their attention from states and institutions (often measured by their ideals and goals rather than their actual accomplishments) to the mechanisms by which they actually functioned, it has become increasingly apparent that the absolutist states of the seventeenth century operated not through the unrelenting imposition of their authority, but through a process of negotiation and cooperation with existing powers. Many scholars have called attention to the ways in which absolutism relied on political patronage and thus signified "a renewed accommodation between monarchy and nobility, not a radical restructuring of their relationship in favour of the former."[5] In the case of Spain, a number of scholars have demonstrated the ongoing ability of representative groups and institutions, as well as royal councils, to limit the practical powers of early modern kings.[6]

Even ordinary people were frequently participants in this system rather than helpless or invisible pawns. Luis Corteguera, for example, has convincingly demonstrated the significance of the political awareness and activity of artisans in seventeenth-century Barcelona.[7] Certainly the most obvious places to look for the political activities of ordinary people are episodes of riot, protest, and rebellion, and there were many of these in Western Europe in the seventeenth century.[8] But what about the regions, such as Castile in the heart of the Spanish empire, that did not experience any substantial violent opposition to the process of absolutism? Are we to understand that the absence of political violence signifies approval or at least indifference? This is too simplistic a solution, but historians are still searching for ways to gain access to the views of the vast majority of the population who experienced these historical changes but did not react in ways extreme enough to leave clear traces in the archival record.[9]

---

5. Zmora, *Monarchy, Aristocracy, and the State*, p. 6, and the discussion of the seventeenth century in Chapter 5. Helen Nader's *Liberty in Absolutist Spain: The Habsburg Sale of Towns 1516–1700* (Baltimore, 1990) is a landmark study on the surprising coincidence of interest between the "absolutist" monarchy and autonomous towns. For the relationship between the crown and local oligarchies in Madrid, see Mauro Hernández, *A la sombra de la Corona: Poder local y oligarquía urbana (Madrid, 1606–1808)* (Madrid, 1995).

6. See the work of I.A.A. Thompson, Charles Jago, José Manuel de Bernardo Ares, Pablo Fernández Albaladejo, and Bartolomé Clavero.

7. Luis Corteguera, *For the Common Good: Popular Politics in Barcelona, 1580–1640* (Ithaca, 2002). Wayne te Brakes' *Shaping History: Ordinary People in European Politics, 1500–1700* (Berkeley, 1998), demonstrates the importance of "taking ordinary people seriously as political actors" throughout early modern Europe, p. 2.

8. See Robert Forster and Jack P. Greene (eds.), *Preconditions of Revolution in Early Modern Europe* (Baltimore, 1970), Yves-Marie Bercé, *Revolt and Revolution in Early Modern Europe* (New York, 1987), Zagorin. *Rebels and Rulers*, and te Brake, *Shaping History*. For Castile, which experienced protests but no serious rebellion, see Pedro L. Lorenzo Cadarso, *Los conflictos populares en Castilla (siglos XVI–XVII)* (Madrid, 1996).

9. An excellent study of the constant negotiations of early modern authority between monarch and people—with and without violence—is Alison Wall, *Power and Protest in England 1525–1640* (New York, 2000).

Early modern society, and especially that of Spain, is frequently described as a society of orders, a clear hierarchy in which every person knew his or her position and corresponding obligations. Paradoxically, the sixteenth and seventeenth centuries were also a period of great uncertainty: the Reformation and subsequent religious wars, the shifting notions of power that accompanied the growth of absolutism, new intellectual views of the world drawn from science and exploration, and changing economic conditions all undermined what people perceived as the familiar foundations of their society. This resulted in a desire for restored stability, what Lawrence Stone has described as an "almost hysterical demand for order at all costs,"[1] but also in a passion for questioning and reevaluating old assumptions and beliefs.[2] Spaniards in the seventeenth century still trusted in the value of a social and political hierarchy, but they wanted to define it clearly, and they wanted to ask questions first. Early modern societies visualized this hierarchy as a system of "interdependent functions and reciprocal duties that formed a body politic of common benefit to all its members, whatever their station,"[3] and many of the challenges and questions posed by Spaniards had to do with defining exactly what those interdependencies were. Ordinary people were aware of and debated nearly every topic related to their changing world: "the state of Spain, kingship, absolutism, Machiavellianism, Tacitism, reason of state,[4] rule by favourite, racial purity, social mobility, honour, the social and professional standing of painting, the rival merits of popular and classicizing literary traditions, the legitimacy of the theatre . . . to name but a handful."[5] Castilians may not have rebelled, but they were active thinkers and questioners and participants in negotiating their place in a changing society.

The Spanish Golden Age has received much attention from literary scholars drawn to the tremendous volume, quality and range of literary work produced in the sixteenth and seventeenth centuries, but these scholars have not always perceived it as an expression of this process of negotiation. The earliest and most thorough studies of Spanish drama in the twentieth century considered Golden Age theater to be the product of a state and an elite culture threatened by political and social instability. José Antonio Maravall, one of the most influential *comedia* scholars of the twentieth century, saw the sixteenth century as a key stage in the evolution from a feudal to a precapitalist society, and noted the social tensions that emerged as a result. Both the state and the nobility saw this evolution as a threat to their established hierarchy of power, and Maravall argued that they consciously used theater as a form of propaganda to stabilize and reinforce the existing order.[6] The *comedia* presented stock

1. Lawrence Stone, *The Family, Sex and Marriage in England, 1500–1800* (London, 1977), p. 653.
2. Jeremy Robbins, *The Challenges of Uncertainty: An Introduction to Seventeenth-Century Spanish Literature* (London, 1998), p. 15: see also Monod, *The Power of Kings*, p. 141.
3. Zagorin, *Rebels and Rulers*, vol. 1, p. 64.
4. Machiavellianism: Renaissance political doctrine based on the writings of Niccolò Machiavelli (1469–1527) that challenged the centrality of morality to rule and instead advocated cunning and deception as necessary in order to preserve the power of the prince. Tacitism: Renaissance political philosophy based on the work of the Roman historian Tacitus (c. 56–117), critical of absolutism. Reason of state: Renaissance political concept that emphasized necessity over morality in the actions of polities [editor's note].
5. Melveena McKendrick, *Playing the King: Lope de Vega and the Limits of Conformity* (London, 2000), p. 4.
6. For Maravall, see pp. 433–45 in this volume [editor's note].

characters representing types of people more than individuals, and these in his view emphasized the inherent honor and dignity of each rank, encouraging subjects to take pride in their place, and consequently to not threaten the system by stepping out of it. Dramatic conflict in the plays was created when the social order was threatened, and resolved when this order was happily restored, often through the assistance of the king himself.[7]

This view of theater as the reactionary tool of an absolutist state has carried a number of consequences for *comedia* studies. Principal among these was the tendency to view dramatic production as an undifferentiated whole, in terms of its meaning and role in society. The assumption was that a *comedia* written by a playwright in Valencia in 1620 would have the same general purpose and meaning as one written by a Sevillian in 1660: they provided a collective answer to a collective problem. The only variations acknowledged by this view were those relating to the two cycles of dramatic production dominated by the century's greatest playwrights, Lope Félix de Vega Carpio (1562–1635) and Pedro Calderón de la Barca (1600–1681), and these are considered to be differences of style rather than substance. Although there were dozens if not hundreds of other playwrights whose work was acclaimed by seventeenth-century audiences, modern scholars recognized them (if at all) as pale imitators of these two giants. Consequently, for the period spanning roughly 1950–1980, there were two approaches to studying the *comedia*: that of studying the characteristics of the genre, and that of studying the works of either Lope or Calderón. Charles Aubrun's classic study of seventeenth-century drama is representative of both; he called theater of that period "a solid whole, consistent and without fissures"[8] and limited his analysis to the most "accessible" plays of Lope and Calderón, meaning those that were most appealing to modern readers and audiences. This pattern held for literary critics as well as for scholars who study literature in its historical context; the methodologies of the most influential studies in *comedia* criticism of the 1970s all approached and analyzed the *comedia* as an undifferentiated whole.[9]

A more specific consequence of viewing theater as a consciously wielded tool of propaganda, and a consequence which is particularly relevant to this study, is the interpretation of the role and nature of kings as presented in the *comedia*. If theater served as a means of promoting the status quo and maintaining the social hierarchy, it stands to reason that it would present a consistently positive picture of kings and their power.

7. Maravall's views on this aspect of theater are most clearly presented in *Teatro y literatura en la sociedad del barroco*, new and rev. edn. (Barcelona, 1990, originally published 1972). This view was influential through the 1980s and beyond in works such as Márquez Villanueva's *Lope: Vida y valores* (Río Piedras, 1988) and Bruce W. Wardropper (ed.), *Historia y crítica de la literatura española*, vol. III, *Siglos de Oro; Barroco* (Barcelona, 1983). McKendrick suggests that its perseverance in Anglo-Saxon criticism as well is due to the Black Legend's insistence on Spain's "resounding devotion to God, King and Country." *Theatre in Spain 1490–1700* (Cambridge, 1989), p. 109.

8. Charles Vincent Aubrun, *La comedia española 1600–1680*, trans. from the French by Julio Lago-Alonso (Madrid, 1968), p. 9.

9. The first and most influential effort to provide a critical approach to the *comedia* as a whole was Alexander A. Parker's essay "The Approach to the Spanish Drama of the Golden Age," *The Tulane Drama Review*, IV (1959): pp. 42–59, revised as "The Spanish Drama of the Golden Age: A Method of Analysis and Interpretation," in Eric Bentley (ed.), *The Great Playwrights*, vol. 1 (New York, 1970).

Comedia scholars recognized that kings often appeared in drama, either as background historical figures or as active protagonists, and their interest was sparked by what they perceived to be the consistent portrayal of a powerful monarchy.[1] Many saw in Spanish drama a tradition of complete submission of Spanish subjects to their king, and echoed Karl Vossler's view was that it was "impossible to find in Lope anything but monarchic absolutism."[2]

*   *   *

In recent years, this interpretation of the "unified whole" of Spanish drama and its unquestioning support of the absolutist monarchy began to fracture along two lines. The first of these cracks appeared when scholars of the two principal seventeenth-century playwrights, Lope and Calderón, began to find elements in their plays that were not as uniformly propagandistic as everyone had believed. Some plays, most notably Lope's *Fuenteovejuna* and Calderón's *La vida es sueño*, had long been the subject of debate over the ambiguities of their messages regarding kingship and rebellion. The immense volume of scholarship devoted to these two plays is evidence of the difficulties of ascribing a single point or message to either. Heated exchanges in scholarly journals have used these plays as examples of very contradictory themes: demonstrating the divinely-given power of the king to resolve any conflict, or proving the equally divinely-given power of the people to take the initiative to correct bad rulers.[3]

What lies behind these debates is the question of the ultimate source of justice and power in the early modern Spanish monarchy. Did Calderón and Lope present the notion that the king was the source of all justice, who must be obeyed by his subjects no matter how unreasonable this obedience may have seemed? Or did they intend to argue, following many contemporary political theorists, that power in fact came from the people, who in turn invested it in a king, retaining the right to remove him in cases of tyranny? Were both readings possible to the seventeenth-century audience, just as they seem to be to modern scholars? Antonio Gómez-Moriana, pursuing these questions, was one of the first to do a systematic study of the political ideas in a wider range of Lope's plays. Working with 14 of Lope's *comedias*, he concluded that they did present stories in which the king was responsible for creating the dramatic conflict of the plot, rather than solving it. In these cases, Gómez-Moriana concluded, Lope argued that the abuse of legitimate authority could be

1. See, for example, Ludwig Pfandl, *Geschichte der spanischen Nationalliteratur in ihrer Blutezeit* (Freiburg, 1929), and Karl Vossler, *Introducción a la literatura española del siglo de oro* (Mexico City, 1941), and *Lope de Vega y su tiempo* (Madrid, 1940).
2. Vossler is quoted in A. Robert Lauer, *Tyrannicide and Drama* (Stuttgart, 1987), p. 11. An even more extreme view is held by Agustín García Calvo, who argued that Golden Age drama was a "depraved and servile" genre dominated by the formation of the Spanish state and its "authoritarian, pyramidal, intimidating structure" which dominated all of its subjects through an all-pervasive fear. García Calvo, "Propuesta de un Auto de Fe para el teatro español del siglo de oro," in *Jornadas de teatro clásico español* (Almagro, 1978), pp. 135–81.
3. See, for example, Robin Carter, "*Fuenteovejuna* and Tyranny: Some Problems of Linking Drama with Political Theory," *Forum for Modern Language Studies*, 13 (1977): 313–35; William R. Blue, "The Politics of Lope's *Fuenteovejuna*," *Hispanic Review*, 59:3 (1991): 295–313; Dian Fox, "Kingship and Community in *La vida es sueño*," *Bulletin of Hispanic Studies*, 58 (1981): 217–28, and "In Defense of Segismundo," *Bulletin of the Comediantes*, 41:1 (1989); Alice Homstad, "Segismundo: The Perfect Machiavellian Prince," *Bulletin of the Comediantes*, 41:1 (1989): 127–39.

considered tyranny, which in turn could be justifiably opposed by the community, or in extreme cases by the individuals whose rights had been violated.[4] Similar work by Stephen Rupp and Dian Fox demonstrates that the work of Calderón also presents arguments for the necessity of good kingship (as opposed to functioning as servile flattery) and evinces a clear concern for the primacy of law over the arbitrary whims of a ruler.[5] This approach, in contrast to that of Maravall, put the ideas of these playwrights squarely in line with those proposed by contemporary political theorists.

Another shift in *comedia* studies came when scholars began to pay attention to Golden Age playwrights other than Lope and Calderón. Although it had long been recognized that the playwright Tirso de Molina had taken a particularly political stance in his plays, and had been reprimanded by the government and threatened with exile from Madrid for his opinions, this seemed to be the exception which proved the rule that theater in general supported the absolutist monarchy. If playwrights who dared to question the status quo were dealt with so harshly, certainly the rest must have learned their lesson. Many studies have explored Tirso's connections to the Madrid court and how his political alliances were expressed in his plays, but always under the assumption that his experience was an anomaly in the world of theater.[6]

Far from being the "illusionist theater serving the conservative myths of the Baroque," as Maravall had claimed, some of these plays were now considered to constitute a serious criticism of seventeenth-century Spanish society.[7]

These discoveries left *comedia* scholars in something of a quandary. First they had a body of work by Lope and Calderón, all supportive of the monarchy, with only a small handful of exceptions, and even those could be explained away with little effort. Finding trends critical of the monarchy in the work of other playwrights, though, complicated the situation. Previously, scholars who wrote surveys of Spanish drama had passed over the minor dramatists, considering them only less-talented imitators of the few who formed the Golden Age canon. Now, though, they faced the question of whether these lesser-known dramatists were fundamentally different from the most famous writers. If they were, this would mean a need to reevaluate the canon; but if in fact they were still mere imitators of Lope and Calderón, this would require a significant revision of our understanding of these two dramatists and their relationship to the absolutist monarchy. One begins to suspect that Tirso de Molina, rather than having been the exception for his political views, was merely the exception in having been punished for them.

4. Antonio Gómez-Moriana, *Derecho de resistencia y tiranicidio: Estudio de una temática en las "comedias" de Lope de Vega* (Santiago de Compostela, 1968), pp. 25–6.
5. Rupp, *Allegories of Kingship: Calderón and the Anti-Machiavellian Tradition* (University Park, PA, 1996) and Fox, *Kings in Calderón: A Study in Characterization and Political Theory* (London, 1986).
6. Ruth L. Kennedy is the principal authority on Tirso and his historical context, particularly his conflicts with the Junta de Reformación. See, for example, "La perspectiva política de Tirso en *Privar contra su gusto*, de 1621, y la de sus comedias políticas posteriores," in *Homenaje a Tirso* (Madrid, 1981), pp. 199–238, and "A Reappraisal of Tirso's Relations to Lope and his Theatre," *Bulletin of the Comediantes*, 18 (1966): 1–13. For a more recent survey of Tirso scholarship, see Ignacio Arellano (ed.), *Tirso de Molina: del Siglo de Oro al siglo XX* (Madrid, 1995).
7. McGaha, "Who was Francisco de Villegas?", p. 174.

Although this particular debate has by no means been settled, one significant outcome of the conflict was a recognition that the "lesser" playwrights of the seventeenth century deserve more attention than they have yet received. This conclusion is probably of greater value to the scholar whose interest is historical more than purely literary, for it is true that most of the thousands of plays written and performed during the Golden Age lack the wit of Lope and the grace of Calderón. Nevertheless, they drew large and enthusiastic audiences, and their creators were well-known and active participants in literary and court circles. There has only been one survey of these "lesser" dramatists to date, and its focus is on the internal structure of the *comedia* rather than its social context.[8] It is important to remember that what we think of as the Golden Age canon does not bear much resemblance to what was actually viewed and read by the Golden Age public. Scholars miss a valuable opportunity when they neglect popular literature because of its perceived lack of literary excellence and insist on "thinking of literature in terms of the highest exemplars of imaginative literature—Virgil, Dante, Shakespeare, Cervantes—and failing to observe that their cultured colleagues are science-fiction addicts, consumers of thrillers, and devourers of newspapers and magazines."[9]

A second outcome of these fissures in the once-solid *comedia* genre was the recognition that the message of popular drama can be far more ambiguous than scholars had believed. Again, this had been clear in a small handful of cases such as Lope's *Fuenteovejuna*, or Calderón's *La vida es sueño* with its seemingly inexhaustible debates about whether the execution of a rebellious character at the end of the play was meant to be Machiavellian, poetic justice, or simply in the interest of the community at large.[1] Now, though, thousands more plays were opened up to scrutiny for the possibility of multiple readings, dramatic irony, and a less direct connection to the ideology of the absolutist government. One possibility is that the apparent inconsistencies that we see in the *comedia* are due to the differences between the modern reader's viewpoint and that of the seventeenth-century Spanish audience. Frank Casa warns that we tend to judge the act of writing according to its roots in the Renaissance tradition of being a particularly individual act, but that the Spanish baroque valued the society over the individual. Playwrights, whatever their personal views, would have felt obliged to defend the prevalent mores of their society. This choice, however, was directed by their own cultural context rather than being intentionally directed by the state. Casa explains the ambiguities of the *comedia* by suggesting that the playwrights occupied a very tenuous position between wanting to please their public and not wanting to endanger themselves by criticizing the government. This conclusion implied that the personal vision of the

8. Vern G. Williamsen, *The Minor Dramatists of Seventeenth-Century Spain* (Boston, 1982).
9. Keith Whinnom, "The Problem of the 'Best-Seller' in Spanish Golden-Age Literature," *Bulletin of Hispanic Studies*, 57 (1980): 195. For additional comments on the non-representative nature of the Golden Age canon, see McGaha, "Who was Francisco de Villegas?", p. 175, and José Sanchis Sinisterra, "La condición marginal del teatro en el Siglo de Oro," in José Mouleón (ed.), *III Jornadas de Teatro Clásico Español* (Madrid, 1981), pp. 106–07.
1. A good overview (and continuation) of the "rebel soldier" debate from the 1960s to the present may be found in A. Robert Lauer, "El leal traidor de *La vida es sueño* de Calderón," *Bulletin of Hispanic Studies*, 77 (2000): 133–44.

playwright tended to be critical of the established order, and that many plays set up plots leading towards this viewpoint. However, they could not bring themselves to follow these plots through to their logical conclusions, so that odd plot twists at the end caused the play to deviate from its original trajectory, landing it in a safer middle ground between the propagandistic and the subversive.[2] Melveena McKendrick has presented the clearest expression of this argument, demonstrating that Lope de Vega used the tools of drama (irony, dialectic, and multiple perspectives) to "support and subvert simultaneously"—to comment on contemporary politics without risking his neck.[3]

These approaches imply that, left to their own devices, playwrights would have expressed opinions and opened discussions rather more subversive than the government would have liked. Audiences were also perfectly aware of the dangers playwrights faced in being overly critical of the monarchy, and these audiences may have been accustomed to seeing past the convenient endings to the real meaning of the play. Careful readings of the *comedia* are crucial to understanding the overall impact of a particular play. Where scholars of previous generations tended to rely on specific passages (often taken out of context) or the positions represented by particular characters to determine the meaning of a play, we now assume that meaning is not so simply revealed.[4] A greater sensitivity to the context in which these plays were produced should lead us to examine the whole of the plot, not just what one character says but how that attitude is borne out and what consequences it holds for the longer term. What at first glance appears to be a happy ending may not be so happy, if the initial conflict has not been truly resolved or if superficial order is maintained at the cost of justice.

The current generation of historians and literary scholars of the *comedia* is therefore much more sensitized to the pressures and limitations which influenced the production of drama.[5] The playwright, rather than being an isolated figure or the puppet of the monarchy, is now located in the midst of his culture, his patrons and his public. Greater attention is being paid to the cooperative effort of author, director, actors, editor, printer and bookseller in the production and distribution of drama. Another factor is the influence of the audience: most previous studies of the *comedia*, even those which focused on the propagandistic or subversive roles of drama in society, entirely neglected to consider the effects of the *comedia's* message on its public, or possibly even the public's influence on the *comedia*.[6] Recently, scholars have begun to consider the audience as an active

2. Frank P. Casa, "Affirmation and Retraction in Golden Age Drama," *Neophilologus*, 62 (1978): 551–64.
3. McKendrick, *Playing the King*, p. 11.
4. See, for example, P. R. K. Halkhoree, who argued that a portrayal of an ideal situation "is not intended to reinforce the stability of the existing order but rather is a threat to it." Halkhoree, in J. M. Ruano de la Haza and Henry W. Sullivan (eds), *Social and Literary Satire in the Comedies of Tirso de Molina* (Ottawa, 1989), p. 31, and McKendrick, *Playing the King*, particularly Chapter 5.
5. For surveys of New Historicist and postmodern trends in *comedia* scholarship, see Enrique García Santo-Tomás (ed.), *El teatro del Siglo de Oro ante los espacios de la crítica: Encuentros y revisiones* (Madrid, 2002), and José A. Madrigal (ed.), *New Historicism and the Comedia: Poetics, Politics and Praxis* (Boulder, 1997).
6. Cynthia Leone Halpern's book on Juan Ruiz de Alarcón, for example, is an excellent study linking the political themes of Alarcón's dramas with contemporary political theory and historical events. It fails, however, to evaluate the impact or consequences these plays may have had.

influence, approaching the *comedia* as a product of the supply-and-demand forces of the marketplace.[7]

*   *   *

Other models from cultural history and anthropology may be fruitfully applied to the Spanish case, such as Roger Chartier's work on representation and the production of meaning, in which he reminds us that

> no matter how forcefully cultural models may have been imposed. they might nevertheless have been received with reactions that varied from mistrust to outright rebellion. A description of the norms, disciplines, discourses, and teachings through which absolutist, Reformation culture may have intended to subject the population does not prove that the people were in fact totally and universally subjected.[8]

For the scholar of theater, one of the greatest advantages to be derived from fields like cultural anthropology is an understanding of the complexities that lay behind politics. Political culture, especially in the early modern period, was imbued with a powerful sense of ritual, and political ceremonies can be understood as "minidramas" or metaphors which underwent a continual process of invention and perpetuation. This process of understanding politics almost as a form of fiction itself (a "master fiction," in anthropologist Clifford Geertz's term) can be helpful in understanding how it can be read in different ways by different parts of society.[9] Language itself becomes an important factor in this process, as we begin to understand it as an active element and not merely a passive vehicle for the mechanisms of power.[1] All of these approaches share an understanding of power as a fluid and negotiated relationship.

The previous paragraphs suggest some of the lines of inquiry which guide this study of the *comedia* and its political voice in seventeenth-century Spain. As we have seen, the principal flaws in older interpretations of the *comedia* are the lack of emphasis on the historical context in which drama was produced, the need for a greater understanding of the cultural forces involved in its creation and its relationship to the power structure, and an incomplete understanding of absolutism. Historians of early modern Europe, in turn, have reevaluated their concepts of the absolute monarchy from an all-powerful centralized government to one whose power was limited to its ability to successfully negotiate with other political, social, and economic power centers in the kingdom, and drama can be understood as a significant part of that negotiation.

The principal obstacle to a thorough understanding of the dramatic production of seventeenth-century Spain and its role in political culture is

---

7. Melveena McKendrick, *Theatre in Spain 1490–1700* (Cambridge, 1989). Although it does not deal principally with the *comedia*, María José del Río Barredo's *Madrid, Urbs Regia: La capital ceremonial de la monarquía católica* (Madrid, 2000) includes valuable attention to the idea of the audience's reception and interpretation of ceremonial events in the court.
8. Chartier, *Forms and Meaning: Texts, Performances, and Audiences from Codes to Computer* (Philadelphia, 1995), p. 86.
9. Sean Wilentz, introduction to *Rites of Power: Symbolism, Ritual, and Politics since the Middle Ages* (Philadelphia, 1985), pp. 3–5. See also Clifford Geertz, "Centers, King, and Charisma: Reflections on the Symbolics of Power," in Joseph Ben-David and Terry Nichols Clark (eds.), *Culture and its Creators: Essays in Honor of Edward Shils* (Chicago, 1977), pp. 150–71.
1. J. H. Elliott's *Lengua e imperio en la España de Felipe IV* (Salamanca, 1994) is an excellent study of the language of power in its broadest sense, including style, metaphor, visual images, and behavior, and the importance of the "art of persuasion" as a factor in power relationships.

its sheer volume. Lope de Vega, probably the best-known dramatist of the Golden Age and certainly its most prolific, claimed in mid-career to have written over a thousand plays, and his biographer, Juan Pérez de Montalván, said that over the course of his lifetime Lope had produced nearly 2,000 full-length plays and 400 one-act religious plays known as *autos sacramentales*.[2] Whether or not this number is exaggerated will never be known, but the 400 *comedias* that have survived and can be attributed with certainty to Lope attest to his remarkable output. Add to this the more than one hundred plays written by Calderón de la Barca, and the thousands more written by playwrights all over Spain, and the estimate of total *comedia* production in the seventeenth century is easily as high as 10,000, greater than that produced by any other nation in the early modern period.[3]

Despite the phenomenal production of Spanish dramatists in the late sixteenth and seventeenth centuries, only a relatively few plays, and even fewer playwrights, are well-known to us today. As we have seen, one studies the Golden Age by reading Lope and Calderón, and even then the same small handful of plays scooped out of their vast literary production appears over and over on course syllabi, in anthologies, and in translation. To an extent this is a justifiable approach, particularly for scholars of literature, because the works that now form the Golden Age canon are arguably of greater and more lasting literary value than the vast majority of the plays that filled the published collections and drew large and enthusiastic audiences to the theaters in the seventeenth century. While a "Best of the Golden Age" selection may be well suited to an appreciation of the height of Spanish baroque culture, it is less useful for the historian. Based on a reading of only these texts, one might easily agree with earlier scholars that Spanish dramatic production is "monolithic" and unvarying in its presentation of society's values and mores. One *comedia* scholar still believes that a fresh examination of one of this small group of plays would be a more valuable contribution "than to rescue from oblivion some potboiler of Diamante or Claramonte—or even Lope—about which little or nothing has found its way into print."[4] But following this logic would result in a completely closed circle of investigation, in which the principal qualification for determining the merit of a particular work would be whether someone else had already studied it. In any case, the taste of the modern scholar is not the same as that of the seventeenth-century popular audience, and if one wishes to understand the perspective of the members of that audience, one must enter into their world and look over their shoulders at the plays which received the greatest attention in their own time, even if these have since been discarded and forgotten. * * *

Although it is impossible for us, more than three centuries later, to capture and recreate this dramatic experience, the plays which commanded

2. Lope's claim is in the *Arte nuevo de hacer comedias en este tiempo* (Madrid, 1609); Pérez de Montalván is cited in Sturgis Elleno Leavitt, "The Popular Appeal of Golden Age Drama in Spain," in *Golden Age Drama in Spain: General Consideration and Unusual Features* (Chapel Hill, 1972), p. 14.
3. Aubrun, *La comedia española*, p. 9; Leavitt, "The Popular Appeal of Golden Age Drama in Spain," p. 13.
4. James Parr, "Criticism and the *Comedia*: Twenty Years Later," in Parr, *After Its Kind: Approaches to the Comedia* (Kassel, 1991), p. 149.

such interest and enthusiasm on the stage were also circulated in published form. *Comedias* in the seventeenth century were nearly as popular in print as they were on the stage. Playwrights, once they had reached a certain degree of fame, often published their own work in collections of 12 *comedias* each. It was also common for publishers to gather collections of the *comedias* of various playwrights and publish them at their own cost. * * * *Comedias* often appeared in printed form shortly after they had ended their theatrical run, and evidence indicates that they were only published once they had received some level of acclaim in the theaters.[5] This suggests that the popularity of drama on stage can be at least roughly measured by its corresponding popularity in print.

This does bring up the question of whether studying theater in print is the same as studying theater on stage, particularly in terms of the audience. Clearly, in the seventeenth century, attending a play in a crowded theater, with dances and songs in between the acts and the spectators paying nearly as much attention to each other as to the actors, would have been a significantly different experience from reading the same play from a book, even though the content of the play would have been the same. Whether or not the audience was the same is a difficult question: literacy rates were very low in the early modern period, though this is not necessarily a good indicator of accessibility to literature. The relatively recent invention of print would not yet have changed substantially the traditional habits of reading aloud and reciting from memory, which were common to all social classes.[6] Contemporary references to the *comedia* described attending a performance by using the verb *oír*, to hear, as often as they used *ver*, to see.[7] Spanish drama of this period relied heavily on words and action to convey meaning rather than using visual elements such as props or stage effects, which made it well suited to being recited or read aloud. Early modern Spaniards were much in the habit of reading aloud chivalric romances and other kinds of novels; it stands to reason that drama, already written in the form of speech, would have been shared in the same manner as well. There is some indication that authors themselves wrote with the expectation that this would happen. Books, including *comedia* collections, often had introductions addressed to "*el vulgo*," the common reader/listener (as opposed to an elite, presumably literate audience). In some cases, a book would have two prefaces—one directed to each level of audience.

Although the experience of seeing a drama performed on stage would have been circumstantially different than reading one (or hearing one read aloud) from print, they do have significant elements in common. Above all, there is an economic argument for evaluating them together in terms of popularity. A playwright's fame came first from the stage; if his plays were successful there, he would have reason to believe they would be popular in print as well. The process of printing collections of plays was

---

5. Aubrun, *La comedia española*, p. 24.
6. Margit Frenk, "'Lectores' y 'oidores': La difusión oral de la literatura en el Siglo de Oro," in Giovanni Bellini (ed.), *Actas del Séptimo Congreso de la Asociación Internacional de Hispanistas* (Roma, 1982), vol. 1, pp. 103–07. See also Chartier, *Forms and Meanings*, p. 16.
7. Municipal orders, for example, required soldiers of the palace guard and other officials "who wish to hear the *comedia*" ("que quisieren oír la comedia") to pay the full ticket price and warned of others who "want to hear them without paying" ("las quieren oír sin pagar"). Archivo Histórico Nacional, Madrid (hereafter AHN), Sala de Alcaldes de Casa y Corte, libro 1269, fol. 276, and libro 1283, fol. 257.

funded either by the playwright himself or by the bookseller, both of whom operated on the hopes of regaining their investment from book sales. Consequently the published collections of plays were not likely to be, for example, personal favorites of a playwright that had not found their way onto a stage. They would most likely be plays that were sure to have a guaranteed audience, proven by the popularity they had already attained. Although there certainly were exceptions to this pattern, and the tastes of the reading audience may have been somewhat different from the tastes of the theatergoing audience, the texts of those plays that received public acclaim on stage would have had a far greater chance of getting into print than those that did not.

As an added factor, the popularity of these plays would then have been perpetuated as a consequence of their publication. As we have noted, literacy was low during the early modern period, but recent studies place it at a higher level than previously believed. Madrid in the seventeenth century logically had a higher literacy rate than the rest of the country, possibly as high as 58 percent.[8] Additionally, the court city was a major market for publishing, producing 40 percent of the items published in all of Spain in the seventeenth century.[9] Although it has generally been assumed that the vast majority of the population did not possess and could not afford books, contemporary references and Inquisition records indicate that book ownership was fairly common, and not just among the highest social classes.[1] We may then assume a fairly wide audience for printed matter, particularly given Madrid's high literacy rates and the cultural conventions favoring the oral transmission of written text. In the absence of consistent information about the performances of particular *comedias* in the seventeenth century, it is reasonable to evaluate their popularity based on their appearance in published form.

* * *

MELVEENA McKENDRICK

Breaking the Silence: Women and the Word in the *Comedia*[†]

* * *

We *comediantes*[1] are certainly still too ready to talk in terms of *comedia* characters being defined by role, as playing parts. Clearly the *comedia*

8. C. Larquié, "L'alphabétisation à Madrid en 1650," *Revue d'histoire moderne et contemporaine*, 28 (1981), p. 152.
9. Cruickshank, "'Literacy' and the Book Trade in Golden-Age Spain," *Modern Language Review*, 73 (1978): 802–03.
1. Sara Nalle, "Literacy and Culture in Early Modern Castile," *Past & Present*, 125 (1989), p. 77. For further information on books and readership in Madrid, see Antonio Castillo (ed.), *Escribir y leer en el siglo de Cervantes* (Barcelona, 1999), Fernando Bouza, "Para qué imprimir: de autores, público, impresores y manuscritos en el Siglo de Oro," *Cuadernos de Historia Moderna*, 18 (1997): 31–50, and María del Carmen González Muñoz, "Datos para un estudio de Madrid en la primera mitad del siglo XVII," *Anales del Instituto de Estudios Madrileños*, 18 (1981).
† From *Revista Canadiense de Estudios Hispánicos*, Vol. 29, Issue 1 (October 2004): 14–30. Reprinted by permission of the publisher.
1. Here, students of the *comedia* [editor's note].

is full of characters who really are playing parts, acting out temporary roles for purposes of their own; and of course it is perfectly legitimate to see such plays metatheatrically as conveying a sense that the world is indeed a theatre, that to the extent that human beings have parts to play and life has a beginning, a middle and an end, they too are actors. The analogue does encapsulate a human truth. But as we are also more than any part we play, than any role we occupy, so *comedia* characters, whether indulging in role play or not, are often more complicated than the categories that appear to define them. The very use of the term "role" or "part," however, contrives to shrink them into something much less than this. It leads us, if we are not careful, to find what we expect to find rather than allowing the detail of the texts to speak for itself. Not even the small core of extensively studied Golden-Age plays has entirely escaped this process, but it is the huge number of underscrutinized plays that constitutes the real problem, conditioning as it does our perception of the nature of the *comedia*. As more good critical editions become available, there will be no excuse for relying any longer on an outdated typology. The general direction the endeavour needs to take seems to me obvious. Since language is at the centre of our humanity, it is the language of the mind that must be explored in the *comedia*, much in the way that Frank Kermode has recently written about the language of Shakespeare. Since language shapes our experience, perception and understanding of the world, language reflects these processes back at the world, making utterance in drama the key to the representation of a complex humanity.

The importance of utterance to the early modern Spanish theatre's representation of the condition of women is a distinct but crucial aspect of this, acquiring definition and significance from the circumstance that female speech was still at the time an activity in principle rationed and controlled by men. Like children and servants, women were enjoined to be silent, to speak when spoken to or otherwise only when absolutely necessary. The idea of silence as a positive, creative state has an important place in religious and philosophical thought—the silence of worship and contemplative prayer in Western Christian spirituality, for example. The silencing of women, servants and children, however, belonged to an allied but oppressive tradition, a tradition where silence signalled order and hierarchy, imposing and implying consent, submission, approval, obedience, subordination, the lack of right to speak, to think, to opine, to decide. Rationing speech meant stifling self-expression, opinion, reaction, thought itself. It tried to exclude women from the life of the mind, the life of an examined and articulated self, to reduce them, effectively, to a sub-human existence. And exclusion from a life of the mind encouraged incompetence, as Maria de Zayas points out in the preface to her *Novelas ejemplares y amorosas* (1636), "la verdadera causa de no ser las mujeres doctas no es defecto del caudal sino falta de la aplicación" (21–22)[2]—*aplicación* in the sense of lack of opportunity to apply themselves. When men categorised women's speech as empty prattle they had only themselves to blame. The prescription of silence was based on the

2. The most prominent female author of seventeenth-century Spain, Zayas was best known for her novella collections *Amorous and Exemplary Novels* (1637) and *The Disenchantments of Love* (1647); "the true cause of women not being learned is no lack in their worth but rather the fact that they do not apply themselves" [editor's note].

assumption that women, children and servants were lesser beings with nothing of value to say, that their views therefore did not count. Any utterance other than the necessary minimum constituted excess, all the more transgressive in women in that, in addition to insolence and presumption, in them it was associated with lack of sexual modesty and continence—the bridled tongue, the closed mouth, was taken as the sign of the chaste body, the roots of this assumption spreading back to Eve's alleged failure of intellection (her inability to see beyond the literal meaning of the serpent's words) and misuse of speech in the Book of Genesis. * * * Even those who regarded learning as not impossible in a woman considered anything more than the instruction necessary to her role in life to be undesirable, to be a dangerous distraction from her true vocation as the help-meet of man.

That the prescription of silence was not nearly as effective as it was intended to be is suggested by the control words traditionally used by men to marginalize and condemn women's speech as garrulousness and verbal bullying—gossip, nag, scold, fish-woman, virago, harridan, witch * * * We must not lose sight of the fact that language was in the past not merely woman's only way of operating socially but her only weapon of defence and attack. The prescription acted nonetheless as a powerful constraint upon the self-expression and witness of women, particularly in the middle and upper social ranks.

* * *

In the context of the official silencing of women's voices, in public record as well as in the domestic sphere, the wholesale emergence of female actors on the Spanish stage (and only on the Spanish stage) at the end of the sixteenth century was a remarkable development, the impact of which, it seems to me, has never been adequately registered. That the new practice was permitted only because it was considered by the authorities to be the lesser of two evils—preferable to continuing to allow boys to play female roles—does not change the fact that the very sex that was supposed to lead a confined, passive and generally silent life within the domestic space was now treading the boards of the playhouses and speaking out, often at great length and with considerable eloquence. The stage of course demands speech, to act is to be neither silent nor passive, but it is the prominence of female voices in the *comedia* which is so striking. Women had been given both a voice and visibility, a public platform no less, from which to represent the condition and experience of being female. Their behaviour on stage might belong to the world of imagination and popular entertainment, but from within that protected fictional space the words they spoke revealed what it was like to be a woman, and specifically what it was like to be a woman in a man's world. That the actresses who embodied the *comedia*'s female characters were neither peasant women abused by noblemen, nor gentlewomen with violent husbands, nor the marriageable daughters of the urban gentry, but came for the most part from relatively humble if often respectable backgrounds made no odds. Not all of them had questionable reputations, as the moral opposition to the theatre held, but as a result of their profession and their peripatetic lives they knew more about the world than most of their sex and were amply equipped to act as forceful spokeswomen for a wide range of female causes. Most importantly, perhaps, the conflation of female role and female player endowed the characters on stage with an illusion of reality which the participation of boy actors could never have achieved. This close fit between presentation and representation must have affected the audience's perception of the relation between cultural practice and the imaginary world, lending added force to the burden of the words. Seeing and hearing a woman lamenting her ill-treatment at the hands of a faithless lover was a very different experience, for both the women and the men in the audience, from seeing and hearing a boy dressed as a woman going through the same motions. Whatever alternative frisson boy actors might have provided, they could not have been entirely credible as persuasive communicators of female experience. If performance is a contingent construction of meaning, as Judith Butler holds (136–37), the female habitation of female roles on stage must inevitably construct different meanings from the male habitation of those roles.

The situation does not fully comply with John Stuart Mill's stipulation in his *The Subjection of Women* (1869): "We may safely assume that the knowledge that men acquire of women even as they have been and what they are, without reference to what they might be, is wretched, imperfect and superficial and will always be so until women themselves have told all they have to tell us" (26). The words that issue from women's mouths in Golden-Age plays were put there by male playwrights. Arguably, however, they were all the more effective for that. The speeches of these characters carry a double weight—the authority of a woman apparently telling her own story, expressing her own opinions, thoughts and responses, and the authority of the male dramatist's voice. Since words from the mouth of a woman carried less authority than the same words from the mouth of a man—because man speaks with the cumulative authority of the dominant group to which he belongs—in the plays the authorial provenance of the speeches did not allow the male spectator the opportunity to dismiss what he heard as special pleading or women's blathering. Female playwrights had to be more careful about the words they placed in their characters' mouths. If "most of the conditions that have to be fulfilled in order for a performative utterance to succeed come down to the appropriateness of the speaker—or, better still, his social function—and of the discourse he utters" (111), as Bourdieu maintains, then the persuasiveness of what the women who speak out in the plays have to say would have gained considerably from their borrowed authority. That authority was constituted not only by the sympathetic authorial shaping of the circumstances which give rise to their utterances, but by the authorial presence behind the thoughts and words themselves, which was a male presence. In the introduction to his edition of Henricus Cornelius Agrippa's *Declamation on the Nobility and Pre-eminence of the Female Sex* (1529), Albert Rabil Jr. has pointed out that in the period 1300 to 1700, against the backdrop of a 3,000-year history of misogyny rooted in the civilizations related to western culture (Hebrew, Greek, Roman and Christian), "questions of female equality and opportunity were raised that still resound and are still unresolved" (ix). For him this questioning constitutes the "other voice" of women and some male supporters, in contradistinction to the "first voice," the voice of the educated men who created western culture. Since by any measure, and certainly by the measure of their time, Lope, Tirso, and Calderón have to qualify as male supporters, the voice of the *comedia*'s women is a composite "other" voice, the fusion of sympathetic male observation and reflection and empathetic female enactment.

Clearly it was by no means the first time that women in Spanish literature had been given a surrogate voice. In Spain, as elsewhere, the late Medieval and Renaissance debate about women and their relationship with men had become a fashionable literary exercise, heavily weighted in women's favour, in which women were often allowed by male writers to "speak for themselves." In the pastoral romance, women play a notably prominent part in the debates—they are portrayed as eloquent in their defence of their sex, perceptive in their analyses of sexual politics and gender prescription, and as capable as the men of intellectual discussion. Florisia's song (sung by Belisa) in Gil Polo's *La Diana enamorada* of 1564 is a brilliant deconstruction of masculine attitudes to women in poetry and in life, written with a mixture of humour, mockery, shrewd analysis and incisive condemnation by a man willing to admit that the literary perspective, indeed the official perspective on everything, is a male perspective. Contemporaneously with the theatre in its early decades, Cervantes placed some equally emphatic and equally nuanced expressions of the female point of view in the mouths of Marcela in the *Quixote* and Preciosa in *La gitanilla*.[3] The difference in terms of impact, however, is bound to have been significant. These women not only inhabited the printed pages of books, but were twice removed from people at large by being located in worlds fashioned by philosophical (neo-Platonic) debate or by idealized romance. What passed for lived reality in the fiction of the age yielded women of a different kind, witches and prostitutes (*La Celestina*)[4] and dysfunctional mothers (the picaresque) whose musings on the condition of women, where they occur, were calculated if anything to confirm traditional stereotypes rather than engage understanding.

In the theatre, by contrast, a socially varied and sexually mixed audience shared a physical space and a present tense with people on the stage, seeing and hearing flesh and blood women reacting to circumstances, pressures and predicaments in an alternative "real" world that, for all the inevitable distortions of art and popular entertainment, presented a recognizable simulacrum of their own, not least because it was inhabited by women as well as men. Women who worked in markets and inns no doubt often expressed themselves very freely indeed, and in the confines of the court Spanish noblewomen—their reputations protected by their rank—acquired a reputation for verbal wit. But most of that was social chaff, proof indeed for many that empty vessels make the most sound. Within their own homes women at all social levels would have thought their own, more subversive, thoughts and sometimes expressed them, particularly amongst themselves. What happened in the playhouses was significantly different. Here, women and men over and over again heard female characters of many kinds and in many situations talking about their lives in ways that challenged orthodox thinking and that were therefore severely disapproved of by churchmen and moralists (even those relatively well disposed towards women) and almost certainly by

---

3. *The Little Gypsy Girl*, one of Cervantes' *Exemplary Novels* (1613) [editor's note].
4. Also known as *The Tragicomedy of Calisto and Melibea*, by Fernando de Rojas (1499) [editor's note].

the majority of men. These characters, furthermore, were by and large characters designed to elicit not condemnation but approval, admiration or at least sympathy. They exhibit no glib association of verbal fluency with easy virtue, although sexual trauma can lead to anguished eloquence— Isabel's rape in *El alcalde de Zalamea* and the infamous treatment to which Dorotea is subjected in *La niña de Gómez Arias*[5] are obvious cases. They enter the discursive masculine space in order to express, explain and justify themselves. Words become the weapon of women constrained and damaged by prejudice and prescription. They have something, not nothing, to say. And what women have to say in the *comedia* is almost invariably validated by the workings of the plays themselves, so that the female voice plays an integral part in what the works are telling us about the world. The *comedia*, in other words, by giving women access to language and action was challenging the authority of tradition and the church by repositioning women in the scheme of things, by reading and representing women in a new way. This strong protofeminist strand can, I think, be partly understood as part of the *comedia*'s complicated oppositional identity, shaped as it was by the urge to pursue its own anti-authoritarian impulses while avoiding damaging confrontation.

It is striking how many of the longest and most memorable speeches in the *comedia* canon are made by women, speeches which reveal more of what it was and felt like to be a woman in that society than a library of history books. They convey the sheer power of words in action, words that illuminate the inner world of the mind and the emotions, words spoken in anguish, in puzzlement, in anger, incomprehension and despair. They are speeches which encourage the habit of mind of seeing the speakers as characters thinking, rather than delivering verse, as debating with themselves rather than reciting poetry. Their structural and linguistic detail then yields patterns, gaps, interruptions and non-sequiturs that are the reflection of mental processes in action. And they betray a humanity as full and complex as that of any man. The dramatists obviously played to what they knew to be the acting companies' strengths, and their actresses were certainly one of these. Sir Richard Wynn, a member of the Prince of Wales's entourage, after an official visit to Madrid in 1623 when the English guests were entertained with a play in the Palace, reported:

> The Players themselves consist of Men and Women. The Men are indifferent Actors, but the Women are very good, and become themselves better than any I ever saw act those Parts, and far handsomer than any Women I saw. To say the truth, they are the only cause their Playes are so much frequented. (Quoted in Shergold 266)

That playwrights gave actresses prominent roles and a lot to say is therefore not surprising. But the nature of the parts those actresses played and of the words they were given to speak could have been very different. * * * The disjunction between what women in plays are perceived as being and expected to be, and what they actually feel and think, is captured in a supplement of words that in terms of the plot need not be included at all. That they are is a tacit acknowledgment that women did have things to say and that they needed to be said.

5. Both by Calderón [editor's note].

How their words from the stage were received is another matter, but in order to evaluate their dramatic purpose and theatrical impact we have to take account of the socio-linguistic context. In the seventeenth century the social world was by and large taken for granted. Vertically and horizontally men and women had a sense of their place in the scheme of things, in terms both of class and gender—a sense of what was permissible and appropriate, a sense of difference, distance and boundaries. Within their own class women's symbolic capital was almost entirely limited to the fulfilment of their role as housekeeper and mother. In the symbolic space of the world outside they lacked political and social authority, power and weight, even when they were contributing financially to the family. The women in the plays often question, reject even, this allocation of social space and the power that goes with it, not in relation to class but to gender. They seek to collapse prevailing categories of difference and distance, to push back boundaries, and in the very process of using language as an instrument of expression and persuasion they are attacking one of the crucial categories of discrimination. Since they are challenging the inevitability and the rightness, not of all the givens by any means— marriage, family and the social hierarchy continue to be taken as primary structures in human life—but certainly of the role and condition of women within those structures, the escape from silence, the right to speak and be heard, is the demand on which all else stands or falls.

The way people, that is men, thought about women in relation to utterance and language suggests that if these stage roles and speeches still make a strong impression upon us today, as they do, then they must have struck audiences at the time as bold at least, often as quite shocking or even absurd. I think we can assume that many of the women in the *cazuelas* and *aposentos*[6] would have approved, because their very presence in the public playhouses marked them out as women of some strength of character. But we must not underestimate the possible weight of female disapproval in society at large. In traditional hierarchical societies, subordinate individuals have always to varying extents shared the system of values that works against them. This was true in terms of sex as well as class or caste. * * * As for the male spectators, those who frequented the court would have been familiar with many of the sentiments being expressed, and therefore probably fairly relaxed about it. But again we must not underestimate the disapproval, the lack of comprehension, the rolled eyes, the derision even, with which the speeches would have been greeted by many men. For a century the constant complaint about the *comedia* was that it put ideas into the heads of impressionable spectators incapable of competent judgement, so I think we can safely assume that to many the presence of women on stage challenging the *status quo* appeared threatening. The plays' endings, of course, provided reassurance of a sort for those literal-minded enough to take comfort from a conventional restoration of the socio-sexual order. Marriage or convent or death would have appeared to reabsorb transgressive thoughts and emotions very nicely into the system. Sharper minds, however, would have grasped the fact that what the speech of women in these plays

6. Enclosed sections of the theater reserved for women and the nobility, respectively [editor's note].

invokes is not some wildly unreal form of rebellion against an immutable universal order, but something all the more dangerous for being more plausible—self-expression, choice, respect, justice and restitution within the system, something which it was largely within men's capacity to give them. The power of their words is therefore never neutralised by the resolution of the action.

It has to be recognised, of course, that we now home in on certain plays and characters because they chime with our own views and sensibilities, and that the dramatic diet of Spanish playgoers would not have included weekly, monthly or even yearly helpings of the sort of riveting female rhetoric that might have caused real disquiet. A great deal of what they saw was routine fare, featuring conventionalised plots and parts that would have been readily absorbed by most theatregoers into their understanding that while the world being created in front of them was a recognisable world, it was not, and could not be, their world. At the same time, we must not be too ready to dismiss its imaginative impact. While the truly outstanding female voices might represent a small if significant minority in the context of such a hugely prolific and long-lived theatre, the vocal and proactive woman was a constant in the *comedia*. There are in fact relatively few plays where her potential in some way, to some extent, is not exploited, and this must mean two things. It must mean, since this was a popular, commercial theatre, that for whatever reasons audiences responded positively to these parts and performances; and it must consequentially mean that the success of the *comedia* and its cultural importance in the life of the nation were in large part due to the presence of women on stage and to the nature of the parts they played. As Jauss observed, "The work does not exist without its effect; its effect presupposes reception, and in turn the audience's judgment conditions the author's production" (138). It is difficult to believe, therefore, that constant exposure of this sort did not affect perceptions, did not familiarise audiences with a different way of being and considering women. If film, sitcom and soap opera now affect social and sexual practice and expectation in the way they undoubtedly do, then there is no reason to believe that the *comedia*'s audience was not also susceptible. Of course the exposure then was not as pervasive nor as relentless, the religious and social controls were much stronger, and the examples and lessons of the stage were not reinforced from other quarters, which is why on the surface of things, at least, little altered. Political and social upheavals are produced not just by revolutions, but by a gradual, almost imperceptible, accumulation of pressures which usually then need some event or circumstance to trigger unstoppable change—in the case of women in Western Europe generally, the First World War followed fifty years later by the arrival of the birth control pill. In Spain itself it would also take the death of one man.[7] The *comedia* was simply ahead of its time.

The playhouses, of course, had their own socio-sexual politics. Men and women, young and old, lowly and noble, rich and poor (albeit not destitute) were gathered together within the same physical space, there to see and be seen, to talk as well as to listen, to react as well as absorb. All had

---

7. I.e., the dictator Francisco Franco, whose death in 1975 ushered in a period of profound social change [editor's note].

paid to see the performance and all were at liberty to respond as they pleased, sharing and expressing the same emotions. Little wonder that this apparent breeding ground for social change alarmed moralists and would-be reformers as much as did the goings-on on stage—traditional separations and assumptions were threatened. And these were the surroundings in which women were portrayed on the boards expressing their thoughts and trying to shape their own destinies, talking back at men, looking back at men, both in character and as actors in real time. The disapproval directed by Spanish commentators at woman's presence on the stage and in the audience may well have been caused in part, as Jean H. Howard observes of the Elizabethan theatre in *The Stage and Social Struggle in Early Modern England* (77), by the perception that her presence in the playhouse put her into circulation in the public world in ways threatening to the larger patriarchal society within which her circulation was in theory a structured and controlled process. In other words, women who went to the theatres (particularly those who stood in the *cazuela*) and women who acted in them were laying claim to a degree of unsupervised freedom that released them from the traditional polarised categories of virtuous woman (silent, reticent, passive, house-bound) and whore. So where did these women fit in? It was a question provoked as well by many a female protagonist. The fact that the situation was one which enabled women in the audience to look as well as to be looked at, and to speak as well as to listen (and we know they could express themselves vigorously), was equally destabilising of traditional attitudes to gender, producing in the playhouse itself a worrying echo of the female activities on stage. Stage and playhouse constituted worlds in flux, each giving to and taking from the other, the old gender rules and divisions no longer being observed. That the areas designated for female spectators themselves were spaces where distinctions became blurred did nothing to assuage anxiety. The *aposentos* doubtless housed courtesans as well as noblewomen, and while the *cazuelas* were occupied largely by women of low degree, and often doubtful morals, as José Maria Diez Borque has stated (143–45), the literature gives us glimpses too of spectators of a different sort. In Zabaleta's *El dia de fiesta por la tarde* (307–23) four sumptuously dressed women with covered faces and underskirts "que chispean oro" (320)—out on a spree one imagines—bribe the *apretador* to allow them into the already packed *cazuela*.[8]

This ambience in the playhouses created a receptive and protected space where acts and utterances did not have to be accounted for. It could therefore be a laboratory for confident and often anarchic exploration and experimentation, for the saying and doing of things that would have been difficult, even impossible, to get away with in the real world; a laboratory where alternative ways of being could be tried out. It was not unlike the acceptable fantasizing and role-playing of children as they learn to understand and come to terms with the real world and their possible place within it. But it also pushed out the boundaries of the imaginable, the potentially realizable, not least because the words and events represented had already taken shape in the mind of their creator and were

---

8. For Zabaleta, see pages 423–27 in this volume; "that sparkle with gold"; *apretador*: an usher for women at the theater [editor's note].

now being enacted by their performers. The *comedia* was effectively engaging in a dialogue with an age-old tradition of misogyny—mediated with renewed energy by Renaissance advice literature on women and their role—now inflecting, now modulating, now disturbing the bland, unquestioning iteration of handed-down certainties. It is skilful at showing the limitations of prescription, at identifying the misfit between prescription and human realities, at negotiating the moral and social nuances of prescription defied. The representation of women in the theatre thus derives its full significance and impact from the debate that implicitly "contains" it, in relation to other forms of representation in the written and oral traditions. Their representation was to a large extent profit and consumer driven, but those very forces were driven in turn by social and cultural circumstances—specifically by intensifying pressures during the early modern period to make woman's place in the scheme of things conform more closely to the hierarchical hegemony of church and state, invested as this was in the idea of the family. The theatre was the only body within the institutional structure which confronted these tendencies and showed them to be problematic—one of the reasons, no doubt, why its enemies were given to accusing it of feminizing Spanish society.[9]

In those speeches that invoke such doctrines and principles as free will, justice, and self-determination, women through the mediation of their creators hijack language, the language of authority, of power, of the symbolic order, and make it their own. * * *

Their command of logic and rhetoric does not imply an abandonment of the broad patterns of woman's existence—marriage and motherhood. However, they do claim and enter into a fully human inheritance at the moment when, through language, they position themselves firmly within the larger philosophical, intellectual and moral structures that transcend their life, in the process revealing how flawed was the commitment of their age to those beliefs. The speaker is entering a discourse that her audience would have identified as being a male discourse (as of course it is, in that it is the dramatist's) and its appropriation by a woman would have been recognised. That element of recognition is central to its impact and therefore to the message, the message that women as well as men are agents in the processes that mediate between principle and reality. Expectations are broken.

* * * The dramatic impact of protofeminist discourse in the plays lay precisely in the fact that it was in this sense both "unauthorised" (and unlikely to succeed) and "authorised" (and consequently effective). Unlike men, women were not mandated to pronounce on religious, philosophical and moral issues; men were the self-appointed regulators of utterance, men, almost never women, were authorised to speak on behalf of the group. However, if their sex rendered these female characters inappropriate speakers, the circumstances that drive them to speak give them an authority that carried weight. Their eloquence and their reasoning, their evident persuasiveness within the fabric of the play's development and resolution, presented audiences with a clear challenge to the belief

9. In 1598 the committee of theologians appointed by Philip II to look into the effects of the playhouses expressed the view that they made men effeminate and unfit for war and work.

that language, and the world of idea and principle to which it gives access, were the exclusive territory of men. In Lope de Vega's *Fuenteovejuna*, Laurencia's defamatory eruption into the rhetoric of leadership is a self-assumed mandate that occupies the vacuum created by the psychological paralysis of the men of the village.[1] * * * The social assumptions upon which such utterances are predicated are turned on their head in this re-presentation of cultural practice. * * * Some form of psychological alienation is a precipitating factor—the women would not be protesting unless they felt ill-used. Rosaura in *La vida es sueño* may have removed herself from her socio-sexual context by pursuing Astolfo from Russia to Poland *vestida de hombre*,[2] but for her extraordinary speech in defence of her honour and her right to reclaim it in the forthcoming battle she repositions herself symbolically by deliberately donning her woman's clothing. These dramatic utterances are empowered by a legitimate sense of injustice, and their rhetorical effectiveness is located not only in the patent validity of arguments that were supposed to transcend gender even in the seventeenth-century (free will and natural justice), but in the circumstances that have given rise to them.

If language formation and use are shaped by social and political practice—and it seems very obvious that they are—then to challenge men's dominance of language is by implication to challenge the socio-sexual order itself. It interferes with power, and is therefore a political act. * * * In a woman rebellious words were rebellious acts—the very process of speaking up and speaking out is an act of insubordination, a challenge to the symbolic power of the male, the father, the head of the family, and therefore of the social order itself.

*   *   *

Silence can be as eloquent as words in the *comedia* in drawing attention to the bleak realities of women's lives.

Bourdieu points out that:

> Among the most effective and best-concealed censorships are all those which consist in excluding agents from communication by excluding them from the groups which speak or the places which allow one to speak with authority. In order to explain what may or may not be said in a group, one has to take into account not only the symbolic relations of power which become established within it and which deprive certain individuals (e.g. women) of the possibility of speaking or which oblige them to conquer that right through force, but also the laws of group formations themselves (e.g. the logic of conscious or unconscious exclusion) which function like a prior censorship. (138)

His inclusion of women here is very apposite. In the (relatively uncensored) *comedia*, the force to which Bourdieu refers takes the form of an explosion of words out of the mouths of women driven way beyond silence by the conditions of their life or the circumstances in which they find

---

1. When Lorca's theatre company, La Barraca, performed the play in Madrid in 1935, Laurencia's speech made a huge impact on an audience unaccustomed to hearing such improprieties from the mouth of a woman. See García Santo-Tomás (352).
2. "Dressed in a man's traveling clothes," from the stage directions [editor's note].

themselves. It is extremity that propels them to break the explicit prescription and the implicit assumption that women should not be heard, certainly not heard using speech as a weapon in defence of their rights and in justification of their transgressive behaviour. As I indicated before, spiritually silence at the time was not an empty, negative state but a positive, productive and fulfilling one. It allowed thought, reflection, contemplation and attention to what really mattered. It was associated with escape into the beauty and bounty of a divine Nature, with closeness to God and the eternal verities. In silence God and God's truth could be heard. This is why restraint in speech was the mark of the serious, *desengañado* man unconcerned by the vanities of life, why it was an intellectual and moral marker as well as a spiritual aid. In the case of women, however, silence was a ghetto, a place to which they were permanently relegated because they were second-class citizens incapable and unworthy of the life of the mind and the exercise of public responsibility that defined men. They had no need to think and speak because they had men to think and speak for them. Depriving them of speech, however, deprived them of witness, and depriving them of witness meant that their point of view was not heard. The *comedia* took them out of their ghetto, put them on a public stage, gave them stories to tell and allowed them to speak, not merely from within the constraints of patriarchy but often against them. It was a profoundly radical initiative.

WORKS CITED

Bourdieu, Pierre. *Language and Symbolic Power.* Ed. John B. Thompson. Trans. Gino Raymond and Matthew Adamson. Cambridge: Polity, 1991.

Butler, Judith. *Gender Trouble. Feminism and the Subversion of Identity.* New York: Routledge, 1999.

Díez Borque, José María. *Sociedad y teatro en la España de Lope de Vega.* Madrid: Antoni Bosch, 1978.

Howard, Jean H. *The Stage and Social Struggle in Early Modern England.* London: Routledge, 1994.

Jauss, Hans Robert. "Theses on the Transition from the Aesthetics of Literary Works to a Theory of Aesthetic Experience." *Interpretation of Narrative.* Ed. Mario J. Valdés and Owen J. Miller. Toronto: U of Toronto P, 1979. 137–47.

Kermode, Frank. *Shakespeare's Language.* London: Allen Lane, 2000.

Mill, John Stuart. *The Subjection of Women,* Ed. Susan M. Okin. Indianapolis: Hackett, 1988.

Rabil Jr., Albert. Introduction. *Declamation on the Nobility and Preeminence of the Female Sex.* By Henricus Cornelius Agrippa. Chicago: U of Chicago P, 1996, ix–xxvii.

Shergold, N. D. *A History of the Spanish Stage from Medieval Times Until the End of the Seventeenth Century.* Oxford: Oxford UP, 1967.

Zabaleta, Juan de. *El día de fiesta por la mañana y por la tarde.* Ed. Cristóbal Cuevas García. Madrid: Castalia, 1983.

Zayas y Sotomayor, María de. *Novelas ejemplares y amorosas.* Ed. Agustín Amezúa y Mayo. Madrid: Aldus, 1948.

URSULA K. HEISE

Transvestism and the Stage Controversy in Spain and England, 1580–1680[†]

* * *

Since actresses were officially allowed to appear on the Spanish stage from the late 1580s on, the issue of transvestism seems at first to have been successfully evaded. But from the time of Lope de Vega on until the late seventeenth century of Calderón de la Barca, plays whose plots require women to dress in men's clothing become so overwhelmingly popular that antitheatrical writers and state legislation see themselves forced again and again to address the question of the legitimacy of female cross-dressing before a public audience. In its arguments for and against women in male attire, this debate offers astonishing parallels with the English controversy over boys in female disguise, and thus allows us to evaluate comparatively some of the historical factors that affect the debate in each country and lead to the exclusion of women from the stage in one case, their admission in the other.

Let me begin by surveying briefly those dates from the beginnings of the Spanish public stage that are relevant to the question at hand.[1] The earliest piece of legislation concerning the Spanish theatre known today is a law decreed in 1534 by Charles V, which specifies that all the content of the *pragmática*,[2] which deals with the prohibition of excessive luxury in clothing, "applies in the same manner to *actors*, men and women, musicians and other persons who take part in the plays singing and playing instruments."[3] Significantly enough, this first law is already concerned with actors' clothing, but beyond that it reveals that at the time it was promulgated, women must have been performing on stage. One of the most well-informed historians of the Spanish theatre, N. D. Shergold, lists a good deal of evidence that women also appear on stage between the 1530s and the 1580s. But sometime during this period, actresses must have been banned, for in 1587 we find the Italian company of the Confidenti applying to Philip II for permission to have their three actresses perform in Madrid, arguing that their representation is impossible to stage without them. Whatever may have been the legal regulation before this date, the permission is granted, and the same law that gives women access to the stage simultaneously forbids boy actors to play female roles. Not for long, however: in 1596 the Council of Castile prohibits women on

---

† From *Theatre Journal* 44.3 (1992): 358–72. © 1992 The Johns Hopkins University Press. Reprinted with permission of Johns Hopkins University Press.

1. The historical data are from N. D. Shergold, *A History of the Spanish Stage from Medieval Times until the End of the Seventeenth Century* (Oxford: Clarendon, 1967), 505–43, and Emilio Cotarelo y Mori, *Bibliografía de las controversias sobre la licitud del teatro en España* (Madrid: Revista de Archivos, Bibliotecas y Museos, 1904), 1–39 and passim. See also the short summary in M. Romera-Navarro, "Las disfrazadas de varón en la comedia," *Hispanic Review* 2 (1934): 269.
2. Law [editor's note].
3. "Item mandamos, que lo que cerca de los trages está prohibido y mandado por las leyes de este titulo, se entienda asimismo con los *comediantes*, hombres y mugeres, músicos y las demás personas que asisten en las comedias para cantar y tañer . . ." (Cotarelo, *Bibliografía*, 619). All translations in this paper are mine.

stage again because "many inconveniences result from it," as the text of the law states[4]—unspecifically but with all the connotations of impropriety that the word *inconveniente* carried at the time. The same formula is used again when Philip II decrees the closing of the theatres in May 1598. After Philip's death in September of the same year, the theatres remain closed for the usual period, and it is only with their re-opening in 1599 that actresses re-appear; their legitimacy is officially decreed again in 1600, once more in conjunction with a prohibition against transvestite boy actors.[5] There is thus considerable vacillation at the beginnings of Spanish public theatre as to whether institutionalized transvestism should be allowed or not—whether it is more unacceptable, that is, to permit boys publicly to take on female disguise, or to admit women to the stage. Strikingly, even during this initial period of indecision the issue of transvestism is a legal problem that occupies and is regulated by Spain's highest legislative authorities—as opposed to England, where the exclusion of women from the stage rests on pure social convention, not official decree.[6] But even these supreme legal instances obviously do not find it easy to lay down a rule in this case. The contradictory regulations within less than ten years from each other reveal that a great deal of unease accompanies either decision.

But the final resolution in 1600 to grant women the permission to act is only the starting point for another, much longer and much more heated controversy over gender and theatre. The Council of Castile's memorandum which contains the prohibition of transvestite boys is presented to the King after the Council has reviewed a report on the subject of the theatre from a committee of ten theologians under the direction of the King's confessor, Fray Gaspar de Córdoba. This report is not extant, but according to a contemporary record it proposed for the first time that actresses not be allowed to dress up as men on stage, but that they be forced to wear long skirts instead, that they should be married, and that they should not be allowed to wear any clothes counter to current sumptuary laws outside the theatre.[7] The Council of Castile retains some of these suggestions in its memorandum: actresses must not wear male attire, and they must be accompanied by their husbands or fathers.[8] From then on, these two preoccupations—with actresses' cross-dressing and their civil status—recur in the legislation of the entire seventeenth century. The interdiction of female transvestism is reiterated in ordinances, laws, and edicts of 1608, 1615, 1641, 1653, 1672, and 1675—a repetition which is in itself evidence enough that the authorities by no means succeed in enforcing its elimination. On the contrary, the pressure exerted by the growing number and popularity of plays which require it ultimately forces the legislation to make some concessions. After repeating the general prohibition, the ordinances of 1641, 1672 and 1675 propose the rather desperate solution that if cross-dressing is absolutely indispensable for the plot, actresses should adopt male attire only from the waist up, keeping their legs and feet decently covered by long skirts or

---

4. ". . . salen mujeres á representar, de que se siguen muchos inconvenietes" (Cotarelo, *Bibliografía*, 620).

5. See Romera-Navarro, "Las disfrazadas de varón," 269; Cotarelo, *Bibliografía*, 619–20.

6. Sue-Ellen Case, *Feminism and Theatre* (London: Macmillan, 1988), 20.

7. Shergold, *A History of the Spanish Stage*, 517.

8. Cotarelo, *Bibliografía*, 164.

a soutane.[9] In 1600, boy actors are forbidden to wear make-up, and in the ordinance of 1641 are again prohibited to play female roles. Similarly, the provision that actresses be married and accompanied by their husbands appears again in 1641 and 1644. The law of 1615 and the ordinance of 1641 decree in addition that if the male actors or *autores* (that is, directors of companies) happen to be married, they too must have their wives with them. In order to enforce these regulations, each *autor* has to send a list of the members of his company to the Protector every year at Easter, specifying which players are married and to whom.[1] These continued attempts at regulating and enforcing a norm in performances as well as in the everyday life of the troupes reveal an intense anxiety over the sexual dynamics of the public theatre and its possible impacts on social order. To theologians, moralists and legislators, theatre always threatens to become a place of legalized promiscuity where sexual norms are publicly flouted. But attempts at controlling this subversiveness by decree invariably fail. In particular, transvestism, the theatre's most most conspicuous disruption of sexual order, proves impossible to control by law: once abolished as an institution, it returns in its inverted form through the plots most favored by playwrights and audience.

Three areas of investigation emerge from this series of legal data. First of all, we must ask why the Spanish authorities show such surprising indecision in the late sixteenth century about whether boys or women should be allowed on stage. What makes this such a difficult legal issue? And how can we account for the fact that English society accepts boys in drag whereas Spanish society ultimately outlaws them? Secondly, we must investigate what preoccupations about gender are at stake in the attempted repression of female transvestism in the second stage of the controversy. And finally, we must take the audience, which consisted of both men and women in Spain as well as in England, into consideration: why is transvestism so popular with audiences in both countries? The following analysis is designed to propose some answers to these questions.

The first problem, why Spanish culture rejects transvestite boys— although after a good deal of hesitation—whereas English society prefers them over women, is not an easy one to solve. There are no specific laws or forms of social organization outside the theatre which would explain the convention in either case.[2] The reasons for this cultural difference must therefore be sought in more general attitudes toward issues

9. Shergold, *A History of the Spanish Stage*, 520.
1. Ibid., 516–21, 529.
2. Sumptuary laws are often assumed to have played a role in the regulation of cross-dressing; but neither English nor Spanish laws of the period even address the question of gender: in England they are concerned with impeding violations of specific dress codes indicating social class or with restricting the excessive display of wealth (Marjorie Garber, *Vested Interests: Cross-Dressing & Cultural Anxiety* [New York: Routledge, 1992], 26–28, 32, 37, where she also discusses the relation between the transgression of class dress codes and transvestism; Stephen Orgel, "Mankind Witches" [unpublished manuscript], 1), and in Spain they serve the same purpose of limiting excessive luxury (silk, gold or silver thread materials) in the attire of all but a few select social groups (for a detailed account see Carmen Bernís, *Indumentaria española en tiempos de Carlos V* [Madrid: Instituto Diego Velázquez del Consejo Superior de Investigaciones Científicas, 1962], passim, as well as Africa León Salmerón and J. Natividad de Diego, *Indumentaria española* [Madrid: San Francisco de Sales, 1915, 113–61]. Another historical factor that suggests itself is the modelling of theatre troupes after guilds, supposedly all-male associations, which would explain why in England, where actors who are members of a guild apprentice boy actors, women have no access to the stage. This assumption has been invalidated by recent historical research which shows that guilds in England were by no means exclusively male; there is evidence that women were practicing craftspeople and full guild members, and in

of gender and sexuality.[3] And it is indeed at this more general level that one finds the most marked differences between English and Spanish Renaissance culture. In England, where antitheatrical tracts express a violent homophobia and intense pre-occupation over the potentially homoerotic implications of male transvestite theatre, society at large seems to be much more concerned with controlling illegal heterosexual activity: although both heterosexual fornication and sodomy (which includes, among other things, intercourse between males) are considered crimes and denounced legally as well as theologically, heterosexual transgressions are in practice punished much more severely, since they can result in illegitimate births or, in the case of married women, endanger the legitimacy of the husbands' heirs. Hence, fornication and adultery are vigorously prosecuted, whereas cases of sodomy, which imply no danger of practical consequences, tend to be discharged with mere admonitions.[4] * * *

Certainly, however, the preoccupation over how to keep women's sexuality under control is not restricted to England, but also affects continental nations where women *are* admitted to the stage.[5] Spain, with its elaborate code of male honor, which depends among other things on the chastity of the women in one's family, and a law which in many cases allows the punishment of adultery with death,[6] seems even more obsessively concerned with such issues. But this tendency is outmatched by what is possibly the most violent history of persecution of homosexuals in Europe. A Castilian edict from the thirteenth century is the first in Europe to prescribe death for homosexual acts and to label sodomy a transgression "against nature";[7] this regulation is repeated and elaborated in *Las siete partidas*, the law code of Alfonso the Wise, drafted in the thirteenth and put into effect in the fourteenth century.[8] It is not easy to know how strictly such laws were enforced, but there is evidence that in the fifteenth century, the death penalty for sodomites is not mere legal theory. García Cárcel reports that during the increasing repression in Valencia during the fifteenth century, there are at least five "killings of sodomites": in 1446 (two deaths), 1447, 1452 (five deaths), 1463 and 1466.[9]

---

some locations constituted a significant percentage of the apprentices (Stephen Orgel, "Call Me Ganymede: Shakespeare's Apprentices and the Representation of Women" [unpublished manuscript], 12–13). In Spain women did not usually have the same membership rights in guilds as men, but the actor's guild, the Cofradía de la Novena, founded in 1631, admitted both men and women (for a discussion of their status, however, see Josef Oehrlein, *Der Schauspieler im spanischen Theater des Siglo de Oro (1600–1681)* [Frankfurt/M.: Vervuert, 1986], 190). Hence guild structure must be ruled out as a conditioning factor in either case.

3. Stephen Orgel, "Nobody's Perfect: Or Why Did the English Stage Take Boys for Women?," *South Atlantic Quarterly* 88 (1989): 18.
4. Orgel, "Nobody's Perfect," 19.
5. Orgel, "Call Me Ganymede," 2.
6. Mary Elizabeth Perry, *Gender and Disorder in Early Modern Seville* (Princeton: Princeton University Press, 1990), 73, 120 and 135.
7. John Boswell, *Christianity, Social Tolerance, and Homosexuality* (Chicago: University of Chicago Press, 1980), 288. The legal texts of the period and historical statistics do not always allow a clear distinction between sodomy understood as sexual acts and what French and Spanish historians generally refer to as "bestiality," intercourse with animals. In the facts and figures that follow, I will distinguish the two whenever the available information allows it. But for the analysis of Spanish attitudes toward homoerotic acts, it is of course also significant that the two types of transgression *do* form part of the same category.
8. Ibid., 289.
9. Ricardo García Cárcel, *Las germanías de Valencia*, 2nd rev. ed. (Barcelona: Península, 1981), 55–56; idem, *Orígenes de la Inquisición española: El tribunal de Valencia, 1478–1530* (Barcelona: Península, 1976), 211.

In 1519, a mob forces the authorities to kill six sodomites at the instigation of preachers.[1] * * *

In 1497, the decrees promulgated by the *Reyes Católicos*[2] state that any person proven to have committed sodomy is to be burned at the stake in the place where the crime has been committed and that his properties are to be confiscated. Burning, as opposed to hanging, was the punishment reserved for the most horrendous crimes, and the introduction of this penalty for sodomy proves in itself that this is considered one of the worst abominations. Philip II's *pragmáticas* of 1598 reinforce the severity of the law by reducing the number of witnesses necessary to "prove" an act of sodomy.[3] Throughout the sixteenth century, but particularly in the second half, there is abundant evidence of trials and sentences against sodomites. * * * Such figures and detailed records of proceedings against sodomites lead the legal historian Tomás y Valiente to claim that "without doubt, the sin-crime which . . . maybe in general caused the greatest horror and scandal in the sixteenth and seventeenth century was sodomy . . . It was commonly called "unspeakable sin" or simply "the sin," as if it were the sin by antonomasia."[4]

* * *

[The Jesuit Father Pedro de] León was chaplain of Seville's Royal Prison at the beginning of the seventeenth century and hence personally met and spiritually advised many of those sentenced by the courts. His account is interesting insofar as it establishes an explicit connection between the *pecado nefando*[5] and effeminate attire and make-up; he argues, for example, that

> not only do honest men have to flee from those beasts—for such I consider those who adorn themselves—but they must attempt with the utmost care not to resemble them in adornments and clothing, for there are some who not only resemble them but who walk around pointing out: Look, I am one of those involved in that vice; and if they are not, they seem to be; and we could tell them, if they are not selling wine why do they have the sign at the door[6] walking around so affectedly, not to mention made-up, that they look like women of bad repute. According to convention, the attire of young men should not give anything to look at or talk about except in the manner common to sons of honest men. For I do not know what there is about these ways of wearing clothes or shoes or curled hair, since in going beyond what is common, what is usual among honest people of good repute, the eyes and even thoughts and words go toward the worst . . . one could ask those who walked around with so much finery and so

1. William Monter, *Frontiers of Heresy: The Spanish Inquisition from the Basque Lands to Sicily* (Cambridge: Cambridge University Press, 1990), 280.
2. Catholic Monarchs; i.e., Ferdinand and Isabel [editor's note].
3. Bartolomé Bennassar, "Le modèle sexuel: L'Inquisition d'Aragon et la répression des péchés abominables,'" in *L'Inquisition Espagnole: XVe–XIXe siècle*, ed. Bartolomé Bennassar (Paris: Hachette, 1979), 342.
4. "Sin duda el pecado-delito que . . . quizá en general, más horrorizaba, y escandalizaba, sobre todo durante los siglos XVI y XVII, era el de sodomía . . . Se le llamaba comunmente el "pecado nefando" o simplemente "el pecado," como si se tratase del pecado por antonomasia"; quoted in Spanish in Monter, *Frontiers of Heresy*, 276.
5. Unspeakable sin (Latin) [editor's note].
6. Literally, "the bunch of flowers at the door." In Spanish, *ramera* (whore) comes from *ramo* (bunch of flowers) or *rama* (branch), since these were used to mark brothels [editor's note].

much fastidiousness, *tu quis es?* Are you by any chance one of those who fly like butterflies together to the light, which in the end get burned?[7]

Now, it is true that many other moralists in the seventeenth century denounce effeminate fashions in male clothing without relating this to the crime of sodomy; nevertheless it is unlikely that Father León's perception is a completely isolated one, especially among those priests and theologians, often Jesuits themselves, who help shape the laws about the public theatre. Obviously, there is an awareness that sodomy typically involves young boys, and that it is a vice linked to and possibly induced or helped by a particular kind of effeminate attire.

These data can of course give only a fragmentary picture; they cover neither the entire Spanish peninsula, nor can they give a comprehensive picture of the practice of secular courts, figures which are much harder to come by than statistics about the extremely well-documented processes of the Inquisition. But what emerges clearly is that homosexual acts in Spain—as opposed to England—are not a minor legal concern either in theory or in practice. Sodomy is not just one aspect of a general nonconformism or seditiousness, but one of the crimes most severely penalized by both inquisitorial and secular courts. The public execution of death and other sentences must have contributed significantly to the public's awareness of the severity of the "crime against nature":[8] it is a violation of social and moral order that justifies torture, is punished harshly and can even lead to execution. All this radically distinguishes the Spanish attitude toward sodomy, and more specifically toward homosexual acts, from the English one, and points to an anxiety over these "unnatural" sexual tendencies infinitely greater than is common in England at the time.

Historians have frequently pointed out that the number of inquisitorial processes, and specifically prosecution of crimes that did not originally fall under the category of "heresy," increase considerably in the second half of the sixteenth century.[9] Whereas the Inquisition had earlier focused its attention mainly on Protestants and converted Jews and Muslims, it puts itself at the service of the Church's massive "re-evangelization" of the Catholic population in the aftermath of the Council of Trent, with the declared aim of substituting strict Tridentine doctrine for the prevalent populist type of Catholicism without very precise moral precepts. In this, the Church finds no resistance from the secular government: Philip II, deeply devoted to the cause of Catholicism, turns the resolutions of the Council of Trent into law for the Spanish nation in the 1560s.[1] The ensuing tightening of moral rules, which, in matters of sexuality, brings

---

7. Pedro de León, *Grandeza y miseria en Andalucía: Testimonio de una encrucijada histórica* (1578–1616), ed. Pedro Herrera Puga [Granada: Facultad de Teología, 1981], 437.
8. For Aragon, however, the Supreme Council of the Inquisition ruled from 1579 on that sodomites were not to appear in public *autos de fe* any more unless they had been condemned to death (Monter, *Frontiers of Heresy*, 296). Apparently, it was felt that minor cases did not relate closely enough to the didactic aim of the *autos* to show victory over heresy and apostasy; see María Victoria González de Caldas, "Nuevas imágenes del Santo Oficio en Sevilla: el auto de fe," in *Inquisición española y mentalidad inquisitorial*, ed. Angel Alcalá (Barcelona: Ariel, 1984), 237–45.
9. Monter, *Frontiers of Heresy*, 287; Bannassar, "Le modèle sexuel," 344–48.
1. J. Contreras, "Contrarreformismo trentino y 'Frente Atlántico,'" in *El conocimiento científico y el proceso histórico de la Institución (1478–1834)*, Vol. I of *Historia de la Inquisición en España y América*, ed. Joaquín Pérez Villanueva and Bartolomé Escandell Bonet (Madrid: Biblioteca de Autores Cristianos/Centro de Estudios Inquisitoriales, 1984), 703–9.

about greater pressure against illicit homosexual acts as well as heterosexual acts, coincides temporally with the emergence of Spanish public
theatre in the 1570s. This theatre, moreover, has throughout its early
history much closer ties with the Church than its English counterpart:
the major theatrical events of the Spanish year are the Corpus Christi
festivities in late spring, processions and religious theatre representations which are performed by some of the public troupes. In addition,
public theatre in its beginnings and throughout the first half of the seventeenth century is often performed in the backyards [and for the bene-
fit] of hospitals run by religious fraternities, and a part of the profit from
these representations goes to the support of the hospitals and their charitable work.[2] Under these circumstances, no change in the policies of the
Church can remain indifferent for theatrical practice.

The heightened moral repressiveness of Spanish society in the second
half of the sixteenth century goes a long way toward explaining the curious legal vacillation in the 1580s and 90s as to whether women should be
allowed to appear on stage, or boys be permitted to wear female make-up
and clothing in public. In a historical context of intense sexual anxiety in
general, it is no wonder that either decision must have seemed baneful to
public morals. If transvestite boys are finally outlawed, this must in large
part be due to the long Spanish history of violent repression of homoerotic tendencies, intensified at precisely this historical juncture by
increased inquisitorial prosecution. The increase of legal procedures
against homosexual acts must have contributed to the cultural awareness of the crime—not least in the minds of those moralists and theologians who advised the king and the Council of Castile. Cultural
perceptions of this kind must have conditioned the final declaration of
the Council of Castile concerning transvestite boys in 1600 stating that
"it seems to the Council that it is of much less inconvenience that women
act, than boys in women's attire even if they do not wear make-up."[3]

But if this declaration closes the debate on boy transvestism, it also
makes possible the abundance of plays featuring women transvestites in
the seventeenth century. This brings us to our second question concerning the cultural preoccupations underlying the controversy over *female*
cross-dressing. These preoccupations by no means express themselves
only in the law texts quoted above; they also surface insistently in a great
number of moral and theological treatises against the theatre during the
period. If the extensive *legislative* concern with transvestism is unique to
Spanish culture, the anxiety of these *religious* stage opponents over the
issue, by contrast, formulates itself in startlingly similar terms in both
England and Spain. Antitheatrical writings in both countries show an
unmistakable family resemblance in their concerns and even in their very
wording. This is true in spite of the fact that they came from opposite
ends of the theological spectrum (from Puritans in England, and, in the
majority of cases, from Jesuits in Spain), from religious groups, that is,

---

2. For a detailed account see Shergold, *A History of the Spanish Stage*, Chs. 4, 7, and 15–17.
3. Cotarelo, *Bibliografía*, 164. One may wonder why women and transvestite boys are considered
   mutually exclusive, as is obvious from this formulation. But if both are deemed moral evils, it
   is no surprise that the authorities would allow at most one of them. The abundance of female
   transvestite roles that are created after boy transvestites are outlawed lends support to Garber's analysis of the close connection between theatre and transvestism (*Vested Interests*,
   48–49).

which might have been expected to take quite different attitudes toward the theatre (the Jesuits regularly used theatrical performances in their seminaries, a custom which would have been anathema to the Puritans), and were directed against exactly the opposite conventions (boys on the stage in England, women on the stage in Spain). Besides the usual general accusation that actors lead lives of sin and dissolution and invite the public by their example to do the same, detractors of the stage in both countries agree that the transvestite actor/actress is an object of irresistible erotic enticement that makes men in the audience burn with lust and detracts them from the duties of work and war, leaving the nation impoverished and helpless before enemies. The tiresome reiteration of this argument has been amply documented in work on antitheatrical currents in England,[4] but it may require some explanation in the Spanish case, since as a twentieth-century observer one might be inclined to think that male disguise would tend to neutralize rather than enhance femininity, and hence diminish the actress's distracting erotic influence on the male audience. Clerics and legislators, opponents and defenders of the *comedia*, however, unanimously assert the contrary throughout the sixteenth and seventeenth centuries: a woman in male attire appears even more attractive than in her usual clothing—so much so, in fact, that she comes to epitomize the dangers of theatre in general. "If a woman acting in her own attire is so dangerous for the chastity of those who watch her, what will occur if she acts in men's clothing, which is so lewd a habit, designed to inflame the hearts in mortal concupiscence?" exclaims Friar José de Jesús María in 1600.[5] Father Juan de Mariana confirms, "Women of excellent beauty, of outstanding grace, movements and postures appear in the theatre to play diverse characters in the shape, clothing and habits of women and even of men, which is something that greatly provokes wantonness and has great power to corrupt men."[6] As late as 1689, the Jesuit Father Ignacio de Camargo fulminates:

> What is there more lewd and enticing than to see such a woman, who was [just] now on stage as a beautiful, painted and affected lady, enter a moment later as a handsome gallant, offering to the eyes of so many men the whole body that nature itself wanted to be always almost entirely withheld from sight? And what if she danced in this outfit, as they often do? What will become of the hearts of the many unfortunates who watched them carefully before in their women's clothing? Truly, these vile and vulgar people, in dishonorable manner, pay no respect to grave and serious people, who buy their pleasure at the price of being scorned . . .

And even a defender of the theatre such as Francisco Ortiz admits in his *Apología de la defensa de las comedias* (1614) that "a man must be more than [just] of ice if he doesn't burn with lust watching a bold and forward woman—sometimes dressed up as a man to this effect—doing things

---

4. See Jonas Barish, *The Antitheatrical Prejudice* (Berkeley: University of California Press, 1981), and Laura Levine, "Men in Women's Clothing: Anti-theatricality and Effeminization from 1579 to 1642," *Criticism* 28 (1986): 121–43.
5. Cotarelo, *Bibliografía*, 381.
6. Cotarelo, *Bibliografía*, 431.

that move [even] a corpse."[7] The reason why male attire makes women so irresistibly attractive is most apparent in Camargo: trousers and breeches reveal female feet, legs, and bottoms which are usually hidden under long skirts; hence the Council of Castile's insistence on wide skirts and long, loose garments. If Ignacio de Camargo claims that "nature itself" wants the female body to be hidden from sight, the controversy over cross-dressing makes it clear that, on the contrary, it is precisely the *culture* of the period that requires female fashion to veil rather than reveal femininity. For such a culture, male attire paradoxically comes to "embody" femininity whereas female apparel is designed to "dis-embody" it.[8]

The paramount danger of a theatre which systematically fosters the representation of such heightened femininity in front of a public audience, detractors of the stage argue, is the *effeminization* of the male spectators—a term which, in the Renaissance, not only refers to excessive concern with sexual matters, but to the actual loss of masculinity.[9] Already in 1589 Rivadeneira complains that "not only are manners corrupted and republics ruined . . . by this kind of performance; but people become idle, luxurious, effeminate and womanish. . . . a recreation that harms good manners and destroys manly vigor and force is not a good one." The theologians' evaluation of public theatre from 1600 insists repeatedly that "the people of Spain become soft, effeminate and inept at work and warfare," so that the Turkish or English could easily attack Spain because the comedians "make the hearts of our Spaniards womanish and feeble so that they do not go to war, or are useless for labors and their execution."[1] The same formulas with almost identical wording are reiterated over and over again in antitheatrical writings. "Another damage [of the theatre] . . . is . . . that with idleness, pleasure, and entertainment the people become soft, effeminate, and inept for matters of work," Ferrer warns.[2]

> On the occasion of these performances, people give themselves over to idleness, pleasure, and entertainment, and distract themselves from the good discipline, and from work and warlike exercise; with the *zarabanda* and other immodest dances, with feasts, banquets, and plays, the men become soft, effeminate and useless for all arduous and difficult enterprises. . . . the Romans themselves lost a great part of their vigor and strength after they conquered Asia, weakened and effeminized with entertainments and intemperance.

José de Jesús María echoes and then adduces a whole list of conquering nations falling into degeneracy because of public entertainment; he does not hesitate even to ascribe the conquest of Spain by the Arabs to such effects.[3] This almost hysterical preoccupation with the effeminizing

---

7. Francisco Ortiz, *La apología en defensa de las comedias que se representan en España*, ed. Louis C. Pérez (Chapel Hill: Estudios de Hispanófila, 1977), 100.
8. Female clothing thus becomes another way of "enclosing" and containing the female body in terms of the analysis proposed by Peter Stallybrass; see his "Patriarchal Territories: The Body Enclosed," in *Rewriting the Renaissance: The Discourses of Sexual Difference in Early Modern Europe*, ed. Margaret W. Ferguson, Maureen Quilligan, and Nancy J. Vickers (Chicago: University of Chicago Press, 1986), 123–42.
9. Thomas Laqueur, *Making Sex: Body and Gender from the Greeks to Freud* (Cambridge, Mass.: Harvard University Press, 1990), 123–25, 128; Levine, "Men in Women's Clothing," passim; Orgel, "Call Me Ganymede," 1.
1. Ibid., 394–95.
2. Ibid., 254.
3. Ibid., 375; see also 376.

influence of the theatre reveals a deep apprehension that female sexuality, which finds a space of its own in the free social intercourse of the actors and actresses, the performance of love plays and the adoption of male disguise, might ultimately not only de-humanize the male spectators by turning them into beasts or dogs but also emasculate them. The assumption seems to be that when the male is confronted with unconcealed, un-covered femininity, he reacts not by asserting his difference but by imitating and adjusting to the female. There is, then, something fundamentally unstable about the male self, which can only keep itself from lapsing into the identity of its sexual other by depriving her of a full expression of what is specifically her own. Theatre, opening up at least temporarily a space for such expression, thus threatens the sexual differentiation on which the nation bases its own identification.

In her discussion of analogous concerns in English attacks on the stage, Levine shows how such arguments rely on the assumption that watching a play will induce the spectators to imitate what they see the actors do, and the almost magical belief that imitation will lead one to actually *being* what one sees.[4] Such a belief implicitly denies the possibility of a stable and well-differentiated identity and betrays cultural fears about the essential nature of selfhood. Two conflicting conceptions of identity, Levine argues, lie at the bottom of this anxiety: there seems to be a deep-seated apprehension that the self, by the very fact that it *can* be so easily altered, may have no inherent substance at all. But since identity is apparently never changed for the better, one can also suppose that the self is by nature monstrous or inferior—maybe even that it is essentially feminine.[5] "By projecting conflicts about monstrosity and indeterminacy onto the stage," Levine claims, "anti-theatrical pamphleteers made the contradictions in themselves more manageable, and in this way the fear of effeminization which came to dominate anti-theatrical tracts disguised a profound conflict about the nature of the self."[6]

＊　＊　＊

But the untiring insistence on the danger of effeminization in the anti-theatrical literature of Spain and England also reveals that in spite of their opposed decisions about acceptable gender constellations on the public stage, the resulting sexual dynamic of theatrical representation remains identical. Fundamentally, this dynamic casts the audience as the male who is attracted, seduced and overcome by the spectacle conceived in essentially female terms.[7] The "femininity" of the spectacle results from a threatening degradation of masculinity embodied by the boy transvestite in England, from the presence of women and specifically the heightened femininity of the transvestite actress in Spain. Strangely enough, then, transvestism in the theatre turns out to be a one-way street:

4. Levine, "Men in Women's Clothing," 124–25.
5. Ibid., 136.
6. Ibid.
7. Lisa Jardine, *Still Harping on Daughters: Women and Drama in the Age of Shakespeare*, 2nd ed. (New York: Columbia University Press, 1989), Ch. 1; Katharine Eisaman Maus, "Horns of Dilemma: Jealousy, Gender and Spectatorship in English Renaissance Drama," *ELH* 54 (1987): 561–83. Whereas Jardine analyzes the convention of male transvestism on the English stage as such, Maus reaches similar conclusions through the consideration of recurring scenes in the plays themselves.

it always leads to greater femininity, never away from it—a femininity, moreover, which always threatens to take over and subdue "the virility of the nation."[8] Thus, while we can agree with analyses which postulate that the gender dynamics of the English Renaissance stage play out profound cultural anxieties about the nature of male identity, it is doubtful whether this is due to the convention of *male* cross-dressing in particular; given the Spanish evidence, one must take into account the real possibility that the same dynamic would have asserted itself had women been admitted to the stage. Since transvestism, male or female, always ultimately feminizes the theatre, it overcodes actual gender constellations on the stage so as to create an erotic interplay between an essentially male audience and a spectacle envisioned as fundamentally female.

This analysis leaves us with the nagging question of how are we to understand this interplay in view of the composition of the *real* audience, in which, in England as well as in Spain, women play a prominent part. What is their place in the dynamics of performance and spectatorship? If transvestism, male or female, is an act conceived for the eyes of men, what pleasure do women find in it? The answer to this question may not be too difficult to find if we just take the logic of the argument one step further. Spanish and English antitheatrical literature by and large ignores the possible influence of the theatre on a specifically female audience. Fantasies analogous to the one of male effeminization occur only rarely; Father Juan Ferrer, who claims that as a consequence of theatrical cross-dressing women actually began to wear masculine clothing in the streets at the beginning of the seventeenth century, remains an exception:[9] most stage detractors waste little time considering how women might be affected by theatre, beyond noting its generally nefarious influence. And yet it is clear that if transvestism sets free powerful erotic energies with the potential to attract and subdue men, this must be a spectacle of the highest interest and pleasure to women who are otherwise locked into social structures which give men power over women. This, according to Stephen Orgel, is precisely what underlies the popularity of the convention in England, where the boy dressed up as a woman can be understood to represent a more manageable, more empowering version of patriarchal structure in the eyes of the female audience.[1]

A similar dynamic is even more obviously at work in the Spanish case. The woman in male attire, escaping from convents, fighting wars, robbing travelers, seducing other women, even attending university lectures (in Lope de Vega's *Escolástica celosa*) or holding public office (in *El Alcalde Mayor*)[2] may, by her physical appearance, appeal to the desires of the male audience, but she also embodies a powerful fantasy of all the social possibilities generally foreclosed to the female spectators in Spanish Renaissance society. Certainly twentieth-century observers might see *both* aspects as falling squarely into the category of patriarchal domination

---

8. J. C. J. Metford, "The Enemies of the Theatre in the Golden Age," *Bulletin of Hispanic Studies* 28 (1951): 87.
9. Cotarelo, *Bibliografía*, 253.
1. Orgel, "Call Me Ganymede," 15.
2. Carmen Bravo-Villasante, *La mujer vestida de hombre en el teatro español (Siglos XVI–XVII)*, 3rd ed. (Madrid: Mayo de Oro, 1988), 46. Bravo-Villasante gives a detailed survey and discussion of the different types of cross-dressing (ibid., 15–69), as does Homero Arjona in "El disfraz varonil en Lope de Vega," *Bulletin Hispanique* 39 (1937): 120–45.

strategies—the actress falls victim to the male gaze at the same time that the female audience is fed a temporary illusion of power—but the fact remains that Spanish authorities of the time attribute to the female transvestite a genuinely disruptive power, as their continued attempts at repressing this particular convention demonstrate.[3] Transvestism in English as well as Spanish theatre thus can be understood to owe its continued existence and popularity to its curious social ambivalence: whereas it enhances on one hand a basically patriarchal structuring of the relationship between audience and performance, it becomes on the other hand precisely the moment which projects an alternative structure as a viable possibility. Hence, the question of whether transvestism on the Renaissance stage is fundamentally "conformist" or "subversive," "patriarchal" or "feminist," and whether it addresses primarily the male or the female audience cannot be given a simple answer. Its power resides precisely in its ability to call up and respond to the desires of both groups.

*   *   *

---

3. Cf. for the English case Katherine E. Kelly, "The Queen's Two Bodies: Shakespeare's Boy Actress in Breeches," *Theatre Journal* 42 (1990): 82, 92–93.

The Plays

WILLIAM R. BLUE

The Politics of Lope's *Fuenteovejuna*†

In a Spanish village in 1476, the people rose up against their overlord and killed him, but exactly why they did it is still undecided. The various versions of the event, the chronicles, the reports, the popular stories that arose, the histories, differ in their explanations, depending on who is telling the story, for what purpose, and from what point of view. The actual event, though perhaps motivated by economic interests, personal grudges, or royal influence, had definite political overtones especially coming as it did in the midst of a long and bitter civil war, a war that determined the future directions not only of the Kingdom of Castile, but, as it turned out, of Spain as well. About one hundred and fifty years later, one of Spain's greatest dramatists took up the story of that small town and wrote what has become his best-known play, *Fuente Ovejuna*. Most of the interpretations of Lope de Vega's drama, in one way or another, speak to its politics.

Overtly political readings of *Fuente Ovejuna* have ranged across the spectrum. The play has been seen as a fervent cry for monarchy, for democracy, for socialism, even for communism. It is a paean to the people, to altruistic love, to harmony, as well as a call to the oppressed to throw off the social, economic, and political chains that bind them to servitude.

*   *   *

The "natural" or "normative" structures in Spain during Lope's life include Catholicism, monarchy, imperialism, and hierarchical class structures. Monarchy seemed as natural to Lope as the Spanish he spoke and wrote. Critics who claim that Lope was a "propagandist" for the monarchy and for the nobility have twisted the point. Against what "organized" opposition was Lope supposedly propagandizing? For Lope and his contemporaries, there was monarchy or there was anarchy. Likewise, those who have seen Lope as a champion of democratic, socialist or communist values and ideologies * * * have made anachronistic, romanticized assertions. Like those who see Lope as a rabid, right-wing monarchist, they tell us more about how they read than about how he wrote.

Monarchy was "natural" for Lope but that does not mean that he could not or would not criticize acts or policies or individuals who occupied important positions and who projected certain styles of governance.

† From *Hispanic Review* 59.3 (Summer 1991): 295–96, 298–315. Reprinted by permission of the University of Pennsylvania Press. Quotations in Spanish have been translated by G. J. Racz.

While avoiding a frontal attack, for he was neither a fool nor a writer of political tracts, Lope could incorporate current critiques into some plays just as he could incorporate praise or joy of a particularly glorious moment into other plays. Lope's *obra* is not of a single piece, artistically or ideologically; it absorbs the trends, thoughts, and feelings of the day and in so doing becomes current for his audience. To examine the relationships between the play and its context as well as to emphasize the questions that the play raises, I present some background material about the play's contemporary context.[1]

During the last years of Philip II's life, a sly pun circulated widely at court: "Si el Rey no acaba, el reino acaba"[2] (Seco Serrano XI). When the infirm old king did pass away (1598), immediately attitudes changed from despondency to excited expectation, confidence, and enthusiastic activity that greeted Philip III. Within a few months, however, many of Philip II's most experienced advisors and administrators had been removed from office. * * *

In place of Philip II's admittedly slow but always careful personal control over the governing process, a process underwritten by studious reports from his councils of qualified advisors, was a government by a bland, indolent king dependent upon and accompanied by his "favorite," the Marquis of Denia, later named Duke of Lerma. In some quarters people sensed that history was repeating itself. Instead of a strong, involved participation by the king, as in the periods of Ferdinand and Isabel, Charles I, and Philip II, Spain had returned to the pre-Catholic Monarch condition of decadence, of government by favorites, reminiscent of John II of Castile's pathetic dependence on Don Álvaro de Luna.[3]

In the previous administration, university-trained bureaucrats and administrators from the lower nobility, who thus owed their post and responsibilities to the king, often held positions of power. Lerma replaced many of these men, especially in the powerful Council of State, with his own men, many of whom were from the higher nobility. Lerma's taking or being given power can thus be seen as an aristocratic, social revolution, and an institutional revolution as well. By 1612, Lerma's own signature had been officially recognized as equal to the king's. The royal bureaucracy, instead of following a merit system, had become an aristocratic client system dominated by Lerma and his subalterns.

Lerma and Philip, not limiting themselves to political appointments, tinkered with all parts of the system, including Spain's legal system.

* * *

As a result, J. H. Elliott notes: "there were endless conflicts between civil and military jurisdiction, in which the municipal authorities were generally worsted, since military tribunals winked at the offences of their men, and the highest tribunal of all, the Council of War, could be relied upon to take the part of its captains and maestres de campo" (*Imperial Spain* 290).

1. I want to acknowledge my debt for the following historical information to Seco Serrano, Pérez Bustamante, Elliott, and Kagan, whose works appear in the bibliography.
2. If there's no end to the king, there will be an end to the kingdom [editor's note].
3. There would be, of course, a tremendous difference between the two in that Álvaro de Luna fought unsuccessfully against powerful nobles who sought to diminish Juan II's power whereas Lerma supports a sycophantic nobility, provided, clearly, that those nobles support him.

All these ills did not pass unnoticed. Within Spain's borders, a number of honorable men, the *arbitristas*[4] tried to analyze their nation's problems. As Elliott states: "it was under the influence of the *arbitristas* that early seventeenth-century Castile surrendered itself to an orgy of national introspection, desperately attempting to discover at what point reality had been exchanged for illusion" (*Imperial Spain* 295). Effectively during the reign of Philip III, public opinion divided into two camps: one that favored the Duke of Lerma and his clients, and another that looked longingly toward powerful, traditional nobles who occupied posts abroad as ambassadors or viceroys. Some of these men, while still respecting the office, saw Philip III more as a symbol, a "rey pintado,"[5] as a satirical poem written after his death called him. For many, Spain had reached the highpoint of its supremacy in 1492 (Elliott, *Imperial Spain* 304–05). The Catholic Monarchs[6] became the mythic symbol of all that had been right with Spain.

One of the principal historical characters in this play set in the time of the Catholic Monarchs is the Maestre de Calatrava, Rodrigo Téllez Girón. Many critics, chief among them C. Anibal, see his presence as one of the keys to understanding what Lope was doing with at least part of the play: writing an oblique homage to one of his patrons. Among those nobles living outside Spain's borders was this patron, Pedro Téllez Girón, the third Duke of Osuna, called *el Gran Duque de Osuna* by his contemporaries. In men like the Gran Duque, some saw a glimmer of what Spain could and should be. * * *

After an infamously wild youth, Osuna went to Flanders, enlisted as a common soldier, rose in rank, and distinguished himself on the field. In 1610 he was named Viceroy of Sicily. There he completely renovated the moth-eaten fleet, attacked pirates, routed the Turks, brought the infantry up to muster, cleaned out nests of bandits, rid the area of counterfeiters and brigands, restored peace, and revived travel and commerce throughout his vicegerency. The Sicilians loved him, his subordinates respected him, and his enemies feared him. Inevitably, opinions in Spain divided between those who saw Osuna as the kind of leader Spain should support, and those who feared or envied his accomplishments and thus saw him as a threat (Rodríguez Marín 1–27). Eventually, and no doubt inevitably, forces in Madrid—principally those centered around Lerma, and later, Olivares—brought Osuna down. Throughout his fall from grace, however, one literary figure stood steadfastly by him, Lope, who even in the darkest moments of Osuna's crisis wrote sincere poems of praise to him.

The picture that Lope paints of the Gran Duque's distant relative, the Maestre, remains nonetheless ambiguous because he and his Order stand in direct opposition to the Catholic Monarchs. Familial, traditional, and personal reasons account for the Maestre's and thus the Order's opposition:

> Upholding past allegiances
> Is vital in the present case
> To honor these progenitors,

4. Advisers or experts [editor's note].
5. Painted king [editor's note].
6. Reyes Católicos; i.e., Ferdinand and Isabel [editor's note].

> So know your kin, since Henry's death,
> Support Alfonso, Portugal's
> Good king, who has inherited
> Castile, your blood contend, because
> His queen, they vow, was Henry's child.
> Prince Ferdinand of Aragon
> Disputes this claim, and through his wife
> And Henry's sister, Isabel,
> Asserts his title to the throne
> Against your family's cause.
>
> (87–99)

[Fernán Gómez] advises the Maestre to take Ciudad Real because of its strategic location and because it will be an easy victory: "You'd hardly need a host of men / To have it fall to your control; / Their only soldiers left there are / Its landowners and citizens / Who still defend Queen Isabel / And follow Ferdinand as king" (111–16) (Kirschner 93).

Lope emphasizes the Maestre's youth throughout, while showing Fernán Gómez [as] a master manipulator of this young and as yet untested leader. The Maestre first wins and later, after the Reyes Católicos counterattack, loses the city; he then retires to Calatrava to rethink his position. He seems already to have assigned blame for his errors when he exclaims, "Ah, youth! / May your deceptions keep me not from Truth!" (1470–71). The Maestre submits to the Catholic Monarchs, once more repenting of his youthful errors: "My tender age may well be one / Defense this loyal heart can use" (2155–56). The Maestre, a valiant though misguided youth, is led astray, makes errors, repents, submits to the King's new order, and finally gains a position of power in the future state.

The Gran Duque was a man who also misspent his youth, made errors, eventually proved himself a great soldier, asked pardon from his king, and was rewarded with a powerful position. A certain parallelism exists between the Gran Duque and his ancestor. * * * [T]he presence of a Téllez Girón in Lope's *Fuente Ovejuna* would doubtless have brought the Gran Duque to the minds of a Madrid audience. * * *

Some of the play's messages, in fact, are less than complimentary. For example, nobles, if led astray by egotism or by self-seeking advisors, might represent a great challenge to the king or might foment dissension, or waste valuable talents if not properly guided by an enlightened monarch. On a more positive note, the play might be affirming that valiant, worthy nobles, with proper guidance from an aware and involved king who understands desire and politics and who can choose and use good men to further the goals of the nation, must be sought out and nurtured. More broadly, the play might be suggesting that the Military Orders,[7] while still of some use to the Monarch, have been left too much to their own devices, have been granted too much independence and privilege, have become a state within the state and thus, as Juan Chamucero y Carrillo noted, may threaten the peace of the republic.

---

7. Powerful military and religious confraternities of Christian knights, originally established to fight against Muslims in Iberia [editor's note].

Fernán Gómez, as many excellent articles have shown, foments disorder on the national, local, and personal levels. I will review briefly Fernán Gómez's role as the manipulator and controller of the young Maestre. Even though the Comendador is below the Maestre in the official hierarchy of the Order of Calatrava, he dominates the young man (D. Larson 91). In the first lines of the play, Fernán Gómez' arrogance flashes through his bitter disappointment that the Maestre did not rush out to tender him an official greeting: "discourtesy between / Two equals is a foolish game," to which he ironically adds, "When men aren't peers, it's . . . / . . . vile, tyrannical and mean" (25–28). In his speech to Rodrigo Téllez Girón, he, the Comendador, takes full credit for the young man being Maestre: "You honor well our bond / As I've done all that's in my power— / Nay, risked my life—to ease affairs / For you, petitioning the pope / To disregard your youth" (55–59). He advises the Maestre to put personal and familial gain above all else in his political considerations of Juana's over Isabel's cause. Should Juana win out, the Maestre will be in a position of power and, of course, the Comendador will further strengthen his position because he is "responsible" for the Maestre's decision to support the Portuguese cause.

Throughout the play, the Comendador cannot see a difference between his role as a man and his role as an official. His title gives him power, entry, and, apparently, the opportunity to manipulate others for his own gain. Rodrigo may be too young and inexperienced to appreciate a gap between man and title, but the villagers are not so naive. After having violated the villagers' rights any number of times, Fernán Gómez cannot understand why the villagers do not accept his offer to redress their grievances, "as a knight." The villagers, in their distrust of his offer as well as in their ironic greeting when he enters the town, mark the difference between signifier and signified, between the man and the title. In the end, they declare him not a true noble despite his birthright and position, but rather a traitor to the proper order both social and political.

The Comendador manipulates the Maestre for personal gain in the same way that he perpetrates violence on the villagers for personal pleasure (Wardropper 170–71). His violence against the villagers derives from, in part, a classist interpretation of a cultural value. He believes that honor belongs only to the high-born, and that since the low-born have no honor he may treat them as the lesser creatures they are, as so many animals.[8] If he wishes to beat one or kill one because he or she frustrated him, so what? If he wishes to share his bed with one, so much the better for her since, for the moment at least, he shares with her his glory, his social rank, and thus his honor.

The people of Fuente Ovejuna see things quite differently. For example, after hearing of the Comendador's adventures and successes on the battlefield, they adopt an ironic attitude * * * They already hate the man, though they still respect the position he holds. They express their disgust in subtle but telling ways. In their song of greeting, they congratulate him for defeating the "Moors" of Ciudad Real, where no Moors live. * * *

---

8. The Comendador constantly dehumanizes his subjects casting them as animals, as hares or does, or worse, as in the words of his servant, Ortuño, who refers to the townswomen as "flesh." In parallel fashion, after seeing the Comendador commit so many violent acts against them, they call him "tiger." There is a mutual descent into animal viciousness. See Wardropper, "*Fuenteovejuna*: 'El gusto' and 'Lo justo'" (*Studies in Philology*, 2, 1956) 159–71, especially 170–71.

Yet even as they take their jabs at the man, they recognize and support class distinction, privileges, rights, and duties (see Frondoso's refusal to kill the Comendador, for example).[9] They believe that honor on its most basic level belongs to everyone because all belong to the same society and all are children of God. People can, of course, lose or squander their honor—such as the women who willingly sleep with the Comendador and the husbands who allow and even encourage such activity—or people can have their honor violently taken from them—as in the cases of Jacinta or Esteban. Those who violate another's honor merit retribution. They have seen the Comendador, over and over, act violently against them; and as his violence grows, the people finally turn against him. "Violence," Lentricchia says, "is a dormant but inherent human disposition" (*Ariel and The Police* 35) that can be awakened by repeated example. Like honor, violence, too, belongs to all; and in this case, the hares or the sheep turn on the tiger and rip him to shreds.

After murdering the Comendador, the villagers know full well that the Reyes Católicos have the right and the duty to employ nonlethal violence against them in order to discover the identity of Fernán Gómez' killers. Their reaction to royal, legitimate violence will not be violence in return, but rather unified passive resistance. Their passivity becomes the other side of the coin whose terrible face Fernán Gómez saw: in his case, they believed that theirs was a just act performed against an untrustworthy tyrant; in the present case, they can, with equal justice, submit passively to the trustworthy Monarchs. The villagers also know that their agreed upon, unifying statement with which they will answer all charges * * * is simultaneously a lie. Not everyone could have killed Fernán Gómez if only because that would have been a physical impossibility. The declaration "Fuenteovejuna did it," for all of its egalitarian strength, functions as an eminently practical decision, based on the trust that even if the Reyes Católicos have the right to kill all of the villagers, they will not do it.

In the Monarchs' decision to send the *pesquisidor*[1] to Fuente Ovejuna, their objective is both to fix blame by discovering the true identity of the person who struck the fatal blow, and to answer the challenge that the villagers' action has posed to royal authority (Carter 329–31). The presumed punishment would be the public, brutal execution of the guilty party or parties whose death would stand as a visible, awful symbol of the Monarchs' justice. Torture was the legal means employed to extract the necessary confession. But the villagers know what is coming: a physical confrontation with their newly proclaimed sovereigns, and they make the necessary preparations.

Lope gives almost equal time to the preparations for and the consummation of the torture as he does to the deliberations about and the commission of the Comendador's murder. The torture episode was perhaps as impressive and certainly more ambiguous for Lope's audience than the murder scene. Two parts constitute the torture scenes: the "play" mounted in Fuente Ovejuna and the actual torture itself. It is altogether appropriate that the villagers "practice" or "dramatize" their torture.

9. Bruce Wardropper makes the point clearly: "The people of Fuenteovejuna do not revolt to change the social organization, but merely to remove an unjust office-holder within the existing social structure. They rise against Fernán Gómez, the man; not against the system of *encomienda* under which they live" (168–69).
1. Investigating judge [editor's note].

*   *   *

Lope creates here a double or triple theatrical effect: the real audience watches the actors in their role as villagers do a tryout and dress rehearsal with the villagers as dramatists, actors, and audience; then later the same villagers surrender control to the *pesquisidor*, a visiting dramatist and director, for the "real" performance.

*   *   *

The villagers' responses as both victims and audience vary. Some feel fear, a fear that someone will tell the truth and thus rend their solidarity. They feel anxiety, love for each other, confidence, and finally joy. In Mengo's response to his pain on the rack and to the investigator's demand for the delinquent's name, the theater of terror becomes first a joke and then a cause for a party: "Here, friend, have a bit to eat / And drink" (2260–2261), "Move food here while he's drinking up" (2265). Even Frondoso and Laurencia join in the black-humored mood with a loving jest:

> FRONDOSO   Who took the town Commander's life?
> LAURENCIA   Who? Fuenteovejuna, dove.
> FRONDOSO   Who killed him?
> LAURENCIA   Stop, you're scaring me!
>   Sure, Fuenteovejuna, churl!
> FRONDOSO   And how did I slay you, sweet girl?
> LAURENCIA   By loving me so tenderly.
>
> (2284–89)

If "normal" responses (how the sign is read) to torture and possible execution are potentially ambiguous, turning torture into a joke flies off the interpretive map. The villagers' joking might signify the recognition of the righteousness of their action, or perhaps their all-encompassing love and respect for each other, or their faith in the Catholic Monarchs. It might signify their belief that they will be exonerated, even though their act was illegal. It might be the laughter of relief or the knowledge of the power they exercise in their solidarity. In any case, Mengo's response offers the key. If the *gracioso*[2] (a role he occupies even though he has shown his bravery in attempting to defend Jacinta) can resist, who can fail?

The *pesquisidor* presents his sovereigns with mutually exclusive alternatives: kill them all or pardon them all * * *

Succinctly put, Ferdinand and Isabel are between a rock and a hard place. That they are at the end of a long and bitter civil war[3] heightens their uncomfortable position; thus they need friends, not more enemies. If they opt for pardon, the nobles of Calatrava will not sit still. Moreover, pardon legitimizes popular rebellion against tyrannical superiors, which, if pushed to its logical ends, might include the king. On the other hand, if they kill all the villagers, they potentially alienate the masses who already know of

---

2. Lower-class comic sidekick [editor's note].
3. According to the play, the events of Fuente Ovejuna and Ciudad Real are essentially contemporaneous with the battle of Toro, 1476. That is true enough, but Lope makes all three of these victories come together in and with the felicitous outcome of the play and with the end of the civil war. The fact is that the war continued until 1479 before the Catholic Monarchs were able once and for all to consolidate their control over rival Christian factions.

Fernán Gómez' terrible treatment of his subjects, and, after all, the villagers did remove a large thorn from the Monarchs' side. The Reyes Católicos must affirm their position as monarchs to preserve themselves from potential violence from the people on the one side and from the nobles and Military Orders on the other.

By sending the *pesquisidor* to Fuente Ovejuna, by attempting through torture to name a guilty party, they have nodded in the direction of the Maestre, the nobles, and the Military Order. They warn the masses that law exists, order exists, that they, the sovereigns, represent order, and that excesses, even if committed in their names, will not be tolerated. Yet after the failure of the mission to produce a punishable guilty party, they defer judgment, but in this case, judgment deferred is not justice lost. They declare the case undecidable and thereby dangle both the sword and the shield over the villagers and over the Maestre and the Order as well.

While the Monarchs tell the Maestre that this matter no longer concerns him, they still in all hold out to him the possible repossession of Fuente Ovejuna sometime in the future. By deferring, they get the Maestre's services because he hopes to reestablish himself in their eyes. In the meantime, they get Fuente Ovejuna and its agricultural wealth. They confirm the people's love and trust in them; they curtail the Order's power yet still draw the Maestre and his followers into their camp. They send messages to both: to the people, we can quickly return you to the not-so-tender mercies of the Maestre should you once more get out of line and we can reopen the case and kill you all if we so wish; to the Order, we can side with the masses against you should you get out of line or we can restore your wealth and fame if you serve us well. They base their Solomonic decision not so much on right or wrong since both parties were right and wrong, but on practical, political convenience (Carter 331).

Ferdinand and Isabel, like all absolute monarchs, stand at the juncture of word and action. Their words can literally kill or save. The king, as the impersonal symbol of social order, expresses its fixed rules and meanings (Eagleton 8–9). He seems able to stand free of that order and dominate it from without but in truth cannot. Barbara Johnson has noted that every act of judgment, like every act of language, manifests not so much the naked, impersonal, absolute truth nor the just value of the person, act, or object, but rather it shows the position of the judge within the system of exchange (107). The king may remake the rules, but the pressures of the situation in which he acts still influence him. He depends upon his subjects, noble and common alike, to support him politically, socially, economically. An understood contract binds the king and his vassals, thus leaving no place outside the lines of force of the particular situation or of the general system where the king can stand to make a "neutral" decision.

If Lope is not writing a historically faithful, archeological piece about events in the fifteenth century, he must be sending decipherable messages to his contemporary audience. The first message says what a good play should be: entertaining, well-constructed, captivating, serious and humorous. Lope writes about love and honor, about the court and the countryside, order and disorder, rights and responsibilities, and about literature, drama in particular. But the political statements are there as well, hidden, subtle, but there.

Order itself, for example, depends upon mutual respect and interdependence, not only among members of the same class but between classes too: thus, those who violate the system ought sooner or later to have to pay for their transgressions. Lope says something about class stereotypes. Not all peasants are ignorant, vulgar, greedy, and gluttonous. They are capable of learning, they value education; they value love, tradition, and respect. Some may be as noble and honorable as their social betters. Despite their peaceful and phlegmatic appearance, they can prove vicious if sufficiently provoked. As for the nobles, some are good, loyal, honest, and understanding men who faithfully serve their king and conscientiously fulfill their duties to their king and to their vassals. Contrarily, others, whose ego knows no bounds, use their position to manipulate, dominate, and abuse everyone from the king down; and they value individual power and personal gain above any virtue. Such men may be noble by birth, but under their finery, they are swine. Youth, inexperience, or overreliance on others easily dupe others. In sum, birth and social position are no guarantors.

Kings, Lope may be saying, should emulate Ferdinand and Isabel. They should be aware, involved, caring and merciful when cases so merit, rigorous and forceful when and where necessary. They should take personal charge. * * * Practicality and efficiency should matter more to kings than the fine print, just as taking care of business, doing their job, should be their first priority. Doing their job requires an even-handed attitude toward all sectors that constitute their kingdom. * * * Rebellious vassals, manipulative and violent nobles, power-grabbing Orders should all be put in their places. The justice system should not be slanted in favor of the wealthy or of the powerful. Monarchy is an ideal system provided that the king and everyone else know, understand, and live up to their rights and responsibilities.

On a wider scale, Lope may be implying the relative nature of secular truth and falsehood. We have, after all, in the villagers' version of events in Fuente Ovejuna and in Flores' version (as earlier in the recounting of events in Ciudad Real by Ortuño and the Regidor) contradictory statements by eye-witnesses. As Melveena McKendricks notes, often in Lope's plays, one man's lie may be another man's truth (94).

But the problem is bigger than that. Critics now believe that Lope was aware of more than one possible source for his play, and the sources do not agree. Thus, given the divergent, and frequently contradictory, "historical" versions of events—Rades, Palencia, Juan de Mariana, Covarrubias, Tunja, Juan de Luna,[4] among others—the "truth" of "history" more often than not depends upon point of view. History, to a very large degree, is a winner's discourse. We certainly can say that acts took place in a small town in Spain in 1476; history was there. But as Frederic Jameson says, history is "an absent cause, it is inaccessible to us except in textual form"; therefore our approach to it and to reality itself "passes through prior textualization, its narrativization in the political unconscious" (35). History, a horizon against which all should be measured, forever recedes. To what then do

4. Various historians and humanist writers of the period who addressed the events of Fuenteovejuna [editor's note].

we turn for the "truth" of Fuente Ovejuna: to history or to poetry? What are the boundaries that absolutely separate one from the other?

Lope was an artist, not a historian; he set out to write an interesting, commercially viable, entertaining play. But politics pervaded him and the language he spoke, shaping everything he wrote. As Jameson states:

> ideology is not something that informs or invests symbolic productions; rather the aesthetic or narrative form is itself ideological, and the production of aesthetic or narrative form is to be seen as an ideological act in its own right, with the function of inventing imaginary or formal "solutions" to unresolvable social contradictions. (79)

Lope, rather than accurately representing the weak, indolent king who ruled Spain, draws from nostalgic popular beliefs and invents strong, involved, practical monarchs who, without reliance on favorites, hold both the common folk and the nobility in check, attracting both into their service. It is the myth of the Reyes Católicos, the myth of the utopian state. In his play, these mythical monarchs unify their ravaged country through the practical politics of punishing wrongdoers, chastising the wayward, forgiving the errant, restoring tranquility, and holding the reins tight in their hands. The dominant political term in this play is monarchy, personal, powerful, active. Lope marginalizes and then eliminates individual, egocentric excess, antimonarchical disorder, and with those, infelicitous social, political, and personal stress: only in harmonic political order can peace exist among all the citizenry. The Monarchs have more concern with order and the power that brings it about than with ultimate truth. Finally, Lope's message to his own contemporaries may be: observe how power and politics worked "once upon a time," it can work thus even in our day. Lope turns "history" into myth, myth into political dream, a dream he may have hoped might be shared by some of his own contemporaries. Lope, neither blind propagandist for his own time and place nor liberal revolutionary, portrays in his best-known play the myth of the past against the background of his own historical moment, depicting things as they ought to be, against things as they are.

WORKS CITED

Anibal, Claude E. "The Historical Elements of Lope de Vega's 'Fuenteovejuna'." *PMLA* 49 (1934): 657–718.

———. "Lope de Vega and the Duke of Osuna." *Modern Language Notes* 49 (1934): 1–11.

Carter, Robin. "*Fuenteovejuna* and Tyranny: Some Problems of Linking Drama with Political Theory." *Forum for Modern Language Studies* 23 (1977): 313–35.

Eagleton, Terry. *William Shakespeare.* Oxford: Basil Blackwell, 1986.

Elliott, J. H. *The Count-Duke of Olivares.* New Haven: Yale UP, 1986.

———. *Imperial Spain, 1469–1716.* New York: St. Martin's, 1964.

Jameson, Frederic. *The Political Unconscious.* Ithaca: Cornell UP, 1981.

Johnson, Barbara. *The Critical Difference.* Baltimore: Johns Hopkins UP, 1980.

Kagan, Richard. *Lawsuits and Litigants in Castile, 1500–1700*. Chapel Hill: U of North Carolina P, 1981.

Kirschner, Teresa. *El protagonista colectivo en* Fuenteovejuna. Salamanca: Ediciones Universidad de Salamanca, 1979.

Larson, Donald. *The Honor Plays of Lope de Vega*. Cambridge, MA: Harvard UP, 1977.

Lentricchia, Frank. *Ariel and the Police*. Madison: U of Wisconsin P, 1988.

———. *After the New Criticism*. Chicago: U of Chicago P, 1980.

McKendrick, Melveena. "Language and Silence in *El castigo sin venganza*." *Bulletin of the Comediantes* 35 (1983): 79–95.

Pérez Bustamante, Ciriaco. *La España de Felipe III*. Vol. 24 of *Historia de España*. Madrid: Espasa-Calpe, 1983.

Rodríguez Marín, Francisco. "El Gran Duque de Osuna." Madrid: R. Velasco, 1920, 1–27.

Seco Serrano, Carlos. "Prólogo." In Ciríaco Pérez Bustamante. *La España de Felipe III*. Madrid: Espasa-Calpe, 1983, ix–lxxxvi.

Wardropper, Bruce. "*Fuenteovejuna:* 'El gusto' and 'Lo justo'." *Studies in Philology* 2 (1956): 159–71.

DUNCAN WHEELER

An (Early) Modern Classic: *Fuente Ovejuna* in Contemporary Spain[†]

In *The Genius of Shakespeare* (1997), Jonathan Bate considers whether it is a matter of chance or destiny that the Bard is considered the world genius of literature. He concludes that the truth lies somewhere in between:

> The apotheosis of Shakespeare was and was not a matter of historical contingency. It was a contingency insofar as it happened to be Shakespeare, not Lope. But it was a necessity because the chosen one had to be a particular kind of genius and could therefore only have been Lope or Shakespeare. (1997, p. 340)

This is the case, Bate argues, because the Spanish playwright is the only other dramatist to have the necessary prerequisites for genius: aspectuality and performativity. The former concept refers to the principle that there are qualities in these works that may ostensibly be mutually exclusive but can nevertheless both be identified, albeit not simultaneously; thus, an 'either/or' dichotomy is replaced by a 'both/and' binary (1997, pp. 314–15). It is not that there is a single truth inherent in the work that the critic can identify; the work is polyvalent to the extent that it can ground heterogeneous interpretations. In relation to Lope or Shakespeare, notions such as revolutionary or conservative are therefore better understood as adverbs, forms of processing information, than adjectives, consubstantial qualities that invariably attach themselves to a play. As an illustrative example, Bate observes: 'Both the Hal aspect (call it the rule of providence) and the

† From *Golden Age Drama in Contemporary Spain: The* Comedia *on Page, Stage and Screen* (Cardiff: University of Wales Press, 2012), pp. 75–104, 230–33. Reprinted by permission of the publisher.

Falstaff aspect (call it the rule of the body) are truths of the *Henry* plays, but you cannot see them both at one and the same time' (1997, p. 328). Performativity, meanwhile, refers to the principle that the truth of a play is to be found in the performance itself. Its genius is not to be found through reference to external determinants such as style, matter, or wisdom: 'It is the process of Shakespeare [or Lope], that which is performed by the performance. As with the later Wittgenstein, the working through does not *lead to a conclusion*, it *performs the point*' (1997, p. 336). Hence, on this reading, a successful staging of a politically contentious Lope play would, for example, not so much refer to revolutionary and/or conservative ideas as it would enact these ideologies on stage through performance.

It is no coincidence that Bate proceeds to single out *Fuente Ovejuna* as possessing both aspectuality and performativity (1997, p. 339).[1] The fact that it is one of the relatively few Golden Age plays to have been translated into readily available modern editions in English is symptomatic of the fact that, in the modern era, it is Lope's best known and most regularly performed play both in Spain and internationally.[2] Furthermore, this (in)famous *comedia*'s standing has largely been forged because it has been read and performed from radically divergent political standpoints. * * *

In this chapter, I will track how the play has been performed and received in modern-day Spain, paying particular attention to how specific interpretations and productions relate to Bate's concepts of aspectuality and performativity. In order to facilitate the comparison of often radically different stagings, I have decided to focus my attention on the performance (or absence) of three specific moments in the play: the central wedding scene, Laurencia's speech and the denouement.

*   *   *

The Rediscovery of Fuente Ovejuna

As Paul E. Larson has recently noted, '*Fuente Ovejuna* has not always been considered a great work, and the development of Lope's play as a masterpiece questions the very concept of how a "masterpiece" is produced, identified and invented' (2001, p. 282). * * *

The play, let us remind ourselves, is the fictional retelling of a real-life historical event where the inhabitants of the eponymous town rose up against, and murdered, their overlord. In Lope's work, the revolt is a consequence of the abuses they suffer at the hands of Comendador Fernán Gómez; among other offences, he interrupts a wedding to abduct the bride, Laurencia, and imprisons Frondoso, the groom. When the former returns, she propels the villagers into action by questioning their

---

1. It is accepted practice to write both *Fuente Ovejuna* and *Fuenteovejuna*. I have opted for the former but, when quoting, I respect the original author's choice.
2. For a general discussion of the play's national and international reception and performance, see Gagen, 1993; García Santo-Tomás, 2000a, pp. 331–72; Kirschner, 1977a and 1979, pp. 13–27; Monleón, 1987; and Pedraza Jiménez, 2002. For details of the play's performance in Russia, see Weiner, 1982; and for Germany, Banús and Barcenilla, 2005, p. 272; and Seliger, 1984. Interesting discussions of specific productions in the UK, the US and Chile are provided by Edwards, 2007; Farrán Gravés, 1989; Hodge, 1963; and Weimer, 2000a and 2000b respectively.

masculinity and accusing her father and local mayor, Esteban, of being unable to protect her. Alongside Jacinta, another victim of the lascivious overlord and his men, Laurencia also raises a female squadron. Following many years in the wilderness, the *comedia* was translated into French in 1822, then into German in 1845. Beyond this philological interest, the country where it first sparked the interest of practitioners was Russia. An 1876 performance was a resounding success and inspired calls for uprisings in the street; subsequently, in the early twentieth century, it became a symbol of the workers' struggle as the uprising was staged as an exemplary and inspirational model to follow (Kirschner, 1977a, pp. 257–9).

By the beginning of the twentieth century, Spanish intellectuals became interested in the classics in so far as they represented what the country had lost and the values that were conspicuously absent from their own period (Garcia Santo-Tomás. 2000a, p. 323). Considering how closely *Fuente Ovejuna* would later be identified with questions of Spanish national identity, it is ironic that its revival would take place far beyond the borders of the Iberian peninsula. Despite its presence on foreign stages, there is no record of the play being performed in Spain during the nineteenth century (Gagen, 1993, p. 5). Equally, as Donald McGrady has noted (1993, p. 23), any mention of Lope's play is conspicuously absent from the historian Rafael Ramírez de Arellano's detailed study of the historical uprising (1901).

This discrepancy prompted Marcelino Menéndez y Pelayo to comment that '[t]al popularidad no sorprende, porque se trata de una de las obras más admirables de Lope, por raro capricho de la suerte, no sea de las más conocidas en España [*sic*]' [popularity of this kind should not surprise us because we are dealing with one of Lope's admirable plays that, were it not for the whimsy of fortune, would be among the best known in Spain] (1925, pp. 194–5). The philologist attempts to reclaim the play and refute any revolutionary dimension: 'este drama, tan profundamente democrático, es también profundamente monárquico. Ambas ideas vivían juntas en el pueblo español; y en Lope, su poeta, su intérprete, tenían que ser inseparables' [this fundamentally democratic drama is also fundamentally monarchical. Both ideas coexisted among the Spanish people; and in Lope—their poet, their voice—they must be inseparable] (p. 201).

Menéndez y Pelayo provided the heuristic model for future interpretations of the play from both ends of the political spectrum. Firstly, he made Lope, *Fuente Ovejuna* and the essence of the Spanish national character virtually synonymous. Secondly, he equated the play's meaning with Lope's intention and assumed that this could be accessed in a direct and reliable manner. The effect of these presuppositions was that *Fuente Ovejuna* came to be equivalent to a positive abstract quality such as goodness, justice or Spanishness: everybody claimed it as their own albeit in radically different guises. This helps to explain why, as Teresa J. Kirschner notes, virtually all of the critical attention paid to the play both in Spain and abroad in the early decades of its rediscovery focussed on its ideological content (1977b, p. 452).

Given the precedent set in Russia where productions either eliminated the Catholic Monarchs or presented them in a negative light, thereby highlighting the righteousness and violence of popular rebellion, it is not surprising that the play was initially adopted by leftist elements. In a work completed in 1923, and first published in 1928, Juan Díaz del Moral notes how among 'el proletariado moderno ha logrado el drama de Lope de Vega singular fortuna' [Lope de Vega's drama has achieved an unprecedented popularity among the modern-day proletariat]. This largely self-taught historian with a strong Marxist bent praises the work because 'se propone en primer término constituir un capítulo de la historia del proletariado' [first and foremost, it constitutes a chapter in the proletariat's history] (1973, pp. 58–9), and cites it as evidence of an unchanging revolutionary spirit among the Cordovan peasantry.

On a wider scale, news of the Soviet performances became increasingly important in Spain following the proclamation of the Second Republic, as the left hoped that Golden Age drama could restore a lost sense of community (Holguín, 2002, p. 86). From 1936 to 1939, *Fuente Ovejuna* was the most frequently staged of all Lope's plays (García Santo-Tomás, 2000a, p. 345). The most important and emblematic production from this period was delivered by Federico García Lorca's theatrical troupe, La Barraca.[3] In a formulation that is equally applicable to Lope's play, Willhem Hortmann has argued:

> For the political potential of Shakespeare's plays to be realised, three things must come together: a political or social situation crying out for critical comment, a director and ensemble willing, able (and also ruthless enough) to use the plays for this purpose; and audiences alive to the sociopolitical climate and therefore primed to catch allusions. (2002, pp. 213–14)

These preconditions were ably satisfied through Lorca and Eduardo Ugarte's version of the play with La Barraca; it was a heavily politicized adaptation that, as in many Russian versions, removed the secondary action involving Ferdinand and Isabella, while offering a direct paean to the inhabitants of Fuente Ovejuna. The Comendador was dressed as a local cacique, while the townspeople wore modern-day peasant clothing.[4] * * * I would not go as far as Victor Dixon who claims that '[t]o adapt can only immeasurably impoverish the work Lope wrote' (1989, p. 7) but, as multiple studies have demonstrated,[5] it is evident that the play's two actions are carefully entwined both aesthetically and politically. The scenes with Ferdinand and Isabella simply cannot be excised without radically altering the play text. Although Lorca clearly had the right to adapt the work for his own purposes, his claims for authenticity and what Jonathan Miller has referred to as the phantom of 'some sort of quantum of intrinsic meaning' are hardly original or convincing (1986, p. 20). They can only

---

3. Jack Weiner has speculated that Lorca may well have heard about these adaptations from Rafael Alberti, who visited the Soviet Union in 1932 to study theatre and staging techniques (1982, p. 220).
4. This information comes from Sáenz de la Calzada, 1976, pp. 65–6, who played the Comendador in this production and whose book tells the story of La Barraca. This production has received more scholarly attention than any other *comedia* performance. For more details of Lorca's version and his work with the classics, see Byrd, 1984; Delgado, 2008, pp. 28–31; Edwards, 2007; Gagen, 1993; Holguín, 2002, pp. 105–67; Huerta, 1987; Oliva, 2008; Stainton, 1998, pp. 403–20; and Suelto de Sáenz, 1964.
5. See, for example, Armas, 2006; Darst, 1995; Fiore, 1966; Hall, 1974; Herrera Montero, 1989; Kirschener, 1979; McCrary 1961; Parker, 1953; Rozas, 1981; Ruiz Ramón, 1997, pp. 50–93; Spitzer, 1955; Varey, 1976; and Wardropper, 1956.

be defended by appealing, as Menéndez Pelayo had done for a different purpose, to a notion of national and individual spirit or soul that is sufficiently abstract and elastic to bypass historical investigation and raise itself into the realm of metaphysics.[6]

Despite these theoretical misgivings, it was undoubtedly a manifestation of political savvy and theatrical instinct to rework the play for a 1930s public who, by all accounts, seem to have been thrilled and energized by classical theatre in a way that few other twentieth-century audiences have been. According to Luis Sáenz de la Calzada, *Fuente Ovejuna* was, alongside Cervantes' *entremeses*, the most frequently performed and popular work in the company's repertoire (1976, p. 75).

The wedding scene was particularly popular and, on one occasion, the troupe even performed it independently from the rest of the play (1976, p. 71). Unlike in the majority of *comedias*, it occurs during rather than after the main action and is therefore afforded an unusual prominence (Strother, 1999, p. 32); Lorca exploited this characteristic to deliver a 'verdadera fiesta' [genuine party].

Another highlight was provided by Laurencia's harangue against the male villagers. The inclusion of the word 'maricones' [queers] (not used by respectable women at the time) invariably provoked a shocked response from audiences. Sáenz de la Calzada claims, however, that at the end of her speech, the actress Carmen Galán would invariably receive a round of applause and the actors would have to pause before recommencing the play (1976, p. 67).

In the struggle for Lope's spirit and legacy, the left may have taken their initial strategic positions with little resistance but, by the centenary of the playwright's death, a counter-attack was in preparation. Objections were raised about staging *Fuente Ovejuna* as it had been in Russia (Tamayo, 1935), and Margarita Xirgu and Enrique Borrás's production became the object of harsh criticism by the Nationalist press which claimed the production was informed by political rather than aesthetic considerations (Kirschner, 1977a, p. 261). * * *

Lope on the Battlefield

Given the prior contention over the performance and reception of *Fuente Ovejuna*, it is hardly surprising that it soon became an ideologically charged prize to be fought over. La Barraca continued to perform during the Civil War albeit without their founder. In 1937, the troupe had to pass by fresh corpses in order to stage *Fuente Ovejuna* alongside Cervantes' *El retablo de las maravillas* in Gajanejos. Sáenz de la Calzada recalls that they were treated well by Spanish soldiers fighting for the Republic due to their political message while members of the International Brigade were

6. This, for example, is the case with Suzanne W. Byrd, who claims, in the most detailed study of the production: 'De ningún modo la supresión del argumento secundario perturba el objetivo primordial de la pieza lopesca . . . En todos los sentidos, La Barraca hizo de *Fuente Ovejuna* una obra maestra del teatro, artística y conmovedora. Tanto que llegó a ser el drama de España en cualquier época, porque expresa verídicamente el brío español ante el vicio y la injusticia' [In no way does the excision of the secondary action distort the primary objective of Lope's piece . . . In every respect, La Barraca's production revealed *The Sheep Well* to be an artful and moving theatrical masterpiece. This is manifest in the fact that the play can embody the drama of Spain in any age; because it genuinely expresses Spanish brio in the face of vice and injustice] (1984, pp. 16–17).

excited to have the opportunity to see a production that had been staged by Lorca (1976, p. 161).[7]

Later, and in a more conventional setting, Manuel González directed a version of the play that was promoted in the news as 'antifascismo del siglo XVII' [anti-fascism from the seventeenth century]. This production was one of only ten plays to have more than a hundred performances in Madrid during 1938 (Collado, 1989, pp. 307–8). Beyond the stage, Republican teachers were also trained to teach the play to the next generation: 'Una obra "de masas", "típicamente antifascista", que los niños deben estudiar, representar y ver es *Fuente Ovejuna*, en la que se puede apreciar "una profunda repulsa a la opresión capitalista"' [A 'characteristically anti-fascist' play 'belonging to the masses' that the children should study, stage and see is *The Sheep Well*, in which they will be able to appreciate a 'profound aversion to capitalist oppression'] (Mayordomo, 1993, p. 79).

The Nationalist counter-attack continued on the page. Kessel Schwartz has examined how the writers of the breakaway Seville *ABC* talked incessantly about the grandeur of Lope and his desecration at the hands of Marxist provocateurs who, according to one editorial, were using the play to make villagers commit the worst kind of atrocities (1969, p. 185). In 1938, Calle Iturrino published a book dedicated exclusively to *Fuente Ovejuna* and its misappropriation. He comments on 'lo mucho que ha influido en la crisis político-social de España la crisis de nuestra poesía' [how the crisis in our poetry has impacted greatly on Spain's sociopolitical crisis] (1938, p. 117), and suggests how the phoenix[8] could help rectify this crisis: 'Su obra es la prueba inequívoca de la "unidad nacional", lograda ya en su tiempo, y no puesta en duda ni negada por ninguno de sus contemporáneos' [His play is the unequivocal proof of 'national unity', already attained at the time and not placed in doubt or refuted by any of his contemporaries] (p. 42).

This same drive for unification that sought to suture both geographical and temporal distances was also manifested on stage, albeit with modest means. Over Christmas 1938, some young men from the nascent SEU[9] performed the play in Cadiz. José María Pemán adopted a deliberately bellicose tone in his partisan review:

> Un *Fuenteovejuna* navideño donde el teatro nacional nacía entre pajas humildes. Pero todo él surcado por una enorme racha de decisión, de valor. Se ha representado *Fueuteovejuna* como se asalta una trinchera. Su 'provisionalidad' era hermana gemela de la de nuestros alféreces. (1939, p. 1)

> [A Christmas version of *The Sheep Well* where the national theatre was born amid humble hay. It was, nevertheless, ploughed with a great surge of determination and valor. *The Sheep Well* was staged as

---

7. Lorca and productions of this kind helped to secure the play's fame in the UK, where Joan Littlewood, for example, staged the play with her Theatre Workshop. Years later, Ruth Fainlight and Alan Sillitoe, who lived for an extended period in Mallorca, would also write a metatheatrical adaptation/translation of the play set in the Teatro Lara in Madrid, in which some Republican soldiers seek refuge to sleep but are recruited to help a depleted troupe of actors perform Lope's play, which tells the story of the people defying the forefathers of fascism who are 'not only the sworn enemies of the Spanish people, but of all the world' (1969, p. 4).
8. I.e., Lope de Vega [editor's note].
9. Sindicato Español Universitario, a Falangist (fascist) association of university students [editor's note].

if it were a trench attack. Its 'provisionality' was the twin brother of our lieutenants in battle.]

As he goes on to say, '[r]epresentar *Fuenteovejuna* es un poco como ganarle una posición al enemigo' [performing *The Sheep Well* is a bit like winning a position from the enemy] (p. 1). The Nationalist side proceeded to win many more positions and, ultimately, the Civil War; the question to which we must now turn is how effectively and decisively they won Lope and his play.

FUENTE OVEJUNA *in* ESPAÑA, UNA, GRANDE Y LIBRE

The 'rescue' of the besieged *Fuente Ovejuna* had been undertaken by the Falange, the military and parafascist wing of Franco's government. Although they were undoubtedly reacting to Republican and Soviet productions of Lope's play, its status also benefited from having been singled out for attention by Menéndez y Pelayo who was adopted by the Nationalist side and '[e]levado a la categoría de arquetipo intelectual del Nuevo Estado' [elevated to the category of the archetypal intellectual of the New State] (Santoveña Setién, 1994, p. 203). Furthermore, the play's narrative arc was particularly well suited to the Falange's political and aesthetic interests. In an attempt to outline the main tenets of fascist ideology, Roger Griffin notes how it:

> fuses the hierarchic elements of *ancien régime* absolutism with the democratic dynamic of revolutionary liberalism and socialism. It promotes the vision of a new state, a new leadership, a new political and economic order born of a revolutionary movement (and not a mere 'party') arising from within the people itself. (1996, p. 16)

The appropriateness of the form and content of *Fuente Ovejuna* to an aesthetic and political agenda of this kind is self-evident. Through a righteous popular uprising forged against a bogus and corrupt form of government, the Falangists aimed to cleanse the country of malevolent intermediaries such as Marxists or caciques, thereby reinvigorating and reuniting true Spaniards in a harmonious brotherhood homologous to a macro *Fuente Ovejuna*. This birth of the nation and national culture was seen to occur in Castile under the reign of Ferdinand and Isabella, which represented 'the Reconquest and myth of unification under Catholicism and the spiritual foundations of Spanish imperialism and conquest' (Herzberger, 1995, p. 24).

This conception can clearly be linked to Benedict Anderson's now ubiquitous formulation of the nation as 'an imagined political community' (1991, pp. 5–6). *Fuente Ovejuna* was unusual in being able to offer two highly valued national icons: Lope de Vega and the Catholic Monarchs. The latter's yoked arrows appeared on the insignia of the Falange, whose propaganda had, from an early stage, differed from most European fascist groups by virtue of its emphasis on religion (Payne, 1961, p. 127). Their presence also served to appeal to the Church, thereby ensuring Lope's work a prominent role in education and prolonging the play's canonical status beyond the wane of Falangist power and influence.[1]

---

1. From the outset of the Civil War, the Church had been awarded responsibility for education and teaching while the Falange largely secured its influence through its appropriation of the mass media (Alted, 2000, p. 217).

Any modern production of *Fuente Ovejuna* must, by necessity, negotiate at least three historical periods: the occurrence of the historical incident on which it is based, the recreation of these events by Lope de Vega and, finally, the moment of its recreation on stage. In theory, additional historical referents might be introduced depending on when and where the modern-day production is set. This latter consideration was bypassed in this period as productions prided themselves on philological fidelity, period costumes and a spurious historical accuracy.[2]

Furthermore, there was an attempt to efface time lapses by submerging both the Early Modern period and the present under the banner of Spanish national identity and historical destiny. This process was exacerbated in relation to *Fuente Ovejuna* because there was rarely any acknowledgement that Lope used fictional devices to tell a story based on an historical event rather than simply relaying facts; in other words, historical and poetic truths are assumed to be synonymous.[3] The Golden Age also becomes a monolithic prism through which to view a long period of history. Expositions of the time rarely if ever acknowledged that, although the seventeenth century was culturally rich, it also coincided with what John Elliott has termed 'an iron age of political and economic disaster' (1989, p. 285). In fact, the psychic and material conditions of the seventeenth century proved to be a closer fit to the post-war years of autarky, 'beset with problems of self-understanding and self-esteem' (Loureiro, 2003: 65), than Spain's earlier imperial phase. In Elliott's words:

> Like other societies, Castile had created an image of itself and of its past, which had helped to shape its expectations and its goals. The disappointments and reverses of the late sixteenth and early seventeenth centuries created a crisis of confidence, because they implied that Castile was falling short of the goals—essentially military and religious—which it had set itself. The failure was then set into the context of *declinación*. (1989, p. 252)

As in Francoist discourse, the answer to this decline was thought to lie in a reawakened Golden Age rather than in radical change (1989, p. 100). This accounts for the 'verdadero culto' [genuine cult] of Ferdinand and Isabella in the early seventeenth century (Pring-Mill, 1962, p. 28). As William R. Blue notes, '[t]he Catholic Monarchs became the mythic symbol of all that had been right with Spain' (1991, p. 301). Lope clearly adapts a poetic rather than historical view of their characters and their relationship with vassals (Caba, 2008, p. 17; Ostlund, 1997, p. 11), and plays such as *Fuente Ovejuna* 'betray a powerful nostalgia for a more personal form of rule, for a time when kings were more actively involved in the processes of justice' (McKendrick, 2000a, pp. 36–7).

This idealization is also extended to a peasant class that, despite or perhaps because of their harsh material conditions, were eulogized in both

---

2. This is particularly clear in this case, considering how little we know about the original staging of the work (Kirschner, 1979, p. 14). For a hypothesis on how the play might have been staged in the seventeenth century, see Takahashi Nagasaka, 2000.
3. In reality, as Peter W. Evans notes, '*Fuenteovejuna* is very much simultaneously a stylised version of history and a complicated aestheticised formulation, both conscious and unconscious, of contemporary political and sociological realities' (1990b, p. 111). For further discussions of the relationship between history and the play, see Cabrera and Morós, 1991; Carter, 1977; Cascardi, 1997; Hall, 1985, pp. 11–18; MacKay and McKendrick, 1986; Marín, 2001; Villegas Ruiz, 1990; and Welles, 2000, pp. 70–115.

periods and held up as the solutions to the nation's ills. In the seventeenth century, as in the 1940s, these idylls would have been enacted on stage primarily for an urban audience perhaps also nostalgic on the individual level for a rural life that many of them or their parents would have left behind (Jones, 1971). Although it would not have been articulated in these terms, *Fuente Ovejuna* was an obvious choice for performance in the early post-war period. Lope had written it in a society proposing many of the same solutions for similar problems and crises; its plot was remarkably amenable to the aesthetics of the Falange; and a definite Spanish version of the play was needed to finally dispel the spectre of 'anti-Spanish' versions.

Fuente Ovejuna *at the* Español

Modesto Higueras toured a version of the play with the Grupo de Teatro Ambulante Lope de Rueda (Teatro Móvil de la Falange) in the early 1940s. It was based on a version by Ernesto Giménez Caballero that is so close to the printed version that the performance script held in the CDT consists of a typed copy of Lope's play text with minor changes indicated by hand-written amendments.[4] These are very minor and are generally introduced to facilitate understanding (e.g. basquiñas [traditional overskirt] is replaced by faldas [skirt]), with the most significant change being Frondoso's final speech being split and delivered by the Maestre and Esteban instead. A note at the end also indicates that these closing lines should be followed by a rendition of the Falangist anthem, *Cara al sol*.

Fuente Ovejuna's major post-war debut took place, however, at the Español, where it opened the 1944–5 season.[5] This production, also based on Giménez Caballero's version, albeit with a few additional cuts,[6] was directed by Cayetano Luca de Tena; it also featured lavish stage sets by Sigfrido Burmann and included a large number of extras for crowd scenes. In what follows, I will argue that it had a blatant fascist subtext.[7] This is not to suggest that it was a fascist production per se but I think it is demonstrable that it went further than any other Spanish *comedia* performance I have encountered in its flirtation with totalitarian aesthetics and politics.

Although Burmann, a German by birth, had provided stage designs for 'anti-Spanish' productions during the Second Republic (Beckers, 1992, p. 211), he had allied himself with the Nationalists in the Civil War. In 1938, he wrote enthusiastically about 'politically correct' productions of *Fuente Ovejuna* and *Peribáñez* that had taken place in the fatherland (Schwartz, 1969, p. 187). The former was the most frequently staged play by Lope in Nazi Germany and a production that opened in Hamburg was clearly envisaged as the Third Reich's official contribution to Lope's centenary celebrations (Gagen, 1993, p. 6).[8] Giménez Caballero, a personal friend of Goebbels and 'the major literary exponent of fascist

4. File no. 1306 in the CDT.
5. For more details on the cast and credits of the major productions of *Fuente Ovejuna* staged between 1939 and 1999, see García Lorenzo, 2000, pp. 103–5.
6. File nos. 1307–8 in the CDT.
7. As Günter Berghaus has noted, our knowledge about theatre orchestrated by the Falange in Spain is heavily under-researched: 'The very existence of a fascist cultural policy and theatrical practice has been repeatedly negated; documents have been destroyed, and access to archival material is often restricted' (1996, p. 6).
8. In further proof of the play's adaptability to different performance contexts, a left-wing version was published by the Dutch during the occupation (London, 2000, pp. 232–3).

thought in Spain' (Labanyi, 1989, p. 36), was invited to attend an official reception. In the presence of various Spanish and German dignitaries, he suggested the parallels between Iberian and Germanic histories and destinies. In a subsequent speech, he went on to highlight 'que Lope afirmaba el principio del caudillaje ('Führerprinzip') y que su obra *Fuenteovejuna* representaba a su vez "el primer drama del socialismo nacional"' [Lope advocated the principle of the strong leader (Führerprinzip) and his play, *The Sheep Well,* constitutes 'the first drama of national socialism'] (Seliger, 1984, p. 400).

The extant records and stills suggest that a similar approach was in operation at the recently baptized Spanish National Theatre.[9] This was clearly a flagship production. There were seven different sets (Beckers 1992, p. 211), while a horizontal bridge and vertical castle at the back of the stage were placed at perpendicular angles so as to give the image of a cross. The set design and directorial style were characterized by geometrical symmetry and precise choreography. As in La Barraca's version, the successful execution of Laurencia and Frondoso's wedding was considered paramount. On this occasion, it was staged below the bridge as befits the villagers' social status (Luca de Tena, 1953a, p. 46), and Manuel Parada de la Puente provided specially commissioned music for scenes that employed a vast number of extras to offer a perfectly synchronized mass spectacle of *castizo* [traditional] village life.[1]

Following her abduction by the Comendador, Laurencia made her return along the bridge where she was raised above the male town council before lowering herself to their level for her speech (1953a, p. 46). As noted, in line with the prevailing aesthetic and ideological norms of the time, Giménez Caballero's version is generally very faithful to Lope's original. Nevertheless, the sexual content of the play text is minimized with, for example, Laurencia's speech being altered so that she says 'maritones' [pansies] rather than 'maricones'. A contemporary audience would have had no problems understanding the latter word—the usual justification for altering Lope's sacred text—and its removal is surely indicative of a sense of sexual propriety and also a concern about the inclusion of a linguistic term deemed inappropriate for a Spanish heroine. Even with this change in place, it is tempting to speculate over what effect Laurencia's words might have had on an audience. Francisco Ruiz Ramón has observed that it is remarkable and unprecedented for a woman who appears to have been raped to be given a voice and centre stage in a seventeenth-century play (1997, p. 77). Given that official discourses of the 1940s were predicated on strictly demarcated and hierarchical gender roles,[2] the mere presence of this vitriolic admonition in the context of a National Theatre is no less remarkable.

9. Multiple stills are available for consultation at the theatre library in the Fundación Juan March.
1. In a recent interview, Luca de Tena recalls how: 'Fue la primera vez que goberné los grupos, grupo por grupo. El movimiento de cada actor, de cada comparsa, estaba planificado. Si eran ocho grupos, numeraba del uno al seis y al ocho cada grupo; cada uno tenía una misión precisa. Dibujé un gran plano de colores con los movimientos, y los encuentros, y las paradas, y las salidas y las entradas' [It was the first time that I controlled groups, group by group. The movement of every actor; every troupe of extras, was planned. If there were eight groups, I numbered each group from one to six, or one to eight; each one had a set mission. I drew up a big plan where different colours indicated the movements, the encounters, the breaks, the exits and the entrances] (cited in Baltés, 2008, p. 178).
2. For a concise overview of the role of women under Franco, see Folguera Crespo, 1997.

Predictably, the reinstatement of the play's original denouement was afforded pride of place. Ferdinand and Isabella were positioned on the bridge and thereby looked down on all the characters so as to highlight their absolute authority (Luca de Tena, 1953a, p. 46). Audiences were directed towards the political significance of these scenes in the theatre programme, which stated:

> Finalmente hemos restablecido la integridad del texto—mutilado o deformado cien veces por sectarismos políticos—tratando de ser fieles a lo que Lope de Vega quiso indudablemente componer: un himno a la unidad española en las personas de sus creadores, los Católicos Reyes Don Fernando y Doña Isabel. (Teatro Español, 1944)

> [We have, at last, re-established the text—mutilated or deformed a hundred times as a result of political sectarianism—in its entirety, in an attempt to be true to what Lope de Vega undoubtedly set out to compose: a hymn to the unity of Spain through those personages who created it, the Catholic Monarchs, Ferdinand and Isabella.]

Elsewhere, in the first issue of a journal produced by young university students, Giménez Caballero discusses this latest production in much the same terms as he had used nearly ten years earlier in Germany. In an extended subsection, entitled 'Exaltación del Rey como símbolo caudillal' [Exaltation of the King as a symbol of the strong leader], he writes:

> Lope de Vega fué [*sic*] el propagandista poético y máximo que tuvo la Monarquía Absoluta Caudillal en España . . . 'Dios', 'Rey', 'Honor', he aquí el trinomio espiritual de la 'Comedia Española', creada por Lope: como reflejo del Estado universo o imperial de España en el mundo. (1944, pp. 6–7)

> [Lope de Vega was the greatest poetic propagandist that the strong rule of the absolute monarchy had in Spain . . . 'God', 'The King', 'Honour'; these constituted the holy trinity of the Spanish 'comedia' created by Lope as a reflection of Spain's universal and imperial standing in the world.]

The vociferous and didactic nature of the extensive written commentary on the play's ending and meaning was indicative of an anger still felt about earlier productions, yet the continued insistence in both critical and performative contexts also implies an unease or anxiety about the play's potential actuality, and is perhaps indicative of an unconscious fear that Lope's message was not as transparent or unequivocal as it was consistently maintained to be. This insecurity was reflected in the anger of a censor at the dress rehearsal who objected to the presence of an onstage sickle that he understood to be a communist symbol; Luca de Tena tried to assuage his anger by explaining that it was a symbol of the *pueblo* but was only successful when the Falangist David Jato came to his aid (cited in Santa-Cruz, 1993, p. 72).

Susan Bennett notes that audiences help produce the meaning of a performance and it is therefore necessary to formulate 'reception as a politically implicated act' (1997, p. 86). Nevertheless, they are never completely free. Just as the academic critic's appraisal is mediated by previous commentaries, so too is the audience by their environment and the field of relations that surround a production: 'In the circumstance of the theatre visit, the spectator takes on his/her role(s) before the performance per se begins' (p. 125). The Español was, in the 1940s, a meeting place for an elite audience who, in this case, had been bombarded with messages in a variety of media on the importance and significance of what they were about to see. While, given the theatrical expertise of those involved, there is no reason to believe that the production was not worthy of merit, these were neither necessary nor sufficient conditions for the production's successful runs (it was revived in 1947), a set of unanimously ecstatic reviews (e.g. Cueva, 1944; Marquerie, 1944b),[3] nor for it being staged in the presence and in honour of Eva Perón during her visit to Spain in 1947 (Burmann, 2009, p. 121). * * *

A Perennial Classic? (1950–98)

Fuente Ovejuna is one of the very rare comedias to have never left the Spanish stage and to have survived various changes in political and cultural moods. In the 1950s it was also performed primarily outside Madrid, often to rural audiences who were not generally accustomed to watching Golden Age drama.[4] There are, I believe, a number of explanations for the play's success in such environments. Firstly, it is a relatively easy comedia for audiences to follow: it is short;[5] its fame meant that it was the Lope play that actors and spectators were most likely to be familiar with; and, at least in performances of this period, there are clearly distinguishable heroes and villains. Secondly, it has a number of set pieces that lend themselves to the kind of folkloric displays that were well suited to both the prevailing ideology and large outdoor spaces. And, thirdly, its ostensible social and political message continued to resonate. It remained an antidote to previous desecration at the hands of the rojos, and the Catholic Monarchs continued to be officially endorsed icons with a strong grip on the popular imagination.[6]

José Tamayo's reputation had largely been forged with Peribáñez, and Fuente Ovejuna was an obvious choice for him to stage. In 1956, he directed a major production in the town itself, featuring one hundred and fifty extras. It also starred two of the most famous actors of the day, Manuel Dicenta and Aurora Bautista.[7] Not surprisingly, these ingredients guaranteed extensive press coverage with all the major critics attending the performance in Fuente Ovejuna alongside the Director General of

3. In its two runs at the Español beginning in October 1944 and June 1947 respectively, the production registered 12,145 spectators. This was, according to records held internally at the CDT, the most for any Spanish comedia in the National Theatres during the dictatorship—it did of course have the advantage of being staged twice—with Lope's La discreta enamorada coming in at a close second with 12,059 spectators over its two runs in 1945 and 1946. I would like to thank Gerardo del Barco for allowing me access to these internal databases.
4. See Marañón, 1952, for an interesting argument about how rural audiences unfamiliar with the comedia were more receptive than their better-educated urban counterparts.
5. 2,453 verses in Marín's edition (Vega Carpio, 2001).
6. The anti-communism that served Spain so well in the Cold War context was one of the few constants in the generally Heraclitean political ideology. So too was an attitude of veneration towards Isabella. The inauguration of the Institute for Hispanic Culture took place symbolically on 12 October 1951 during the quincentennial of her birth (Resina, 2005, p. 168), and in 1958 attempts were made for her beatification (Caba, 2008, p. 176). As late as 1972, an official document was sent to Rome with the hope yet again that she might be declared a saint. This document is reprinted in Álvar Ezquerra, 2002, pp. 274–85.
7. A recording of the play with much of the same cast and based on the same version was later issued by RCA records, and is available for consultation at the Sala Barbieri in the Biblioteca Nacional; the actors are impressive both in their mastery of verse and emotional range.

Cinema and Theatre. One reviewer, who began by praising the 'villa blanca, limpia y empinada' [pure, clean and elevated village] and its pretty young girls, noted how Nicolás González Ruiz had simplified and modernized the text before moving on to the following analysis of the performance and its rapt audience:

> Como espectáculo, lo más logrado es la escena de la boda, con bailes y cantares interpretados por chicas y chicos cordobeses: ellas, creo, de la Sección Femenina. Hay también una aparición del comendador a caballo verdaderamente teatral. El público entra en seguida en la pieza; cada vez que el comendador aparece se oye decir: '¡Ese es el malo!', y como es malo se aplaude su defenestración. (Torrente, 1956)

> [As a live performance, the highlight is the wedding scene complete with dances and songs performed by Cordovan boys and girls: the latter, I believe, from the Sección Femenina.[8] There is also the genuinely theatrical appearance of the commander on horseback. The audience is engaged from the outset; every time the commander appears, you hear them say: 'There's the villain' and, as he is the villain, his defenestration is met with applause.]

As with the classics, the recuperation of popular music and dances was a trend with origins in the Second Republic that was subsequently co-opted under Francoism with a largely predetermined political agenda. Furthermore, this appropriation of different regional dances also constituted what Jo Labanyi has characterized as 'a particularly interesting attempt at defusing the separatist implications of regional culture by incorporating it into a popular vision celebrating "national essences"' (1989, p. 41). Hence, while Tamayo's spectacle was not overtly political in the manner of earlier productions, it was nevertheless complicit in an ideological agenda that was far from neutral.[9] This was also the case with the production directed in the town itself by José Osuna, which was the subject of a special report by the official Spanish newsreel service, NO-DO, projected in cinemas before the commencement of the main feature.[1]

It is proof that the times were however changing, that when Tamayo resurrected the work in 1962, as part of the centenary celebrations of Lope's birth, it received a lukewarm reception. The traditional and conservative Marqueríe gave it a positive review as he spoke of the various ovations that Tamayo received at the premiere in the Español; even he, however, noted that a number of young people in the audience tried to heckle the director (1962). The majority of reviewers were less positive and criticized the actors' complete inability to recite verse and the production's general approach, which was seen to be the relic of a bygone age.[2]

---

8. "Female section" of the Falange, the Spanish fascist movement [editor's note].
9. The director occupies an ambivalent place in Spanish theatrical history for he was construed as a plaything of the regime yet he was also instrumental in having controversial foreign playwrights staged. Francisco Umbral has argued convincingly that, as an impresario, he was an expert strategist who knew how to negotiate under difficult circumstances: 'fue dúctil y sabio con la censura, jugó al posibilismo, les daba un *Fuenteovejuna* a cambio de un rojo y un Buero Vallejo a cambio de una legión romana de Pemán' [he was flexible and clever with the censor, he played with the possibilities contained within the system. He would offer them a production of *The Sheep Well* so as to stage a work by a left-wing playwright; a Buero Vallejo play for one of Pemán's Roman legions] (cited in Valverde, 2006).
1. No. 1040A, 1962.
2. For an overview of the critical reaction, see Álvaro, 1963, pp. 78–83.

There were, however, a number of productions of the play in the 1960s that began to engage with an alternative performance and political tradition. At the beginning of the decade, La Pipironda, a theatre group led by Ángel Carmona, and including playwright José María Rodríguez Méndez, performed a very liberal version of the play alongside Cervantes's *entremeses*. This modest project, aimed at working-class audiences in the poorer areas of Barcelona (predominantly Castilian-speaking immigrants from other parts of Spain), was a small-scale precursor, to the TEI.[3] Their performances, generally including songs, dances, discussions and workshops on popular theatre, were normally free and tended to take place in community centres, bars or in the open air (Thompson, 2007, pp. 45–6).

In 1963, the first meeting on the state of university theatre was held in Murcia. It was decided that there ought to be a return to the ideals of the Second Republic, more specifically La Barraca, and that they needed to try and rectify the middle-class domination of their current audiences (Oliva, 1999, pp. 20–1). In 1964, Alberto Castilla took Cervantes's *El retablo de las maravillas* to the Nancy Festival in France (Pérez Rasilla, 1999, p. 50), and then returned there in 1965 with a heavily politicized version of *Fuente Ovejuna*.

According to the director, they were aware of Russian productions, but it was Lorca's version that they chose to follow, ending as it does with the villagers resisting torture (1992, p. 51). Castilla also sought to eulogize a simple and just form of Spanish traditionalism that was seen to have its roots in the *pueblo*. Although this is not too far removed from the logic underpinning Tamayo or Luca de Tena's versions, its exposition was radically different. Music was employed in the wedding scene, for example, but in an anachronistic fashion so as to distance the audience and make them think about the relationship between past and present (p. 53). In terms of performance style, Castilla claims he was trying to move away from the histrionics that were a staple of most Spanish productions. He notes, for example, how Laurencia's monologue was habitually used as a showcase for the lead actress to shine, but that he made sure it was understated (p. 54).

With Franco's death, the analytical frame whereby the presence or absence of the Catholic Monarchs indicated the political affiliation of the production had suddenly disappeared. Unlike *Peribañéz* and *El villano en su rincón*, Lope's other famous peasant honour dramas, *Fuente Ovejuna* was able to outlive the dictator on the Spanish theatrical stage. Its canonical status was also assured by a high-profile television adaptation directed by Mario Camus and a musical version for the Teatro de la Zarzuela in 1981.[4] Beyond its intrinsic merits, this process of (un)natural selection is predicated on a number of factors. The play's contested legacy and actuality fascinate practitioners and have often made it one of the most 'politically correct' *comedias,* if not the most. Its cause has also been aided by the possibility it offers to deconstruct one of the chief Francoist

---

3. Teatro Experimental Independiente, avant-garde Spanish theater company that straddled the last years of the Franco regime and the transition to democracy [editor's note].
4. For more details, see Álvaro, 1982, pp. 224–85.

icons through the Catholic Monarchs,[5] and its amenability to being interpreted as a universal call for basic human rights.

Fuente Ovejuna made its post-Franco debut during 1978 in a version
directed by Vicente Sainz de la Peña and starring María Paz Ballesteros.
Laurencia, who now uttered the once taboo 'maricones', was raped on
stage and there was full frontal nudity. In this respect, it marked an arguably unfortunate precedent: the heroine's sexual violation is taken as a
given and exploited in an opportunistic manner to disrobe a young
actress.[6] This tendency is rarely criticized in a post-dictatorship culture
that has increasingly negated the possibility that sexual permissiveness
can in itself be a sexist practice. The denouement was retained but
changes were made. While most of the villagers claim that they want to
be placed under the jurisdiction of the Catholic Monarchs, Frondoso and
Mengo object and exit the stage through the auditorium in an abrupt and
violent manner. According to contemporary reviews, the production was
lacking in almost every respect: verse was badly recited, it lacked any
overall direction and was theatrically inept.[7]

Another trend that would develop over the coming years was the tendency to pinpoint the Comendador's sexual depravity through, for example, draping him in black leather costumes. This was the case, for example,
in José Osuna's 1984 production that visualized his threat to Jacinta that
'del bagaje / del exército has de ser' [you will form part of the army's booty]
(2001, vv. 1269–70). We see the soldiers rip her clothes off onstage and she
is then tied with her arms outstretched on a giant wheel in a crucifixion
pose. The actress convulses naked while the character is violated and
humiliated as she is wheeled offstage with phallic spears attacking her.

This is, however, relatively tame in comparison to a version of the play
based on the German filmmaker Rainer Werner Fassbinder's adaptation,
directed for the stage by Rafael Bermúdez in 1992.[8] The Catholic Monarchs are complicit with the Comendador and force the villagers into
choosing between submission and subversion; Laurencia at least temporarily chooses the latter and enjoys sadomasochistic sexual relations with
her overlord. The play ends with the villagers killing their oppressors and
eating them as part of a stew. Although the production was performed to

5. Even before 1975 this had been a popular trend. Then, in the post-1975 period, irreverent
works were frequently staged (Hernanz Ángulo, 1999, p. 102).
6. There has been some critical debate over whether Laurencia is actually raped. Her disheveled
appearance on her return seems to suggest that she has been, although Dixon has offered a convincing argument that, for a contemporary audience, Lope's precise physical descriptions would
not have warranted this conclusion (1988). The narrative of *El mejor alcalde, el rey* (see chapter
four [not included here]) proves that, at least in Lope's dramatic universe, it was possible for a
man to marry a woman who has been sexually violated. Frondoso later suggests that this was not
the case here (2001, vv. 2410–13). This is, however, said in front of the other villagers and, if the
assault did in fact take place, it is still plausible that she has not told her husband and/or that he
does not want his neighbours to know. A more cynical reading is offered by Robert Archer who
suggests that she deceives the villagers by crying rape so as to propel them into action (1990,
pp. 117–18).
7. Antonio Valencia claimed that 'se quiso original y puesta al día y ha resultado un indigesto
experimento, penoso de contemplar de principio a fin' [it has tried to be original and contemporary, but it has resulted in an indigestible experiment, painful to watch from start to fin-
ish] (cited in Álvaro, 1979, pp. 244), while Ángel Fernández Santos was even more scathing in
his attack: 'Montar *Fuenteovejuna* en estas condiciones linda con la irresponsabilidad' [Staging
The Sheep Well in these conditions borders on the irresponsible] (cited in Álvaro, 1979, p. 246).
8. A copy of the script is available in German (Fassbinder, 1976). For more details of the original
production, see Iden, 1976.

sell-out audiences in Geneva, it was not selected for the Festival de Otoño in 1992, the year when Madrid was named City of Culture (Monleón, 1992). In that year Spanish audiences were, however, able to see the CNTC's[9] production which, according to set designer Carlos Cytrynowski, was designed as an antidote to 'ese universo "tipico" lleno de "color local"' [that 'typical' universe full of 'local colour'] (cited in CNTC, 2006b, p. 132). This aim was certainly realized in a set design that resembled the dystopian universe of a science-fiction film replete with wire fences, metallic ramps, cubic structures and leather-clad protagonists. Characters enter and exit the stage on a metal passageway that passes through the auditorium. This invasion of the audience's public space alongside ubiquitous low lighting and the sound of deafening whistles yields what Susan Fischer has termed 'a dramatic interrogation of multiple carnivals of terror' (2009, p. 93).

In spite of manifest differences, two common characteristics can be attributed to many productions of the early democratic period. Firstly, there was a move away from the idealization of rural life. This was often manifested through a focus on the brutality committed against and by the villagers that placed a greater emphasis on the ritualistic and sexual aspects of violence. Secondly, the scenes with Ferdinand and Isabella were generally retained but their mythic status was deconstructed and they were often ridiculed and/or had their motives interrogated. Interestingly, these were among the very same themes and approaches that were being rehearsed in academic studies around the same time.[1]

Fuente Ovejuna *at the* CAT

Emilio Hernández directs an all-female cast in this turn of the century co-production between the Jerusalem-based Teatro Al-Kasaba and CAT.[2] The heavily edited version of the text, by Ana Rossetti, is complimented by a riotous soundtrack provided by Bishara Khilly and Paco Aguilera and choreography by the dancer Ana María Bueno, '[para] mostrar la fiesta de una victoria de las libertades sobre el poder tiránico' [in order to show the celebration of the victory of freedom over tyrannical power] (cited in Tamayo, 1998).

The project arose from the director's interest in Spain's Arabic roots and his experiences in Palestine where he spent time teaching actors and touring refugee camps.[3] Hernández knew that he wanted to direct a collaborative project with CAT—of which he was artistic director at the time—and the Palestinian theatre company with a focus on the oppression suffered in that land. He was also keen to work with actresses from Palestine as he claims that they were more accomplished than their male counterparts.

Given its politically charged narrative and strong female characters, *Fuente Ovejuna* was, perhaps, an obvious choice. The director was also persuaded by his discovery of a nineteenth-century Arabic translation of the play. In her heavily updated version of the text often rendered in

---

9. Compañía Nacional de Teatro Clásico, founded 1986 [editor's note].
1. On the first point see, for example, Allatson, 1996; Camino, 2004; Cañadas, 2005, pp. 137–83; Larson, 1991; López Estrada, 1989; Smith, 1993; Swietlicki, 1992; Weimer, 1996; and Worley Jr., 2003. On the second, Carter, 1977; Herrera Montero, 1989; Lauer, 1997; and Stroud, 2008.
2. Centro Andaluz de Teatro, founded 1988 [editor's note].
3. Unless otherwise noted, all of the information about this production comes from an interview between the author and Emilio Hernández conducted in Madrid on 16 September 2008.

prose, Rossetti includes dialogue in Arabic; the content of these phrases is, however, always clarified and contextualized by having another character paraphrase or repeat them in Spanish. The production shows little or no interest in even speculating over authorial intention or in engaging with Golden Age poetics, focussing instead on those elements of the plot that are considered relevant, and the dramatic tension inherent in some of its scenarios. The scenes with Ferdinand and Isabella are, for example, removed. No apology is made for the fact that the playwright is at the service of the performance rather than vice versa. In line with Hernández's preference, there are only actresses on stage (seven Spaniards and five Palestinians) and the production engages in what Philip Auslander has defined as 'postmodern theatrical practice' through its use of gender crossing and intercultural casting (2004, p. 102).

*   *   *

Fortunately, in performance, *Fuente Ovejuna* is far more complex and sensitive as it interrogates the audience's relationship with women who suffer, but also perpetrate, violence in a visceral and intelligent manner. Although the set is not realistic, and there are no concrete geographical markers, it is clearly meant to resemble a camp in Palestine. There is dark ominous lighting, the Comendador wears a similar black leather costume and whistles are also blown. In general, the *mise en scène* resembles a more minimalist version of Marsillach's production, and it also undergoes the process Keir Elam has characterized as the attempt 'to transform architectural fixity as far as possible into dynamic proxemic informality' (1980, p. 63). Hernández's production has, however, far more impact, largely as a result of the kinetic onstage dynamism and activity which, as will be discussed, relate to events happening in the real world and bestow the production with a sense of genuine political commitment.

The actresses enter one by one, each holding a bag, and introduce themselves to the audience with their real names and say where they are from. A wire fence physically separates them from their public, yet complicity between stage and auditorium is central to the production's success. The women proceed to sing about Fuente Ovejuna and it is immediately evident that their vocal dexterity far exceeds what one is accustomed to hearing in Spanish theatre. A character then reads from a paper of the Comendador's taking of the village by force in 1478 (an obvious interpolation by Rossetti) and that he committed so many outrages the village decided to rebel. As she recounts the story, the others beat drums to an increasingly furious rhythm. This cacophony of regimented arms and deafening noise reaches a climax as the narrator furiously screws up the paper and the principal action is synaesthetically propelled into motion.

The rhythm and tone of the drums and music help determine the mood throughout. While they are played in a soothing and non-threatening manner as Mengo expounds his theories on love, they then become louder, faster and more ominous as the Comendador interrupts this harmonious scene to make his first appearance. This is complemented in visual terms as the villagers throw themselves to the floor where they remain rigidly still as they are regaled with stories of military triumphs and receive scraps of food that are condescendingly flung down to their presumably starving mouths.

A similar, albeit intensified, aesthetic dynamic is in operation during the wedding scenes which are lit, as is most of the production, in simple blue light and benefit from the actresses' tight control over their bodies that is equally suited to frenetic kinetic activity as it is to comatose rigidity. Laurencia appears in a white wedding dress and stands centre stage as confetti is dropped on her from above while the drums pound a festive beat and the villagers sing. This idyll is shattered as the Comendador reappears. Frondoso tries to escape but is caught and assaulted; he is then left hanging on the metal fence.

The bride's reappearance is handled in a sensitive and effective manner. Earlier in the production, Jacinta had hardly been able to articulate her words when she returned to the village, and now Laurencia begins her monologue calmly but gradually becomes more animated. As she speaks, Frondoso remains in view to the audience as he is left hanging on the fence as a martyred visual icon. The villagers all have long wooden sticks, and as her harangue reaches its crescendo, they begin to beat them in a synchronized manner. This becomes a battle cry as their voices become louder and louder and they move with the demeanour of a highly disciplined military unit towards the Comendador who is now on stage.

Their former oppressor is now trapped between them and the fence. Facing the audience, he begs for mercy and begins to climb but is impaled from behind by the sticks which all strike simultaneously, thereby emphasizing the collective aspect of the execution. Although the audience morally applauds their actions, this is the only production I have seen that makes the inhabitants of the town sufficiently ferocious that they also inspire genuine fear.

As noted, Ferdinand and Isabella do not appear and the play ends with the villagers resisting torture. It is perhaps unfortunate that, while being assaulted, they are tied to the fence blindfolded and topless. Although there is a case for suggesting that this is a means of suggesting how sexuality is used as a weapon against women in warfare, I am not convinced that specularizing this means of oppression is the most ethical or effective form of condemnation.[4]

Their response on being pardoned is far more interesting: after chanting 'vivan muchos años' [may they live many years] in animalesque fashion, they begin to break down the fence that provided a physical barrier between them and their public. The drums roll and initiate an extended dance sequence that incorporates the curtain call.

*　*　*

Most audience members will, presumably, sympathize with the plight of their onstage counterparts, but the anger, unpredictability and agency that it unleashes is also liable to occasion genuine unease. There is a visceral thrill to this production's denouement that, I would suggest, is the result of both fear and admiration. One is impressed about the villagers' achievements but, equally, we are scared about them breaking down the fence and emerging from their enclosed compound into 'our' world. Racda Ghazaleh, the deputy director of Al-Kasaba, has

4. This issue is exacerbated when an all-female cast is being directed by a man who is also in charge of the company.

argued that this aspect of the play and the production had particular relevance for women living in Palestine:

> Las doce actrices se convierten aquí en un único narrador, suman toda su energía y eso es lo más interesante de la obra . . . Cuando hay problemas, la sociedad necesita que la mujer sea fuerte, luche y tome decisiones, pero cuando todo ha pasado quieren que vuelva a casa. Contra eso estamos luchando en la calle y en el teatro. (cited in Molina, 1999)[5]
>
> [The twelve actresses here form a single narrator; they combine all their energy and this is what is most interesting about the production . . . When there are problems, society requires women to be strong, to fight and to take decisions, but when everything has calmed down, men want them to go back home. It is this that we are fighting against in the street and in the theatre.]

This staging revealed (at least to this spectator) the complex and often contradictory emotions provoked by justifiable and righteous outbreaks of violence by subaltern groups who are oppressed on the grounds of their race, gender and/or class. In the manner of an amputee who only becomes conscious of a limb once it has been removed, the absence of the traditional ending made me appreciate some of the psychological and theatrical reasons underpinning the restoration of order in Lope's play text. By presenting an onstage reality that, following conflicts in the Balkans and the Middle East, resembles a world that is familiar, albeit through the media, we are able to feel the fear occasioned by the breakdown of traditional hierarchies and the desire for some semblance of order. These heady emotions suddenly make Lope's ambivalence over ostensibly irreconcilable drives towards revolution and order appear both logical and human(e).

The production inspired an equally fervent emotional response in other spectators as the preconditions for communicating the political aspect of Lope's play text were once again in place. On the night I attended, the audience was visibly more engaged in the onstage action than I have seen at any other *comedia* performance in Spain. As a result of the deliberate conflation of the actresses and their roles, it was not clear whether their extended standing ovation was directed towards the former's performances or the latter's actions. The critical response was also enthusiastic. Gonzalo Pérez de Olaguer wrote of a performance in Barcelona, for example, that it was 'uno de los mejores espectáculos presentados aquí en los últimos años' [one of the best productions to be staged here in recent years] (1999b).[6] After touring Spain, Hernández took the production to New York but, perhaps unsurprisingly, he was unsuccessful in his attempts to perform it in Palestine.[7]

---

5. This has resulted in women suffering on multiple levels: 'Palestinian women living in the West Bank . . . face the oppression of two systems: the patriarchal (sociocultural) and Israeli occupation (political). Palestinian women have been expected to combat the occupying forces to accept patriarchal hegemony' (Shalhoub-Kevorkian, 2003, p. 584).
6. For a representative selection of reviews of the productions, see Urzáiz Tortajada, 2006.
7. Subsequent to Arafat being elected President in 1996 and the formation of the Palestinian National Authority, all sports, cultural and social events required a police permit (Aburish, 1998, p. 312). Hernández claims that Arafat's Minister of Culture came to watch the production in Seville and said that it would be impossible to perform in Palestine not as a result of the violence but due to the onstage nudity. An unfortunate side effect of this decision is that it in all likelihood consolidated the director's association of nudity with artistic freedom.

The Repoliticization of Fuente Ovejuna *(1999–2008)*

With eight documented productions between 1999 and 2008, *Fuente Ovejuna* was more frequently staged than at any time in its history. This is not altogether surprising. Firstly, its fame and legacy makes it a popular choice for amateur and student groups who have been increasingly active. Secondly, Spanish politics have become increasingly polarized at the beginning of the twenty-first century as there has been a renegotiation of the *pacto de olvido*[8] that had tacitly underpinned mainstream Spanish politics since the transition. This came to the fore with the passing of the Law of Historical Memory, first proposed by the PSOE in 2004, published in 2006 and approved by congress in 2007.[9] * * *

This climate has been readily discernible in many productions which have been politicized to an extent not seen since the 1960s. What has changed, however, is that the liberal factions of Spanish society now appear to have the monopoly on the play and its meaning.[1] This is largely a result of the political allegiances of most Spanish cultural practitioners but it is also because the left have more to gain from re-engaging with the play's performance tradition. Their opponents may not want to condemn Francoism outright, but neither do they generally want to directly associate themselves with it. A number of productions have, for example, self-consciously sought to make the play's performance history part of the theatrical experience.

Hence in 1999, for example, Achiperre Coop. Teatro staged their version of the play titled *Fuente Ovejuna 1476–1999*. This production, based on an adaptation by Michel Van Loo and directed by Carlos Herans, is something of an anomaly: an updated version of a *comedia* by a Belgian dramaturge influenced by Brecht and Marx and aimed at teenagers. Set in an occupied factory in the midst of strike action, Lope's drama provides the means by which four fictional workers articulate their thoughts. The polyvalence of *Fuente Ovejuna* is suggested by the way in which each of the workers interprets it differently and in accordance with their own preoccupations and experiences. Clara, who has been studying the play at the Universidad Popular [Workers' University], uses it to explain the Marxist doctrine that she believes holds the key to her co-workers' emancipation. In contrast, Isabel and Pedro, who only have vague recollections from school, gradually recall the plot as they identify with different narrative strands: the central love story and the popular uprising respectively. The action switches between their commentary and the acting out of individual scenes. This short production (barely over an hour) ends with a discussion about Lope's inclusion of Ferdinand and Isabella.

A similar approach would be advanced ten years later by Samarkanda Teatro in *Chrónica de Fuente Ovejuna* under the direction of the well-respected veteran, José Carlos Plaza.[2] This relatively modest production

---

8. "Pact of Forgetting": political agreement not to prosecute those responsible for repression during the Franco regime; basis for 1977 amnesty law [editor's note].
9. Partido Socialista Obrero Español [Spanish Socialist Workers' Party] [editor's note].
1. Hence, for example, one of Spain's most outspoken communists, the dancer Antonio Gades, has performed a ballet based on the play with the Spanish National Ballet, both at home and abroad, since the early 1990s. The company he founded has continued to include it in their repertoire since his death in 2004.
2. For a more detailed analysis of the production, see Wheeler, 2011b, pp. 191–6.

is the antithesis of Francoist productions for it seeks to disperse rather than condense historical time. *Fuente Ovejuna* is theatrically unstitched and the audience's knowledge (or lack thereof) of the play text and its stage history are woven into the very fabric of the theatrical action. Hence, for example, the performance opens with a number of actors struggling to perform the scene where the Catholic Monarchs ostensibly restore order. The apparent lack of professionalism on display does not bode well but, fortunately, it soon becomes evident that this is a staged rehearsal. The performance comes full circle at the end as the house lights are raised after the torture scenes, which are shown on rather than off stage. The onstage director says that this is where Lorca's version ends and they debate whether their version should follow this example or remain faithful to Lope's play text.

A more traditional staging of the play was undertaken by the TNC[3] in 2005, which nevertheless engaged with aspects of the play that have often been sidelined; as J. B. Hall reminds us, 60 per cent of the verses are written in *redondillas*[4] and this underlies the importance of love in the play (1985, pp. 75–6).[5] One of the most detrimental effects of a lack of a continuous performance tradition in Spain is that both actors and audiences have lost their sensitivity to verse as a semiotic device. As early as 1940, Karl Vossler lamented this breakdown in communication: 'Era un compositor de fina sensibilidad. No es culpa suya que el lector actual carezca de oído para sus ritmos y sus rimas' [He was a composer with a refined sensibility. It is not his fault that the modern-day reader does not have an ear for his rhythms and rhymes] (1940, p. 327). Consequently, the theme of love has largely been ignored in productions that want to focus more heavily on the political and ideological aspects of the play. In this case, however, love is ubiquitous and not construed to be the exclusive preserve of romantic couples; harmonious relationships of all kinds are afforded a privileged role. In the wedding scenes, for example, all of the villagers happily sing and dance; Laurencia and Frondoso canoodle at the side before being dragged into a communal dance.

In sharp contrast, the revolt is violently staged and the Comendador's decapitated head is kicked around the stage as if it were a football. Laurencia, seated on a chair, tends it in an almost cannibalistic manner before throwing it on the floor as she kisses Frondoso in a savage romantic exchange in which the lips of both are coated with blood. Mengo then jumps off a chair to land on the Comendador's head, which is subsequently placed on a spike. At the end of this dark celebratory scene, all of the villagers leave the stage and Laurencia and her father are left alone. She is crying and he hugs her with the words 'mi hija' [my daughter]. By showing the villagers as loving and loved human beings, without shying away from the carnivalesque savagery of their actions, the production inspires that mixture of pity, fear and compassion that is axiomatic to the play's dramatic potential.

---

3. Teatre Nacional de Catalunya [National Theater of Catalonia] [editor's note].
4. Stanzas of four lines of eight syllables each, rhyming *abba* [editor's note].
5. These are not restricted to the village scenes and are, as Marsillach's production intelligently picked up on, frequently used in exchanges between Ferdinand and Isabella. Critics who argue that the play is essentially about love include Feito, 1981; Pring-Mill, 1962; Spitzer, 1955; and Wardropper, 1956 and 1978.

Ferdinand and Isabella are presented as a young and loving couple dressed in elegant ball gowns; they are seen to be cynical but neither cruel nor perverse. This is rather unnecessarily vocalized at the end when he says: 'A estos cansados villanos bien podemos perdonar, pues vinieron a dejar Calatrava en nuestras manos' [We can easily forgive these exhausted villagers, as they have come to leave Calatrava in our hands]. Then, in line with the prominence given to female characters throughout, the queen delivers the lines uttered by her husband in Lope's play text (2001, vv. 2442–9). This is the least successful part of the production and is symptomatic of the way in which Spanish theatre has an apparent inability to satisfactorily incorporate the secondary action into the body of the play.

*　*　*

Following what appeared to be a ceasefire, *Fuente Ovejuna* has once again become a symbolic and strategic prize to be fought over. The battle is clearly more civilized than it had been in the 1930s and 1940s, and the weapons and objectives have changed. Culture is no longer evoked as a form of praxis but as a manifestation of civilization. This has resulted in some dramatically effective and balanced productions, yet the equation can easily become as deceitful and politically charged as earlier attempts to patent Lope. Nevertheless, the play's iconic status and associations with key moments in national history afford it a privilege hardly ever bestowed on Golden Age plays: an almost guaranteed presence on the Spanish stage.

Conclusion

Fuente Ovejuna is arguably the only *comedia* to have a genuine performance tradition in the modern era. *El alcalde de Zalamea* and *La vida es sueño*[6] may be staged on a regular basis but, with the occasional exception, productions tend not to enter into an active dialogue with their predecessors. In contrast, virtually every performance of Lope's play is engaged in a process Marvin Carlson refers to as 'ghosting', whereby 'the external associations that the continually recycled material of theatre brings in from the external world as well as from previous performances' perform a constitutive role (2004, p. 58).

Even before it was revived for the Spanish stage, *Fuente Ovejuna* was a haunted play. That this 'ghosting' has exerted an incredible force field is undeniable; how and to what extent this has enabled or stifled creativity and/or engagement with Lope and the nation's cultural past is more open to debate. It is paradoxical that the play text's actuality has ensured its continual presence on the Spanish stage, yet in performance this actuality has so often been resisted in an attempt to deliver a single univocal meaning. It is easy, therefore, to see Lope as a sacrificial lamb delivered as an offering to the grand political ideals of the last hundred years. Does the play, therefore, need to be rescued from the ghosts of its performance history?

---

6. *The Mayor of Zalamea* and *Life Is a Dream*, both by Calderón [editor's note].

This certainly appeared to be the view of a recent Spanish production directed by Laurence Boswell, associate director of the RSC, which followed the play text very closely and boasted of its post-ideological credentials in the programme: 'Fuenteovejuna no pertenece a nadie, y es y siempre será de todos y cada uno de nosotros y de vosotros' [The Sheep Well does not belong to anyone in particular; it is, and will always be, the property of all of us and all of you] (Compañía Rakatá, 2009). On attending this version in Madrid just prior to completing this chapter, I realized that I had never seen a version of the play text which was not heavily cut performed in a way that did not appear anachronistic. In this case, despite being imaginatively staged and reasonably well acted, the onstage action was unengaging and the audience was visibly bored for the duration.

What is it that has prevented philologically faithful versions from triumphing on the modern Spanish stage? I would like to suggest that it is because Fuente Ovejuna presents two specific challenges that have not been adequately addressed. Firstly, in order for the two actions to have the unity many textual critics see as central to the play's artistry, practitioners and audiences alike would require a conceptual and intuitive knowledge of verse forms and seventeenth-century philosophical and political ideals that have been rendered obsolete by the absence of a wider performance tradition. Secondly, the vicissitudes of Spanish history have converted the Catholic Monarchs into such volatile icons that a hermeneutical chasm separates seventeenth- and twenty-first-century spectators. As a result, it seems difficult to see how a literal interpretation of the denouement could make dramatic or ethical sense to a contemporary Spanish audience. This is not to imply that a talented director will not discover a way of successfully performing the play in its entirety, but I suspect they will only be able to do so if and when they discover ingenious solutions to the challenges outlined above.

The most successful performances of the play, from La Barraca to CAT, have been those where the production has a strong personal vision and message to communicate. If we return to Bate's postulate that Fuente Ovejuna is open to multiple interpretations that can nevertheless not be perceived simultaneously, does this therefore imply that it is the role of the theatre practitioner to decide on a reading that they will then perform to an audience? This would accord with Howard Mancing's belief that 'the experience of reading a book is comparable not to the watching of a play but to participation in its performance' (2006, p. 196). The problem with this division of labour is that it makes the audience passive, when in reality the play's performance history suggests that the most affecting productions have been those that have actively encouraged the audience's response(s) to perform an unusually decisive role in the theatrical experience.

As we have seen, the play contains individual scenes that retain their effect even when removed from the wider dramatic edifice. Fuente Ovejuna may have been staged so frequently because of its amenability to different ideological agendas, but it would have had little or no propagandistic worth if it were not for its theatrical virtues which clearly have the capacity to stir audiences in a unique way. Paradoxically, as we speculated in the case of Luca de Tena's production and saw in the case of Hernández's, those characteristics that make the play a potentially valuable political tool also ensure that it communicates multiple and even contradictory messages. In other words, the play's performability, performativity and actuality are inextricably linked. It is surely in these relationships that, as Bate suggests, Lope's genius is to be found.

WORKS CITED

Aburish, Said K. (1998). *Arafat: From Defender to Dictator*. London: Bloomsbury.

Allatson, Paul (1996). 'Confounding convention: "women" in three Golden Age plays'. *Bulletin of the Comediantes*, 48.2: 261–73.

Alted, Alicia (2000). 'Notas para la configuración y el análisis de la política cultural del franquismo en sus comienzos: la labor del Ministerio de Educación Nacional durante la guerra'. In Josep Fontana (ed.), *España bajo el franquismo*. Barcelona: Editorial Crítica, pp. 215–29.

Álvar Ezquerra, Alfredo (2002). *Isabel la Católica: una reina vencedora, una mujer derrotada*. Madrid: Temas de hoy.

Álvaro, Francisco (ed.) (1963). *El espectador y la crítica: el teatro en España en 1962*. Valladolid: Francisco Álvaro.

——(ed.) (1979). *El espectador y la crítica: el teatro en España en 1978*. Valladolid: Francisco Álvaro.

——(ed.) (1982). *El espectador y la crítica: el teatro en España en 1981*. Valladolid: Francisco Álvaro.

Anderson, Benedict (1991). *Imagined Communities: Reflections on the Origin and Spread of Nationalism*, 2nd ed., London: Verso.

Archer, Robert (1990). 'El pueblo, los reyes y el público: el pragmatismo dramático en *Fuente Ovejuna*'. In Roy Boland and Alun Kenwood (eds.), *War and Revolution in Hispanic Literatura*. Melbourne: Voz Hispánica, pp. 109–19.

Armas, Frederick A. de (2006). 'A woman hunted, a city besieged: Spanish emblems and Italian art in *Fuenteovejuna*'. In Margaret R. Greer and Laura R. Bass (eds.), *Approaches to Teaching Early Modern Spanish Drama*. New York: MLA, pp. 45–52.

Auslander, Philip (2004). 'Postmodernism and performance'. In Steven Connor (ed.), *The Cambridge Companion to Postmodernism*. Cambridge: Cambridge University Press, pp. 97–115.

Baltés, Blanca (2008). 'Cayetano Luca de Tena: dirigir en los años cuarenta'. *ADE*, 120: 171–82.

Banús, Enrique and María C. Barcenilla (2005). '¿Vive el teatro del Siglo de Oro? Los "clásicos" en la programación de los teatros europeos'. In Carlos Mata and Miguel Zugasti (eds.), *Actas del Congreso 'El Siglo de Oro en el nuevo milenio'*, vol. 1. Barañáin: Ediciones Universidad de Navarra, pp. 263–74.

Bate, Jonathan (1997). *The Genius of Shakespeare*. London: Picador.

Beckers, Ursula (1992). 'La escenografía teatral de Sigfrido Burmann'. Unpublished dissertation, Universidad Complutense.

Benach, Joan-Antón (2005). '*Fuente Ovejuna*', review. *La vanguardia*, 23 April: 53.

Bennett, Susan (1997). *Theatre Audiences: A Theory of Production and Reception*, 2nd ed. London: Routledge.

Berghaus, Günter (1996). 'Introduction'. In Günter Berghaus (ed.), *Fascism and Theatre: Comparative Studies on the Aesthetics and Politics of Performance in Europe (1925–1945)*. Providence: Berghahn Books, pp. 1–10.

Blue, William R. (1991). 'The politics of Lope's *Fuenteovejuna*'. *HR*, 59.3: 295–315.

Burmann, Conchita (2009). *La escenografía teatral de Sigfrido Burmann*. Madrid: Fundación Jorge Juan.

Byrd, Suzanne W. (1984). *La Fuente Ovejuna de Federico García Lorca*. Madrid: Editorial Pliegos.

Caba, María Y. (2008). *Isabel la Católica en la producción teatral española del siglo XVII*. Woodbridge: Támesis.

Cabrera, Emilio and Andrés Morós (1991). *Fuenteovejuna: la violencia antiseñorial en el siglo XV*. Barcelona: Editorial Crítica.

Camino, Mercedes (2004). '"¡Volvióse en luto la boda!": ritual, torture and the technologies of power in Lope's *Fuente Ovejuna*'. *Modern Language Review*, 99.2: 382–93.

Cañadas, Ivan (2005). *Public Theater in Golden Age Madrid and Tudor-Stuart London*. Aldershot: Ashgate.

Carlson, Marvin (2004). *Performance: A Critical Introduction*, 2nd ed. London: Routledge.

Carter, Robin (1977). '*Fuenteovejuna* and tyranny: some problems of linking drama with political theory'. *Forum for Modern Language Studies*, 13: 313–35.

Cascardi, Anthony J. (1997). 'The Spanish *comedia* and the resistance to historical change'. In Anthony J. Cascardi, *Ideologies of History in the Spanish Golden Age*. Pennsylvania: The Pennsylvania State University Press, pp. 17–46.

Castilla, Alberto (1992). 'Teatro universitario: *Fuenteovejuna* 65'. In Heraclia Castellón, Agustín de la Granja and Antonio Serrano (eds.), *En torno al teatro del Siglo de Oro: Actas de las Jornadas VII–VIII celebradas en Almería*. Granada: Instituto de Estudios Almerienses and Diputación de Almería, pp. 39–58.

CNTC (2006b). *20 años en escena (1986–2006)*. Madrid: CNTC.

Collado, Fernando (1989). *El teatro bajo las bombas en la Guerra Civil*. Madrid: Kayeda Ediciones.

Compañía Rakatá (2009). 'Theatrical programme for *Fuente Ovejuna*'. Madrid: Compañía Rakatá.

Cueva, Jorge de la (1944). '*Fuenteovejuna*', review. *Ya*, 13 October: 9.

Darst, David H. (1995). 'Las analogías funcionales en *Fuenteovejuna*'. *Neophilologus*, 79.2: 245–52.

Delgado, María M. (2008). *Federico García Lorca*. London: Routledge.

Díaz del Moral, Juan (1973). *Historia de las agitaciones campesinas andaluzas: antecedentes para una reforma agraria*. Madrid: Alianza Universidad.

Dixon, Victor (1988). '"Su majestad habla, en fin, como quien tanto ha acertado": la conclusión ejemplar de *Fuente Ovejuna*'. *Criticón*, 42: 155–68.

———(1989). 'Introduction'. In Lope de Vega, *Fuente Ovejuna*, ed. and trans. Victor Dixon. Warminster: Aris and Phillips, pp. 1–52.

Elam, Keir (1980). *The Semiotics of Theatre and Drama*. London: Methuen.

Elliott, J. H. (1989). *Spain and Its World (1500–1700)*. New Haven: Yale University Press.

Evans, Peter William (1990b). 'Civilisation and its discontents in *Fuenteovejuna*'. In Peter William Evans (ed.), *Conflicts of Discourse: Spanish Literature in the Golden Age*. Manchester: Manchester University Press, pp. 110–29.

Fainlight, Ruth and Allan Sillitoe (1969). *All Citizens are Soldiers*. London: Macmillan.

Farrán Graves, Natalia (1989). 'Adrian Mitchell y su versión de *Fuenteovejuna*'. *Cuadernos de teatro clásico*, 4: 175–80.

Fassbinder, Rainer Werner (1976). *Stücke 3: Die biteren Tränen der Petra von Kant, Das brenne onde Dorf, Der Müll, die Stadt und der Tod*. Frankfurt: Edicion Suhrkamp.

Feito, Francisco E. (1981). '*Fuenteovejuna* o el álgebra del amor'. In Manuel Criado de Val (ed.), *Lope de Vega y los orígenes del teatro español*. Madrid: EDI, pp. 391–98.

Fiore, Robert (1966). 'Natural law in the central ideological theme of *Fuenteovejuna*'. *Hispania*, 49.1: 75–80.

Fischer, Susan L. (2009). *Reading Performance: Spanish Golden Age Theatre and Shakespeare on the Modern Stage*. Woodbridge: Támesis.

Folguera Crespo, Pilar (1997). 'El franquismo: el retorno a la esfera privada (1939–1975)'. In Elisa Garrido, Pilar Folguera Crespo, Margarita Ortega López and Cristina Segura Graíño (eds.), *Historia de las mujeres en España*. Madrid: Síntesis, pp. 527–48.

Gagen, Derek H. (1993). *Coming to Terms with the Civil War. Modern Productions of Lope de Vega's* Fuenteovejuna *(University College of Swansea Inaugural Lecture)*. Swansea: University College of Swansea.

García Lorenzo, Luciano (2000). 'Puesta en escena y recepción de *Fuente Ovejuna* (1940–1999)'. In M. G. Profeti (ed.), *Otro Lope no ha de haber: atti del Convegno Internazionale su Lope de Vega 10–13 febbraio*, vol. 2. Florence: Alinea, pp. 85–105.

García Santo-Tomás, Enrique (2000a). *La creación del Fénix: recepción crítica y formación canónica del teatro de Lope de Vega*. Madrid: Gredos.

Giménez Caballero, Ernesto (1944). '¡Fuenteovejuna, todos a una!'. *Cuadernos de teatro*, 1: 4–7.

Griffin, Roger (1996). 'Staging the nation's rebirth: the politics and aesthetics of performance in the context of fascist studies'. In Günter Berghaus (ed.), *Fascism and Theatre: Comparative Studies on the Aesthetics and Politics of Performance in Europe (1925–1945)*. Providence: Berghahn Books, pp. 11–29.

Hall, J. B. (1974). 'Theme and structure in Lope's *Fuente Ovejuna*'. *Forum for Modern Language Studies*, 10: 57–66.

——(1985). *Critical Guides to Spanish Texts (Lope de Vega: Fuenteovejuna)*. London: Grant and Cutler/Támesis.

Hernanz Angulo, Beatriz (1999). 'Aproximación a una teoría de la puesta en escena del teatro histórico español'. In José Romera Castillo and Francisco Gutiérrez Carbayo (eds.), *Teatro histórico (1975–1998)*. Madrid: Visor Libros, pp. 93–109.

Herrera Montero, Bernal (1989). '*Fuenteovejuna* de Lope de Vega y el maquiavelismo'. *Criticón*, 45: 131–51.

Herzberger, David K. (1995). *Narrating the Past: Fiction and Historiography in Post-War Spain*. Durham: Duke University Press.

Hodge, Francis (1963). 'Fuente Ovejuna on the American Stage'. *The Texas Quarterly*, 6.1: 204–13.

Holguín, Sandie (2002). *Creating Spaniards: Culture and National Identity in Republican Spain*. Madison: University of Wisconsin Press.

Hortmann, Wilhem (2002). 'Shakespeare on the political stage in the twentieth century'. In Stanley Wells and Sarah Stanton (eds.), *The Cambridge Companion to Shakespeare on Stage*. Cambridge: Cambridge University Press, pp. 212–29.

Huerta, Teresa (1987). 'Tiempo de iniciativa en la *Fuenteovejuna* de García Lorca'. *Hispania* 80.3: 480–87.

Iden, Peter (1976). 'Making an impact: Rainer Werner Fassbinder and the theatre'. In Tony Rayns (ed.), *Fassbinder*. London: BFI, pp. 17–23.

Iturrino, Calle (1938). *Lope de Vega y la clave de* Fuenteovejuna. Bilbao: Casa Dochao.

Jones, R. O. (1971). 'Poets and peasants'. In David A. Kossoff and José Amor y Vázquez (eds.), *Homenaje a William L. Fichter: estudios sobre el teatro antiguo hispánico y otros ensayos*. Madrid: Castalia, pp. 341–55.

Kirschner, Teresa J. (1977a). 'Sobrevivencia de una comedia: historia de la difusión de *Fuenteovejuna*'. *Revista canadiense de estudios hispánicos*, 1.3: 255–71.

——(1977b). 'Evolución de la crítica de *Fuenteovejuna* de Lope de Vega en el Siglo XX'. *Cuadernos hispanoamericanos*, 320–1: 450–65.

——(1979). *El protagonista colectivo en* Fuenteovejuna *de Lope de Vega*. Salamanca: Ediciones Universidad de Salamanca.

Labanyi, Jo (1989). *Myth and History in the Contemporary Spanish Novel*. Cambridge: Cambridge University Press.

Larson, Catherine (1991). '"Violent hierarchies": the deconstructive voice and writing undone in *Fuenteovejuna*'. In Catherine Larson, *Language and the Comedia: Theory and Practice*. London: Associated UP, pp. 109–25.

Larson, Paul E. (2001). '*Fuente Ovejuna*: history, historiography and literary history'. *Bulletin of Comediantes*, 53.2: 267–90.

Lauer, A. Robert (1997). 'The recovery of the repressed: a neo-historical reading of *Fuenteovejuna*'. In José A. Madrigal (ed.), *New Historicism and the Comedia: Poetics, Politics and Praxis*. Colorado: Society of Spanish and Spanish American Studies, pp. 15–28.

London, John (2000). 'Non-German drama in the Third Reich'. In John London (ed.), *Theatre Under the Nazis*. Manchester: Manchester University Press, pp. 222–61.

López Estrada, Francisco (1989). 'Músicas y letras: más sobre los cantares de *Fuente Ovejuna*'. *Cuadernos de teatro clásico*, 3: 45–52.

Loureiro, Angel. G. (2003). 'Spanish nationalism and the ghost of empire'. *Journal of Spanish Cultural Studies*, 4.1: 65–76.

Luca de Tena, Cayetano (1953a). 'Ensayo general: notas, experiencias y fracasos de un director de escena, III'. *Teatro*, 3: 45–48.

MacKay, Angus and Geraldine McKendrick (1986). 'The crowd in theater and the crowd in history: *Fuenteovejuna*'. *Renaissance Drama*, 17: 125–47.

Mancing, Howard (2006). 'See the play, read the book'. In Bruce McConachie and F. Elizabeth Hurt (eds.), *Performance and Cognition: Theatre Studies and the Cognitive Turn*. London: Routledge, pp. 189–206.

Marañon, Gregorio (1952). 'Más no el honor'. *Teatro*. 1: 4–5.

Marín, Juan María (2001). 'Introducción'. In Lope de Vega, *Fuente Ovejuna*, ed. Juan María Marín. Madrid: Cátedra, pp. 13–78.

Marquerie, Alfredo (1944b). '*Fuenteovejuna*', review. *ABC*, 13 October: 17.

——(1962). '*Fuenteovejuna* de Lope de Vega, en el Español', review. *ABC*, 1 May: 65.

Mayordomo, Alejandro (1993). *Vencer y convencer: educación y política, España 1936–1945*. Valencia: Universitat de València.

McCrary, William C. (1961). '*Fuenteovejuna*: its platonic vision and execution'. *Studies in Philology*, 58: 179–92.

McGrady, Donald (1993). 'Prólogo'. In Lope de Vega, *Fuente Ovejuna*, ed. Donald McGrady. Barcelona: Crítica, pp. 3–38.

McKendrick, Melveena (2000a). *Playing the King: Lope de Vega and the Limits of Conformity*. London: Tamesis.

Menéndez y Pelayo, Marcelino (1925). *Estudios sobre el teatro de Lope de Vega*, vol. 5. Madrid: Librería General de Victoriano Suárez.

Miller, Jonathan (1986). *Subsequent Performances*. London: Faber and Faber.

Molina, Margot (1999). 'La intifada del Siglo de Oro', review of *Fuente Ovejuna*. *El País*, 2 January.

Monleón, José (chair) (1987). 'Debate sobre la representación actual de los clásicos'. *PA*, 217 (supplement): 2–24.

——(1992). '*Fuenteovejuna* por Fassbinder. Ginebra: talento, escándalo y herejía'. *PA*, 243: 112–15.

Oliva, César (1999). 'La escena universitaria española'. In Luciano García Lorenzo (ed.), *Aproximación al teatro español universitario (TEU)*. Madrid: Consejo Superior de Investigaciones Científicas, Instituto de la Lengua Española, pp. 15–30.

——(2008). 'García Lorca y la puesta en escena de los clásicos'. *Gestos*, 45: 31–46.

Ostlund, DeLys (1997). *The Re-Creation of History in the Fernando and Isabel Plays of Lope de Vega*. New York: Peter Lang.

Parker, A. A. (1953). 'Reflections on a new definition of "Baroque drama"'. *BHS*, 30: 142–51.

Payne, Stanley G. (1961). *Falange: A History of Spanish Fascism*. Stanford: Stanford University Press.

Pedraza Jiménez, Felipe B. (2002). 'El resurgir escénico de las comedias de comendadores'. In Enrique García Santo-Tomás (ed.), *El teatro del Siglo de Oro ante los espacios de la crítica: encuentros y revisiones*. Frankfurt and Madrid: Iberoamericana and Vervuert, pp. 379–404.

Permán, José María (1939). '*Fuenteovejuna* en la provincia'. *ABC de Sevilla*, 1 January: 1–3, 5.

Pérez de Olaguer, Gonzalo (1999b). 'Las mujeres, unidas y todas a una', review of *Fuente Ovejuna*. *El periódico*, 23 May.

Pérez-Rasilla, Eduardo (1999). 'La situación del teatro universitario en España desde 1939 a 1967'. In Luciano García Lorenzo (ed.), *Aproximación al teatro español universitario (TEU)*. Madrid: Consejo Superior de Investigaciones Científicas, Instituto de la Lengua Española, pp. 31–53.

Pring-Mill, R. D. F. (1962). 'Sententiousness in *Fuente Ovejuna*'. *Tulane Drama Review*, 7.1: 5–37.

Ramírez de Arellano, Rafael (1901). 'Rebelión de Fuente Obejuna contra el Comendador mayor de Calatrava, Fernán Gómez de Guzmán'. *Boletín de la Real Academia de la Historia*, 39: 446–512.

Resina, Joan Ramón (2005). 'Whose hispanism? Cultural trauma, disciplined memory, and symbolic dominance'. In Mabel Moraña (ed.), *Ideologies of Hispanism*. Nashville: Vanderbilt University Press, pp. 160–86.

Rozas, José Manuel (1981). '*Fuente Ovejuna* desde la segunda acción'. In Alberto Navarro González (ed.), *Actas del I Simposio de Literatura Española*. Salamanca: Universidad de Salamanca, pp. 173–92.

Ruiz Ramón, Francisco (1997). *Paradigmas del teatro clásico español*. Madrid: Cátedra.

Sáenz de la Calzada, Luis (1976). '*La Barraca*': *Teatro Universitario*. Madrid: Biblioteca de la Revista de Occidente.

Santa-Cruz, Lola (1993). 'Cayetano Luca de Tena. Director del Teatro Español de 1942 a 1952'. In Andrés Peláez Martín (ed.), *Historia de los Teatros Nacionales (1939–1962)*. Madrid: CDT, pp. 69–79.

Santoveña Setién, Antonio (1994). *Menéndez Pelayo y las derechas en España*. Santander: Ayuntamiento de Santander y Ediciones de Librería Estudio.

Schwartz, Kessel (1969). *The Meaning of Existence in Contemporary Hispanic Literature (Hispanic-American Studies, no. 23)*. Miami: University of Miami Press.

Seliger, H. W. (1984). '*Fuenteovejuna* en Alemania: de la traducción a la falsificación. *Revista canadiense de estudios hispánicos*, 8.3: 381–403.

Shalhoub-Kevorkian, Nadera (2003). 'Re-examining femicide: breaking the silence and crossing "scientific" borders'. *Signs*, 28.2: 581–608.

Smith, Alan E. (1993). 'Ritual y mito en *Fuenteovejuna* de Lope de Vega y los casos de la honra'. *Sociocriticism*, 9.2: 141–66.

Spitzer, Leo (1955). 'A central theme and its structural equivalent in Lope's *Fuenteovejuna*'. *HR*, 23.4: 274–92.

Stainton, Leslie (1998). *Lorca: A Dream of Life*. London: Bloomsbury.

Strother, Darci L. (1999). *Family Matters: A Study of On- and Off-Stage Marriage and Family Relations in Seventeenth-Century Spain*. New York: Peter Lang.

Stroud, Matthew D. (2008). 'The play of means and ends: justice in Lope's *Fuenteovejuna*'. *Neophilologus*, 92.2: 247–62.

Suelto de Sáenz, Pilar G. (1964). 'El teatro universitario español en los últimos treinta años'. *Thesaurus: boletín del Instituto Caro y Cuervo*, 19.3: 543–57.

Swietlicki, Catherine (1992). 'Close cultural encounters: speech and writing in *Fuenteovejuna*'. *HR*, 60.1: 33–53.

Takahashi Nagasaki, Hiroyuki (2000). 'Una hipótesis sobre la escenificación de *Fuente Ovejuna*'. *La palabra y el hombre: revista de la Universidad Veracruzana*, 114: 37–47.

Tamayo, Nuria (1998). 'El CAT muestra su grito contra el poder'. *Diario de Andalucía*, 30 December: 29.

Tamayo, Victoriano (1935). 'Información teatral. Ante el tricentenario de Lope'. *La voz*, 2 February: 3.

Teatro Español (1944). 'Theatrical Programme for *Fuente Ovejuna*'. Madrid: Teatro Español.

Thompson, Michael (2007). *Performing Spanishness: History, Cultural Identity and Censorship in the Theatre of José María Rodríguez Méndez*. Bristol: Intellect Books.

Torrente (1956). 'Fuenteovejuna de Lope en Fuente Obejuna', review. *Arriba*, 8 July: 29.

Urzáiz Tortajada, Héctor (2006). 'Fuente Ovejuna CAT, 1999'. In Javier Huerta Calvo (ed.), *Clásicos entre siglos*. Madrid: CNTC, pp. 243–47.

Valverde, Fernando (2006). 'Un maestro del teatro'. *El País*, 8 February: 11.

Varey, J. E. (1976). *La inversión de valores en 'Fuenteovejuna'*. Santander: Universidad Internacional Menéndez Pelayo.

Vega Carpio, Lope de. (2001). *Fuente Ovejuna*, ed. Juan María Marín. Madrid: Cátedra.

Villegas Ruiz, Manuel (1990). Fuenteovejuna: *el drama y la historia*. Córdoba: Adisur.

Vossler, Karl (1940). *Lope de Vega y su tiempo*. Madrid: Revista de Occidente.

Wardropper, Bruce W. (1956). 'Fuente Ovejuna: el gusto and lo justo'. *Studies in Philology*, 53: 159–71.

——(1978). 'La comedia española del Siglo de Oro'. Appendix to Elder Olson, *Teoría de la comedia*. Barcelona: Ariel, pp. 181–242.

Weimer, Christopher B. (1996). 'Desire, crisis and violence in *Fuenteovejuna*: a Girardian perspective'. In Barbara Simerka (ed.), *El arte nuevo de estudiar comedias: Literary Theory and Golden Age Drama*. Cranbury: Bucknell and Associated UPs, pp. 162–86.

——(2000a). 'El arte de la refundición y (de) la protesta política: la comedia española en el Chile de Pinochet'. In Bárbara Mújica and Anita K. Stoll (eds), *El texto puesto en escena: estudios sobre la comedia del Siglo de Oro en honor a Everett W. Hesse*. Woodbridge: Támesis, pp. 193–204.

——(2000b). 'The politics of adaptation: *Fuenteovejuna* in Pinochet's Chile'. In Barbara Simerka and Christopher B. Weimer (eds.), *Echoes and Inscriptions: Comparative Approaches to Early Modern Spanish Literatures*. Lewisburg: Bucknell University Press, pp. 234–49.

Weiner, Jack (1982). 'Lope de Vega's *Fuenteovejuna* under the tsars, commisars and the second Spanish Republic (1931–39)'. *Annali Istituto Universitario Orientale Sezióne Romanza*, 24.1: 167–223.

Welles, Marcia L (2000). *Persephone's Girdle: Narratives of Rape in Seventeenth-Century Spanish Literature*. Nashville: Vanderbilt University Press.

Wheeler, Duncan (2011b). 'From the town with more theaters than taxis: Calderón, Lope and Tirso at the 2008 Almagro Festival (part one)'. *Comedia Performance*, 8.1: 151–200.

Worley Jr, Robert D. (2003). 'La inversión de funciones en *Fuente Ovejuna*'. In Aurelio González et al. (eds.), *Estudios del teatro áureo: texto, espacio y representación*. Mexico: Universidad Autónoma Metropolitana y Aitenso, pp. 199–209.

BRUCE W. WARDROPPER

Comic Illusion: Lope de Vega's
El perro del hortelano[†]

* * *

The obsession with the nature of reality is a characteristic of this, and every other, *comedia de capa y espada*.[1]

The title—reflecting the proverb about the dog in the manger who neither eats nor lets any other dog eat[2]—leads the spectator or reader directly to the mystery of Diana. Why does she behave so unpredictably? Teodoro, her humble lover, charges her with a dog-in-the-manger attitude to their relationship:

> When I don't love you, you grow mad,
> But when I do, you grow irate.
> You call me when I don't attend,
> But act offended when I do.
> You'd have me fathom your desires,
> But later treat me like a fool.
>
> (2330–35)

But her motivation remains inscrutable. The servant Anarda, in a dark image, expresses her mistress' fearful choleric irrationality:

> The surges wait till night to break
> When angry seas grow choppier.
>
> (159–60)

Over and over we hear of Diana's *secretos*, the unfathomable depths of her puzzling psyche. The superficial explanation, never quite lost sight of, is that she acts as she does because of what she naturally is: a dog in the manger, unintelligible in her selfish capriciousness.[3] It is true of course that she is a woman. This fact may also help explain her inconstancy to Teodoro. In this play all the characters, not excluding Diana, are somewhat misogynous, regarding woman as weak and fickle by nature.[4] Diana says of herself:

[†] From *Kentucky Romance Quarterly* 14.2 (1967): 103–11. Reprinted by permission of Taylor & Francis, Ltd. Quotations in Spanish have been translated by G.J. Racz.

1. Literally, a cloak-and-sword play—a term applied to the subgenre of *comedias* that deals with love among the nobility, i.e., those who would sport cloaks and swords [editor's note].

2. For variants and literary uses of the proverb see Kohler's introduction (B.—Signification du titre), pp. xv–xvii and Francis C. Hayes, "The Use of Proverbs as Titles and Motives in the *Siglo de Oro* Drama: Lope de Vega," *HR*, VI (1938), 305–323. According to the OED the English expression dates from 1573.

3. Cf. Teodoro to Diana: "This moral tale about the dog / That guards the manger comes to mind" (2193–94). Teodoro to Tristán: "by nature she's / The dog in the manger" (2296–97). Teodoro to Tristán: "Say, I don't think this dog's half bad; / It bites, but later licks the wound" (2355–56). Dorotea to Anarda: "It seems Diana's come to be / The dog in the manger, indeed. /—She took his hand with no great speed. /—No other eats, but nor does she" (3070–73). Dorotea to Anarda: "So, what will happen now? /—I own / We'll hardly see the countess play / The dog in the manger much more.—She'll eat, then? /—There's much food in store! /—Then let her burst with it, I say!" (3154–58).

4. Cf. Anarda: "You cruelly torment me to test / My secret-keeping in this way, / Aware that I'm a woman, too" (215–17). Diana to Anarda, on her inability to resist love: "Does not a woman yearn?" (1616)

> Besides that, I'm a woman prone
> To making errors in what I write
> And not the cleverest one in sight,
> (807–09)

Teodoro regards her as the personification of all womankind: "she's / That lady she had spoken of" (853–54). But he immediately corrects himself, recognizing that she, unlike most women, is discreet and free from ambition. Some other explanation of her conduct must be sought.

The dog-in-the-manger and anti-feminist theses are based on appearances and on the most superficial appeal to folk experience. They just will not do for the aristocratic Diana, with her hidden depths. In any case, appearances are deceptive. Gradually the people surrounding Diana come to understand her behavior as dictated by an interior conflict between love and honor. She loves passionately, but the object of her love—her secretary, a hired servant—is impossible, unattainable. To love him publicly, to want to marry him would be to expose herself to open ridicule. Such mockery would not just be inadmissible to her as a person. It would reflect badly on the good and noble name she has inherited from her forebears. It would deprive her family of the respect, the *honra*,[5] in which it is held. It would dishonor her. Her first concern must be for her name, however much she might wish to ignore it under the prompting of an irresistible love:

> Lest love, though general to all, disarm,
> My name comes first, commanding pride of place.[6]

Teodoro, though at times he forgets, is truly aware of Diana's dilemma:

> Accommodate
> Diana with some way to lift this threat
> Of honor lost, and we'll be married yet.
> Till then, though, fearing for her name, the more
> She burns, the more I'm coldly spurned.
> (2538–42)

Tristán, the most clear-sighted of the characters, puts it even more categorically:

> But when so grand a lady leaves
> Her lack of self-respect so bared,
> The conduct is most base, indeed.
> (2286–88)

It is not to be expected, then, that Diana will demean herself to the level of a servant. If a solution is to be found, it must be on the basis of the commoner's elevation.

---

5. Honor, reputation [editor's note].
6. 329–330. Diana is nevertheless capable of inveighing (probably but not certainly in a soliloquy) against her inherited aristocracy: "I curse my titled name / For not allowing me to claim / The one my fond soul would possess" (2650–52); and against honor (clearly in an aside): "Oh, curse you, honor!" (2623).

It is clear in any case that the solution to Diana's dilemma does not rest in her hands. The only alternatives open to her provide no solution at all: she might suppress her passion, or she might jeopardize her good name. If she can count on the cooperation of her lover, a further solution—the almost equally unsatisfactory one of cutting the Gordian knot—does indeed exist: Teodoro might go away, thus removing her object of temptation while protecting the good name of Belflor. For lack of any better idea, the lovers adopt this remedy. Teodoro is prepared to leave Naples for Spain from the time of his "ground put in between" sonnet (Act III, 2563–76) until the final denouement.

Now, if *El perro del hortelano* had been set entirely in the quasipastoral world with which the peasant plays (including *El villano en su rincón*)[7] begin, this solution would have been the only one possible. It is the essence of pastoral that the lovers exists on a desert island of love, insulated from the existential entanglements of parents, honor, everyday business: they are exempt from social commitments. But because the play is not set in an idealized world, Diana and Teodoro are not alone. They live in a fictitious Naples which, resembling the real one, reflects a crowded world of jealous rivals, paid assassins, Greek merchants, mailmen, markets, and busy streets. Their love exists in a social context. In society all men are members of one another; each act affects, and may be calculated to affect, another's life. Diana's and Teodoro's fate is thus determined not only by their own decisions but also by those of others. For this reason there are other possible solutions to Diana's dilemma than the ones already considered. Ricardo's and Federico's plot to have Teodoro killed would—if it had been successful—have provided another solution to her dilemma; Marcela's scheme for marrying Teodoro would—if he had acquiesced in it—have provided yet another. The solution finally arrived at—Tristán's fraudulent passing off of Teodoro as the noble Ludovico's long-lost son—was indeed successful, but only with the connivance of a dramatist who, since he was writing a comedy, needed a happy ending.

The plot, then, is contrived. But because the plot underpins the play, the whole drama is also contrived. This is true of all *comedias de capa y espada*. They are artifacts, artistically constructed, quite unlike the more problematic plays in which each event in the plot emerges naturally from the preceding events. The artificial quality of *El perro del hortelano* is evident at a first reading from its multiple sonnets, its rejection of verisimilitude in the fake ending, its introverted style.[8]

If Lope's serious plays, such as *Fuente Ovejuna*, convince by the natural sequence—the essentially historical sequence—of the events presented for our inspection, his comedies use other means. In them art imposes its will on nature. In the play under discussion Diana is "by nature . . . / The dog in the manger" (2297–98) cholerically rebellious by nature. Love, even between unequals, is "común naturaleza" (329),[9]

---

7. Lope's *The Countryman and the King* [editor's note].
8. The most important clues to the artificiality of the work are found in its self-conscious style. Here are some examples from Act I: the parody of a serious baroque *desengaño* (119–32). Marcela to Diana: "He translates feelings to his lips. /—He translates! There's a curious word" (260–61); Tristán: "All lovers magnify / Their troubles" (366–67); Diana's obliging Teodoro to repeat his banal *requiebro* to Marcela (1055–65); her questioning of trite pseudo-Petrarchan imagery (1113–17).
9. Common nature [editor's note].

thwarted by, yet capable of transcending, the artificial barriers created by social distinctions between the classes. The characters artfully control their movements and their speech, but their natural sentiments are revealed by their blushes.[1] Nature is ever ready to burst out of the confines imposed on it by the artificiality of society. But it never succeeds. Society, with its arts of politics, of government, and of etiquette, keeps a firm hand on nature's reins. The magnetic field between art and nature is not the least of the dynamic tensions of the baroque.

It may be said, then, that the social convention regarding the inequality of man, seen from the perspective of natural love, is artificial. But, as Tristán observes. "All know-how conquers love in turn" (380), including the lesser forms of art which we call artificiality. In the *comedia de capa y espada* one art regularly defeats another in order to rescue nature. The active skillful art of Tristán's deception overcomes the inert, stagnant artificiality of a social convention. He contrives his *engaño*[2] in such a way as to eliminate the *appearance* of social incompatibility between Diana and Teodoro. Teodoro will appear, as a result of this artificial trick, to be as noble as Diana. Society, the product of the art of civilization, is always satisfied if appearances are saved. But will love—"común naturaleza"—be equally satisfied? No, love and nature will make no accommodation with the social arts because they flourish on truth. Given his sincere nature, Teodoro must not practice on his beloved Diana the art of telling falsehoods. Yet civilization, however false the premises on which it is founded, is a useful art. Diana and Teodoro, not being fictional shepherds, cannot survive—and their love cannot survive—without it. So Diana, who is herself not deceived by social artifices, decides to conspire with Teodoro to perpetuate Tristán's trick on society, to add this extra strand to the web of society's self-deception. Tristán's hoax, once it has been generally accepted by the Neapolitans, will be reduced to the same inert, unrenewed status as any other convention.

Out of Tristán's artistic lie, however, a natural truth emerges. Art, when successful, acts as a catalyst to precipitate a new intuition about nature. At the same time that Diana associates herself with a public lie to preserve a private truth, she perceives the "nobleza natural" of her lover. Teodoro tells her:

> Though the count believes
> That I'm his son and we could wed,
> Both nobles now, to live out all
> Our days in happiness henceforth,
> My natural nobility
> Forbids imposture of this sort
> Since I am by my nature one
> Who only can profess the truth.

> DIANA You've been both wise and foolish, then:
> Wise in declaring this to me,

---

1. For example, Teodoro: "a trace / Of shyness made her cheek turn red" (867–68). And Diana to Teodoro: "You're blushing, Teodoro. Look! / The color in your cheeks is proof / Of sentiments your tongue denies" (1101–03).
2. Trick [editor's note].

As it reveals a noble soul,
But foolish in that you assume
I wouldn't marry you for that,
For now I've just the right excuse
To overlook your humble state
Since pleasure's not in noble parts
But in the mind once it conforms
To what a person's wishes are.

(3290–97, 3302–11)

This is Diana's instant of epiphany. Nobility, she realizes, does not have to do with society's recognition of an accident of birth but with character, the spiritual product of birth and life. Nature reveals its truth, as does man, by its blushing, its "color." Teodoro's nature is thus liberated from the artificiality to which it has been enthralled. The true nobility of nature triumphs over the artificial nobility which is all that society can admit.

So Teodoro tells Diana the truth about his humble origin when he might have feigned a noble birth as Ludovico's son. In so doing, he risks a rebuff from the Countess in spite of his overweening ambition. More than anything else he wanted to rise in the world. It was by no means certain until near the end of the play that his love for Diana was greater than his loathing of his lowly status as a secretary. To him too comes a revelation: he is prepared to sacrifice a feasible, though feigned, social improvement to a sincere natural love. Teodoro's ambition goes, in the play, under the names of *imaginación* and *pensamiento*.[3] His soliloquy to ambition discloses a magnificent dynamic ruthlessness:

Don't flee me, fancy, brave new thought
Upon imagination's wind!
You're crazy and undisciplined!
I laugh at what my folly's sought
But fear my mind is overwrought,
So slow down while I press your speed.
If my intent is daft, indeed,
I see but what my mind espies:
To come away with such a prize,
A little daring's what I'll need.

(1278–87)

He plans to create, as a playwright might on paper, a new role for himself on the stage of life, that of the husband of the Countess of Belflor. Tristán—the schemer, the organizer of the natural, the artist—insists that the creative imagination can be disciplined by a kind of spiritual exercise; one may use an artist's selectivity on the material offered by the imagination (453–502). By thinking only of the ugly parts present even in a beautiful woman, for example, one may channel love into an alternate route. Natural love may be replaced by an artificial independence. Teodoro, the spontaneous man of nature, rejects this theory; he knows he is incapable of such a calculated plan (503–505). It therefore falls to Tristán's

3. Imagination and thought [editor's note].

lot to impose the formalism of art on Teodoro's highflying ambitious imagination. The final resolution will be the result of a magical fusion of Teodoro's imagination and Tristán's art. The denouement, the betrothal of the Countess and the secretary, may properly be called a work of art in itself. A truth based on a lie, it is a half-believed fiction, a fictional ending to a work of fiction.

The artistic means employed by Tristán to accomplish this fictional ending is masquerading or impersonation, that is to say, the artistic means of the theatre itself. He changes his own personality artificially with each change of circumstance: at one time or another he is the servant of a secretary, a hired assassin, and a Greek merchant. Like an actor, he changes his style, his speech, and his manner to accord with each part he plays; like an actor, he controls these changes of personality with art, the histrionic art. Teodoro also changes character: now he is a servant, now a nobleman; now an ambitious social-climber, now a sincere lover. Unlike an actor, however, he effects these changes naturally in accordance with his changes of whim and circumstance. Teodoro's various roles are not the result of an actor's masquerading. When he puts away his servant's clothes at the end to don the habit of a nobleman, it is a poetically symbolic act, the outward recognition of an inner transformation. Tristán, by changing clothes, merely changes appearances. Whether wearing his filthy old hat at the beginning or his new finery at the tavern or his pseudo-Greek costume at Ludovico's house, he is still the same old rascal at heart. He deals in appearances and superficialities. This is his kind of art or at least his conception of art. Yet, by applying to Teodoro the superficiality of a new appearance, that of nobility, he succeeds unwittingly in transforming his master into a new man. He has invoked the alchemy of artistic creation. Teodoro, once a vain, lying, ambitious philanderer, has become at the end of the play an integral man, honest, truthful, noble. As in all poetic creation, art has transformed nature.

This artistry within the action corresponds to the artistry with which Lope de Vega manipulated the action from the outside. The poetic world which at the outset he presents to us is exempt from the baroque doubt and chiaroscuro which, as we have seen, beset the opening scene in serious works. Each character in *El perro del hortelano* knows his station in society and the role assigned to him in the theatre of life. The reality of sense perception is affirmed in a pleasant burlesque of standard baroque *desengaño*. When Diana muses about the conversion of the feathers of Tristán's hat into the dust of mortality, Fabio makes the comparison *de rigueur* about Icarus' prideful scorching. Diana then dashes cold water on this overdone comparison: "You turn my mood to jest this way. / We've much to do to solve this crime" (133–134). But if these feathers of a servant's hat were not "resolved into dust" (121), by the beginning of Act III men in love *are*: "remains . . . laid beneath that ground" (2575). A world of such utter certainty that perceived objects are true starts to disintegrate. By the end of the play it is a world of total uncertainty for those who are most intimately involved in the problem of Teodoro's nobility: Teodoro himself, Diana, her suitors, and the reader or spectator. It is considered highly likely by all of these that Teodoro may be Ludovico's son. The rest of Naples is sure that he is. Only Tristán knows that he is not, and even he expresses some doubt:

TRISTÁN   It couldn't possibly be right
That Teodoro is his son?

FURIO   A lie like that could have a grain
Of truth in it, so don't be shocked.

                                        (2901–04)

The thin line dividing truth from falsehood is as hard to distinguish at
the end of *El perro del hortelano* as it is at the beginning of *La vida es
sueño*. Even the artist may doubt the artificiality of his creation.

   To persuade the reader to accept fiction as reality is the ultimate objective of all who write fiction. In other words, the fiction writer, to be successful, must magically turn illusion into reality. Tristán accomplishes
this transmutation in the fictional world of *El perro del hortelano*—in the
"real life" of fiction. Lope de Vega achieves the same thing in the "real
life" of the theatre, inducing into the imagination of his spectator or
reader the acceptance of a purely imaginary reality. Tristán in the poetic
world of the play performs the same function as Lope de Vega in the real,
or perhaps not so real, world in which he lived, the baroque world of
time, with its shifting appearances, and its uncertainty about the line
separating truth and falsehood. In this world, so accurately represented
at the end of the comedy, only moral values ("nobleza natural"[4] as opposed
to social appearances) are valid. Though the revelation of this true nature
of the temporal world pursues a different pattern from that used in the
serious plays, the lesson is the same: the world is an illusion, but this fact
is no excuse for behaving immorally.[5]

MERCEDES MAROTO CAMINO

"Esta sangre quiero": Secrets and Discovery in Lope's *El perro del hortelano*[†]

Mostly interpreted as a work which confronts the contradictions of the
Baroque code of honor, *El perro del hortelano* is also a play about the process of discovery.[1] Indeed, the theme of discovery runs through the
argument and, as will be seen below, associates the play's structure and
layers of meaning. The multiple aspects of the discovery *topos* help organize
the play from its beginning, when the Countess of Belflor, Diana, searches
in the dark for the intruders who have dared to enter her chambers. More
importantly, issues related to the revelation of secrets also implicate the

---

4. Natural nobility [editor's note].
5. After this article was submitted for publication Roy O. Jones, "*El perro del hortelano* y la visión
   de Lope," *Filología*, X (1964), 135–142 has appeared (actually in 1966). Jones' interpretation of
   Diana as a perverter of the natural order of things is correct as far as it goes; but it does not
   grapple with what seem to me to be more fundamental questions raised by the play.
† From *Hispanic Review* 71.1 (Winter 2003): 15–30. Reprinted by permission of the author and
   the University of Pennsylvania Press. ("Esta sangre quiero": I want this blood.) Quotations in
   Spanish have been translated by G. J. Racz.
1. *El perro del hortelano* was published in 1618. Morley and Bruerton think it was written
   between 1613 and 1615.

audience members who, at the play's end, are called upon to be accessories to the maintenance of "el secreto de Teodoro."[2]

From beginning to end, then, *El perro* foregrounds *anagnorisis* in its Aristotelian dimension, especially stressing the welcome transition between ignorance and knowledge.[3] There is, however, not a unified process of discovery concerning a single protagonist. Diana, Teodoro, Tristán, and Ludovico all deploy various strategies to uncover or discover the world of the other and of the self at various stages of the play. These "discoveries" ultimately lead to the harmonious resolution of the conflict presented. Discovery and knowledge, then, act as a means to overcoming the constraints of a code of honor that stifles the developing passion of Diana and her secretary, Teodoro. But, as will be shown in this article, to discover and to uncover, in this case, do not lead to the vindication of either truth or reality.

Although discovery, in the sense of recognition and access to knowledge, is important in *El perro*, other aspects of this process are equally central to the play. Discovery in *El perro* is extended to embrace also the recognition both of oneself and of the role and situation of others. It is, consequently, interesting to note that probably the more important discovery of the play is the result of Tristán's invention of Teodoro's wealthy parentage. Along the way to this fabrication and Ludovico's *anagnorisis*, however, some important sacrifices are made. The more prominent of these are, for a contemporary audience, Marcela's feelings and future. Sacrifices are also made on the moral level, where truth is the first and the last victim of the play's "happy" discoveries. Nevertheless, in spite of these sacrifices, as Pilar Miró's recent rendition of the play shows, a director can manage to keep the audience's sympathy with its main protagonists.[4] Although switching our allegiance from Marcela's plight to Diana's and Teodoro's confusing relationship, a skillful director may have viewers endorse and even enjoy the play's denouement.

Suitably for a play dealing with discovery, recognition, and deception both within the play and between the play and its audience, the initial scene reveals that appearances are not what they seem. When searching for those intruders whose presence within her chambers threatens to undermine her reputation, Diana stresses the dimensions of her deception. Using her own sense of vision as a way of describing the access to knowledge, she informs her servants that the scene is not the product of her own imagination. She then insists and qualifies her assertion that she has not been a victim of Baroque "desengaño" [disillusion] and has seen neither a

---

2. Pring-Mill highlights the role of *anagnorisis* and (mis)recognition in the construction of the play. He describes the "delicious irony of the ending" which, he believes, is precisely one of the play's main successes (xxviii). [Teodoro's secret—editor's note.]

3. The role played by *anagnorisis* in the final scenes has been observed by Rothberg, who traces it to Aristotle's precepts regarding Greek tragedy:

> Anagnorisis is . . . as old as Aristotle's analysis of Greek tragedy in the *Poetics* where he defines it along with peripeteia in chap 11: "A Discovery is, as the very work implies, a change from ignorance to knowledge, and thus to either love or hate, in the personages marked for good or evil fortune. The finest form of Discovery is one attended by Peripeties." (95)

4. Pilar Miró directed and wrote the script of this movie, released in 1995 before she died. The roles of Diana, Teodoro, Marcela, and Tristán were played by Emma Suárez, Carmelo Gómez, Ana Duato, and Fernando Conde respectively. The film was awarded seven Goya awards, including Best Director for Miró.

dream nor a shadow: "I'm sure I didn't see a ghost / Or dream what passed before my eyes" (11–12). Diana is determined to find out the identity of the men who use their own capes to disguise themselves. Quite like Don Juan, who will use Mota's cape to try to usurp his place in Doña Ana's bed, these men depart from a possible scene of seduction covering themselves with a cape. Both a sign of their class and an indicator of their masculinity, the cape also underscores their deceitfulness.[5] Not only do Teodoro and his servant run away under cover of darkness but they "kill" the light on their way in a scene which is echoed in Don Juan's seduction of Isabella in the palace.[6] The "sombrero" that is used to suffocate the torch will, Diana believes, provide a clue to the discovery of the intruders' secret identity: "He won't remain beyond my ken: / The culprit's hat had plumes on it / And may have fallen when he took / Those steps to flee" (80–83).[7] The hat, however, reveals to Diana something she was not prepared for: the poverty of its bearer. As will be emphasized later on in the play, the owner of the pitiful hat that disabuses Diana is one of her own servants or, rather, a servant of her own secretary, Teodoro.

More effective than the hat as a means to discovery is Diana's loyal servant, Anarda. In a private conversation, Anarda, who quickly names the culprits of the intrusion, justifies her own loquacity by making it a feature of her own sex: "You cruelly torment me to test / My secret-keeping in this way, / Aware that I'm a woman, too" (215–17). No "tormento" has, however, been necessary for Anarda to show her disregard for a fellow worker, Marcela. Anarda willingly reveals to Diana that the visitor was courting one of her own private servants, her protégée and relation Marcela. Also, Anarda informs Diana that Marcela's suitor is precisely a person Diana would be expected to trust completely, her own secretary Teodoro.[8]

Both a writer and a keeper of the household "secrets," Teodoro holds an office that is more intimate than that of a modern secretary. As the private letters of Diana corroborate thereafter, the secretary is a servant holding a privileged position regarding the private and public information of the household. Not only was the private secretary important as a keeper of the household's secret documents, but his role was often associated with the very items related to secrecy such as locks, keys, and closets. As Richard Rambuss has illustrated with reference to contemporary manuals, secretaries were urged to keep under lock and key a household's "hidden secrets." Angel Day, the writer of a letterwriting manual entitled *The English Secretary*, remarks that a secretary is, above all, "a keeper or conserver of the secret unto him committed" (qtd. in Rambuss 314).

The same notions are stressed by the Venetian Francesco Sansovino in another letterwriting manual, *Il Secretario* (1564). According to Adam Stewart, "Sansovino devotes the opening pages to a brief theoretical outline of the ideal secretary, noting that he must be faithful and secretive,

---

5. In *El burlador* Don Juan uses Mota's cape to disguise himself before Mota's fiancée, Doña Ana. Mota offers Don Juan his cape (1524–25) and Catalinón hints towards the outcome of the event when he tells Don Juan: "Echaste la capa al toro" ["you've thrown your cape at the bull"— editor's note] (1541).

6. In the very first scene of the play Don Juan says to Isabella "Mataréte la luz yo" ["I'll kill that light"—editor's note] (13) and only then Isabella realises he is not her fiancé, Octavio.

7. "Plumas" [plumes] is the first reference to the myth of Icarus, which underscores the play. Herrero studies in detail the development of this myth throughout the play (56–58).

8. Weber de Kurlat classes *El perro* as a "comedia de secretario" [secretary play] (348) and compares it with *Arminda celosa* (347).

serving his prince not only with his body and his secretarial skills but also with his soul" (84). Secretaries should also ensure that secrets are kept as though they are precious commodities, that is, locked away safely. In the words of the Clerk to the English Privy Council, Robert Beale, secrets belonged in "a speciall Cabinett, whereoff he [the secretary] is himself to keepe the Keye, for his signetts, Ciphers and secrett intellingences" (qtd. in Rambuss 320). This advice was taken literally by Day, who associates the secretary's own body with the household's private administration, documents, and the very spaces where these may be kept. The secretary is seen by Day as nothing "but the closet, whereof another hath both the key, use and commandment . . . a thick plated doore, where no man may enter, but by the locke which is the tongue, and that to be of such efficacies, as whereof no counterfeity key should bee able to make a breache" (qtd. in Rambuss 321).

The secretary's work and body are thus feminized in that they are under the control of the master, normally a man, and are also to be controlled by him. The items associated with women, with the closet, and with the secretary are door, key, and lock, which are all icons of a long tradition dating from the medieval era. The control necessary to keep secrets echoes the mode of thought underlying the concern with female sexuality. Woman's chastity or virginity, many believed, ought to be protected precisely as a household secret: under lock and key. According to this view, female chastity is associated with a fortress, a door, the *porta clausa*, or an enclosed garden, the *hortus conclusus*.[9] Interestingly, these are symbols pertaining to the Virgin Mary's inviolate virginity and perhaps find a source in the Song of Songs.[1] Within this tradition, female virginity is perceived as a closed chamber, much as Diana wishes hers had remained at the beginning of the play. The keeping of secrets and secret places can therefore be read as the protection of female "secrets," that is to say, female genitalia and, by implication, their sexuality.

The feminization of the "keeper of secrets," the secretary, and the masculinization of the master are clearly apparent in *El perro*. This role reversal is corroborated by Teodoro's attitude throughout the play, as well as by Diana's threats and power displays. As Roy O. Jones has observed, "Mientras Diana muestra la iniciativa de un hombre, Teodoro revela un cierto carácter femenino" (141).[2] This femininity is remarked upon by Tristán, who, commenting on the changeability of Teodoro's affections towards Marcela, associates it with female mutability: "Well, this change of heart / Lets Tedoro act the part / Of certain women"

9. Strong traces the representation of the *hortus conclusus* to the Song of Solomon: "The *hortus conclusus* is a symbol of the Immaculate Conception and is borrowed from the Song of Solomon . . . Medieval paintings and illuminations depict the Virgin and Child seated within this garden surrounded by the horticultural attributes of the Virgin: the violet, the lily, the white and red rose" (49). This motif, as Fumerton has noted, recurs in renaissance and early modern representations of the Annunciation to the Virgin Mary: "two topoi are commonly depicted in perspective behind the foreground scene in annunciations: the enclosed garden (*hortus conclusus*) and closed door (*porta clausa*)" (149).

1. Ziegler has suggested that "From St. Bernard in the twelfth century, the Virgin was associated with images of enclosure—the bride chamber, the door, and the garden—taken from the Song of Songs" (76–77).

2. While Diana displays a man's initiative, Teodoro reveals a certain feminine character [editor's note].

(1489–91). The same inversion of gender roles is experienced by Diana when she tells Teodoro that she will pay dearly for his blood "So I can keep dear blood near me" (2341). Tristán clarifies Diana's words and deeds a few lines below, explaining to Teodoro how Diana has literally made him a "maiden" who can be "made" and "unmade" by his master's power: "Don't rue that virgin nose she slapped; / Deflowering it has cost her dear" (2353–54).

Within Lope's contemporary society, feminization amounts to a personal debasement. However, the feminization and humiliation of the job of the secretary is not the only debasement to which Teodoro is submitted. His intelligence and abilities are treated contemptuously in various ways throughout the play. * * *

Tristán's poverty, stressed in the scene of the hat at the beginning of the play, is also a means of reminding us of Teodoro's own lack of financial means. In fact, Tristán goes on to say directly that the *criado*[3] is the mirror of the master, thereby highlighting the poverty of Teodoro and the meanness of their master, Diana. Lope presents these ideas through Tristán's address to Diana as follows:

> *   *   *
>
> Now you'll agree an honest man's
> Remiss to leave his footman frayed.
> A servant is his looking glass,
> Reflecting shield and harbinger
> So can't be shabbily attired.
>
> (606–10)

Tristán's words, Herrero observes, are Lope's way of presenting the particular as the universal and criticizing the contemporary treatment of intellectuals.

Tristán's ensuing tirade corroborates Herrero's assertion when he goes on to add that things are not what they used to be. The lowly position occupied by the arts in his contemporary society comes under fire in the following terms:

> An expert painter, doing all
> To turn a lifelike portrait out,
> Will use each last bit of his skill,
> Yet any half-wit can pronounce
> The striking likeness valueless.
>
> (629–33)

Teodoro, as he himself recognizes, owes his life to belonging to Diana's household. But, as Tristán insists, masters can be ignorant, not valuing the intelligence of their servants or paying their skills according to their merits. In Herrero's words, Tristán is insisting here that "las clases medias intelectuales, los escritores, los artistas no son pobres por ser disolutos

---

3. Servant [editor's note].

bohemios, sino simplemente porque la riquísima nobleza, poderosa y necia, no les paga" (67).[4]

It is, therefore, suitable in this context of dependence, servitude, and property that Diana feel the invasion of her private chamber to be a double violation. Firstly, because of the obvious concern with her own security and reputation; and, secondly, because the intimate involvement of her own, private secretary is a potential disclosure of her "secrets." Diana abhors the possible revelation of her "secret" chamber as well as the loss of the exclusive control over the possessor of those secrets. However self-interested and arrogant, Diana's initial fit of jealousy is not as whimsical as it may appear to contemporary readers. The invasion of her chamber also amounts to a potential violation of Diana's own body, that is, her virginity, as well as her own intimacy, subjectivity and, above all, her private property. Therefore, she does not hesitate to qualify the intrusion into her rooms as a "traición."[5]

The paradigm created from the play's onset clearly associates the entrance into private rooms with the violation of the inner self. The gravity of the situation, along with the revelation of the identity of the intruder, make Diana argue for secrecy in Marcela's and Teodoro's affair. In an apparently contradictory statement, Diana argues to Marcela for the need to keep their relationship secret. At the same time, however, Diana offers herself as the guarantor of the legitimacy of the relationship and as a go-between to arrange Marcela's marriage to Teodoro. Although the audience has not been given reasons to doubt Diana's sincerity at this point in the play, her confusing words to Marcela arouse suspicion. Diana invites Marcela to keep their affair secret while claiming she will legitimize it and allow it to continue: "You, in the interim, might pursue / Your courtship more judiciously" (310–11). Diana finally believes that her own privacy and reputation rest on the secrecy of Marcela's and Teodoro's love affair and opts for the radical measure of imprisoning Marcela. She now holds the key that confers her power over the bodies of her servants and orders Dorotea:

> take
> This key and leave Marcela pent
> Inside my chambers a few days,
> As she's some needlework to do.
> (1011–14)

Somehow more cautious is Teodoro, who promptly attempts to refuse Diana's invitation to further disclose her "secrets" when she asks him to read the contents of a sonnet she has written. Diana coyly requests that he judge the poem of a female friend of hers who is in love with a man below her station. To this, Teodoro answers that he does not wish to "see" and

---

4. Herrero further illustrates the nobility displayed by Teodoro regarding his profession (66–68) and associates this with Lope's own position as secretary of the Duke of Sessa. Lope's financial strictures were often so extreme that he had to appeal directly to the generosity of the dissolute Sessa (69–70). [The intellectual middle classes, the writers, the artists are not poor because they are dissolute bohemians, but simply because the richest of nobles, powerful and ignorant, do not pay them—editor's note.]

5. Early in the play, Diana asks: "who / Committed treason by this deed" (23–24), and Anarda also refers to the intrusion as "treachery" (195).

thus know its contents: "I've no need to review your turn / Of phrase. Please give it to your friend" (527–28).

Secrecy and discovery thus figure at the forefront of Diana's assertion of her authority over and above her servants. This is also corroborated in the allusion to a secret "book of remedies" (676),[6] which she deploys to threaten Tristán. * * *

Diana suggests to Tristán that she can seize the occasion to take away not only his opportunities but his own life-blood. In this way, she emphasizes her primacy over her servants' time as well as life, as she has already shown in her tyrannical decision to imprison Marcela. Diana underscores her dominion over "ocasión"[7] when she offers herself to Teodoro. As she does, she falls in front of him in a scene full of sexual innuendo. When Teodoro hesitates to intervene and offers his covered arm, Diana, again assuming a masculine, dominant role, asks him to uncover himself. At the same time, however, she threatens him not to reveal her own weakness. Her own fall, Diana tells Teodoro, has to be treated with discretion if he wants to raise himself above his status: "So listen to this sound advice: / I'd guard the secret of my fall / If ever it's your hope to rise" (1170–72).

Interwoven with the notions of secrecy and discovery is that of the truth. The enlightenment of "la verdad," it is expected, ought to be the end result of the process of discovery that underlies the play's argument. Throughout the play, then, the concepts of truth, reality and discovery are closely related to "traición," "engaño," "sospecha," and "confesión."[8] These terms appear repeatedly and are even sequentially alternated in the key dialogue between Diana and Anarda early in the play. To Anarda's qualification of the invasion of Diana's chamber as a "traición" (196), Diana answers: "Wait. Step aside. As I reflect / Upon your answer, I suspect—/ Unless this story was designed / To fool—our breacher came to meet / The maid with whom he trysts inside" (198–202). Anarda then replies that she is telling the truth (206) and Diana describes her statement as a "confesión" (213).

Teodoro also uses truth as a means of presenting his own honesty. After his less-than-honorable treatment of Marcela we are, however, far from taking him at his word when he contrasts his "verdad" with the possible "engaño" or "mentira" [deception or lie] he could coin. He protests to Diana that:

> I wouldn't lie to you on this,
> Though I might well invent some ruse,
> For nothing in the world enlists
> A highborn person's favor more
> Than speaking plainly, I'm convinced.
>
> (988–92)

Besides the obvious sycophancy implied by his calling Diana "una persona discreta," our suspicion is heightened when Teodoro answers Diana's question about the way to flatter women "Come, Tedoro, how do men / Woo women with their flowery speech?" [1050–51]). He replies bluntly

---

6. The editor of the play, Armiño, glosses "libro de secretos" as "libro de recetas médicas" [book of medical remedies—editor's note] (71n).
7. Chance, opportunity [editor's note].
8. "La verdad": truth; "traición": betrayal; "engaño": deception; "sospecha": suspicion; "confesión": confession [editor's note].

that, when dealing with matters of the heart, truth itself needs to be dressed, that is to say, "covered," in lies. What is more, Teodoro insists that anything that rings true can only be remotely hinted at. In a statement deserving of Don Juan, Teodoro remarks that a man conquers women by presenting himself falsely, as though he were loving and pleading. Nevertheless, Teodoro confesses, the seducer is obviously lying to the woman: "Well, when you love, you have to beg, / And wrap a thousand lies around / The truth, should this be voiced or not" (1052–54). * * * [T]he direct references to lies show Teodoro as a dishonest would-be lover for any woman. Such attitude does not go unnoticed by Diana, who hopes to inspire (or command) a different response than what Teodoro presents as a rather staple and hypocritical seductive technique.

Teodoro is also at his lowest when, to Diana's question about how a high-class woman could enjoy a man of an inferior social class, he unhesitatingly proposes "engaño" as the best alternative. What is more, he insists, by means of this deception, the woman can disguise her identity and "enjoy" the man she wants: "Then let her come up with some ruse / By which she'd, say, in some disguise, / Delight in him" (1125–27). Sexual innuendo notwithstanding, this dialogue already shows this couple to have some important moral flaws that can work to distance the audience from their predicament. Their errors are, however, human and no malice is shown either by a Countess trying to combat her amorous desire for her servant or a servant aspiring to "medrar"[9] in a difficult social environment. However, their selfishness and moral laxity will be only partly corrected during a play that ends with both lovers pledging to keep secret the very lie that enables them to marry without flaunting social expectations.[1]

Cleverness and cunning are also confused when Teodoro recurs to the image of the classical navigator Ulysses. First, Teodoro remembers Ulysses when he feels he may be tricked: "Is it so odd a pair of eyes / This utterly enravishing / Should lead to thoughts so ill-advised / When they'd have fooled Ulysses, too?" (1701–04). In a further allusion to Ulysses as the spirit of "engaño" Teodoro commends Tristán's resourcefulness in devising a trick to take him out of his predicament. Tristán questions Teodoro about what he will answer if he is able to provide a remedy for the situation: "Now what / If I took care of that?" (2542–43). Teodoro replies that, by so doing, Tristán is acquiring not just Ulysses's technique but his spirit: "I'd swear you bore / More wiles in you than old Ulysses" (2543–44).

Truth and secrecy also underline the subplot surrounding the suitors of the Countess, Conde Federico and Marqués Ricardo. Secrecy is involved in their ill-fated choice of Teodoro's would-be killer, who happens to be his own servant, Tristán. Their decision to murder Teodoro is aimed at keeping secret Diana's potential fall so that Diana's bloodline (and that of her relation, Ricardo) may remain untainted. Federico voices the concern with decorum and contemporary notions of honor when he enlists his rival to prevent the secret from being revealed:

9. To do well, to prosper [editor's note].
1. Rothberg sees the ending as a commentary on the contemporary convention of "happy endings." In Rothberg's own words: "the solution is a comment on the hollowness of the honor concept as public reputation" (89).

> Before all Naples starts to prate
> About this base indignity
> And your good name's dragged through the mud—
> If true, if false, it's all the same—
> The man must die. (2398–2402)

As with Teodoro's and Diana's before, Federico's words emphasize that secrecy is needed regardless of whether the possible discovery would reveal a truth or a lie. Federico therefore underlines the importance of blood and family honor, the very notions that hinder Diana's resourcefulness in this play. However, Federico foregrounds a different notion of blood than the outlook given by Diana who, only in the previous scene, has referred to Teodoro's blood as an item of consumption when she carries away Teodoro's bloodied handkerchief.

This crucial scene positions Diana as a bloodthirsty woman who doubly subjects her servant, Teodoro, firstly to her strikes and, secondly, to her compliance. It is, therefore, suitable that Lope associate Diana at this point with the ruthless, mythical women of Classical Rome. Diana's unbridled sexual desire is emphasized when Lope matches her with Faustina, the wife of Roman emperor Marcus Aurelius. Faustina was given the blood of a suitor by her husband in the belief that only this would soothe her luxurious passion:

> Marcus Aurelius, men claimed,
> Dispelled his wife Faustina's itch—
> Her gladiator lover slain—
> By giving her his blood to drink.
> But Roman remedies are frowned
> Upon today in Christian lands. (1130–35)

The sadistic overtones of this comparison have been rightly underscored by Herrero. * * * Herrero goes on to propose that, by comparing Diana with Faustina, Teodoro is censoring her desire to kill him. To kill the unlucky social inferiors who are love objects is, Lope suggests, a behavior proper of corrupted Roman aristocrats. Thus, by threatening him, Diana is debasing herself to their level and is not only acting like a pagan (as opposed to a true Christian) but playing out overtly the myth of female sexual insatiability.

Diana corroborates the notion that she can be as cruel as her Roman predecessors up to the end of the play. With the action rapidly approaching its happy ending, she realizes that Tristán holds the key to revealing the secret of the plot he has engineered to raise the status of Teodoro. There is no hesitation when Diana suggests to Teodoro a possible solution to keep Tristán silent: kill him,

> And, just to make sure Tristán keeps
> Our secret hidden all our days,
> [I] will bid the guards, once he's asleep,
> To throw his body in the well
> And have him drowned. (3313–17)

To a surprised Tristán, who is hidden behind the nearest bush, Diana's words convey an unfair treatment for his generous solution to the lovers' dilemma. Diana will literally bury Teodoro's secret by physically interring its maker: the garden's well will hearse Tristán for ever. She easily relents, however, when listening to Tristán's own protestations, but she assures herself that he will remain silent, reminding him that, as the maker of the plot, Tristán could be liable to punishment by others too: "But you will need to keep this scheme / A secret, though it was all yours" (3331–32).

Tristán's invention is that of a "noble" Teodoro who, thanks to a lie, finds himself a wealthy father. Old Ludovico, whose vision is blurred by his desire, finally "knows" his son, when he sees him. The knowledge he has acquired by Tristán's verbal entrapment (and his own visual and cognitive deception) is, however, as false as the eyesight that sees nobility written in Teodoro's face when he exclaims: "God bless you, what a noble mien you have! / How finely Nature stamped gentility, / Brave Teodoro, on that high-born brow!" (3114–16).

Like the face of Teodoro, writing and interpreting are, in this play, subject to endless deceptions and ironies. Not the least of these is the fact that the audience is urged to become an accomplice in keeping Teodoro's secret: "And so, dear public, on this note, / I beg you to keep mum this truth / That Tedoro's secret holds" (3378–80). * * * Like Teodoro, the audience is free to make what they like of the play's discoveries for they have the freedom of choice that comes from knowing, seeing, and securing one's own secrets.

The ideas expounded in this last scene sum up the correspondences I have been tracing throughout this article between the various dimensions of the notions of discovery and secrecy that inform the play. These range, as I have suggested, from intellectual and sexual "knowledge" to the undertones and complexities of the "sangre." The blood that gives Diana her social status is the same blood against which she rebels in her love for Teodoro. At the same time, this blood is extracted and revealed in the scene of the "rape" of Teodoro and is paid for by Diana in a display of power that also, paradoxically, reveals her weakness. The "sangre" that Diana so keenly desires is the embodiment of her own social and sexual identity. This blood exposes Teodoro as the social fraud that he is and makes him, like the audience, an accomplice of the questioning of contemporary social mores. The discovery and exposure of the truth and the lies that underscore this play subtly and efficiently create indissoluble links between the characters, the play, the author, and the audience. Contemporary readers cannot but take part in this baroque game where they expose and are exposed by the contradictions inherent in both reinforcing and contesting the hypocritical codes on which social hierarchies rest.

WORKS CITED

Fumerton, Patricia. *Cultural Aesthetics: Renaissance Literature and the Practice of Social Ornament.* Chicago: U of Chicago P, 1991.

Herrero, Javier. "Lope de Vega y el Barroco: La degradación del honor." *Sistema* 6 (1974): 49–71.

Jones, Roy O. "*El perro del hortelano* y la visión de Lope." In *Lope de Vega: El teatro II.* Ed. A. Sánchez Romeralo. Madrid: Taurus, 1989. 323–32.

Lope de Vega, Félix. *El perro del hortelano*. Ed. Mauro Armiño. Madrid: Cátedra, 1997.

Molina, Tirso de. *El burlador de Sevilla*. Ed. Alfredo Rodríguez López-Vázquez. Madrid: Cátedra, 1991.

Morley, Sylvanus Griswold, and Courtney Bruerton. *Cronología de las comedias de Lope de Vega*. Madrid: Gredos, 1968.

Pring-Mill, Robert D. F. Introduction. *Five Plays*. Trans. Jill Booty. Ed. Robert D. F. Pring-Mill. New York: Hill and Wang, 1961, vii–xii.

Rambuss, Richard. "The Secretary's Study: The Secret Designs of *The Shepheardes Calendar*." *English Literary History* 59 (1992): 313–35.

Rothberg, Irving P. "The Nature of the Solution in *El perro del hortelano*." *Bulletin of the Comediantes* 29.1 (1977): 86–96.

Stewart, Alan. "'The Early Modern Closet Discovered." *Representations* 50 (1995): 76–100.

Strong, Roy. *The Renaissance Garden in England*. London: Thames and Hudson, 1979.

Weber de Kurlat, Frida. "*El perro del hortelano*, comedia palatina." *Nueva Revista de Filología Hispánica* 25 (1975): 339–63.

Ziegler, Georgianna. "'My Lady's Chamber': Female Space, Female Chastity in Shakespeare." *Textual Practice* 4 (1990): 73–90.

MICHAEL ARMSTRONG-ROCHE

(The) *Patria* Besieged: Border-Crossing Paradoxes of National Identity in Cervantes's *Numancia*[†]

Cervantes's *La destruición de Numancia* (ca. 1581–1585)[1] is a play about a heroic last stand waged by the Celtiberian Numantines against Rome. Numancia—capital of the *arevaci*, near today's Soria in northern Castile—was indeed destroyed by Scipio Aemilianus in 133 B.C. but won an enduring reputation for courage.[2] Only a few years before Cervantes wrote *Numancia*, Philip II's chronicler Ambrosio de Morales celebrated this Celtiberian legacy as a decisive moment in Spanish history (in the *Corónica general de España*, 1574), although ancient Numancia and Habsburg Spain shared little more than the accident of geography and a reputation for warrior audacity and prowess, preoccupation with honor, pride, and, above all, courage.[3] Because *Numancia* dramatizes an historical event that had begun to acquire the status of an origin story for sixteenth-century Habsburg Spain, the play lends itself to an exploration of the conceptual shortcuts needed for imperial and national myth-making. The role of violent conflict, selective memory, and nostalgic idealization in the fashioning

† From *Border Interrogations: Questioning Spanish Frontiers*, ed. Benita Sampedro Vizcaya and Simon Doubleday (New York: Berghahn Books, 2008), pp. 204–27. Reprinted by permission of the publisher.
1. On the likely dates of composition, see Canavaggio (1977, 20). Hereafter, Cervantes's play is referred to as *Numancia*.
2. On Scipio Aemilianus ("Scipio Africanus the Younger") and Numancia, see Astin (1967, 35–60, 137–160).
3. Ambrosio de Morales's account of the siege of Numancia appears in book 8 of his *Corónica general de España* (1574). I refer to the following edition: Ambrosio de Morales, *Corónica general de España*, vol. 4 (Madrid: 1791).

of a narrative that draws on a past thought exemplary for the present, is starkly highlighted in this siege of Celtiberians identified as ancient Spaniards. In part, this is because the event itself pits two ancestral peoples taken to be foundational for modern Spain against one another, the Celtiberians and the Romans locked in a bitter fight to the death. But the play also prompts questions about the use of history to define national identity (Which past is ours? The Celtiberian or the Roman?), the value of literature—in this case, public theater—for imagining the past and restoring nuances omitted in official histories, and the dramatic possibilities of that contested past as a mirror for the contemporary Habsburg adventure of world-straddling dominion.

A question that remains alive is whether Cervantes participates unabashedly in the myth-making use of Numancia to celebrate sixteenth-century Habsburg Spain or whether the play is to be read as a cautionary tale about the wages of empire. Readings that regard *Numancia* as an untroubled celebration of Spanish heroism, and Cervantes himself as a patriot for whom Numancia's destruction heralds Spanish imperial glory, are authorized explicitly in prophecies voiced by the Duero river in Act 1, War (*Guerra*) in Act 4, and Fame (*Fama*) as she brings the curtain down (Vivar 2000). These personifications appear on the stage to immortalize the heroic valor of the Numantines seen as a precursor people for Habsburg Spain and to promise future renown and the humiliation of Rome by a long series of invasions capped by the Sack of 1527 and the defeat of the Franco-Papal alliance in 1557. The destruction of Numancia is taken by these prophetic voices for a providential death, necessary sacrifice, and historical tragedy resurrected, redeemed, and avenged by the rise of sixteenth-century Spain. Numancia's body politic dies like Christ on the cross only to live again in the spirit associated insistently with courage, the renown for valor won by the Spanish sword from Ferdinand of Aragon (vv. 1997–1999).[4] Its Second Coming is cast, among other ways, as the fulfillment of the old dream of peninsular union with Philip II's inheritance of the Portuguese crown in 1581.[5] No longer prevalent in Cervantes scholarship, this line of interpretation remains a theme in accounts of Spanish history that draw on "the national author" as a resounding voice for *patria* (fatherland), who sooner reinforces than questions symbols and myths of patriotic fervor (Alcalá de Zamora Queipo de Llano 2000, 104–105). Although such readings are grounded in the providential accounts of history voiced by Duero, War, and Fame, their drawback is that they claim these voices for the play's or Cervantes's last word.

Other readers have ventured to interpret the play allegorically, not as a fundamentally antiquarian exercise whose connection to the author's present is limited by what Duero, War, and Fame "foretell," but also as in some sense about the actual rather than the anticipated world of Philip II's Habsburg Spain. Avalle-Arce (1975), for example, identifies the Roman consul Scipio and his army with Philip II and his forces, relies on

---

4. I cite the following edition: Miguel de Cervantes, *La destruición de Numancia*, ed. Alfredo Hermenegildo (Madrid: Clásicos Castalia, 1994). All references to *Numancia* in this chapter are to verse number(s) from this edition. Translations are my own, unless otherwise indicated.
5. I date the Spanish Habsburg annexation of Portugal from the Estatuto de Tomar (April 1581), which settled Philip's claims to the Portuguese throne. See Bouza (1998).

the Duero river's and Fame's expression of faith in imperial ideals, and suggests that the Romans newly disciplined under Scipio will make themselves worthy of empire, to be revitalized with even greater glory by sixteenth-century Spaniards. This argument reminds us that Cervantes's contemporaries were liable to recognize themselves in both Numancia and Rome. Because of the sheer extent of his dominions and the resources at his command, Philip II—though shorn of the imperial title, which passed to his uncle Ferdinand of Austria in 1556—was among the few sovereigns since Charlemagne who could plausibly aspire to revive Augustus's *pax romana*[6] in the new guise of a united Christendom, an imperial ambition routinely underlined by Habsburg royal iconography.[7]

Now dominant in political readings of *Numancia* is the appeal to historical allegory that presses the identification between Scipio and Philip II (and therefore between Rome and Spain), but acknowledges features of the play that cast doubt on the imperial ideal. Taking a cue from its prophetic thrust, the invitation to look ahead and to conjure "future" audiences (especially Spanish legatees of Numancia) and to make them implied characters in the larger historical drama being lived under Philip II, this tendency finds powerful textual support in Plague's (*Enfermedad*'s) and Famine's (*Hambre*'s) Act 4 descriptions of Numancia in flames like a new Troy (vv. 2020, 2024–2025, 2050–2055). The Trojan resonances evoke the epic discourse of *translatio imperii*, the transfer of political and cultural authority in a movement that was said, by convention, to follow the sun (Johnson 1980, 80–81). Virgil's *Aeneid* locates the legendary and heroic origins of Roman imperial glory in the destruction of the Trojans by the Greeks, much as the Duero's prophetic speech in Cervantes's play traces the origins of the Spanish empire to Numancia's defeat. We are thus invited to step both backward and forward in time beyond the limits of the play's action, when history takes over and providentialism leaves off.

If Troy's destruction is to the Roman Empire as Numancia's is to Spain's, and if Rome is heir to and subjugates Greece as Spain is heir to and subjugates Rome, the play's deep sense of history as a set of (political and cultural) translations invites us to wonder what Habsburg Spain's contemporary Numancias might be. It should come as no surprise to us that, in the late 1970s—a period marked especially in the US by ubiquitous images of the horrors of Vietnam, renewed questions about established authority, and concerns about "imperial quagmire" and the threat to republican ideals— *Numancia* should have drawn seminal scholarly readings more disposed to recognize evidence of royal arrogance, injustice, and imperial overreach than had been the case in earlier scholarship. For Alfredo Hermenegildo, the play's siege recalled the bloody suppression of the morisco revolt that took place in the mountains of Granada in 1568–1570,[8] led by Philip II's half-brother Don John of Austria (Hermenegildo 1976, 47–74). Willard

6. Roman Peace (Latin): prolonged period of peace and stability in the early Roman empire, from the reign of Augustus to that of Marcus Aurelius (27 B.C.E.–120 C.E.) [editor's note].
7. On the imperial theme in Habsburg iconography see Checa Cremades (1987, 185–187 and 195–258) and Tanner (1993).
8. The moriscos, or "little Moors," were Muslims forcibly converted to Christianity after the fall of Granada in 1492 and their descendants. In 1568–70, they revolted against culturally repressive legislation [editor's note].

King suggested that the play could well have served its early Madrid *corral* audiences as a painful reminder of the notoriously brutal, interminable, and costly war in Flanders, especially the Duke of Alba's failed campaign of terror between 1567 and 1573 (King 1979, 202, 214–217). Because of the play's borrowings from Alonso de Ercilla's New World epic, *La Araucana*, King also wondered whether Scipio's siege of Numancia could not have evoked Habsburg operations against the *Araucos* of southern Chile led by García Hurtado de Mendoza. Carroll Johnson developed the parallel with the Revolt in Flanders in compelling detail, drawing on the soldier-chronicler don Bernardino de Mendoza's account of the Duke of Alba's campaign (Johnson 1981). In both cases—Numancia and Flanders—a vastly superior military force is projected abroad to a remote province far from central authority, where the customs are different, and where recent imperial representatives are regarded as tyrannical. Other analogies with contemporary Flanders include the practice of siege warfare on walled cities situated on wide rivers, a commander (Alba) more interested in winning than in personal display of courage or shedding of his own troops' blood, terrible famines, and a mutiny.

Although the voices of Duero and Fame make Rome the evil oppressor and Numancia—identified with Spain (*España*) and Spaniards (*españoles*)— the courageous yet woefully outmanned resistors, these kinds of historical readings remind us that the prophetic mode in the play, neo-Roman dynastic propaganda promoting the Habsburg House as imperial Rome's rightful successor, and the realities of Spanish power in the 1580s all conspire to declare that the tables have been turned and Numancia is now Rome. And if Rome once played enemy to Numancia (and therefore to Spain), the irony of history has now cast sixteenth-century Habsburg Spain as a new Rome to contemporary Numancias, such as Flanders, the *moriscos,* and the *Araucos*. In the light of this historical role reversal, the apparently triumphant tale of Numancia's historical defeat), becomes a cautionary tale for Habsburg Spain. Spain is not only the glorious reincarnation of Ancient Numancia, but also now the New Rome; not only Numancia avenged, but also now the tyrannical oppressor. And Rome's fate in the sixteenth century—crushed twice under the Habsburg boot—could be Spain's tomorrow.

Since the 1970s, some scholars (e.g. Simerka 2003, 77–128) have pursued one or another of the historical allegories outlined (Numancia as Flanders, the *moriscos,* or the *Araucos* among other New World peoples). By and large, however, *Numancia* scholarship has retreated from or subordinated the play's politics to genre criticism, asking whether it should be categorized with classical tragedy, historical tragedy, secular tragedy, tragicomedy, comedy, history or epic (Bergmann 1984; Lewis-Smith 1987; Tar 1990; Rey Hazas 1991; Martín 1996; Karageorgou Bastea 1997; Armas 1998; and Maestro 2004).[9] In the pages that follow, I return to the possibilities raised in those earlier readings of *Numancia*'s politics by exploring how the text makes visible the later historical role reversal that would put Numancia (Spain) in Rome's place. The play's chief strategy is, as I will argue, its paradoxical handling of identity. I mean paradox in its root sense here, as a proposition contrary to received opinion. And rather

---

9. Graf proposes a new political reading of Numancia's sacrifice as an allegory for Philip II's persecution of heretics.

than defend a triumphalist patriotic or anti-imperial critical reading of the play as has already been done very well, I am interested in drawing attention to the way the text plays those implications off one another in the light of Numancia's sixteenth-century consolidation as a proto-national myth for Spain.

By emphasizing the complexity of the play's approach to history and national identity, I am proposing that it engages in a kind of debate with historical and royal discourses keen to advance national or dynastic interests by appeal to an idealized version of the past, whether Numancia's or Rome's. And its chief contribution to this debate is, as I see it, to answer the moral certainties and pieties of patriotic discourse about Numancia and Rome by highlighting not only the continuities, but also the discontinuities between precursor and current communities imagined as making up a *patria*. It will become apparent that *Numancia* defeats any single-minded effort to identify Habsburg Spain with Numancia (promoted by such contemporary historians as Morales) or Rome (promoted by Habsburg royal iconography), because both are presented as morally suspect. Nevertheless, since the triumphalist view of Numancia (and Spain) is supported explicitly by key speeches, my emphasis is on countervailing voices, actions, and characterizations that convey a reiterated impulse to muddy what seems on the face of it to be clear. The play's profiles in courage unsettle facile appropriations, undercutting the easy identification between either Numancia or Rome and early Spanish audiences, the homogeneity within what passes for Numantine and Roman "culture" (as we might call it), and the clean-cut polarization of Numancia and Rome.

What does Cervantes make of this emergent national myth of Spanish courage and liberty? And how does the play explain the link between ancient Numancia and sixteenth-century Spain, the developing sense of a *patria* or national identity continuous in time? The play's several references to *patria* are to the city-state of Numancia (vv. 717, 2369, 2399) and it finds many occasions to identify that Numantine *patria* explicitly with Spaniards (*españoles*) and Spain (*España*) set over against Romans and Rome. The Roman consul Scipio speaks of Numantines as "Spaniards" (españoles; v.115), "this puny hispanic people" (*este pequeño pueblo hispano*; v. 126), and "these rebellious, barbaric Hispanics" (*estos rebeldes, bárbaros hispanos*; v. 164). He also declares that by crushing Numantine pride, all of Spain will submit to the Roman senate (vv. 350–351). For this reason, when the boy Bariato denies Scipio his official triumph by killing himself—one Numantine survivor is needed to prove victory at home—Scipio predicts that his courage will bring glory not only to Numancia, but also to the whole of Spain (vv. 2403–2404).

The Numantines themselves participate in this identification of themselves and their *patria* with Spaniards, Spain, and the Hispanic: the warrior Caravino declares his faith in the "courage of the Spanish arm" (*valor de la española mano*; v. 565) to lift the siege despite overwhelming Roman superiority in numbers. The personification of War speaks of Numantines as "Hispanics" (*hispanos*; v. 1989) and anticipates the day—from the reign of Ferdinand of Aragon (v. 1999)—when Numancia's "hispanic courage" (*valor hispano*) will be known to all the world. Cervantes here follows the lead of the humanist historian Ambrosio de Morales, whose *Corónica general de España* (1574) calls the Numantines "Spaniards" (*españoles*) just as both Romans and Numantines do in the play.[1] This usage suggests that, well before Cervantes, the destruction of the Celtiberian city had come to be regarded as an episode of Spanish national history, a milestone in the history of what John Armstrong has called *Nations before Nationalism* (Armstrong 1982; Johnson 1980, 76).

Numancia's conception of that Numantine *patria* identified with sixteenth-century "Spain" and "Spaniards" is as varied (or confused) as was the range of contemporary reflection on a collective reality still very much in ferment and far from consolidation (Barton 1993; Thompson 1995; Rodríguez Salgado 1996 and 1998). One measure of the play's model of *patria*, and of a patriotism directed to it, is the personification of Spain (*España*). At the end of Act 1, Spain speaks out for Numancia and against perfidious Rome, addressing her lament of Numancia's lost cause to the heavens and to posterity. The stage direction—which describes her as "crowned with several towers, bearing a castle in one hand, representing Spain" (Cervantes 1994, 72)—clearly identifies Spain with the iconography of its leading peninsular kingdom, Castile. This reflex is imitated by the personified Duero river, the besieged Numancia's only lifeline to the wider world and hope for relief. Duero looks ahead to that moment when the "Lusitanian tatter"—once ripped from "the garments of illustrious Castile"—will be restored to her "old self" (*antiguo ser; Numancia* vv. 517–520), Duero's vivid sartorial image for Philip II's annexation of Portugal in 1581. Spain in her lamentation speech (vv. 361–392), and especially Duero in her consolation speech (vv. 473–480), offer yet another vision of what constitutes the *patria* near the end of Act 1, a broadly territorial *ius solis*[2] that embraces the variety of peoples settled and kingdoms established within what is today known as the Iberian peninsula. Such a conception of Spain remained something of an abstraction even in 1581, given the comparative lack—by later standards—of institutional, legal, monetary, and linguistic unity of the chief peninsular kingdoms (Castile, Aragon, and Portugal) that owed the Habsburg Philip II fealty.

Addressing and consoling the personified Spain, the Duero river ends Act 1 by delivering the most elaborate reflection on the historical relation between ancient Numancia and sixteenth-century Spain. Although Duero predicts that Spain's leading champion will be the Habsburg Philip II following the annexation of Portugal and its seaborne empire, it enumerates key themes in the formation of an emerging sense of a "Spanish" community defined by more than loyalty to house and home or even fealty to monarch or dynasty. For instance, it announces the coming of Christianity and insists on associating the key attribute of "courage" (*valor*) with the "Hispanic name" (*nombre hispano*). Indeed, other than geography, the principal link between ancient Numancia and Habsburg Spain is a transhistorical ethopoeia[3] that includes a shared reputation for warrior audacity (vv. 572, 644, 2382, 2384), preoccupation with honor (vv. 592, 593, 605, 1295, 1298, 2143, 2147, 2183), military prowess (v. 2252), and arrogance and pride (vv. 114, 352, 1115, 2201, 2230, 2246). The salient virtue of Numancia is, of

---

1. On Cervantes's historical and legendary sources, including Ambrosio de Morales's *Corónica*, see especially Cervantes (1922, 6: 34–62): Canavaggio (1977, 40–46; and 1979, 3: 647–653).
2. The right of the soil (Latin); i.e., birthright citizenship [editor's note].
3. A figure of speech that involves putting one person in the place of another [editor's note].

course, courage (vv. 1753, 1761, 2376, 2431, 2434, 2440, 2445), a *topos* in sixteenth-century descriptions of Habsburg Spain and Spaniards for those writers who took the warrior code of the nobility for a national virtue.[4]

The character Spain also gives voice to a more troubling attribute destined to a long life as one of the enduring myths of modern Spain: the house eternally divided against itself. She blames internecine strife and even simple discord for the "tyranny" of earlier successive waves of barbarian invaders (she names the Phoenicians and the Greeks in her review of "Spanish" history; vv. 361–384), a Spain divided having made herself easy prey to others only too prepared to enslave her inhabitants. Alone in Spain, Numancia has traded her blood for "liberty" (v. 388). And yet Spaniards too will prove traitors to Numancia. The Numantine chief Theogenes laments the "Spaniards" allied with Rome and prepared to slit Numancia's throat (vv. 545–548), referring to turncoat Celtiberian tribes as if to confirm Spain's and Duero's diagnosis of the *patria*'s historical ill: treachery of Spaniard against Spaniard, disunity of Peninsular kingdoms and peoples. It is in this light that we may understand the providential hopes Duero attaches to the union of Portugal to Castile (and Aragon) in 1581, cast as a fulfillment of the promise of liberty from foreign invasion with the apparently definitive achievement of internal peace.

What national identity is *not* characterized by is equally interesting, because it breaks with attributes that have come to define nationalism. Ethnicity, religion, the law, and key political institutions are neither decisive for marking peoples held essentially to be antagonists for all time (Numancia and Rome), nor certainly a guarantee of unity or peace. Only in the Duero speech does the play identify historical Spaniards ethnically, and it waffles: in part, it looks back to the Visigoths and the heroic deeds with which they will breathe new life into Spain following their invasion (vv. 477–480). It also links Spanish royalty (from Ferdinand and Isabella) with the Visigoths (vv. 503–504), in consonance with dynastic propaganda that promoted identification of the ruling families of Spain with a kind of Visigothic prelapsarian golden age, a nostalgic vision of peace, unity, and Christian orthodoxy shattered by the Muslim invasion.[5] Spain is otherwise associated with the various peoples, especially but not only the Celtiberian Numantines (v. 459), who inhabited the peninsula—many of them, as we noted, traitors to Numancia. Duero envisions "peoples" (*gentes*; vv. 473–476) arriving from "remote nations" (*remotas naciones*) to inhabit Spain's "sweet bosom" (*dulce seno*), peoples joined chiefly by their opposition to Rome (vv. 475–476).

The mere coincidence between Numancia and Rome of crucial "cultural" and political features such as religion, the law, and the senate thematizes the complexities and limits of Spanish historical identification with a Numancia pitted against Rome in the nationalist rhetoric voiced especially by Duero and Fame. Although Cervantes here sometimes follows historical sources, such evidence that Numancia and Rome are more like each other than not fits into a larger pattern peculiar to this play (as we shall see) that

---

4. Herrero García (1966, 15–103) reviews sixteenth- and seventeenth-century texts that followed this rhetorical convention, repeated to the point of cliché.
5. A useful overview of medieval and sixteenth-century Spanish discussions of ancestors, including the Celtiberians and the Visigoths, is to be found in Lupher (2003, 195–226).

knocks the wind out of this myth-making reliance on anti-Roman diatribe. The play's ethnography does indeed Romanize Numancia. Romans and Numantines pray and offer oblations to and sacrifice for the same gods, including Jupiter (vv. 561, 634, 670, 773, 782, 810, 829, 1231, 1936, 2211), Diana (v. 2105), Pluto (vv. 864, 962), Ceres (v. 868), and Charon (v. 971). The debate whether love undermines or steels martial valor, translated into the mythological terms of Mars (vv. 89, 154, 713) and Venus (vv. 89, 123), is first engaged in the Roman Act 1 only to be echoed by the Numantine Act 2. The parallels remind us of what these sworn enemies have in common, and there is no little poignancy in the repeated Numantine invocation of Roman deities called on to defeat the Romans. To be sure, a shared pantheon of non-Christian deities could convey a generic paganism and this may have been sufficient historical accuracy for Cervantes's purposes. Yet the potential dramatic and thematic effect of such a choice is to blur the boundary dividing apparently irreconcilable foes.

Much the same can be said for the handling of the law. The Numantines are political tributaries to Rome, who sue for peace alleging the tyranny of previous consuls. The ambassadors want justice, not independence, citing the avarice, lust, and otherwise unlawful rule of earlier consuls to legitimize their rebellion. In the final scenes of the play, the Numantine Bariato will throw an accusation of broken "treaties and agreements" in Scipio's face (v. 2363). The play here agrees with Roman and Spanish historical sources, including Guevara's account in Letter 5 of the *Epístolas familiares* (1545), which portray an unjust war initiated when the Roman senate authorized Scipio to break a truce and renew hostilities (Guevara 1950, 1, 46–47). The link between the two peoples is reinforced by a shared political institution: the senate was originally Roman, not Numantine, of course, and yet, like Rome (v. 2), the play's Numancia is governed by its own senate (v. 1739). A senate in Golden Age theater often simply meant the audience, addressed through the fourth wall, the sense glossed by Berganza's drummer in Cervantes's own *Coloquio de los perros* (Cervantes [1613] 1989, 2: 335). More pointedly, Alonso de Ercilla calls the governing assembly of the *Araucos* of southern Chile a senate in his epic poem *La Araucana* (1569–1589), about the Habsburg war against this confederation of Amerindian peoples, endowing the governing council of indigenous "others" with a Roman name much as Cervantes does with his Numantine "barbarians" (*bárbaros*).[6] What might otherwise pass for a stylistic convention acquires a potentially charged meaning in a context where the boundary between peoples has been drawn so deep. In both camps, moreover, the senate is associated with an injustice. As the Roman senate authorizes an unjust war, so in the final Act we learn that the Numantine senate is responsible for the decree that orders all women, children, and elderly killed (vv. 1680–1681, 1944–1945). Ostensibly a glorious collective suicide, it will meet with internal resistance and will more than once be given the name of homicide.

Despite evidence that Rome and Numancia have more in common than their deep enmity would suggest, so far we have confirmed there is no lack of grist for the patriotic mill in Cervantes's version of the legend of

---

6. Ercilla (1993, canto 8, oct. 11, verse 2). On Cervantes's possible debts to Ercilla in this play, see King (1979, 200–221).

Numancia. Act 1 plunges the spectator and reader into the Roman camp as Scipio prepares a renewed siege of the city, speeches on both sides tell us that ancient Numantines are Spaniards whose common enemy is Rome, and personifications of Spain and Duero end the act by praising Numancia's courage and love of liberty and by foretelling its death and resurrection in sixteenth-century Habsburg Spain. For good reason the play, like the legend, has been invoked as a resoundingly patriotic defence of Spanish heroism, as an effort to promote the consolidation and celebration of this emergent national myth. Act 2, however, situates us squarely in the Numantine camp, where the exalted views floated in Act 1 are put to severe tests. Up close from Act 2, *Numancia* begins to dwell on typical actions, attributes, and characterizations that undermine the heroic identification of contemporary Spaniards with Numancia. It does so by presenting features of Numancia. It does so by presenting features of Numancia that could only distance most Spaniards of around 1581, thereby heading off a too facile complacency about a selectively idealized version of past "selves."

First, there is the characteristic Numantine mode of warfare. The Numantine warrior Caravino, chafing at being enclosed "like women" (v. 570), proposes the stand-off between Numancia and Rome be resolved through single combat (v. 574). The motion is seconded by an anonymous Numantine soldier (vv. 613–616) and in Act 3, Caravino puts it to Scipio directly (vv. 1152–1160). The offer of single combat is in part a desperate measure meant to move the war to a terrain on which the outnumbered Numantines might have a chance. Early Spanish audiences may well also have responded to an idealized, mythic image of themselves as swashbuckling heroes determined to die honorably rather than waste away miserably from hunger. As is well-known, long after the mounted, armorbearing knight had ceased to be an effective military force, the major courts of Europe were swept by a taste for knightly accoutrements, rituals, and rhetoric copied from the late flowering of chivalric literature, especially Garci Rodríguez de Montalvo's *Amadís de Gaula* (1508) and Ariosto's *Orlando furioso* (1516) (Checa Cremades 1987, 187–232). Rivals Francis I and Charles V[7] were not immune to the fashion and, in 1528, made a ceremonial gesture of agreeing to settle the war between them through single combat (Tomás y Valiente 1992, 58–61). In 1596, the extravagant English Earl of Essex stood before the walls of Lisbon during its siege and challenged his counterpart to single combat, asserting the justice of his lord's cause and the greater beauty of his mistress (Meron 1998, 125; Braudy 2003, 150–157).

But such theatrical gestures and bravado were far removed from the realities of military combat as it was actually waged. We might reasonably wonder whether the archaic touch of single combat was not designed to achieve historical plausibility about an ancient people. Indeed Cervantes reveals his concern about, and perhaps also a general disregard in directors and audiences for, elementary verisimilitude when a stage direction in Act I requests that the Roman host gathered before Scipio dress "as in Antiquity, without harquebuses" (Cervantes 1994, 60). And yet, the Numantines are cast as throwbacks by contrast not only to late sixteenth-century

---

7. Francis I of France (1494–1547) and Charles V, Holy Roman Emperor and King of Spain (1500–1558) were long-term enemies, particularly warring over influence in Italy [editor's note].

warfare, but also to classical Roman standards. Roman strategy in the play involves large-scale troop movements and engineering for siege warfare. Scipio not only renews his insistence on unconditional surrender, he scoffs at the challenge to single combat as if it were a joke and a fool's errand (vv. 1179–1184). Indeed Roman strategy would have struck a resonantly "modern" note to contemporary audiences, since fortress-building and siege warfare (especially in the Netherlands) had come into their own by the end of the sixteenth century, much as cannon in the late fifteenth century had lent the advantage to offensive war (Keegan 1994, 325–328). In this same vein, Spaniards in 1581 were renowned for an infantry formation—the *tercio*—that had been regarded as the most effective land force on European battlefields for a century (Elliott 1990, 134). Certainly on that historical score, early Spanish audiences and readers would have seen themselves sooner in Scipio and Rome than in Caravino and the Numantines.

More problematic still for the impulse to embrace Numancia as an idealized *patria* projected into the past is the representation of Numantine religious rituals and beliefs in Act 2. They conspicuously draw attention to the fact that second-century B.C. Celtiberian Numancia and sixteenth-century Habsburg Spain were divided by religion. Two ceremonies are performed in succession and the sequence mimes the contrapuntal relationship between a Roman Act 1 that explicitly emphasizes Numantine Spanishness and a Numantine Act 2 that implicitly emphasizes Numancia's difference from sixteenth-century Spain. The first ceremony, officiated by "priests" (*sacerdotes*), involving water, wine, incense, and a live ram to be sacrificed, strongly suggests a primitive version of the Catholic mass and the Eucharistic sacrament as verisimilar "antique" touch, anticipation, or parody (Cervantes 1994, 89). It clearly departs from them when the priests perform a series of divinatory rites on a sacred fire, read avian and celestial augurs and portents (imperial eagles fighting overhead, thunder, and lightning), and invoke Pluto and the forces of hell in an attempt to divine and then alter Numancia's fate. The attempted propitiatory sacrifice of a ram is thwarted by a demon (vv. 885–886) who emerges from the ground to sieze the ram and scatter the fire and offerings. The second ceremony is officiated by the diviner Marquino and his acolyte Milvio. Marquino's black hair, vials of black water, and black staff, and the reference to "the evil spirits" with which he communes (Pluto, Ceres, Cerberus, and other denizens of the Underworld) sensationally evoke sorcery or black magic. This effect culminates in an act of necromancy, the ritual revival of a corpse to elicit a prophecy that foretells Numancia's fated death by near and dear. The Numantine Leoncio becomes a kind of spokesman for late sixteenth-century Catholic orthodoxy when he dismisses the whole spectacle as "diabolical inventions," "illusions," and "chimeras and fantasies / omens and sorcery" (vv. 1097–1100), at odds with his conception of knowledge (*ciencia*: v. 1102) and the power of the will to defeat portents.

Such staged rituals no doubt serve in part the straightforward theatrical function of evoking a diffuse, pre-Christian paganism while providing its audiences a voyeuristic *frisson* of heterodoxy. This is especially the case here since the portrayal of these ostensibly ancient Spanish religious practices recalls decidedly pagan literary models for necromancy in the witch Erichtho of Lucan's *Pharsalia*, the witch who resurrects her son to divine the future in Heliodorus's *Ethiopian History* (newly translated into Spanish in 1554), and Amerindian sorcery in Ercilla's epic *La Araucana* (1569–1589).[8] Yet following an Act 1 so insistent about the "Spanishness" of Numancia and the Numantines, it can also be seen as a means to achieve a thematic distancing from the emerging national myth of Numancia. Many Spaniards around 1581 may have recognized idealized versions of themselves in Numancia's fierce commitment to courage and honor, but at least officially they would have been hard-pressed to see themselves in its religious rituals and beliefs. By drawing attention to such features, the play spotlights a more historically mixed legacy from Numancia than the Spain, Duero, War, and Fame speeches acknowledge. They expose the shortcuts at work when a myth-making narrative white-washes features of a past that could not be claimed by historical heirs.

The Spanish identification with the Numantine is especially complicated in the portrayal of collective suicide. It must have turned up the moral heat for those early audiences since Church doctrine declared it a mortal sin.[9] Indeed, in this light it might appear at first glance that the Numantines are never more Roman and less Christian than when they choose honorable suicide over death on the battlefield, continued resistance, suffering, or even dishonor. Roman law opposed any moral condemnation of suicide and hence provided no sanctions against it. Christian authority took the opposite position from Roman law and custom, though gradually. The fullest treatment long remained St. Augustine's in *The City of God* (I.16–27), which argues against the standard Roman teaching with the aim of dissuading Christian women, threatened by barbarians, from preferring suicide to rape—much the same situation that leads the women of Numancia to ask their men to remain with them.[1]

And yet, even within the Christian tradition, there developed a defence of self-sacrifice for the *patria*—the *topos* of *pro patria mori*[2]—of heroic acts, including suicide, whose objective was to head off enslavement, religious conversion or death by the enemy. Medieval historians were liable to compare such self-sacrifice for the fatherland to Christ's for the salvation of humanity.[3] * * * There are moments of Numantine self-sacrifice in Act 4 that do, indeed, seem to fit a kind of proto-Christian virtue of self-sacrifice as *caritas*.[4] A starving mother no longer able to breastfeed her child urges her son to take her body and blood, as if she were herself a literal prefiguration of the Eucharistic offering (vv. 1708–1723). Then again, Marandro and his friend Leoncio die in a raid on the Roman camp designed to procure Marandro's beloved Lira some crumbs of bread, once again to stave off starvation. Leoncio never makes it back, and Marandro himself dies handing over the "bitter bread" (*amargo pan*) to "sweet" (*dulce*) Lira (vv. 1804–1827). Marandro's last words to Lira underline the Eucharistic resonances of the offering, bread mixed with his own and his friend's spilled blood (vv. 1844–1847). Nevertheless, what differentiates these acts of self-sacrifice from the medieval tradition of *pro*

---

8. Armas (1998, 136–153) reviews literary models for this episode.
9. On what was known as the "sin of despair," see Murray (2000, 2: 369–395).
1. For an account of patristic views of suicide, see Murray (2000, 2: 98–121).
2. To die for one's country (Latin) [editor's note].
3. For the *topos* of *pro patria mori*, see Kantorowicz (1957, 232–272).
4. Charity (Latin) [editor's note].

patria mori is that they are personal (mother to child, friend to friend, lover to beloved), rather than patriotic in motivation.

*   *   *

The apparently noble act of collective suicide understood as patriotism is shadowed by evidence in Act 4 that the decision does not reflect a unanimous, voluntary giving of self. We are shown an enforced participation that has, by no means, won the consent of all Numantines. Moreover, the play's most insistent response to Numancia's bid for liberation through suicide is to call it "homicide," a reality of escalating horror not argued rhetorically, but named explicitly and displayed graphically. The first instance of this sober evaluation is voiced by the soldier the Numantine diviner Marquino revives in Act 2. His baleful prediction is that there will be no peace, neither Romans nor Numantines will triumph, and that Numantines will perish at the hands of near and dear: "A friendly dagger will prove Numancia's murderer [*homicida*]" (vv. 1079–1080). The revived corpse then hurls himself into the grave, and Marquino follows suit, preferring to take his own life than bear witness to such a prospect. Marquino's personal suicide anticipates Numancia's collective suicide much as Bariato's recapitulates it at the end. It may be questionable in the light of Church doctrine, because it cannot be excused even as a patriotic act—unlike Bariato's jump from the tower at the end of the play, by which he denies Scipio his human trophy—but it is not homicide, nor does it enforce consent with a particular idea of collective glory.

We are made to witness a variation of this more troubling facet of collective suicide as two unnamed Numantines look on the spectacle of their valuables going up in holocaust (vv. 1648–1671). What is worse, says one to the other, is that we must die by "cruel" sentence and act as our own "executioners" because the Numantine senate has decreed, now that hunger is stalking the city, "that no woman, child or elder be left with life" (vv. 1680–1681). With that decree, the apparent Numantine commitment to chivalry in Act 2—to the bravery and dexterity in arms of single combat and the protection of children and women—is thrown by the board. Rather than give quarter especially to women, children, and the elderly, the senate singles them out for murder. Famine emphasizes the point that famine, fury, and rage have turned Numantines against themselves, and that they have come to find happiness in death, with one objective only: to deny Romans a victory over living Numantines (vv. 2021–2023).

The play is not content merely to announce or describe the senate's resolution. A particularly poignant display of its implications takes place in Act 4 when a Numantine soldier gives chase to a Numantine woman across the stage, hellbent on killing her in line with "the senate decree that no woman's life be spared" (vv. 1944–1945). Lira, mourning her beloved Marandro and brother, has resolved to take her own life before hunger does. She catches sight of the soldier and begs him to kill her instead: "Let her who prizes life keep her own / And take mine now that it is a burden" (vv. 1942–1943), a plea that highlights the effective breach of consent with which the Numantine senate decree of collective suicide is being put into practice. The Numantine woman who does not want to die is spared, but the soldier's perverse sense of duty is thwarted by the power of Lira's beauty rather than reason or principle (vv. 1946–1951). Bewitched, the soldier refuses to be her "murderer" (v. 1949) and helps Lira bury Marandro and her brother (the Roman Mario again uses "homicide" to describe Numancia's self-immolation at v. 2278). The soldier is prepared to kill a Numantine woman who does not want to die, but is unable to kill a woman who does. There is a neoplatonic hint of a beauty capable of eliciting virtue, of civilizing a barbaric impulse, not unlike the effect of Rosaura on the "barbaric" Segismundo in the mountain tower fastness of Calderón's *La vida es sueño* [Life is a dream]. And yet this paradoxical moment also illustrates the arbitrariness of Numancia's collective decision to do away with itself before surrendering to Scipio's Rome, the breakdown of moral order in which—as Lira puts it—"mercy" (*piedad*) becomes "rigor" (vv. 1952, 1955).

The taboo-shattering bloodbath, chaos, and confusion that ensue from the Numantine senate's decree—which pits husbands against wives, sons against mothers, and parents against children—are given their most luridly gruesome expression by Famine in that same chilling Act 4 (vv. 2024–2055). Indeed, Famine's speech could be set against the Duero's Act 1 prophecy as a kind of pendant; that is, alongside Duero's unvarnished patriotism, we would have to place Famine's alarmingly clear-eyed, counter-patriotic response. Pairing off those speeches (and Acts 1 and 4), each of which in isolation might be cited to make exactly opposite cases for the play's take on the heroism of Numancia and its possible legacy to sixteenth-century Habsburg Spain, starkly highlights what is lost in moral complexity when we reduce this play's voices to one. It also illustrates the thematic and structural counterpoint through which Cervantes achieves that complexity about an issue—suicide in the name of patriotism—that in his own day divided his contemporaries. Famine's speech is worth quoting in full for the cumulative impact of its searing detail:

> Hark to the wailings terrible and dire / Of beauteous women, who to death go down; / Their tender limbs in flame and ashes lie, / No father, friend, or love to heed their cry! / As timid sheep, upon their careless way, / Whom some ferocious wolf attacks and drives, / Go hurrying hither, thither, all astray, / With panting dread to lose their simple lives; / So, fleeing from the swords upraised to slay. / Do these poor children, and these tender wives, / Run on from street to street, O fate insane! / To lengthen out their certain death, in vain, / Within the breast of his belovèd bride / The husband sheathes his keen and glittering brand; / Devoid of pity, and of filial pride, / The son against the mother turns his hand; / The father, casting clemency aside, / Against his very offspring takes his stand, / And while with furious thrusts to death they bleed, / He finds a piteous pleasure in the deed! / No square, or street, or mansion can be found. / That is not filled with blood and with the dead; / The sword destroys, the fierce fire blazes round. / And Cruelty with fearsome step doth tread! / Soon will ye see upon the level ground / The strongest and the loftiest turrets spread. / The humble dwellings, and the temples high. / Shall turn to dust and ashes by and by![5] (vv. 2028–2055)

As if to underscore the horror of the Numantine senate's decree, a little later in the same Act, two boys (Bariato and Servio) sneak on stage

---

5. I use Gibson's Victorian translation for this passage (Cervantes 1885, 96–97). Although his version often reads like a parody of Jacobean verse, here, the fustian works.

wondering which way to escape certain death. Their concern is not the fury of the Roman enemy, but their fellow, murderously rampaging countrymen given permission to kill women, children, and the elderly. Bariato plaintively asks Servio: "Sad boy, do you not see we are pursued / By two thousand swords intent on slaying us?" (vv. 2120–2121). To which Servio responds: "There is no escaping / Those who hound us" (vv. 2122–2123). Servio is too hungry to go on, but Bariato decides to take cover in his father's tower. Like the unnamed woman saved by Lira, their desire to flee—both acts of civil disobedience—brings home the diversity of reactions to the Numantine senate's decree, departures from a genuine consent that might lend it a measure of legitimacy.

⁂

Theogenes and Scipio, leaders of the Numantine and Roman camps, come to incarnate the dark side of Numantine and Roman exemplarity: Theogenes exemplifies what becomes of courage and noble self-sacrifice when they turn homicidal, Scipio exemplifies what becomes of prudence and moderation—his self-professed virtues (vv. 13–24, 81–168, 1748, 2258)—when they turn blindly arrogant and willful.[6] In their characterizations, they illustrate particularly well the paradoxes of identity portrayed in the play and the morally ambiguous reality of its patriotism. At strategic moments, the two leaders are associated with the rhetoric of a kind of border-crossing conversion, and for those moments they become vehicles for the play's otherwise largely implicit recasting of the patriotic certainties of a Duero or Fame. The Numantine chief Theogenes is closely associated with the two most morally suspect decisions undertaken by Numancia during the siege, the two that would cut most deeply against the grain of Spanish self-perception in 1581. It is Theogenes who proposes in Act 2 that the Numantines draw and quarter, share out, and cannibalize their Roman prisoners to stave off hunger. Framed as his "honorable intention," the language suggests a sinister parody of the Last Supper and the Eucharist: "Our cruel, necessary meal / Will some day be celebrated by Spain" (vv. 1431, 1434–1441). Neither ritual human sacrifice nor customary practice, this survival cannibalism nonetheless departs from other less doctrinally questionable solutions such as Marandro's and Leoncio's raid on the Roman camp for bread.

Theogenes also takes credit for the Numantine senate's motion to enact collective suicide. What is more, he proudly claims paternity for it just as he is preparing to murder his wife and children in the name of liberty and honor (vv. 2081, 2085–2087, 2092–2097). This too, like the survival cannibalism, stands alongside less problematic alternatives proposed by other Numantines, such as rushing the Roman lines, hunkering down behind the city's defensive walls, or even allowing famine to take its course. The women of Numancia, notably Lira, time and again become mouthpieces for a cool-headed prudence and pragmatism opposed to Theogenes's rash,

---

6. In Armstrong-Roche (2005), I examine *Numancia*'s Scipio as a caustic, revisionary turn on his early modern reception as exemplary statesman of the Roman Republic (promoted by Macrobius, Machiavelli, and Juan Luis Vives), who sacrifices the cardinal virtues in the quest for reputation through conquest. I link this portrayal with the political abuse of the humanist rhetoric of virtue by apologists for the Habsburg monarchy.

bloody-minded bravado (vv. 1370–1401) and even Marandro's futile heroism (vv. 1522–1545). They give voice to the kinds of doubts raised elsewhere in *Numancia* implicitly about the value and virtue of the cult of
self-sacrifice that sometimes passes for patriotism and love in the Numantine camp.

Finally, Theogenes consistently associates honor, glory, liberty, and
contentment with death (vv. 2165–2167, 2172–2173, 2180–2183). As if
to highlight his more questionable impulses, he is brought out onto the
stage "with two drawn swords, and blood on his hands" (Cervantes 1994,
145). He has turned his own hand—as he puts it—against himself, to spill
blood "with honorable and cruel vigor" (vv. 2140–2143). After killing his
wife and children off-stage, he challenges his fellow Numantines to fight
him as if he were a Roman, staging his own death with the characteristic
language and action of a revenge tragedy: "O valiant Numantines, do as
if / I were a perfidious Roman / And avenge your disgrace on my breast / By
bloodying sword and hand" (vv. 2148–2151). We cannot be surprised that
Theogenes, chief spokesman for the Numantine senate's choice of collective suicide over surrender to Scipio, would ask his compatriots to kill him
nor that he would choose so sensational a way to dramatize his death (and
himself) for posterity. And yet the rhetorical form it takes—Theogenes not
only asks his fellows to dispatch him, but to do so *as if* he were Roman—
figuratively models the play's broader impulse to notice the telling ways
in which peoples otherwise poles apart come to resemble one another, if
often unwittingly.

Indeed, Theogenes's "Roman" moment foreshadows Numancia's historical "translation" into the New Rome of sixteenth-century Habsburg Spain,
repeatedly announced by the prophetic voices in the play and here given a
sinister turn. In case we miss the point, Plague calls on a comparable sim-
ile to underscore the paradox of Numantine ire run amok, turning on itself
as if Numantines were the Roman enemy: "Fierce madness and rage, [fam-
ine's] attendant brood, / Have taken possession of every [Numantine] breast
/ Such that, as if they were Roman battle lines, / They thirst for [Numan-
tine] blood" (vv. 2016 2019). Theogenes, appealing to fellow Numantines to
sacrifice him, spells out the topsy-turvy ethical implications of his version
of patriotic glory: where once there was tenderness toward friends, there is
to be rabid rage as if against the foe (vv. 2162–2163).

That the boundary between Roman and Numantine becomes increasingly blurred under the stress of war is brought home when, in the final
act of the play, Scipio, Roman consul, experiences his own momentary
conversion, appearing—if only rhetorically—to recognize himself in the
Numantines. Following the mayhem of Numancia's frenzied self-
destruction, a pall of silence descends on the city. The Romans, baffled,
scale the walls and find corpses and ashes where the city once flourished.
Scipio stands there gazing on the carnage, his hope of winning an official
triumph at Rome by bearing home at least one live Numantine no more
than a charred ruin (vv. 2244–2246, 2261–2263, 2282–2284). Having
failed to grasp that the Numantines' collective attachment to honor—the
difference between conditional and unconditional surrender—is greater
even than his own, Scipio has a rare moment of self-examination. Here is
Scipio:

Was my breast perchance filled / With barbaric arrogance and deaths / And devoid of the most just mercy? / Is it so foreign to my condition / To treat the vanquished with benevolence, / As befits the victor who is kind? / Poorly did Numancia know the valour in my breast, / Born to conquer and to forgive! (vv. 2306–2314)

Initially, the speech offers the hope that Scipio may have learned to acknowledge his own moral failure to show mercy and compassion to the vanquished—*piedad* and *benignidad con el rendido*—but the self-recognition is fleeting and finally denied in the last tercet. It is not Scipio, of course, but the play through him that diagnoses the overweening confidence (*bárbara arrogancia*) that led him to underestimate his foe, to badly misread their desperation and pronounced code of honor, and to rebuff their bid for peace in exchange for justice. The last Numantine, Bariato, however, confirms the play's judgment of Scipio expressed in this speech. Scipio's peremptory Act 1 response to the Numantine ambassadors—"Too late do you show repentance!" (v. 267)—is met in Act 4's final scene with Bariato's equally unyielding answer to his entreaties: "Too late, cruel one, do you offer clemency" (v. 2342).

✳   ✳   ✳

It only gradually emerges from the soaring rhetoric of virtue, liberty, and patriotism that Theogenes and Scipio—bitter foes to the end—are bound together by their chief failing: they are joined at the hip of fame. Their primary motivation, it turns out, is the overriding concern with reputation, the hunger for which becomes their defining attribute and leads them to destroy what they most cherish. Theogenes comes to stake everything on the testimony of "history" (vv. 1418–1421) and "fame" (vv. 2291–2296). Scipio puts fame first too, for instance to justify his "cowardly" choice of siege warfare in the name of winning (vv. 1197–1200). Over the course of the play, Scipio reveals himself less interested in securing a peace for Rome than in personal triumph. As we saw, this blinds him to his enemy and leads to the refusal of key virtues—compassion and clemency—that, he himself recognizes at least rhetorically, may have partially saved the day. Scipio suffers the consequences directly in the play's historical time, namely, he fails to achieve his official triumph, which requires that he return to Rome with at least one live Numantine as a trophy. But even Theogenes's ostensible victory in historical memory is overshadowed by the price paid for glory: not only total destruction, but also the combination of cannibalism and homicidal turning of Numantine against Numantine that, in Act 4, passes for Numantine patriotic courage.

The trajectory undergone personally by the Roman Scipio and the Numantine Theogenes—who figuratively trade places—has its collective counterpart, under the species of history, in the process by which second-century BC Celtiberian Numancia becomes sixteenth-century New Rome or Habsburg Spain. Even if we fail to recognize how much alike Numancia and Rome already are on the theatrical stage, the larger stage of history—as Fame asserts—will ensure that political roles are reversed and that they do in this sense become one another. It is because of the play's unflinching gaze on these dramatic and historical ironies, on the yawning distance between the patriotic certainties of a Duero or Fame, and the cannibalistic and homicidal horrors of Acts 3 and 4, that we can say there is a *Numancia* resoundingly patriotic, fully engaged in the creation of a national myth of courage and providential mission, and another *Numancia* skeptical about that legacy and, by indirection, critical of Habsburg Spain and imperial adventurism. The first tendency suggests that Numancia's self-sacrifice is in the service of a higher good that redeems it; the second, that Numancia is for many reasons less apt an ancestor than Rome and that even its apparent act of patriotic charity is marred by homicidal degeneration and a dehumanizing quest for fame. In the voices of Duero and Fame, the play most insistently presents that higher good as sixteenth-century Habsburg Spain. But who has the last word on that score? The triumphalist rhetoric of Duero and Fame or Famine's rather less flattering, blood-drenched portrait of homicidal Numantines? The backdrop of smoking ruins and human carnage, or the uncertain promise that the imperial wheel of fortune will come to a grinding halt in 1581?

Alongside full-throated hymns to *patria* and monarch and nation, *Numancia* also makes conspicuous how patriotic sentiment—confused with virtue, and driven by the imperative of fame—can lead to atrocity, to a betrayal of the principles that a *patria* may otherwise hold most dear in its ideal self-conception. For this reason, the play ultimately defeats any single-minded effort to make it speak for Rome or Numancia, for empire or against it. But if we are prepared to recognize its urge to blur boundaries, it offers us something perhaps more compelling. Seen in all its complexity *Numancia* would seem to treat national identity as a question rather than as a foreordained answer, and the question it raises implicitly is whether the *patria* embodies key virtues or betrays them. It especially draws attention to the moral responsibility incumbent on those who would answer the question "who are we?" by invoking remote ancestors. As we have seen, the play discourages facile replies predetermined by ethnicity, religion, the law, or language. Instead, it responds by dramatizing a pair of conditionals: If we are Numantine, then we are courageous, but also primitive, cannibalistic, and homicidal. If Roman, then we are prudent, accomplished, and Lords of all the World, but also proud, tyrannical, and doomed to be trampled underfoot by once and future Numancias.

BIBLIOGRAPHY

Alcalá de Zamora Queipo de Llano, José. 2000. "Idea y realidad de España en los siglos XVI y XVII." In *España como nación*. Barcelona: Real Academia de la Historia.

Armas, Frederick A. de. 1998. *Cervantes, Raphael, and the Classics*. Cambridge: Cambridge University Press.

Armstrong, John. 1982. *Nations before Nationalism*. Chapel Hill, NC: University of North Carolina Press.

Armstrong-Roche, Michael. 2005. "Imperial Theater of War: Republican Virtues under Siege in Cervantes's *Numancia*." *Journal of Spanish Cultural Studies* 6, no. 2 (July), 185–203.

Astin, A. E. 1967. *Scipio Aemilianus*. Oxford: Oxford University Press.

Avalle-Arce, Juan Bautista, 1975. "'*La Numancia*': Cervantes y la tradición histórica." In *Nuevos deslindes cervantinos*. Barcelona: Editorial Ariel, 247–275.

Barton, Simon F. 1993. "The Roots of the National Question in Spain." In Mikulás Teich and Roy Porter, eds., *The National Question in Historical Context*. Cambridge: Cambridge University Press, 106–127.

Bergmann, Emilie. 1984. "The Epic Vision of Cervantes' *La Numancia*." *Theatre Journal* 36, 85–96.

Bouza, Fernando. 1998. "De archivos y antiguas escrituras en la pretensión al trono portugués de Felipe II: La unión de coronas ibéricas de un fin de siglo a otro." In *Imagen y propaganda: Capítulos de historia cultural del reinado de Felipe II*. Madrid: Ediciones Akal, 121–152.

Braudy, Leo. 2003. *From Chivalry to Terrorism: War and the Changing Nature of Masculinity*. New York: Alfred A. Knopf.

Canavaggio, Jean. 1977. *Cervantes dramaturge: Un théâtre à naître*. Paris: Presses Universitaires de France.

———. 1979. "Le dénouement de 'Numance': Jalons d'une tradition." In *Les cultures ibériques en devenir: Essais publiés à la mémoire de Marcel Bataillon (1895–1977)*. Vol. 3. Paris: Fondation Singer-Polignac, 1979.

Cervantes, Miguel de. 1885. *Numantia: A Tragedy*. Tr. James Gibson. London: Kegan Paul, Trench, & Co.

———. 1922. *Comedias y entremeses*, vol. 6. Eds. Rodolfo Schevill and Adolfo Bonilla. Madrid: n.p.

———. 1989. "El coloquio de los perros," in Harry Sieber, ed., *Novelas ejemplares*. Vol. 2. Madrid: Ediciones Cátedra.

———. 1994. *La destruición de Numancia*. Ed. Alfredo Hermenegildo. Madrid: Clásicos Castalia.

Checa Cremades, Fernando. 1987. *Carlos V y la imagen del héroe en el Renacimiento*. Madrid: Taurus Ediciones.

Elliott, J. H. 1990 [1963]. *Imperial Spain: 1469–1716*. London: Penguin Books.

Ercilla, Alonso de. 1993. *La Araucana*. Ed. Isaías Lerner. Madrid: Ediciones Cátedra.

Graf, Eric C. 2003. "Valladolid *delenda est*: La política teológica de *La Numancia*." In Jesús C. Maestro, ed., *Theatralia*. No. 5, *El teatro de Miguel de Cervantes ante el IV Centenario*, 273–282.

Guevara, Fray Antonio de. 1950. *Libro primero de las epístolas familiares*. Ed. José Maria Cossio, vol. 1. Madrid: Aldus.

Hermenegildo, Alfredo. 1976. *La 'Numancia' de Cervantes*. Madrid: Sociedad General Española de Librería.

Herrero García, Miguel. 1966. *Ideas de los españoles del siglo XVII*. Madrid: Editorial Gredos.

Johnson, Carroll. 1980. "The Structure of Cervantine Ambiguity." *Ideologies and Literature* 3. no.12 (March–May), 75–94.

———1981. "*La Numancia* y la estructura de la ambigüedad cervantina." In Manuel Criado de Val., ed., *Cervantes, su obra y su mundo (Actas del I Congreso International sobre Cervantes)*. Madrid: EDI, 309–316.

Kantorowicz. Ernst H. 1957. *The King's Two Bodies: A Study in Medieval Political Theology*. Princeton: Princeton University Press.

Karageorgou Bastea, Christina. 1997. "El texto especular y sus implicaciones ideológicas en *La Numancia*." In Aurelio González Pérez, ed., *Texto y representación en el teatro del Siglo de Oro*. México: El Colegio de México, 23–43.

Keegan, John. 1994. *A History of Warfare*. New York: Vintage Books.

King. Willard F. 1979. "Cervantes' *Numancia* and Imperial Spain." *Modern Language Notes* 94, 200–221.

Lewis-Smith, Paul. 1987. "Cervantes' *Numancia* as Tragedy and Tragicomedy." *Bulletin of Hispanic Studies* 64, no. 1 (January), 15–26.

Lupher. David A. 2003. *Romans in a New World: Classical Models in Sixteenth-Century Spanish America.* Ann Arbor, MI: The University of Michigan Press.

Maestro, Jesús G. 2004. *La secularización de la tragedia. Cervantes y 'La Numancia'.* Madrid: Ediciones Clásicas y University of Minnesota.

Martín, Francisco J. 1996. "EI desdoblamiento de la *hamartia* en *La Numancia.*" *Bulletin of the Comediantes* 48, no. 1 (summer), 15–24.

Meron, Theodor. 1998. *Bloody Constraint: War and Chivalry in Shakespeare.* Oxford: Oxford University Press.

Morales, Ambrosio de. 1791. *Corónica general de España,* vol. 4. Madrid.

Murray, Alexander. 2000. *Suicide in the Middle Ages,* vol. 2. Oxford: Oxford University Press.

Rey Hazas, Antonio. 1991. "Algunas reflexiones sobre el honor como sustituto funcional del destino en la tragicomedia barroca española." In Manuel V. Diago and Teresa Ferrer, eds., *Comedias y comediantes: Estudios sobre el teatro clásico español.* València: Departament de Filologia Espanyola, 253–258.

Rodríguez Salgado, María José. 1996. "Patriotismo y política exterior en la España de Carlos V y Felipe II." In Felipe Ruiz Martín, ed. *La proyección europea de la monarquía hispánica.* Madrid: Editorial Complutense, 49–105.

———. 1998. "Christians, Civilised and Spanish: Multiple Identities in Sixteenth-Century Spain." *Transactions of the Royal Historical Society,* sixth series. no. 8, 233–251.

Simerka, Barbara. 2003. *Discourses of Empire: Counter-Epic Literature in Early Modern Spain.* University Park, PA: Pennsylvania State University Press.

Tanner, Marie. 1993. *The Last Descendant of Aeneas: The Habsburgs and the Mythic Image of the Emperor.* New Haven, CT: Yale University Press.

Tar, Jane. 1990. "*Hamartia* in Cervantes' *La Numancia.*" *Aleph* 5, 22–28.

Thompson, I. A. A. 1995. "Castile, Spain and the Monarchy: The Political Community from *Patria Natural* to *Patria Nacional*" In Richard L. Kagan and Geoffrey Parker, eds, *Spain, Europe and the Atlantic World: Essays in Honour of John H. Elliott.* Cambridge: Cambridge University Press, 125–159.

Tomás y Valiente, Francisco. 1992 [1969]. *El derecho penal de la monarquía absoluta: siglos XVI, XVII y XVIII.* Reprint ed. Madrid: Editorial Tecnos.

Vivar, Francisco. 2000. "El ideal *pro patria mori* en *La Numancia* de Cervantes." *Cervantes* 20, no. 2, 7–30.

ANA LAGUNA

Life is a Dream and the Fractures of Reason[†]

> *Virtue!* a fig! . . . If the balance of our lives had not one scale of *reason* to
> poise another of sensuality, the blood and baseness of our natures would
> conduct us to most preposterous conclusions: but *we have reason to cool*
> our raging motions, our carnal stings, our unbitted lusts.
>
> (emphasis added, *Othello* I.1.3)

Although, as one of the most unreliable characters in literature, Iago can
seldom be trusted when articulating his intentions, his speech often conveys fascinating insights into the competing arguments of the early 1600s.
In the above quote, the ensign holds the common view that "virtue" as a
transformative attribute can be negated and substituted by the individual
power of reason, which alone is capable of determining and altering human
behavior. This idea was not new and had become somewhat common at the
turn of the century, as writers of every genre and religious creed—perhaps
less emphatically than Iago—increasingly invoked the glorifying power of
reason to escape the constraints of passion. But now, this substitution conveyed an entire cultural shift: the displacement of a moral framework by a
rational one, a process that would arouse and reenergize an old (and powerful) philosophical friction: the debate over the limits of human capacities,
either to obtain a true knowledge of this world and/or to achieve ultimate
salvation in the other. Situated within the asymmetric axes of theology and
natural philosophy, Iago's reasoning—and the secular line of inquiry it
implies—would prove to be an idiosyncratic and progressively perilous contention for Renaissance thinkers. The experiments and theories of Galileo
(1564–1642), Descartes (1596–1650), Kepler (1571–1630), Hobbes (1588–
1679), and Bacon (1561–1626) anticipated a mindset that would alter "universal" orders and cosmologies, thus becoming a threat to both the State
and Church of Christians and Reformists[1] alike. Soon, the awakening of
man's rational and scientific capacities would decenter and desanctify heavenly realms by subjecting the skies to very human and material laws and
experiments.

While European philosophers, theorists, and empiricists reversed traditional worldviews or reflected, like Shakespeare or Racine[2] on newly emerging paradigms, writers of the Spanish Baroque have been traditionally
considered to be too entrenched in their Catholic dogmas to participate in
or even consider such transformative discussions. However, critical works
of the last three decades have challenged this perception by revealing the
extent to which the Spanish literary tradition—even with its inquisitorial
constraints and honor-code pledges—also took part in the moral and

[†] From *Modern Language Notes* 129.2 (2014): 238–54. © 2014 The Johns Hopkins University
Press. Reprinted with permission of Johns Hopkins University Press. Quotations in Spanish
have been translated by G. J. Racz.

1. Galileo Galilei and Johannes Kepler were astronomists who based their work on scientific
observation and the development of optics; René Descartes, Thomas Hobbes, and Francis
Bacon were philosophers associated with empiricism, rationalism, and the scientific revolution. Reformists: members of the Reformed (i.e., Protestant) churches [editor's note].
2. French tragedian (1639–1699) [editor's note].

philosophical frictions that preceded the paradigm shifts of modernity. Even a play as emblematic as *La vida es sueño (Life is a Dream)* (1635), heralded once as the icon of conservatism, might also expose the attrition between moral and rational (pre-scientific) frameworks. Pedro Calderón de la Barca (1600–81), often considered a representative of the Spanish honor paradigm as the "dramatist who authoritatively answers all the questions that he poses"[3] is now approached as an author of questionable assumptions rather than universal principles, and this emphasis on instability is now allowing us to draw new or, at least, stimulating implications from his work.

It is from this more open perspective that this reading of *La vida es sueño* explores the role of reason in the main protagonist's thought and restitution process. Dispelling the cynicism of Iago's view, Segismundo—a prince abandoned and unjustly imprisoned by his father—regains his natural and symbolic order through a lengthy negotiation between rational thought and the moral, virtuous prerogative of "obrar bien" (do the right thing). * * *

Renaissance, Scholasticism, and the New Limits of Reason

Calderón holds the unique position in literature of being the "dramatist of Scholasticism in general" (Parker 68). * * * Indeed, using a dialogic disputation[4]—the Scholastic method of inquiry *par excellence*—allows Calderón to investigate various sides and implications of one theme. The approach is especially pertinent for his treatment of religious dogmas, since Scholastic inquiry, rather than questioning the truth of a statement, only subjects it to a partial analysis (Weijer 148). In turn, Calderón instills a new fluidity in Scholastic *disputatio,* providing it with an unprecedented dramatic power.

With regard to the question associated with free will, Calderón's predilection for Saint Thomas is still more fitting; since the playwright explores "the precise roles which the *reason* and the *will* must play" in human freedom/salvation (emphasis added, Parker 70). The roles of these capacities are somewhat limited in Saint Thomas Aquinas,[5] since for him man can only get to know God imperfectly through unaided reason. However, Saint Thomas does defend reason as a tool of philosophical and personal inquiry: "dará su Fe verdadera / a quien quiera, y como quiera, / . . . *que a todos dotó / de razón para buscar / la mejor . . . que nos dé testimonio* de él" (God will give his faith to anyone as He pleases . . . since He gave us all reason to look for the good argument that . . . would render proofs of his existence) (emphasis added, *A Dios por razón de estado* 1077–78, 1082–86). The assertion of this human limit was key in the reconciliation of faith and reason of thirteenth-century philosophies, and one could easily see a

---

3. McKendrick invokes this stereotype only to dispel the negative, traditional view of critics like Menéndez Pelayo (12). David Thacher Gies claims that Calderón as a playwright has been mostly rescued from his traditional image of guarantor of the national Spanish spirit of values—decisively emphasized by Menéndez Pelayo—mostly after the centennial of 1981 (269–71). Indeed, the works of Alexander Parker, Frederick De Armas, Margaret Greer, Bruce Wardropper, Evangelina Rodríguez and Kurt Levy have been highly influential in the rediscovery of Calderón's complexity and its relevance to post-modernity.
4. A medieval theological and philosophical system with a strong basis in religious dogma, Scholasticism used a formal debate (*disputatio*) between scholars to determine the validity of a claim [editor's note].
5. Influential medieval philosopher (1224–1275) who attempted to reconcile Scholasticism and the Aristotelian tradition [editor's note].

conflicted playwright of the seventeenth century return to this rationale in an attempt to find viable solutions for the dogmatic frictions eroding Catholicism on the Reformist front. However, even though the resurrection of Scholasticism four centuries after its birth offered new possibilities, the approach also faced new and demanding challenges.[6] The deductive process of logic and reason which had proved sufficient for the reaffirmation of faith in the thirteenth century had became an insufficient argument in the Baroque, when Spaniards faced the effects of the Protestant Reformation and the instabilities and disillusionment of an insecure world (Wright 537). Against Protestantism, the Baroque man now had to defend the existence of his free will while preserving his belief—despite new scientific evidence—in an ordered, infinite, and harmonious cosmos. These convictions proved increasingly difficult to maintain and reconcile in a practical world of rapid change and political decline which seldom afforded any opportunity for social mobility.

Although Golden Age writers often recurred to works of religious instruction such as the *Autos*[7] in an effort to recuperate confidence in man's own road to salvation, this dogmatic exaltation was not the only way they coped. Other authors turned to the endorsement of human reason as the capacity that could allow man to navigate the chaos that surrounded him, a rational turn that was ironically not devoid of doubt or distress. As William Egginton has reminded us, "the Baroque is the cultural expression of a deep and abiding anxiety regarding the nature and extent of human reason," and it is in "its philosophical expression, [that] this anxiety takes the form of a paradox that hinges on the problem of truth as a function of appearances" (186). Thus, this view, which regarded reason as a channel of anguish, inherently problematizes the later, enlightened myth that reason constituted the civilizing light of the intellect. In the mid 1600s, writers engaged in the exploration of reason often detached it from "the promise of human liberation," relating it instead to a profound cultural apprehension (Castillo and Lollini ix–xxiii). Yet, in *Life is a Dream,* both designations are at play; whereas, following a traditional Thomistic view, Segismundo locates the promise of his freedom in reason, he also finds in this rational competence the frustrating channel for self-doubt and the ultimate justification for his self-denial.

This latter conflict, between man's most profound instincts to (both) assert his desires and to rationalize (or suppress) them, points to Segismundo's idiosyncratic self-conflict, but such frictions are also paradigmatic of an entire era. Whereas in the Middle Ages, man's free will had been derailed by an external monster (devil, woman, or temptation), in the early modern world, man was hindered by his *own* internal turmoil and confusion.[8] Thus, one could argue that Segismundo embodies one of the great battles of the time, not the blunt—and stoic—struggle against man's

---

6. To evaluate these changes, see David Jonathan Hilder. His study—also on reason—is quite different from this one. He believes that "reason" in the Calderonean *opera* defends and alludes to not only a mental capacity, but also a social and moral order. "Both reason and exalted passions," he states, "become the preserve of noble blood in Calderón's plays. Whether he is dealing with vengeful husbands, monarchs . . . the concern of his characters that they not commit 'a bajeza' a 'low' action is not simply a Christian concern . . . but a case of aristocracy" (10).
7. Short, allegorical religious plays [editor's note].
8. To see more on moral confusion and its weight in *La vida,* see Mary Wilson 172–76.

violent passions, but the more sensitive one against the interferences of his thought-process.

Matthew Stroud has identified some of these interferences as purely epistemological. For him, even those straightforward murder plays of the *Comedia*, where the truth of a perception seems irrelevant to the action, reveal that an ongoing epistemological preoccupation is at the core of the plot conflict, since the question of how a party knows that his/her honor has been affronted is largely undermined by an uncertainty about our own knowledge and perceptions (116). Continually testing the limits of human reason and perception, *Life is a Dream* is a prime example of this epistemological instability. Knowledge seems to be Segismundo's preoccupation from the start, as evident in his first striking soliloquy: "what horrid crime / Was perpetrated at the time / When I, offending you, was born" (104–06).[9] The pursuit of knowledge does not only inform the climatic soliloquy of "¿Qué es la vida?" (2182) ("What's life?"), it also permeates Segismundo's journey, either to nurture his arrogance and certainty—"What could remain for me to know / When knowing my identity" (1296–97)—or to plague his mind with doubt when conditions around him do not match his perception—"I'm awed and not untouched by fear / But can't be sure what to believe" (1226–27). As the action unfolds, Segismundo reveals his endemic cerebral nature when he blames, time and again, the confusion of his state on the tricks that his own mind is playing on him.

Perhaps these are some of the aspects and instances of the play that made Christopher Soufas conclude that "what the prince actually confronts in the palace is the confused structure of his thought" (293). For Soufas, Calderón's emphasis on the prince's mental process leads this character away from reality and into indulging an obsessive and "overdeveloped reasoning ability . . . at the expense of his sensitive development" (290). Ironically, this critic censors Segismundo's mode of thinking for the same reasons that humanists criticized late Scholasticism—"the extreme rationalization of the external world" (Soufas 291)[1]—reinforcing the idea that Calderón had indeed made of Segismundo an icon—or an exploration—of the scholastic mind. To the characteristic "sic et non" scholastic *disputatio* (that so often defines Segismundo's "logical" thinking), Calderón adds the lingering question of "How do you know for sure if it is a yes or a no?" which throws Segismundo's mind into deeper levels of epistemological volatility.

Segismundo might only escape such volatility through the moral compass of "obrar bien" (doing the right thing). Reaching a moral epiphany that is still highly intellectual, Segismundo affirms that

> Be careful or your logic might
> Convince you this is fact again!
>   . . . I've learned

---

9. Unless specified, all textual references to the play are from Ciriaco Morón's edition.
1. By the fifteenth and sixteenth centuries, the scholastic *disputatio* had turned into a mechanized method of discussion that Humanists often criticized and mocked. However, as Erika Rummel has shown, Humanism also benefitted from its dialectic method, especially when examining controversies: while Scholastics used the *sic et non* method, it is easy to see in the Humanists' dialogues—as a form of exploration of confronting views—an adaptation of the Scholastic mechanic (153–92).

That pleasure is a lovely flame
The merest breath of air blows out
So only wafting ash remains—
Let's look toward the eternal, then,
And seek renown that never dies
Where joy will not succumb to sleep
Or splendor ever napping lie!

(2967–68, 2978–85)

Following this rational voice, which affirms the lasting values of virtue and restraint, the prince achieves a victory against himself. Thomas O'Connor argues that this personal triumph translates into the three great victories of the play: Segismundo's dominion over violence and lust; the restoration of Rosaura's honor; and Basilio's pardon. Reason is so pivotal in Segismundo's success, that, in O'Connor's view, it stands in the play as a guiding principle for human behavior. Similar views abound; for Jacinto Rivera Rosales, for example, it is precisely the prince's rational reflection that allows him to emerge as a hero despite all previous uncertainty about his stature as man/prince. Reason becomes a liberating moral paradigm in line with a Thomistic prerogative, "a razón prudente o de la fe considerada verdadera" (prudent reason or faith assumed to be true) with which the character is able to escape the nihilism of a paralyzing *desengaño (disenchantment)* (7).

But not all readings need to be this positive. While Segismundo's mode of thinking might free him from the idiosyncratic baroque *desengaño*, it also allows him to assert—for himself and others—the very irrational code of honor which immediately interrupts his pursuit of happiness. While his renunciation of Rosaura and his forced union to Estrella comply with the return to order prescribed in the *comedia*, such decisions also connote a self-cancellation that shapes the deep structure of the play through the very negative imperatives of honor (O'Connor 101).

* * *

The New Cosmologies of Reason: Towards a New Assessment in Life is a Dream

Embedded in the ideological reevaluations of the seventeenth century are not only new, emerging rationalist epistemes, but also a whole new cosmology. At the dawn of a Galilean era, the best attempts to reconcile reason with revelation seemed to still come from Saint Thomas, with his ineffable defense of reason and experimentation with the natural world. Conveniently enough, reason, for Saint Thomas, included not only man's logical thought processes but also the empirical observation and experimentation of the physical world. For him, it was the combination of these perspectives (logical and experimental) which afforded men their cognition of the world (Tarnar 172). Reason, then, for Aquinas, was not only the central tenet of faith, as the philosopher famously declared, it also constituted the first principle of science.[2] It was through reason that he defended the truth of

2. "Not only does faith hold that there is creation, but reason also demonstrates it" (*De potentia Dei* 3.5).

scientific paradigms as significant as Aristotle's Ptolemaic idea of the universe. Aristotle believed, with Ptolemy, that the universe entailed a harmonic entity where all planets (Moon, Mercury, Venus, Sun, Mars, Jupiter, and Saturn) were set into motion by a *Primum Mobile*[3] in perfectly concentric orbs. This idea was accurate for Saint Thomas since it was the "*most reasonable*," just as it was "*reasonable* that the stars pertain to the nature of the sphere in which they are situated" (emphasis added, *De Caelo* Book 2, Lect. 10). Science in Scholasticism is consequently a very "rational" matter, and this rationality affects the ill-defined areas like astronomy and astrology, the sciences that occupied such a central role in *Life is a Dream* and were intimately related to Thomism.

Both disciplines experienced an unprecedented development in the 1600s and Calderón's life span allowed him to be a direct witness of such expansion; *Life is a Dream* was published in 1635, only twelve years after the publication of Galileo's revolutionary *Assayer*, and only three years after the appearance of the *Dialogue Concerning the Two Chief World Systems*. Such circumstances seemed conducive to an ideological cross-pollination between science and literature, which—as Enrique García Santo Tomás has explored in the context of optic inventions—was not only unavoidable but also highly significant for the study Spain's "uneven modernity" (72).

As a play, *Life* is particularly immersed in the contemporary discussions that attempted to define what was physically plausible and/or religiously acceptable. This distinction was not always as clear as writers and philosophers desired, even in Inquisitorial Spain. Astronomical and astrological prognostications had not disappeared from early modern intellectual life, even in Iberia, despite the 1585 Bull *Coeli et Terrae* (Of Heaven and Earth) by Pope Sixtus V that—even before Galileo—forbade some astrological practices. Current studies in science in the Spain of the 1500s and 1600s have demonstrated that seventeenth-century Iberia did not always follow inquisitorial mandates regarding astronomy, especially in those cases regarding astronomical predictions, perhaps because prophecy from astronomy "was not only seen as a form of divine inspiration, but also as a *rational* or *scientific* way of understanding the regularities of nature and predicting future events" (Lanuza-Navarro and Avalos-Flores). It might be remembered that this had not even been the first attempt to stop such beliefs and practices; the Council of Trent[4] Session on December 4, 1563 had issued a prohibition against writing or reading any book of magic, sorcery, or other divinatory art. Yet, the popular and academic endurance of these practices indicates that "the ecclesiastic authorities of the time mainly followed the practical posture of Saint Thomas Aquinas: astrology was legitimate as long as it did not deny the human free will" (Lanuza-Navarro and Avalos-Flores).[5] And in his normal guise, Thomas had elaborated his argument in his *Summa* by first appealing to reason: "Some have said that the stars signify rather than cause what is going to happen in the future. But this is *not reasonable*. Every corporeal sign is the effect of that which manifests." Then, he adds:

3. Prime mover [editor's note].
4. Council of the Roman Catholic Church (1545–63), held in response to the Protestant Reformation that established the principles of the Counter-Reformation [editor's note].
5. For a story of the reception of Copernican and Galilean theses in Spain, see García Santo Tomás 69–70.

We can as safely say that there is no knowledge of the future to be had from the heavenly bodies except that in which effects are foreknown from causes. Now there are two kinds of effects which are not caused by celestial bodies. The first ones are all of those which happen by accidents

. . . The second kind . . . includes acts of man's freedom, his faculty of will and reason. His mind or reason is not corporeal, nor is the act of a bodily organ; consequently neither is *his will, which is in his reason* . . . so it is impossible for the heavenly bodies directly to make an impression on man's mind or his free will.

. . . [T]o conclude, if anyone attempts from the stars to foretell future contingent or chance events . . . he is acting under a false and groundless presupposition, and opening himself to the intrusion of diabolic powers. Consequently, this kind of foretelling is superstitious and wrong. But if someone uses astronomic observations to forecast future events, which are actually determined by physical laws, for instance, drought or rainfall, and so forth, then this is neither superstitious nor sinful. (*Summa Theologica* 55; Vol. 40, Question 51, Article 5)

By distinguishing the realm of human choice from the purely mechanical processes of nature, Aquinas is thus able to defend scientific inquiry and reconcile it with traditional Catholic theology.

However, throughout the *Summa,* one can attest the theologian's strong anxiety about the interaction of divination and superstition, astronomy and astrology. Attempting to explain the "frequent accuracy of astrologists in predicting future contingents," Aquinas claims that when "men follow their emotions . . . the heavenly bodies influence them through their bodies and senses" (*Summa* 55; Vol. 40, Question 51, Article 5). That is to say, there is some external effect on man's choice, especially on men driven by emotions rather than reason, who tend to be the majority because "[f]ew are the wise who control themselves by the dictates of reason. This is why astrological forecasts often come off, especially with regard to public events which depend on the masses" (*Summa* 55; Question 51, Article 5).

Life is a Dream demonstrates iconically such anxiety about the accuracy of astrological predictions and the real influence of stars on human will. The idea is, of course, discredited because of Basilio, "a fine astrologer" able to produce accurate predictions—"How famous an astrologer / Would that man be who only spied / Disasters for, without a doubt, / These always manage to transpire!" (1728–31)[6]—does not prove to be a wise, "docto" (learned) (606) monarch given the choices he makes with his son and the government of this kingdom. This characterization of unwise scientists is consistent with others in Calderón, and has been interpreted as the author's negative view of science. Vincent Martin, for example, argues that Calderón often points at "the limits of man's *sophia* and *logos* with regard to the great mysteries of life" (126), as if only God

---

6. The text leaves the nature of these predictions (mechanical processes or events) conveniently undefined in the generic word "casos" (cases), either avoiding the specific definition provided by Saint Thomas between predictions on events or purely mechanical processes, thereby demonstrating the practical impossibility of making that distinction.

were the supreme scientist: "En todas las ciencias insigne; y en todos los estudios Docto" (*Loa El pintor* 372). As Martin has amply explored, the sciences are commonly depicted in the Calderonian *opera* as "Magical" or "Diabólicas," often leading the characters involved with them to the edge of perdition.[7] Certainly, in certain milieus, there is an undeniable disregard for science in general, and astrology in particular. Notorious advisors, like Juan de Mariana (1536–1624), had warned kings about the dangers of astrology (for him, an art rather than a science): "No por eso queremos que . . . venga á caer en supersticiones que manchen su majestad, agora escudriñando los eventos futuros por medio de alguna arte adivinatoria (si arte puede llamarse á lo que antes bien es ludibrio de hombres vanísimos)" (We don't want that Your Majesty . . . should fall prey to superstitions that though some form of divinatory art (if such a ludicrous, vain entertainment could be called art) might undermine Your dignity with the scrutiny of future events) (398).[8]

However, in the case of Basilio, and in a play that so carefully avoids political mentions or religious overtones, the characterization of the unwise scientist might be articulated through a Thomistic—rather than purely traditional—reference. Basilio's troubled decisions are not based on "rational," Ptolemaic calculations of the universe, but on a very emotional response, the fear of losing his power. The way in which the text describes the extent to which he embraces that fear—imprisoning his own son—suggests a tyrannical drive, repeatedly hinted by Segismundo as he addresses his father as "tyrant to my will" (1504). The accusation is echoed by the kingdom in general, given the promptness with which the mob rises to support him against Basilio (engaging in a civil war), and the anonymous comments, like that of "2nd Servant," who after hearing Segismundo's charge of tyranny against his father simply censors Segismundo for judging the king, not for being wrong in his appreciation (1324–2).[9]

Basilio and Segismundo, by themselves or opposed to one another, demonstrate the negative effects of this lack of rationality, thereby exposing throughout the play their profound flaws as men. Ironically, even though in many regards they do complement and correct one another, they share the same equivocal cosmology. Invoking the ethnocentric paradigm *à propos de* Rosaura's beauty, for example, Segismundo alludes to the beauty of the heavenly realm, composed of "esferas perfetas" (1604–1606), clearly suggesting a shared perception of the Ptolemaic universe that has captured Basilio's judgment and imagination. Thus, although in exemplary way, Basilio is humbled as a scientist and king ("But this time in my crown's defense I'll trust / Cold steel where once my hapless science vied" [2486–87]), Segismundo inherits from his father this same deluded cosmovision, and with it, perhaps, a similar inability to resolve the deepest issues with which he is confronted in his government, the questions of treason (he

---

7. Basilio reenacts the message explicitly when he recognizes, upon Clarín's death:

> "persuade / nuestro error, nuestra ignorancia, / a mayor conocimiento / este cadaver que habla . . . que son diligencias vanas / del hombre, cuantas dispone / contra mayor fuerza y causa!" (how convincingly this [Clarín's] corpse / reflects upon our error / showing . . . how vain are / men's deliberations when set / against a higher will and cause) (3099–3102, 3105–06).

8. See Vilvalda 383–396.
9. For more on treason in the play, see Heiple "Tradition," and Laguna.

forgives the father that attacked him while imprisoning the soldier that liberated him) and restitution (of his power and Rosaura's honor).

In presenting an unflattering depiction of kingship, Calderón thus devaluates the Church/God/King scheme that had dominated previous centuries (and the theater of the previous generation emblematized in Lope). In fact, Calderón's propensity to portray "irrational," fallible monarchs (be it Basilio, Henry VIII in *La cisma de Inglaterra* or Herod, in *El mayor monstruo los celos*) who can no longer act as fair representatives of divine justice among men has been identified with a new attitude regarding the role of monarchy (Forcione 10; Ed Wilson 160). Alban Forcione explains this new political sensibility arguing that, in the Golden Age, "what had been a mere abstraction in the medieval *speculum principis*[1] tradition, the real educable body of the monarch, seamlessly transferable to its royal dignity, became a preoccupation and paradoxically a source of anxiety in its glorious elevation to the suprapersonal and immortal majesty" (1).[2] The anxiety that translates into recurring, forced abdications on the stage invokes for Forcione not only the stepping down of the royal figure, but also—perhaps more importantly— the search for a humanness in the monarch that had been lost in all levels of society. The frequent disrobing of a king thus points at the need for the crowning of a recovered—and perhaps more rational—humanity across the social spectrum.[3] Indeed, only a redefined rationality might be able to reconcile the inherited honor-ridden structures with the emerging reason-bound mindsets that would end up dominating the late 1600s.

Situated in a transitional period that has not yet defined its own physics of power, *Life is a Dream* demonstrates how in Iberia, while the traces of the old cosmology embodied in Basilio are certainly shut, the doors to the Galilean universe are not yet open. What becomes painfully clear is how the cosmic ordering of the universe coined by the (neo) Scholastics is now rendered insufficient and incomplete. In the absence of an explicit divine allegory able to resolve such epistemological rupture, the heavens, to which Segismundo prays and to which Galileo turns, witness a humbling moment for the traditional worldview that had dominated the Spanish Baroque. Suspended between Iago's cynicism and Segismundo's uncertainty, *Life is a Dream* does not present Iberia as the self-contained inquisitorial country traditionally assumed, but as a porous and vulnerable state too aware of the doubts and fractures implied in the very earthy art of government.

WORKS CITED

Aquinas, Thomas. *The Summa Theologica*. Trans. Thomas Franklin O'Meara and Michael John Duffy. Cambridge: Cambridge UP, 2006.

———. *De Caelo. By Aristotle*. Trans. J. L. Stocks. *The Works of Aristotle*. Ed. W. D. Ross. Vol. 2. Oxford: Clarendon Press, 1930.

1. "Mirror for princes": a medieval and Renaissance genre of advice and instruction for rulers [editor's note].

2. See also Anita Howard, when she studies the progressive humanization of the king figure whose flaws "come to signify the fragmentation of a changing world rather than the completeness of older concepts of ideal harmony." For her, Calderón comes to emblematize how "monarchs are challenged to face and acknowledge their likeness with their subjects whilst resolving their imperfections" (37).

3. This disrobing also "emphatically remind[s] the audience that the central regal identity— institutionalized, legal, executive, political, requires analysis and critical inspection" (Forcione 186).

Castillo, David, and Massimo Lollini. "Reason and Its Others in Early Modernity (A View from the South)." *Reason and Its Others: Italy, Spain, and the New World*. Eds. Castillo and Lollini. Nashville: Vanderbilt UP, 2006. ix–xxiii.

Calderón de la Barca, Pedro. *La vida es sueño*. Ed. Ciríaco Morón. Madrid: Cátedra, 1986.

———. *Autos sacramantales alegóricos e historiales del insigne poeta español Don Pedro Calderón de la Barca*. Ed. Pedro Pando y Mier. Madrid: Manuel Ruiz de Murga, 1717.

De Armas, Frederick, ed. *The Prince in the Tower: Perceptions of* La vida es sueño. Lewisburg, PA: Bucknell UP, 1993.

Egginton, William. "Reason's Baroque House (Cervantes, Master Architect)." Castillo and Lollini 186–203.

Forcione, Alban K. *Majesty and Humanity: Kings and Their Doubles in the Political Drama of the Spanish Golden Age*. New Haven: Yale UP, 2009.

Galilei, Galileo. "The Assayer." *The Essential Galileo*. Ed. Maurice A. Finocchiaro. Indianapolis: Hackett, 2008. 179–89.

García Santo-Tomás, Enrique. "Fortunes of the *Occhiali Politici* in Early Modern Spain: Optics, Vision, Points of View." *PMLA* 124.1 (2009): 59–75.

Gies, David Thacher: *Cambridge History of Spanish Literature*. Cambridge: Cambridge UP, 2005.

Greer, Margaret. *The Play of Power: Mythological Court Dramas of Calderón de la Barca*. Princeton: Princeton UP, 1991.

———. "An (In)convenient Marriage? Justice and Power in *La vida es sueño*, comedia and auto sacramental." *Bulletin of Spanish Studies* 85.6 (Fall 2008): 55–68.

———. "Mirror Neurons, Theatrical Mirrors and the Honor Code." *Anuario calderoniano* (2012): 85–100.

———. "Los estudios calderonianos: los retos para dentro y para fuera." *Calderón: del manuscrito a la escena*. Eds. Frederick A. de Armas and Luciano García Lorenzo. Frankfurt: Iberoamericana, 2011. 109–23.

Heiple, Daniel. "The Tradition Behind the Punishment of the Rebel Soldier in *La vida es sueño*." *Bulletin of Hispanic Studies* 50 (1973): 1–17.

———. "Life as Dream and the Philosophy of Disillusionment." De Armas, *Prince* 118–131.

Hilder, David Jonathan. *Reason and the Passions in the Comedias of Calderón*. West Lafayette: Purdue U Monographs, 1983.

Howard, Anita. *The King Within: Reformation of Power in William Shakespeare and Pedro Calderón de la Barca*. New York: Peter Lang, 2010.

Laguna, Ana M. "Antonio Pérez and the Art of Influence." *Signs of Power in Habsburg Spain and the New World*. Eds. Jason McCloskey and Ignacio López. Lewisburg, PA: Bucknell UP, 2013. 133–52.

Lanuza-Navarro, Tayra M. C., and Ana Cecilia Avalos-Flores. "Astrological Prophecies and the Inquisition in the Iberian World." *Proceedings of the 2nd ICESHS, Cracow. Poland, 6–9 Sept., 2006: The Global and the Local: The History of Science and the Cultural Integration of Europe*. Ed. Michal Kokowski. Cracow: P of the Polish Academy of Arts and Sciences, 2007. 681–88. Web. 13 Oct. 2010. <http://www.2iceshs.cyfronet.pl/proceedings.html>.

Levy, Kurt L., Jesús Ara and Gethin Hughes, eds. *Calderón and the Baroque Tradition*. Waterloo, ON: Wilfrid Laurier UP, 1986.

McKendrick, Melveena. "The Reign of Calderón." *Theatre in Spain 1490–1700*. Cambridge: Cambridge UP, 1989. 140–77.

Mariana, Juan. *Del rey y de la institución real*. Barcelona: Selecta, 1880.

Martin, Vincent. *El concepto de "representación" en los Autos Sacramentales de Calderón*. Pamplona: Reichenberg-Kassel, 2007.

———. "Experiencia y ciencia en Calderón" *Hacia un nuevo inventario de la ciencia española*. Eds. Gonzalo Capellán de Miguel and Xavier Agenjo Bullón. Santander: Sociedad Menéndez Pelayo, 2000. 91–105.

Menéndez Pelayo, Marcelino. *Calderón y su teatro*. Madrid, 1881.

O'Connor, Thomas. *"La vida es sueño*. Reason and Renunciation, Versus *La estatua de Prometeo*, Love and Fulfillment." De Armas, *Prince* 97–110.

Parker, Alexander. *The Allegorical Drama of Calderón*. Oxford: Dolphin, 1943.

———. *The Mind and Art of Calderón*. Cambridge: Cambridge UP, 1988.

Rivera Rosales, Jacinto. "El idealismo práctico de Calderón: de Descartes a Kant." *Signos filosóficos* 10 (2009): 41–67.

Rodríguez, Evangelina and Antonio Tordera. *Calderón y la obra corta dramática del siglo XVII*. London: Tamesis, 1983.

Rummel, Erika. *The Humanist-Scholastic Debate in the Renaissance and Reformation*. Cambridge, MA: Harvard UP, 1995.

Soufas, Jr., C. Christopher. "Thinking in *La vida es sueño*." *PMLA* 100.3 (1985): 287–99.

Stroud, Matthew. *Fatal Union: A Pluralistic Approach to the Spanish Wife-Murder Comedias*. Lewisburg, PA: Bucknell UP, 1990.

Tarnar, Richard. *The Passion of the Western Mind. Understanding the Ideas that Have Shaped our Worldview*. New York: Ballantine, 1991.

Vilvalda, Nicolás. "Basilio o el ocaso del monarca-astrólogo: Juegos de la similitud e inconveniencias políticas en *La vida es sueño*." *Hacia la tragedia áurea: lecturas para un nuevo milenio*. Eds. Frederick De Armas, Luciano García Lorenzo and Enrique García Santo-Tomás. Frankfurt: Iberoamericana; Vervuert, 2008. 383–96.

Wardropper, Bruce, ed. *Criticial Essays on the Theater of Calderón*. New York: New York UP, 1965.

Weijer, Olga. "The Medieval Disputatio." *Traditions of Controversy*. Ed. Marcelo Dascal and Hamliang Zhang. Amsterdam: John Benjamins, 2007. 141–50.

Wilson, Mary, *Calderón*. Oxford: Pergamon, 1969.

Wilson, Edward. M. "On *La vida es sueño*." Wardropper 63–89.

Wright, Diane M. "Finding One's Way into the Counter Reformation: Thomistic Thought in Tirso de Molina and Calderón de la Barca." *Hispanic Studies in Honor of Robert L. Fiore*. Eds. Chad M. Gasta and Julia Domínguez. Newark, DE: Juan de la Cuesta, 2009, 537–59.

DANIEL L. HEIPLE

Life as Dream and the Philosophy of Disillusionment[†]

The Spanish seventeenth century was a period of deep disillusionment and pessimism. While it is easy to correlate the advent of pessimism with the decline of Spanish political power, it is important to remember that disillusionment was not limited to Spain, but was a general European phenomenon (Bréhier 1966, 1–17). One cause clearly lies in a reaction against the extreme optimism of the previous century. Accompanying the expansion of empire and the consolidation of national states was the revival of Platonic idealism and the concepts of peace, harmony, and utopian dream permeate sixteenth-century writings. Particularly important was the concept of the perfectibility of the individual through education and moral reform, as advocated by humanist learning and teaching. The seventeenth century witnessed the failures of this idealism: the desire for reform had turned into extreme intolerance, the desire for peace was broken by the cruel Thirty Years War and various rebellions and religious wars. And for the Spaniards, the wealth, military power, and organization of empire clearly began to decline. Religious persecution and wars had produced a fear of confidence and discrete thinkers avoided involved worldly entanglements, looking to the stability of eternity and personal values as guides in this life. This introspective withdrawal produced a great deal of literature in Spain, where the severe political and economic decline seemed to imprint the message that the affairs of the world were indeed risky. Literature dealing with *desengaño*[1] is extremely pessimistic, describing worldly existence in the bleakest of terms through comparisons with death, decay, sickness, old age, shipwrecks, etc.

Both terms, *desengaño* and disillusionment, imply a previous deception. In seventeenth-century thought, the *engaño* consisted of an infatuation with the things of the world, believing them to be real when their existence is precarious and transitory. *Desengaño* is an act of realization that the things of the world cannot be held, for they decay and pass into ruin (Green 1968, 4: 44). This idea easily relates to the movement of the Counter-Reformation, calling for spiritual reform and less worldly values. *Desengaño*, however, placed more emphasis on recognizing the deception of the world than on the benefits resulting from such a recognition. The end result was to be the superior individual of Stoic philosophy, the person who, while realizing the falseness of the world, does not form an attachment to it and remains indifferent to both success and failure.

The distrust of the things of the world was also extended to fellow humans and to social dealings. In this period the word "discretion" passed—in English as well as in Spanish—from its use as a favored synonym for prudence and intelligence to its modern meanings of circumspection and wariness, and, at times, even secrecy. Not only was it a suspicious, distrustful age

---

[†] From *The Prince in the Tower: Perceptions of* La vida es sueño, ed. Frederick A. de Armas (London: Associated University Presses, 1993), pp. 118–31. Reprinted by permission of the publisher. All translations of Golden Age poets are by Daniel L. Heiple. All footnotes are by the editor of this Norton Critical Edition.

[1] As applied to seventeenth-century Spain, a generalized feeling of disillusion or disenchantment.

regarding human relationships, but in other countries, it produced the great skeptical philosophers. Descartes and Hume, and even Calderón's thought process is imbued with skeptical methodology and terminology, from Segismundo's education through experience to the methodological doubting of the devil figure in Calderón's religious allegories (*autos sacramentales*). While most writers on *desengaño* do not explore the parameters of doubt, they do express much awareness of the paradoxes and contradictions of existence. The spirit and themes of *desengaño* are most familiar from lyrical poetry. At times it seems as if the poets engaged in a competition to see who could reduce life to its most miserable terms. The rantings of Quevedo against the brevity of life are quite well known, as he tried to reduce the limits of life to nothing or even less than nothing:

> Fue sueño ayer, mañana será tierra:
> poco antes nada, y poco después humo.
> (1963, 5)

> It was a dream yesterday; tomorrow it will be earth:
> a little before, nothing; and a little after, vapor.

> Ayer se fue, mañana no ha llegado,
> hoy se está yendo, sin parar un punto,
> soy un fue, y un será, y un es cansado.
> En el hoy, y mañana, y ayer, junto
> pañales, y mortaja. . . .
> (1963, 4)

> Yesterday has gone, tomorrow has not arrived,
> Today is going, without stopping a bit,
> I am a *was*, and a *will be*, and a tired *is*.
> In the today, and tomorrow, and yesterday, together
> diapers and death shroud . . .

*   *   *

Desengaño was not a developed philosophical system, but an attitude brought about by the realization of the vanity of the world. Such a realization should logically lead to a spiritual reform and asceticism, but this theme is less prevalent in the literary manifestations of seventeenth-century disillusionment than the desire to recreate and convey to the reader the sense of the unsubstantiality of the world. Rather than present the glories of retirement from the active life, Quevedo's moral sonnets portray his bitter disillusionment with the world and the sense of futility of life. Less clear are the alternatives to be pursued after realizing that the world is a deception. * * *

Among the metaphors of *desengaño* are those of the self-consciousness of life: the Calderonian metaphors of life as a dream and life as theater. López de Zárate bitterly summed up the importance of life in three essential acts: birth, death and a moment of consciousness:

> Estas tan consecuentes brevedades:
> nacer, morir, dar cuenta de haber sido;
> (1947, 2: 71)

These such meaningful moments:
to be born, to die, to realize one has existed;

Employing the traditional metaphor of life as a theater, he views human
existence as a show or spectacle observed by other actors:

Espectáculos son todos los hombres,
unos de otros y teatro el mundo
donde humanas tragedias se eternizan.
                    (1947, 2: 58).

All men are spectacles,
everyone of each other, and the world a theater
where human tragedies are made eternal.

This idea of one as actor, observer, and evaluator of one's own actions—
in short, self-consciousness—can only be terribly inhibiting, further
reducing the desire for action. Even though *desengaño* as a philosophical
attitude has its logical extension in actions, as a literary movement it
seemed to exaggerate the obstacles of life and to preach futility of action.

La vida es sueño recreates the negative arguments of futility, but goes
on to supersede the limitations implied in poetic *desengaño*. Like
Gracián's *Criticón*, Calderón begins by showing how nature serves as a
school for basic education. Both Basilio and Segismundo can be con-
trasted as readers and interpreters, not of books, but of the signs of
nature. Basilio interprets the configurations of the stars and Segismundo
receives his education through the observation of nature:

. . . las letras
humanas que le ha enseñado
la muda naturaleza
de los montes y los cielos,
en cuya divina escuela
la retórica aprendió
de las aves y las fieras.
                    (1027–33)

those humane studies taught him
by silent nature under skies
and mountains, that holy school where
he'd learned rhetoric from birds and beasts.
                    (35)

As readers, Segismundo and Basilio have opposite responses. Reading
the forecasts of doom, as would any reader of Quevedo and the *concep-
tistas*;[2] Basilio tends to despair and inaction. He tries to avoid the disaster by putting it off or preventing it. Segismundo, on the other hand,
throws himself into life and into action, be it his destructive trial in the
palace or as leader of the rebellion to achieve his rights.

2. Early seventeenth-century poets in Spain who strove for concentrated and exact expression—
i.e., wits.

In this respect *La vida es sueño* differs from other works of Spanish Baroque in that it does not rely on the otherworldly to make its point. Although a number of critics in the past have assumed the play is a religious work, there are in fact few references to the deity (mostly in oaths). The other references to Christianity are minimal: one to original sin, one to Christian charity, two to Catholic education, and only two to an afterlife. Segismundo dialogues with the impersonal "cielos,"[3] not God, throughout the play. In this context, the high number of references to secular philosophers is also noteworthy. Calderón has carefully avoided references to religion in order to demonstrate that nature and experience by themselves are sufficient to instruct human intelligence in this life. Segismundo looks at the world and extracts from his experiences a morality for this world. In this play, there are no references to the Church, and the Church does not instruct and does not teach—quite the contrary, experience (nature) itself proves to be an adequate guide and instructor in this world. Calderón's position on education seems to be a step towards that of the *philosophes*[4] of the following century, for whom nature was sufficient unto itself as a teacher and model. Starting from the *tabula rasa* of the skeptic philosopher, Calderón reaffirms traditional philosophy and Christianity, but, by replacing the Church with experience and reason as necessary steps in Segismundo's education, he seems to anticipate the philosophical positions of the eighteenth century.

In the second act, Segimundo's failure in the palace leads the spectator through the arguments of poetic *desengaño*. Following a basic distinction of scholasticism, seventeenth-century writers distinguished three types of goods in the world: the goods of nature, the goods of fortune, and the spiritual goods of virtue and knowledge. "Los bienes de la naturaleza"[5] referred to given things that cannot be changed, such as one's race, stature, physical characteristics, mental ability, etc. Thus, if one is a genius, or blind, or extremely handsome, nothing can be done to change these natural qualities. "Los bienes de la fortuna"[6] referred to all things that can be acquired and lost against one's will, such as wealth, power, station, honors, etc. The third category, spiritual goods, had no general name but consisted of two transcendental goods: Virtue and Wisdom. They are the only goods that one can acquire and not be deprived of either against one's will or at death, for since they are acquired by the spirit, they transcend death. Moral philosophy taught that happiness comes from relinquishing the love of the goods of fortune and turning to the transcendental goods of Wisdom and Virtue. Otherwise one will live a life of constant turmoil worrying about the possession of acquisitions and suffering for their loss.

This distinction forms the basis of Segismundo's disillusionment and the empirical lesson he learns in the play. In the palace, Segismundo's error consists of confusing the unchangeable goods of nature with those of fickle fortune:

> Mi padre eres y mi rey;
> luego toda esta grandeza

---

3. Heavens.
4. French Enlightenment intellectuals.
5. What nature grants us.
6. What fortune grants us.

> me da la naturaleza
> por derechos de su ley.   (1508–11)

> You're my father and my King.
> And so all this majesty
> is what justice and the law
> of nature already grant me.   (51)

When his father suggests he may be dreaming, Segismundo states he is certain of his sense perceptions and concludes:

> sé quien soy, y no podrás,
> aunque suspires y sientas,
> quitarme el haber nacido
> desta corona heredero.   (1538–41)

> I know who I am, and however
> you bemoan it and regret it,
> you cannot rob me of the fact
> that I am the born heir to this throne.   (52)

Segismundo has yet to understand the precariousness of the goods of fortune, and, even though his argument is impeccable—he is indeed the heir to the crown—he fails to realize the limitations of his own statement. Being the heir does not mean he will inherit or actually possess the crown and rule. His bloodline does make him the crown prince, but ruling itself is subject to the whims of fortune and the circumstances of occasion.

By the end of act 2 when he awakens in prison and is told he had a dream, Segismundo has mastered this distinction. From his experience he concludes that all life is a dream—not in the Cartesian sense that he doubts or affirms his existence, but in the sense that the goods of the world, riches and power, are illusory because they can be taken from him against his will. Thus, people do not dream *that* they are, but rather *what* they are (in Spanish: no sueña *que* es, sino *lo que* es):

> . . . el vivir sólo es soñar;
> y la experiencia me enseña,
> que el hombre que vive, sueña
> lo que es, hasta despertar.
> Sueña el rey que es rey, y vive
> con este engaño mandando,
> disponiendo y gobernando;
> y este aplauso, que recibe
> prestado, en el viento escribe
> y en cenizas le convierte
> la muerte . . .   (2154–64)

> that to live is but to dream.
> And all that's happened to me tells me
> that while he lives man dreams
> what he is until he wakens.

> The king dreams he's a king,
> and so he lives with this illusion,
> making rules, putting things in order,
> governing, while all the praise
> he's showered with is only lent him,
> written on the wind, and by death,
> his everlasing sorrow,
> transformed to dust and ashes.   (76)

He concludes from this argument that life—not that one exists, but what one is and what one owns—is a fiction and a fantasy, possessing all the insubstantiality of a dream. This is the stage reached in lyric poetry of *desengaño* in the seventeenth century. As a philosophical situation, however, it implies a lack of sense and purpose to existence. A rational corollary to the statement that the things of this life are a dream would be that one's actions in this life lack meaning and purpose.

The third act of *La vida es sueño* denies this sense of futility and affirms a commitment to life and action. When faced with the call to action in the third act, Segismundo concludes that virtue is a good that can never be lost:

> Que estoy soñando, y que quiero
> obrar bien, pues no se pierde
> obrar bien, aun entre sueños.   (2399–2401)

> I am dreaming, and I want
> to do right, since one does not lose
> a good deed, even in dreams.
>
> (translation mine)

With this precept, he forgives Clotaldo and comes to govern his passions. Dressed in skins like a beast, he finds himself alone with Rosaura and questions if he should follow his instincts to take advantage of the situation and violate her, but he concludes that it is a prince's duty to protect the helpless, not to abuse them. He hopes that doing right will prevent his suffering the shock of waking up again in the tower, and he decides to continue acting out the dream, but this time with the awareness that he could awaken at any moment and his world could disappear (2359–65; 84). Following the division of the goods of the world into categories, he decides virtue can never do harm:

> Mas sea verdad o sueño,
> obrar bien es lo que importa;
> si fuere verdad, por serlo;
> si no, por ganar amigos
> para cuando despertemos.
>
> (2423–27)

> but whether real
> or not, to do the right thing
> is all that matters. If it's true,
> then for truth's sake only;

if not, then to win some friends
against the time when we awaken.
(86–87)

This is of course the essence of Segismundo's reform. He accepts the possibility that he can fail, or that everything may prove to be insignificant or illusory, but all the same, he throws himself into the action, hoping that by doing right he can escape further setbacks. He has concluded from his experiences that the world is deceptive, but that doing right, at least, will not cause harm.

In *La vida es sueño*, Calderón takes up the complex question of destiny in order to assert the importance of individual freedom. An evil omen hangs over the play, since the stars have predicted that Segismundo will lead a revolution against his father, conquer him in battle, and stand triumphant in an emblematic stance of victory with his foot on his father's neck.

This prophecy was not only predicted by the stars, but Segismundo himself comes to know it through his own imagination when he accuses his father of unnaturally imprisoning him:

querer que tenga yo respeto a canas;
pues aun ésas podría
ser que viese a mis plantas algún día,
porque aún no estoy vengado
del modo injusto con que me has criado.
(1715–19)

Such futile nonsense—expecting me
to honor someone's white hairs! . . .
Perhaps some day you'll see your own
become a carpet for my feet.   (60)

And later on awakening in the tower, he mutters in his drugged stupor: "bese mi padre mis pies" (2067: "and my father kiss my feet" [72]).

In spite of the prophecy, known to all the characters, the play maintains that the individual has freedom of action and that the stars only incline the will, but do not force it. Basilio explains this before exposing Segismundo to the court (787–91; 27). At the end of the play, Segismundo reiterates the idea of a fate awaiting the individual, but maintains that such a fate can be overcome with prudence and moderation, not injustice and vengeance:

la fortuna no se vence
con injusticia y venganza,
porque antes se incita más;
y así, quien vencer aguarda
a su fortuna, ha de ser
con prudencia y con templanza.
(3214–19)

no vengeance nor injustice
would alter the course of fate,
but, if anything, would incite it.

> And so, the man who wishes
> to control his fate must use
> judgment and be temperate.   (112)

The idea of destiny is complemented by that of valor, which is worked out positively in Segismundo and Rosaura and negatively in Clarín, whose cowardice is ultimately compared to Basilio's refusal to face his own destiny and to Clotaldo's refusal to recognize his daughter. From the very first scene, Clarín shows his cowardice, the inversion of valor, in contrast to the other characters. When Segismundo asks if the person who heard his monologue was Clotaldo, Clarín advises Rosaura to say yes, but she responds truthfully who she is (176). When Segismundo threatens to kill them because they heard his confession of grief, Clarín says: "Yo soy sordo, y no he podido/escucharte," 'I'm deaf, I couldn't hear a word/you said' (186–87; 9). Such cowardice is typical of the materialistic values of the comic servant in the Golden Age theater, but in this play Calderón extracts a major theme from it. In act 3, when the two forces join in battle, Clarín, following his cowardly instincts, decides to hide and save himself. Paradoxically, he is the only one who is killed, being hit by a stray bullet. Falling from his hiding place at the feet of the fleeing Basilio, he laments the errors of having tried to avoid destiny.

> Soy un hombre desdichado,
> que por quererme guardar
> de la muerte, la busqué.
> Huyendo della, topé
> con ella, pues no hay lugar,
> para la muerte secreto.   (3075–80)

> A man whose luck ran out.
> Trying to hide from death,
> I ran straight into it.
> I discovered it by fleeing it;
> for death, no place is secret.   (108)

And he concludes:

> y así, aunque a libraros vais
> de la muerte con huir,
> mirad que vais a morir
> si está de Dios que muráis.   (3092–95)

> So if by fleeing you now attempt
> to free yourselves from death, remember,
> you die when it's God's will you die.
>   (108)

His speech is not lost on the fleeing Basilio. Repeating Clarín's dying words, he realizes that he has spent his life trying to avoid the inevitable.

> Pues yo, por librar de muertes
> y sediciones mi patria,

> vine a entregarla a los mismos
> de quien pretendí librarla.   (3108–11)

> So in endeavoring to free
> my country of murder
> and sedition, I succeeded
> only in giving it away
> to murderers and traitors.   (108–9)

Fleeing from the battle was only the last act in a series of many in which he tried to avoid his destiny by refusing to act. He realizes they began with fearing his son and imprisoning him, and have continued until that moment in which he was fleeing from a prefigured event. Thus, all of Basilio's precautions and attempts to save his kingdom (and himself) are compared to Clarín's cowardice, to a failure to act and to meet life and destiny heroically. He decides to return against the superior odds of the enemy and surrender:

> Si está de Dios que yo muera,
> o si la muerte me aguarda
> aquí, hoy la quiero buscar,
> esperando cara a cara.   (3132–35)

> If God intends that I should die here,
> or death awaits me somewhere nearby,
> I should like to meet it face to face.   (109)

And Basilio himself fulfills the prophecy freely throwing himself at his son's feet by his own will, not forced as he had imagined.

> Si a mí buscándome vas,
> ya estoy, príncipe, a tus plantas,
> sea dellas blanca alfombra
> esta nieve de mis canas.
> Pisa mi cerviz, y huella
> mi corona . . .   (3146–51)

> If you've come to find me, Prince,
> here I am now, at your feet. . . .
> Here's a snowy carpet for you,
> made out of my white hair.
> Here's my neck—stamp on it!
> Here's my crown—trample on it!   (110)

The moment that was predicted in the prophecy and has been repeated throughout the play has arrived. The question is how will Segismundo meet his destiny, as he did on his first attempt at playing prince or as the reformed individual who has conquered unruly passions? He first points out the error of his education. He says that, even though astrology is a true science and it is possible to know the future, his father's error consisted in trying to act on that information. But where the father failed as a reader of nature, the son will succeed:

Sentencia del cielo fue;
por más que quiso estorbarla,
él no pudo; ¿y podré yo,
que soy menor en las canas,
en el valor y en la ciencia,
vencerla?—Señor, levanta,
dame tu mano; que ya
que el cielo te desengaña
de que has errado en el modo
de vencerle, humilde aguarda
mi cuello a que tú te vengues:
rendido estoy a tus plantas.   (3236–47)

          For such was
Heaven's verdict and, do what he might,
he could not change it. How then can I,
with fewer white hairs, less courage,
and less knowledge, conquer fate
when he could not?
(*to the* KING)
          Rise, Sir,
and give me your hand. Now
that Heaven's disabused you
of the illusion that you knew the way
to overcome it, I offer
myself to you. Take
your vengeance. I kneel before you.
                              (113)

From the theme of valor Segismundo has turned to the theme of liberty, asserting that one is never obliged to commit a wrong action. Segismundo and Basilio must fulfill their destiny, but they are never forced to commit evil. Although the prophecy is fulfilled, it never in fact obliged Segismundo to do wrong.

Calderón's drama clearly achieves a philosophical coherence. Education is necessary in order to separate human beings from the beasts, to civilize them, and to teach them the benefits of civilization. With education, one can see through the deceits of the world and see life for the sham it is. But the realization that life is a dream carries a negative implication. The central theme, stated in the title *La vida es sueño*, implies that if life is a dream, an illusion, and a fantasy, then of course it has no importance, and the individual person has no purpose except the pursuit of pleasure.

Desengaño as a literary theme is dangerously pessimistic. While trying to advocate indifference to the world, it focuses on the failures and deceptions of life, and the implications move from indifference to inaction. Thus Calderón saw the inherent dangers of this world view, and, in *La vida es sueño*, he undertook the further step of adding the call to action in the face of pessimistic nihilism. At the end of the second act in his famous soliloquy, Segismundo settles back to face the rest of his life in jail, and his consolation of philosophy[7] is that life is a dream, that everyone is an actor playing a

---

7. Heiple invokes the famous sixth-century work of this title by Boethius, which reflects on the possibility of happiness and the fickleness of fortune.

role whose outcome is unimportant in the final score. In the third *jornada* (act) he is called upon to act—and it is action, *right* action—that resolves his dilemma. The cowardly avoidance of action by Basilio, Clotaldo, and Clarín are refuted as inappropriate, and the valorous righteous actions of Segismundo and Rosaura are rewarded. It is the people who refuse to act, who refuse to face destiny—Basilio, Clotaldo, and Clarín—who face defeat. Segismundo learns to act, but with the lessons of *desengaño* at hand. He is prepared to face defeat, but aspires through action to the resolution of his problems. As a philosophical play, *La vida es sueño* addresses the inherent failings of *desengaño* and argues not for an extreme optimism, but, accepting the pessimism of disillusionment, it advocates a heroic action in face of defeat and futility—a right action that does not create the utopia of the optimist, but a compromised world suitable to a pessimistic age of disillusionment.

WORKS CITED

Bréhier, Emile. *The History of Philosophy: The Seventeenth Century*. Vol. 4. Translated by Wade Baskin. Chicago: University of Chicago Press, 1966.

Green, Otis H. "Desengaño." *Spain and the Western Tradition: The Castilian Mind in Literature from "El Cid" to Calderón*. Vol. 4. Madison: University of Wisconsin Press, 1966: 43–76.

López de Zárate, Francisco. *Obras varias*. Edited by José Simón Díaz. 2 vols. Madrid: CSIC, 1947.

Quevedo, Francisco de. *Poesía original*. Edited by José Manuel Blecua. Barcelona: Editorial Planeta, 1963.

SIDNEY DONNELL

From Cross Gender to Generic Closure: Sor Juana Inés de la Cruz's *Los empeños de una casa*†

Although the nature of Baroque studies began to change radically at the end of the twentieth century, there remain several interpretative impasses due to our adherence to the teachings of the past. For *comedia* scholars, one of the more significant obstacles stems from conservative assumptions about certain discursive practices that are commonly used to define the genre and the period in which they were deployed. The most salient is the ubiquitous wedding scene (or promise of marriage) at the close of countless theatrical productions in the early modern era. For traditionalists, nuptials at the end of any given play symbolize an affirmation of church and state, that is, an intensification of the "social order" or status quo, and for this reason, wedding bells have represented a discursive element essential to defining the *comedia* as a monolithic literary genre. But are there no exceptions to the rule? Does the institution of marriage resolve every conflict on the Baroque stage? Do promises of marriage

† From *Revista Canadiense de Estudios Hispánicos* 33.1 (Fall 2008): 177–93. Reprinted by permission of the publisher. Page references in the editor's notes refer to this Norton Critical Edition.

ever have the potential to result in the opposite effect, that is, lead to a disorderly, open-ended story or a subversion of the status quo? And if so, what do we do with the long-lived model of the *comedia* as monolith?

In response to these questions, I will offer a reading of Sor Juana Inés de la Cruz's *Los empeños de una casa* [*Trials of a Noble House*],[1] a play in which cross-dressing disrupts conventional understandings of the relationship between story and discourse, particularly generic closure.[2] The focus of the present study is on how the play's comic figure, the *gracioso*, exerts new societal power by masquerading a different gender, class and ethnicity during the final act of the play. Through what Nathalie Zemon Davis calls a "woman-on-top" subversion of societal norms in the early modern period, the cross-dressed comic figure overturns the conflictual hierarchy within this noble household by standing it on its head (Davis 136).[3] Clothes mark not only one's gender but also one's class and ethnicity in society; so, if we rethink traditional readings of the *comedia* as a conformist genre, we discover that representations of gender identity in Imperial Spain are more fluid than previously thought. Through the manipulation of vestments and other markers of masculinity and femininity, categories of man and woman are exposed as performative gender identities. In the words of Judith Butler, they are "repetitions" that have no essential nature.[4] The mimetic process of making a reproduction of what is frequently taken for granted as being an "original" or stable referent—specifically, the *gracioso* Castaño's successful imitation of the play's heroine—extends to and subverts literary binaries as well. Therefore, we will also look at the Baroque themes of original (the real thing) and reproduction (copy) in the context of Sor Juana's parody of the *comedia* as a genre. For these reasons my study of Sor Juana's *Los empeños* pays close attention to the power that the male cross-dresser derives from cultural anxiety over instability in gender. In so doing, I will offer a more inclusive understanding of the Baroque by examining how the *gracioso* undermines conventional hierarchies of a patriarchal society by replacing women with men, nobles with servants, and in Sor Juana's colonial example, white Europeans with people of color born in New Spain.

Today *Los empeños* is perhaps the most canonical *comedia* with a male-to-female transvestite protagonist. Sor Juana's play was intended for performance in aristocratic palaces in Mexico (Paz 433) and was premiered at the home of the Mexico City tax collector in 1683.[5] The work is set in Spain in a very reduced space—within the walls of the home of a young nobleman, Pedro. Regardless of the fact that the play is set in Toledo,

---

1. The title of Sor Juana's work is a play on words, proving elusive to direct translation as evidenced by the following: The House of Trials (Pasto), House of Desires (Boyle), and Pawns of a House (Hernández Araico and McGaha).
2. Edward Friedman cogently advocates a narratological approach to comedia studies.
3. Davis' focus is France, but through her discussion of comic figures in the early modern period, we can see how Castaño's meta-theatrical powers are joined with a perceived criminal element associated with his cross-dressing, servant-class status, and racialized ethnicity. Passing as a European noblewoman undermines the essentialized characteristics that made whites an elite group.
4. Here, as in other instances, Butler uses the stage as a metaphor for gendered performance: "Significantly, if gender is instituted through acts which are internally discontinuous, then the *appearance of substance* is precisely that, a constructed identity, a performative accomplishment which the mundane social audience, including the actors themselves, come to believe and to perform in the mode of belief" (*Gender* 141). However, Butler also warns that "there is no necessary relation between drag and subversion" (*Bodies* 125).
5. For a discussion of the discrepancies in the historical record as to the year that *Los empeñas* debuted, see Hernández Araico ("Problemas").

Pedro's home could be almost anywhere. The only local color comes from references to Mexican popular culture, chiefly from the play's Mexican-born *gracioso*, Castaño (Paz 436).

*   *   *

Although seventeenth-century drama ostensibly aligned itself ideologically with the state, many critics are open to alternative interpretations that look beyond the parameters that have been imposed on the genre. Without dismissing the significance of the Maravall school, Catherine Connor ("Toward" 377) proposes a case-by-case socio-cultural approach to the *comedia*, arguing that state propaganda and subversion of the same were often intermingled on the early modern stage. This is precisely the type of strategy that several scholars have adopted when approaching the topic of closure. For his part, José M. Regueiro (28–29) demonstrates the inherent weaknesses of always reading for the same traditional generic codes in the Spanish *comedia*, inviting us to ask if a particular play could lead to open-ended interpretations of its story.[6] In many respects, the versatility of the *comedia* as a genre—whether staged in public or in court—can be attributed to the Spanish theater's popular origins and its maintenance of popular practices. Mariscal (25–26) argues that dramatic spectacle relies on the physical conditions of the theater, making it flexible in areas where poetry and the novel are not. Drag performance, in particular, coincides with what Mariscal has called the "contestatory responses" and "carnivalesque inversions" (21) found in the public stage's sixteenth-century beginnings. And so, in this investigation on closure in the *comedia*, I privilege Sor Juana's *Los empeños* and its transvestite subject because it is my contention that cross-dressing in both text and stage performance served as one of the principal means of exploring variant signs of identity and of interrogating the dominant discourse that supported the ruling elite in the Baroque.

As way of summary, *Los empeños* parodies aspects of the *comedia de enredo* and the *comedia de capa y espada* (comedies of "intrigue" or "cloak and dagger").[7] The principal love triangle in the play involves three nobles: Don Carlos and Dona Leonor who love each other and want to marry, and Don Pedro who also wants to make Leonor his wife. At the beginning of the play, Pedro's armed men foil Carlos and Leonor's elopement, permitting Pedro (in collusion with his sister Doña Ana) to lock the would-be bride in his home. When Castaño becomes involved on behalf of his master Don Carlos, he penetrates the home and transforms himself into a replica of Leonor. His entry on stage in drag successfully redirects the antagonist's desire, allowing the so-called "real" Leonor and Carlos to marry. When Castaño reveals his manipulation of a feminine gender identity, the unhappy love triangle is broken up, and the institution of marriage places an obstacle in the way of Pedro's pursuit of Leonor. At the end, Castaño asks for the hand of the maid, Celia, but—still in drag—he also repeats his promise to wed Pedro. In my reading of the play, the disorderly consequences of gender parody disrupt the traditional paradigm of orderly closure through marriage in the *comedia*.

6. For others who propose to revise the concept of generic closure in the comedia, see Carreño, Guimont and Pérez Magallón, Connor ("Marriage"), and Barber.
7. For more information on Sor Juana's parody of the *comedia de enredo* and *capa y espada* tradition, see Feustle (147), Rivers (636–37), and Canavaggio (139).

Dressed as a woman, the *gracioso* is no longer a character in the subplot but becomes the play's central figure. At the beginning of the third act, Castaño changes clothes and his gender identity on stage. During his speech he lists numerous articles that noblewomen of his day typically use to adorn their bodies. Some he chooses to use; others he does not: a cloth and head scarf for his hair (2414–15, 2426), petticoats (2418), jewels (2423), something to serve as a bustier or brassiere (2429), a skin-lightening cream (2430), a corset (2441–42), gloves (2450–53), and a silk cloak (2454–57). A closer examination of a few of these objects will help us to better understand the process of gender transformation and (re)construction. For instance, Castaño must cover his hands with gloves in order to completely mask, one supposes, his rather unfeminine, hairy features: "Los guantes: / aquesto sí, / porque las manos no vean, / que han de ser las de Jacob / con que a Esaú me parezca"[8] (2450–53). The comic figure inverts the story from Genesis 27 in which Rebecca hides Jacob's identity from a blind Isaac by covering the boy's soft hands with kidskin (García Valdés 237). For Jacob, what was hairless is now mature and hairy. In the reverse attempt to give the illusion of soft, lady-like hands and youth, Castaño resorts to high fashion in order to conceal one truth (based on appearances that are gendered masculine) and flaunt another (based on appearances that are gendered feminine). By "donning" a feminine gender and passing for Doña Leonor, Castaño seems both to adhere to and subvert the Baroque union of opposites, a theme that Dopico Black (182) and Horswell (70) also discuss elsewhere in the play.

This crossing of gender barriers leads to the crossing of other barriers that mark class and ethnicity. Indeed, Castaño's monologue serves to explore this premise. While he is having fun with Leonor's inner and outer garments, the *gracioso* addresses the ladies of the court and the Viceroy—a move that crosses theatrical barriers as well (Feustle 148). Here the class of the actor becomes apparent in addition to the class of the character he plays. He begins somewhat subtly, mocking ladies' court fashion: "¿Qué les parece, señoras, / este encaje de ballena?"[9] (2440–41). Then he attempts to delineate between the nobility he parodies in the plot and the nobility he entertains during the course of the performance, a type of apologia that Dopico Black (189–92) explains well. In this context, the break with theatrical illusion and the resultant suspension of the audience's disbelief are masking elements (like clothes) that provide both an acceptance of colonial Mexico's nobility and a veiled repudiation of their class practices.

Apart from intersecting gender and class identities, a racialized ethnic identity plays an explicit role in the reinscription of the comic figure's body. Castaño (which means "chestnut colored" or "brown") also needs to conceal his brown skin (Rivers 634; Kenworthy 104; Horswell 72–73). The word "moreno/a" certainly appears often enough in the play in reference to Castaño, and he also claims to have been born in "las Indias" (2385–87).[1] We should remember that he is a manservant from Mexico, not of noble birth, and in all likelihood not of two European parents. In

---

8. These gloves should keep my hands from view / As well as add a touch of charm, / For how can I boast Jacob's limbs / When I've got Esau's hairy arms? (p. 348) [editor's note].
9. Hey ladies, take a look at this: / My collar's truly lovely lace (p. 348) [editor's note].
1. "Moreno/a" (Spanish): dark-skinned. "Las Indias": the Indies; i.e., the Americas [editor's note].

this light, the reference to "solimán" (2430)—which is a mercury-based cosmetic—suggests one popular strategy to attain greater whiteness and to pass for European. Nevertheless, Castaño still feels compelled to completely cover his face. A silk cloak provides him with the perfect disguise to conceal his skin color, which, the *gracioso* claims, gives him a means of both defense and deception: "¡Válgame Dios! cuánto encubre / esta telilla de seda, / que ni foso que así guarde, / ni muro que así defienda, / ni ladrón que tanto encubra, / ni paje que tanto mienta, / ni gitano que así engañe, / ni logrero que así venda"² (2456–63).

In keeping with aristocratic women's fashion, which revealed little of the body's surface in public, cross-dressing not only reinscribes Castaño's gender and class, but also his racialized ethnicity, which he explains through a curious shift in metaphor. He begins to compare the "telilla" to sanctioned objects of protection (i.e. "foso," "muro") but then moves to marginalized artists of deception (i.e. "ladrón," "gitano").³ Particularly striking is the comparison of the cloak with a gypsy—a racialized, stereotypical trickster whose skills Castaño now rivals through cross-dressing. Despite the apparent contradiction, that is to say, an acceptance and repudiation of a racialized other in this instance, the dramatic representation of a person of color in the act of dressing as a noblewoman also serves to highlight miscegenation in the colonial era.

During the staged transformation, Castaño reveals an awareness of his newly acquired external allure for attracting a suitor as he puts on Leonor's "basquiñas"⁴ (2418). At first glance, this seems a shame because the blue of the undergarments sets off his beautiful skin pigmentation: "No hay duda que me esté bien, / porque como soy morena / me está del cielo lo azul"⁵ (2420–22). This statement, however, goes deeper than what appears on the surface because Castaño begins to wonder what it would be like to show someone what is underneath his petticoats. His verses are both declarative ("I am a brown woman" or "my name is Morena") as well as contemplative ("blue looks heavenly on me"), signaling an internal transformation and self-awareness of how this assumed identity goes well with his "true colors." Castaño in drag—whom I will now call Morena—plays up the advantages of "her" recently inscribed identity to a coquette extreme. *She* begins to refer to herself in the feminine: "morena" (2421), "revuelta" (2425), "hermosa" (2444), and "bella" (2445),⁶ indicating an entanglement of psychological and linguistic changes accompanying the change of clothes. Morena is also narcissistic, taking for granted that men will fall in love with her: "¿Quién duda / que en el punto que me vean / me sigan cuatro mil lindos?" (2478–80). She also fears that a suitor could win her heart in her feminine gender role: "Temor llevo de que alguno / me enamore"⁷ (2496–97).

---

2. This little piece of silk sure does / The trick! Lord, has there ever been / A gaping chasm more obscured / Or thief more muffled in the night; / A rampart offering more defense / Or page boy telling bigger lies; / A gypsy who deceived as much / Or profiteer with greater scams? (pp. 348–49) [editor's note].
3. "Telilla": cloak; "foso": moat; "muro": wall; "ladrón": thief; "gitano": gypsy [editor's note].
4. Petticoats or skirts [editor's note].
5. This shade of blue could only make / My stunning self more beautiful / As I lean toward a dusky hue (p. 348) [editor's note].
6. Adjectives in Spanish vary according to the gender of the person or thing described. When Castaño uses "dusky," "pretty," and "stunning," s/he uses the feminine form [editor's note].
7. No doubt four thousand pretty boys / Will follow me in hot pursuit (p. 349); I fear I'll break some hearts, but what's / A gal to do? (p. 349) [editor's note].

In addition to feminine conventions of word choice during her encounters with others, Morena has to be careful to avoid the Mexican usage that distinguishes Castaño in other parts of the play. Particularly, she has to pay attention to the verbal customs and etiquette of the nobility, not those of the servant class. During her encounter with Don Pedro, Morena is still perfecting her feminine identity: "Mas pues por Leonor me marca, / yo quiero fingir ser ella"[8] (2508–09). But her surface appearance is not enough. While in the process of transformation, the Leonor look-alike must mask her speech and demeanor—in addition to the pitch of her voice—in order to climb the social ladder: "Que quizá atiplando el habla / no me entenderá la letra" (2510–11).[9] She thinks that treble may disguise verbal content, but in practice with Don Pedro, she has trouble coming across as "lady-like," as it were, and needs to be more discreet. Fortunately, Pedro believes that Morena is Leonor simply attempting to be rude in order to make him feel less attracted to her. At this point Morena realizes her limitations. She can adjust for content better than she can change her expression even though she tells herself, "Mejor es mudar de estilo / para ver si así me deja" (2612–13). Adopting a "desaire" here and a "fineza" there (2617–18), her coarse speech does change somewhat.[1] She also comes to terms with the content of her speech. Sex, in particular, is at stake in her verbal negotiations with Pedro: "¡Notable aprieto, por Dios! / Yo pienso que aquí me fuerza"[2] (2610–11). With all puns aside ("aprieto," "me fuerza"), the *gracioso*-cum-*dama* ("comic figure as damsel") desists in discussing how hungry she feels (2550–59, 2570–71, 2588–92) and begins to sweet talk Pedro by promising to become his wife (2621–22, 2640): "Que seré vuestra / como dos y dos son cuatro" (2623–24).[3]

One's demeanor and one's words are as necessary to a socially constructed gender identity as the clothes one wears. In short, Doña Morena's European femininity consists of clothes that mask signs of her former identity (as regards gender, class, and skin color). Just as importantly, she effects a successful readjustment in the way she speaks, what she talks about, and how she carries herself in order to imitate a white noblewoman. These elements show that the representation of gender identity is performative in *Los empeños*, revealing the essentialism in conventional social constructs. Upon revealing her so-called "true," masculine identity at the close of the play, Castaño—still in Leonor's clothing—reveals the secret to dressing for success: "No soy sino el perro muerto / de que se hicieron los guantes" (3307–08). By paying attention to every detail, Castaño is able to restructure his identity. As he jokingly says, he is nothing more than "the dead dog from which the gloves were made," proving that one can "make a silk purse" (a Leonor imitation) "of a sow's ear" (his former state). However, the sexual innuendo and deception in this process disappear from both my direct translation and use of an analogous English-language adage. As David

8. But since he's taken me for her, / I'll juggle two identities (p. 350) [editor's note].
9. And raise my voice's pitch a bit / To keep this ruse from being discerned (p. 350) [editor's note].
1. [I'll] change my tune and fast! / Let's see if this will do the trick (p. 352); *desaire*: snub; *fineza*: gallantry [editor's note].
2. I'm really in a pickle now! / He'll have his way with me, I think (p. 352) [editor's note].
3. Why not say, "como uno y uno son dos"? Besides observing the rules of rhyme and meter, Sor Juana's amusing choice of words invites further analysis about concepts of racial mixing in colonial Mexico. [I'll] be yours tonight / As sure as two plus two make four (p. 352)—editor's note.]

Pasto explains, "el perro muerto" is probably a reference to the "the bed trick," that is, "when people are tricked into having sex with someone other than the person they expect" (150 n32). In addition, "guantes de perro" may be an allusion to a beauty aid that women used in order to keep their hands lily white.[4]

Reminiscent of the sexually charged conclusion to *As You Like It* in which the boy-heroine addresses the audience, the ending of *Los empeños* leaves us with more questions than answers. In Shakespeare's work, "the ambiguities of the conclusion to that play involve not only gender but sex itself, and not only the character Rosalind but also the boy actor who played her part" (Rackin 36). The marvelous discovery of the transvestite subject's "true" identity privileges the actor in the roles of Castaño and Morena by allowing the "dead dog" to dominate the stage from the moment of anagnorisis until the final bows when s/he announces to the audience the "fin" ("end") of the play. Castaño's words and gestures during the final recognition scene introduce this final break in theatrical illusion by indirectly reminding audience members of their complicity during the *gracioso*'s earlier aside to the "Señoras." Breaks in illusion are characteristic of the Baroque because they interrogate what is "original" and what is "copy" as regards the actor and his craft.[5] On a more "lowbrow" level, the *gracioso* also implicates audience members through sexual innuendo. Castaño gives signs that he may pursue the advantages of his feminine identity by maintaining his relationship with Don Pedro once the play ends. These are all discursive moves toward an open ending, which underscore the chains of mimicry in daily repetitions and respective performances of gender identities.

✳ ✳ ✳

To see an actor's transformation from bumpkin comic figure to damsel in distress is to witness the power of the transvestite subject.[6] In order to highlight both performance and gender performativity associated with the *gracioso*'s role, I will now speak of "Castaño/Morena" because s/he exerts newly-acquired societal power by masquerading a different gender, class and ethnicity: "¡Gran cosa es el ser rogadas! / . . . / Ahora bien, de vuelta y media / he de poner a este tonto" (2540–46).[7] And although Don Pedro may be played as a fop (Stroud 141–58), he is no idiot—unless, of course, all the noblemen on stage are fools—because Castaño/Morena's performance convinces others of her feminine likeness to Leonor. During a sword fight between Don Carlos and a secondary rival, Don Juan, Castaño-cum-Leonor coquettishly asks, "¿Mas si por mí se acuchillan / los que mi beldad festejan?" (2674–75).[8] At a later moment in the play, as Carlos and Pedro fight over Leonor's hand, Castaño/Morena's aside makes it clear that both duelers think she is Leonor: "Pues por mí quieren matarse" (3288).[9] It

---

4. For a summary of the connotations of "guantes de perro," see García Ruiz (212).
5. For more on Castaño's asides to the audience, see Larson (186, 192–93).
6. Alberto González played the role of Castaño in the Teatro Repertorio Latinoamericano's production of *Los empeños* at the Festival Internacional de Teatro del Siglo de Oro held in 1999 at the Chamizal National Memorial in El Paso, Texas.
7. It's quite a thrill to be pursued! / I'll never be surprised again / To see gals vaunting haughty pride. / There's nothing in the world like woo / To swell one's head with vain conceit. / It's time I made this lovesick fool's / Own head spin round from cockiness (p. 350) [editor's note].
8. Is this the way they'd celebrate / My beauty, trading fatal blows? (p. 353) [editor's note].
9. [T]hey'd do battle over me (p. 366) [editor's note].

is not necessary for the actor playing Morena to achieve "realness," that is, to pass for a woman *vis-à-vis* the audience; in fact, she can be played in sloppy butch drag. The point is that the player's corporeal reproduction of Leonor be a "sufficient" likeness for the male rivals to accept her on stage, underscoring the general absurdity of the social construction of a noble-woman's feminine identity in the 1680s.

As the patriarch of the Toledan home where the action takes place, we witness how the Old World native, Don Pedro, helps the New World Castaño/Morena assert her feminine, European identity. Pedro perceives the cultural codes that he also helps to generate in society—the same codes Castaño manipulates in order to become Morena. These codes con-sist of clothes, voice, speech, and gestures, which—when combined and performed—are gendered feminine. As a consequence, Don Pedro loses his claim to Doña Leonor when Castaño reveals his purportedly "true" identity, that is to say, his previous state as Don Carlos' manservant. Pedro's honour is besmirched by falling for a body that is gendered feminine but is anatomically male. Horswell cogently argues, "Pedro's desire for the hybrid ends in an anxiety-ridden abjection of that which is now part of the Span-ish imperial identity, both in its gendered and its racial dimensions" (75). In this regard, if Pedro's home is read as a symbol for the metropolis, then a Mexican manservant has thoroughly feminized the head of the household, resulting in a suggestive parody of Hapsburg decadence to which Horswell (76) also refers.[1] In so doing, the consequences of Castaño/Morena's so-called "trick" reveal a great deal about Don Pedro and other empowered men's gender identities in Imperial Spain.

* * * Having "almost" obtained full possession of Leonor (by placing her under his roof and attempting to take advantage of her liminal status), Pedro becomes the swindled party because he chases the wrong version of Leonor. According to Castaño/Morena, "Y Don Pedro enamorado / de mi talle y de mi aseo, / de mi gracia y de mi garbo, / me encerró en este apo-sento" (3332–35).[2] By abducting Leonor's look-alike, Castaño/Morena, Pedro hijacks the components of the white male elite's definition of femi-ninity. He is driven to try to possess the parts that make up Leonor's generic identity: her "figure," "cleanliness," "grace" and "allure." What he really pos-sesses is the reproduction of these elements, not Leonor. However, this statement assumes that the female protagonist is a stable referent when she herself may not be. In fact, *Los empeños* takes the Leonor imitation at least one step further. Is Leonor herself a copy lost in social reproduction? In this way, drag performance affects a disruption in the gender binary man-woman as well as other binary systems common to the study of Baroque aesthetics, specifically the opposition of "original" with "reproduction."

According to traditional approaches to reading the *comedia*, if there has been any disruption to social norms during the course of a play, conven-tional closure dictates a reestablishment of a hegemonic normativity; in the case of a character whose identity is counterhegemonic, the comedic forms of the genre mandate the reinscription of said character as a legitimate hus-band or wife.[3] If cross-dressing leads to a denaturalization of masculinity or

1. For more on feminization in the comedia, see Donnell (*Feminizing*).
2. Don Pedro took a shine to me / And, quickly falling in a swoon / About my looks, grace, style and charm, / Had me sequestered in these rooms! (p. 367) [editor's note].
3. In tragedy, according to the same model, the offender is duly punished, sometimes by death.

femininity, then definitive closure requires a renaturalization of the same by the play's end. It might be argued that Sor Juana wants to have it both ways: the open-endedness of destabilized identities and decentralized subjectivities, and the neatly closed ending where order is reestablished and all referents recover their univocal "nature." However, the *gracioso*'s putative social reintegration, like that of the *pícaro* Lazarillo de Tormes[4] would be "based upon false premises and self-delusion" (Babcock III). In other words, we find a simultaneous acceptance and repudiation of norms until the very end of Sor Juana's play, but we also discover that one of the work's objectives is to parody everything about the genre, including its form.

✳   ✳   ✳

When the dark-skinned manservant Castaño cross-dresses, we can see how he reconstructs his identity in reference to gender, class and ethnicity, and also how he redirects pursuit in the links of the amatory chain, reverting the elements to something closer to the original order by redirecting Pedro's affections. Patricia Kenworthy points out that "from Calderón's *Los empeños de un acaso* . . . Sor Juana adapted the title and the comic complications of a *ménage à cinq*:[5] two pairs of lovers and an 'odd man out,' the brother of one of the ladies" (104). In other words, there is one too many men, Don Pedro. To this extent, a position approximating the original order prior to the outset of the play is reestablished and fixed through marriage, but this is done by means of what the dominant culture "normally" considers to be a transgressive act. Quite simply, it takes a cross-dressed man attracting another man to reestablish order. Ironically, ambiguity and confusion in gender roles—not stability—resolves several of the play's conflicts and appears to restore much, but not all, of its heteronormativity.

At the outset of the play, we learn of a preexisting love relationship between Juan (Leonor's cousin) and Ana (Pedro's sister). When the lovers Carlos and Leonor enter the home that Ana shares with her brother, Ana spurns Juan and chooses to pursue the more attractive Carlos. Her brother Pedro, in turn, pursues Leonor. So, rather than represent desire throughout the course of *Los empeños* as a series of love triangles, a single amatory chain proves useful:

Juan → Ana → Carlos ↔ Leonor ← Pedro

✳   ✳   ✳

According to Dopico Black, "Castaño as (a second) Leonor provides, temporarily, the extra wife's body required so that the various overlapping triangles of desire . . . can give way to binary symmetries (Leonor-Carlos, Ana-Juan, and, most importantly, Pedro-Castaño as Leonor)" (199–200). But what of Celia and her relationship with Castaño? And if Castaño's entry in drag successfully redirects Pedro's desire for Leonor, is the effect truly temporary? To the contrary, one very unconventional love triangle (Pedro-Castaño-Celia) survives conventional closure, which permits the corresponding love that existed prior to the outset of the play to succeed

---

4. The anonymous *Lazarillo de Tormes* (1554) is the first Spanish picaresque novel [editor's note].
5. A play on the French expression *ménage à trois* (three people in a sexual relationship, generally in the same household), here expanded to five participants [editor's note].

(that is, Carlos-Leonor). In the presence of Leonor's father (3336–44), the institution of marriage ostensibly protects Carlos and Leonor's union by breaking the links of the amatory chain to unwanted suitors (i.e., Ana and Pedro, respectively), thus facilitating the reestablishment of Juan's liaison with Ana, which is sanctioned by her brother Pedro. The newly broken chain is as follows:

$$\text{Juan} \leftrightarrow \text{Ana} \quad \text{Carlos} \leftrightarrow \text{Leonor} \quad \text{Pedro} \leftrightarrow \text{Castaño} \leftrightarrow \text{Celia}$$

When Don Pedro threatens to kill Castaño in retaliation for undermining his plans, the *gracioso* (still in drag) replies that he will remain true to his word and marry the dishonored patriarch: "Cuando te di / palabra de casamiento, / que ahora estoy llano a cumplirte, / quedamos en un concierto" (3312–15).[6] Though comical, Castaño appears unwilling for their relationship to end so abruptly, acknowledging his drag persona's betrothal to Pedro even after his masculine identity has been revealed. In response, Pedro remains neutral: "Mas disimular importa / que ya no tiene remedio / el caso" (3348–50).[7] So, in the context of generic closure, does every wedding promise carry the same weight? Do some promises intensify church and state, and do others subvert the same?

As for Castaño and Celia's future relationship, the two characters speak metonymically about the possibility of marriage, never negating the bonds between Castaño and Pedro. The *gracioso* asks for the maid Celia's "hand," and she answers by offering him her "dedo" ("finger") in its place (3361–65). Castaño then underscores the phallic symbolism of the substitution: "Daca, que es el dedo malo, / pues es él con quien encuentro"[8] (3366–67). According to the *Diccionario de Autoridades*, "el dedo malo"[9] is a vulgar reference to someone who has fallen into disgrace. It is impossible to say if Castaño is referring to himself as character in terms of his ambiguous relations with Celia and Don Pedro, or to himself as an actor who loses face or transgresses societal norms in the "real world" of the audience, but his disgrace, nonetheless, also highlights Celia's agency. Without a patriarch (such as a father or brother) to give her hand away and formally acknowledge her marital union to Castaño, her finger becomes a powerful phallic symbol, suggesting that she is the "butch" and the feminized *gracioso* (still in drag) is the "femme" in their relationship. In this context, Castaño's reiteration of his vow to wed Don Pedro could be taken seriously if patriarchal conventions and law were to permit such an act between men, especially since the *gracioso*'s bond to Celia is neither formally named nor made symbolically sacrosanct by a patriarchal guardian. The happy ending to which many critics ascribe never erases Pedro's, Castaño's and Celia's respective unwillingness or inability to consent to a heteronormative, monogamous relationship, which is a luxury reserved for Carlos and Leonor as well as the possibly loveless Juan and Ana. In this way, Sor Juana

---

6. But why, sir? When I gave my word / Of honor that we'd soon be wed—/ A promise that I'd still fulfill— / You tendered me your solemn pledge (p. 367) [editor's note].
7. In any case, I'd best conceal / My deep chagrin, as it's too late / To change things now (p. 367) [editor's note].
8. As long as you're attached to it, / I'll take a finger, if I must! (p. 368) [editor's note].
9. The bad finger [editor's note].

leaves her play formally closed but contextually open, thus maintaining the work's fundamental ambiguity.[1]

Through the identity transformations portrayed in *Los empeños*, the subjectivity of a servant-class "moreno/a" is substituted for that of an upperclass, white woman. Consequently, an aristocratic man attempts to marry the servant in drag who has copied (reproduced) the elite's definition of "woman." In so doing, the primacy of desire between men—what Eve Kosovsky Sedgwick calls "male hom(me)osocial relations"—is subverted.[2] What happens when there are not enough white women to go around? Patriarchs—desperate from the rivalry and power struggles between themselves—grab male servants in drag. Copy has called into question the legitimacy of original, rendering the conventional closure of a reestablished order impossible. There is simply no turning back for the foppish patriarch, the butch maid, or the colorful manservant still standing on stage in his blue petticoats.

Finally, is *Los empeños de una casa* a mere exception to the "order-disturbed-to-order-restored" model of the *comedia*? Is Sor Juana's secular comedy just an extreme example? I think not. A growing number of scholars—especially those studying gender and genre—now point to both canonical and non-canonical Baroque plays in which, like *Los empeños*, the formal telling (particularly the discursive moves signaling generic closure) does not necessarily reduce the content of what has been told to a single, definitive interpretation.

☆   ☆   ☆

WORKS CITED

Babcock, Barbara. "'Liberty's a Whore': Inversions, Marginalia, and Picaresque Narrative." *The Reversible World: Symbolic Inversion in Art and Society.* Ed. Barbara Babcock. Ithaca: Cornell UP, 1978. 95–116.

Barber, Amy Rebecca. "Validating the Marginal: Characterization and Closure in Ruiz de Alarcón." Diss. Pennsylvania State U, 2003.

Boyle, Catherine M., trans. *House of Desires.* By Juana Inés de la Cruz. London: Oberon, 2004.

Butler, Judith. *Bodies that Matter: On the Discursive Limits of "Sex."* New York: Routledge, 1993.

———. *Gender Trouble: Feminism and the Subversion of Identity.* New York: Routledge, 1990.

Canavaggio, Jean. "Los disfrazados de mujer en la comedia." *La mujer en el teatro y la novela del siglo XVII. Actas del Segundo Coloquio del Grupo de Estudios sobre Teatro Español.* Toulouse: France-Ibérie Recherche, 1979. 135–45.

Carreño, Antonio. "Hacia una poética del final de comedia: de Lope a Calderón." *Actas del II Congreso de la Asociación Internacional de Teatro Español y Novohispano de los Siglos de Oro.* Ed. Ysla Campbell. Ciudad Juárez: U Autónoma de Ciudad Juárez, 1994. 175–99.

---

1. For more on the problematic ending of the picaresque novel, see Babcock (111).
2. For her definition of the "homosocial," see Sedgwick (2–3).

Connor (Swietlicki), Catherine. "Marriage and Subversion in Comedia Endings: Problems in Art and Society." *Gender, Identity, and Representation in Spain's Golden Age.* Ed. Dawn L. Smith and Anita K. Stoll. Lewisburg: Bucknell UP, 2000. 23–46.

———. "Toward a New Socio-Cultural Theory of Baroque Theater." *Hispanic Essays in Honor of Frank P. Casa.* Ed. A. Robert Lauer and Henry W. Sullivan. New York: Peter Lang, 1997. 375–87.

Davis, Nathalie Zemon. "Women on Top." *Society and Culture in Early Modern France: Eight Essays.* Stanford: Stanford UP, 1975. 124–51.

Donnell, Sidney. *Feminizing the Enemy: Imperial Spain, Transvestite Drama, and the Crisis of Masculinity.* Lewisburg: Bucknell UP, 2003.

Dopico Black, Georgina. "Sor Juana's *Empeños*: The Imperfect Wife." *Perfect Wives, Other Women: Adultery and Inquisition in Early Modern Spain.* Durham: Duke UP, 2001. 164–204.

Feustle, Joseph A., Jr. "Hacia una interpretación de *Los empeños de una casa* de sor Juana Inés de la Cruz." *Explicación de Textos Literarios* 1.2 (1972): 143–49.

Friedman, Edward H. "Theorizing the *Comedia*: The Impact of Narratology." *A Society on Stage: Essays on Spanish Golden Age Drama.* Ed. Edward H. Friedman, H. J. Manzari, and Donald D. Miller. New Orleans: UP of the South, 1998. 73–87.

García Ruiz, Victor. "Una nota explicativa a *El lindo Don Diego*, de Moreto: Mosquito revela la impotencia sexual de Don Diego." *La edición de textos: Actas del I Congreso Internacional de Hispanistas del Siglo de Oro.* Ed. Dolores Noguera Guirao, Pablo Jauralde Pou, y Alfonso Reyes. London: Tamesis, 1990. 209–18.

Guimont, Anny, and Jesús Pérez-Magallón. "Matrimonio y cierre de la comedia en Lope." *Anuario Lope de Vega* 4 (1998): 139–64.

Hernández Araico, Susana. "Problemas de fecha y montaje en *Los empeños de una casa* de sor Juana Inés de la Cruz." *Sor Juana Inés de la Cruz y las vicisitudes de la crítica.* Ed. José Pascual Buxó. México DF: Universidad National Autónoma de México, 1998. 161–77.

———, and Michael D. McGaha, trans. *Los empeños de una casa / Pawns of a House.* By Juana Inés de la Cruz. Tempe: Bilingual, 2007.

Horswell, Michael. "Transatlantic Performances of Hybridity in Sor Juana's Baroque Festival, *Los empeños de una casa.*" *Crosscurrents: Transatlantic Perspectives on Early Modern Hispanic Drama.* Ed. Mindy E. Badía and Bonnie L. Gasior. Lewisburg: Bucknell UP, 2006. 64–84.

Kenworthy, Patricia. "The Spanish Priest and the Mexican Nun: Two Views of Love and Honor." *Calderón de la Barca at the Tercentenary: Comparative Views.* Ed. Wendell M. Aycock and Sydney P. Cravens. Lubbock: Texas Tech UP, 1982. 103–17.

Larson, Catherine. "Writing the Performance: Stage Directions and the Staging of Sor Juana's *Los empeños de una casa.*" *Bulletin of the Comediantes* 42 (1990): 179–98.

Mariscal, George. *Contradictory Subjects: Quevedo, Cervantes, and Seventeenth-Century Spanish Culture.* Ithaca: Cornell UP, 1991.

Pasto, David, trans. *The House of Trials.* By Juana Inés de la Cruz. New York: Peter Lang, 1997.

Paz, Octavio. *Sor Juana Inés de la Cruz o las trampas de la fe.* México: Fondo de Cultura Económica, 1985.

Rackin, Phyllis. "Androgyny, Mimesis, and the Marriage of the Boy Heroine on the English Renaissance Stage." *Publications of the Modern Language Association of America* 102 (1987): 29–41.

Regueiro, José M. "Textual Discontinuities and the Problems of Closure in the Spanish Drama of the Golden Age." *Cultural Authority in Golden Age Spain.* Ed. Marina S. Brownlee and Hans Ulrich Gumbrecht. Baltimore: The Johns Hopkins UP, 1995. 28–50.

Rivers, Elias L. "Indecencias de una monjita mejicana." *Homenaje a William L. Fichter.* Ed. A. David Kossof and José Amor y Vázquez. Madrid: Castalia, 1971. 634–37.

Sedgwick, Eve Kosofsky. *Between Men: English Literature and Male Homosocial Desire.* New York: Columbia UP, 1985.

Stroud, Matthew D. "Comedy, Foppery, Camp: Moreto's *El lindo don Diego* and Sor Juana's *Los empeños de una casa.*" *Plot Twists and Critical Turns: Queer Approaches to Early Modern Spanish Theater.* Lewisburg: Bucknell UP, 2007. 141–58.

CATHERINE BOYLE

Los Empeños de una Casa by Sor Juana Inés de la Cruz: Translation, Cultural Transmission and Staging[†1]

Empty Perfection?

THE PLOT: "Doña Leonor, a young noblewoman, has fled with her lover, Don Carlos, fearing that her father is about to choose a more suitable husband for her. Unbeknownst to them, Don Pedro, one of Leonor's luckless suitors, knows of their plans to elope and has arranged for an ambush, the success of which will have Don Carlos take flight and will lead Leonor to take refuge in his house, in the care of his sister, Doña Ana. When the two women meet, Leonor is prompted to tell her story, and Doña Ana soon finds out that she is in the company of a rival, for she too has fallen in love with Don Carlos, forsaking her own love, Don Juan. Thus begins three days of intrigue and deceit, which do finally end in the couples being suitably paired off. All, that is, except for Don Pedro, who has lost his Leonor, but who had easily mistaken a disguised Castaño (Don Carlos's manservant) for Leonor."[2] The result is a comedy of errors and mistaken identities, as Octavio Paz says:

> A world of shadows and masks: A falls in love with the beautiful B, but at the masked ball, or in the shadows of the garden by night, he

† From *Forum for Modern Language Studies* 35.3 (1999): 227–37. Reprinted by permission of the publisher, Oxford University Press. Quotations in Spanish have been translated by G. J. Racz.

1. *Los empeños de una casa* by Sor Juana Inés de la Cruz [1651?–1695] was first performed in Mexico City in 1683 for the viceregal court in the palace of one of its officials, during a celebration for the viceregal couple, the Marquis and Marquise de la Laguna. The celebration was also in recognition of the arrival of the new Archbishop, Francisco Aguiar y Seijas. This article is based on my involvement, as dramaturg (or literary adviser), in the One Horse production of *Los empeños de una casa*, *The House of Desires*. It was directed by Gaynor Macfarlane in a new version for the stage by Peter Oswald, and ran at Battersea Arts Centre, London, from 3rd to 21st December 1997.
2. C. Boyle & G. Macfarlane, "From Response to Reproduction: Three Centuries of Sor Juana Inés de la Cruz", *Journal of Latin American Cultural Studies, Travesía* 4, 2 (1995), 191–5 (pp. 192–3).

confuses her with C; meanwhile in the darkness, B, who actually loves A, takes him for D, who loves her but is abhorred by her. Fate shuffles the cards again and again until truth triumphs. The plot, the humor, the dialogues of the comic character and the lovers, the beautiful verses, are perfection. Empty perfection. Sor Juana is a typical author of the period but, unlike Rojas or Moreto, she is locked into its conventions and it would be futile to seek in the comedy the slightest transgression of the aesthetic of decorum.[3]

One of the first steps towards the performance of the play in English was the production of a literal translation. I quote from notes that I made at the time (with apologies for the language): "is this a piss-take?". Perhaps this is the same question as Paz's much more eloquently expressed sense of the play as "empty perfection". My question arose because it seemed to me that Sor Juana was, more than anything else, having great fun with the codes—of behavior and of the theatre—of her time. That what she had created was a merciless game with her hapless and not very commendable characters. As Paz says, there is no transgression of the "aesthetic of decorum", but within it, I believe, she elaborates a transparent game of revelation. Codes are laid bare to the point of emptiness. But, if this is the case, where does that leave the modern production: how can it be played (the next question in my notes)?

Working on the literal translation, I constantly found myself questioning the nature of the exercise. I aimed for what I called "the linguistic facts", that is, I aimed to unravel Sor Juana's baroque syntax in order to make the sense more immediately clear. This was also a means of making sure of the facts of the drama: as Octavio Paz's description makes clear, it is, at times, head-scratchingly difficult to work out who is where, how they got there, who actually sees whom, to whom speeches are addressed, and who actually hears or overhears them. I eventually saw my job as establishing the grammar of the piece, establishing a familiarity with its linguistic and dramatic syntax, with its shapes of language, movement, light and darkness. For this purpose the poetry became subsumed into what I imagined to be rhythmic paragraphs: the language, the grammar of the piece, was ironed out, made linear.

In this sense, the literal translation became an exercise in disintegration, in demolition. It unravels what the author has written, it is a shocking meeting place for languages, codes, periods, and it produces a type of non-language that is the expression of the space in between. This "interlingua" comes across as a violence to both language and the original.[4] The literal translation, then, is part of a circular process: it is up to the translation or adaptation and production to "ravel" it all together again, to give the play back its shape.

If we linger a little more on this question of unraveling, of the shocking intermediate space, where does it take us? What happens with this unraveling is that a clear sight of Sor Juana's edifice of language is achieved.

3. Octavio Paz, *Sor Juana or, The Traps of Faith*, trans. Margaret Sayers Peden (Cambridge, Mass, 1988), p. 327.
4. Here I use as my reference point George Steiner's concept of an "interlingua": George Steiner, *After Babel. Aspects of language and translation*, 2nd edn (Oxford, 1992), p. 332.

My sense, on disentangling the language, was that the language itself, lexically, was quite simple. Syntactically it is a constant and wonderful delight. It relies heavily on wit and deceit and there are many seemingly impenetrable cultural allusions, but these rely on intellectual dexterity, on the cultural familiarity with these allusions of the contemporary court audience, and, for the modern translator, some research and ingenuity.[5] The dialogues are largely explicative, the soliloquies likewise provide information, or describe a state of mind at certain moments in the whole chaos, but these are generally without great depth, for they express largely standard, coded emotions. And there are few moments of elevated poetry. The play, to an almost absurd degree, and one that certainly verges on the farcical, relies on asides. There is a great lack of seemingly crucial direct dialogue between the characters, but, by the end, everyone knows all they need to know for their own good, and order is restored (almost). In the vertiginous speed of the drama, we would be hard pushed to say how.

Embedded in their linguistic expression, the rigid codes of behavior, courtship and honour rule supreme, and, indeed, each of these characters is happily inserted into that code. What Sor Juana has invented here is an edifice of language around an empty core. There is a sameness of voice; the characters have recourse to the same figures and tropes, the same codes. Their language is a consequence of their insertion in that world. The language, I would say, is intended to be transparent on one level in order to allow access to a "futile perfection", not its own, but that of what it is representing: codes of honour at court. In this process of disentangling the play, the creation of modern linearity destroys the edifice of the late baroque circuitousness.

What then becomes apparent is that this is a very clever play, that the plot itself may be ultimately conventional, but that what lies behind it has a wonderful geometry of its own. It is witty in its use of space, in its use of the dynamics of light and dark, hearing and not hearing, seeing and not seeing, and the myriad combinations these allow for. Its dynamic lies in the movement and shapes that emerge, are revealed and then disintegrate. One of the key examples of this is the garden scene, stage-managed by Doña Ana and her maidservant Celia, together and independently, where the characters listen to a song of the greatest pains of love. They can all see and hear the singing, but can only see what the two engineers of the scene wish them to, that is, the seeming deceit of their respective lovers. They are the audience at a scene that only mirrors their own worst fears, which they each express, within their discrete group, that is, ultimately to themselves. Sor Juana creates and manipulates this imaginary dramatic space gloriously. For in a sense it does remain empty—the focus of the drama is scattered, the protagonists become the shadows in which they are all semi-hidden—and we, the audience, are left with that emptiness to ponder. We are entertained while being given sight of emptiness. It is very modern: we may not recognize this precise emptiness, but we have no trouble in identifying the empty core.

---

5. In his version for the stage, Peter Oswald deliberately avoided clarifying some of the more obscure cultural allusions, to hilarious effect.

Sor Juana's Space[6]

* * * Safety is the space for the main action of *Los empeños de una casa*. When she enters the house of Doña Ana, Leonor enters a space that she perceives as being safe, but that is, in fact, potentially dangerous. This house seems to be dominated by women but bows irrevocably to the codes and power of men, which, as we will see, do not always follow the famed codes of honour.

Los empeños de una casa sees Sor Juana at her most mischievous and self-confident, and in it she clearly demonstrates her awareness of the space she occupies and of a sense of constant performance from within it. What I mean to suggest by that is that, on working on this "unraveling" of the play, and then seeing the process of "reconstruction" for performance, I have become aware of how magnificently and with what humour Sor Juana imagines space, and my interpretation of that rests in a sense on the way that she manipulated her own given place in society and manoeuvred herself through it for most of her life. For me, *Los empeños de una casa* is as much a dramatization of this as it is "about" anything.

On entering the Convent of Saint Paula of the Hieronymite Order in 1669, at the age of twenty, Sor Juana had followed the advice of her confessor, Father Antonio Núñez de Miranda. This was to be her place in society: in the court she had found some freedom, but court life would normally lead to marriage, and as Sor Juana said in her famous defence of her right to study and write poetry, her "Respuesta a Sor Filotea",[7] marriage was abhorrent to her. The other space in society that might shelter a woman of her studious inclinations was, of course, the convent. In 1683, Sor Juana was confident and assured: she had, in effect, created an excellent creative and intellectual space in the convent. Her works had been produced beyond Mexico, she continued to be in the favour of the present viceregal couple, and was especially sure of the protection of the Countess of Paredes, the Marquise de la Laguna. This protection against the disapprobation of the hierarchy of the Church was crucial, and she had no reason to doubt it.

Such is Sor Juana's confidence in these years that it seems that in 1681 or '82 she issued a challenge to her confessor, Father Antonio Núñez de Miranda. In an extraordinary letter that anticipates but, in its passionate and unguarded language, goes far beyond the later "Respuesta", Sor Juana attacks Miranda openly and passionately for his disapproval of her writing. And she names his attitude as being born from the fact that she is a woman:

> I am not unaware that to study publicly in schools is not seemly for a woman's honour, because this gives occasion for familiarity with men, and is sufficient for barring them from public studies, and that if women may not challenge men in such studies as pertain to them alone, it is because the body politic, having no need of women for

---

6. For a discussion of Sor Juana and space, see Jean Franco, "Sor Juana Explores Space", in Jean Franco, *Plotting Women. Gender and Representation in Mexico* (London, 1989), pp. 23–54. For a wider discussion of the use of the space on stage, see Aurelio González, "El espacio teatral en *Los empeños de una casa*", in: *Y diversa de mi misma entre plumas ando. Homenaje internacional a Sor Juana Inés de la Cruz*, ed. Sara Poot Herrera (Mexico, 1993), pp. 269–77.
7. See Sor Juana Inés de la Cruz, *Poems, Protest and a Dream*, translated with notes by Margaret Sayers Peden (London, 1997). The "Respuesta" was written in 1691.

government by magistrates (from which service, for the same reason of honor, women are excluded) has not provided for them; but private and individual study, who has forbidden that to women? Like men, do they not have a rational soul? Why then shall they not enjoy the privilege of the enlightenment of letters? Is a woman's soul not as receptive to God's grace and glory as a man's? Then why is she not as able to receive learning and knowledge, which are the lesser gifts? What divine revelation, what regulation of the Church, what rule of reason framed for us such a severe law?[8]

She demands of Miranda a response to the question of how to deal with the unsolicited fame and attention to which she is subject, and compares her obedience to the commands of the viceregal court to his own. And finally she commands him that if he cannot accept her nature—"I was born with it and with it I shall die" (Paz, p. 499)—then he must think of her no more. Her dismissal of her confessor is bold and daring, perhaps even foolhardy. But it is an amazing declaration of her own being: it is direct and passionate, and it demands that she be recognised for what she is and not given impossible goals to achieve. It is open and unguarded: she is confident, aware of the difficulties, but determined to fight on.

It is this spirit that she invests in Leonor: she will command her own destiny. But her heroine loves and is loved, and as such can forge her own destiny within the parameters of an accepted female existence. As Margo Glantz shows, in her verbal portrait of herself to Doña Ana at the beginning of the play, Leonor does not dwell on her beauty, contrary to the conventions of theatrical portraiture: "I don't suppose I need to say / That I was born a lovely girl, / As you can see that for yourself" (283–285). In Margo Glantz's words, "by calling attention—through the silence that surrounds it and underlines it—to exterior narcissism, that of simple physical beauty, Sor Juana enters into its other, perhaps more dangerous, aspect, that of the arrogance that is engendered in the exaggerated consciousness of one's own worth. The interior look, faced with the mirror that the world creates, is deformed. Who to love but the masculine reflection of one's self, built with the same ingredients and nuanced in the same way as one's own image?"[9] Leonor, whose later portrayal of Don Carlos paints him in physical, moral and intellectual glory, will, through this reflection of herself in another, find a place in society. The character is autobiographical in the creation of a portrayal of spirit, of womanhood beyond the ordinary: Leonor is the dramatisation of an imagined alternative space. But the character is not just an easy autobiographical device, nor does her portrayal suggest the love of a man as the only alternative to the convent (although she does threaten flight there if she loses Don Carlos). For it is not love that Leonor has ultimately succumbed to, but correspondence, the mirroring of her soul by another soul. This is part of Sor Juana's quest—an image in society that would legitimate and validate her

8. The letter was found by Father Aureliano Tapia Méndez and published by him in *Autodefensa espiritual de Sor Juana* (Monterrey, 1981) (reproduced in Paz, p. 491).
9. My translation. See Margo Glantz, "De Narciso a Narciso o de Tirso a Sor Juana: *El vergonzoso en palacio* y *Los empeños de una casa*", in Margo Glantz, *Borrones y borradores. Reflexiones sobre el ejercicio de la escritura (Ensayos de literatura colonial, de Bernal Díaz del Castillo a Sor Juana)* (Mexico, 1992), p. 167.

self, a type of community where she would be safe. The play makes reference to this in much more subtle ways, largely by the manipulation of its audience.

Sor Juana's Audience

Los empeños de una casa was written as a *festejo* (a celebration). In this sense, the play is part of a much wider celebration. It is preceded by a *loa* (a brief piece in praise of a saint or of a newly-arrived dignitary) and there is a *sainete* (a short satirical piece) between each of the acts or *jornadas* (days, of which there were three). At the end there would be a *fin de fiesta*, a celebration in the form of a dance or a musical piece. So, the play was not a dramatic event in isolation: it was part of a wider programme, a more diffuse event than now, when we play the three acts together and concentrate on one line of dramatic action. The relationship to time and space is different, there is a suggestion of more room, a more spacious entertainment, one in which wit and leisure play equally important roles.

Sor Juana loved this space: it was the concrete recreation of her own intellectual space. In it she could exercise her wit and ingenuity, elaborate precise and sophisticated poetic schemes, and satisfy her appetite for fun. In it she could experiment, and, at this time in her life, that is exactly what she did. Sor Juana occupied this space as she did all others: testing out its every possibility, pushing both at its boundaries and beyond them. This is especially true in terms of how she develops the relationship with her audience.

The audience, the key interlocutor for the collective of the actors, seems to be, constantly, also the key interlocutor for each individual character. They barely talk to each other. Except for Carlos and Leonor, their dialogue with each other is largely unhelpful, being full of deceit, betrayal and the desire to keep others in the dark. But their speeches, as I have said, are littered with asides. Take this example from Act I, Scene vii, when the whole contrived episode seems on the point of collapse as the key players meet:

CELIA   I wonder, has my mistress come?
I'll need to relocate Don Juan,
Whom I've kept hidden in her rooms.
But look—what's this before my eyes?

DOÑA LEONOR [*Aside.*]   What's this I see here? By God's wounds!
Is that not Carlos I espy?

DON CARLOS [*Aside.*]   Have my nerves got the best of me
Or is that Leonor?

DOÑA ANA [*Aside.*]   Don Juan?
In this house? I can hardly breathe!

DON JUAN [*Aside.*]   Don Carlos de Olmedo, here?
He's Doña Ana's lover! All
Signs point to it and that's why she—

Perfidious, inconstant, false—
Feels free to treat me with disdain.

DOÑA LEONOR: [*Aside.*]   How can it be that Carlos dwells
Among our number, heavens, when
I've wept to think him in a cell?
Concealed, instead, inside these rooms,
He now makes amorous assaults
On me, whom he deems someone else!
So he's that lady's lover! All
Signs point to it. But can it be?
(Am I imagining these things
I see?) The man was taken off
To jail and I lodged here within.
My life's one cruel abyss of grief
And pain!

                                        (868–94)

The characters are in a situation, in semi-darkness, where they must believe their eyes and ears. From the asides we learn that, apart from Leonor and Carlos, the rest are trapped by what they see or believe they see. Sight has been their instrument of love, and they are trapped by it. Leonor and Carlos will not trust sight alone: they will look beyond the evidence of their eyes, no matter how many times "fate", as Octavio Paz calls it, proves otherwise.

From Celia's asides, we learn of the mysteries that the plot does not solve through action; for example, how it happens that Doña Ana's suitor is already hiding in the house:

> Before I'd heard all this, I had
> That Don Juan hidden in her room!
> For some time he'd been noticing
> Cold treatment from her run its course.
>   (167–170)

Her asides remind us time and again of her duplicity, of her awareness of herself in the hierarchy of servants, and of her ruthless disregard for "decorum":

> Just look at her, so gripped by fears
> She quite forgot to ask me how
> Don Juan contrived to enter here.
> Now that she's out of danger, though,
> I'll come up with some pale excuse,
> Attributing the blame for it
> To some dishonest servant's ruse.
> When many maids work side by side,
> A lot of them you just can't trust,
> For they'll protect their kind with lies
> Or else make accusations up.
>   (962–72)

The asides suspend action, but move it along in terms of informing the audience. They are virtually Brechtian *placards*.[1] We are never allowed to forget that we are watching an artifice. Sor Juana suggests the futility of the fourth wall, which she virtually destroys. We are invited to collude with the characters one by one, but are rarely asked to enter into a world of emotional closeness with them. Each character elicits a response, but no response carries more moral weight than the other: Celia's double-dealings as the servant are greeted as knowingly as Doña Ana's gleeful bitching; Castaño's cursing and "cowardice" gloriously unveil the absurdities of his master's code of honour and decorum. In a world where the communication is encoded to a great degree and, furthermore, is situated in a world of envy and ritual games, where real passions are rare, the characters speak "outwards", beyond their immediate possible interlocutor on stage to the normally barely acknowledged interlocutor beyond the stage. These characters circling and hounding and missing each other, are locked into their own individuality, and the only possible interlocutor is this "invisible" one. We have distance, direct communication with the audience; we have, as it were, an insight into their inner monologues, and we have a play that is utterly conscious of itself and its absurdities. (The London production showed the strength of these devices: the audience entered the game from the first—perhaps after initial consternation—and people surprised themselves by laughing from the beginning to the end of a play written by a seventeenth-century Mexican nun). The place of *Los empeños de una casa* seems to be somewhere between Brecht, Pirandello[2] and Hollywood ham.

If the asides are almost Brechtian, then the *sainetes* anticipated Pirandello, as has been noted elsewhere (Paz, p. 328). In the second *sainete*, two characters comment on the play so far, which they criticise for being too long and tedious; they decide to "murmurar" [criticize] (p. 132),[3] to hiss and make a noise, wondering who has deceived the owner of the house in which the play takes place, and suggesting that it would have been better to choose a play by, for example, Calderón (Spanish imports being vastly superior to the substandard native effort). Their whistling brings out the "author"—the male dramatist, Acevedo—and he swears he will not write again, preferring "death by whistling" to death by the garrotte.

Within the constraints of the modern production, this is not a scene that would be included since it is not necessary to the development of the play. But for Sor Juana, as the author of all the elements of the *festejo*, this was her opportunity to indulge her imagination and playfulness. From this perspective she names her own space. As I have said, this, in 1683, is one of fulfillment, the creative space being filled exuberantly. But it is also a space in which a sense of threat sits on the margins of the author's consciousness, yet at the centre of her condition. One of the key functions of the incident in the *sainete* is to take us directly to the heart of Sor Juana's femininity. In it, she is "disguised" as a male dramatist (one, moreover, that did exist). In typical style, she is drawing attention to her sex by hiding it,

---

1. Bertolt Brecht (1898–1956), German playwright, director, and critic, advocated the use of placards (signs) to convey clear messages to the audience as part of his didactic, socially engaged "epic theater" [editor's note].
2. Luigi Pirandello (1867–1936), Italian writer best known for his plays, which interrogate the relationship between illusion and reality [editor's note].
3. References in Spanish to the play are to *Los empeños de una casa* (Mexico, 1994).

drawing attention to the fact that she would be required to "change"—become a man—in order to be recognized properly and legitimately as a poet. And she audaciously names the stakes: the garrotte or silence.

This theme—perhaps the main subtext of the play—is carried over to gloriously humorous effect in the final act. Castaño is bid by his master (who has learned that Leonor is to be married to Don Pedro in her father's mistaken belief that it was they who had eloped as lovers) to take a letter of confession to Leonor's father, convinced that once the truth is known it is he who will be honour bound to marry her. Castaño is reluctant to do this, in the highly probable belief that he will be made to pay for his master's errors. In his desperation he hits on the idea of dressing as Leonor, whose clothes he has been carrying around * * * and proceeds to be "transformed" by taking off the "shapeless trappings of a man". This he does in full view of the audience with a running conversation with them that gloriously unveils the mechanisms and results of "change".

What is it that Sor Juana is doing here? She is, in fact, entering dangerous territory. By having Castaño subject to the realities of being a woman, she creates a new transparency in our awareness of these codes. On his immediate encounter with Don Pedro (who, because of his trust in what he sees rather than the evidence of reason and what he hears, believes he has found Leonor), Castaño discovers the easy power of femininity. At first he delights in the power woman has over man:

> It's quite a thrill to be pursued!
> I'll never be surprised again
> To see gals vaunting haughty pride.
> There's nothing in the world like woo
> To swell one's head with vain conceit.
> (2540–44)

But Don Pedro persists in his pursuit of her, and it becomes clear that the power of women is superficial, and ultimately insignificant. With his greater physical power, Don Pedro is a threat to "Leonor", and will use this when "she" tries to leave. Castaño's cry of "I'm really in a pickle now! / He'll have his way with me, I think, / If I don't change my tune and fast!" (2610–12) unveils what we have seen before in the play (for example, Leonor's encounter with Don Juan, who mistakes her for his lover, Doña Ana), but has not been named: the power of the men and the easy recourse to the threat of sexual violence. The "aesthetics of decorum" are not transgressed, but they are transfigured into a much uglier reality. Castaño saves himself by promising marriage, and the slapstick humor of the scene is quickly reimposed, but Castaño relentlessly plays to the audience, inviting their complicity in the unveiling of the real Don Pedro. And at the end, Sor Juana mischievously leaves one element undone in her hasty resolution of the intrigues: Don Pedro is now "betrothed" to a false Leonor. She has left the audience a final reminder of the tricks that she has been playing in the course of the play. The question of the "changing" of gender has not been entirely resolved. The audience is a witness to this.

In the theatrical experience, Sor Juana does not lose sight of her position—one filled with satire and easy laughter, and one in which the audience is supreme. For she is constantly aware of the audience, not only as spectator, but as possible site for the reception (and understanding, mirroring?) of her intellectual and human fears. Even in the protection of the viceregal couple she cannot but be aware of the condemnation that murmurs "offstage". In her letter to her confessor she had written, "for even having a reasonably good handwriting has caused me worrisome and lengthy persecution, for no other reason than they said it looked like a man's writing, and that it was not proper, whereupon they forced me to deform it purposely, and of this the entire community is witness" (Paz, p. 497). *Los empeños de una casa* makes reference to this constant need for disguise, for change, for bending to an outside authority. Here, in the protection of the court audience, but in full view of the Church, she names her persecution and names the need for abandoning her gender, adopting another to be herself. She identifies the gendered space into which she is forced, and she suggests the possibility of alternative spaces. From our perspective as possible interlocutors for her at that point in her life, we can glimpse the dream of multiple possibilities for women. And from our modern perspective we also know that it was one that she was forced to abandon in appearance if not in spirit. Let us not forget that the *festejo* of which *Los empeños de una casa* is a part was performed partly in honour of the new Archbishop, who hated theatre and abhorred women, and who would be instrumental less than ten years later in silencing Sor Juana Inés de la Cruz.

Selected Bibliography

• indicates works included or excerpted in this Norton Critical Edition

Criticism: The Comedia

Albrecht, Jane. *The Playgoing Public of Madrid in the Time of Tirso de Molina*. New Orleans: University Press of the South, 2001.

Bass, Laura R. *The Drama of the Portrait: Theater and Visual Culture in Early Modern Spain*. University Park: Pennsylvania State University Press, 2008.

———. "Introduction" and "The *Comedia* and Cultural Control: The Legacy of José Antonio Maravall." *Bulletin of the Comediantes* 65.1 (2013): 1–13.

Bayliss, Robert Elliott. *The Discourse of Courtly Love in Seventeenth-Century Spanish Theater*. Lewisburg: Bucknell University Press, 2008.

Burningham, Bruce R. *Radical Theatricality: Jongleuresque Performance on the Early Spanish Stage*. Purdue Studies in Romance Literatures. Vol. 39. West Lafayette: Purdue University Press, 2007.

• Campbell, Jodi. "Plays and Politics." *Monarchy, Political Culture, and Drama in Seventeenth-Century Madrid: Theater of Negotiation*. Aldershot: Ashgate, 2006. 1–29.

Carreño-Rodríguez, Antonio. *Alegorías del poder. Crisis imperial y comedia nueva (1598–1659)*. London: Támesis, 2009.

Carrión, Gabriela. *Staging Marriage in Early Modern Spain: Conjugal Doctrine in Lope, Cervantes, and Calderón*. Lewisburg: Bucknell University Press, 2011.

Carrión, María M. *Subject Stages: Marriage, Theatre and the Law in Early Modern Spain*. Toronto: University of Toronto Press, 2010.

Cruz Peterson, Elizabeth M. "A Mindful Audience: Embodied Spectatorship in Early Modern Madrid." Isabel Jaéan and Julien Jacques Simon, eds. *Cognitive Approaches to Early Modern Spanish Literature*. Oxford: Oxford University Press, 2016. 111–30.

De Armas, Frederick A., Luciano García Lorenzo, and Enrique García Santo-Tomás, eds. *Hacia la tragedia áurea. Lecturas para un nuevo milenio*. Biblioteca Áurea Hispánica, 55. Madrid: Iberoamericana, 2008.

Donnell, Sidney. *Feminizing the Enemy: Imperial Spain, Transvestite Drama, and the Crisis of Masculinity*. Lewisburg: Bucknell University Press, 2003.

Dopico-Black, Georgina. *Perfect Wives, Other Women: Adultery and Inquisition in Early Modern Spain*. Durham: Duke University Press, 2001.

Fischer, Susan L. "Aspectuality, Performativity, and 'Foreign' *Comedia*: (Re) Iteration of Meaning for the Stage." Catherine Boyle and David Johnston, eds. *The Spanish Golden Age in English: Perspectives on Performance*. London: Oberon, 2007. 31–48.

García Santo-Tomás, Enrique. *Espacio urbano y creación literaria en el Madrid de Felipe IV*. Madrid: Iberoamericana, 2004.

———, ed. *El teatro del Siglo de Oro ante los espacios de la crítica. Encuentros y revisiones*. Madrid: Iberoamericana, 2002.

Gasta, Chad M. *Imperial Stagings: Empire and Ideology in Transatlantic Theater of Early Modern Spain and the New World*. Chapel Hill: University of North Carolina Press, 2013.

Greer, Margaret R. "Authority and Theatrical Community: Early Modern Spanish Theater Manuscripts." *Renaissance Drama* 40.1 (2012): 101–12.

———. "Place, Space and Public Formation in the Drama of the Spanish Empire." Angela Vanhaelen and Joseph P. Ward, eds. *Making Space Public in Early Modern Europe: Performance, Geography, Privacy*. New York: Routledge, 2013. 76–97.

———. "Spanish Golden Age Tragedy: From Cervantes to Calderón." Rebecca Bushnell, ed. *A Companion to Tragedy.* Malden: Blackwell Publishing, 2005. 351–70.

———. "A Tale of Three Cities: The Place of the Theatre in Early Modern Madrid, Paris and London." *Bulletin of Hispanic Studies* 77.1 (2000): 391–419.

• Greer, Margaret R., and Andrea Junguito. "Economies of the Early Modern Stage." *Revista canadiense de estudios hispánicos* 29.1 (2004): 31–46.

Hegstrom, Valerie. *Engendering the Early Modern Stage: Women Playwrights in the Spanish Empire.* New Orleans: University Press of the South, 1999.

• Heise, Ursula. "Transvestism and the Stage Controversy in Spain and England, 1580–1680." *Theatre Journal* 44.3 (1992): 357–74.

Kallendorf, Hilaire, ed. *A Companion to Early Modern Hispanic Theater.* The Renaissance Society of America Texts and Studies Series, 2. Leiden: Brill, 2014.

• Maravall, José Antonio. "The Social Role of Artifice." *Culture of the Baroque: Analysis of a Historical Structure*, trans. Terry Cochran. Minneapolis: University of Minnesota Press, 1986. 233–40.

———. *Teatro y literatura en la sociedad barroca.* Madrid: Seminarios y Ediciones, 1972.

• McKendrick, Melveena. "Breaking the Silence: Women and the Word in the *Comedia*." *Revista canadiense de estudios hispánicos* 29.1 (2004): 13–30.

———. "The Corrales and Their Audience." *Theatre in Spain, 1490–1700.* Cambridge: Cambridge University Press, 1989. 178–208.

———. "Honour/Vengeance in the Spanish *Comedia*: A Case of Mimetic Transference?" *The Modern Language Review* 79.2 (1984): 313–35.

———. *Identities in Crisis: Essays on Honour, Gender and Women in the Comedia.* Teatro del Siglo de Oro, Estudios de Literatura. Vol. 77. Kassel: Edition Reichenberger, 2002.

———. *Woman and Society in the Spanish Drama of the Golden Age: A Study of the* mujer varonil. Cambridge: Cambridge University Press, 1974.

Mujica, Barbara. *A New Anthology of Early Modern Spanish Theater: Play and Playtext.* New Haven: Yale University Press, 2015.

Mujica, Barbara, and Anita K. Stoll. *El texto puesto en escena: estudios sobre la comedia del Siglo de Oro en honor a Everett W. Hesse.* London: Támesis, 2000.

Quintero, María Cristina. "Women and Drama in Early Modern Spain." *Gendering the Crown in the Spanish Baroque* Comedia. Aldershot: Ashgate, 2012.

Stoll, Anita K., and Dawn L. Smith, eds. *Gender, Identity, and Representation in Spain's Golden Age.* Lewisburg: Bucknell University Press, 2000.

Stroud, Matthew D. *Plot Twists and Critical Turns: Queer Approaches to Early Modern Spanish Theater.* Lewisburg: Bucknell University Press, 2007.

Taylor, Scott K. *Honor and Violence in Golden Age Spain.* New Haven: Yale University Press, 2008.

Thacker, Jonathan. *A Companion to Golden Age Theatre.* Woodbridge: Tamesis, 2007.

———. "Rethinking Golden-Age Drama: The *Comedia* and Its Contexts." *Paragraph* 22.1 (1999): 14–34.

———. *Role-Play and the World as Stage in the* Comedia. Liverpool: Liverpool University Press, 2002.

Weimer, Christopher B. "Beyond Canvas and Paint: Falling Portraits in the Spanish Comedia." *Objects of Culture in the Literature of Imperial Spain.* Frederick A. de Armas and Mary Barnard, eds. Toronto: University of Toronto Press, 2013. 99–121.

Criticism: Plays and Playwrights

Alatorre, Antonio. *Sor Juana a través de los siglos (1668–1910).* 2 vols. México: Colegio de México, Colegio Nacional, UNAM, 2007.

Arenal, Electa. "The Convent as Catalyst for Autonomy: Two Hispanic Nuns of the Seventeenth Century." *Women in Hispanic Literature: Icons and Fallen Idols* (1983): 147–83.

• Armstrong-Roche, Michael. "(The) *Patria* Besieged: Border-Crossing Paradoxes of National Identity in Cervantes' *Numancia*." Benita Sampedro

Vizcaya, ed. *Border Interrogations: Questioning Spanish Frontiers.* New York: Berghahn Books, 2008. 204–27.

Avilés, Luis F. "War and Material Conditions for Suffering in Cervantes' *Numancia.*" Frederick A. De Armas, and Mary Barnard, eds. *Objects of Culture in the Literature of Imperial Spain.* Toronto: University of Toronto Press, 2013. 253–76.

Benabu, Isaac. *Reading for the Stage: Calderón and His Contemporaries.* Woodbridge: Támesis, 2003.

Bergmann, Emilie. "The Epic Vision of Cervantes' *Numancia.*" *Theatre Journal* 36.1 (1984): 85–96.

• Blue, William. "The Politics of Lope's *Fuenteovejuna.*" *Hispanic Review* 59.3 (1991): 295–315.

• Boyle, Catherine. "*Los empeños de una casa* by Sor Juana Inés de la Cruz: Translation, Cultural Transmission and Staging." *Forum for Modern Language Studies* Vol. 35, No. 3 (1999): 227–37.

Briones, A. J. Valbuena. "El concepto del hado en el teatro de Calderón." *Bulletin Hispanique* 63.1 (1961): 48–53.

Cruickshank, Don William. *Don Pedro Calderón.* Cambridge: Cambridge University Press, 2009.

• Donnell, Sidney. "From Cross Gender to Generic Closure: Sor Juana Inés de la Cruz's *Los empeños de una casa.*" *Revista Canadiense de Estudios Hispánicos* (2008): 177–93.

El Saffar, Ruth. "Way Stations in the Errancy of the Word: A Study of Calderón's *La vida es sueño.*" *Renaissance Drama* 17 (1986): 83–100.

Fischer, Susan L. "Montaigne, Lying and Early Modern Self-Fashioning: A Discursive Dialogue with Lope's *El perro del hortelano* on the Page and on Stage." *Bulletin of Spanish Studies* 90.4–5 (2013): 577–98.

Fulton, J. Michael. "In Defense of Clotaldo: Reconsidering the Secondary Plot in Calderón's *La vida es sueño.*" *Rocky Mountain Review of Language and Literature* (2002): 11–23.

García Santo-Tomás, Enrique. "Calderón en el 'Memorial Literario': coordenadas de una poética, fragmentos de una canonización." *Criticón* 80 (2000): 169–86.

Greer, Margaret. "An (In)convenient Marriage? Justice and Power in *La vida es sueño, comedia* and *auto sacramental.*" *Bulletin of Spanish Studies* 85.6 (2008): 55–68.

• Heiple, Daniel L. "Life as Dream and the Philosophy of Disillusionment." Frederick De Armas, ed. *The Prince in the Tower: Perceptions of La vida es sueño.* Lewisburg: Bucknell University Press, 1993. 118–31.

Johnson, Carroll B. "*La Numancia* and the Structure of Cervantine Ambiguity." *I. and L. (Ideologies and Literature): Journal of Hispanic and Luso-Brazilian Literatures* 3.12 (1980): 75–94.

Kahn, Aaron M. *The Ambivalence of Imperial Discourse: Cervantes's La Numancia Within the "Lost Generation" of Spanish Drama (1570–90).* Hispanic Studies: Culture and Ideas. Vol. 14. Bern: Peter Lang, 2008.

King, Willard F. "Cervantes' *Numancia* and Imperial Spain." *MLN* 94.2 (1979): 200–221.

• Laguna, Ana. "*Life Is a Dream* and the Fractures of Reason." *MLN* 129.2 (2014): 238–54.

Maroto Camino, Mercedes. "'En distintas cuadras': Gender, Exile and Shipwreck in Sor Juana's *Los empeños de una casa.*" *Romance Studies* 20.2 (2013): 155–64.

———. "'Esta sangre quiero': Secrets and Discovery in Lope's *El perro del hortelano.*" *Hispanic Review* 71.1 (2003): 15–30.

McKendrick, Melveena. "Calderón and the Politics of Honour." *Bulletin of Hispanic Studies* 70.1 (1993): 135–46.

———. *Playing the King: Lope de Vega and the Limits of Conformity.* London: Támesis, 2000.

———. "Writings for the Stage." Anthony J. Cascardi, ed. *The Cambridge Companion to Cervantes.* Cambridge: Cambridge University Press, 2002. 131–59.

O'Brien, Eavan. "Sor Juana's *Los empeños de una casa* [*The Trials of a Noble House*]: Theatrical Exchange Between Europe and New Spain." Helen Hackett, ed. *Early Modern Exchanges: Dialogues Between Nations and Cultures, 1550–1800.* Farnham: Ashgate, 2015. 201–22.

Paden, Jeremy. "Interrupting Augustine: Hermeneutics, Allegory, and Irony in *El perro del hortelano*." *Romance Quarterly* 61.4 (2014): 238–53.
Samson, Alexander, and Jonathan Thacker. *A Companion to Lope de Vega*. Woodbridge: Támesis, 2008.
Schmidhuber, Guillermo. *The Three Secular Plays of Sor Juana Inés de la Cruz: A Critical Study*. Lexington: University Press of Kentucky, 2015.
• Wardropper, Bruce. "Comic Illusion: Lope de Vega's *El perro del hortelano*." *Kentucky Romance Quarterly* 14.1 (1967): 101–11.
• Wheeler, Duncan. "An (Early) Modern Classic: *Fuente Ovejuna* in Contemporary Spain." *Golden Age Drama in Contemporary Spain: The Comedia on Page, Stage and Screen*. Cardiff: University of Wales Press, 2012.
Wright, Elizabeth R. *Pilgrimage to Patronage: Lope de Vega and the Court of Philip III, 1598–1621*. Lewisburg: Bucknell University Press, 2001.

Modern Translation, Adaptation, Teaching, and Performance

Bass, Laura R., and Margaret Greer, eds. *Approaches to Teaching Early Modern Spanish Drama*. New York: Modern Language Association of America, 2005.
Boyle, Catherine, and David Johnston, eds. *The Spanish Golden Age in English: Perspectives on Performance*. London: Oberon, 2007.
Erdman, Harley, and Susan Paun De García, eds. *Remaking the Comedia: Spanish Classical Theater in Adaptation*. Woodbridge: Támesis, 2015.
Fischer, Susan L. *Reading Performance: Spanish Golden Age Theatre and Shakespeare on the Modern Stage*. Woodbridge: Támesis, 2009.
Martin, Vincent, and Rosie Seagraves. "Restaging the Classroom: A Multidisciplinary Approach to Teaching Early Modern Hispanic Theater." *Bulletin of the Comediantes* 66.2 (2014): 211–27.
Mujica, Barbara, ed. *Shakespeare and the Spanish Comedia: Translation, Interpretation, Performance: Essays in Honor of Susan L. Fischer*. Lewisburg: Bucknell University Press, 2013.
Paun de García, Susan, and Donald R. Larson, eds. *The Comedia in English: Translation and Performance*. Woodbridge: Támesis, 2008.
Simerka, Barbara. *El arte nuevo de estudiar comedias: Literary Theory and Spanish Golden Age Drama*. Lewisburg: Bucknell University Press, 1996.
Vidler, Laura L. *Performance Reconstruction and Spanish Golden Age Drama: Reviving and Revising the Comedia*. Basingstoke: Palgrave Macmillan, 2014.
Wheeler, Duncan. "Contextualising and Contesting José Antonio Maravall's Theories of Baroque Culture from the Perspective of Modern-Day Performance." *Bulletin of the Comediantes* 65.1 (2013): 15–43.
———. *Golden Age Drama in Contemporary Spain: The Comedia on Page, Stage and Screen*. Cardiff: University of Wales Press, 2012.